Lecture Notes in Computer Science 15931

Founding Editors

Gerhard Goos
Juris Hartmanis

Editorial Board Members

Elisa Bertino, *Purdue University, West Lafayette, IN, USA*
Wen Gao, *Peking University, Beijing, China*
Bernhard Steffen, *TU Dortmund University, Dortmund, Germany*
Moti Yung, *Columbia University, New York, NY, USA*

The series Lecture Notes in Computer Science (LNCS), including its subseries Lecture Notes in Artificial Intelligence (LNAI) and Lecture Notes in Bioinformatics (LNBI), has established itself as a medium for the publication of new developments in computer science and information technology research, teaching, and education.

LNCS enjoys close cooperation with the computer science R & D community, the series counts many renowned academics among its volume editors and paper authors, and collaborates with prestigious societies. Its mission is to serve this international community by providing an invaluable service, mainly focused on the publication of conference and workshop proceedings and postproceedings. LNCS commenced publication in 1973.

Ruzica Piskac · Zvonimir Rakamarić
Editors

Computer Aided Verification

37th International Conference, CAV 2025
Zagreb, Croatia, July 23–25, 2025
Proceedings, Part I

Editors
Ruzica Piskac
Yale University
New Haven, CT, USA

Zvonimir Rakamarić
Amazon (United States)
Seattle, WA, USA

ISSN 0302-9743　　　　　　ISSN 1611-3349 (electronic)
Lecture Notes in Computer Science
ISBN 978-3-031-98667-3　　　ISBN 978-3-031-98668-0 (eBook)
https://doi.org/10.1007/978-3-031-98668-0

© The Editor(s) (if applicable) and The Author(s) 2025, corrected publication 2025. This book is an open access publication.

Open Access This book is licensed under the terms of the Creative Commons Attribution 4.0 International License (http://creativecommons.org/licenses/by/4.0/), which permits use, sharing, adaptation, distribution and reproduction in any medium or format, as long as you give appropriate credit to the original author(s) and the source, provide a link to the Creative Commons license and indicate if changes were made.
The images or other third party material in this book are included in the book's Creative Commons license, unless indicated otherwise in a credit line to the material. If material is not included in the book's Creative Commons license and your intended use is not permitted by statutory regulation or exceeds the permitted use, you will need to obtain permission directly from the copyright holder.
This work is subject to copyright. All rights are solely and exclusively licensed by the Publisher, whether the whole or part of the material is concerned, specifically the rights of translation, reprinting, reuse of illustrations, recitation, broadcasting, reproduction on microfilms or in any other physical way, and transmission or information storage and retrieval, electronic adaptation, computer software, or by similar or dissimilar methodology now known or hereafter developed.
The use of general descriptive names, registered names, trademarks, service marks, etc. in this publication does not imply, even in the absence of a specific statement, that such names are exempt from the relevant protective laws and regulations and therefore free for general use.
The publisher, the authors and the editors are safe to assume that the advice and information in this book are believed to be true and accurate at the date of publication. Neither the publisher nor the authors or the editors give a warranty, expressed or implied, with respect to the material contained herein or for any errors or omissions that may have been made. The publisher remains neutral with regard to jurisdictional claims in published maps and institutional affiliations.

This Springer imprint is published by the registered company Springer Nature Switzerland AG
The registered company address is: Gewerbestrasse 11, 6330 Cham, Switzerland

If disposing of this product, please recycle the paper.

Preface

It was our privilege to serve as the program chairs for CAV 2025, the 37th International Conference on Computer-Aided Verification. CAV 2025 was held in Zagreb, Croatia, on July 23–25, 2025, and the pre-conference workshops were held on July 21–22, 2025.

CAV is an annual conference dedicated to the advancement of the theory and practice of computer-aided formal analysis methods for hardware and software systems. The primary focus of CAV is to extend the frontiers of verification techniques by expanding to new domains such as security, quantum computing, and machine learning. This puts CAV at the cutting edge of formal methods research. This year's program is a reflection of this commitment.

CAV 2025 received 305 submissions. We accepted 24 tool papers, 4 case-study papers, and 51 regular papers, which amounts to an acceptance rate of roughly 25.9% overall. The accepted papers cover a wide spectrum of topics, from theoretical results to applications of formal methods. These papers apply or extend formal methods to a wide range of domains such as concurrency, machine learning and neural networks, quantum systems, as well as hybrid and stochastic systems. The program featured keynote talks by Corina Păsăreanu (Carnegie Mellon University, USA), Emina Torlak (Amazon Web Services and University of Washington, USA), and Roderick Bloem (Graz University of Technology, Austria). In addition to the contributed talks, CAV 2025 also hosted the CAV Award ceremony, and a report from the Synthesis Competition (SYNTCOMP) chairs. Furthermore, we continued the tradition of Logic Lounge, a series of discussions on computer science topics targeting a general audience. This year's Logic Lounge speakers were Moshe Y. Vardi (Rice University) and Henry Shevlin (University of Cambridge) who invited us to examine the nature of mind itself and whether artificial intelligence met its defining criteria.

In addition to the main conference, CAV 2025 hosted the following workshops: Verification Mentoring Workshop (VMW), Workshop on Synthesis (SYNT), Workshop on Verification of Quantum Computing (VQC), Workshop on Automated Reasoning for Tensor Compilers (AR4TC), International Workshop on Trustworthy Cyber-Physical Systems (TACPS), Workshop on Hyperproperties: Advances in Theory and Applications (HYPER), Symposium on AI Verification (SAIV), Meeting on String Constraints and Applications (MOSCA), Workshop on Horn Clauses for Verification and Synthesis (HCVS), and Workshop on Verification of Probabilistic Programs (VeriProP). Furthermore, CAV 2025 also included the following events dedicated to two prominent members of the CAV community: Ken McMillan Celebration and Allen Emerson Memorial.

Organizing a flagship conference like CAV requires a great deal of effort from the community. The Program Committee for CAV 2025 consisted of 122 members and two co-chairs—a committee of this size ensures that each member has to review only a reasonable number of papers in the allotted time. In all, the committee members wrote 958 reviews while investing significant effort to maintain and ensure the high quality of the conference program. We are grateful to the CAV 2025 Program Committee for their outstanding efforts in evaluating the submissions and making sure that each paper got a fair chance.

Like recent years in CAV, we made artifact evaluation mandatory for tool paper submissions, but optional for the rest of the accepted papers. This year we received 68 artifact submissions, all of which received at least one badge. We rejected 5 tool papers because the associated artifacts did not meet the functional badge criteria. The Artifact Evaluation Committee consisted of 83 members and two co-chairs, who put in significant effort to evaluate each artifact. The goal of this process was to provide constructive feedback to tool developers and help make the research published in CAV more reproducible. We are also very grateful to the Artifact Evaluation Committee for their hard work and dedication in evaluating the submitted artifacts.

CAV 2025 would not have been possible without the tremendous help we received from a number of individuals, and we would like to thank everyone who helped make CAV 2025 a success. First, we would like to thank our area chairs Anthony Widjaja Lin, Azadeh Farzan, Erika Ábrahám, Eva Darulova, Guy Katz, Peter Müller, Philipp Rümmer, and Roderick Bloem. Moreover, we would like to thank Matthias Heizmann and Tanja Schindler for chairing the Artifact Evaluation Committee. We also thank Grigory Fedyukovich for chairing the workshop organization. Ferhat Erata and Hadar Frenkel for leading publicity efforts, Ning Luo as the fellowship chair, Borzoo Bonakdarpour and Jana Hofmann as sponsorship chairs, and Jordan Schmerge as the website chair. Steve Siegel helped prepare the proceedings, while Alan Jović spearheaded the local organization. We also thank Grigory Fedyukovich, Mukund Raghothaman, Elizabeth Polgreen, Kaushik Mallik, and Thom Badings for organizing the Verification Mentoring Workshop. Last but not least, we would like to thank the members of the CAV Steering Committee (Kenneth McMillan, Aarti Gupta, Orna Grumberg, and Daniel Kroening) for helping us with several important aspects of organizing CAV 2025.

We hope that you will find the proceedings of CAV 2025 scientifically interesting and thought-provoking!

June 2025

Ruzica Piskac
Zvonimir Rakamarić

Organization

Steering Committee

Orna Grumberg	Technion, Israel
Aarti Gupta	Princeton University, USA
Daniel Kroening	Amazon, USA
Kenneth McMillan	University of Texas at Austin, USA

Conference Co-chairs

Ruzica Piskac	Yale University, USA
Zvonimir Rakamarić	Amazon Web Services, USA

Artifact Evaluation Co-chairs

Matthias Heizmann	University of Stuttgart, Germany
Tanja Schindler	University of Basel, Switzerland

Local Chair

Alan Jović	University of Zagreb, Croatia

Area Chairs

Anthony Widjaja Lin	Technical University of Kaiserslautern, Germany
Azadeh Farzan	University of Toronto, Canada
Erika Ábrahám	RWTH Aachen University, Germany
Eva Darulova	Uppsala University, Sweden
Guy Katz	Hebrew University of Jerusalem, Israel
Peter Müller	ETH Zurich, Switzerland
Philipp Rümmer	University of Regensburg, Germany
Roderick Bloem	Graz University of Technology, Austria

Workshop Chair

Grigory Fedyukovich　　　　　Florida State University, USA

Fellowship Chair

Ning Luo　　　　　University of Illinois Urbana-Champaign, USA

Publicity Chairs

Ferhat Erata　　　　　Yale University, USA
Hadar Frenkel　　　　　Bar Ilan University, Israel

Publication Chair

Stephen Siegel　　　　　University of Delaware, USA

Website Chair

Jordan Schmerge　　　　　Yale University, USA

Program Committee

Aarti Gupta　　　　　Princeton University, USA
Ahmed Bouajjani　　　　　Université Paris Cité, France
Aina Niemetz　　　　　Stanford University, USA
Alan J. Hu　　　　　University of British Columbia, Canada
Alberto Griggio　　　　　Fondazione Bruno Kessler, Italy
Alessandro Cimatti　　　　　Fondazione Bruno Kessler, Italy
Alexander J. Summers　　　　　University of British Columbia, Canada
Alexander Nadel　　　　　Technion & Intel, Israel
Alfons Laarman　　　　　Leiden University, Netherlands
Aman Goel　　　　　Amazon Web Services, USA
Anastasia Isychev　　　　　TU Wien, Austria
Anastasia Mavridou　　　　　KBR/NASA Ames Research Center, USA
Anca Muscholl　　　　　LaBRI, Université Bordeaux, France

Andreas Pavlogiannis	Aarhus University, Denmark
Andreas Podelski	University of Freiburg, Germany
Anna Lukina	TU Delft, Netherlands
Anne-Kathrin Schmuck	Max Planck Institute for Software Systems, Germany
Anthony Widjaja Lin	TU Kaiserslautern, Germany
Anton Wijs	Eindhoven University of Technology, Netherlands
Arie Gurfinkel	University of Waterloo, Canada
Armin Biere	University of Freiburg, Germany
Azadeh Farzan	University of Toronto, Canada
Barbara Jobstmann	Cadence Design Systems, Switzerland
Benjamin Kaminski	Saarland University, Germany
Bernd Finkbeiner	CISPA Helmholtz Center for Information Security, Germany
Bettina Könighofer	Graz University of Technology, Austria
Borzoo Bonakdarpour	Michigan State University, USA
Burcu Kulahcioglu Ozkan	Delft University of Technology, Netherlands
Cesar Sanchez	IMDEA Software Institute, Spain
Christoph M. Wintersteiger	Imandra, UK
Christoph Matheja	University of Oldenburg, Germany
Clark Barrett	Stanford University, USA
Claudia Cauli	Huawei Ireland Research Center, Ireland
Corina Pasareanu	NASA Ames Research Center, USA
Cristina David	University of Bristol, UK
Damien Zufferey	NVIDIA, Switzerland
Daniel Kröning	Amazon, USA
Daniel Stan	LRE EPITA Research Laboratory, France
Dirk Beyer	LMU Munich, Germany
Dominik Winterer	ETH Zurich, Switzerland
Đorđje Žikelić	Singapore Management University, Singapore
Dorra Ben Khalifa	ENAC – University of Toulouse, France
Duc-Hiep Chu	Google Research, USA
Elizabeth Polgreen	University of Edinburgh, UK
Elvira Albert	Complutense University of Madrid, Spain
Enrico Magnago	Amazon Web Services, Germany
Erika Ábrahám	RWTH Aachen University, Germany
Eva Darulova	Uppsala University, Sweden
Gidon Ernst	LMU Munich, Germany
Guowen Xu	University of Electronic Science and Technology of China, China
Guy Amir	Cornell University, USA
Guy Katz	Hebrew University of Jerusalem, Israel

Hadar Frenkel	Bar Ilan University, Israel
Haoze (Andrew) Wu	Amherst College, USA
Harald Ruess	SRI International, USA
Hari Govind Vediramana Krishnan	University of Waterloo, Canada
Hazem Torfah	Chalmers University of Technology, Sweden
He Zhu	Rutgers University, USA
Hossein Hojjat	Tehran Institute of Advanced Studies, Iran
Ichiro Hasuo	National Institute of Informatics, Japan
Jana Hofmann	Max Planck Institute for Security and Privacy, Germany
Ji Guan	Institute of Software, Chinese Academy of Sciences, China
Jianan Yao	Amazon Web Services, USA
Jingbo Wang	Purdue University, USA
Jocelyn (Qiaochu) Chen	New York University, USA
Joey Dodds	Amazon Web Services, USA
Joost-Pieter Katoen	RWTH-Aachen University, Germany
Jorge A. Pérez	University of Groningen, Netherlands
Junkil Park	Aptos Labs, USA
Kaushik Mallik	IMDEA Software Institute, Spain
Kedar Namjoshi	Bell Labs, Nokia, USA
Kshitij Bansal	Google, USA
Kyungmin Bae	POSTECH, South Korea
Laura Kovacs	TU Wien, Austria
Magnus Myreen	Chalmers University of Technology, Sweden
Marco Faella	University of Naples Federico II, Italy
Marieke Huisman	University of Twente, Netherlands
Mark Santolucito	Barnard College, Columbia University, USA
Michael Emmi	Amazon Web Services, USA
Mihaela Sighireanu	University Paris-Saclay, France
Mirco Giacobbe	University of Birmingham, UK
Natasha Sharygina	University of Lugano, Switzerland
Nian-Ze Lee	National Taiwan University, Taiwan
Ning Luo	University of Illinois Urbana-Champaign, USA
Ondřej Lengál	Brno University of Technology, Czech Republic
Pablo Castro	Universidad Nacional de Río Cuarto - CONICET, Argentina
Pavithra Prabhakar	Kansas State University, USA
Peter Müller	ETH Zurich, Switzerland
Philipp Ruemmer	University of Regensburg, Germany
Qinxiang Cao	Shanghai Jiao Tong University, China
Ravi Mangal	Colorado State University, USA

Rayna Dimitrova	CISPA Helmholtz Center for Information Security, Germany
Roderick Bloem	Graz University of Technology, Austria
S. Akshay	Indian Institute of Technology Bombay, India
S. Krishna	Indian Institute of Technology Bombay, India
Shaobo He	Amazon Web Services, USA
Shibashis Guha	Tata Institute of Fundamental Research, India
Soham Chakraborty	TU Delft, Netherlands
Stefan Leue	University of Konstanz, Germany
Stefan Zetzsche	Amazon Web Services, UK
Stephen F. Siegel	University of Delaware, USA
Subhajit Roy	Indian Institute of Technology Kanpur, India
Sylvie Putot	Ecole Polytechnique, France
Sébastien Bardin	CEA List, Université Paris Saclay, France
Tachio Terauchi	Waseda University, Japan
Tatjana Petrov	University of Trieste, Italy
Thomas Wahl	Trusted Science and Technology, Inc., USA
Tim King	Amazon Web Services, USA
Timos Antonopoulos	Yale University, USA
Tom van Dijk	University of Twente, Netherlands
Tomas Vojnar	Masaryk University, Czech Republic
Vijay Ganesh	Georgia Tech, USA
Viktor Kunčak	EPFL, Switzerland
Wenxi Wang	University of Virginia, USA
William Hallahan	Binghamton University, USA
Xi (James) Zheng	Macquarie University, Australia
Yakir Vizel	Technion, Israel
Yedi Zhang	National University of Singapore, Singapore
Yu-Fang Chen	Academia Sinica, Taiwan
Yuting Wang	Shanghai Jiao Tong University, China
Yuxin Deng	East China Normal University, China
Yuyang Sang	Alibaba Cloud, USA

Artifact Evaluation Committee

Abdalrhman Mohamed	Stanford University, USA
Abhishek Kr Singh	National University of Singapore, Singapore
Adwait Godbole	UC Berkeley, USA
Akshatha Shenoy	Università della Svizzera italiana, Switzerland
Alejandro Hernández-Cerezo	Complutense University of Madrid, Spain
Ameer Hamza	Florida State University, USA

Amit Samanta	University of Utah, USA
Anna Becchi	Fondazione Bruno Kessler, Italy
Annelot Bosman	Universiteit Leiden, Netherlands
Avaljot Singh	University of Illinois Urbana-Champaign, USA
Avraham Raviv	Bar Ilan University, Israel
Benjamin F. Jones	Amazon Web Services, USA
Bruno Andreotti	Federal University of Minas Gerais, Brazil
Calvin Chau	Technische Universität Dresden, Germany
Cayden Codel	Carnegie Mellon University, USA
Chenyu Zhou	University of Southern California, USA
Christoph Weinhuber	University of Oxford, UK
Clara Rodríguez-Núñez	Universidad Complutense de Madrid, Spain
Daniel Ajeleye	University of Colorado, Boulder, USA
Diptarko Roy	University of Birmingham, UK
Ehsan Kafshdar Goharshady	Institute of Science and Technology, Austria
Enrico Magnago	Amazon Web Services, Germany
Filip Cano	Graz University of Technology, Austria
Filip Macák	Brno University of Technology, Czech Republic
Filipe de Arruda	Universidade Federal de Pernambuco, Brazil
Florian Sextl	TU Wien, Austria
Frédéric Recoules	CEA LIST, France
Geunyeol Yu	Pohang University of Science and Technology, South Korea
Guangyu Hu	Hong Kong University of Science and Technology, China
Hichem Rami Ait-El-Hara	Université Paris-Saclay, France
Idan Refaeli	Hebrew University of Jerusalem, Israel
Jacqueline Mitchell	University of Southern California, USA
Jaime Arias	CNRS, LIPN, Université Sorbonne Paris Nord, France
Jiong Yang	Georgia Institute of Technology, USA
Joseph Tafese	University of Waterloo, Canada
Kadiray Karakaya	Paderborn University, Germany
Konstantin Britikov	University of Lugano, Switzerland
Konstantin Kueffner	Institute of Science and Technology, Austria
Leni Aniva	Stanford University, USA
Lutz Klinkenberg	RWTH Aachen University, Germany
Mahboubeh Samadi	Tehran Institute for Advanced Studies, Iran
Mahyar Karimi	Institute of Science and Technology, Austria
Marek Chalupa	Institute of Science and Technology, Austria
Mário Pereira	NOVA School of Science and Technology, Portugal

Mathias Fleury	University of Freiburg, Germany
Mehrdad Karrabi	Institute of Science and Technology, Austria
Miguel Isabel	Complutense University of Madrid, Spain
Mihai Nicola	Stevens Institute of Technology, USA
Mihály Dobos-Kovács	Budapest University of Technology and Economics, Hungary
Mikael Mayer	Amazon Web Services, USA
Muqsit Azeem	Technical University of Munich, Germany
N. Ege Saraç	Institute of Science and Technology, Austria
Neea Rusch	Augusta University, USA
Nicolas Koh	Princeton University, USA
Omar Inverso	Gran Sasso Science Institute, Italy
Omkar Tuppe	IIT Bombay, India
Omri Isac	Hebrew University of Jerusalem, Israel
Oyendrila Dobe	Amazon Web Services, USA
Pablo Gordillo	Complutense University of Madrid, Spain
Patrick Trentin	Amazon Web Services, USA
Pei-Wei Chen	UC Berkeley, USA
Peixin Wang	Nanyang Technological University, Singapore
Philipp Kern	Karlsruhe Institute of Technology, Germany
Pinhan Zhao	University of Michigan, USA
Po-Chun Chien	LMU Munich, Germany
Rajarshi Roy	University of Oxford, UK
Sankalp Gambhir	EPFL, Switzerland
Sascha Klüppelholz	Technische Universität Dresden, Germany
Shantanu Kulkarni	IIT Bombay, India
Simon Guilloud	EPFL, Switzerland
Stefan Zetzsche	Amazon Web Services, UK
Timo Lang	Huawei Ireland Research Center, Ireland
Xuan Xie	University of Alberta, Canada
Yanju Chen	University of California, Santa Barbara, USA
Yannik Schnitzer	University of Oxford, UK
Yibo Dong	East China Normal University, China
Yizhak Elboher	Hebrew University of Jerusalem, Israel
Yogev Shalmon	Technion, Israel
Yuning Wang	Rutgers University, USA
Yusen Su	University of Waterloo, Canada
Zhengyang John Lu	University of Waterloo, Canada
Zhiyang Chen	University of Toronto, Canada
Zunchen Huang	CWI, Netherlands

Additional Reviewers

Abha Chaudhary
Adam Husted Kjelstrøm
Adam Rogalewicz
Alejandro Luque-Cerpa
Alejandro Villoria Gonzalez
Alex Ozdemir
Alexander Bork
Alexander C. Wilton
Alexander Stekelenburg
Andoni Rodriguez
Andrew Reynolds
Anja Petkovic Komel
Anton Varonka
Antonina Skurka
Antonio Casares
Arend-Jan Quist
Áron Ricardo Perez-Lopez
Arshia Rafieioskouei
Ashwani Anand
Benedikt Maderbacher
Benjamin Monmege
Che Cheng
Chia-Hsuan Su
Christian Lidström
Christina Gehnen
Christophe Chareton
Christopher Brix
Christopher Watson
Corto Mascle
Cruise Song
Daniela Kaufman
David Boetius
Dimitrios Thanos
Fabio Mogavero
Faezeh Labbaf
Felix Stutz
Filip Cano
Gianluca Redondi
Grigory Fedyukovich
Grégoire Menguy
Hangcheng Cao
Henrik Wachowitz
Igor Walukiewicz

Irmak Saglam
Iwo Kurzidem
Jan Martens
Jannick Strobel
Jasper Nalbach
Jia Hu
Jingyi Mei
Jinhua Wu
Johannes Haring
Joonhwan Yoo
Konstantin Britikov
Ling Zhang
Lutz Klinkenberg
Marc Farreras I Bartra
Marek Jankola
Marian Lingsch-Rosenfeld
Marvin Brieger
Massimo Benerecetti
Mathias Preiner
Matthew Davis
Matthias Kettl
Matthieu Bovel
Matthieu Lemerre
Michal Hečko
Milad Rabizadeh
Min Wu
Mingyu Huang
Muhammad Mahmoud
Pengzhi Xing
Pierre Ganty
Piyush Jha
Po-Chun Chien
Pranshu Gaba
Prithwish Jana
Rachel Cleaveland
Rafael Dewes
Raffael Senn
Ritam Raha
Robert Mensing
Roy Hermanns
Satya Prakash Nayak
Simon Guilloud
Steef Hegeman

Stefan Pranger
Subhajit Bandopadhyay
Thomas Hader
Thomas Lemberger
Tian-Fu Chen
Timm Spork
Tobias Winkler
Tomas Kolarik
Tomáš Dacík
Tzu-Han Hsu
Valentin Promies
Xieting Chu
Xin Hong
Xinyuan Qian
Yanis Sellami
Yicheng Ni
Yizhou Mao
Zhengyang Lu
Zhengyu Li
Zihao Li

Keynote Talks

Through the Looking Glass: Semantic Analysis of Neural Networks

Corina Păsăreanu

Carnegie Mellon University, USA

Abstract. Neural networks are known for their lack of transparency, making them difficult to understand and analyze. In this talk, we explore methods designed to interpret, formally analyze, and even shape the internal representations of neural networks using human-understandable abstractions. We review recent techniques including the use of vision-language models to investigate perception modules, the application of probing and steering vectors to identify vulnerabilities in code models, and an axiomatic approach for validating mechanistic interpretation of transformer models.

Bio. Corina Păsăreanu is an ACM Fellow working at NASA Ames. She is affiliated with KBR and Carnegie Mellon University's CyLab. Her research interests include model checking, symbolic execution, compositional verification, AI safety, autonomy, and security. She is the recipient of several awards, including an ETAPS Test of Time Award and an ACM Impact Paper Award. She has served as Program/General Chair for several conferences, including CAV in 2015, and more recently ICSE in 2025. More information can be found on her website: https://www.andrew.cmu.edu/user/pcorina/.

Cedar: A New Language for Expressive, Fast, Safe, and Analyzable Authorization

Emina Torlak

Amazon Web Services and University of Washington, USA

Abstract. Authorization is the problem of deciding who has access to what in a multi-user system. Every cloud-based application has to solve this problem, from photo sharing to online banking to health care. This talk presents Cedar, a new language for authorization that is designed to be ergonomic, fast, safe, and analyzable by reduction to SMT. Cedar's simple and intuitive syntax supports common authorization use-cases with readable policies, naturally expressing concepts from role-based, attribute-based, and relation-based access control models. Cedar's policy structure enables authorization requests to be decided quickly. Its policy validator uses optional typing to help policy writers avoid mistakes, but not get in their way. Cedar's design has been finely balanced to allow for a sound, complete, and decidable logical encoding, which enables precise policy analysis, e.g., to ensure that policy refactoring preserves existing permissions. We have implemented Cedar in Rust and used Lean to formally verify important properties of its design. Cedar is used at scale in Amazon Verified Permissions and Amazon Verified Access, and it is freely available at https://github.com/cedar-policy.

Bio. Emina Torlak is a Senior Principal Scientist at Amazon Web Services and an Affiliate Professor at the University of Washington. Emina works on new languages and tools for program verification and synthesis. She received her Bachelors (2003), Masters (2004), and Ph.D. (2009) degrees from MIT. Emina is the creator of Rosette and Kodkod, and leads the development of Cedar. Rosette is a solver-aided language that powers verification and synthesis tools for all kinds of systems, from radiation therapy control to Linux JIT compilers. Kodkod is a solver for relational logic, used widely in tools for software analysis and design. Cedar is an expressive, fast, and analysable language for authorization, used at scale at Amazon Web Services and beyond. Emina is a recipient of the Robin Milner Young Researcher Award (2021), NSF Career Award (2017), Sloan Research Fellowship (2016), and the AITO Dahl-Nygaard Junior Prize (2016).

Side Channel Secure Software: A Hardware Question

Roderick Bloem

Graz University of Technology, Austria

Abstract. We will present a method to prove the absence of power side channels in systems that are protected using masking. Power side channels may allow attackers to discover secret information by measuring electromagnetic emanations from a chip. Masking is a countermeasure to hide secrets by duplication and addition of randomness. We will discuss how to formally prove security against power side channel techniques for circuits. We will then move on to software running on a CPU, where hardware details can have surprising effects. We will present some vulnerabilities on a small CPU and how to fix them, and we will talk about contracts that take side channels into account.

Bio. Roderick Bloem is a professor at Graz University of Technology. He received his M.Sc. degree in Computer Science from Leiden University, the Netherlands, in 1996, and his Ph.D. degree in Computer Science from the University of Colorado at Boulder in 2001. From 2002 until 2008, he was an Assistant at Graz University of Technology, Graz, Austria. From 2008, he has been a full professor of Computer Science at the same university. He is a co-editor of the *Handbook of Model Checking* and has published over 140 peer reviewed papers in formal verification, reactive synthesis, Safe AI, and security.

References

1. Bloem, R., Gigerl, B., Gourjon, M., Hadzic, V., Mangard, S., Primas, R.: Power contracts: provably complete power leakage models for processors. In: Yin, H., Stavrou, A., Cremers, C., Shi, E. (eds.) Proceedings of the 2022 ACM SIGSAC Conference on Computer and Communications Security, CCS 2022, Los Angeles, CA, USA, 7–11 November 2022. pp. 381–395. ACM (2022). https://doi.org/10.1145/3548606.3560600
2. Bloem, R., Gross, H., Iusupov, R., Könighofer, B., Mangard, S., Winter, J.: Formal verification of masked hardware implementations in the presence of glitches. In: Nielsen, J., Rijmen, V. (eds.) EUROCRYPT 2018. LNCS, vol. 10821, pp. 321–353. Springer, Cham (2018). https://doi.org/10.1007/978-3-319-78375-8_11

3. Hadzic, V., Bloem, R.: COCOALMA: a versatile masking verifier. In: Formal Methods in Computer Aided Design, FMCAD 2021, New Haven, CT, USA, 19–22 October 2021, pp. 1–10. IEEE (2021). https://doi.org/10.34727/2021/ISBN.978-3-85448-046-4_9
4. Haring, J., Hadzic, V., Bloem, R.: Closing the gap: Leakage contracts for processors with transitions and glitches. IACR Trans. Cryptogr. Hardw. Embed. Syst. 2024(4), 110–132 (2024). https://doi.org/10.46586/TCHES.V2024.I4.110-132

Contents – Part I

Data Structure Verification

Verifying Tree-Manipulating Programs via CHCs 3
   Marco Faella and Gennaro Parlato

Automated Verification of Monotonic Data Structure Traversals in C 29
   Matthew Sotoudeh

Arithmetizing Shape Analysis 56
   Sebastian Wolff, Ekanshdeep Gupta, Zafer Esen, Hossein Hojjat,
   Philipp Rümmer, and Thomas Wies

Raven: An SMT-Based Concurrency Verifier 81
   Ekanshdeep Gupta, Nisarg Patel, and Thomas Wies

Fifteen Years of Viper 107
   Marco Eilers, Malte Schwerhoff, Alexander J. Summers, and Peter Müller

Model Checking

Efficient Probabilistic Model Checking for Relational Reachability 127
   Lina Gerlach, Tobias Winkler, Erika Ábrahám, Borzoo Bonakdarpour,
   and Sebastian Junges

Verifying PETSc Vector Components Using CIVL 148
   Venkata Dhavala, Jan Hückelheim, Paul D. Hovland,
   and Stephen F. Siegel

Compositional Abstraction for Timed Systems with Broadcast
Synchronization 162
   Hanyue Chen, Miaomiao Zhang, and Frits Vaandrager

The rIC3 Hardware Model Checker 185
   Yuheng Su, Qiusong Yang, Yiwei Ci, Tianjun Bu, and Ziyu Huang

HornStr: Invariant Synthesis for Regular Model Checking as Constrained
Horn Clauses 200
   Hongjian Jiang, Anthony W. Lin, Oliver Markgraf, Philipp Rümmer,
   and Daniel Stan

Infinite-State Liveness Checking with rlive 215
   Alessandro Cimatti, Alberto Griggio, Christopher Johannsen,
   Kristin Yvonne Rozier, and Stefano Tonetta

Deeply Optimizing the SAT Solver for the IC3 Algorithm 237
   Yuheng Su, Qiusong Yang, Yiwei Ci, Yingcheng Li, Tianjun Bu,
   and Ziyu Huang

Property Directed Reachability with Extended Resolution 258
   Andrew Luka and Yakir Vizel

Introducing Certificates to the Hardware Model Checking Competition 281
   Nils Froleyks, Emily Yu, Mathias Preiner, Armin Biere,
   and Keijo Heljanko

BTOR2-SELECT: Machine Learning Based Algorithm Selection
for Hardware Model Checking 296
   Zhengyang Lu, Po-Chun Chien, Nian-Ze Lee, Arie Gurfinkel,
   and Vijay Ganesh

Cryptography and Security

Automated Verification of Consistency in Zero-Knowledge Proof Circuits 315
   Jon Stephens, Shankara Pailoor, and Isil Dillig

Integer Reasoning Modulo Different Constants in SMT 339
   Elizaveta Pertseva, Alex Ozdemir, Shankara Pailoor, Alp Bassa,
   Sorawee Porncharoenwase, Işil Dillig, and Clark Barrett

Structural Operational Semantics for Functional and Security Verification
of Pipelined Processors 363
   Robert J. Colvin and Roger C. Su

Relational Hoare Logic for Realistically Modelled Machine Code 389
   Denis Mazzucato, Abdalrhman Mohamed, Juneyoung Lee,
   Clark Barrett, Jim Grundy, John Harrison, and Corina S. Păsăreanu

Correction to: Efficient Probabilistic Model Checking for Relational
Reachability C1
   Lina Gerlach, Tobias Winkler, Erika Ábrahám, Borzoo Bonakdarpour,
   and Sebastian Junges

Author Index 415

Data Structure Verification

Verifying Tree-Manipulating Programs via CHCs

Marco Faella[1](✉) and Gennaro Parlato[2]

[1] University of Naples Federico II, Naples, Italy
m.faella@unina.it
[2] University of Molise, Pesche, Isernia, Italy
gennaro.parlato@unimol.it

Abstract. Programs that manipulate tree-shaped data structures often require complex, specialized proofs that are difficult to generalize and automate. This paper introduces a unified, foundational approach to verifying such programs. Central to our approach is the *knitted-tree encoding*, modeling each program execution as a tree structure capturing input, output, and intermediate states. Leveraging the compositional nature of knitted-trees, we encode these structures as constrained Horn clauses (CHCs), reducing verification to CHC satisfiability. To illustrate our approach, we focus on *memory safety* and show how it naturally leads to simple, modular invariants.

1 Introduction

Ensuring automatic or semi-automatic verification of programs that manipulate dynamic memory (heaps) presents numerous challenges. First, heap can grow unboundedly in size and store unbounded data, requiring expressive logics to capture intricate invariants, preconditions, and postconditions. Next, dynamic shape changes complicate the maintenance of structural constraints, such as binary search tree ordering or balance. Aliasing further obscures these constraints and breaks invariants. Unbounded recursion and loops, common in tree algorithms, add complexity by making termination reasoning non-trivial. Finally, incomplete or missing specifications often force verifiers to infer properties on-the-fly, and integrating various verification techniques (e.g., SMT-solving, abstract interpretation, and interactive theorem proving) remains a nontrivial task.

This paper presents a foundational approach for automated analysis of heap-manipulating programs, particularly those involving tree data structures. By combining automata and logic-based methods, we reduce verification to checking satisfiability of constrained Horn clauses (CHCs). This reduction allows us to capitalize on advancements in CHC solvers [3,16]. We demonstrate our approach on the *memory safety problem*, ensuring that no execution causes crashes (e.g., null-pointer dereferences, use-after-free, or illegal frees) or nontermination.

The core of our methodology maps an entire program execution π on an input data tree T into a single tree data structure called a **knitted-tree**. This structure encapsulates the input, output, and all intermediate configurations of π. Its underlying tree, or *backbone*, is derived from T by adding a fixed number of inactive nodes to allow dynamic node allocation. Each node is labeled by a sequence of records, or *frames*, connected in a global linear sequence called the *lace*, where consecutive frames may belong to the same node or adjacent nodes, resembling a knitting tree. Each frame describes changes to the associated node (e.g., pointer updates) and records the current program state, preserving the backbone's original structure while also representing the final heap that may differ graph-wise. However, the knitted-tree's parameters – the number of extra nodes added to the backbone and the number of frames per node – may not capture every possible execution, potentially excluding some from our analysis.

```
        pointer head, prev, cur, tmp
        int key
 0 :    cur :− head ;
 1 :    while (cur ≠ nil && cur → val ≠ key) do
 2 :        tmp :− cur → next ;
 3 :        cur → next :− prev ;
 4 :        prev :− cur ;
 5 :        cur :− tmp ;
        od ;
 6 :    if (cur ≠ nil) then    We found the key
 7 :        tmp :− cur → next ;
 8 :        head → next :− tmp ; Rewind for head
 9 :        head :− cur ;  Rewind for cur
        else
10 :        head :− prev ;
        fi ;
11 :    exit ;
```

Fig. 1. Running example.

Example. We illustrate our encoding method with a simple program shown in Fig. 1 that manipulates a singly linked list, specifically designed to highlight the key features of our encoding methodology. The program takes a list of integers with *head* pointing to the first node and a value stored in *key*. It reverses the list up to and including the first node containing the key, then appends the remaining nodes. For example, given the input list $1 \to 2 \to 3 \to 4 \to 5$ and $key = 3$, the output list is: $3 \to 2 \to 1 \to 4 \to 5$. The knitted-tree corresponding to this program execution is shown in Fig. 2.

The knitted-tree's structure matches the input list. The label of each node is displayed next to it, with the lace being depicted by red arrows and numbers. In our example, the lace starts at the frame with ordinal 1 of node u_1, takes two local steps to the frames with ordinals 2 and 3, then moves to the frame numbered 4 in node u_2, and so on. Note that consecutive frames in the lace either belong to the same node, or to adjacent nodes. Due to space constraints, only a selection of the information contained within each frame is displayed.

Our encoding's main innovation is how it handles pointer fields and variables:

1. an update to a pointer field is stored in its node;
2. an update to a pointer variable is stored in the node it points to.

For example, the lace's first frame includes the event $\langle head :- \mathbf{here} \rangle$, indicating that *head* initially points to the first node of the input structure. This initial assignment is implicit. The second frame corresponds to the execution of $cur :- head$ at line 0. According to rule 2, when a pointer is dereferenced, it may be necessary to traverse the lace backward to find its latest assignment, a process called *rewinding*. In our example, the first rewinding occurs at line 8 when the current value of *head* is needed. In the knitted-tree, frame 15 in node

u_4 reaches line 8, but since the label of u_4 does not contain information about $head$, rewinding is triggered. Frames 16 and 17 are then added to the lace to go back to node u_1, where $head$ currently points, and frame 18 in u_1 reports the effect of the instruction at line 8, consisting in the event $\langle next :\!\!- tmp \rangle$.

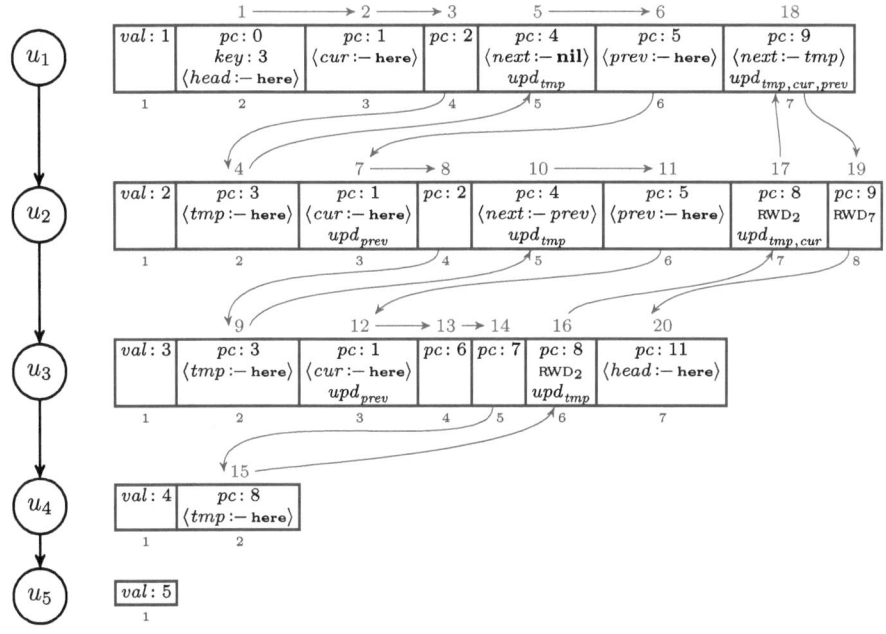

Fig. 2. A knitted-tree of the program in Fig. 1 on the input list $1 \to 2 \to 3 \to 4 \to 5$ and $key = 3$. Blue numbers below the frames represent positions within the label, while red numbers and arrows refer to the lace. (Color figure online)

Knitted-trees enjoy **compositional properties** that are essential for our CHC-based verification method. These properties allow subtree replacement: a subtree rooted at node v in one knitted-tree can be swapped with a subtree rooted at node v' in another, provided that the labels of v and v' satisfy a local consistency condition expressible in a quantifier-free first-order data theory. This replacement rule enables us to build a CHC system whose minimal model precisely captures the set of valid node labels for the knitted-trees, allowing the detection of any reachable error configuration during execution. If our analysis reports no errors, we need to check whether any execution was truncated by the current choice of parameters. With a small modification, the same CHC system can also reveal whether that is the case; if so, we can increase the parameters to encompass more executions. While verification is undecidable and may not terminate, our method significantly broadens the class of programs and properties amenable to automation. In particular, executions of several well-known programs are fully captured by knitted-trees with suitable parameters, as they traverse nodes a bounded number of times and admit simple CHC solutions.

Organization of the Paper. The rest of the paper is structured as follows. Section 2 introduces notation and definitions. Section 3 defines the knitted-tree encoding, and Section 4 details its compositionality. Section 5 describes our reduction to the CHC satisfiability problem, presents a sound procedure to solve the memory safety problem, and analyzes the structure and complexity of the required invariants. Section 6 reviews related work, and Section 7 concludes with future directions. An extended version of this paper [25] includes substantial supplementary material.

2 Preliminaries

Let $\mathbb{N}$ denote the natural numbers that include 0, $[i, j] \stackrel{\text{def}}{=} \{k \in \mathbb{N} \mid i \leq k \leq j\}$, and $[j] \stackrel{\text{def}}{=} [1, j]$.

Trees. A k-ary tree T is a finite, prefix-closed subset of $[k]^*$, where $k \in \mathbb{N}$. Each element in T is a *node*, with the *root* represented by the empty string ε. The tree *edge relation* is implicit: for any $d \in [k]$, if both v and $v.d$ are nodes in T, then $(v, v.d)$ is an *edge*, making $v.d$ the dth child of v, and v the *parent* of $v.d$.

Data Signatures. A *data signature* $\mathcal{S}$ consists of pairs $\{id_i : type_i\}_{i \in [n]}$, defining field names and their types (e.g., integers, Booleans $\mathbb{B}$). An *evaluation* ν of $\mathcal{S}$ assigns each field name id a type-specific value, denoted $\nu.id$. The *language* of $\mathcal{S}$, $L(\mathcal{S})$, is the set of all its evaluations.

Data Trees. A *data tree* with data signature $\mathcal{S}$, or $\mathcal{S}$-*tree*, is a pair (T, λ) where T is a tree and λ is a labeling function $\lambda : T \to L(\mathcal{S})$ that assigns an evaluation of $\mathcal{S}$ to each node $t \in T$. To simplify notation, the value of a field id at node t can be written as $t.id$ when λ is clear from the context.

Constrained Horn Clauses. We use standard first-order logic (FOL) with equality [46] and formulas from a many-sorted, quantifier-free first-order theory $\mathcal{D}$ that includes program-relevant data types like arithmetic, reals, and arrays. We refer to $\mathcal{D}$ as the *data theory*.

Definition 1. *Let R be a set of uninterpreted fixed-arity relation symbols representing unknowns. A **constrained Horn clause** (CHC) is a formula of the form $H \leftarrow C \wedge B_1 \wedge \cdots \wedge B_n$ where: (i) C is a constraint, a formula of the data theory $\mathcal{D}$ without symbols from R; (ii) each B_i is an application $r(v_1, \ldots, v_k)$ of a relation symbol $r \in R$ to first-order variables $v_1, \ldots, v_k$; (iii) H (the* head*) is either false, or an application $r(v_1, \ldots, v_k)$ as in B_i. A CHC is a* fact *if its body is only C and a* query *if its head is false. A finite set $\mathcal{C}$ of CHCs forms a* system *by conjoining all CHCs with free variables universally quantified. We assume the constraint semantics is predefined as a structure.* □

A CHC system $\mathcal{S}$ with relation symbols R is *satisfiable* if there exists an interpretation for each $r \in R$ that makes all clauses in $\mathcal{S}$ valid. Any such interpretation is called a *solution* of $\mathcal{S}$. The CHC *satisfiability problem* is the computational task of determining whether a given system $\mathcal{S}$ of CHCs is satisfiable.

Each CHC system $\mathcal{S}$ has a unique minimal model under subset ordering,[1] computable as the fixed-point of an operator derived from its clauses [19,36]. We use this fixed-point semantics to ensure the correctness of our reductions.

Heap-Manipulating Programs. The *heap* is essential for dynamic memory allocation, allowing memory blocks (*nodes*) to be allocated and deallocated during execution. We assume that nodes have a single data field and one or more pointer fields. A *specific heap state* is defined as follows.

Definition 2. *A* **heap** *is a tuple* $\mathcal{H} = (N, \mathcal{S}, \mathbf{data}, PF)$ *where*

- N *is a finite set of nodes, including a unique element* **nil** *for free memory.*
- $\mathcal{S}$ *is a data signature defining the type of data that can be stored in a node.*
- $\mathbf{data} : N \setminus \{\mathbf{nil}\} \to L(\mathcal{S})$ *is a map modeling the data field of each node.*
- PF *is a finite sequence of distinct pointer fields, each defined as a function of type* $(N \setminus \{\mathbf{nil}\}) \to N$, *representing the pointers of each node.* □

We define k as the number of pointer fields. For example, in Fig. 1, $PF = \{next\}$ and $k = 1$, while for binary trees use $PF = \{left, right\}$ and $k = 2$.

Syntax. The syntax of our programming language is shown on the right. Programs begin with declarations of pointer and data variables, followed by labeled instructions. Instructions include assignments, control flow, and heap operations. Data assignments are of the form

$$\begin{aligned}
Program &\stackrel{\text{def}}{=} decl\ block \\
decl &\stackrel{\text{def}}{=} (\mathbf{pointer}\ id(,id)^*)^*\ (\mathbf{type}\ id(,id)^*)^* \\
block &\stackrel{\text{def}}{=} (pc : (ctrl\_stmt\ |\ heap\_stmt)\ ;)^+ \\
ctrl\_stmt &\stackrel{\text{def}}{=} d :\!\!-\ exp\ |\ d_{\text{bool}} :\!\!-\ heap\_cond\ |\ \mathbf{skip}\ |\ \mathbf{exit} \\
&\quad |\ \mathbf{if}\ cond\ \mathbf{then}\ block\ \mathbf{else}\ block\ \mathbf{fi} \\
&\quad |\ \mathbf{while}\ cond\ \mathbf{do}\ block\ \mathbf{od}\ |\ \mathbf{goto}\ pc \\
heap\_stmt &\stackrel{\text{def}}{=} \mathbf{new}\ p\ |\ \mathbf{free}\ p\ |\ p :\!\!-\ \mathbf{nil}\ |\ p :\!\!-\ q\ |\ p :\!\!-\ q \to pfield \\
&\quad |\ p \to pfield :\!\!-\ \mathbf{nil}\ |\ p \to pfield :\!\!-\ q \\
&\quad |\ p \to dfield :\!\!-\ exp\ |\ d :\!\!-\ p \to dfield \\
exp &\stackrel{\text{def}}{=} d\ |\ f(exp, \ldots, exp) \\
cond &\stackrel{\text{def}}{=} r(exp, \ldots, exp)\ |\ (\neg)?\ heap\_cond \\
heap\_cond &\stackrel{\text{def}}{=} p = q\ |\ p = \mathbf{nil}\ |\ p \to pfield = q\ |\ p \to pfield = \mathbf{nil}
\end{aligned}$$

$d :\!\!-\ exp$, where d is a data variable set to the value of the data expression exp. Data expressions are built from data variables and combined using function symbols of the data theory $\mathcal{D}$. Control flow instructions include **skip**, **exit**,

---

[1] See [19] for logic programs and [36, Prop. 4.1] for constr. logic programs (or CHCs).

if-then-else statements, and **while** loops. Boolean conditions (*cond*) are exclusively either *data conditions* or *heap conditions*. Heap conditions can be assigned to a Boolean variable with $d_{\text{bool}} :- heap\_cond$, integrating them into Boolean theory. Heap operations include **new** p (creates a new node, initializes its fields to undefined or **nil**, and assigns it to p) and **free** p (deallocates the node pointed by p and sets all pointers pointing to the node to **nil**). We also allow assignment and retrieval of pointer fields (i.e., $pfield \in PF$) and data fields (i.e., $dfield \in \mathcal{S}$). Programs are **valid** if they are well-formed, type-correct, uniquely labeled, and terminate with **exit**. Figure 1 shows an example of a program.[2] For a program P, PC_P, PV_P, and DV_P represent program counters, pointer variables, and data variables, respectively. The function *succ* defines the successor(s) of a program counter. Statements can have from 0 to 2 successors: most statements have a single successor, denoted by $succ(pc)$; the **exit** statement has no successor; **if-then-else** and **while** have two successors based on a Boolean condition: $succ(pc, true)$ and $succ(pc, false)$. The language does not support function calls directly: non-recursive calls are inlined, and limited recursion, typical in tree-based algorithms, can be simulated (see the extended version [25] for details).

Semantics. A program P operates on a specialized heap called a *P-heap*, that includes all its pointers and data. A *configuration* of P is a tuple $(\mathcal{H}, \nu_p, \nu_d, pc)$ consisting of a P-heap, an evaluation of the pointer variables, an evaluation of the data variables, and next instruction label. Focusing on tree-based programs, a configuration c is *initial* if it meets the following conditions:

- $\mathcal{H}$ is *isomorphic* to a data tree $\mathcal{T}$ via a bijection ρ that maps each node in $\mathcal{H}$ to a node in $\mathcal{T}$, such that for all nodes x, y in $\mathcal{H}$ and $i \in |PF|$, $y = pf_i(x)$ iff $\rho(y) = \rho(x).i$, where pf_i is the i-th pointer field in PF. We refer to $\mathcal{T}$ as the data tree of c, and may use $\mathcal{T}$ in place of $\mathcal{H}$.
- ν_p maps the first pointer variable declared in P, conventionally denoted by $\hat{p}$, to the $\mathcal{H}$ node corresponding to the root of $\mathcal{T}$ and maps the other pointer variables to **nil**.
- ν_d assigns each variable a non-deterministic value.
- pc is the label of the first statement in P.

A *transition* $c \rightarrow_P c'$ in P occurs by executing the instruction at pc using standard semantics unless noted otherwise. If pc is an **exit** statement, c becomes a *final configuration* with no further transitions. Attempting to dereference or deallocate a **nil** pointer makes c an *error configuration*. An **execution** π of P is a (possibly infinite) sequence of configurations $c_0 c_1 \ldots$ where: **(i)** c_0 is initial, and **(ii)** $c_{i-1} \rightarrow_P c_i$ for each $i \in \mathbb{N}$. A finite π that ends in a final or error configuration is a *terminating* or *buggy execution*, respectively. We aim to solve the following (undecidable) problem:

Problem 1. A program P is *memory safe* if all its executions terminate without reaching an error configuration. The **memory safety problem** asks whether a given program is memory safe.

---

[2] The **while** condition goes beyond our syntax but is easily translatable into it.

3 Knitted-Trees: Representing Executions as Data Trees

Our approach to solving the memory safety problem uses the knitted-tree encoding, which models a program execution as a single data tree capturing inputs, outputs, and intermediate configurations.

We first fix notation and assumptions. The encoding uses two parameters $m, n \in \mathbb{N}$, explained later. For simplicity, we assume that heap nodes have a single data field *val* of an arbitrary type $\mathcal{D}$. We consider a fixed program P and omit it from most notations and statements. Let π be an execution of P starting from an initial configuration c_0, where $\mathcal{T} = (T, \lambda)$ is a k-ary data tree of c_0 with signature $\mathcal{S}^{\Sigma} = \{val : \mathcal{D}\}$, and $\hat{p}$ points to the root of $\mathcal{T}$. The encoding maps π to a set of data trees $kt(\pi, m, n)$, called the (m, n)-*knitted-trees* of π. We now describe a generic knitted-tree $\mathcal{K} = (K, \mu)$ from the set $kt(\pi, m, n)$.

The Backbone. The *backbone* K of $\mathcal{K}$ is the smallest tree such that: (i) the input tree T is a subset of K ($T \subset K$), (ii) all nodes from T are internal nodes in K, (iii) each internal node of K has degree $k + m$, and (iv) K has at least one internal node. Note that, in the special case where T is empty, the backbone K is a full tree of height 2, consisting of a root and its $k + m$ children.

Each node of K represents a distinct heap node. Initially, all nodes in T are active, and the rest are inactive; freeing an active node makes it inactive.

The Node Signature. The backbone of a knitted-tree depends only on the input data tree and parameters m, n, independent of the execution it represents. Each backbone node is labeled with a sequence of *frames* (a *log*) tracking changes along π. Frames form a doubly linked list called *lace*, to maintain chronological order and enable bidirectional navigation. When consecutive operations involve different nodes, frames are inserted along the backbone path connecting them. The data signature $\mathcal{S}_{\mathcal{K}}$ of an (m, n)-knitted-tree is the following:

$$\mathcal{S}_{\mathcal{K}} = \left\{ \begin{array}{ll} avail^i : \mathbb{B}, & \text{Is this frame available?} \\ active^i : \mathbb{B}, & \text{Is this node allocated?} \\ val^i : \mathcal{D}, & \text{Current value of this node's data field} \\ pc^i : PC_P, & \text{Program counter} \\ \{d^i : \mathcal{D}_d\}_{d \in DV_P}, & \text{Current value of the data variables} \\ \{upd_p^i : \mathbb{B}\}_{p \in PV_P}, & \text{Has } p \text{ been updated since the frame } i-1? \\ \{isnil_p^i : \mathbb{B}\}_{p \in PV_P}, & \text{Is } p \text{ nil?} \\ event^i : Event, & \text{A pointer update, rewind, or error} \\ active\_child^i : \mathbb{B}^{k+m} & \text{Is each child allocated?} \\ next^i : Dir \times [2, n+1], & \text{Link to the next frame} \\ prev^i : Dir \times [2, n], & \text{Link to the previous frame} \end{array} \right\}_{i \in [n+1]},$$

where $Dir = \{-, \uparrow\} \cup [k+m]$ encodes the position of an adjacent frame relative to the reference frame. Each node's label, or *log*, has $n+1$ indexed frames in time order. Once a frame f in a log σ is named, its fields are referenced without the index (e.g., $f.pc$ instead of $\sigma.pc^i$). The last frame of a log handles *label overflow* (if more than n frames are needed), via the $(n+1)^{\text{th}}$ frame. The *prev* field holds a value from $Dir \times [n]$, since a frame with index $n+1$ has no successor. The *event* field holds an *event* taken from:

$$Event = \{\langle pfield :- p \rangle, \langle pfield :- \textbf{nil} \rangle, \langle p :- \textbf{here} \rangle \mid pfield \in PF, p \in PV_P\}$$
$$\cup \; \{\text{RWD}_i \mid i \in [n]\} \cup \{\text{RWD}_{i,p} \mid i \in [n], p \in PV_P\} \cup \{\text{NOP}, \text{ERR}, \text{OOM}\}.$$

The first group represents updates to pointer fields and variables. RWD_i and $\text{RWD}_{i,p}$ represent *lace rewinding* events. Other symbols denote the empty event (NOP), null-pointer dereference (ERR), and out-of-memory error (OOM) caused by excessive use of the statement **new**.

3.1 The Labeling Function

The labeling function μ of $\mathcal{K}$ is defined inductively on the length of π.

Base Case. π consists of an initial configuration, say $(\mathcal{T}, \nu_p, \nu_d, pc)$. We encode the input tree $\mathcal{T} = (T, \lambda)$ into the backbone by setting the first frame of each node $t \in K$ as follows:

$$\mu(t).avail^1 = false, \qquad \mu(t).active^1 = \begin{cases} true & \text{if } t \in T \\ false & \text{otherwise} \end{cases}$$

$$\mu(t).val^1 = \begin{cases} \lambda(t).val & \text{if } t \in T \\ \text{unspecified} & \text{otherwise} \end{cases} \qquad \mu(t).active\_child^1_j = \begin{cases} true & \text{if } t.j \in T \\ false & \text{otherwise.} \end{cases}$$

All other fields of the first frame are unspecified.

The root's *second* frame stores π's initial configuration: $\mu(\varepsilon).avail^2 = false$, $\mu(\varepsilon).prev^2 = (-, 2)$ (a self-loop), $\mu(\varepsilon).pc^2$ is the first statement's label in P, and $\mu(\varepsilon).isnil^2_q = true$ for all pointer variables q different from $\hat{p}$. If T is not empty, $\mu(\varepsilon).event^2 = \langle \hat{p} :- \textbf{here} \rangle$ and $\mu(\varepsilon).isnil^2_{\hat{p}} = false$; otherwise, $\mu(\varepsilon).event^2 = \text{NOP}$ and $\mu(\varepsilon).isnil^2_{\hat{p}} = true$. All other frames are marked as available. The root's second frame also copies *active*, *val*, and *active_child* from the first frame.

Inductive Case. We start with an overview of the encoding method, its properties, and the required notation. Let $\pi = \overline{\pi} c$, where c is a configuration and $\overline{\pi}$ is a non-empty execution. Assume that $\overline{\mathcal{K}} = (K, \overline{\mu})$ is a knitted-tree in $kt(\overline{\pi}, m, n)$. We define the labeling μ for π by extending the lace of $\overline{\mathcal{K}}$ based on the last instruction executed in π. To aid understanding, we list some invariants for all knitted-trees, providing an informal explanation for brevity.

The Lace. Besides individual node logs, we maintain a chronological order of all frames across all nodes. All the unavailable frames in the knitted-tree with index greater than 1 form a doubly linked list called the *lace* using the *next* and *prev* fields of the frames. The first frame in the lace is the root's second frame. Each frame is identified by a pair (u, i), where u is a node and $i \in [n+1]$ is the frame's index. A frame (v, j) is the *lace successor* of frame (u, i), denoted $(u, i) \rightarrow_{next} (v, j)$ (and (u, i) is the *lace predecessor* of (v, j), written $(v, j) \rightarrow_{prev} (u, i)$) if $i, j > 1$ and one of the following holds:

- $u = v$, $j = i + 1$, $\mu(u).next^i = (-, j)$, and $\mu(v).prev^j = (-, i)$;
- v is the lth child of u, $\mu(u).next^i = (l, j)$, and $\mu(v).prev^j = (\uparrow, i)$;
- u is the lth child of v, $\mu(u).next^i = (\uparrow, j)$, and $\mu(v).prev^j = (l, i)$.

Available frames' unspecified fields contribute to $kt(\pi, m, n)$'s non-determinism.

Properties of the Frame Fields. In our inductive definition, we obtain the knitted-tree for π by extending that of $\overline{\pi}$ by appending frames for π's final step. This helps us assign meanings to fields like upd_p, $isnil_p$, d, val, pc, and $active\_child$ for the unavailable frames. The upd_p flag tracks changes to the pointer p outside the current node: it is set to *true* in frame (u, i) (for $i > 1$) if p was assigned a non-**nil** value in the part of the lace between frames $(u, i-1)$ and (u, i) (excluding these frames). Thus, if frames $(u, i-1)$ and (u, i) are adjacent in the lace (i.e., $(u, i-1) \rightarrow_{next} (u, i)$, aka an *internal step*), all upd_p flags in (u, i) are *false*. The $isnil_p$ flag is *true* in a frame if $p =$ **nil** at that point in the execution. The $active\_child$ flags help track the allocation of the child nodes of the backbone. Other fields preserve their usual meanings.

Pushing a Frame. Appending a frame to a log involves: *(1)* finding the smallest index i with $avail^i$ is *true*, and *(2)* adding the new frame at position i. Hence, a log behaves like a stack, with the bottom frame at index 1 and the *top frame* being the highest-index frame where $avail$ is *false*.

Default Values for a Frame. Any frame pushed onto a log assumes default values unless specified otherwise. When pushing a frame f on a node u, default values come from the preceding frame in the lace, f^{prev}, or the frame below f in u's log, f^{below}. Note that f^{prev} and f^{below} can be the same. The default values for the fields of f are as follows: for all $p \in PV_P$ and $d \in DV_P$,

- $avail = false$, $event = \text{NOP}$, and $upd_p = false$;
- $active$ and val are copied from f^{below};
- $isnil_p$, d, and pc are copied from f^{prev};
- $active\_child_j$ is copied from $f^{\text{prev}}.active$ if f^{prev} belongs to the jth child of u; otherwise, it is copied from $f^{\text{below}}.active\_child_j$;
- $prev$ points to f^{prev};
- $next$ is unspecified and can take any value in different knitted-trees for the same execution.

Moreover, $f^{\text{prev}}.next$ is updated to point to f, eliminating the non-determinism of the $next$ field of the previous frame.

Despite the non-determinism in the $next$ field, identifying the last frame f in a lace can be done by checking f and its lace successor f'. Specifically, f is the last frame of the lace if f' is available or f' precedes f in the lace, which happens when field of $f'.prev$ does not point to f.

Henceforth, assume that $\overline{f}$ is the final lace last frame in $\overline{\mathcal{K}}$, located as the top frame of node $\overline{t}$. We first present the encoding of the statements that push a single new frame f on the current node $\overline{t}$. The fields of f are set to default values, except for those specified below.

Encoding of $p :-$ nil: $f.pc = succ(\overline{f}.pc)$ and $f.isnil_p = true$.

Encoding of $d :-$ exp: $f.pc = succ(\overline{f}.pc)$ and $f.d$ is set to the value of exp, with variables in DV_P evaluated using their values from $\overline{f}$.

Encoding of skip: $f.pc = succ(\overline{f}.pc)$.

The other statements may operate on different nodes in addition to $\overline{t}$. The main reasons to move to another node are to dereference a pointer or identify the node a pointer field refers to. To get this information, we *rewind the lace* by moving backward to find the most recent assignment to the relevant pointer. For example, to identify the node a pointer variable p points to, we rewind the lace until we find a frame with the event $\langle p :-$ **here**$\rangle$.

Lace Rewinding Function. To enable rewinding, we define the auxiliary function $find\_ptr(p, id)$, which takes a pointer $p \in PV_P$ and a frame ID and returns a sequence of frame IDs by traversing the lace backward from id, until the most recent assignment to p. The sequence uses *shortcuts*, including only the IDs where the lace moves between nodes and where such moves are *relevant* to track p, as indicated by the upd_p flags. For example, in Fig. 2, rewinding from frame 15 to resolve *head* gives the following:[3]

$$find\_ptr(head, (u_4, 2)) = find\_ptr(head, 15) = ((u_3, 2), (u_2, 2), (u_1, 2)) = (9, 4, 1).$$

Frames 9 and 4 have a predecessor that belongs to another node; moreover, they represent the earliest occurrence of their node in the lace. Contrast this with frame 12, which also follows a frame in another node, but is *not* in the sequence because 12 is not the first visit to u_3, and upd_{head} is false in 12. Frame 1 is included as the value of *head* in frame 15 was established in frame 1. Thus, rewinding from 15 adds frames 16, 17 and 18 for these IDs.

Null Pointer Dereference. If the instruction located at $\overline{f}.pc$ dereferences a pointer p, and p is **nil**, it indicates an error. Thus, if the flag $isnil_p$ is *true* in $\overline{f}$, we push a new frame with the event ERR onto the current node $\overline{t}$ to indicate a runtime error. We now present the encoding for the other types of statement.

Encoding of $p \rightarrow pfield :-$ nil. We rewind the lace to find the latest assignment to p. Let $(\overline{t}, \overline{i})$ be the identifier of $\overline{f}$, and $id_1 = (u_1, i_1), \ldots, id_l = (u_l, i_l)$ be the sequence $find\_ptr(p, (\overline{t}, \overline{i}))$. We push a new frame for each element of the sequence $id_1, \ldots, id_l$, to keep a faithful record of the movements necessary to simulate the current statement: for each $j \in [l-1]$, we push a frame onto u_j with the event RWD_{i_j}, without advancing the program counter. Finally, we push a frame f onto u_l with $f.pc = succ(\overline{f}.pc)$ and $f.event = \langle pfield :-$ **nil**$\rangle$.

Encoding of $p \rightarrow pfield :- q$. Same as the encoding for $p \rightarrow pfield :-$ **nil**, but the final frame's event is set to $\langle pfield :- q \rangle$.

---

[3] Using the global lace positions as frame IDs (red numbers in Fig. 2).

Encoding of $p := q$. If $isnil_q$ evaluates to $true$ in $\overline{f}$, we push a new frame onto $\overline{t}$ with $isnil_p$ set to $true$. Otherwise, a rewinding operation takes the lace to the node pointed by q, where we push a frame with $\langle p := \textbf{here} \rangle$. In either case, the last frame also updates the program counter.

Encoding of new p. Let j be the smallest index in $[k+1, k+m]$ such that $active\_child_j$ is $false$. If no such index exists, we push a frame on $\overline{t}$ with the event OOM, representing an out-of-memory error. Otherwise, the lace moves to the jth child of $\overline{t}$ and pushes a frame f there with $f.pc = succ(\overline{f}.pc)$, $f.event = \langle p := \textbf{here} \rangle$, $f.active = true$, and $f.isnil_p = false$.

Encoding of free p. A rewinding operation takes the lace to the node u pointed by p, where we push a frame f with $active = false$ and an updated pc. In the new frame, $isnil_q$ is set to $true$ for every pointer q that currently points at u, including p. To find such pointers, let (u, i) be the id of f. Then, q points at u if the log of u contains another frame (u, j) such that: $j < i$, (u, j) contains $\langle q := \textbf{here} \rangle$, and the upd_q flag is $false$ in all frames from $(u, j+1)$ to (u, i).

Encoding of $p := q \rightarrow pfield$. First, the lace moves to the node u pointed by q through a rewinding process. Then, we search in u's log for the most recent assignment to $pfield$. We look for the largest index i s.t. the frame (u, i) is in use and contains an event of the form $\langle pfield := \alpha \rangle$, for some α. If no such index exists, $pfield$ is interpreted as having its default value pointing to a child in the original input tree. We then distinguish the following cases:

[$\alpha = $ **nil**] We push a frame with $isnil_p = true$ on u.
[$\alpha = r$, **for some** $r \in PV_P$] If $isnil_r$ is $true$ in the current frame, the lace pushes a frame with $isnil_p = true$. Otherwise, the lace moves again to the node pointed by r, and there it pushes a frame with $\langle p := \textbf{here} \rangle$.
[**The log of** u **does not contain an explicit assignment to** $pfield$] If $pfield$ is the jth field in PF, $u.j \in T$, and $u.j$ is active (as encoded in the flag $active\_child_j$), the lace moves to $u.j$ and pushes a frame with event $\langle p := \textbf{here} \rangle$ there. Otherwise, a frame with $isnil_p = true$ is pushed on u.

The last pushed frame always updates the program counter.

Encoding Boolean Conditions and Control-Flow Statements. Data conditions are evaluated locally using variable values in the current frame $\overline{f}$. For heap conditions, we may need to traverse the lace. We focus on conditions of the form $p = q$, since others (e.g., $p \rightarrow pfield = q$) can be reduced to this form using auxiliary variables. To evaluate $p = q$, we first check the $isnil$ flags: if both pointers have their $isnil$ flags set to true, the condition is true; if the flags differ, it is false. If this is inconclusive, we rewind the lace to find an assignment to p or q. For example, upon finding $\langle p := \textbf{here} \rangle$ in frame (u, i), we search in u's log for the largest index $j < i$ where frame (u, j) has $\langle q := \textbf{here} \rangle$. If none exists, the condition is false. If found, the condition holds if q was unchanged between (u, j) and (u, i), verified via $\neg \bigvee_{l \in [j+1, i]} upd_q^l$. A new frame is then pushed, updating the program counter accordingly. The process is symmetric if $\langle q := \textbf{here} \rangle$ is found first.

Table 1. Summary of the encodings.

Statement	Movement	Information stored
$p \rightarrow \textit{pfield} := \mathbf{nil}$	Find p or fail	$\langle \textit{pfield} := \mathbf{nil} \rangle$
$p \rightarrow \textit{pfield} := q$	Find p or fail	$\langle \textit{pfield} := q \rangle$ or $\langle \textit{pfield} := \mathbf{nil} \rangle$
$p := q$	Find q	$\langle p := \mathbf{here} \rangle$ or set $\textit{isnil}_p$
$p := q \rightarrow \textit{pfield}$	Find q or fail, then find last assignment to $\textit{pfield}$	$\langle p := \mathbf{here} \rangle$ or set $\textit{isnil}_p$
$p \rightarrow \textit{val} := \textit{exp}$	Find p or fail	Update $\textit{val}$
$d := p \rightarrow \textit{val}$	Find p or fail	Update d
new p	Move to the first inactive child or fail	$\langle p := \mathbf{here} \rangle$ and set $\textit{active}$
free p	Find p or fail	Reset $\textit{active}$

On the Choice of Parameters m and n. Parameter m bounds the number of allocations: $m = 0$ for programs without allocations, while $m = 1$ is adequate for programs that insert a single new node. The parameter n limits the passes and instructions executed per node; while some programs need unbounded labels, typical tree-like algorithms work with moderate n (usually ≤ 10).

3.2 Relations with Program Executions

Our first result establishes that knitted-trees provide an accurate and faithful representation of program executions.

Theorem 1. *Given a program P and parameters m, n, $kt(\cdot, m, n)$ is computable. Moreover, there is a computable function exec such that, for any data tree $\mathcal{K}$ that is a knitted-tree of P, $\text{exec}(\mathcal{K})$ is an execution π of P s.t. $\mathcal{K} \in kt(\pi, m, n)$.*

Notice that the relation between executions π and knitted-trees $\mathcal{K}$ defined by $\mathcal{K} \in kt(\pi, m, n)$ is neither injective nor functional. It is not functional due to the non-determinism in the encoding. It is not injective because a knitted-tree ending in a label overflow represents only a prefix of an execution and thus relates to all executions sharing that prefix.

Exit Status of a knitted-tree. To distinguish how knitted-trees terminate, we introduce the notion of *exit status* for individual frames and for the entire knitted-tree. Each frame f of a knitted-tree is assigned one of five statuses in $\textit{ExStatus} = \{\mathbf{C}, \mathbf{E}, \mathbf{O}, \mathbf{M}, \mathbf{N}\}$, with the following meanings:

- Clean exit: The program counter (pc) of f points to an **exit** instruction.
- Runtime **E**rror: $f.\textit{event} = \text{ERR}$, indicating a null-pointer dereference.
- Label **O**verflow: The index of f in its label is $n+1$, indicating log overflow.

– Out of Memory: $f.event = \text{OOM}$, indicating a failed attempt to allocate a node with the **new** statement due to the absence of inactive nodes.
– None: Indicates that frame f is not a terminal frame.

A frame f is *terminal* if its status is not **None**. Indeed, the exit statuses different from **N** terminate the lace, hence only the last frame in the lace may have an exit status different from **N**. The *exit status* of a knitted-tree $\mathcal{K}$, denoted $exit(\mathcal{K})$, is the status of the last frame in its lace. The theorem below links knitted-tree's exit status to its corresponding executions.

Theorem 2. *For all executions π and $\mathcal{K} \in kt(\pi, m, n)$, the following holds:*

1. *If $exit(\mathcal{K}) = \mathbf{E}$, then π ends in an error configuration.*
2. *If π ends in an error configuration, then $exit(\mathcal{K}) \in \{\mathbf{E}, \mathbf{O}, \mathbf{M}\}$.*
3. *If π is infinite, then $exit(\mathcal{K}) = \mathbf{O}$.*

4 Properties of Knitted-Trees

Prefix of a knitted-tree. An (m,n)-knitted-tree is a knitted-tree associated with an execution π in $kt(\pi, m, n)$. A *prefix* of a knitted-tree $\mathcal{K}$ is a data tree obtained from $\mathcal{K}$ by truncating its lace at a frame f, setting $f'.avail$ to *true* for all subsequent frames, and leaving $f.next$ unconstrained.

Locality. For a label σ and $i \in \mathbb{N}$, we define $\sigma^{<i}$ (resp., $\sigma^{\leq i}$) as the label obtained by setting *avail* to true in all frames of σ with indices $\geq i$ (resp., $> i$).

The following lemma states that each new frame in a knitted-tree depends only on *local* information from neighboring nodes. We use $f_1 \equiv f_2$ to indicate that frames f_1 and f_2 differ only in their *next* field.

Lemma 1 (Locality). *There exist functions $Up, Down, Internal$ such that for logs $\sigma, \tau_1, \ldots, \tau_{k+m}$ of a node u and of its children in a knitted-tree prefix:*

– *For all steps $(u.j, b) \rightarrow_{next} (u, a)$ in the lace, it holds $\sigma^a \equiv Up(\tau_j^{\leq b}, j, \sigma^{<a})$.*
– *For all steps $(u, a) \rightarrow_{next} (u.j, b)$ in the lace, it holds $\tau_j^b \equiv Down(\sigma^{\leq a}, j, \tau_j^{<b})$.*
– *For all steps $(u, a) \rightarrow_{next} (u, a+1)$ in the lace, it holds $\sigma^{a+1} \equiv Internal(\sigma^{\leq a})$.*

Compositionality. Using the functions Up and $Down$ from Lemma 1, we define the predicate $consistent\_child(\tau, j, \sigma)$. This predicate is meant to check whether two logs σ and τ may belong to the same knitted-tree as the logs of a node and its jth child. Specifically, it verifies that all pairs of consecutive frames, linked by *next* and *prev*, with one frame belonging to τ and the other frame belonging to σ, adhere to the functions Up and $Down$. A detailed definition of $consistent\_child$ is in the extended version [25].

From $consistent\_child$ and knitted-tree prefix definitions, the next lemma follows, ensuring that $consistent\_child$ holds on all parent-child log pairs.

Lemma 2. *For all labels $\sigma, \tau \in L(\mathcal{S}_{\mathcal{K}})$ and indices $j \in [k+m]$, if there exists a knitted-tree prefix where σ and τ are the logs of a node and its jth child respectively, then $consistent\_child(\tau, j, \sigma)$ holds.*

The following lemma establishes a key property of *consistent_child* for our verification approach, enabling knitted-tree composition from different subtrees.

Lemma 3 (Compositionality). *Let $\sigma_1, \sigma_2 \in L(\mathcal{S}_\mathcal{K})$ be the logs of nodes t_1, t_2 in (m,n)-knitted-tree prefixes $\mathcal{K}_1, \mathcal{K}_2$. If consistent_child$(\sigma_2, j, \sigma_1)$ holds true for some $j \in [k+m]$, then there is an (m,n)-knitted-tree prefix $\mathcal{K}$ where σ_1 is the log of a node and σ_2 is the log of its jth child. Moreover, $\mathcal{K}$ is obtained by replacing the jth subtree of t_1 in $\mathcal{K}_1$ with the subtree rooted at t_2 in $\mathcal{K}_2$.*

Proof. Let $\mathcal{K}$ be the data tree obtained by replacing the subtree rooted at the jth child of t_1 in $\mathcal{K}_1$ with the subtree rooted at t_2 in $\mathcal{K}_2$. We prove that $\mathcal{K}$ is a knitted-tree prefix by induction on the number of pairs (a,b) where frames σ_1^a and σ_2^b are adjacent in the lace, each such pair representing an interaction between the parent's and the child's labels.

When the above number is zero, there are no interactions between t_1 and its jth child in $\mathcal{K}_1$. Let π_1 be an execution s.t. $\mathcal{K}_1$ is a prefix of a knitted-tree representing π_1. It is direct to show that $\mathcal{K}$ is a knitted-tree prefix for an execution π following the same steps as π_1, starting with the input tree of $\mathcal{K}$. Since π_1 never visits the jth child of t_1, and this subtree is the only difference between $\mathcal{K}_1$ and $\mathcal{K}$, π is a valid execution of P.

For the inductive case, consider the last interaction (a,b) between σ_1^a and σ_2^b. First, assume that such interaction is a step *up* from frame σ_2^b to σ_1^a. Let $\mathcal{K}_1'$ be derived from $\mathcal{K}_1$ by truncating its lace to end just before σ_1^a. Clearly, $\mathcal{K}_1'$ is still a knitted-tree prefix, and the modified label σ_1' of t_1 is obtained from σ_1 by removing the frames with index at least a, by setting their *avail* flags to true. We can now apply the inductive hypothesis to the labels σ_1' and σ_2, because we have removed one interaction between them. Hence, we can assume that there is a single knitted-tree prefix $\mathcal{K}'$ containing both labels as the logs of a parent and its jth child. We then obtain the desired knitted-tree prefix $\mathcal{K}$ from $\mathcal{K}'$ by reintroducing the sequence of frames removed from $\mathcal{K}_1$. We need to prove that adding those frames respects all rules of knitted-trees. The correctness of the first added frame, σ_1^a, is ensured by *consistent_child*(σ_2, j, σ_1), because it applies the function *Up* to all upward interactions between σ_2 and σ_1. In turn, Lemma 1 ensures that adhering to that function is sufficient to establish the correctness of the next frame. Subsequent frames can be reintroduced due to the unchanged surroundings. Lemma 1 ensures that no other information is relevant.

The other case to prove is when the last interaction is a step *down* from the parent's frame σ_1^a to the child's frame σ_2^b. Define σ_2' as the label obtained from σ_2 with the frames of indices b and above removed. Similar to the previous case, we apply the inductive hypothesis to the shortened label σ_2' and its shortened knitted-tree prefix $\mathcal{K}_2'$, resulting in a knitted-tree prefix $\mathcal{K}'$. We then reintroduce the frames removed from $\mathcal{K}_2$ into $\mathcal{K}'$. The correctness of the first reintroduced frame is ensured by *consistent_child* checking the function *Down* on every downward interaction. The subsequent reintroduced frames are still valid because there are no steps returning to the parent of t_2, and their surroundings remain unchanged from $\mathcal{K}_2$. □

Example 1. Consider the knitted-tree in Fig. 2, with node labels $\sigma_1, \ldots, \sigma_5$, and another knitted-tree of the same program on the input list $7 \to 8 \to 9 \to 3 \to 10 \to 11 \to 12$ and $key = 3$. Let v_4 be the node of the second knitted-tree with value 3, and let τ_4 be its label. By inspecting the second knitted-tree, one can observe that the occupied frames of τ_4 (i.e., those with $avail = false$) contain the same information as the occupied frames of σ_3. Therefore, $consistent\_child(\tau_4, 1, \sigma_2)$ holds, and by Lemma 3, the two knitted-trees can be composed at nodes u_2-v_4 to construct a knitted-tree for the input list $1 \to 2 \to 3 \to 10 \to 11 \to 12$.

5 Reasoning About Knitted-Trees with CHCs

We introduce a CHC system $\mathcal{C}_{kt}(P, m, n)$ for a program P with parameters $m, n \in \mathbb{N}$. It employs a single uninterpreted relation symbol, $\mathbf{Lab}(\sigma)$, where σ matches the data signature $\mathcal{S}_{\mathcal{K}}$ of knitted-trees, ensuring the following:

Theorem 3. *In the minimal model of $\mathcal{C}_{kt}(P, m, n)$, $\mathbf{Lab}(\sigma)$ holds for a label σ iff σ labels a node in some (m, n)-knitted-tree prefix $\mathcal{K}$ of P.*

We define $\mathcal{C}_{kt}(P, m, n)$ using the knitted-tree rules constructing constructing partial knitted-trees (impractical for enumerating all knitted-trees). Instead, we rely on the compositionality lemma (Lemma 3), which states that two consistent labels imply the existence of a knitted-tree where those labels are logs of an internal node and one of its children, and the locality lemma (Lemma 1) to extend the lace involving these nodes. This lemma entails that constructing a knitted-tree involves adding frames to node logs so that any two consecutive frames belong to the same node or to neighboring backbone nodes. We use this property in the CHC system, employing independent CHCs to simulate adding a single frame. In the CHC system, we simulate adding a single frame via *Up* (upward), *Down* (downward), and *Internal* (within the same log). We define predicates $\Psi_{Down}(\sigma, j, \tau_j, f), \Psi_{Up}(\tau_j, j, \sigma, f)$, and $\Psi_{Internal}(\sigma, f)$ to constrain logs accordingly, with f as the resulting frame.

Figure 3 details the CHCs of $\mathcal{C}_{kt}(P, m, n)$. While describing each CHC, we establish the "only if" direction of Theorem 3, by induction on the number of CHC applications needed to insert σ into the minimal interpretation of $\mathbf{Lab}$. The proof of the "if" direction appears in the extended version [25].

Before detailing the CHCs, we introduce some notation. Let $\sigma \in L(\mathcal{S}_{\mathcal{K}})$ and $i \in \mathbb{N}$. The formula $len(\sigma, i)$ is true if all frames with indices in $[i]$ are unavailable and all other frames are available, i.e., $len(\sigma, i) \stackrel{def}{=} \neg \sigma^i.avail \land \bigwedge_{j=i+1}^{n+1} \sigma^j.avail$. With an abuse of notation, we write $\sigma^{<i}$ in a CHC as a shorthand for a fresh variable θ, together with the conjunct $\bigwedge_{\ell \in [i-1]}(\theta^\ell = \sigma^\ell) \land \bigwedge_{\ell \in [i, n+1]} \theta^\ell.avail$.

CHCs **I** and **II** ensure that $\mathbf{Lab}$ includes labels of all knitted-trees of 0-length executions of P, forming the base case for the "only if" direction of Theorem 3, since both are facts. CHC I defines non-root labels with all but the first frame available, and consistent $active/active\_child$, while CHC II defines root labels by disabling the first two frames and using $start(\sigma)$ for the second frame, as per the base-case labeling (Section 3.1).

(I)	$\mathbf{Lab}(\sigma) \leftarrow len(\sigma, 1) \wedge \textit{first\_frame}(\sigma^1)$	*Initializing non-root nodes*
(II)	$\mathbf{Lab}(\sigma) \leftarrow len(\sigma, 2) \wedge start(\sigma)$	*Initializing the root node*
(III)	$\mathbf{Lab}(\sigma) \leftarrow len(\sigma, i) \wedge \mathbf{Lab}(\sigma^{<i}) \wedge \Psi_{Internal}(\sigma^{<i}, \sigma^i)$	*Internal step*
	A step from the jth child to its parent	
(IV)	$\mathbf{Lab}(\sigma) \leftarrow\ len(\sigma, i) \wedge \mathbf{Lab}(\sigma^{<i}) \wedge \mathbf{Lab}(\tau)$	
	$\wedge\ consistent\_child(\tau, j, \sigma^{<i}) \wedge \Psi_{Up}(\tau, j, \sigma^{<i}, \sigma^i)$	
	A step from a node to its jth child	
(V)	$\mathbf{Lab}(\tau) \leftarrow len(\tau, i) \wedge \mathbf{Lab}(\sigma) \wedge \mathbf{Lab}(\tau^{<i})$	
	$\wedge\ consistent\_child(\tau^{<i}, j, \sigma) \wedge \Psi_{Down}(\sigma, j, \tau^{<i}, \tau^i)$	
(VI)	$\bot \leftarrow \mathbf{Lab}(\sigma) \wedge label\_exit(\sigma, Ex)$	*Lace ends with status in Ex*

Fig. 3. CHCs (I)-(V) form the CHC system $\mathcal{C}_{kt}(P, m, n)$, while the CHC system $\mathcal{C}_{ex}(\mathcal{I})$ includes all the CHCs in the figure. Here, $i \in [2, n]$ and $j \in [k + m]$.

The remaining CHCs extend each node's log frame by frame, following the inductive knitted-tree label definition. For Theorem 3 ("only if" direction), we assume inductively that the body labels satisfy the claim, i.e., they label a node in a (m, n)-knitted-tree prefix, and show that the head label does too.

CHC III handles *internal steps*, where σ^i follows σ^{i-1} in the lace. Here, $\mathbf{Lab}(\sigma^{<i})$ ensures that $\sigma^{<i}$ labels a node in an (m, n)-knitted-tree prefix, while $\Psi_{Internal}(\sigma^{<i}, \sigma^i)$ constrains σ^i to encode the next internal step, as per Lemma 1.

CHC IV handles cases where the lace extends with a new frame pushed to the parent of the previous frame, typically during a rewind phase. The predicate *consistent_child* ensures that $\sigma^{<i}$ and τ belong to the same knitted-tree prefix, as the log of a parent and its jth child (Lemma 3). Then, Ψ_{Up} extends the lace by adding a frame to $\sigma^{<i}$, following the topmost frame of τ.

CHC V handles the reverse of CHC IV, where the current lace extends from a parent to its jth child. Using Ψ_{Down}, it ensures that τ_j correctly extends $\tau_j^{<i}$ with a new frame for the latest step.

The Exit Status Problem. We present a method to check whether a program can lead to a memory safety error via an execution that can be represented by an (m, n)-knitted-tree. This reduces to solving a CHC system: if unsatisfiable, such an execution exists. We formalize this as the following decision problem.

Problem 2. An instance of the **exit status problem** is a tuple (P, m, n, Ex), where P is a program, $m, n \in \mathbb{N}$, and Ex is a set of exit statuses excluding $\mathbf{N}$. The exit status problem asks whether there exists an (m, n)-knitted-tree of P whose exit status is in Ex.

We solve the exit status problem using the CHC system $\mathcal{C}_{\text{ex}}(\mathcal{I})$ (Fig. 3), which includes (i) all CHCs from $\mathcal{C}_{\text{kt}}(P, m, n)$, crucial for Theorem 3, and (ii) a single query, CHC VI, to check for a knitted-tree corresponding to a program execution with an exit status in Ex. Combining Theorem 3 with the definition of CHC VI yields the main result of this section.

Theorem 4. *Let $\mathcal{I}$ be an instance of the exit-status problem. Then, $\mathcal{I}$ admits a positive answer if and only if the CHC system $\mathcal{C}_{\text{ex}}(\mathcal{I})$ is unsatisfiable.*

5.1 Verifying Memory Safety

We begin by establishing two key theorems linking the exit status problem to memory safety, forming the basis for our method's correctness.

Theorem 5. *If the answer to the exit status problem $(P, m, n, \{\mathbf{E}\})$ is positive, then the answer to the memory safety for P is negative.*

Theorem 6. *If the answer to the exit status problem $(P, m, n, \{\mathbf{O}, \mathbf{M}, \mathbf{E}\})$ is negative, then the answer to the memory safety problem for P is positive.*

Algorithm MEMSAFETY: We outline our algorithm on the right. We are given a program P and initial values m_0 and n_0 for the two parameters m and n of knitted-trees. Verification starts by solving the problem EXITSTATUS$(P, m, n, \{\mathbf{E}\})$ to detect null-pointer dereference errors. If the answer is positive, by Theorem 5 P violates memory safety. Otherwise, memory safety is not guaranteed, as the current values of m and n may not cover all executions. To address this, we solve EXITSTATUS(P, m, n, X) with:

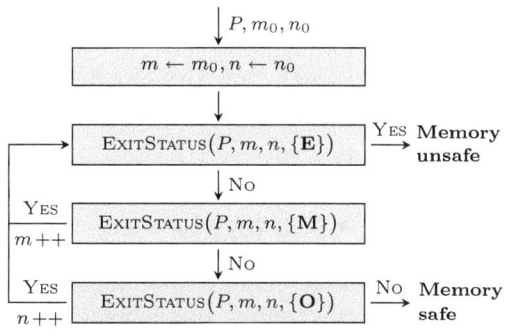

1. $X = \{\mathbf{M}\}$ to detect out-of-memory failure from **new** allocations, and
2. $X = \{\mathbf{O}\}$ to detect label overflow errors.

If both instances are negative, Theorem 6 ensures that P is memory-safe. Otherwise, we increment m or n to broaden coverage and restart. This may continue indefinitely if the semi-algorithm never terminates (due to undecidability) or no parameter values suffice to establish memory safety.

Theorem 7. *Algorithm MEMSAFETY is a sound solution to the memory safety problem, i.e., if it terminates, it yields the correct answer.*

5.2 Invariant Structure

In this section, we examine the essential properties that a solution to the CHC system presented in Fig. 3 must satisfy, with particular emphasis on the structure and complexity of the required invariants. To ground the discussion, we refer to the running example introduced in Section 1 and shown in Fig. 1, representative of a broad class of procedures manipulating tree data structures. This example highlights both the challenges and the recurring structural patterns encountered in the synthesis of suitable invariants for CHC systems.

The minimal model of **Lab** for logs of knitted trees (from lists containing the *key* value) results in labels that can be classified as follows:

Initial Node: the first node of the lists is shaped as u_1 (see Fig. 2).
Intermediate Nodes: one or more nodes like u_2 (depending on the length of the input list).
Target Node: the node containing the special value, u_3.
Post-Target Node: the node immediately following the special value, u_4.
Subsequent Nodes: remaining nodes, similar to u_5.

Labels associated with nodes of the same category differ only in their data fields (*val* and *key*), while all other fields (e.g., program counters) are equal across nodes (for instance, nodes like u_2 consistently exhibit program counter 3 in the second frame). Only the data fields *val* and *key* depend on the input list, and their constraints are simple:

- In each node, both *val* and *key* retain the same value across all frames.
- In an intermediate node, $val \neq key$;
- In the target node (u_3), $val = key$.

Input lists that do not contain the *key* induce additional node types, subject to analogous constraints. In Section 7, we briefly outline how the regularities discussed above could be exploited in an implementation of our framework.

6 Related Work

Our work is related to many works in the literature in different ways. Here we focus on those that seem to be the closest to the results presented in this paper.

Our approach uses CHC engines for backend analysis, similar to other verification methods [12,21,23,24,26,28–30,32,34,38,39,50]. CHCs serve as an intermediate language, allowing us to focus on proof rules while solvers implement algorithms within a standard framework. A primary challenge is encoding heap-allocated mutable data structures. While array theory is often used (e.g., [15,40]), it can result in complex CHCs. Our approach uses simple theories for basic data types, avoiding array theory unless necessary. Traditional heap program analysis often relies on abstractions like shape analysis [59] to scale. Refinement types and invariants can be used to transform complex data structures, avoiding array theory (e.g. [10,37,51,58]). This can lead to over-approximation in CHCs and false positives by replacing heap operations with local object assertions, potentially missing global invariants but enabling efficient verification when local invariants suffice. A recent proposal suggests using an SMT-LIB theory of heaps for CHCs to standardize heap data-structure representation [20].

Our technique relates to tree automata, automata with auxiliary storage, and bounded tree-width graphs representing their executions. It also relates to Courcelle's theorem (proof), which reduces analysis to tree automata emptiness [27]. Inspired by Alur and Madhusudan's nested words to represent pushdown automata executions [2], and their extensions for multistack and distributed automata by Madhusudan and Parlato [44], we represent tree-manipulating program executions as knitted-trees, where nodes are frames and edges are *next* and *prev* frame fields. Similar to La Torre et al. [41] for multistack pushdown automata, our approach provides tree decompositions with a bounded tree width. Instead of using tree automata emptiness for reachability analysis, we leverage CHC solvers to enable a tree automata-like method with enhanced data reasoning. Additionally, like Heizmann et al. [31], we use automata for program analysis but replace counterexample-guided abstraction refinement with precise knitted-tree representations and CHC solvers for approximation and refinement.

Our work extends decidable methods for bounded-pass heap-manipulating programs by supporting a broader range of properties, potentially at the cost of undecidability. Mathur et al. [49] achieve decidable memory safety for forest-like initial heaps and single-pass traversals, building on uninterpreted coherent programs [47, 48]. They handle memory freeing but leave support for more complex postconditions for future work. Alur and Černý [1] reduce assertion checking of single-pass list-processing programs to data string transducers, achieving decidability with a single advancing variable. This approach is less flexible than Mathur et al.'s, as it doesn't address memory safety or heap shape changes and is limited to data ordering and equality without handling explicit memory freeing.

Heap verification has been extensively studied using decidable logics such as first-order logic with reachability [43], LISBQ in the HAVOC tool [42], and fragments of separation logic [7, 18, 55]. Some approaches interpret bounded tree width data structures on trees [33, 45]. While these logics are often restrictive, other methods handle undecidable cases using heuristics, lemma synthesis, and programmer annotations [4–6, 8, 9, 11, 13, 14, 17, 35, 52–54, 56, 60]. In contrast, our knitted-tree encoding promotes a separation of concerns, offloading the algorithmic burden to the underlying CHC solver.

7 Conclusions and Directions for Future Research

We presented a foundational, compositional approach to verifying programs that manipulate tree data structures. By modeling executions as knitted-trees and encoding them as CHCs, verification reduces to CHC satisfiability. This enables modular reasoning and supports simple invariants. Overall, our method offers a uniform and scalable framework for automating the verification of a broad class of tree-manipulating programs.

Future Work. Our approach opens multiple research directions.

Efficient Implementation. Labels are currently handled by a single predicate, **Lab**. Performance can be improved via case splitting—encoding enumerated fields into predicate names—to simplify invariants (see Section 5.2). Moreover, precomputing all possible configurations of the enumerated fields arising in every possible frame of the program, together with (an overapproximation of) the within-node and across-neighbor adjacency relations between frames would produce a larger set of significantly simplified CHCs that enforce consistency of the data with the enumerated structure of the knitted tree.

Beyond Memory Safety. Full correctness requires verifying structural and functional properties. Using *symbolic data-tree automata* (SDTAs), which integrate well with CHC-based verification [22], we can formally specify pre/postconditions–e.g., that inputs form a red-black tree and outputs a sorted list. Preconditions are easy to encode as they involve only the first frame of each node in the knitted-tree, while postconditions require more effort due to the complexity of encoding the output heap within the knitted-tree structure. For set-like trees, it is also important to verify that operations such as insertion, deletion, and search preserve key invariants, which can be checked via knitted-tree logs. Termination can be verified by ensuring that labels do not overflow.

Deductive Verification. Our methodology is particularly suited for deductive verification of procedures with linear-time complexity—i.e., those that traverse each node a bounded number of times. We aim to develop a verification framework where program correctness is established by breaking down verification conditions into preconditions and postconditions for code segments, with each segment provably executable in linear time. This would bridge the gap between our approach and classical deductive verification techniques.

More Structures. Our approach naturally extends to programs manipulating multiple data structures, especially those with bounded treewidth. While there is no general method for all combinations, many can be handled with suitable encodings. For example, a program that traverses a red-black tree in-order and inserts values into a singly linked list can be modeled using knitted trees with bounded labels; our method can then verify that the output list contains the input values in non-increasing order. Some scenarios require more inventive encodings. For instance, checking equality of two lists via separate dummy roots leads to unbounded log growth. Instead, modeling both as a single list of paired elements keeps the log size bounded and tractable.

As noted in the previous section, the graphs induced by knitted-trees have bounded treewidth, suggesting applicability to a broad range of structures, including arrays, doubly-linked lists, trees with parent pointers, and, more generally, any structure with bounded treewidth and a canonical tree decomposition.

Program Synthesis. We also plan to explore syntax-guided synthesis (SyGuS) of tree-manipulating code. By expressing correctness properties as SDTAs and reducing synthesis to CHC solving, we aim to generate correct-by-construction procedures, extending recent work on synthesis from specifications [57].

Acknowledgements. We sincerely thank the anonymous reviewers for their insightful feedback and constructive suggestions, which significantly improved the quality of this paper. This work was partially supported by INdAM-GNCS Project 2025 - CUP: E53C24001950001, and the MUR projects SOP (Securing sOftware Platforms, CUP: H73C22000890001) as part of the SERICS project (n. PE00000014 - CUP: B43C22000750006), and MUR project FAIR (Future AI Research, CUP: E63C22002150007).

Disclosure of Interests. The authors have no competing interests to declare that are relevant to the content of this article.

References

1. Alur, R., Cerný, P.: Streaming transducers for algorithmic verification of single-pass list-processing programs. In: Ball, T., Sagiv, M. (eds.) Proceedings of the 38th ACM SIGPLAN-SIGACT Symposium on Principles of Programming Languages, POPL 2011, Austin, TX, USA, January 26-28, 2011, pp. 599–610. ACM (2011). https://doi.org/10.1145/1926385.1926454
2. Alur, R., Madhusudan, P.: Adding nesting structure to words. J. ACM **56**(3), 16:1–16:43 (2009). https://doi.org/10.1145/1516512.1516518
3. Angelis, E.D., Hari Govind, K.H.: CHC-COMP 2022: competition report. Electron. Proc. Theor. Comput. Sci. **373**, 44–62 (2022). https://doi.org/10.4204/eptcs.373.5
4. Banerjee, A., Barnett, M., Naumann, D.A.: Boogie meets regions: a verification experience report. In: Shankar, N., Woodcock, J. (eds.) Verified Software: Theories, Tools, Experiments, Second International Conference, VSTTE 2008, Toronto, Canada, October 6-9, 2008. Proceedings. Lecture Notes in Computer Science, vol. 5295, pp. 177–191. Springer, Berlin, Heidelberg (2008). https://doi.org/10.1007/978-3-540-87873-5_16
5. Banerjee, A., Naumann, D.A., Rosenberg, S.: Regional logic for local reasoning about global invariants. In: Vitek, J. (ed.) ECOOP 2008 - Object-Oriented Programming, 22nd European Conference, Paphos, Cyprus, July 7-11, 2008, Proceedings. Lecture Notes in Computer Science, vol. 5142, pp. 387–411. Springer, Berlin, Heidelberg (2008). https://doi.org/10.1007/978-3-540-70592-5_17
6. Banerjee, A., Naumann, D.A., Rosenberg, S.: Local reasoning for global invariants, part I: region logic. J. ACM **60**(3), 18:1–18:56 (2013). https://doi.org/10.1145/2485982
7. Berdine, J., Calcagno, C., O'Hearn, P.W.: A decidable fragment of separation logic. In: Lodaya, K., Mahajan, M. (eds.) FSTTCS 2004: Foundations of Software Technology and Theoretical Computer Science, 24th International Conference, Chennai, India, December 16-18, 2004, Proceedings. Lecture Notes in Computer Science, vol. 3328, pp. 97–109. Springer, Berlin, Heidelberg (2004). https://doi.org/10.1007/978-3-540-30538-5_9
8. Berdine, J., Calcagno, C., O'Hearn, P.W.: Smallfoot: Modular automatic assertion checking with separation logic. In: de Boer, F.S., Bonsangue, M.M., Graf, S., de Roever, W.P. (eds.) Formal Methods for Components and Objects, 4th International Symposium, FMCO 2005, Amsterdam, The Netherlands, November 1-4, 2005, Revised Lectures. Lecture Notes in Computer Science, vol. 4111, pp. 115–137. Springer, Berlin, Heidelberg (2005). https://doi.org/10.1007/11804192_6

9. Berdine, J., Calcagno, C., O'Hearn, P.W.: Symbolic execution with separation logic. In: Yi, K. (ed.) Programming Languages and Systems, Third Asian Symposium, APLAS 2005, Tsukuba, Japan, November 2-5, 2005, Proceedings. Lecture Notes in Computer Science, vol. 3780, pp. 52–68. Springer, Berlin, Heidelberg (2005). https://doi.org/10.1007/11575467_5
10. Bjørner, N.S., McMillan, K.L., Rybalchenko, A.: On solving universally quantified horn clauses. In: Logozzo, F., Fähndrich, M. (eds.) Static Analysis - 20th International Symposium, SAS 2013, Seattle, WA, USA, June 20-22, 2013. Proceedings. Lecture Notes in Computer Science, vol. 7935, pp. 105–125. Springer, Berlin, Heidelberg (2013). https://doi.org/10.1007/978-3-642-38856-9_8
11. Calcagno, C., Distefano, D., O'Hearn, P.W., Yang, H.: Compositional shape analysis by means of bi-abduction. J. ACM **58**(6), 26:1–26:66 (2011). https://doi.org/10.1145/2049697.2049700
12. Champion, A., Chiba, T., Kobayashi, N., Sato, R.: Ice-based refinement type discovery for higher-order functional programs. J. Autom. Reason. **64**(7), 1393–1418 (2020)
13. Chin, W., David, C., Nguyen, H.H., Qin, S.: Automated verification of shape, size and bag properties via user-defined predicates in separation logic. Sci. Comput. Program. **77**(9), 1006–1036 (2012). https://doi.org/10.1016/J.SCICO.2010.07.004
14. Chu, D., Jaffar, J., Trinh, M.: Automatic induction proofs of data-structures in imperative programs. In: Grove, D., Blackburn, S.M. (eds.) Proceedings of the 36th ACM SIGPLAN Conference on Programming Language Design and Implementation, Portland, OR, USA, June 15-17, 2015, pp. 457–466. ACM (2015). https://doi.org/10.1145/2737924.2737984
15. De Angelis, E., Fioravanti, F., Pettorossi, A., Proietti, M.: Program verification using constraint handling rules and array constraint generalizations. Fundam. Informaticae **150**(1), 73–117 (2017). https://doi.org/10.3233/FI-2017-1461
16. De Angelis, E., K., H.G.V.: CHC-COMP 2023: competition report. CoRR abs/2404.14923 (2024). https://doi.org/10.48550/ARXIV.2404.14923
17. Distefano, D., O'Hearn, P.W., Yang, H.: A local shape analysis based on separation logic. In: Hermanns, H., Palsberg, J. (eds.) Tools and Algorithms for the Construction and Analysis of Systems, 12th International Conference, TACAS 2006 Held as Part of the Joint European Conferences on Theory and Practice of Software, ETAPS 2006, Vienna, Austria, March 25 - April 2, 2006, Proceedings. Lecture Notes in Computer Science, vol. 3920, pp. 287–302. Springer, Berlin, Heidelberg (2006). https://doi.org/10.1007/11691372_19
18. Echenim, M., Iosif, R., Peltier, N.: Unifying decidable entailments in separation logic with inductive definitions. In: Platzer, A., Sutcliffe, G. (eds.) Automated Deduction - CADE 28 - 28th International Conference on Automated Deduction, Virtual Event, July 12-15, 2021, Proceedings. Lecture Notes in Computer Science, vol. 12699, pp. 183–199. Springer, Cham (2021). https://doi.org/10.1007/978-3-030-79876-5_11
19. van Emden, M.H., Kowalski, R.A.: The semantics of predicate logic as a programming language. J. ACM **23**(4), 733–742 (1976)
20. Esen, Z., Rümmer, P.: An SMT-LIB theory of heaps. In: Déharbe, D., Hyvärinen, A.E.J. (eds.) Proceedings of the 20th Internal Workshop on Satisfiability Modulo Theories co-located with the 11th International Joint Conference on Automated Reasoning (IJCAR 2022) part of the 8th Federated Logic Conference (FLoC 2022), Haifa, Israel, August 11-12, 2022. CEUR Workshop Proceedings, vol. 3185, pp. 38–53. CEUR-WS.org (2022)

21. Esen, Z., Rümmer, P.: TRICERA: verifying C programs using the theory of heaps. In: Griggio, A., Rungta, N. (eds.) 22nd Formal Methods in Computer-Aided Design, FMCAD 2022, Trento, Italy, October 17-21, 2022, pp. 380–391. IEEE (2022). https://doi.org/10.34727/2022/ISBN.978-3-85448-053-2_45
22. Faella, M., Parlato, G.: Reasoning about data trees using CHCs. In: Shoham, S., Vizel, Y. (eds.) Computer Aided Verification - 34th International Conference, CAV 2022, Haifa, Israel, August 7-10, 2022, Proceedings, Part II. Lecture Notes in Computer Science, vol. 13372, pp. 249–271. Springer, Cham (2022). https://doi.org/10.1007/978-3-031-13188-2_13
23. Faella, M., Parlato, G.: Reachability games modulo theories with a bounded safety player. In: Williams, B., Chen, Y., Neville, J. (eds.) Thirty-Seventh AAAI Conference on Artificial Intelligence, AAAI 2023, Thirty-Fifth Conference on Innovative Applications of Artificial Intelligence, IAAI 2023, Thirteenth Symposium on Educational Advances in Artificial Intelligence, EAAI 2023, Washington, DC, USA, February 7-14, 2023, pp. 6330–6337. AAAI Press (2023). https://doi.org/10.1609/AAAI.V37I5.25779
24. Faella, M., Parlato, G.: A unified automata-theoretic approach to LTLf modulo theories. In: Endriss, U., Melo, F.S., Bach, K., Diz, A.J.B., Alonso-Moral, J.M., Barro, S., Heintz, F. (eds.) ECAI 2024 - 27th European Conference on Artificial Intelligence, 19-24 October 2024, Santiago de Compostela, Spain - Including 13th Conference on Prestigious Applications of Intelligent Systems (PAIS 2024). Frontiers in Artificial Intelligence and Applications, vol. 392, pp. 1254–1261. IOS Press (2024). https://doi.org/10.3233/FAIA240622
25. Faella, M., Parlato, G.: Verifying tree-manipulating programs via CHCs (2025). https://arxiv.org/abs/2505.14092
26. Fedyukovich, G., Ahmad, M.B.S., Bodík, R.: Gradual synthesis for static parallelization of single-pass array-processing programs. In: Proceedings of the 38th ACM SIGPLAN Conference on Programming Language Design and Implementation, PLDI 2017, Barcelona, Spain, June 18-23, 2017, pp. 572–585. ACM (2017)
27. Flum, J., Grohe, M. (eds): Parameterized Complexity Theory. TTCSAES, Springer, Heidelberg (2006). https://doi.org/10.1007/3-540-29953-X
28. Garoche, P., Kahsai, T., Thirioux, X.: Hierarchical state machines as modular horn clauses. In: Proceedings 3rd Workshop on Horn Clauses for Verification and Synthesis, HCVS@ETAPS 2016, Eindhoven, The Netherlands, 3rd April 2016. EPTCS, vol. 219, pp. 15–28 (2016)
29. Gurfinkel, A.: Program verification with constrained horn clauses (invited paper). In: Shoham, S., Vizel, Y. (eds.) Computer Aided Verification - 34th International Conference, CAV 2022, Haifa, Israel, August 7-10, 2022, Proceedings, Part I. Lecture Notes in Computer Science, vol. 13371, pp. 19–29. Springer, Cham (2022). https://doi.org/10.1007/978-3-031-13185-1_2
30. Gurfinkel, A., Kahsai, T., Komuravelli, A., Navas, J.A.: The SeaHorn verification framework. In: Kroening, D., Păsăreanu, C.S. (eds.) CAV 2015. LNCS, vol. 9206, pp. 343–361. Springer, Cham (2015). https://doi.org/10.1007/978-3-319-21690-4_20
31. Heizmann, M., Hoenicke, J., Podelski, A.: Software model checking for people who love automata. In: Sharygina, N., Veith, H. (eds.) Computer Aided Verification - 25th International Conference, CAV 2013, Saint Petersburg, Russia, July 13-19, 2013. Proceedings. Lecture Notes in Computer Science, vol. 8044, pp. 36–52. Springer, Berlin, Heidelberg (2013). https://doi.org/10.1007/978-3-642-39799-8_2

32. Hojjat, H., Konečný, F., Garnier, F., Iosif, R., Kuncak, V., Rümmer, P.: A verification toolkit for numerical transition systems. In: Giannakopoulou, D., Méry, D. (eds.) FM 2012. LNCS, vol. 7436, pp. 247–251. Springer, Heidelberg (2012). https://doi.org/10.1007/978-3-642-32759-9_21
33. Iosif, R., Rogalewicz, A., Simácek, J.: The tree width of separation logic with recursive definitions. In: Bonacina, M.P. (ed.) Automated Deduction - CADE-24 - 24th International Conference on Automated Deduction, Lake Placid, NY, USA, June 9-14, 2013. Proceedings. Lecture Notes in Computer Science, vol. 7898, pp. 21–38. Springer, Berlin, Heidelberg (2013). https://doi.org/10.1007/978-3-642-38574-2_2
34. Itzhaky, S., Shoham, S., Vizel, Y.: Hyperproperty verification as CHC satisfiability. In: Weirich, S. (ed.) Programming Languages and Systems - 33rd European Symposium on Programming, ESOP 2024, Held as Part of the European Joint Conferences on Theory and Practice of Software, ETAPS 2024, Luxembourg City, Luxembourg, April 6-11, 2024, Proceedings, Part II. Lecture Notes in Computer Science, vol. 14577, pp. 212–241. Springer, Cham (2024). https://doi.org/10.1007/978-3-031-57267-8_9
35. Jacobs, B., Smans, J., Philippaerts, P., Vogels, F., Penninckx, W., Piessens, F.: VeriFast: a powerful, sound, predictable, fast verifier for C and java. In: Bobaru, M.G., Havelund, K., Holzmann, G.J., Joshi, R. (eds.) NASA Formal Methods - Third International Symposium, NFM 2011, Pasadena, CA, USA, April 18-20, 2011. Proceedings. Lecture Notes in Computer Science, vol. 6617, pp. 41–55. Springer, Berlin, Heidelberg (2011). https://doi.org/10.1007/978-3-642-20398-5_4
36. Jaffar, J., Maher, M.J.: Constraint logic programming: a survey. J. Log. Program. **19**(20), 503–581 (1994)
37. Kahsai, T., Kersten, R., Rümmer, P., Schäf, M.: Quantified heap invariants for object-oriented programs. In: Eiter, T., Sands, D. (eds.) LPAR-21, 21st International Conference on Logic for Programming, Artificial Intelligence and Reasoning, Maun, Botswana, May 7-12, 2017. EPiC Series in Computing, vol. 46, pp. 368–384. EasyChair (2017). https://doi.org/10.29007/ZRCT
38. Kahsai, T., Rümmer, P., Sanchez, H., Schäf, M.: **JayHorn**: a framework for verifying java programs. In: Chaudhuri, S., Farzan, A. (eds.) CAV 2016. LNCS, vol. 9779, pp. 352–358. Springer, Cham (2016). https://doi.org/10.1007/978-3-319-41528-4_19
39. Kobayashi, N., Sato, R., Unno, H.: Predicate abstraction and CEGAR for higher-order model checking. In: Proceedings of the 32nd ACM SIGPLAN Conference on Programming Language Design and Implementation, PLDI 2011, San Jose, CA, USA, June 4-8, 2011, pp. 222–233. ACM (2011)
40. Komuravelli, A., Bjørner, N.S., Gurfinkel, A., McMillan, K.L.: Compositional verification of procedural programs using horn clauses over integers and arrays. In: Kaivola, R., Wahl, T. (eds.) Formal Methods in Computer-Aided Design, FMCAD 2015, Austin, Texas, USA, September 27-30, 2015, pp. 89–96. IEEE (2015). https://doi.org/10.1109/FMCAD.2015.7542257
41. La Torre, S., Napoli, M., Parlato, G.: A unifying approach for multistack pushdown automata. In: Csuhaj-Varjú, E., Dietzfelbinger, M., Ésik, Z. (eds.) Mathematical Foundations of Computer Science 2014 - 39th International Symposium, MFCS 2014, Budapest, Hungary, August 25-29, 2014. Proceedings, Part I. Lecture Notes in Computer Science, vol. 8634, pp. 377–389. Springer, Berlin, Heidelberg (2014). https://doi.org/10.1007/978-3-662-44522-8_32
42. Lahiri, S.K., Qadeer, S.: Back to the future: revisiting precise program verification using SMT solvers. In: Necula, G.C., Wadler, P. (eds.) Proceedings of the 35th

ACM SIGPLAN-SIGACT Symposium on Principles of Programming Languages, POPL 2008, San Francisco, California, USA, January 7-12, 2008, pp. 171–182. ACM (2008). https://doi.org/10.1145/1328438.1328461
43. Lev-Ami, T., Immerman, N., Reps, T.W., Sagiv, M., Srivastava, S., Yorsh, G.: Simulating reachability using first-order logic with applications to verification of linked data structures. Log. Methods Comput. Sci. **5**(2) (2009)
44. Madhusudan, P., Parlato, G.: The tree width of auxiliary storage. In: Ball, T., Sagiv, M. (eds.) Proceedings of the 38th ACM SIGPLAN-SIGACT Symposium on Principles of Programming Languages, POPL 2011, Austin, TX, USA, January 26-28, 2011, pp. 283–294. ACM (2011). https://doi.org/10.1145/1926385.1926419
45. Madhusudan, P., Parlato, G., Qiu, X.: Decidable logics combining heap structures and data. In: Ball, T., Sagiv, M. (eds.) Proceedings of the 38th ACM SIGPLAN-SIGACT Symposium on Principles of Programming Languages, POPL 2011, Austin, TX, USA, January 26-28, 2011, pp. 611–622. ACM (2011). https://doi.org/10.1145/1926385.1926455
46. Manna, Z., Zarba, C.G.: Combining decision procedures. In: Formal Methods at the Crossroads. From Panacea to Foundational Support, 10th Anniversary Colloquium of UNU/IIST, the International Institute for Software Technology of The United Nations University, Lisbon, Portugal, March 18-20, 2002, Revised Papers. LNCS, vol. 2757, pp. 381–422. Springer, Berlin, Heidelberg (2002). https://doi.org/10.1007/978-3-540-40007-3_24
47. Mathur, U., Madhusudan, P., Viswanathan, M.: Decidable verification of uninterpreted programs. Proc. ACM Program. Lang. **3**(POPL), 46:1–46:29 (2019). https://doi.org/10.1145/3290359
48. Mathur, U., Madhusudan, P., Viswanathan, M.: What's decidable about program verification modulo axioms? In: Biere, A., Parker, D. (eds.) Tools and Algorithms for the Construction and Analysis of Systems - 26th International Conference, TACAS 2020, Held as Part of the European Joint Conferences on Theory and Practice of Software, ETAPS 2020, Dublin, Ireland, April 25-30, 2020, Proceedings, Part II. Lecture Notes in Computer Science, vol. 12079, pp. 158–177. Springer, cham (2020). https://doi.org/10.1007/978-3-030-45237-7_10
49. Mathur, U., Murali, A., Krogmeier, P., Madhusudan, P., Viswanathan, M.: Deciding memory safety for single-pass heap-manipulating programs. Proc. ACM Program. Lang. **4**(POPL), 35:1–35:29 (2020). https://doi.org/10.1145/3371103
50. Matsushita, Y., Tsukada, T., Kobayashi, N.: RustHorn: CHC-based verification for rust programs. ACM Trans. Program. Lang. Syst. **43**(4), 15:1–15:54 (2021). https://doi.org/10.1145/3462205
51. Monniaux, D., Gonnord, L.: Cell morphing: from array programs to array-free horn clauses. In: Rival, X. (ed.) Static Analysis - 23rd International Symposium, SAS 2016, Edinburgh, UK, September 8-10, 2016, Proceedings. Lecture Notes in Computer Science, vol. 9837, pp. 361–382. Springer, Berlin, Heidelberg (2016). https://doi.org/10.1007/978-3-662-53413-7_18
52. Murali, A., Peña, L., Blanchard, E., Löding, C., Madhusudan, P.: Model-guided synthesis of inductive lemmas for FOL with least fixpoints. Proc. ACM Program. Lang. **6**(OOPSLA2), 1873–1902 (2022). https://doi.org/10.1145/3563354
53. Nguyen, H.H., Chin, W.: Enhancing program verification with lemmas. In: Gupta, A., Malik, S. (eds.) Computer Aided Verification, 20th International Conference, CAV 2008, Princeton, NJ, USA, July 7-14, 2008, Proceedings. Lecture Notes in Computer Science, vol. 5123, pp. 355–369. Springer, Berlin, Heidelberg (2008). https://doi.org/10.1007/978-3-540-70545-1_34

54. Pek, E., Qiu, X., Madhusudan, P.: Natural proofs for data structure manipulation in C using separation logic. In: O'Boyle, M.F.P., Pingali, K. (eds.) ACM SIGPLAN Conference on Programming Language Design and Implementation, PLDI '14, Edinburgh, United Kingdom - June 09 - 11, 2014, pp. 440–451. ACM (2014). https://doi.org/10.1145/2594291.2594325
55. Piskac, R., Wies, T., Zufferey, D.: Automating separation logic using SMT. In: Sharygina, N., Veith, H. (eds.) Computer Aided Verification - 25th International Conference, CAV 2013, Saint Petersburg, Russia, July 13-19, 2013. Proceedings. Lecture Notes in Computer Science, vol. 8044, pp. 773–789. Springer, Berlin, Heidelberg (2013). https://doi.org/10.1007/978-3-642-39799-8_54
56. Piskac, R., Wies, T., Zufferey, D.: Automating separation logic with trees and data. In: Biere, A., Bloem, R. (eds.) Computer Aided Verification - 26th International Conference, CAV 2014, Held as Part of the Vienna Summer of Logic, VSL 2014, Vienna, Austria, July 18-22, 2014. Proceedings. Lecture Notes in Computer Science, vol. 8559, pp. 711–728. Springer, Cham (2014). https://doi.org/10.1007/978-3-319-08867-9_47
57. Polikarpova, N., Sergey, I.: Structuring the synthesis of heap-manipulating programs. Proc. ACM Program. Lang. **3**(POPL), 72:1–72:30 (2019). https://doi.org/10.1145/3290385
58. Rondon, P.M., Kawaguchi, M., Jhala, R.: Liquid types. In: Gupta, R., Amarasinghe, S.P. (eds.) Proceedings of the ACM SIGPLAN 2008 Conference on Programming Language Design and Implementation, Tucson, AZ, USA, June 7-13, 2008, pp. 159–169. ACM (2008). https://doi.org/10.1145/1375581.1375602
59. Sagiv, S., Reps, T.W., Wilhelm, R.: Parametric shape analysis via 3-valued logic. In: Appel, A.W., Aiken, A. (eds.) POPL '99, Proceedings of the 26th ACM SIGPLAN-SIGACT Symposium on Principles of Programming Languages, San Antonio, TX, USA, January 20-22, 1999, pp. 105–118. ACM (1999). https://doi.org/10.1145/292540.292552
60. Ta, Q., Le, T.C., Khoo, S., Chin, W.: Automated mutual explicit induction proof in separation logic. In: Fitzgerald, J.S., Heitmeyer, C.L., Gnesi, S., Philippou, A. (eds.) FM 2016: Formal Methods - 21st International Symposium, Limassol, Cyprus, November 9-11, 2016, Proceedings. Lecture Notes in Computer Science, vol. 9995, pp. 659–676 (2016). https://doi.org/10.1007/978-3-319-48989-6_40

Open Access This chapter is licensed under the terms of the Creative Commons Attribution 4.0 International License (http://creativecommons.org/licenses/by/4.0/), which permits use, sharing, adaptation, distribution and reproduction in any medium or format, as long as you give appropriate credit to the original author(s) and the source, provide a link to the Creative Commons license and indicate if changes were made.

The images or other third party material in this chapter are included in the chapter's Creative Commons license, unless indicated otherwise in a credit line to the material. If material is not included in the chapter's Creative Commons license and your intended use is not permitted by statutory regulation or exceeds the permitted use, you will need to obtain permission directly from the copyright holder.

Automated Verification of Monotonic Data Structure Traversals in C

Matthew Sotoudeh[✉]

Stanford University, Stanford, USA
sotoudeh@stanford.edu

Abstract. Bespoke data structure operations are common in real-world C code. We identify one common subclass, *monotonic data structure traversals* (MDSTs), that iterate monotonically through the structure. For example, `strlen` iterates from start to end of a character array until a null byte is found, and a binary search tree `insert` iterates from the tree root towards a leaf. We describe a new automated verification tool, SHRINKER, to verify MDSTs written in C. SHRINKER uses a new program analysis strategy called *scapegoating size descent*, which is designed to take advantage of the fact that many MDSTs produce very similar traces when executed on an input (e.g., some large list) as when executed on a 'shrunk' version of the input (e.g., the same list but with its first element deleted). We introduce a new benchmark set containing over one hundred instances proving correctness, equivalence, and memory safety properties of dozens of MDSTs found in major C codebases including Linux, NetBSD, OpenBSD, QEMU, Git, and Musl. SHRINKER significantly increases the number of monotonic string and list traversals that can be verified vs. a portfolio of state-of-the-art tools.

Keywords: Verification · Data Structures · Small Model Property

1 Introduction

The C language's lack of generics and focus on performance encourages bespoke, application-specific data structures. Bugs in these data structures can threaten safety and correctness of the entire codebase. Hence, we desire a tool to automatically prove the correctness of such data structure code written in C.

This paper focuses on a subclass of data structure code we call *monotonic data structure traversals* (MDSTs). MDSTs are programs that take finitely many monotonic sweeps through the structure, where each sweep starts at some root or head element and moves forward on each loop iteration[1]. Examples of MDSTs include classic implementations of `strlen` (start at the first character and iterate forward until a null byte is found), `list-search` (start at the head and iterate forward until the desired element is found), and `bst-insert` (start at the root and iterate down until a null pointer is found, then insert the new node).

---
[1] We give no strict definition of MDST; it is merely intuition guiding the design of our analysis. Our tool remains sound (but incomplete) when applied to any C program.

Benchmarks and Empirical Results. Existing benchmarks sets are either not focused on MDSTs, or involve crafted benchmarks that are not necessarily representative of real-world code. Hence, we constructed a new program verification benchmark consisting of over one hundred instances verifying temporal memory safety, spatial memory safety, and correctness properties of dozens of MDSTs extracted from major C projects. For example, one instance checks that the Linux and OpenBSD implementations of strcmp return numbers with the same sign for every pair of input strings; another checks that appending to a GNOME list increases its length by one.

Our tool, SHRINKER, nearly triples the number of string instances solved (58 vs. 20) and more than doubles the number of list instances solved (20 vs. 9) compared to the second-best solver. SHRINKER solves the second-most number of tree instances among the tools evaluated, including one not solved by any other tool. Our results indicate SHRINKER would make a strong addition to a portfolio solver and can significantly improve the state-of-the-art in verifying string and list MDSTs.

Scapegoating Size Descent. SHRINKER is based on our new *scapegoating size descent* technique for verifying safety properties, i.e., that no execution trace of a given input program crashes (dereferences null, makes a false assertion, etc.).

Traditional program verifiers execute the program on all possible inputs at once, tracking sets of possible program execution traces. If fixedpoint is reached without any of the sets containing a crashing trace, the verifier can conclude that the program is safe. Because most programs have infinitely many possible traces, to ensure termination the verifier must overapproximate the set of possible traces. E.g., rather than record that there are traces where a certain variable might have values 0, or 2, or 4, ..., the verifier might track only that the value is nonnegative. While needed to make the verifier terminate, this overapproximation can make the abstract interpreter think a crash might be possible even when it is not.

Scapegoating size descent gives the verifier a new option: when it finds an overapproximated trace that might crash, instead of giving up and reporting a potential error, it is allowed to instead prove that, *if* there is a reachable crashing trace of this form, then there *also* exists some strictly smaller reachable trace that also crashes. In other words, the verifier establishes that, for every possible program execution trace either: (1) the trace does not crash, or (2) if the trace crashes, then there exists some smaller trace that crashes as well. Together, these facts constitute a proof by infinite descent that no trace crashes.

Our verification tool, SHRINKER, is based on these ideas. Instead of running the program on a single abstract input, it runs two (or more) copies of the program side-by-side, one on an abstract input x and another on a *shrunk* version x' of that input. For example, x might be a nonempty linked list, and x' might be formed by dropping the first node in x. Any time the abstract trace executing on x potentially crashes (reaches a failure state), SHRINKER merely needs to prove that the 'scapegoat trace' executing on x' also crashes and is smaller.

Why Does It Work for MDSTs? The basic difficulty in automated verification of heap-manipulating programs is that the heap can be arbitrarily large, so the verifier must track facts involving an unknown number of values. Scapegoating size descent can sidestep this problem because many MDSTs do almost the same thing when run on an input x as when run on a shrunk version of that input x'. Consider a loop over a linked list: other than the very first iteration, every subsequent iteration does exactly the same thing when run on a list x as when run on the tail list $x' = x$.next formed by dropping the first element in the list. Thus, SHRINKER only needs to track precise facts about the finitely many memory locations that actually differ between the executions on x and x'.

Contributions and Outline. We make the following contributions:

1. *Scapegoating size descent* framework for program analysis (Sect. 4).
2. SHRINKER tool for automated verification of C programs (Sect. 5).
3. Evaluation of SHRINKER and multiple baseline verifiers on our new benchmark set of MDSTs extracted from major C projects (Sect. 6).

Section 2 gives preliminaries, Sect. 3 works through a motivating example, and Sect. 7 describes related work. Appendix C describes limitations, future work, and a motivating connection to the small scope hypothesis. The SHRINKER homepage is located at https://lair.masot.net/shrinker/ and an archival version is located at https://doi.org/10.5281/zenodo.15225947. The full version of this paper, with appendices, is available at https://doi.org/10.48550/arXiv.2505.18818.

2 Preliminaries and Traditional Abstract Interpretation

We now formalize our notion of a program and what it means for a program to be safe, then describe a variant of abstract interpretation, which Sect. 4 builds on to form scapegoating size descent as used by SHRINKER. In addition to distinguishing names, we use blue for concrete states/traces and red for abstract.

2.1 Preliminary Definitions

We model the program to be verified as a transition relation on uninterpreted states. We make no formal assumption about what a state is, but in practice it represents the state of the registers and heap at a given point during program execution. For the duration of this paper we assume a single, fixed program.

Definition 1. *We assume the program to be verified is defined by a transition relation $\to$ on states: $s_1 \to s_2$ means "state s_1 can transition to state s_2 in one program step." A trace $s_1, \ldots, s_n$ is a sequence of states. We assume the verification conditions are specified by a (possibly infinite) set of initial traces I, each of length 1, and a (possibly infinite) set of failure traces F.*

SHRINKER automatically extracts the program relation $\to$, initial traces I, and failure traces F from C code. We use the terms 'fails' and 'crashes' equivalently in this paper. We distinguish between *traces* (any sequence of states) and *reachable traces* (those that can actually result from an execution of the program).

Definition 2. *A trace* $s_1, \ldots, s_n$ *is a* reachable trace *if every step is a valid program transition (i.e.,* $s_1 \to s_2 \to \cdots \to s_n$*) and the singleton prefix of the trace (i.e., just* s_1*) is in the set of initial traces* I*. We use* R *to notate the set of reachable traces. The program to be verified is safe if* $R \cap F = \emptyset$*.*

Finally, we introduce notation for executing the program for one additional timestep, i.e., extending traces by one state. We allow nondeterminism, so the result will be a set of possible subsequent traces.

Definition 3. *Given a trace* $t = (s_1, s_2, \ldots, s_n)$*,* $\mathrm{Step}(t)$ *is the possible traces reachable after one timestep, i.e.,* $\mathrm{Step}(t) = \{(s_1, s_2, \ldots, s_n, s_{n+1}) \mid s_n \to s_{n+1}\}$*.*

2.2 Trace Abstractions

Real computers are finite, but abstract interpreters must reason about a potentially infinite number of possible program traces. Hence, we need a finite representation of infinite sets of traces. This representation is formalized as an *abstract domain* [41]. This paper only uses abstract domains as a representation of infinite sets, and we do not place many requirements on our abstract domain (e.g., we do not require a Galois connection).

Definition 4. *An* abstract trace domain $\mathcal{A}^T$ *is a set of* abstract traces *along with a concretization function* γ^T *that maps abstract traces to sets of traces.*

The concretization function is merely used for the theoretical results: it need not be implemented or even implementable. We make no other formal assumption about the abstract traces. In practice, they usually contain constraints about states in the trace, e.g., "the value of variable i at the last state in the trace is positive," and the concretization function γ^T gives the set of all traces satisfying those constraints. For the abstract interpreter to construct, manipulate, and reason about abstract domain elements, the analysis designer must implement:

1. $I^\sharp$: overapproximates the possible initial traces, i.e., $I \subseteq \gamma^T(I^\sharp)$
2. $\mathrm{CanFail}(a)$: tests for possible failure traces; must be true if $\gamma^T(a) \cap F \neq \emptyset$.
3. $\mathrm{Step}^\sharp(a)$: applies Step to all of the represented traces, i.e., for any $t \in \gamma^T(a)$ and $t' \in \mathrm{Step}(t)$, we have $t' \in \gamma^T(\mathrm{Step}^\sharp(a))$.
4. $\mathrm{MorePrecise}(a, b)$: true only when $\gamma^T(a) \subseteq \gamma^T(b)$.
5. $\mathrm{Widen}(a)$: introduces overapproximations to ensure termination; it can return anything as long as $\mathrm{MorePrecise}(a, \mathrm{Widen}(a))$.
6. $\mathrm{Split}(a)$: splits a set of traces into subsets, often to introduce flow-, path-, or context-sensitivity into the analysis; it returns a list of abstract traces $a'_1, a'_2, \ldots, a'_n$ such that $\gamma^T(a) \subseteq \bigcup_i \gamma^T(a'_i)$.

Data: A program (Section 2.1) and an abstract trace domain (Section 2.2).
Result: SAFE if the program is definitely safe, or UNKNOWN.
1 worklist ← $\{I^\sharp\}$, seen ← $\{\}$;
2 **while** worklist *is not empty* **do**
3       $a \leftarrow$ worklist.pop();
4   **if** CanFail(a) **then return** Unknown ;
5   seen.add(a);
6   **foreach** $a'_i \in \mathrm{Split}(\mathrm{Step}^\sharp(a))$ **do**
7           $a'_i \leftarrow \mathrm{Widen}(a'_i)$;
8   **if** *there exists* $b \in$ seen $\cup$ worklist *with* $\mathrm{MorePrecise}(a'_i, b)$ **then**
9   continue;
10   worklist ← (worklist $\setminus \{b \in$ worklist $\mid \mathrm{MorePrecise}(b, a'_i)\}) \cup \{a'_i\}$;
11 **return** Safe;

Algorithm 1: Variant of Traditional Abstract Interpretation

The tool designer can instantiate this framework with different choices to reach different points on the completeness–performance–termination tradeoff curve, but as long as the above constraints are met soundness is guaranteed.

2.3 Variant of Traditional Abstract Interpretation

Algorithm 1 shows an automated verification algorithm based on the traditional abstract interpretation framework. It repeatedly calls $\mathrm{Step}^\sharp$ to explore the set of reachable traces. If CanFail reports that any one might involve a failure trace, it reports a possible error. Otherwise, once fixedpoint is reached, the program is guaranteed to be safe. Widen and MorePrecise are used to encourage convergence, while Split is used to case split abstract traces to improve precision.

The key Lemma 1 guarantees that every reachable trace is represented by some abstract trace processed on an iteration of the main loop in Algorithm 1.

Lemma 1. *If the algorithm returns* Safe, *then for any reachable trace t there exists some abstract trace $a \in$ seen with $t \in \gamma^T(a)$.*

Proof. Induct on the length of $t = (s_1, s_2, \ldots, s_n)$. The first iteration handles everything with $n = 1$. Otherwise, by inductive hypothesis, the prefix $t' = (s_1, \ldots, s_{n-1})$ was added to seen on line 5 during some iteration. On that iteration, one of the a'_is must have $t \in \gamma^T(a'_i)$, which gets added to the worklist on line 10, hence processed and added to seen in a future iteration. Alternatively, a less-precise b might have been found already (line 9), but then $t \in \gamma^T(b)$ already, as desired. Finally, a'_i might be removed from the worklist in a future execution of line 10, but that only occurs if something less precise (hence also containing t in its concretization set) is added to replace it. □

Theorem 1. *If Algorithm 1 reports* Safe, *then the program is safe.*

Proof. Otherwise there must be a reachable trace $t \in F$, hence by Lemma 1 there is a $a \in$ seen with $t \in \gamma^T(a)$. But everything added to seen passed the check on line 4, i.e., CanFail(a) is false, contradicting the definition of CanFail. □

3 Motivating Example

This section works through a concrete example showing how traditional abstract interpretation (Sect. 2.3) with a precise enough abstract domain can prove correctness of a simple heap manipulating program. We then describe some issues that make this difficult to do reliably and sketch how our technique, scapegoating size descent (Sect. 4), would approach the same verification task. Consider the code below, where we want to prove the __VERIFIER_fail() call is unreachable.

```
1   struct arr { int *data; int n_data; };
2   void test(struct arr arr) {
3       for (int i = 0; i < arr.n_data; i++)
4           arr.data[i] = 0;
5       for (int i = 0; i < arr.n_data; i++)
6           if (arr.data[i] != 0)
7               __VERIFIER_fail(); }
```

The example is simplified for expository purposes, ignoring techniques like loop fusion that can solve this instance but do not generalize as well. For space reasons we are somewhat informal; see Appendix B for a more complete worked example.

3.1 Traditional Abstract Interpretation (Algorithm 1)

Recall that Algorithm 1 explores sets of possible program traces (each set represented by an abstract trace a_i) and checks that none includes a failing trace (i.e., one reaching line 7). On termination, Lemma 1 guarantees that every reachable trace lies in the concretization set of one of those abstract traces added to seen. The exact behavior depends on the abstraction used, but below we have visualized one possible result. Each node represents an abstract trace in the final seen set. An edge $a_i \to a_j$ means a_j was added to the worklist while processing a_i, i.e., applying Step to a trace in $\gamma^T(a_i)$ might result in a trace in $\gamma^T(a_j)$.

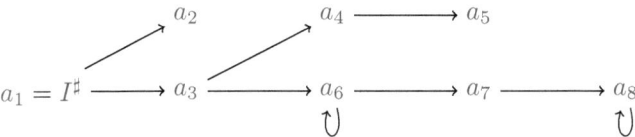

Below, we describe each abstract trace as a set of constraints. The concretization set consists of every trace satisfying those constraints. We assume executing lines 3 and 5 checks the corresponding loop condition and either executes the loop body or exits the loop.

- a_1: About to execute line 3. arr.data points to arr.n_data integers, i=0
- a_2: About to execute line 5. arr.n_data=0, i=0
- a_3: About to execute line 3. arr.n_data>=1, arr.data[0]=0, i=1
- a_4: About to execute line 5. arr.n_data=1, arr.data[0]=0, i=0

- a_5: About to execute line 5. `arr.n_data=1, arr.data[0]=0, i=1`
- a_6: About to execute line 3. `arr.n_data>1, 2<=i<=arr.n_data, arr.data[0]=0, ..., arr.data[i-1]=0`
- a_7: About to execute line 5. `arr.n_data>1, i=0, arr.data[0]=0, ..., arr.data[arr.n_data-1]=0`
- a_8: About to execute line 5. `arr.n_data>1, 1<=i<=arr.n_data, arr.data[0]=0, ..., arr.data[arr.n_data-1]=0`

Algorithm 1 can prove that traces represented by a_8 never reach the crash on line 7, because all of those traces satisfy `arr.data[0]` = `arr.data[1]` = ... = `arr.data[arr.n_data-1]` = 0, so the `if` condition is never taken. This analysis, however, **requires the abstract domain to reason about constraints involving an unknown number of memory locations**, specifically the constraints asserting that some subset of `arr.data` entries are zero (the "..."s in the above constraints for a_6, a_7, and a_8). If the abstract domain used was not able to represent such constraints, the analyzer would report a false positive because it would not be able to guarantee that the `if` condition on line 6 is not taken.

Some abstract domains can handle constraints like this [74], but the larger search space makes automatically synthesizing useful invariants harder than when restricted to only constraints that involve a finite number of memory locations. By contrast, the abstract traces for a_1 through a_5, which only constrain the values of finitely many memory locations, tend to be simpler to reason about and synthesize. **The key goal of scapegoating size descent is to avoid having to track precise constraints about an unknown number of memory locations.** Instead, we want to only track constraints about the (often finitely many) memory locations that *differ* when executing on a full input vs. some related, smaller input.

3.2 Scapegoating Size Descent

At a high level, our scapegoating size descent approach also explores sets of program traces that together account for every possible reachable trace and checks whether they reach failure. In fact, its handling of the traces with inputs of size 0 or 1 (i.e., a_1 through a_5) is essentially identical to traditional abstract interpretation: we track constraints on the finitely many memory locations `arr.n_data`, `arr.data[0]`, and `i` to verify that line 7 is never reached on any such small-sized input. The difference comes in handling a_6 through a_8, which represent traces that go through the loops an arbitrary (larger than 1) number of times and which, in traditional abstract interpretation, required an abstract domain capable of handling constraints on an unknown number of memory locations.

Instead of directly proving that line 7 can never be reached on such traces, scapegoating size descent tries to prove that it can *only* be reached if some smaller trace reaches it as well. This conditional proof is often easier to synthesize and can avoid needing to track precise constraints on arbitrarily many memory locations, as in a_6, a_7, a_8 above. We do this by associating each such abstract trace with a *scapegoat trace* that has very closely related behavior to the *primary trace* we are concerned with. Usually, the scapegoat trace is the result of running the program on a shrunk version of the input for one fewer iteration of each loop: if a trace is the result of running the program on input array [3, 4, 10, 8], the scapegoat trace might result from running the program on [4, 10, 8]. For example, the equivalent of a_6, a_7, and a_8 are the following:

- a_6: About to execute line 3. `arr.n_data>1, 2<=i<=arr.n_data, arr.data[0]=0`.
  For any reachable trace satisfying those constraints, there exists another reachable trace (the *scapegoat*) where the last state is identical except: `arr.data[0]` was removed, and both `arr.n_data` and `i` were decremented by 1.
- a_7: About to execute line 5. `arr.n_data>1, i=0, arr.data[0]=0`.
  For any reachable trace satisfying those constraints, there exists another reachable trace where the last state is identical except: `arr.data[0]` was removed and `arr.n_data` was decremented by 1.
- a_8: About to execute line 5. `arr.n_data>1, 1<=i<=arr.n_data, arr.data[0]=0`.
  For any reachable trace satisfying those constraints, there exists another reachable trace where the last state is identical except: `arr.data[0]` was removed, and both `arr.n_data` and `i` were decremented by 1.

Crucially, the constraints for a_8 imply that if some trace satisfying the constraints of a_8 *were* to fail (reach line 7) on the next iteration, its corresponding scapegoat trace would *also* fail. So we have actually proved: if some input of size `arr.n_data` leads to a failing execution, then there is another input of strictly smaller size `arr.n_data - 1` that *also* reaches failure. In this way, because the size is nonnegative, we can apply *proof by infinite descent* (Theorem 2, essentially induction on input size) to conclude that no input causes a failure.

4 Scapegoating Size Descent

This section formalizes our scapegoating size descent variant of abstract interpretation, as used in SHRINKER. Traditional abstract interpretation tracks a set of possible traces. Scapegoating size descent modifies this framework to track a set of *herds* of traces; each herd is a *primary trace* t_1 along with a number of *scapegoat traces* $t_2, t_3, \ldots$ resulting from different inputs or different nondeterministic choices[2]. When the abstract interpreter thinks it might be possible for the primary trace to have crashed, scapegoating size descent allows the abstract interpreter to avoid giving up by transferring the blame onto one of the scapegoat traces. To blame a scapegoat trace, it must prove that, if the primary trace has crashed, then the scapegoat trace has also crashed and is smaller than the primary trace (for some definition of size; see Sect. 4.1). In this way, scapegoating size descent proves that every reachable trace either does not crash, *or*, if it

---

[2] Apparently, some call a group of goats a 'trip' or a 'tribe,' but unfortunately 't'-starting names overload with 'trace.'.

does crash, then there is some strictly smaller reachable trace that also crashes. If the size measure is *well-founded* (e.g., natural numbers), proof by infinite descent (Theorem 2) ensures that no traces crash, i.e., the program is safe. A detailed worked example is provided in Appendix B.

4.1 Trace Sizes and Infinite Descent

We assume the tool designer provides a measure of the *size* of a trace.

Definition 5. *A trace size function* $\langle \cdot \rangle$ *maps traces t to a size* $\langle t \rangle \in \mathbb{N}$.

SHRINKER currently uses a measure of size that essentially counts the number of allocated items on the heap. But SHRINKER is fairly robust to the exact measure of size; we expect that the number of bytes allocated or even the length of the trace itself would work as well (see Appendix A.9 for further discussion). The choice of trace size affects only completeness, not soundness. Since our trace sizes are natural numbers, we can use *proof by infinite descent*.

Theorem 2. *(Proof by Infinite Descent) Let $P(n)$ be any statement parameterized by $n \in \mathbb{N}$. Suppose that whenever $P(n)$ is false, there exists $m \in \mathbb{N}$ such that $m < n$ and $P(m)$ is also false.*[3] *Then, $P(n)$ is true for all $n \in \mathbb{N}$.*

In fact, our results generalize to any measure of size as long as the comparison relation admits no infinite descending chains, i.e., there exists no infinite sequence of traces $\langle t_1 \rangle > \langle t_2 \rangle > \dots$.

4.2 Trace Herds and Abstract Trace Herds

Rather than tracking sets of traces, scapegoating size descent tracks sets of *herds* of traces. In addition to distinguishing names, we will color herds in teal and abstract herds in purple.

Definition 6. *A* herd *is an ordered tuple of traces. If h is a herd, then $|h|$ is the size of h and $h[1], \dots, h[|h|]$ are all traces. We use $h = (h[1], \dots, h[n])$ to indicate a herd of size $|h| = n$. We call $h[1]$ the* primary trace *of the herd, and $h[2], \dots, h[n]$ the* scapegoat traces *of the herd.*

The size $|h|$ of a herd is just the number of traces in it; there is no relation to the size of an individual trace in the herd. The first trace in the herd plays the role of the primary trace we are trying to prove things about; in fact, scapegoating size descent restricted to size-1 herds is identical to traditional abstract interpretation (Algorithm 1). HSingle constructs a singleton herd from a trace:

Definition 7. *Given a trace t, we define* $\texttt{HSingle}(t) = (t)$ *to be the herd of size 1 consisting of only the primary trace t and no scapegoats. Given a set of traces T, we overload* $\texttt{HSingle}(T)$ *to mean the set* $\{\texttt{HSingle}(t) \mid t \in T\}$.

---
[3] Inparticular, this implies $P(0)$ is not false, as 0 has no predecessor in $\mathbb{N}$.

Given a herd, we need notation for modifying individual traces in the herd.

Definition 8. *Given a herd h, index i, and trace t, we define the* update-index *function* $\text{HUpdate}(h, i, t) = (h[1], \ldots, h[i-1], t, h[i+1], \ldots, h[n])$. *We also define the* drop-index *function* $\text{HDrop}(h, i) = (h[1], \ldots, h[i-1], h[i+1], \ldots, h[n])$.

Finally, we need to be able to extend traces in the herd by executing the program on that trace for one timestep.

Definition 9. *Given a herd h and a number $i \in \mathbb{N}$, we define the function* $\text{HStep}(h, i) = \{\text{HUpdate}(h, i, t) \mid t \in \text{Step}(h[i])\}$, *or* $\text{HStep}(h, i) = h$ *if i is not between 1 and $|h|$.*

4.3 Herd Abstractions

As with Algorithm 1, the tool designer must provide an abstract domain to represent sets of herds along with a number of abstract domain operations.

Definition 10. *An* abstract herd domain $\mathcal{A}^{\mathcal{H}}$ *is a set of abstract herds along with a concretization function γ^H that maps abstract herds to sets of herds.*

Once again, we make no assumptions about what the abstract herds are, and the concretization function is only needed for the theoretical results; it does not need to be implementable. The tool designer does still need to provide a number of operations for working with abstract herds.

The following operations are essentially lifting ones we used in Sect. 2.2 to abstract herds rather than abstract traces:

1. $I^{H\sharp}$: represents all herds where the primary trace is a starting trace, i.e., $\text{HSingle}(I) \subseteq \gamma^H(I^{H\sharp})$.
2. $\text{HCanFail}(a)$: must be true if any of the herds has a failing primary trace, i.e., true whenever there exists $h \in \gamma^H(a)$ with $h[1] \in F$.
3. $\text{HStep}^\sharp(a)$: runs the primary trace in each herd forward, i.e., for every $h \in \gamma^H(a)$ and $h' \in \text{HStep}(h, 1)$, we have $h' \in \gamma^H(\text{HStep}^\sharp(a))$.
4. $\text{HMorePrecise}(a, b)$: true only when $\gamma^H(a) \subseteq \gamma^H(b)$.
5. $\text{HWiden}(a)$: returns anything as long as $\text{HMorePrecise}(a, \text{HWiden}(a))$.
6. $\text{HSplit}(a)$: returns abstract herds $a'_1, a'_2, \ldots, a'_n$ such that $\gamma^H(a) \subseteq \bigcup_i \gamma^H(a'_i)$.

The following are new operations only used in scapegoating size descent:

1. $\text{MaybeAddScapegoats}(a)$ adds candidate scapegoat traces to the herd. These candidate scapegoat traces must be reachable traces whenever the primary trace is reachable. In practice, the scapegoat traces are constructed by modifications to the input in the main trace, e.g., dropping the first node in a linked list input argument. Formally, for every herd $h \in \gamma^H(a)$, either
   (a) $h[1]$ is not a reachable trace, or
   (b) there exists $h' \in \gamma^H(\text{MaybeAddScapegoats}(a))$ extending h, i.e., where $h' = (h[1], \ldots, h[|h|], t_1, \ldots, t_n)$ and $t_1, \ldots, t_n$ are all reachable traces.

Data: A program (Section 2.1) and an abstract herd domain (Section 4.3).
Result: SAFE if the program is definitely safe, or UNKNOWN.
1 worklist ← $\{I^{H\sharp}\}$, seen ← $\{\}$;
2 **while** worklist *is not empty* **do**
3   a ← worklist.pop();
4   **if** HCanFail(a) *and there is no* $i > 1$ *with* CanBlame(a, i) **then**
5 | return Unknown;
6   seen.add(a);
7   **for** $a'_i \in$ HSplit(HStep$^\sharp$(a)) **do**
8   a'_i ← MaybeAddScapegoats$^\sharp$(a'_i);
9   **for** j ← StepperHeuristic() *with* $j > 1$ **do** a'_i ← HStep$^\sharp_\exists$(a'_i, j) ;
10   a'_i ← HWiden(a'_i);
11   **if** *there exists* $b \in$ seen $\cup$ worklist *with* HMorePrecise(a'_i, b) **then**
12 | continue;
13   worklist ← (worklist $\setminus \{b \in$ worklist $\mid$ HMorePrecise(b, a'_i)$\}$) $\cup \{a'_i\}$;
14 **return** Safe;

Algorithm 2: Scapegoating size descent. For soundness, StepperHeuristic may return any sequence of numbers greater than 1.

2. HStep$^\sharp_\exists$(a, i) runs the ith trace in the herd (must be a scapegoat, i.e., $i > 1$) forward for one timestep. If multiple subsequent states are possible, e.g., because a nondeterministic choice was made by the program, it may pick any one of the choices (we only need to guarantee the existence of at least one scapegoat trace, not analyze all possible scapegoat traces). Alternatively, it may drop a scapegoat trace, e.g., if no successors exist. Formally, for any $h \in \gamma^H(a)$, either:
   (a) there exists a $h' \in$ HStep(h, i) such that $h' \in \gamma^H($HStep$^\sharp_\exists(a, i))$, or
   (b) HDrop(h, i) $\in \gamma^H($HStep$^\sharp_\exists(a, i))$.

3. CanBlame(a, i) determines whether we can blame the ith scapegoat in the herd, i.e., whether it represents a trace that reached failure on a strictly smaller input. Formally, returns true only if for every $h \in \gamma^H(a)$ both:
   (a) $\langle h[i] \rangle < \langle h[1] \rangle$, and
   (b) $h[i] \in F$.

4.4 Algorithm

The scapegoating size descent algorithm is presented in Algorithm 2. It is almost identical to Algorithm 1, except (1) the verifier can add and step forward scapegoat traces arbitrarily, i.e., according to the heuristics MaybeAddScapegoats and StepperHeuristic; and (2) the verifier can ignore a possibly failing herd if one of the scapegoat traces can be successfully blamed.

Correctness Proof. In traditional abstract interpretation, Lemma 1 guaranteed that every reachable trace was in the concretization set of some seen abstract trace. But in scapegoating size descent, the abstract elements represent sets of herds, not sets of traces, so we need to be more precise about what we mean when we say an abstract herd seen by the algorithm accounts for a given trace. We will say that an abstract herd a accounts for a trace t if there is some herd in the concretization set of a where (i) t is the primary, and (ii) everything in the herd is reachable. The following definition makes this precise.

Definition 11. *An abstract herd a accounts for a trace t if there exists some herd $h \in \gamma^H(a)$ with $h[1] = t$ and all of the traces in h are reachable. In that case, we say h witnesses that a accounts for t.*

Lemma 2 observes that none of the new, scapegoat-only operations that Algorithm 1 performs can decrease the set of traces accounted for.

Lemma 2. *Let a be an abstract herd and suppose t is a trace accounted for by a. Then, after computing $a' = \text{HWiden}(a)$, $a' = \text{MaybeAddScapegoats}(a)$, or $a' = \text{HStep}_\exists^\sharp(a, i)$ for any $i > 1$, t is still accounted for by a'.*

Proof. Let $h \in \gamma^H(a)$ be the herd witnessing that a accounts for t (Definition 11). We must show there exists some h' witnessing that a' accounts for t as well. For $a' = \text{HWiden}(a)$, the definition guarantees that $\gamma^H(a) \subseteq \gamma^H(a')$ so in particular we can take h' to be h. For $a' = \text{MaybeAddScapegoats}(a)$, we know that a valid h' exists by the requirements on case (b) of the definition of MaybeAddScapegoats in Sect. 4.3. For $a' = \text{HStep}_\exists^\sharp(a, i)$ with $i > 1$, we know that there exists some $h' \in \gamma^H(a')$ such that either (i) a $h' \in \text{HStep}(h, i)$, or (ii) $h' \in \text{HDrop}(h, i)$. In either case, h' satisfies the desired conditions. □

We can now prove the equivalent of Lemma 1 in almost exactly the same way as Sect. 2.3, except replacing "$t \in \gamma^T(a)$" with "a accounts for t."

Lemma 3. *If Algorithm 2 returns Safe, then for any reachable trace t there exists an abstract herd $a \in$ seen accounting for t.*

Proof. Induct on the length of $t = (s_1, s_2, \ldots, s_n)$. For the base case, if $n = 1$ then it is accounted for by a when line 6 is reached on the first iteration. Otherwise, by inductive hypothesis, the prefix $t' = (s_1, \ldots, s_{n-1})$ was accounted for by some a added to seen on line 6 during some iteration. On that iteration, one of the a_i's must account for t and get added to the worklist, and hence processed and added to seen in a future iteration (Lemma 2 guarantees that it still accounts for t even after executing MaybeAddScapegoats, $\text{HStep}_\exists^\sharp$, and HWiden in the inner loop). Alternatively, a less-precise b might have been found already (line 12), but then t will be accounted for by b already, as desired. Notably, it is possible for a_i' to be removed from the worklist in a future execution of line 13 but that only occurs if something less precise (hence also accounting for t) is added to replace it. □

Lemma 4. *If Algorithm 2 reports Safe, then for every reachable trace t either $t \notin F$ or there is another reachable trace $t' \in F$ with $\langle t' \rangle < \langle t \rangle$.*

Proof. From Lemma 3 an abstract herd a was added to `seen` with some herd $h \in \gamma^H(a)$ having primary trace $t = h[1]$ and reachable scapegoats $h[2]$, ..., $h[n]$. But for Algorithm 2 to return `Safe`, it must have passed the `HCanFail` and `CanBlame` check on line 4, i.e., either $t \notin F$ or some scapegoat $t' = h[i]$ is smaller and also fails, i.e., $t' \in F$ and $\langle t' \rangle < \langle t \rangle$ as desired. □

Theorem 3. *If Algorithm 2 reports* `Safe`, *then the program is safe.*

Proof. Using Lemma 4 we can apply proof by infinite descent (Theorem 2) to the claim "no reachable trace of size n is in F" and conclude that no reachable trace (of any size) is in F, i.e., the program is safe.

5 The Shrinker Tool

This section describes our scapegoating size descent implementation SHRINKER. The SHRINKER homepage is located at https://lair.masot.net/shrinker/ and an archival version with benchmarks and baseline tools is located at https://doi.org/10.5281/zenodo.15225947.

5.1 User Interface.

Verification goals are provided by the user to SHRINKER as a C file defining a special `test` function. This function may take parameters, and it may call the special methods `__VERIFIER_ignore()` and `__VERIFIER_fail()`. SHRINKER tries to prove that no input to `test` produces a trace that calls `__VERIFIER_fail()` without first calling `__VERIFIER_ignore()`. It is useful to wrap those methods in `assume(X)` and `assert(X)` macros that check a condition before ignoring or failing. This lets the user express program-specific correctness properties without requiring the user to learn a complicated logical notation. SHRINKER automatically instruments pointer operations to check memory safety properties. Optional overflow checking can also be implemented by instrumentation. We also support `__VERIFIER_nondet_type()` methods to get nondeterministic values. We do not support VLAs or explicit C array types, but the user can specify that an input pointer points to an arbitrarily sized array of items (Appendix A.11).

Subset of C Supported. SHRINKER supports a usable subset of C including structs, pointers, loops, nonrecursive and tail-recursive function calls, and the standard integer types. We throw an error immediately upon seeing unsupported parts of C, such as union types, function pointers, and array types.

Assumption that Inputs Point to Disjoint Heaps. For linked structures, SHRINKER verifies the correctness condition under the additional assumption that the inputs to the function point to disjoint, acyclic heaps, i.e., we only consider tree-shaped input structures. This only affects *inputs* to the function; the function can itself modify the input into any form it wishes and call other functions with cyclic inputs. This is how, e.g., we verify doubly and cyclicly linked structures: the test harness first rewrites the acyclic input into a cyclic list and only then is the relevant operation performed. See Appendix A.10 for more details.

Array and String Inputs. Array inputs are specified by a struct type having two fields, one integer length field named n_X and one pointer field named X (see Appendix A.11 for an example). SHRINKER verifies the program under the assumption that all instances of such structs reachable from the input arguments are initialized with a nonnegative value for the n_X field and an allocated memory region of exactly n_X items pointed to be the X field. String inputs can be specified by declaring an array-of-chars input, then having the test harness iterate over it at the start of the test harness and call __VERIFIER_ignore() if it is not a properly formatted string.

5.2 Tool Organization and Trusted Code Base

SHRINKER is unusually small, having fewer than 7 thousand lines total of C and Python code, with no runtime dependence on third-party libraries. A small trusted codebase can improve maintainability and confidence in its soundness.

SHRINKER includes a parser written in Python that lowers C code to a simple intermediate representation. Each operation in this intermediate representation has corresponding implementations of abstract transformers (i.e., $\text{HStep}^\sharp$ and $\text{HStep}^\sharp_\exists$) that together encode the semantics of the program. To keep the implementation manageable, we do not support array types, unions, or function pointers. We also inline all function calls, hence we only support nonrecursive and tail-recursive function calls. When unsupported syntax is encountered, we provide a line number and descriptive error message to the user.

The remainder of the tool is organized as described in Sect. 4, using an abstract domain we wrote with core operations implemented in C for efficiency. One other major optimization was to parallelize the tool (see Appendix A.8).

5.3 Abstract Herd Domain

We represent abstract herds as constraints on the values of memory locations in different states in each trace. Constraints can relate valuess across different states, memory locations, and traces in the herd. They can also constrain the possible values of trace metadata, e.g., what the 'program counter' (next instruction to be executed) is. Examples of constraints include:

- "The value of i in the first state of trace 1 is one less than the value of i in the first state of trace 2,"
- "The value of j in the last state of trace 5 is positive,"
- "If x is positive in the second-to-last state of trace 1, then the program counter in the last state of trace 1 is instruction 10 in the intermediate representation of the program; otherwise it is instruction 20."

The abstraction can be queried, e.g., to ask questions like:

– "Can j be nonzero in the last state of trace 5?"
– "What are the possible program counter values in the last state of trace 1?"

Memory Abstraction. The above informal examples refer to local variables in the program. But to verify heap-manipulating code, we need the ability to refer to locations in the heap. This is done using heap addresses, i.e., constraints can refer to a term representing "the value at memory address X in the ith state of trace j." We use a memory abstraction inspired by the three-valued logic analyzer [77]. We track facts about two types of locations in memory: either *concrete* locations that represent a specific address in memory (e.g., the first node in a linked list), or a *summary* location that represents multiple addresses in memory (e.g., all of the remaining nodes in the list). We implement this with a two-level memory abstraction: every memory location has both a *major* and *minor* address, and summary locations refer to a group of memory locations that share the same major address. We implement linked structures of arbitrary size by adding a summary node to represent all nodes beyond a certain depth. We prevent this addressing scheme from leaking into the program, e.g., by disallowing the casting of non-NULL pointers into integers. We implement arrays by giving all entries in the array a single major address, introducing concrete nodes for the first few entries in the array, and then introducing a summary node to represent the remainder of the array (the number of entries to make concrete nodes for is a user-configurable parameter).

Numerical Reasoning. SHRINKER only adds a small number of constraints, e.g., applying HStep to a program about to execute a line `i=j;` will add a constraint saying that `i` in the last state has the same value as `j` in the second-to-last state (along with other constraints asserting that no other memory location has changed). These often imply additional implicit constraints, e.g., if we also know that `j>k` in the second-to-last state, we can infer `i>k` in the last state (after applying `i=j`). To make such inferences, we wrote a standard integer difference logic (IDL) solver to determine all relations implied by constraints of the form $x - y \leq c$ where x and y are terms and c is a constant offset [40]. All terms in the state (even nonnumerical ones) are represented in the IDL solver; boolean terms can be encoded as 0 for false and 1 for true. Additional rules infer basic numerical and logical properties, e.g., when $a = b$ and some fact $F(a)$ is true, the fact $F(b)$ can be deduced. Additional checks are added to properly model unsigned `int` overflow and casting behavior according to the C standard, even though the underlying solver treats all variables as mathematical integers.

5.4 Widening (HWiden)

HWiden(a) is implemented by dropping constraints in a heuristically. SHRINKER only widens at loop iteration points, and only once the loop has been unwound for a certain (user-controlled) number of times or a summary region has been accessed during an earlier iteration of that loop. We first remove all constraints referring to anything other than the very first and last states in the trace. We then search through the `seen` and `worklist` lists for other abstract trace herds with the same abstract path (essentially, about to execute the same line; see Appendix A.1 for more details), and weaken any constraints that are not shared by all of those herds to just store the sign of the difference (e.g., if one implies $a - b < -4$ and another implies $a - b < -7$, we weaken to the constraint $a - b < 0$). Because there are only finitely many major addresses in our memory abstraction, we exempt constraints describing the major address portion of a pointer and instead try to track the precise list of all possibilities (a threshold is used to overapproximate if even this gets too large).

Scapegoating and Other Heuristics. For space reasons, details of our other heuristics, e.g., for adding and stepping scapegoats, are deferred to Appendix A. Briefly stated, we keep the analysis precise up to a certain unrolling depth for each loop. Then, we add scapegoats corresponding to traces formed by dropping elements from the input structure (e.g., the first element of an array or list). We step those scapegoats forward until the two loops come in-sync, i.e., pointers to input nodes point to the same thing in the primary and the scapegoat, and integer loop indices into arrays differ by one. Then we step the scapegoats in lockstep with the primary trace until the loop is exited.

6 Evaluation

This section describes our benchmark set and empirical evaluation. Experiments were run on a Debian 12 virtual machine on an Intel i9-13900. Benchexec was used to limit RAM to 32 GB and wallclock to 3 h per instance–tool pair.

6.1 Benchmarks

We collected a set of benchmarks verifying correctness, memory safety, and equivalence properties of dozens of MDSTs from major real-world C projects. The full list of projects we extracted data structure traversals from are: Linux [2], NetBSD [3], OpenBSD [7], Musl [6], GLib [5], QEMU [8], Redis [9], Zsh [10], Git [4], and GLibC [1]. We divided the benchmarks into three classes: strings, lists, and trees. Our set is more heavily weighted towards string benchmarks because all the operations shared a standard string representation so we could construct many benchmark instances by cross-checking them. Examples of instances include checking:

1. The Linux and NetBSD implementations of `strcmp` agree on all inputs.
2. After inserting into an instance of Redis' linked list, using Redis' list-search routine to search for the item just inserted always succeeds.
3. If a search for `x` in the `glibc` implementation of red-black trees succeeds, then after rotating a node in the tree, a subsequent search for `x` still succeeds.

Table 1. Evaluation Table. For each benchmark, the 'solved' row shows how many instances that tool solved, the 'unique' row shows how many instances were solved only by that tool, and the 'fastest' row shows how many instances that tool solved faster than any other tool. "Port. w/o" shows the number solved by a virtual-best portfolio of all tools except SHRINKER, while "Port. w/" shows the number solved by a virtual-best portfolio including SHRINKER.

Benchmark	Count	Kind	SHRINKER	VeriAbsL	PredatorHP	2LS	Port. w/o	Port. w/
strings	62	solved	**58**	20	0	0	20	**58**
		unique	**38**	0	0	0		
		fastest	**51**	7	0	0		
lists	26	solved	**20**	4	6	9	14	**23**
		unique	**9**	1	0	1		
		fastest	**9**	2	6	6		
trees	17	solved	13	0	0	**16**	16	**17**
		unique	1	0	0	**4**		
		fastest	3	0	0	**14**		

We tried to specialize the test harnesses to the tools' preferred format. E.g., SHRINKER expects the input to the operation to be taken as an argument to the test harness, while the baseline tools expect this input to be constructed by the harness itself. Meanwhile, one of the baseline tools does not support tail recursion, so for the benchmarks using recursion we provided it versions that were manually transformed into a loop. We also performed some tuning of the encodings, e.g., finding that the baseline tools performed better when strings were allocated using `malloc` rather than as VLAs on the stack, so we used those encodings. We configured all tools to check only memory safety and user assertion properties. We have provided the full benchmark set with this submission.

6.2 Baseline Tools

We report comparisons against the baseline tools VeriAbsL [42], PredatorHP [79], and 2LS [69]. We tried to represent the state-of-the-art in verification of heap-manipulating C code, excluding tools like Astree [23] without public executables, but including tools like VeriAbsL that are publicly available only in binary form.

We also considered MemCAD [80] and Ultimate Taipan [50]. Although it worked for small test programs, MemCAD threw many errors when we tried to run it on our benchmark instances, apparently due to the use of C features like initializing a struct pointer in a for loop. Because of this, we could not run most of the benchmarks on MemCAD, and its errors/documentation were not descriptive enough for us to adapt them in time for this submission. While Ultimate Taipan did properly parse and begin verifying our benchmarks, it timed out or returned `Unknown` on all of them. In both cases, we assume that the tools are probably tuned for different classes of inputs and so we exclude them from our experiments and do not report such negative results further.

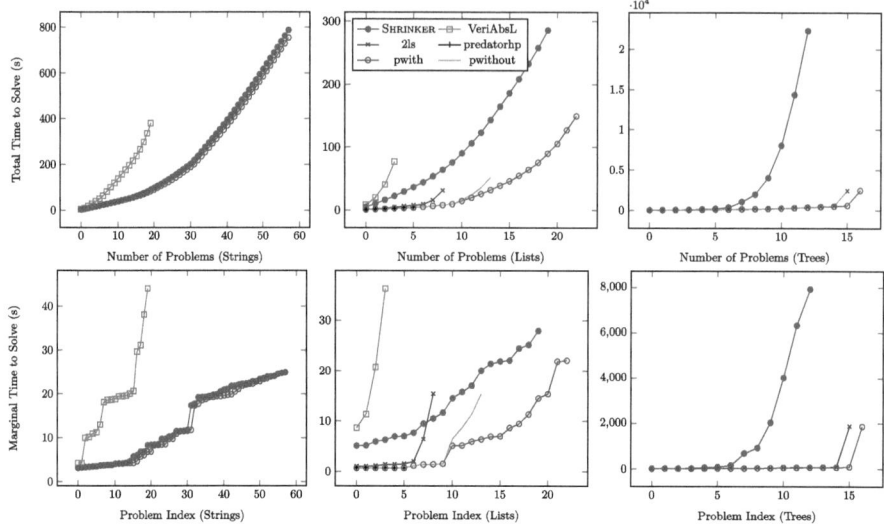

Fig. 1. Cactus plots. A point (n, t) on the top row indicates the tool can solve n of the benchmarks in t total seconds. A point (i, t) on the bottom row indicates the tool can solve the ith easiest (for it) benchmark in t seconds; prefix-summing the bottom row gives the top row. In all cases, curves lower (faster) and to the right (solving more problems) are better. We also give curve corresponding to the virtual-best portfolio (i.e., assuming a perfect heuristic that picks the best solver out of the four for that instance) both with (**pwith**) and without (**pwithout**) SHRINKER (for strings and trees, only one other tool solved any instances so the "portfolio without" line is identical to the other tool's curve). For both strings and lists, SHRINKER on its own always solves more instances than any other tool, is within the same order of magnitude of time as the other tools (sometimes faster), and leads to significant improvements in the portfolio performance. For trees, SHRINKER is considerably slower than the best tool (2ls), but its inclusion in the portfolio results in solving one additional benchmark.

It is also important to note that VeriAbsL, PredatorHP, and 2LS are competitors in the SV-COMP competition, which involves detecting unsafe programs quickly in addition to verifying safe ones. Our evaluation considers only the verification of safe programs, as we suggest detecting unsafety using a dedicated bounded model checking or fuzzing tool. Hence, it should be kept in mind that these baseline models might perform better if optimized to our setting.

6.3 Results

Our results are summarized in Table 1 and visualized as cactus plots in Fig. 1.

For both the string and list benchmark classes, SHRINKER is the single best solver. It is able to solve more than double the number of instances compared with the second-best solver. In fact, in both cases SHRINKER is able to solve many benchmarks that were not solved by any other baseline solver. Furthermore, it does so in a reasonably small (≤ 30 s) amount of time per benchmark. There remain only four string instances unsolved, all of which involve `strcat`, which is implemented in a complicated way for SHRINKER to follow (namely, the loop iterates simultaneously from the middle of the destination array and the start of the source array). On the whole, however, these results indicate SHRINKER is particularly good at solving monotonic string and list instances.

On tree benchmarks, SHRINKER performs quite well, solving over 75% of the tree benchmarks while neither VeriAbsL nor PredatorHP solved any. However, 2LS performs surprisingly well (solving all but one), hence SHRINKER takes second-place when looking at individual solvers. SHRINKER took longer to solve the tree benchmarks than the string and list benchmarks because it performs path splitting up to a certain unrolling depth, and tree-manipulating programs have an extra exponential blowup in the number of paths (because there is a choice between left/right child during each traversal). This path splitting is not strictly required by scapegoating size descent, but is needed for SHRINKER to increase precision in lieu of a more precise abstract domain (see Appendix C.5 for more discussion). Nonetheless, SHRINKER was able to solve the one instance left unsolved by 2LS.

In fact, for all three classes of benchmarks we find that adding SHRINKER to a virtual-best portfolio solver would allow it to solve more benchmarks than would be possible without SHRINKER (compare the "Port. w/o" and "Port. w/" columns in Table 1 and the 'pwith' and 'pwithout' curves in Fig. 1). Hence, in addition to being a compelling stand-alone solver for monotonic string and list benchmarks, SHRINKER could make a good addition to a portfolio like VeriAbsL.

7 Related Work

Induction on Input Size. [32,33] (integrated into the VeriAbsL portfolio) use rules to rewrite array programs P_N into a tail recursive form $P_N = \delta P_N; P_{N-1}$ and prove correctness by inducting on the size of the input. [55] describe a similar approach for array verification. Scapegoating size descent generalizes these ideas to a framework parameterized by data type, measure of size, and abstraction.

Cyclic Proof Systems. Proof by infinite descent also forms the basis of *cyclic proof systems* [27,28,67]. Our main contribution is scapegoating size descent, which is a general framework for combining proof by infinite descent with abstract interpretation to form a parameterized, general method of automatically proving properties about imperative programs.

Abstract Interpretation. Traditional static analysis is formalized by abstract interpretation [23,26,41], and we described one formulation of it in Sect. 2. Abstract interpreters use special abstractions of the heap [31,72,77]. [77] introduced the summary nodes idea we adapted in Sect. 5. Unfortunately, the space of such heap invariants is large, making discovering them hard. Scapegoating size descent builds on this framework to verify monotonic data structure traversals even without complicated heap abstractions.

Relational Verification. Reasoning about pairs of traces is part of the broader field of *relational program verification* [20] of *hyperproperties* [38]. The standard method for relational program verification is to reduce it to nonrelational program verification on a *product program* that simulates both traces together [19,65,83]. The approach taken in this paper is more similar to tools that verify relational properties directly, without constructing a product program [44,62,81].

Ordering States. Partial order reduction, abstraction, bisimulation, symmetry-breaking, and state merging all involve establishing an order on program states [11–15,24,35,36,47,54,82]. These methods generally require much stronger orderings on the traces, and give much stronger guarantees. E.g., [14] guarantees completeness when there is a well-ordering between reachable traces. In particular, ordering traces according to their length, heap size, or input size does not meet their requirements. As their results generally apply to temporal analyses, our scapegoating size descent approach is orthogonal and complementary.

Completeness Thresholds and Small Model Properties. Our approach of reducing the size of crash traces is similar the goal of *completeness thresholds* research [29,37,63]. Existing work in that area does not immediately apply to heap-manipulating C programs. *Small model properties* are a similar notion in the automated reasoning community [75] including some results for polymorphic programs [22,45] and theories modeling the heap [43,68,76].

Non-temporal Analyses. [21] use concrete tests to prove program properties, where the tests are generated dynamically by a verification engine. [16] show how to soundly infer static types from finitely many test executions. [70,71] show that proving properties of a restricted class of heap-manipulating imperative programs is decidable. [60] translates the program to a set of recurrence relations and tries to find a closed-form solution implying correctness properties.

Testing and BMC. Testing [30,46,49,53,58,59,61,66,78] cannot directly rule out the existence of bugs on inputs not tested. Ways to pick test inputs are known [18,51,57,64,73], and our work can be interpreted as a method for proving, for a particular program, that the small scope hypothesis holds [17,58]. Bounded model checking tools can prove a property holds for *every* program trace up to a certain length [59,61]. When used as a bug checker, scapegoating size descent tends to report bugs quicker than BMC because it uses an abstraction, i.e., it is allowed to report false alarms. But in practice BMC can usually detect buggy variants of our MDSTs in a few seconds, and gives counterexamples. Hence the real challenge for these instances, and benefit of SHRINKER, is in proving safety.

Manual Program Analysis. Tools for manually proving correctness require annotating the code with loop invariants [25,34,39,48,52,56,72,74].

Acknowledgements. I would like to thank the anonymous reviewers (whose suggestions have dramatically improved the quality of the paper) as well as Dawson Engler, Alex Ozdemir, Clark Barrett, David K. Zhang, Geoff Ramseyer, Alex Aiken, Martin Brain, Aditya V. Thakur, Zachary Yedidia, Akshay Srivatsan, and attendees of the Stanford software lunch, who provided helpful insights, conversations, and proofreading.

Disclosure of Interests. This work was generously funded via grants NSF DGE-1656518 and Stanford IOG Research Hub 281101-1-UDCPQ 298911.

References

1. The GNU C library (glibc) (2023). https://www.gnu.org/software/libc/
2. The Linux Kernel archives (2023). https://kernel.org/
3. The NetBSD project (2024). https://www.netbsd.org/
4. Git (2025). https://git-scm.com/
5. GNOME/glib (2025). https://gitlab.gnome.org/GNOME/glib
6. musl libc (2025). https://musl.libc.org/
7. OpenBSD (2025). https://www.openbsd.org/
8. QEMU (2025). https://www.qemu.org/
9. Redis - the real-time data platform (2025). https://redis.io/
10. Zsh (2025). https://www.zsh.org/
11. Abdulla, P.A., Aronis, S., Jonsson, B., Sagonas, K.: Optimal dynamic partial order reduction. In: Jagannathan, S., Sewell, P. (eds.) The 41st Annual ACM SIGPLAN-SIGACT Symposium on Principles of Programming Languages, POPL '14, San Diego, CA, USA, 20–21 January 2014, pp. 373–384. ACM (2014). https://doi.org/10.1145/2535838.2535845
12. Abdulla, P.A., Atto, M., Cederberg, J., Ji, R.: Automated analysis of data-dependent programs with dynamic memory. In: Liu, Z., Ravn, A.P. (eds.) ATVA 2009. LNCS, vol. 5799, pp. 197–212. Springer, Heidelberg (2009). https://doi.org/10.1007/978-3-642-04761-9_16
13. Abdulla, P.A., Bouajjani, A., Cederberg, J., Haziza, F., Rezine, A.: Monotonic abstraction for programs with dynamic memory heaps. In: Gupta, A., Malik, S. (eds.) CAV 2008. LNCS, vol. 5123, pp. 341–354. Springer, Heidelberg (2008). https://doi.org/10.1007/978-3-540-70545-1_33
14. Abdulla, P.A., Cerans, K., Jonsson, B., Tsay, Y.: General decidability theorems for infinite-state systems. In: Proceedings, 11th Annual IEEE Symposium on Logic in Computer Science, New Brunswick, New Jersey, USA, 27–30 July 1996, pp. 313–321. IEEE Computer Society (1996). https://doi.org/10.1109/LICS.1996.561359
15. Abdulla, P.A., Haziza, F., Holík, L.: Parameterized verification through view abstraction. Int. J. Softw. Tools Technol. Transf. **18**(5), 495–516 (2016). https://doi.org/10.1007/s10009-015-0406-x
16. An, J.D., Chaudhuri, A., Foster, J.S., Hicks, M.: Dynamic inference of static types for ruby. In: Ball, T., Sagiv, M. (eds.) Proceedings of the 38th ACM SIGPLAN-SIGACT Symposium on Principles of Programming Languages, POPL 2011, Austin, TX, USA, 26–28 January 2011, pp. 459–472. ACM (2011). https://doi.org/10.1145/1926385.1926437
17. Andoni, A., Daniliuc, D., Khurshid, S., Marinov, D.: Evaluating the "small scope hypothesis". In: Popl, vol. 2. Citeseer (2003)

18. Ball, T.: A theory of predicate-complete test coverage and generation. In: de Boer, F.S., Bonsangue, M.M., Graf, S., de Roever, W.-P. (eds.) FMCO 2004. LNCS, vol. 3657, pp. 1–22. Springer, Heidelberg (2005). https://doi.org/10.1007/11561163_1
19. Barthe, G., Crespo, J.M., Kunz, C.: Relational verification using product programs. In: Butler, M., Schulte, W. (eds.) FM 2011. LNCS, vol. 6664, pp. 200–214. Springer, Heidelberg (2011). https://doi.org/10.1007/978-3-642-21437-0_17
20. Beckert, B., Ulbrich, M.: Trends in relational program verification. In: Principled Software Development, pp. 41–58. Springer, Cham (2018). https://doi.org/10.1007/978-3-319-98047-8_3
21. Beckman, N.E., Nori, A.V., Rajamani, S.K., Simmons, R.J., Tetali, S., Thakur, A.V.: Proofs from tests. IEEE Trans. Softw. Eng. **36**(4), 495–508 (2010). https://doi.org/10.1109/TSE.2010.49
22. Bernardy, J.-P., Jansson, P., Claessen, K.: Testing polymorphic properties. In: Gordon, A.D. (ed.) ESOP 2010. LNCS, vol. 6012, pp. 125–144. Springer, Heidelberg (2010). https://doi.org/10.1007/978-3-642-11957-6_8
23. Blanchet, B.: Design and implementation of a special-purpose static program analyzer for safety-critical real-time embedded software. In: Mogensen, T.Æ., Schmidt, D.A., Sudborough, I.H. (eds.) The Essence of Computation. LNCS, vol. 2566, pp. 85–108. Springer, Heidelberg (2002). https://doi.org/10.1007/3-540-36377-7_5
24. Boonstoppel, P., Cadar, C., Engler, D.: RWset: attacking path explosion in constraint-based test generation. In: Ramakrishnan, C.R., Rehof, J. (eds.) TACAS 2008. LNCS, vol. 4963, pp. 351–366. Springer, Heidelberg (2008). https://doi.org/10.1007/978-3-540-78800-3_27
25. Boutillier, P., et al.: Coq 8.4 Reference Manual. Research report, Inria (2014). https://inria.hal.science/hal-01114602, the Coq Development Team
26. Brat, G., Navas, J.A., Shi, N., Venet, A.: IKOS: a framework for static analysis based on abstract interpretation. In: Giannakopoulou, D., Salaün, G. (eds.) SEFM 2014. LNCS, vol. 8702, pp. 271–277. Springer, Cham (2014). https://doi.org/10.1007/978-3-319-10431-7_20
27. Brotherston, J.: Cyclic proofs for first-order logic with inductive definitions. In: Beckert, B. (ed.) TABLEAUX 2005. LNCS (LNAI), vol. 3702, pp. 78–92. Springer, Heidelberg (2005). https://doi.org/10.1007/11554554_8
28. Brotherston, J., Gorogiannis, N., Petersen, R.L.: A generic cyclic theorem prover. In: Jhala, R., Igarashi, A. (eds.) APLAS 2012. LNCS, vol. 7705, pp. 350–367. Springer, Heidelberg (2012). https://doi.org/10.1007/978-3-642-35182-2_25
29. Bundala, D., Ouaknine, J., Worrell, J.: On the magnitude of completeness thresholds in bounded model checking. In: Proceedings of the 27th Annual IEEE Symposium on Logic in Computer Science, LICS 2012, Dubrovnik, Croatia, 25–28 June 2012, pp. 155–164. IEEE Computer Society (2012). https://doi.org/10.1109/LICS.2012.27
30. Cadar, C., Ganesh, V., Pawlowski, P.M., Dill, D.L., Engler, D.R.: EXE: automatically generating inputs of death. In: Juels, A., Wright, R.N., di Vimercati, S.D.C. (eds.) Proceedings of the 13th ACM Conference on Computer and Communications Security, CCS 2006, Alexandria, VA, USA, 30 October–3 November 2006, pp. 322–335. ACM (2006). https://doi.org/10.1145/1180405.1180445
31. Calcagno, C., Distefano, D., O'Hearn, P.W., Yang, H.: Compositional shape analysis by means of bi-abduction. In: Shao, Z., Pierce, B.C. (eds.) Proceedings of the 36th ACM SIGPLAN-SIGACT Symposium on Principles of Programming Languages, POPL 2009, Savannah, GA, USA, 21–23 January 2009, pp. 289–300. ACM (2009https://doi.org/10.1145/1480881.1480917

32. Chakraborty, S., Gupta, A., Unadkat, D.: Verifying array manipulating programs with full-program induction. In: TACAS 2020. LNCS, vol. 12078, pp. 22–39. Springer, Cham (2020). https://doi.org/10.1007/978-3-030-45190-5_2
33. Chakraborty, S., Gupta, A., Unadkat, D.: DIFFY: inductive reasoning of array programs using difference invariants. In: Silva, A., Leino, K. (eds.) CAV 2021. LNCS, vol. 12760, pp. 911–935. Springer, Cham (2021). https://doi.org/10.1007/978-3-030-81688-9_42
34. Chen, H., Ziegler, D., Chajed, T., Chlipala, A., Kaashoek, M.F., Zeldovich, N.: Using crash hoare logic for certifying the FSCQ file system. In: Miller, E.L., Hand, S. (eds.) Proceedings of the 25th Symposium on Operating Systems Principles, SOSP 2015, Monterey, CA, USA, 4–7 October 2015, pp. 18–37. ACM (2015). https://doi.org/10.1145/2815400.2815402
35. Clarke, E.M., Grumberg, O., Browne, M.C.: Reasoning about networks with many identical finite-state processes. In: Halpern, J.Y. (ed.) Proceedings of the Fifth Annual ACM Symposium on Principles of Distributed Computing, Calgary, Alberta, Canada, 11–13 August 1986, pp. 240–248. ACM (1986). https://doi.org/10.1145/10590.10611
36. Clarke, E.M., Grumberg, O., Long, D.E.: Model checking and abstraction. ACM Trans. Program. Lang. Syst. **16**(5), 1512–1542 (1994). https://doi.org/10.1145/186025.186051
37. Clarke, E., Kroening, D., Ouaknine, J., Strichman, O.: Completeness and complexity of bounded model checking. In: Steffen, B., Levi, G. (eds.) VMCAI 2004. LNCS, vol. 2937, pp. 85–96. Springer, Heidelberg (2004). https://doi.org/10.1007/978-3-540-24622-0_9
38. Clarkson, M.R., Schneider, F.B.: Hyperproperties. J. Comput. Secur. **18**(6), 1157–1210 (2010). https://doi.org/10.3233/JCS-2009-0393
39. Cohen, E., et al.: VCC: a practical system for verifying concurrent C. In: Berghofer, S., Nipkow, T., Urban, C., Wenzel, M. (eds.) TPHOLs 2009. LNCS, vol. 5674, pp. 23–42. Springer, Heidelberg (2009). https://doi.org/10.1007/978-3-642-03359-9_2
40. Cormen, T.H., Leiserson, C.E., Rivest, R.L., Stein, C.: Introduction to Algorithms, 3rd edn. The MIT Press, Cambridge (2009)
41. Cousot, P., Cousot, R.: Abstract interpretation: a unified lattice model for static analysis of programs by construction or approximation of fixpoints. In: Graham, R.M., Harrison, M.A., Sethi, R. (eds.) Conference Record of the Fourth ACM Symposium on Principles of Programming Languages, Los Angeles, California, USA, January 1977, pp. 238–252. ACM (1977). https://doi.org/10.1145/512950.512973
42. Darke, P., Chimdyalwar, B., Agrawal, S., Kumar, S., Venkatesh, R., Chakraborty, S.: Veriabsl: Scalable verification by abstraction and strategy prediction (competition contribution). In: Sankaranarayanan, S., Sharygina, N. (eds.) Tools and Algorithms for the Construction and Analysis of Systems - 29th International Conference, TACAS 2023, Held as Part of the European Joint Conferences on Theory and Practice of Software, ETAPS 2022, Paris, France, 22–27 April 2023, Proceedings, Part II. Lecture Notes in Computer Science, vol. 13994, pp. 588–593. Springer, Heidelberg (2023).https://doi.org/10.1007/978-3-031-30820-8_41
43. David, C., Kroening, D., Lewis, M.: Propositional reasoning about safety and termination of heap-manipulating programs. In: Vitek, J. (ed.) ESOP 2015. LNCS, vol. 9032, pp. 661–684. Springer, Heidelberg (2015). https://doi.org/10.1007/978-3-662-46669-8_27

44. Farina, G.P., Chong, S., Gaboardi, M.: Relational symbolic execution. In: Komendantskaya, E. (ed.) Proceedings of the 21st International Symposium on Principles and Practice of Programming Languages, PPDP 2019, Porto, Portugal, 7–9 October 2019, pp. 10:1–10:14. ACM (2019). https://doi.org/10.1145/3354166.3354175
45. (Favonia), K.H., Wang, Z.: Logarithm and program testing. Proc. ACM Program. Lang. **6**(POPL), 1–26 (2022). https://doi.org/10.1145/3498726
46. Fioraldi, A., Maier, D., Eißfeldt, H., Heuse, M.: AFL++ : combining incremental steps of fuzzing research. In: Yarom, Y., Zennou, S. (eds.) 14th USENIX Workshop on Offensive Technologies, WOOT 2020, 11 August 2020. USENIX Association (2020). https://www.usenix.org/conference/woot20/presentation/fioraldi
47. Flanagan, C., Godefroid, P.: Dynamic partial-order reduction for model checking software. In: Palsberg, J., Abadi, M. (eds.) Proceedings of the 32nd ACM SIGPLAN-SIGACT Symposium on Principles of Programming Languages, POPL 2005, Long Beach, California, USA, 12–14 January 2005, pp. 110–121. ACM (2005). https://doi.org/10.1145/1040305.1040315
48. Floyd, R.W.: Assigning meanings to programs. American Mathematical Society (1967)
49. George, B., Williams, L.A.: An initial investigation of test driven development in industry. In: Lamont, G.B., Haddad, H., Papadopoulos, G.A., Panda, B. (eds.) Proceedings of the 2003 ACM Symposium on Applied Computing (SAC), Melbourne, FL, USA, 9–12 March 2003, pp. 1135–1139. ACM (2003). https://doi.org/10.1145/952532.952753
50. Greitschus, M., Dietsch, D., Podelski, A.: Loop invariants from counterexamples. In: Ranzato, F. (ed.) SAS 2017. LNCS, vol. 10422, pp. 128–147. Springer, Cham (2017). https://doi.org/10.1007/978-3-319-66706-5_7
51. Grochtmann, M., Grimm, K.: Classification trees for partition testing. Softw. Test. Verificat. Reliab. **3**(2), 63–82 (1993). https://doi.org/10.1002/stvr.4370030203
52. Hoare, C.: An axiomatic basis for computer programming. Commun. ACM **12**(10), 576–580 (1969). https://doi.org/10.1145/363235.363259
53. Howden, W.E.: Program testing versus proofs of correctness. Softw. Test. Verificat. Reliab. **1**(1), 5–15 (1991). https://doi.org/10.1002/stvr.4370010103
54. Ip, C.N., Dill, D.L.: Better verification through symmetry. Formal Methods Syst. Des. **9**(1/2), 41–75 (1996). https://doi.org/10.1007/BF00625968
55. Ish-Shalom, O., Itzhaky, S., Rinetzky, N., Shoham, S.: Putting the squeeze on array programs: loop verification via inductive rank reduction. In: Beyer, D., Zufferey, D. (eds.) VMCAI 2020. LNCS, vol. 11990, pp. 112–135. Springer, Cham (2020). https://doi.org/10.1007/978-3-030-39322-9_6
56. Itzhaky, S., Banerjee, A., Immerman, N., Nanevski, A., Sagiv, M.: Effectively-propositional reasoning about reachability in linked data structures. In: Sharygina, N., Veith, H. (eds.) CAV 2013. LNCS, vol. 8044, pp. 756–772. Springer, Heidelberg (2013). https://doi.org/10.1007/978-3-642-39799-8_53
57. Ivankovic, M., Petrovic, G., Just, R., Fraser, G.: Code coverage at google. In: Dumas, M., Pfahl, D., Apel, S., Russo, A. (eds.) Proceedings of the ACM Joint Meeting on European Software Engineering Conference and Symposium on the Foundations of Software Engineering, ESEC/SIGSOFT FSE 2019, Tallinn, Estonia, 26–30 August 2019, pp. 955–963. ACM (2019). https://doi.org/10.1145/3338906.3340459
58. Jackson, D.: Alloy: a language and tool for exploring software designs. Commun. ACM **62**(9), 66–76 (2019). https://doi.org/10.1145/3338843

59. Khazem, K., Tautschnig, M.: CBMC path: a symbolic execution retrofit of the C bounded model checker. In: Beyer, D., Huisman, M., Kordon, F., Steffen, B. (eds.) TACAS 2019. LNCS, vol. 11429, pp. 199–203. Springer, Cham (2019). https://doi.org/10.1007/978-3-030-17502-3_13
60. Kincaid, Z., Reps, T., Cyphert, J.: Algebraic program analysis. In: Silva, A., Leino, K. (eds.) CAV 2021. LNCS, vol. 12759, pp. 46–83. Springer, Cham (2021). https://doi.org/10.1007/978-3-030-81685-8_3
61. King, J.C.: Symbolic execution and program testing. Commun. ACM **19**(7), 385–394 (1976). https://doi.org/10.1145/360248.360252
62. Kolesar, J.C., Piskac, R., Hallahan, W.T.: Checking equivalence in a non-strict language. Proc. ACM Program. Lang. **6**(OOPSLA2), 1469–1496 (2022). https://doi.org/10.1145/3563340
63. Kroening, D., Ouaknine, J., Strichman, O., Wahl, T., Worrell, J.: Linear completeness thresholds for bounded model checking. In: Gopalakrishnan, G., Qadeer, S. (eds.) CAV 2011. LNCS, vol. 6806, pp. 557–572. Springer, Heidelberg (2011). https://doi.org/10.1007/978-3-642-22110-1_44
64. Kuhn, R., Kacker, R.N., Lei, Y., Simos, D.E.: Input space coverage matters. Computer **53**(1), 37–44 (2020). https://doi.org/10.1109/MC.2019.2951980
65. Lahiri, S.K., McMillan, K.L., Sharma, R., Hawblitzel, C.: Differential assertion checking. In: Meyer, B., Baresi, L., Mezini, M. (eds.) Joint Meeting of the European Software Engineering Conference and the ACM SIGSOFT Symposium on the Foundations of Software Engineering, ESEC/FSE'13, Saint Petersburg, Russian Federation, 18–26 August 2013, pp. 345–355. ACM (2013). https://doi.org/10.1145/2491411.2491452
66. Li, J., Zhao, B., Zhang, C.: Fuzzing: a survey. Cybersecurity **1**(1), 1–13 (2018). https://doi.org/10.1186/s42400-018-0002-y
67. Lucanu, D., Roşu, G.: CIRC: a circular coinductive prover. In: Mossakowski, T., Montanari, U., Haveraaen, M. (eds.) CALCO 2007. LNCS, vol. 4624, pp. 372–378. Springer, Heidelberg (2007). https://doi.org/10.1007/978-3-540-73859-6_25
68. Madhusudan, P., Parlato, G., Qiu, X.: Decidable logics combining heap structures and data. In: Ball, T., Sagiv, M. (eds.) Proceedings of the 38th ACM SIGPLAN-SIGACT Symposium on Principles of Programming Languages, POPL 2011, Austin, TX, USA, 26–28 January 2011, pp. 611–622. ACM (2011). https://doi.org/10.1145/1926385.1926455
69. Malík, V., Hruska, M., Schrammel, P., Vojnar, T.: Template-based verification of heap-manipulating programs. In: Bjørner, N.S., Gurfinkel, A. (eds.) 2018 Formal Methods in Computer Aided Design, FMCAD 2018, Austin, TX, USA, 30 October–2 November 2018, pp. 1–9. IEEE (2018). https://doi.org/10.23919/FMCAD.2018.8603009
70. Mathur, U., Madhusudan, P., Viswanathan, M.: Decidable verification of uninterpreted programs. Proc. ACM Program. Lang. **3**(POPL), 46:1–46:29 (2019). https://doi.org/10.1145/3290359
71. Mathur, U., Murali, A., Krogmeier, P., Madhusudan, P., Viswanathan, M.: Deciding memory safety for single-pass heap-manipulating programs. Proc. ACM Program. Lang. **4**(POPL), 35:1–35:29 (2020). https://doi.org/10.1145/3371103
72. O'Hearn, P., Reynolds, J., Yang, H.: Local reasoning about programs that alter data structures. In: Fribourg, L. (ed.) CSL 2001. LNCS, vol. 2142, pp. 1–19. Springer, Heidelberg (2001). https://doi.org/10.1007/3-540-44802-0_1
73. Ostrand, T.J., Balcer, M.J.: The category-partition method for specifying and generating functional tests. Commun. ACM **31**(6), 676–686 (1988). https://doi.org/10.1145/62959.62964

74. Piskac, R., Wies, T., Zufferey, D.: Automating separation logic using SMT. In: Sharygina, N., Veith, H. (eds.) CAV 2013. LNCS, vol. 8044, pp. 773–789. Springer, Heidelberg (2013). https://doi.org/10.1007/978-3-642-39799-8_54
75. Pnueli, A., Rodeh, Y., Strichman, O., Siegel, M.: The small model property: how small can it be? Inf. Comput. **178**(1), 279–293 (2002). https://doi.org/10.1006/inco.2002.3175
76. Ranise, S., Zarba, C.G.: A theory of singly-linked lists and its extensible decision procedure. In: Fourth IEEE International Conference on Software Engineering and Formal Methods (SEFM 2006), Pune, India, 11–15 September 2006, pp. 206–215. IEEE Computer Society (2006). https://doi.org/10.1109/SEFM.2006.7
77. Sagiv, S., Reps, T.W., Wilhelm, R.: Parametric shape analysis via 3-valued logic. In: Appel, A.W., Aiken, A. (eds.) POPL '99, Proceedings of the 26th ACM SIGPLAN-SIGACT Symposium on Principles of Programming Languages, San Antonio, TX, USA, 20–22 January 1999, pp. 105–118. ACM (1999). https://doi.org/10.1145/292540.292552
78. Sen, K.: DART: directed automated random testing. In: Namjoshi, K., Zeller, A., Ziv, A. (eds.) HVC 2009. LNCS, vol. 6405, pp. 4–4. Springer, Heidelberg (2011). https://doi.org/10.1007/978-3-642-19237-1_4
79. Soková, V., Peringer, P., Vojnar, T., Kinst, O.: Predatorhp (version 3.1415) (2023). https://doi.org/10.5281/zenodo.10183805
80. Sotin, P., Rival, X.: Hierarchical shape abstraction of dynamic structures in static blocks. In: Jhala, R., Igarashi, A. (eds.) APLAS 2012. LNCS, vol. 7705, pp. 131–147. Springer, Heidelberg (2012). https://doi.org/10.1007/978-3-642-35182-2_10
81. Tiraboschi, I., Rezk, T., Rival, X.: Sound symbolic execution via abstract interpretation and its application to security. In: Dragoi, C., Emmi, M., Wang, J. (eds.) Verification, Model Checking, and Abstract Interpretation - 24th International Conference, VMCAI 2023, Boston, MA, USA, 16–17 January 2023, Proceedings. Lecture Notes in Computer Science, vol. 13881, pp. 267–295. Springer, Heidelberg (2023). https://doi.org/10.1007/978-3-031-24950-1_13
82. Wesley, S., Christakis, M., Navas, J.A., Trefler, R., Wüstholz, V., Gurfinkel, A.: Compositional verification of smart contracts through communication abstraction. In: Drăgoi, C., Mukherjee, S., Namjoshi, K. (eds.) SAS 2021. LNCS, vol. 12913, pp. 429–452. Springer, Cham (2021). https://doi.org/10.1007/978-3-030-88806-0_21
83. Zaks, A., Pnueli, A.: CoVaC: compiler validation by program analysis of the cross-product. In: Cuellar, J., Maibaum, T., Sere, K. (eds.) FM 2008. LNCS, vol. 5014, pp. 35–51. Springer, Heidelberg (2008). https://doi.org/10.1007/978-3-540-68237-0_5

Open Access This chapter is licensed under the terms of the Creative Commons Attribution 4.0 International License (http://creativecommons.org/licenses/by/4.0/), which permits use, sharing, adaptation, distribution and reproduction in any medium or format, as long as you give appropriate credit to the original author(s) and the source, provide a link to the Creative Commons license and indicate if changes were made.

The images or other third party material in this chapter are included in the chapter's Creative Commons license, unless indicated otherwise in a credit line to the material. If material is not included in the chapter's Creative Commons license and your intended use is not permitted by statutory regulation or exceeds the permitted use, you will need to obtain permission directly from the copyright holder.

Arithmetizing Shape Analysis

Sebastian Wolff[1]*, Ekanshdeep Gupta[1], Zafer Esen[2], Hossein Hojjat[3], Philipp Rümmer[4,2], and Thomas Wies[1]

[1] New York University, New York, USA
ekansh@nyu.edu
[2] Uppsala University, Uppsala, Sweden
[3] TeIAS, Khatam University, Tehran, Iran
[4] University of Regensburg, Regensburg, Germany

Abstract Memory safety is a fundamental correctness property of software. For programs that manipulate linked, heap-allocated data structures, ensuring memory safety requires analyzing their possible shapes. Despite significant advances in shape analysis, existing techniques rely on hand-crafted domains tailored to specific data structures, making them difficult to generalize and extend. This paper presents a novel approach that reduces memory-safety proofs to the verification of heap-less imperative programs, enabling the use of off-the-shelf software verification tools. We achieve this reduction through two complementary program instrumentation techniques: space invariants, which enable symbolic reasoning about unbounded heaps, and flow abstraction, which encodes global heap properties as local flow equations. The approach effectively verifies memory safety across a broad range of programs, including concurrent lists and trees that lie beyond the reach of existing shape analysis tools.

1 Introduction

One of the most severe and common types of flaws in software systems are memory safety violations. Memory safety violations typically happen in unsafe languages such as C and C++, for instance when the program tries to use a pointer to a memory location that has already been freed or that is out of bounds.

In this paper, we focus on *automatic* methods to prove the memory safety of programs operating on *linked mutable data structures*. We explicitly ignore issues related to the use of low-level patterns such as pointer arithmetic, union types, and casts as these are of orthogonal concern.

The key difficulty to verifying memory safety in this context is to determine the expected *shape* of the data structures, a challenge that has led to the field of *shape analysis* [37,13] and a plethora of different methods; for instance, based on three-valued logic [59], automata techniques [31], separation logic [16,5,15,17], bi-abduction [12,33], and other tailor-made abstract domains [57,14,2,10,18,34,62,22]. Today, the best tools competing in the *MemSafety* category of the software verification competition SV-COMP are based on an intricate combination of shape analysis techniques, including abstract interpretation, symbolic execution, and model checking.

---

* This work was completed prior to the author's employment at Amazon.

The mentioned approaches have in common that they generally need to be carefully tuned for a particular class of linked data structures to obtain good performance. As a result, practical shape analyses often make trade-offs such as targeting only specific data structures, e.g., linked lists. The engineering effort involved in developing and maintaining these sophisticated analyses makes an extension to other classes of data-structures (e.g., to trees), support for concurrency in programs [49,64], or an integration with techniques that target properties unrelated to memory safety (e.g., reasoning about data [10]) highly non-trivial. At SV-COMP, shape analysis-based tools largely form a class of their own, whereas software model checkers that aim at general safety properties provide only very limited support for reasoning about pointers. State-of-the-art verifiers, even though they might perform well on general verification tasks, can fail even on simple memory safety benchmarks involving singly-linked lists.

The goal of this paper is to provide a new avenue for adding shape reasoning to general-purpose verification tools, bypassing the need to develop and integrate sophisticated shape analysis domains. To this end, we propose a reduction-based approach that can be implemented in a preprocessing step for static analyzers targeting heap-free programs. The reduction builds on recent advances on local reasoning techniques for heap-manipulating programs. Specifically, we combine ideas from the *flow framework* [42,43,50], an approach based on separation logic for node-local reasoning about inductive properties of general heap graphs, with *space invariants* [38], which can summarize heap properties using node-local invariants. We formalize the approach in terms of rewrite rules that translate heap-manipulating programs to heap-less programs, and thus effectively *arithmetize* shape analysis for memory safety verification.

Compared to bespoke shape analysis methods, our reduction-based approach has several advantages. (i) Our approach is not tailored to any specified class of data-structures, but can handle, e.g., lists, nested lists, and trees out of the box. By plugging in different flow domains, the precision of the analysis can be controlled and increased on demand. (ii) Since the final analysis is carried out by an off-the-shelf verification tool, our approach inherits all capabilities for reasoning about data from the back-end tool; similarly, the approach is agnostic of the control structure (e.g., recursion) present in programs. (iii) Our approach is easy to extend to concurrent programs, which can be analyzed in a thread-modular way. We show that the reduction method can handle yield points and locks, and thus analyze challenging concurrent programs fully automatically. (iv) Our approach is simple to implement, since the required symbolic reasoning is offloaded to the off-the-shelf verification tool used as back-end.

For evaluation, we have implemented our approach in a prototype verification tool TRICERATOPS, utilizing the off-the-shelf software model checkers SEAHORN [23] and TRICERA [20] as back-ends, and evaluate using a set of benchmarks from the SV-COMP [7], as well as implementations of standard data structures written by us. The benchmarks include both sequential and concurrent programs and cover a variety of different shapes, including singly-linked lists, doubly-linked lists, and trees. We find that TRICERATOPS is able to verify

```
1  Node* List = new_dummy();                12  void insert() {
2  void pop() {                              13    Node* curr = List; lock(curr);
3    lock(List);                             14    while (havoc && curr->next != NULL) {
4    Node* item = List->next;                15      Node* next = curr->next;
5    if (item != NULL) {                     16      lock(next); unlock(curr);
6      lock(item);                           17      curr = next; }
7      List->next = item->next;              18    Node* item = malloc;
8      unlock(item);                         19    item->next = curr->next;
9      free(item); }                         20    curr->next = item;
10   unlock(List);                           21    unlock(curr);
11 }                                         22  }
```

Figure 1. A NULL-terminated singly-linked list implementation that pops elements from the front and inserts elements at a non-deterministically chosen position. Adding the colored lines turns the sequential implementation into a concurrent one that supports arbitrarily many concurrent pops and inserts.

memory safety effectively on such a diverse range of problems. In comparison with PREDATOR-HP [56,30], the 2024 SV-COMP gold medalist in the memory safety category [7], we observe that TRICERATOPS tends to exhibit longer runtimes, but is able to cover a wider range of problems than the more specialized tool PREDATOR-HP.

The *main contributions* of our paper are (i) a new reduction-based approach to shape analysis that combines space invariants (§3) with flow reasoning (§4) and extends to concurrent programs (§5); (ii) an *implementation* of our approach, resulting in the TRICERATOPS tool; and (iii) an *empirical evaluation* of the approach using a diverse set of sequential and concurrent programs (§6). The paper presents the overarching ideas of our new shape analysis and takes an operational view that lends itself to an implementation via program transformation. For a formalization of the analysis, we direct the reader to [68].

2 Motivating Example

We address the challenge of proving *memory safety* for heap-manipulating programs. Our goal is to fully automate the verification of the following properties:

(M1) Absence of unsafe accesses: heap reads and writes happen only through valid pointers, i.e., pointers that reference memory addresses that are allocated and have not been freed.
(M2) Absence of double frees: no memory is deallocated more than once.
(M3) Absence of memory leaks: all allocated memory is eventually deallocated.

Ensuring memory safety is a foundational aspect of program correctness but is often challenging due to the inherent complexity of understanding and capturing the shape of heap-allocated structures.

Running Example. We use the singly-linked list implementation from Fig. 1 as the running example (ignore the colored lines for a moment). The implementation includes a shared pointer List that references a dummy node whose successor is the head of the list. Initially, the list is empty and List's next field is NULL. This initialization is performed by new_dummy() on Line 1, which we elide.

New elements are added using the insert function. The insertion location is denoted by pointer curr, which is chosen by traversing the list for a non-deterministic number of steps, Lines 14–17. A new node item is allocated using malloc and its next field is set to curr's current successor, curr->next, on Line 19. Then, the new item is inserted after curr on Line 20 by updating curr's next field to item.

The pop function removes the head of the list. It begins by reading the current head into the pointer item, Line 4. If item is non-null, its successor becomes the new head, Line 7, and item is deallocated using free, Line 9.

Figure 2 illustrates a possible heap graph after inserting three nodes and popping one. Concretely, node a_1 represents the dummy node referenced by List. Nodes a_2, a_3, and a_4 have been inserted into the list in that order. Node a_2 has been unlinked (Line 7) and freed (Line 9) while pointer item from pop is still referencing it.

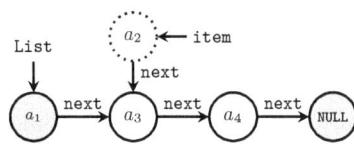

Figure 2. A possible heap resulting from three inserts and one pop.

We are working in the regime of whole-program analysis. When we refer to the *program* in Fig. 1 below, we mean the most general client of the given functions.

Although simple, verifying the program automatically turns out to be surprisingly challenging. To establish memory safety, we have to identify the following invariant that the program maintains: the allocated heap objects that have not yet been deallocated are precisely those reachable from List by traversing next links. Deriving this invariant automatically is non-trivial, as it requires global reasoning about the structure of the heap graph. While existing shape analysis techniques can derive such invariants, they rely on carefully designed shape domains to achieve efficiency and are typically precise only for specific shapes they are tailored to. Additionally, these techniques are often difficult to combine with other static analysis methods, such as those needed to reason about data [10,22]. Consequently, many software model checkers and automatic verification tools are unable to verify memory safety of our running example.

Our Approach. We present a source-to-source code transformation (*instrumentation*) that carries out the required shape analysis in a *completely local* way, making it both easy to automate and easy to integrate with other automatic verification methods. After instrumentation, we obtain a heap-less program that can be verified using off-the-shelf verification tools, such as the software model checker SEAHORN [23]. To achieve heap-lessness, our approach is based on two main reasoning principles: *space invariants* [38] and *flow abstraction* [42,43]. While both space invariants and flow abstraction have been developed in previous works, we are the first to combine them in order to obtain a fully automatic approach for verifying memory safety of programs like the one in Fig. 1. We stress that neither of the two approaches, by itself, is able to (automatically) verify such programs.

Space invariants over-approximate the heap: they capture all possible values that the fields of the object at a given address may have. This means that space invariants are per-object invariants. Materializing them for the addresses referenced by the pointers in the program allows us to mirror in the stack the (finitely many) heap locations that are accessible at any given program location. Hence, reads and writes targeting the heap can be mimicked by equivalent reads and writes targeting the stack. Since space invariants can be encoded using uninterpreted predicates [20,66], they can be automatically inferred by verification tools.

Flow abstraction, intuitively, performs a data-flow analysis on the heap graph. That is, the *flow* at a node is computed by propagating some initial flow value from a set of root nodes along the links in the heap. Hence, the flow captures global properties of the heap graph in a node-local way. We can use this abstraction, for instance, to capture the number of paths starting in a set of roots that a given node lies on. Flows like this path count can reveal shape information such as reachability (path count ≥ 1) and tree-ness (path count at most 1 at all nodes). To access the flow in our instrumentation, we treat it as ghost field flow on every object that is updated whenever there are writes to the heap.

Using the above abstractions, our instrumentation is capable of checking for memory safety. For (**M1**), we add assertions prior to dereferencing a pointer x to ensure that x is neither NULL nor freed. For the latter, we extend all objects with a special free flag that is raised by free. That is, x is not freed if x->free is not raised. For (**M2**), we do the same prior to freeing a pointer x. For (**M3**), we rely on the path counting flow and let our instrumentation assert that the space invariant is strong enough to imply that every object is either reachable or has been freed.

Figure 3 gives the instrumentation of function pop from Fig. 1. The accessible heap locations are mirrored using stack variables, one for each field of each object. For example, field next of pointer List is mirrored in List_next, and similarly for all other pointers. Dereferences like List->next on Line 4 in Fig. 1 are then replaced with the corresponding stack variable List_next on Line 26. The memory safety (**M1**) of this dereference is ensured by the assertion on Line 25. Similarly, an instance for checking (**M2**) is on Line 39. Checking (**M3**) is wrapped within function sync on Line 43, detailed in Fig. 6. In the following sections we elaborate on the ingredients of our instrumentation and discuss how to obtain the one in Fig. 3.

3 Core Instrumentation

We present an idealized version of our code instrumentation for rewriting the input program into a new program that does not use dynamically allocated heap memory. Our instrumentation conservatively overapproximates the behavior of the original program by overapproximating the actual values that it may read from or write to the heap. Later, we incorporate orthogonal techniques for the instrumentation to handle flow reasoning (§4) and concurrency (§5).

```
23  void pop() {
24    // Line 4: Node* item = List->next;
25    assert(List != 0 && List_free == 0);  avail(List)
26    int item = List_next;                                    Fmaterialize(item)
27    int item_next = havoc, item_free = havoc, item_flow = havoc;
28    assume(Inv(item, item_next, item_free, item_flow));  materialize(item)
29    int item_0_next = item_next, item_0_flow = item_flow;
30    assume(item_flow >= 1);  Fprop(List,item)
31    // Line 5: if (item != NULL) { ... }
32    if (item != 0) {
33      // Line 7: List->next = item->next;
34      assert(List != 0 && List_free == 0);  avail(List)
35      assert(item != 0 && item_free == 0);  avail(item)
36      List_next = item_next;
37      if (List == item) { item_next = List_next; }  dyn_up(List,next)
38      // Line 9: free(item);
39      assert(item != 0 && item_free == 0);  avail(item)
40      item_free = 1;
41      if (item == List) { List_free = 1; }  dyn_up(List,next)
42      // combined push site for Lines 7 and 9  Fpush(List), Fpush(item)
43      sync(List, item);
44      assert(Inv(List, List_next, List_free, List_flow));  push(List),
45      assert(Inv(item, item_next, item_free, item_flow));  push(item)
46      List_0_next = List_next; List_0_flow = List_flow;
47      item_0_next = item_next; item_0_flow = item_flow;
48  } }
```

Figure 3. Instrumentation of function pop from Fig. 1. The instrumentation is heap-less, mirroring the accessed heap locations in the stack by materializing the space invariant Inv. Moreover, the instrumentation ensures memory safety by inserting appropriate assertions. Helper sync on Line 43 performs flow reasoning and is discussed in detail in §4.

3.1 Overview

The instrumentation closely follows the structure of the original program, retaining control structures such as loops and branching. Primitive commands and expressions are rewritten to *not* use the heap. To make this precise, we assume that programs adhere to the following EBNF:

$$st ::= \text{while (havoc) } \{ st \} \mid \text{if (havoc) } \{ st \} \text{ else } \{ st \} \mid st^* \mid com;$$
$$com ::= \text{int x} \mid \text{T* x} \mid \text{x = y} \mid \text{x = y->f} \mid \text{x->f = y} \mid \text{x = malloc}$$
$$\mid \text{free(x)} \mid \text{assert(x} \oplus \text{y)} \mid \text{assume(x} \oplus \text{y)}$$

Both while and if statements are non-deterministic, as indicated by their conditions being havoc. This way, only primitive commands require rewriting. The

Rule	Input *com*	Instrumentation *com* ⤳ ...
INTRO	T* x;	int x; int x_f$_1$, ..., x_f$_n$, x_free, x_flow;
INTRO2	int x;	int x;
ASSIGN	x = y;	x = y; x_f$_1$ = y_f$_1$; ...; x_f$_n$ = y_f$_n$;
		x_free = y_free; x_flow = y_flow;
READ	x = y->f;	avail(y); x = y_f; materialize(x);
WRITE	x->f = y;	avail(x); x_f = y; dyn_up(x, f); push(x);
FREE	free(x);	avail(x); x_free = 1; dyn_up(x, f); push(x);
MALLOC	x = malloc;	x = ++ALLOC; x_f$_1$ = havoc; ...; x_f$_n$ = havoc;
		x_free = 0; x_flow = 0; no_alias(x); push(x);
ASSUME	assume(x ⊕ y);	prf(⊕, x, y); assume(x ⊕ y);
ASSERT	assert(x ⊕ y);	prf(⊕, x, y); assert(x ⊕ y);

```
49  avail(x)          ≡ assert(x != 0 && x_free == 0);
50  materialize(x)    ≡ if (x is not a pointer) { /* no-op */ } else {
51     x_f_1 = havoc; ...; x_f_n = havoc; x_free = havoc; x_flow = havoc;
52     assume(Inv(x, x_f_1, ..., x_f_n, x_free, x_flow)); }
53  push(x)           ≡ assert(Inv(x, x_f_1, ..., x_f_n, x_free, x_flow));
54  dyn_up(x, f)      ≡ for i in 1..k: if (x == y_i) { y_i_f = x_f; }
55  no_alias(x)       ≡ for i in 1..k: assume(x != y_i && ⋀_{j=1}^{m} x != y_i_ptr_j);
56  prf(⊕, x, y)      ≡ if (⊕ is other than ==) { /* no-op */ } else {
57     assert(x == 0 || y_free == 0); assert(y == 0 || x_free == 0); }
```

Figure 4. Instrumentation rules (top) and abbreviations (bottom). For a streamlined presentation, we assume that pointers are of type T* and have fields f$_1$, ..., f$_n$, of which ptr$_1$, ..., ptr$_m$ are those that are pointers themselves. We also assume that y$_1$, ..., y$_k$ are all pointers in scope other than x. We use `for` loops to syntactically repeat code.

primitive commands include variable declarations for integers and pointers T, variable assignments, reads from the heap, writes to the heap, heap memory allocation and deallocation, as well as assertions and assumptions that compare variables using an operator ⊕. Note that assumptions enable this language to model standard conditional loops and branching.

Our instrumentation is a relation $st_o \rightsquigarrow st_i$ among statements, where st_o is from the original program and st_i is the instrumented version of st_o. As mentioned earlier, statements themselves need no rewrite, only the primitive commands do. An overview of the rewriting rules is given in Fig. 4 and further detailed in the remainder of this section.

3.2 Heap Abstraction

Our instrumentation abstracts from the actual heap by overapproximating it with a *space invariant*. The space invariant is a family of uninterpreted predicates $\mathsf{Inv}_T(a, f_1, \ldots, f_n, \mathsf{free}, \mathsf{flow})$, one for each pointer type T in the program, indicating whether or not the fields of the object at address a may have the given values. The invariant takes all fields $f_1, \ldots, f_n$ of type T as well as the special fields free and flow.

A crucial aspect of our approach is the fact that the space invariant is uninterpreted. This allows us to pose requirements to it without explicitly specifying it, relying on the back-end solver to synthesize an appropriate invariant when verifying our instrumented program. While uninterpreted predicates are no standard feature, they are supported by tools like SEAHORN [23,66] and TRICERA [20].

3.3 Reading from the Heap

The original program accesses the heap with dereferences, such as x->f to access field f of the address a that x points to. These accesses are replaced to refer to the stack. To that end, our instrumentation mirrors the heap portion referenced by x by introducing a program variable x_f, for each field f of x. This is implemented by rule INTRO. The dereference x->f is then simply replaced with x_f.

To ensure the memory safety of dereferences (**M1**), our instrumentation inserts assertions prior to every dereference x->f that ensure that x is neither NULL nor freed. This check is implemented by avail(x) from Fig. 4.

For the newly introduced stack variables x_f to appropriately mirror the actual heap portions they correspond to, we materialize their values from the space invariant. Hence, we refer to those variables as materialization variables. Concretely, when a pointer x receives a new address (is assigned to) from a heap read, rule READ non-deterministically chooses new values for all materialization variables associated with x and then constrains them to satisfy the space invariant, implemented by materialize(x) from Fig. 4. This guarantees that subsequent accesses to the fields of x, including the special fields flow and free, overapproximate the values that the actual heap may hold.

Example 1. Consider the assignment Node* item = List->next; on Line 4 of our running example from Fig. 1. The instrumentation of this assignment is on Lines 25–28 from Fig. 3 and proceeds as follows. First, Line 25 ensures that dereferencing List is safe (avail(List)). Second, Line 26 updates item to its new value as read from List's materialization variable List_next. Last, Line 27 havocs the materialization variables for item and Line 28 materializes them from the space invariant Inv (materialize(List)).

Note that Line 27 deviates from materialize(List) in that it declares the materialization variables for item. This is because our running example does not separate the declaration of item from its assignment, which is why we combine rules INTRO and READ. □

3.4 Writing to the Heap

In the instrumentation, updates to the heap are reflected by updates to the materialization variables, rule WRITE. As expected, we replace writes to the heap, say to x->f, with writes to the corresponding materialization variables, x_f. Since we store materialization variables for every pointer, simply updating x_f may result in an inconsistent state where the materialization variable y_f of an alias y of x does not reflect the update. To overcome this, we perform a *semantic alias analysis* and mirror the update on aliasing pointer's materialization variables. The alias analysis is semantic in the sense that we encode it into the instrumentation such that it is performed by the back-end solver. Concretely, we use dyn_up(x,f) from Fig. 4 which adds conditionals that, for every pointer y, check if it aliases x and, if so, update y_f to x_f.[5]

Besides updating the materialization variables, our instrumentation has to reconcile heap updates with the space invariant, ensuring that it conservatively overapproximates all possible heap values. To that end, we simply assert the space invariant for the updated pointer and its materialization variables, cf. push(x) from Fig. 4. We refer to the program locations where this happens as *push sites*.

In practice, it is beneficial not to push each update on its own, but collect multiple updates and push them together. Coarse-grained pushes lead to more *sensible* space invariants as they avoid capturing intermediate states.

Technically, we require a push site for an update to x->f after updating the corresponding materialization variable x_f and before x_f becomes inaccessible. Materialization variable x_f may become inaccessible if it goes out of scope, i.e., if x goes out of scope, or if x is assigned to, i.e., x_f represents a potentially different memory portion. Due to space constraints, we do not detail this optimization.

Example 2. Consider the heap update List->next = item->next; on Line 7. The instrumentation in Fig. 3 proceeds as follows. First, Lines 34 and 35 ensure that it is safe to dereference pointers List (avail(List)) and item (avail(item)), respectively. Second, Line 36 updates the materialization variable List_next corresponding to List->next in order to reflect its new value, item_next. Third, Line 37 mirrors the update on aliases of List (dyn_up(List, next)). In the example, item is the only potential aliasing pointer in scope. Last, Line 44 asserts the invariant for List with its updated field values (push(List)).

In Fig. 3, the push site for List is deferred until the subsequent free of item from Line 9, the instrumentation of which is detailed below. Combining the push sites for these two commands alleviates the space invariant from capturing the intermediate state where item has been unlinked but not yet freed, improving the precision of our analysis. □

3.5 Frees

The instrumentation of memory reclamation free(x) by rule FREE is straightforward: we treat it as if it was an ordinary heap update to the special field free, i.e.,

---

[5] The attentive reader readily realizes that reading from the heap may result in pointers being aliases of the same object, which our materialization does not detect. Since this does not affect soundness, we omit an improved READ rule. Extending READ with a semantic alias analysis such as the one discussed here follows naturally.

we treat it as x->free = 1. Consequently, the instrumentation of frees ensures that x is neither NULL nor freed. This, in turn, ensures that x is not freed twice **(M2)**.[6]

It is worth pointing out that in order to check for double frees, the instrumentation does not need to consider the free field of pointers y that alias x. This is because heap updates to y keep the materialization variables of x consistent, i.e., freeing y sets the free materialization variables associated with both x and y.

Example 3. The instrumentation in Fig. 3 of free(item) on Line 9 proceeds as expected: Line 39 ensures memory safety (avail(item)), Line 40 performs the deletion by setting the free flag to 1, and Line 41 frees List should it alias item. The push site for the deletion is on Line 45. □

3.6 Allocation

Instrumenting allocations, rule MALLOC, is similar to materializing from the space invariant: we assign a new value to the receiving pointer x and havoc its materialization variables, except for the special field free which is set to 0 (not freed). We do not assume the space invariant because allocations do not initialize fields but leave them unspecified. For the address that the allocation returns we use a global allocation counter ALLOC to produce a new address for every allocation. Moreover, we use no_alias(x) to add assumptions that guarantee that the returned address is distinct from all pointers and all materialization variables of pointer type in scope. This resembles a garbage-collected semantics and not a standard C/C++ semantics where previously freed memory can be reused. For this to be sound, we require that the program cannot distinguish whether or not memory is actually reclaimed [25,32,51,52]. This requirement boils down to proving that the program satisfies memory safety properties **(M1)** and **(M2)** and, additionally, that pointers referencing freed memory are not compared to other pointers (except NULL). These assertions are implemented by the helper prf from Fig. 4 used in rules ASSERT and ASSUME. Note that this means that our instrumentation inlines an analysis akin to [25,32].

Similar to heap updates, pushing new allocations to the space invariant immediately will pollute the space invariant with states of uninitialized objects. In practice, we thus follow standard verification practice [63,65] and treat new allocations as *owned*, deferring their push until they are published into the shared heap so that the space invariant captures only *shared* objects. Due to space constraints and the fact that this optimization is not relevant for soundness, we refrain from making it explicit here.

Example 4. Consider the allocation of a Node into pointer item on Line 18. The instrumentation for item = malloc is given in Fig. 5. Line 58 assigns the next available address to item and increases the allocation counter ALLOC, which is declared along the shared pointer List. Line 59 havocs the fields of item and initializes the special fields free and flow. Lines 60 and 61 ensure that the allocation for item is fresh, i.e., distinct from List, curr, and any of their pointer fields. □

---

[6] This is stricter than necessary as it prevents freeing NULL, which is allowed and simply does nothing in C/C++. We ignore this technicality here.

```
58  int item = ++ALLOC;
59  int item_next = havoc, item_free = 0, item_flow = 0;
60  assume(item != List && item != List->next);
61  assume(item != curr && item != curr->next);
62  // assert(Inv(item, item_next, item_free, item_flow)); // push deferred
```

Figure 5. Instrumentation of `malloc`, Line 18. The allocation returns a *fresh* address. It is treated as owned memory and not pushed immediately.

4   Flows Instrumentation

We extend our instrumentation with flows. Flows provide light-weight shape information so that we can detect memory leaks, **(M3)**. Together with the assertions for **(M1)** and **(M2)** discussed in the previous section, this completes our memory safety analysis. Additionally, the shape information provided by flows increases the overall precision of our technique.

The changes required to integrate flow reasoning into our instrumentation are summarized in Fig. 6. We elaborate on the key components.

Flow Abstraction. The flow framework [42,43,50] associates a flow value with each node in the heap graph. Similar to forward data flow analyses, the flow values are computed by solving a fixed-point equation: each node is assigned an initial value and propagates updated values along its outgoing edges (pointers) based on its current flow value. This enables the flow framework to express inductive, global properties such as reachability in a local way, through the flow values of individual nodes.

To illustrate the reasoning carried out by our approach, we associate a *path count* with each node, a natural number that counts the number of paths starting in a root node and leading to the respective node on the heap. In terms of the running example from Fig. 2, we associate numbers $f_1, \ldots, f_4 \in \mathbb{N}$ with the nodes $a_1, \ldots, a_4$, respectively. The fixed-point equations for each node are derived by summing the path counts of the incoming `next` links:

$$f_1 = 1, \qquad f_2 = 0, \qquad f_3 = f_1 + f_2, \qquad f_4 = f_3.$$

The unique solution to these equations is $f_1 = f_3 = f_4 = 1$ and $f_2 = 0$, which enables us to differentiate between nodes that are still reachable (path count > 0) and nodes that are not part of the list (path count 0). Note that a_1 receives $f_1 = 1$ despite having no predecessors because it is the root of the list.

Towards detecting memory leaks **(M3)**, observe that the path-counting flow characterizes reachability: nodes with a path count of 0 are no longer reachable from the roots. Consequently, property **(M3)** is satisfied if all nodes with a path count of 0 have been reclaimed when the program under scrutiny terminates.

To perform this flow reasoning within our instrumentation, we extend the heap by adding a field `flow` to each object. In our example, field a_i->flow represents value f_i. The `flow` fields are updated dynamically by the instrumentation whenever heap objects or the heap graph change.

Localizing Flow Updates. The challenge in incorporating flows into the instrumentation arises because they are defined as fixed points over the entire heap graph, making a straightforward recomputation intractable.

We refer to the set of nodes whose flow values are affected by a heap update as the *footprint* of the update. A key observation that helps to address the issue of recomputing flow values is that the footprint is often localized to a small bounded region in the vicinity of the update. It then suffices to recompute the flow only in this bounded region, avoiding a recomputation of the full fixed point.

The key idea for this localization of the flow update is thus to (i) guess a bounded set of nodes (the footprint) for which the flow values are changed by the update, (ii) compute new flow values, but just within the footprint, (iii) verify that the update is really local to the chosen footprint.

Identifying a footprint that is guaranteed to localize the recomputation (i.e., step (i) above) is algorithmically challenging and oftentimes not possible to do statically. Instead, we use a heuristic for choosing the footprint: we include objects whose fields are updated by the program and neighboring objects with a statically fixed distance to the updated objects. In our implementation, we include only the immediate successors of updated objects.

We explain step (ii) below. Step (iii) guarantees the soundness of the localization to a given footprint. It requires our instrumentation to ensure that the flow at the boundary of the footprint is not changed by the update [42,43,50]. To be precise, for all objects y outside the footprint, we have to ensure that the total flow they receive from the footprint is exactly the same before and after the update. If so, the flow update is indeed local to the footprint and does not change outside of the footprint. Otherwise, verification fails.

Revisited Instrumentation. In order to compare the footprint before and after the update, we have to duplicate the materialization variables of all pointers before any update is performed. Our instrumentation creates such duplicates whenever a pointer is declared, rule FINTRO from Fig. 6. For pointer x and field f, the duplicate is x_0_f. (We do not duplicate the free field, it is not needed.) Whenever x is materialized (Fmaterialize), the duplicates x_0_f are set to the corresponding original x_f to reflect that no updates have been performed so far.

The main change for integrating flows concerns pushing updates as part of rules WRITE and FREE. Our revised instrumentation from Fig. 6 employs Fpush to do this. To present it in a way that does not rely on the actual flow that is being used, we use the following placeholders: $I(\text{x})$ produces the initial flow value for object x, $E_{\text{pre}}(\text{x}, \text{y})$ produces the flow that y receives from x before the update (using the duplicates x_0_f), and $E_{\text{post}}(\text{x}, \text{y})$ produces the flow that y receives from x after the update (using the originals x_f). Note that E_{pre} and E_{post} produce the sum of all edges between the nodes, should there be multiple. For an instantiation of these placeholders to the path-counting flow, refer to Example 5 below.

After choosing some footprint $x_1, \ldots, x_k$, e.g., according to the above heuristic, the most interesting part of Fpush is sync. It computes the new flow in the footprint (step (ii) above) and checks that the updates did not change the flow at the boundary of the footprint (step (iii)). Intuitively, to compute the new flow, we

Rule	Input com	Flow-aware instrumentation com ⤳ ...
FINTRO	T* x;	int x; int x_f$_1$, ..., x_f$_n$, x_free, x_flow;
		int x_0_f$_1$, ..., x_0_f$_n$, x_0_flow;
FASSIGN	x = y;	x = y; x_f$_1$ = x_f$_1$; ...; x_f$_n$ = x_f$_n$;
		x_0_f$_1$ = y_0_f$_1$; ...; x_0_f$_n$ = y_0_f$_n$;
		x_free = y_free; x_flow = y_flow; x_0_flow = y_0_flow;
FREAD	x = y->f;	avail(y); x = y_f; Fmaterialize(x); Fprop(y, x);
FMALLOC	x = malloc;	x = ++ALLOC; x_f$_1$ = havoc; ...; x_f$_n$ = havoc;
		x_free = 0; x_flow = 0; no_alias(x);
		x_0_f$_1$ = x_f$_1$; ...; x_0_f$_n$ = x_f$_n$;
		x_0_flow = x_flow; push(x);

63 Fprop(y, x) ≡ if (x is a pointer) { assume(x_flow >= E_{post}(y, x)); }
64 Fmaterialize(x) ≡ materialize(x); if (x is a pointer) {
65   x_0_f$_1$ = x_f$_1$; ...; x_0_f$_n$ = x_f$_n$; x_0_flow = x_flow; }
66 Fpush(x) ≡ let x$_1$, ..., x$_k$ = footprint of x; sync(x$_1$, ..., x$_k$);
67   for i in 1..k, j in 1..n: push(x$_i$); x$_i$_0_f$_j$ = x$_i$_f$_j$;
68 sync(x$_1$, ..., x$_k$) ≡
69   for i in 1..k: int x$_i$_in = havoc; x$_i$_flow = havoc;
70   for i in 1..k: assume(x$_i$_0_flow == x$_i$_in + I(x$_i$) + $\sum_{j=1}^{k} E_{\text{pre}}$(x$_i$,x$_j$));
71   for i in 1..k: assume(x$_i$_flow == x$_i$_in + I(x$_i$) + $\sum_{j=1}^{k} E_{\text{post}}$(x$_i$,x$_j$));
72   int out = havoc; assume(out > 0 && $\bigwedge_{i=1}^{k}$ out != x$_i$);
73   assert($\sum_{i=1}^{k} E_{\text{pre}}$(x$_i$, out) == $\sum_{1 \le i \le k} E_{\text{post}}$(x$_i$, out));

Figure 6. Revision of the core instrumentation from Fig. 4 to support flow reasoning. Changes to the rules (top) are colored. The F-prefixed abbreviations (bottom) replace the ones from Fig. 4 in all remaining and otherwise unchanged rules. In sync, functions $E_{\text{pre}}(\mathtt{x},\mathtt{y})$ and $E_{\text{post}}(\mathtt{x},\mathtt{y})$ encode the flow-specific values that are sent from x to y before and after the update, respectively.

havoc the new flow values and constrain them to guarantee that they are a fixed point (lines 69-71). We explain the relevant steps in more detail.

Since we compute the flow fixed point only for the footprint, we have to account for the flow that the footprint receives from objects outside the footprint. To that end, sync introduces x$_i$_in, for each x$_i$, which reflects that flow x$_i$ receives from the outside. The value of x$_i$_in is chosen non-deterministically on Line 69, and then constrained by the flow from before the update on Line 70. Intuitively, Line 70 performs one step of a Kleene fixed point iteration and assumes that the result equals the expected flow. Technically, the Kleene iteration for x$_i$ sums up the initial value $I(\mathtt{x}_i)$, the flow x$_i$_in that x$_i$ receives from outside the footprint, and the flow x$_i$ receives from within the footprint (via E_{pre}).

Next, sync computes the flow after the update on Line 71. While we could explicitly implement a standard least fixed point computation to do so, we found it to be more efficient to non-deterministically choose new flow values and enforce on Line 71 that they are *a* fixed point, analogous to the Kleene iteration above.

Step (iii) is implemented on lines 72-73. Similar to the previous step, we found it to be more efficient to perform this final check for a non-deterministically chosen object outside the footprint, rather than iterating over all the links that the objects in the footprint have to the outside. Concretely, Line 72 first havocs a node outside the footprint (this is variable out). Then Line 73 asserts that the flow that this node receives from within the footprint has remained unchanged, i.e., the flow it received before the update is the same as after the update.

Example 5. Consider the updates pop performs, namely unlinking and freeing item on Lines 7 and 9, respectively. The instrumentation of pop in Fig. 3 implements the flow reasoning presented so far. The interesting part is the combined push site for both updates on Lines 43–47. First, it invokes sync to recompute the flow after the update and check that choosing {List, item} as the footprint is a sound, local update. Then, it asserts the invariant for each node participating in the footprint, Lines 44 and 45. Finally, it resets the duplicated materialization variables, Lines 46 and 47.

The implementation for sync follows the blueprint from Fig. 6. We instantiate the flow-specific helpers according to our intuition for the path-counting flow, initializing the path count (flow) at root nodes and forwarding it along next links:

$$I(\mathtt{x}) \equiv \mathtt{x} == \mathtt{List}\ ?\ 1\ :\ 0$$
$$E_{\text{pre}}(\mathtt{x, y}) \equiv \mathtt{x\_0\_next} == \mathtt{y}\ ?\ \mathtt{x\_0\_flow}\ :\ 0$$
$$E_{\text{post}}(\mathtt{x, y}) \equiv \mathtt{x\_next}\ \ \ == \mathtt{y}\ ?\ \mathtt{x\_flow}\ \ \ :\ 0$$

Note that the above definitions need to be copied verbatim into sync, because the instrumentation has to *dynamically* compute the flow. □

Lastly, it is worth noting that we also change rule FREAD. When reading a pointer field y->f into x, then flow may propagate along the f edge if y receives flow. We capture this propagation using Fprop from Fig. 6, which assumes that the flow in x is at least what it receives from y, $E_{\text{post}}(\mathtt{y, x})$. In the running example, the read on Line 4 leads to the flow propagation on Line 30 in the instrumentation, where item is guaranteed to receive at least path count 1 from List because the shared List pointer is the root of the structure.

Memory Leaks. With the flow instrumentation in place, we are ready to check for memory leaks. To that end, we rely on the space invariant: we require that all objects, as captured by the space invariant, are either deleted or have a flow other than 0. The universal quantifier in this requirement is resolved by non-deterministically choosing some object with some field values, assuming the object satisfies the space invariant, and then asserting the above requirement. The following code implements this check for a type with fields $\mathtt{f}_1, \ldots, \mathtt{f}_n$:

```
int x = havoc; int x_f₁, ..., x_fₙ, x_free, x_flow; materialize(x);
assume(x != NULL); assert(x_flow > 0 || x_free == 1);
```

It does not matter where exactly this code is inserted because it only poses a requirement to the invariant. If the back-end solver cannot satisfy this requirement, verification fails. Our prototype tool inserts the check at the end of main.

Rule	Input *com*	Flow-aware instrumentation *com* ⇝ ...
YIELD	yield(x);	if (x_lock != 1) { Fmaterialize(x);
		assume(x_lock != 1); }
LOCK	lock(x);	avail(x); assume(x_lock == 0); x_lock = 1;
UNLOCK	release(x);	avail(x); assert(x_lock == 1); x_lock = 0;
CWRITE	x->f = y;	avail(x); assert(x_lock == 1); x_f = y;
		dyn_up(x, f); push(x);

Figure 7. Instrumentation for verifying concurrent programs using a thread-modular abstraction. New rules and changes to existing ones are colored. The instrumentation uses locks to avoid unnecessary materializations when no interference is possible.

5 Concurrency

Our instrumentation is readily extended to perform a thread-modular abstraction [6,21,36,55], allowing us to verify the program as if it was executed concurrently by an arbitrary number of threads. To that end, our instrumentation verifies the program from the point of view of an isolated thread that is subject to *interference*, i.e., heap updates, from other threads. The interference is applied whenever the isolated thread may be preempted, at so-called *yield points*. The possible heap updates from interfering threads are dictated by the space invariant: we continue to enforce that all atomic updates maintain the space invariant, so we can rely on it to always hold even in the presence of concurrency. For our instrumentation, summarized in Fig. 7, this simply means that we re-materialize all pointers at every yield point.

To make this precise, we assume that the yield points of the program under scrutiny are annotated with commands yield x, for every pointer x in scope. Annotating yield points in a given program is straightforward as they are required after every atomic command. Note that this approach easily supports applying standard moverness arguments [45,19,24,40] to reduce the number of yields, thereby increasing both precision and performance. Our instrumentation then replaces these yield x with Fmaterialize(x).

To improve the precision of our instrumentation, we make it lock-aware, with the goal of reducing unnecessary materializations. To that end, we equip all objects x with a lock x->lock, which can be acquired and released using commands lock(x) and unlock(x). To distinguish which thread is holding a lock, our instrumentation uses value 0 to indicate that the lock is available, value 1 to indicate that the isolated thread holds the lock, and any other value to indicate that an interferer is holding the lock. Hence, the instrumentation for acquiring x->lock sets its value to 1 if it is currently available (rule LOCK), and releasing x->lock reverts it back to 0 if it is currently held (rule UNLOCK).

Using locks, we can now elide materializing x at a yield point if the isolated thread holds x->lock, rule YIELD. Since interferers cannot acquire the lock on behalf of the isolated thread, it is safe for the rule to include an assumption stating that the newly materialized lock of x is distinct from 1.

Table 1. Each cell gives the number of solved benchmarks and average time over 10 runs. TRICERA and SEAHORN use instrumented benchmarks, while PREDATOR uses uninstrumented ones. "Broom" and "Shape" denote `memsafety-broom` and standard shape analysis benchmarks, respectively.

Properties	Benchmark Set	TRICERA	SEAHORN	PREDATOR	Total
sequential, safe	Broom	20 (9.4s)	21 (9.2s)	30 (0.8s)	31
sequential, safe	Shape1	9 (10.1s)	9 (4.3s)	8 (0.9s)	9
sequential, unsafe	Shape2	4 (4.8s)	4 (3.2s)	4 (0.9s)	4
concurrent, safe	Concurrent	4 (17.4s)	4 (39.6s)	0 (–)	5

To ensure that eliding materializations is sound, we add assertions to updates of x to guarantee that its lock is held during the update, rule CWRITE. This enforces that all threads adhere to this policy, so that holding x->lock indeed prevents interferers from updating x. More involved locking strategies are straightforward to integrate, but are beyond the scope of this paper.

Example 6. Consider the `pop` function from Fig. 1, including the concurrent extension in pink color. Line 4 reads `item` from the locked `List`'s next field. Between this line and the subsequent locking of `item` on Line 6, there is a yield point. At this yield point, `item` is re-materialized because it is not locked. However, `List` is not re-materialized because it is locked, Line 3. In particular, this allows our instrumentation to *remember* that `item` equals `List->next` on Line 7, which is crucial to derive the fact that `item` is being unlinked. □

Our instrumentation enabled us to verify complex concurrent structures, such as lock-based linked lists and trees (cf. §6), substantiating the merit of our approach. Notably, it generalizes far more easily to various settings compared to traditional, hand-crafted shape analyses.

6 Evaluation

We have implemented our proposed approach in a tool called TRICERATOPS. TRICERATOPS accepts programs in a C-like language, performs the instrumentation from the previous sections, and analyzes the instrumented program with an off-the-shelf solver to verify the assertions added through instrumentation, thereby proving memory safety. The supported solver toolchains are SEAHORN [23,66] with Z3/SPACER [39] as well as TRICERA [20] with ELDARICA [29,28]. Our tool currently requires manual preparation of input programs to match its simplified input language, such as separating chained pointer dereferences into individual ones. While automating this manual preprocessing step is conceptually straightforward, we did not prioritize it in the prototype.

Our instrumentation relies on several constructs and operators not native to C but widely supported by verification tools: (i) `havoc` for non-deterministically choosing values, (ii) `assert` for raising a runtime error if a given condition fails, and (iii) `assume` for blocking the execution if the given condition is not satisfied. Additionally, our encoding of space invariants Inv depends on (iv) uninterpreted predicates [20,66], which are less commonly supported. Our back-end solvers, SEAHORN and TRICERA, support all of these features. While we are not aware of a general method to encode uninterpreted predicates in any verification tool, we believe it is straightforward to do so in Horn clause-based tools.

Limitations of the current implementation are that we rely on a simplified acyclicity requirement for the localized flow update instrumentation instead of running a fixed point computation, for performance reasons. This precludes handling of data structures like circular lists. Currently, we also only support the path-counting flow domain. Neither of these are inherent limitations of the technique; our implementation can be extended to support different flow domains, but we decided to focus on the path-counting flow domain since it suffices to handle a large variety of data structures most relevant in practice, and to demonstrate the usefulness of our technique. As mentioned previously, our analysis is a whole-program analysis—if the input program has no `main` function, TRICERATOPS inserts one that implements a most general client by invoking the remaining program functions in a nondeterministic order and analyzes it.

We evaluated TRICERATOPS on a set of benchmarks that covers a variety of shapes, including singly-linked, doubly-linked, and nested lists, as well as trees, to substantiate that our approach is capable of verifying programs where this task inherently relies on shape information. Our benchmark set is divided into three parts: (1) 31 sequential `memsafety-broom` [1] examples from SV-COMP [7,8], featuring singly-linked, doubly-linked, and nested lists. Amongst these, four examples feature circular queues and three more examples feature pointer arithmetic and are thus incompatible with TRICERATOPS. We limit our evaluation to the `memsafety-broom` subset of the `MemSafety-LinkedLists` sub-category of SV-COMP due to the manual preprocessing of benchmarks required by TRICERATOPS. (2) 13 standard sequential shape analysis examples with singly- and doubly-linked lists and binary trees, including four with memory-safety violations, to stress-test TRICERATOPS. (3) Five memory-safe examples of concurrent singly-linked lists and binary trees, designed for memory safety verification; they non-deterministically generate, traverse (and possibly modify), and free dynamic structures in the heap.

We compare TRICERATOPS with the state-of-the-art shape analysis tool PREDATOR-HP [56,30], the 2024 SV-COMP gold medalist in the memory safety category [7]. Table 1 summarizes the number of sequential and concurrent benchmarks solved by TRICERATOPS using TRICERA and SEAHORN, and the number solved by PREDATOR-HP. Detailed results for the concurrent benchmarks are in Table 2. All experiments were conducted on an Apple M1 Pro.

The experiments show that our approach is capable of verifying intricate memory safety tasks. As expected, the runtimes are slower than those of a fine-tuned shape analysis tool like PREDATOR-HP. PREDATOR-HP is able to handle a wider variety of linked list examples than TRICERATOPS. It is able to correctly solve 30 of the 31 examples from the `memsaftey-broom` benchmark with runtimes

Table 2. Concurrent benchmarks with runtimes averaged over 10 runs. The TRICERATOPS column shows instrumentation time. TRICERA and SEAHORN columns show solving times using those backends. LoC = lines of code; LoI = lines after instrumentation. Symbols ✓ and ✗ indicate if the tool produced a correct verification verdict.

Benchmark	LoC	LoI	TRICERATOPS	TRICERA	SEAHORN
Running Example (Fig. 1)	37	303	0.77s	15.73s ✓	0.99s ✗
Coarse Stack	38	260	0.42s	8.37s ✓	4.39s ✓
Fine List [26, §9.5]	60	392	2.25s	30.56s ✓	92.19s ✓
Internal BST (no maintenance)	41	281	1.73s	14.77s ✓	5.78s ✓
Internal BST (simple removal)	78	441	6.04s	122.62s ✗	55.93s ✓

of less than one second, whereas TRICERATOPS can only handle 21. Seven of the examples from this set are incompatible with TRICERATOPS because they involve circular lists or pointer arithmetic. Another three examples fail due to unbounded flow updates. We note that swapping the order of two operations in each of these three benchmarks makes the resulting flow updates bounded, without changing the semantics. Such transformations could be implemented with a simple heuristic. Overall, the better performance of PREDATOR-HP on these benchmarks is expected since it is a highly specialized and mature tool.

However, our adaptable approach verifies sequential and concurrent tree benchmarks that are beyond PREDATOR-HP's capabilities. We believe that extending PREDATOR-HP to handle trees or concurrency would be non-trivial and labor intensive. This substantiates the usefulness of arithmetizing shape analysis to leverage a broader range of verification tools.

Notably, runtimes for sequential and concurrent benchmarks are comparable, likely due to materializing the space invariant, yielding similarly precise shape information in both cases, and the re-materialization required for concurrent instrumentation (cf. rule YIELD) can be dealt with efficiently by the solvers.

Finally, our over-approximate analysis may produce spurious counter-examples. However, these often allow reconstructing *why* a failing assertion was added, revealing actual bugs in the input program. Although not automated, this approach was effective during the development of TRICERATOPS and our experiments.

7 Related Work

Shape Analysis. We briefly survey existing approaches in shape analysis that our work is related to; for a more in-depth overview, we refer the reader to [13].

A parametric framework based on three-valued logic was introduced in [59] and later reformulated in terms of predicate abstraction in [57]. The effectiveness of this approach depends on manually chosen predicates tailored to each program.

The tool PREDATOR [18] uses an abstract shape domain for lists. PREDATOR can report spurious counterexamples, which is addressed in the version PREDATOR-HP [53] by running additional instances of PREDATOR without heap abstraction in parallel. PREDATOR only provides limited support for non-pointer data, and cannot handle programs with trees, skip-lists, or concurrency in a sound way. The approach of PREDATOR is also used by CPACHECKER [3] in combination with symbolic execution [9] for the purpose of checking unbounded memory safety. MEMCAD [62,34,22] combines sequence and shape abstractions and supports lists and trees. The sequence abstraction enables the tracking of data constraints on such data structures, like value ranges and lengths of sequences.

Several studies employ expensive global reasoning about heap memory, but deliberately stay within decidable logics in order to enable automation [35,44,46,67].

More generally, many points-to domains have been proposed to reason abstractly about pointers and linked data-structures stored on the heap, e.g., [61,27]. Such domains are less precise, but can be implemented more efficiently than shape analysis domains. Space invariants resemble points-to analysis in that they summarize the possible states of objects using a symbolic invariant; the inference of space invariants is carried out symbolically using a model checker, however, and not with the help of abstract interpretation. Refined versions of space invariants [38] are related to recency-abstraction [4], which distinguishes objects based on allocation sites and summarizes object states separately for the most recent allocation and all earlier allocations.

Separation Logic and the Flow Framework. Separation logic (SL) [54,58] is widely used for reasoning about memory safety and functional properties. It enables compositional reasoning by partitioning the heap into smaller regions, allowing properties for different heap regions to be expressed locally, such that modifications to one region do not invalidate properties about other regions.

The flow framework [42,43,50], which we build on in this paper, endows the (heap) graph with a flow that allows global properties to be specified in terms of node-local invariants by referring to that flow. Flows augment the nodes in the heap with additional ghost information, and are computed inductively over the graph structure using data-flow equations. The flow framework has been used in the verification of sophisticated algorithms that are difficult to handle by other techniques, such as the Priority Inheritance Protocol, object-oriented design patterns, and complex concurrent data structures [41].

A general proof technique for reasoning about global graph properties using the flow framework is presented in [43]. The framework automatically checks that each modified heap region preserves invariants, and is implemented using the tool VIPER. In this setting, invariants must be manually provided but can then be verified automatically. Similarly, [48,49,47] devise (semi-)automatic flow framework-based techniques for fine-grained concurrent data structures.

Bi-abduction-based Shape Analysis. Bi-abduction [12] is an SL-based shape analysis technique that simultaneously identifies both the missing preconditions required for safe code execution and the portions of memory that remain unchanged after execution. This enables a compositional analysis strategy that analyzes parts of a program independently and later combines the results, leading to improved scalability, as demonstrated by the success of the INFER tool [11].

The BROOM tool implements a bi-abduction analysis for low-level C code [33]. Classical bi-abduction often yields imprecise invariants for loops. The authors of [60] address this limitation by introducing "biabductive loop acceleration", which directly constructs and verifies candidate loop invariants, complemented by a shape extrapolation heuristic that leverages locality in list-like data structures.

Our technique has strengths and weaknesses orthogonal to those of bi-abduction-based approaches. On the one hand, our reduction-based approach enables easy integration into existing software verification tool chains. The approach also promises to be more easily extensible, e.g., by instantiating the flow abstraction with different flow domains to track different kinds of shape properties. In particular, we can use the same flow domain to prove memory safety of both concurrent and sequential programs manipulating lists and trees.

On the other hand, our approach reduces the verification problem to a whole program analysis that is not immediately amenable to the more efficient compositional reasoning that underlies biabduction techniques. Exploring a combination of the two approaches is an interesting direction for future work.

8 Conclusions

We have presented a new automatic shape analysis method based on two reasoning principles: *flow abstraction,* which reduces global properties of the heap graph to local flow equations that are required to hold for every object on the heap, and *space invariants,* for representing an unbounded number of heap objects using symbolic invariants. As our approach is implemented through a source-to-source transformation, it can be used in conjunction with different verification back-ends, and is able to leverage all data types and language features supported by the back-end tool. Our experiments show that the analysis approach covers a wide range of shapes and can even be extended to concurrent programs.

Several avenues for future work exist. At the moment, concurrency support in TRICERATOPS is only experimental, more research is needed to work out the details of how to analyze concurrent programs operating on linked data structures using our approach. We also plan to investigate the use of other flow domains, beyond path counting, to obtain more precise shape analysis. Lastly, the details of how to combine shape analysis with data analysis (e.g., sortedness of lists or well-formedness of search trees) remain to be investigated.

Acknowledgements. This work is funded in parts, by the National Science Foundation under grant GS1000000012304758 and by the Swedish Research Council (VR) under the grant 2021-06327. The first author was supported by a Junior Fellowship from the Simons Foundation (855328, SW).

Disclaimers. The authors have no competing interests to declare that are relevant to the content of this article.

References

1. c/memsafety-broom benchmark suite of SV-COMP 2024. https://gitlab.com/sosy-lab/benchmarking/sv-benchmarks/-/tree/svcomp24-final/c/memsafety-broom, [Accessed 04/08/2025]
2. Abdulla, P.A., Bouajjani, A., Cederberg, J., Haziza, F., Ji, R., Rezine, A.: Shape analysis via monotonic abstraction. In: Beyond the Finite: New Challenges in Verification and Semistructured Data. Dagstuhl Seminar Proceedings, vol. 08171. Schloss Dagstuhl - Leibniz-Zentrum für Informatik, Germany (2008)
3. Baier, D., Beyer, D., Chien, P., Jankola, M., Kettl, M., Lee, N., Lemberger, T., Rosenfeld, M.L., Spiessl, M., Wachowitz, H., Wendler, P.: Cpachecker 2.3 with strategy selection - (competition contribution). In: TACAS (3). Lecture Notes in Computer Science, vol. 14572, pp. 359–364. Springer (2024)
4. Balakrishnan, G., Reps, T.W.: Recency-abstraction for heap-allocated storage. In: Yi, K. (ed.) Static Analysis, 13th International Symposium, SAS 2006, Seoul, Korea, August 29-31, 2006, Proceedings. Lecture Notes in Computer Science, vol. 4134, pp. 221–239. Springer (2006). https://doi.org/10.1007/11823230_15, https://doi.org/10.1007/11823230_15
5. Berdine, J., Calcagno, C., Cook, B., Distefano, D., O'Hearn, P.W., Wies, T., Yang, H.: Shape analysis for composite data structures. In: CAV. Lecture Notes in Computer Science, vol. 4590, pp. 178–192. Springer (2007)
6. Berdine, J., Lev-Ami, T., Manevich, R., Ramalingam, G., Sagiv, S.: Thread quantification for concurrent shape analysis. In: CAV. Lecture Notes in Computer Science, vol. 5123, pp. 399–413. Springer (2008)
7. Beyer, D.: State of the art in software verification and witness validation: SV-COMP 2024. In: TACAS (3). Lecture Notes in Computer Science, vol. 14572, pp. 299–329. Springer (2024)
8. Beyer, D.: Sv-benchmarks: Benchmark set for software verification (SV-COMP 2024) (version svcomp24). https://doi.org/10.5281/zenodo.10669723 (Mar 2024). https://doi.org/10.5281/ZENODO.10669723, https://doi.org/10.5281/zenodo.10669723, accessed on YYYY-MM-DD.
9. Beyer, D., Lemberger, T.: Cpa-symexec: efficient symbolic execution in cpachecker. In: ASE. pp. 900–903. ACM (2018)
10. Bouajjani, A., Dragoi, C., Enea, C., Rezine, A., Sighireanu, M.: Invariant synthesis for programs manipulating lists with unbounded data. In: CAV. Lecture Notes in Computer Science, vol. 6174, pp. 72–88. Springer (2010)
11. Calcagno, C., Distefano, D.: Infer: An automatic program verifier for memory safety of C programs. In: NASA Formal Methods (NFM). Lecture Notes in Computer Science, vol. 6617, pp. 459–465. Springer (2011). https://doi.org/10.1007/978-3-642-20398-5_33, https://doi.org/10.1007/978-3-642-20398-5_33
12. Calcagno, C., Distefano, D., O'Hearn, P.W., Yang, H.: Compositional shape analysis by means of bi-abduction. In: POPL. pp. 289–300. ACM (2009)
13. Chang, B.E., Dragoi, C., Manevich, R., Rinetzky, N., Rival, X.: Shape analysis. Found. Trends Program. Lang. **6**(1-2), 1–158 (2020)
14. Chang, B.E., Rival, X.: Relational inductive shape analysis. In: POPL. pp. 247–260. ACM (2008)
15. Chang, B.E., Rival, X., Necula, G.C.: Shape analysis with structural invariant checkers. In: SAS. Lecture Notes in Computer Science, vol. 4634, pp. 384–401. Springer (2007)

16. Distefano, D., O'Hearn, P.W., Yang, H.: A local shape analysis based on separation logic. In: TACAS. Lecture Notes in Computer Science, vol. 3920, pp. 287–302. Springer (2006)
17. Dudka, K., Peringer, P., Vojnar, T.: Predator: A practical tool for checking manipulation of dynamic data structures using separation logic. In: CAV. Lecture Notes in Computer Science, vol. 6806, pp. 372–378. Springer (2011)
18. Dudka, K., Peringer, P., Vojnar, T.: Byte-precise verification of low-level list manipulation. In: SAS. Lecture Notes in Computer Science, vol. 7935, pp. 215–237. Springer (2013)
19. Elmas, T., Qadeer, S., Tasiran, S.: A calculus of atomic actions. In: POPL. pp. 2–15. ACM (2009)
20. Esen, Z., Rümmer, P.: Tricera: Verifying C programs using the theory of heaps. In: FMCAD. pp. 380–391. IEEE (2022)
21. Flanagan, C., Qadeer, S.: Thread-modular model checking. In: SPIN. Lecture Notes in Computer Science, vol. 2648, pp. 213–224. Springer (2003)
22. Giet, J., Ridoux, F., Rival, X.: A product of shape and sequence abstractions. In: SAS. Lecture Notes in Computer Science, vol. 14284, pp. 310–342. Springer (2023)
23. Gurfinkel, A., Kahsai, T., Komuravelli, A., Navas, J.A.: The seahorn verification framework. In: CAV (1). Lecture Notes in Computer Science, vol. 9206, pp. 343–361. Springer (2015)
24. Hawblitzel, C., Petrank, E., Qadeer, S., Tasiran, S.: Automated and modular refinement reasoning for concurrent programs. In: CAV (2). Lecture Notes in Computer Science, vol. 9207, pp. 449–465. Springer (2015)
25. Haziza, F., Holík, L., Meyer, R., Wolff, S.: Pointer race freedom. In: VMCAI. Lecture Notes in Computer Science, vol. 9583, pp. 393–412. Springer (2016)
26. Herlihy, M., Shavit, N.: The art of multiprocessor programming. Morgan Kaufmann (2008)
27. Hind, M., Pioli, A.: Assessing the effects of flow-sensitivity on pointer alias analyses. In: Levi, G. (ed.) Static Analysis, 5th International Symposium, SAS '98, Pisa, Italy, September 14-16, 1998, Proceedings. Lecture Notes in Computer Science, vol. 1503, pp. 57–81. Springer (1998). https://doi.org/10.1007/3-540-49727-7_4, https://doi.org/10.1007/3-540-49727-7_4
28. Hojjat, H., Konecný, F., Garnier, F., Iosif, R., Kuncak, V., Rümmer, P.: A verification toolkit for numerical transition systems - tool paper. In: FM. Lecture Notes in Computer Science, vol. 7436, pp. 247–251. Springer (2012)
29. Hojjat, H., Rümmer, P.: The ELDARICA horn solver. In: FMCAD. pp. 1–7. IEEE (2018)
30. Holík, L., Kotoun, M., Peringer, P., Soková, V., Trtík, M., Vojnar, T.: Predator shape analysis tool suite. In: Haifa Verification Conference. Lecture Notes in Computer Science, vol. 10028, pp. 202–209 (2016)
31. Holík, L., Lengál, O., Rogalewicz, A., Simácek, J., Vojnar, T.: Fully automated shape analysis based on forest automata. In: CAV. Lecture Notes in Computer Science, vol. 8044, pp. 740–755. Springer (2013)
32. Holík, L., Meyer, R., Vojnar, T., Wolff, S.: Effect summaries for thread-modular analysis. CoRR **abs/1705.03701** (2017)
33. Holík, L., Peringer, P., Rogalewicz, A., Soková, V., Vojnar, T., Zuleger, F.: Low-level bi-abduction. In: ECOOP. LIPIcs, vol. 222, pp. 19:1–19:30. Schloss Dagstuhl - Leibniz-Zentrum für Informatik (2022)
34. Illous, H., Lemerre, M., Rival, X.: A relational shape abstract domain. Formal Methods Syst. Des. **57**(3), 343–400 (2021)

35. Itzhaky, S., Banerjee, A., Immerman, N., Nanevski, A., Sagiv, M.: Effectively-propositional reasoning about reachability in linked data structures. In: CAV. Lecture Notes in Computer Science, vol. 8044, pp. 756–772. Springer (2013)
36. Jones, C.B.: Tentative steps toward a development method for interfering programs. ACM Trans. Program. Lang. Syst. **5**(4), 596–619 (1983)
37. Jones, N.D., Muchnick, S.S.: Flow analysis and optimization of lisp-like structures. In: POPL. pp. 244–256. ACM Press (1979)
38. Kahsai, T., Kersten, R., Rümmer, P., Schäf, M.: Quantified heap invariants for object-oriented programs. In: LPAR. EPiC Series in Computing, vol. 46, pp. 368–384. EasyChair (2017)
39. Komuravelli, A., Gurfinkel, A., Chaki, S., Clarke, E.M.: Automatic abstraction in smt-based unbounded software model checking. In: CAV. Lecture Notes in Computer Science, vol. 8044, pp. 846–862. Springer (2013)
40. Kragl, B., Qadeer, S.: Layered concurrent programs. In: CAV (1). Lecture Notes in Computer Science, vol. 10981, pp. 79–102. Springer (2018)
41. Krishna, S., Patel, N., Shasha, D.E., Wies, T.: Verifying concurrent search structure templates. In: PLDI. pp. 181–196. ACM (2020)
42. Krishna, S., Shasha, D.E., Wies, T.: Go with the flow: compositional abstractions for concurrent data structures. Proc. ACM Program. Lang. **2**(POPL), 37:1–37:31 (2018)
43. Krishna, S., Summers, A.J., Wies, T.: Local reasoning for global graph properties. In: ESOP. Lecture Notes in Computer Science, vol. 12075, pp. 308–335. Springer (2020)
44. Lahiri, S.K., Qadeer, S.: Back to the future: revisiting precise program verification using SMT solvers. In: POPL. pp. 171–182. ACM (2008)
45. Lipton, R.J.: Reduction: A method of proving properties of parallel programs. Commun. ACM **18**(12), 717–721 (1975)
46. Madhusudan, P., Qiu, X., Stefanescu, A.: Recursive proofs for inductive tree data-structures. In: POPL. pp. 123–136. ACM (2012)
47. Meyer, R., Opaterny, A., Wies, T., Wolff, S.: nekton: A linearizability proof checker. In: CAV (1). Lecture Notes in Computer Science, vol. 13964, pp. 170–183. Springer (2023)
48. Meyer, R., Wies, T., Wolff, S.: A concurrent program logic with a future and history. Proc. ACM Program. Lang. **6**(OOPSLA2), 1378–1407 (2022)
49. Meyer, R., Wies, T., Wolff, S.: Embedding hindsight reasoning in separation logic. Proc. ACM Program. Lang. **7**(PLDI), 1848–1871 (2023)
50. Meyer, R., Wies, T., Wolff, S.: Make flows small again: Revisiting the flow framework. In: TACAS (1). Lecture Notes in Computer Science, vol. 13993, pp. 628–646. Springer (2023)
51. Meyer, R., Wolff, S.: Decoupling lock-free data structures from memory reclamation for static analysis. Proc. ACM Program. Lang. **3**(POPL), 58:1–58:31 (2019)
52. Meyer, R., Wolff, S.: Pointer life cycle types for lock-free data structures with memory reclamation. Proc. ACM Program. Lang. **4**(POPL), 68:1–68:36 (2020)
53. Müller, P., Peringer, P., Vojnar, T.: Predator hunting party (competition contribution). In: TACAS. Lecture Notes in Computer Science, vol. 9035, pp. 443–446. Springer (2015)
54. O'Hearn, P.W., Reynolds, J.C., Yang, H.: Local reasoning about programs that alter data structures. In: CSL. Lecture Notes in Computer Science, vol. 2142, pp. 1–19. Springer (2001)
55. Owicki, S.S., Gries, D.: An axiomatic proof technique for parallel programs I. Acta Informatica **6**, 319–340 (1976)

56. Peringer, P., Soková, V., Vojnar, T.: Predatorhp revamped (not only) for interval-sized memory regions and memory reallocation (competition contribution). In: TACAS (2). Lecture Notes in Computer Science, vol. 12079, pp. 408–412. Springer (2020)
57. Podelski, A., Wies, T.: Boolean heaps. In: SAS. Lecture Notes in Computer Science, vol. 3672, pp. 268–283. Springer (2005)
58. Reynolds, J.C.: Separation logic: A logic for shared mutable data structures. In: LICS. pp. 55–74. IEEE Computer Society (2002)
59. Sagiv, S., Reps, T.W., Wilhelm, R.: Parametric shape analysis via 3-valued logic. ACM Trans. Program. Lang. Syst. **24**(3), 217–298 (2002)
60. Sextl, F., Rogalewicz, A., Vojnar, T., Zuleger, F.: Compositional shape analysis with shared abduction and biabductive loop acceleration. In: Programming Languages and Systems - 34th European Symposium on Programming (ESOP). Lecture Notes in Computer Science, Springer (2025), to appear
61. Steensgaard, B.: Points-to analysis in almost linear time. In: Boehm, H., Jr., G.L.S. (eds.) Conference Record of POPL'96: The 23rd ACM SIGPLAN-SIGACT Symposium on Principles of Programming Languages, Papers Presented at the Symposium, St. Petersburg Beach, Florida, USA, January 21-24, 1996. pp. 32–41. ACM Press (1996). https://doi.org/10.1145/237721.237727, https://doi.org/10.1145/237721.237727
62. Toubhans, A., Chang, B.E., Rival, X.: Reduced product combination of abstract domains for shapes. In: VMCAI. Lecture Notes in Computer Science, vol. 7737, pp. 375–395. Springer (2013)
63. Vafeiadis, V.: Modular fine-grained concurrency verification. Ph.D. thesis, University of Cambridge, UK (2008)
64. Vafeiadis, V.: Automatically proving linearizability. In: CAV. Lecture Notes in Computer Science, vol. 6174, pp. 450–464. Springer (2010)
65. Vafeiadis, V., Parkinson, M.J.: A marriage of rely/guarantee and separation logic. In: CONCUR. Lecture Notes in Computer Science, vol. 4703, pp. 256–271. Springer (2007)
66. Wesley, S., Christakis, M., Navas, J.A., Trefler, R.J., Wüstholz, V., Gurfinkel, A.: Inductive predicate synthesis modulo programs. In: ECOOP. LIPIcs, vol. 313, pp. 43:1–43:30. Schloss Dagstuhl - Leibniz-Zentrum für Informatik (2024)
67. Wies, T., Muñiz, M., Kuncak, V.: An efficient decision procedure for imperative tree data structures. In: CADE. Lecture Notes in Computer Science, vol. 6803, pp. 476–491. Springer (2011)
68. Wolff, S., Gupta, E., Esen, Z., Hojjat, H., Rümmer, P., Wies, T.: Arithmetizing shape analysis. CoRR **abs/2408.09037** (2024). https://doi.org/10.48550/ARXIV.2408.09037, https://doi.org/10.48550/arXiv.2408.09037

Open Access. This chapter is licensed under the terms of the Creative Commons Attribution 4.0 International License (http://creativecommons.org/licenses/by/4.0/), which permits use, sharing, adaptation, distribution, and reproduction in any medium or format, as long as you give appropriate credit to the original author(s) and the source, provide a link to the Creative Commons license and indicate if changes were made.

The images or other third party material in this chapter are included in the chapter's Creative Commons license, unless indicated otherwise in a credit line to the material. If material is not included in the chapter's Creative Commons license and your intended use is not permitted by statutory regulation or exceeds the permitted use, you will need to obtain permission directly from the copyright holder.

Raven: An SMT-Based Concurrency Verifier

Ekanshdeep Gupta[1], Nisarg Patel[*,2], and Thomas Wies[1]

[1] New York University, New York, USA
ekansh@nyu.edu
[2] Certora, Tel Aviv, Israel

Abstract This paper presents Raven, a new intermediate verification language and deductive verification tool that provides inbuilt support for concurrency reasoning. Raven's meta-theory is based on the higher-order concurrent separation logic Iris, incorporating core features such as user-definable ghost state and thread-modular reasoning via shared-state invariants. To achieve better accessibility and enable proof automation via SMT solvers, Raven restricts Iris to its first-order fragment. The entailed loss of expressivity is mitigated by a higher-order module system that enables proof modularization and reuse. We provide an overview of the Raven language and describe key aspects of the supported proof automation. We evaluate Raven on a benchmark suite of verification tasks comprising linearizability and memory safety proofs for common concurrent data structures and clients as well as one larger case study. Our evaluation shows that Raven improves over existing proof automation tools for Iris in terms of verification times and usability. Moreover, the tool significantly reduces the proof overhead compared to proofs constructed using the Iris/Rocq proof mode.

1 Introduction

We present Raven, a new language and SMT-based tool for deductive verification of concurrent programs. Raven is designed as an intermediate verification language (IVL) that can be used for building *front-end* verifiers for other programming languages.

Several existing SMT-based IVLs such as Why3 [13], Boogie [3], and Viper [37] have been used successfully to build concurrent program verifiers. However, none of these IVLs provide direct support for reasoning about concurrency. As a consequence, front-end tool developers are left with building their own concurrency support from scratch [6, 43, 49]. This requires an extra layer of encoding that can be a source of subtle soundness bugs [44].

Raven aims to fill this gap by providing inbuilt support for concurrency that is based on a solid theoretical foundation, yet builds on the lessons learned from existing IVL developments. Raven's design allows us to do the soundness reasoning for concurrency once at the IVL level rather than having to do it anew for each verification frontend. This argument extends to implementation bugs: eliminating redundancy in the verification tool pipeline reduces sources of potential soundness bugs.

Raven's meta-theory is based on the concurrent separation logic Iris [20, 22]. Iris is parametric in the underlying programming language. It is also very expressive due to its higher-order features that can be used to define new verification methodologies and

---

[*] Work started while at NYU

prove them sound within the logic itself. Thus, the logic can be thought of as an IVL in its own right. In fact, several efforts exist to build verification tools for real-world programming languages on top of Iris, including C [32] and Rust [15].

So why is there a need for a new tool? The answer is twofold. First, Iris is complex. This complexity is a key prerequisite to some of the logic's most impressive success stories [19]. But on the flip side, this complexity comes at the cost of a steep learning curve. This is despite the fact that many of Iris's advanced features are usually not needed for more mundane program verification tasks. In fact, in such cases, they can get in the way of a seamless user experience. Raven's design therefore restricts Iris's features to a subset that is geared towards these common use cases. The goal of this design is to make the logic more accessible and aid proof automation.

This brings us to the second point. The existing tooling effort in the Iris ecosystem has centered on its Rocq mechanization and accompanying proof mode [26]. While the proofs constructed with these tools provide strong foundational correctness guarantees, they also tend to be much more laborious compared to those done using SMT-based deductive verifiers. Recent efforts, notably the Diaframe project [34, 35] aim to provide better automation for Iris within Rocq. Diaframe already achieves impressive results and is able to almost fully automate linearizability proofs of small but intricate data structures. However, using this tool effectively requires a deep understanding of not just Iris, but also the intricacies of its low-level mechanization in Rocq. Moreover, Diaframe does not help with the automation of theory reasoning.

Overview and Contributions. In §2 we introduce Raven's core features. These include (i) a basic imperative programming language with concurrency primitives, (ii) a higher-order module system that aids proof modularization and reuse, (iii) an Iris-based specification language with invariants for thread-modular reasoning about shared state, and (iv) user-definable ghost state based on Iris's notion of resource algebras. In §3 we provide an overview of the proof automation support for these core features and discuss aspects of the SMT encoding. §4 covers some of Raven's advanced features such as atomic contracts for modular reasoning about linearizability, support for iterated separating conjunctions, and heuristics for dealing with quantifier alternations in specifications. In §5 we discuss implementation details and our evaluation of Raven. Finally, §6 discusses related work in more detail and §7 concludes.

We end here with a brief summary of the key findings of our evaluation. First, we compare Raven against Diaframe on Diaframe's verification benchmark suite of concurrent data structures and accompanying client programs. The takeaway is that Diaframe generally requires fewer proof annotations for these benchmarks. However, Raven's verification times are 1-2 orders of magnitude faster, resulting in a more agile interactive user experience. To assess the scalability and usability of the tools, we also reimplemented a more complex existing Iris linearizability proof in Raven. The original proof consists of several thousand lines of Rocq code and was done without the help of Diaframe. Compared to the original proof, Raven achieves a reduction in proof overhead by a factor of 12, and runs 8 times faster. We also used Diaframe to automate aspects of the original Iris development but quickly ran into usability issues with the tool's current proof automation support. Finally, we also compare Raven with Viper, another SMT-based IVL, on a subset of sequential examples and find the two tools' performance to be comparable.

In summary, we believe that Raven provides a solid foundation for the development of concurrent program verifiers and is a useful verification tool in its own right.

2 Overview of Core Functionality

We introduce Raven's language and core functionality by using the verification of a ticket lock implementation as an illustrative example.

Module System. Raven programs are organized as modules. The members of a module include data type definitions, pure functions and values defined over these data types, fields that introduce (shared) heap-allocated state, procedures that perform computations over this state, as well as additional members related to specification and verification. The module system also supports nested and higher-order modules (or *functors*) that take other modules as parameters. The types of functor parameters are specified by *interfaces*. An interface is like a module but is allowed to have *abstract* members that are declared but not yet defined.

Figure 1a shows the signature of the interface Lock that specifies the operations supported by a lock instance l. The inbuilt type Ref of l represents references to heap locations. Lock abstracts over a module R that implements the interface LockResource. This interface declares the abstract predicate resource(r), which represents a shared resource that can be protected by a lock. The value r of the representation (or **rep**) type T is used to uniquely identify this resource. Each module and interface can have at most one **rep** type member. A module is identified with its **rep** type when its name is used in a context that expects a type expression. For instance, the occurrence of R on Line 15 implicitly expands to R.T.

Specification Language. Raven provides a rich specification language based on concurrent separation logic with (abstract) predicates, shared invariants, user-definable ghost state, axioms, lemmas, etc. In our example, the axiom LockResource.exclusive(r) states that resource(r) cannot be duplicated. In particular, this means that the predicate can only be owned by one thread at a time. Note that in Raven the operator && is interpreted as *separating conjunction*, which we denote by $*$ outside of code snippets. When a module implements an interface, all such axioms must be turned into lemmas that are supported by proofs. The tool simplifies this task by attempting to automatically complete the proofs of all axioms that have been omitted in a module implementation by discharging them directly to the SMT solver.

Thread modular reasoning is enabled via (shared) invariants like lock_inv(l,r) declared on Line 13 of interface Lock. Invariants specify *global* data structure-level logical invariants about shared resources such as the heap representation of the lock. They are themselves duplicable resources that can be freely shared between threads. For this to be sound, a thread can only access the underlying resources of an invariant for one atomic step at a time after which the invariant must be reestablished.

The procedure create(r) initializes a new ticket lock instance l and *binds* the resource r to l via the invariant lock_inv(l,r). The invariant then governs the ownership transfer of R.resource(r) between threads that share l. The actual transfer is realized via

```
1  interface LockResource {
2    rep type T
3    // Resource protected by a lock
4    pred resource(r: T)
5    axiom exclusive(r: T)
6      requires resource(r) && resource(r)
7      ensures false
8  }
9
10 interface Lock {
11   module R: LockResource
12
13   inv lock_inv(l: Ref, r: R)
14
15   proc create(r: R) returns (l: Ref)
16     requires resource(r)
17     ensures lock_inv(l, r)
18
19   proc acquire(l: Ref, ghost r: R)
20     requires lock_inv(l, r)
21     ensures resource(r)
22
23   proc release(l: Ref, ghost r: R)
24     requires lock_inv(l, r) && resource(r)
25     ensures true
26 }
```

(a) Lock interface

```
27 module TicketLock[R: LockResource] : Lock {
28   field next: Int; field curr: Int
29
30   module DisjInts = Library.DisjSet[IntType]
31   module AuthDisjInts = Library.Auth[DisjInts]
32   ghost field tkts: AuthDisjInts
33
34   inv lock_inv(l: Ref, r: R) {
35     exists n: Int, c: Int, b: Bool ::
36       own(l.next, n) && n >= 0 && own(l.curr, c)
37       && own(l.tkts, •[0, n-1])
38       && (b ? own(l.tkts, ○{c}) : resource(r))
39   }
40
41   proc acquire(l: Ref, ghost r: R)
42     requires lock_inv(l, r)
43     ensures resource(r)
44   {
45     ghost var lockAcq: Bool;
46     unfold lock_inv(l, r)[lockAcq := b];
47     val nxt := faa(l.next, 1);
48     fpu(l.tkts, •[0,nxt-1], •([0, nxt], {nxt}));
49     fold lock_inv(l, r)[b := lockAcq];
50     var crr := -1;
51     while (crr != nxt)
52       invariant lock_inv(l, r) &&
53         crr == nxt ? resource(r) : own(l.tkts, ○{nxt})
54     {
55       unfold lock_inv(l, r)[lockAcq := b];
56       crr := l.curr;
57       fold lock_inv(l,r)[b := crr == nxt || lockAcq];
58     }
59   }
60   ...
61 }
```

(b) TicketLock module

Figure 1: Raven implementation of a ticket lock

the procedures acquire and release. For instance, the contract of acquire specifies that if lock l satisfies loc_inv(l,r) upon entry to the procedure, then acquire will guarantee access to resource(r) upon return. Because the invariant is duplicable, calls to acquire and release do not actually consume it, even though the contracts do not explicitly specify that ownership of the invariant is returned back to the calling context. Note that the parameter r is declared as **ghost** for these two procedures to indicate that it is only used for verification.

Implementation Language. Raven's underlying programming language is a first-order concurrent imperative language supporting primitive atomic statements such as fetch-and-add (**faa**), compare-and-set (**cas**), thread spawning, etc. Figure 1b shows a functor that implements the interface Lock using the ticket lock algorithm. You may ignore the code highlighted in gray for now in the implementation of acquire as it is only relevant for the proof, which we discuss later.

A ticket lock instance l maintains a logical FIFO queue of threads that are waiting to acquire the lock. The queue is represented by two counters stored in the heap fields next and curr. The counter next tracks the next available ticket number. When a thread calls acquire(l) it reads and increments l.next in one atomic step using an **faa** operation (Line 47). The read integer value nxt represents the ticket number that determines the thread's place in the queue.

The counter l.curr always trails l.next and tracks the ticket number of the thread whose turn it is to acquire the lock and obtain ownership of resource(r). After a thread has obtained its ticket number, it enters a loop that continuously reads l.curr until this counter has caught up to nxt, indicating that the thread has acquired the lock. The implementation of release (omitted in the figures) simply increments l.curr, signaling to the next thread in the queue that its turn has come.

Resources and Resource Algebras. The invariant lock_inv(l, r) for the ticket lock is defined on Line 34. In Raven, access to heap fields like next and curr is governed via fractional permission resources [7]. These provide a multi-reader, single-writer access control mechanism. In general, for a reference x, a heap field f:T, a value v of type T, and a rational $q \in (0,1]$, the predicate own$(x.f, v, q)$ indicates that $x.f$ stores value v and gives fractional access permission q to this location. A fraction $q > 0$ provides read access and $q = 1$ additionally gives write access to the location. If q is omitted, then it defaults to 1. The first three conjuncts of the invariant, thus, specify that the invariant provides the permission to read and write the locations l.next and l.curr and that the value n stored in l.next is positive.

The remaining two conjuncts of the invariant govern the ownership transfer of the protected resource using an auxiliary ghost field. Ghost fields allow users to augment the program state with logical *ghost resources* that track auxiliary information conducive to verification. Ghost resources a are drawn from a *resource algebra* (of which fractional permissions are one example). Formally, a resource algebra (RA) is a tuple:

$$\langle M, \mathcal{V}\colon M \to \mathbb{B},\ \varepsilon \in M,\ (\cdot)\colon M{\times}M \to M,\ (\backslash)\colon M{\times}M \to M,\ (\rightsquigarrow)\colon M{\times}M \to \mathbb{B} \rangle$$

that satisfies the axioms laid out in Fig. 2. In particular, $\langle M, (\cdot) \rangle$ is a commutative monoid with unit ε. For a reference x and ghost field g and value $a \in M$, the predicate own$(x.g, a)$ states ownership of fragment a of the total ghost resource value stored at $x.g$. The monoid operation $(\cdot) : M \times M \to M$ provides meaning to separating conjunction of such owned fragments:

$$\text{own}(x.g, a) \ast \text{own}(x.g, b) \dashv\vdash \text{own}(x.g, a \cdot b) \ .$$

The predicate $\mathcal{V}(a)$ states that the fragment a is *valid*. Only valid fragments can be owned: own$(x.g, a) \vdash \mathcal{V}(a)$. The relation $a \rightsquigarrow b$ indicates that an owned fragment own$(x.g, a)$ can be updated to own$(x.g, b)$ in a frame-preserving way, i.e., without invalidating ownership of other fragments own$(x.g, c)$ of the same ghost location (FPU-VALID). The *subtraction* function $(\backslash)$ can be understood as the right inverse of $(\cdot)$. Its inclusion in the definition of RAs deviates from Iris's notion of an RA. It is used for automating the *frame rule* of separation logic using an SMT solver. We discuss this in more detail in §3.

An example of a resource algebra that we use in the invariant of the ticket lock is DisjSet$[T]$, which consists of subsets $S \in \wp(T)$ of some carrier set T with disjoint set

$$\mathcal{V}(\varepsilon) \qquad \text{(ID-VALID)}$$
$$\forall a,b,c :: (a \cdot b) \cdot c = a \cdot (b \cdot c) \qquad \text{(COMP-ASSOC)}$$
$$\forall a,b :: a \cdot b = b \cdot a \qquad \text{(COMP-COMM)}$$
$$\forall a :: a \cdot \varepsilon = a \qquad \text{(COMP-ID)}$$
$$\forall a,b :: \mathcal{V}(a \cdot b) \implies \mathcal{V}(a) \wedge \mathcal{V}(b) \qquad \text{(COMP-VALID)}$$
$$\forall a :: a \setminus \varepsilon = a \qquad \text{(FRAME-ID)}$$
$$\forall a,b :: \mathcal{V}(a \setminus b) \implies (a \setminus b) \cdot b = a \qquad \text{(COMP-FRAME-INV)}$$
$$\forall a,b :: \mathcal{V}(a \cdot b) \implies \mathcal{V}((a \cdot b) \setminus b) \qquad \text{(FRAME-COMP-VALID)}$$
$$\forall a,b,c :: a \leadsto b \wedge \mathcal{V}(a \cdot c) \implies \mathcal{V}(b \cdot c) \qquad \text{(FPU-VALID)}$$

Figure 2: Axioms defining a resource algebra

union as composition:

$\mathsf{DisjSet}[T] ::= S \mid \xi \quad \mathcal{V}(a) = (a \neq \xi) \quad a \cdot b = (\mathcal{V}(a) \wedge \mathcal{V}(b) \wedge a \cap b = \emptyset) \,?\, a \cup b : \xi$
$\varepsilon = \emptyset \qquad a \setminus b = (\mathcal{V}(a) \wedge \mathcal{V}(b) \wedge b \subseteq a) \,?\, a - b : \xi \qquad a \leadsto b = \mathit{false}$.

Raven allows users to define their own proof-specific RAs using modules that implement the predefined interface Library.ResourceAlgebra. This interface defines the signature of the RA operations along with their axioms. When specifying a new RA, it often suffices to define only the operations, and Raven automatically verifies that the axioms are satisfied. To further simplify the definition of new RAs, the standard library defines specialized variants *cancellative* RAs and *lattice-based* RAs, which satisfy stronger properties.

As certain reasoning patterns often recur across proofs, Raven ships with several predefined RAs as well as RA functors that construct new RAs from existing ones. In fact, DisjSet[T] is predefined as Library.DisjSet[T].

The second common RA construction that we use in the invariant is that of the *authoritative RA* [22]. This construction is useful whenever we want to track an updatable ghost resource a in an invariant, but allow fragments of a to be owned by individual threads. Formally, given an RA M, the authoritative RA Auth[M] is defined as:

$$\mathsf{Auth}[M] ::= \bullet(a,b) \mid \circ a \mid \xi \qquad \varepsilon = \circ M.\varepsilon$$
$\bullet(a,b) \cdot \circ c = \circ c \cdot \bullet(a,b) = \bullet(a, b \cdot c) \qquad \circ a \cdot \circ b = \circ(a \cdot b) \qquad \_\cdot\_ = \xi \text{ otherwise}$
$\mathcal{V}(\bullet(a,b)) = \mathcal{V}(a) \wedge \mathcal{V}(b) \wedge \mathcal{V}(a \setminus b) \qquad \mathcal{V}(\circ a) = \mathcal{V}(a) \qquad \mathcal{V}(\xi) = \mathit{false}$
$\bullet(a_1,b_1) \leadsto \bullet(a_2,b_2) = \mathcal{V}(\bullet(a_2,b_2)) \wedge (\forall c :: a_1 = b_1 \cdot c \Rightarrow a_2 = b_2 \cdot c)$

where $a,b,c \in M$. We omit the definition of ($\setminus$). Intuitively, $\bullet(a,b)$ denotes the authoritative resource a with a fragment b of a that can still be handed out. On the other hand, $\circ c$ denotes a fragment c of a that has already been handed out. We write just $\bullet a$ for $\bullet(a, M.\varepsilon)$. The authoritative RA is predefined as Library.Auth[M].

The invariant lock_inv(l,r) uses the ghost field tkts of type Auth[DisjSet[$\mathbb{Z}$]] (lines 30-32) to track the authoritative set of tickets [0,n-1] that have been in use so far (Line 37). When a thread attempts to acquire the lock and increments `next` to `n+1`, the authoritative set of tickets is increased to include `n`. The fragment `o{n}` is given to the thread as proof that it exclusively owns ticket `n` while it is waiting for its turn to acquire the lock. Once the value `c` of `curr` has caught up to `n`, the thread can exchange `o{n}` for `resource(r)`. This ownership transfer is realized via the conjunct on Line 38. That is, the Boolean `b` indicates whether the lock is presently held by a thread. When the thread releases the lock and increments `curr`, then Line 38 forces the thread to relinquish ownership of `resource(r)` back to the invariant because the thread does not also own `o{c+1}`.

Raven as an IVL. Raven's module system and user-definable ghost state provide the flexibility to model a wide range of front-end language features, thus increasing its usefulness as an IVL. The module system facilitates rapid prototyping of various features, while custom resource algebras can be used to encode language features that are not directly supported by Raven. As a concrete example, user-definable ghost resources can be used to encode deallocation obligations for reasoning about languages with manual memory management [5]. Additionally, Raven includes explicit `inhale` and `exhale` commands for direct manipulation of the proof state. Raven also supports atomic triples, which are discussed in §4. Invariants and atomic triples can be used to define new atomic primitives. When developing frontend verifiers, one only needs to reason about the encoding of the concurrency primitives (e.g. that they satisfy their atomic specifications), but not the soundness of the entire underlying concurrent program logic.

3 Proof Automation

Proofs in Raven deploy a combination of user-provided ghost code annotations and SMT-based proof automation. We demonstrate the mechanics using the proof of `acquire` (Fig. 1b with ghost code highlighted in gray). We first discuss the role of the annotations and then explain the SMT encoding that enables proof automation.

Proof Annotations. As discussed earlier, a thread executing `acquire(l,r)` first reads and increments `l.next` using an **faa**. This statement requires read and write access to `l.next`, which is granted by Line 36 of the invariant `lock_inv(l, r)`. In order to retrieve the relevant permission from the invariant, the proof author needs to manually unfold the invariant, which is achieved by the **unfold** statement on Line 46. The statement instructs the verifier to exchange the symbolic resource denoting ownership over the invariant, with the resources contained in the *body* of the invariant. The statement also assigns the value of the existentially quantified b in the body of the invariant to the ghost variable `lockAcq` so that we can subsequently refer to it in the proof.

As the invariant is shared between all threads that have access to `l`, other threads may interfere between each atomic access to `l.next`. The verifier therefore enforces that the invariant is *closed* again between any two such atomic steps. This is achieved using the **fold** statement as used on Line 49. The verifier is able to automatically compute witnesses for the existentially quantified variables n and c in the invariant, as these can be inferred from the heap state. However, the value of b needs to be supplied manually. Here, we set it to `lockAcq` since the current thread has not yet acquired the lock. When the verifier executes the **fold** statement, it first checks that the invariant indeed holds again for the computed and supplied existential witnesses. Then it exchanges the related resources with the symbolic resource representing the closed invariant.

Most of the remaining ghost code is similarly related to unfolding and folding the invariant around atomic accesses to the underlying resources. The one exception is Line 48, which we discuss in more detail.

Suppose that after the value of l.next has been incremented to nxt+1 by the faa, we immediately attempted to fold the invariant. Then the fold statement would fail because the invariant is no longer satisfied: the ghost location l.tkts still holds •[0, nxt-1] but needs to hold •[0, nxt]. To bring l.tkts back into sync with the value stored at l.next, Line 48 performs a frame-preserving update (fpu) that replaces the fragment •[0, nxt-1] of l.tkts with •([0, nxt], {nxt}). The updated fragment can be split into the fragments •[0, nxt] and ○{nxt}. The first part is folded into the invariant on Line 49. The second part stays with the thread and is the proof of ownership of ticket nxt that is later traded for resource(r) with the invariant (Line 57 if crr == nxt).

SMT Encoding. Raven automatically checks the proof outline by generating a verification condition that is discharged using an SMT solver.

Raven's first-order logic encoding maintains for each field f a *field heap* f#heap, which maps references ℓ to values of the resource algebra associated with f. The value f#heap$[\ell]$ represents the total fragment of the location $\ell.f$ that is presently owned by the thread. Heap fields and ghost fields are treated uniformly: the RA associated with a heap field is that of fractional permissions over the values of the field's underlying type.

Similarly, the encoding maintains *invariant heaps* and *predicate heaps* that track all instances of invariants and predicates owned by the thread. The representation of these heaps is similar to that of field heaps but relies on specialized RAs. In particular, for an invariant $inv(\overline{x})$, the invariant heap inv#heap maps a valuation $\overline{v}$ of the parameters $\overline{x}$ to a Boolean flag that indicates whether $inv(\overline{v})$ is owned by the current thread.

Ghost statements like fold, unfold, and fpu are then translated to updates of the various heaps to reflect the changes to the owned resources affected by the execution of the statement. The encoding maintains the property that all heaps are valid with respect to the underlying RA. Note that unfolding and folding an invariant does not change the invariant heap since invariants are duplicable resources. Instead, a separate atomicity analysis guarantees that the same invariant cannot be unfolded twice in a row without folding it in between.

To build intuition for the reduction to SMT, we discuss the encoding of the frame-preserving update on Line 48 in more detail:

```
1 /* Encoding of fpu(l.tkts, •[0, nxt-1], •([0, nxt], {nxt})); */
2 // 1. Check that fpu is valid
3 assert •[0, nxt-1] ⤳ •([0, nxt], {nxt});
4 // 2. Exhale own(l.tkts, •[0, nxt-1])
5 tkts#heap := tkts#heap[l := (tkts#heap[l] \ •[0, nxt-1])];
6 assert V(tkts#heap[l]);
7 // 3. Inhale own(l.tkts, •([0, nxt], {nxt}))
8 tkts#heap := tkts#heap[l := (tkts#heap[l] · (•[1, nxt], ○{nxt}))];
```

Since the fpu updates l.tkts, only the field heap tkts#heap is affected. Line 3 first checks that the update is indeed frame-preserving by utilizing the (⤳) relation of the underlying RA, Auth[DisjSet[$\mathbb{Z}$]]. The actual update then proceeds in two steps, first we *exhale* ownership of the fragment •[0, nxt-1] by removing it from the field heap at 1 (Line 5). This step uses the function (\) to compute the residual fragment that is still owned by the thread after the removal of •[0, nxt-1]. Because the fpu may be executed in a state where the thread does not actually own •[0, nxt-1], Line 6 asserts that the resulting heap remains valid. Together with the RA axiom COMP-FRAME-INV, this check also ensures that the newly computed fragment tkts#heap[1] is indeed a residual of •[0, nxt-1] and the old tkts#heap[1]. That is, own(l.tkts,•[0, nxt-1]) actually holds before the update.

The second step composes the new fragment (•[1, nxt], ∘{nxt}) of the fpu to the computed residual (Line 8). The axiom FPU-VALID and the check on Line 3 guarantee that the resulting field heap is again valid. The fpu involves an implicit application of the frame rule in separation logic with the residual fragment acting as the frame.

The SMT reduction then utilizes a standard SSA encoding of this intermediate representation of the program, using the theory of arrays to reason about the updates to heap fields. To automate reasoning about RAs, the axioms from Fig. 2 are annotated with appropriate E-matching patterns. If a module abstracts over a generic RA, then during the verification of the module, the axioms are given directly to the SMT solver. For concrete user-defined instantiations of RAs, the tool provides the SMT solver with axioms that define the RA operations as specified by the user, as well as the RA axioms (except for COMP-ASSOC). Providing the RA axioms for user-defined RAs is usually redundant from a completeness perspective but we find that it improves solver performance. The associativity axiom is omitted because of its cubic instantiation cost in the number of RA terms. (That is, we rely on the SMT solver being able to infer associativity from the definitional axioms of the RA operations.)

With this encoding, Raven verifies the full implementation of the ticket lock in less than one second. We emphasize that Fig. 1b comprises all annotations that the user must provide for the proof of acquire. The annotation burden for release is similar.

4 Additional Features

In this section, we discuss several additional features of Raven that aim to further increase its expressivity and usability.

Atomic Procedure Contracts. A common usage of concurrent program logics is to prove linearizability of concurrent data structures. Logics like Iris provide the notion of an *atomic triple* [43] to enable compositional reasoning about linearizability. While atomic triples can be encoded using standard Hoare triples and invariants, Raven supports them directly via atomic procedure contracts.

An atomic triple takes the form $\langle \overline{x}. P \rangle$ st $\langle \overline{r}. Q \rangle$. Intuitively, the atomic precondition P acts like an invariant up to the linearization point of statement st. That is, before the linearization point, st has access to the resources provided by P, but it needs to ensure that P is maintained by each of its atomic steps. The logical variables $\overline{x}$ should be thought of as representing the abstract state of the data structure that st operates on. Importantly, between any two steps of st the values of $\overline{x}$ for which P holds may change due to interferences by other threads. At its linearization point, st must transform P into

```
1  pred is_lock(l: Ref; r: R, b: Bool) {
2    exists n: Int, c: Int ::
3      own(l.next, n) && n >= 0
4      && own(l.curr, c)
5      && (b ? own(l.tkts, ∘{c}) : resource(r))
6      && own(l.tkts, •[0, n-1])
7  }
8
9  proc wait_loop(l: Ref, x: Int,
10     implicit ghost r: R,
11     implicit ghost b: Bool
12 )
13   requires own(l.tkts, ∘{x})
14   atomic requires is_lock(l, r, b)
15   atomic ensures is_lock(l, r, true)
16       && b == false && resource(r)
17 {
18   ghost val phi := bindAU();
19   r, b := openAU(phi);
20   unfold is_lock(l);
21   val c: Int := l.curr;
22
23   if (x == c) {
24     fold is_lock(l, r, true);
25     commitAU(phi);
26     return;
27   } else {
28     fold is_lock(l, r, b);
29     abortAU(phi);
30
31     r, b := openAU(phi);
32     wait_loop(l, x);
33     commitAU(phi);
34   }
35 }

36 proc acquire(l: Ref,
37    implicit ghost r: R,
38    implicit ghost b: Bool)
39    atomic requires is_lock(l, r, b)
40    atomic ensures is_lock(l, r, true)
41        && b == false && resource(r)
42 {
43   ghost val phi := bindAU();
44
45   r, b := openAU(phi);
46   unfold is_lock(l);
47   val nxt: Int := l.next;
48   fold is_lock(l, r, b);
49   abortAU(phi);
50
51   r, b := openAU(phi);
52   unfold is_lock(l);
53   val res: Bool := cas(l.next, nxt, nxt+1);
54
55   if (res) {
56     fpu(l.tkts, •[0,nxt-1], •([0, nxt], {nxt}));
57     fold is_lock(l, r, b);
58     abortAU(phi);
59
60     r, b := openAU(phi);
61     wait_loop(l, nxt);
62     commitAU(phi);
63   } else {
64     fold is_lock(l, r, b);
65     abortAU(phi);
66     r, b := openAU(phi);
67     acquire(l);
68     commitAU(phi);
69   }
70 }
```

Figure 3: Atomic triple specification for TicketLock.acquire

Q in one atomic step. The variables $\overline{r}$ are the values that st returns upon termination. After the linearization point, the transformed resources Q are then no longer accessible by st. That is, the atomic triple captures the effect of st on the underlying data structure at its linearization point in relationship to its return values.

We explain Raven's support for atomic triples using the variant of the ticket lock example shown in Fig. 3. An atomic triple for a procedure is specified by marking its requires and ensures clauses as **atomic**. Such atomic pre/postconditions can be mixed with regular pre/postconditions (as on Line 13), which retain their usual semantics. The variables $\overline{x}$ of the atomic triple are specified as *implicit ghost* parameters in the atomic contract. Note that unlike the invariant-based specifications used in Fig. 1a, the atomic contract of acquire now allows us to directly refer to the state b of the lock. It specifies that, at acquire's linearization point, the state of the lock changes from b == false (unlocked), to b == true (locked). To demonstrate the interplay between atomic contracts of different procedures, we split the loop in the original implementation of acquire into a separate recursive procedure wait_loop.

Raven's atomic contracts work as follows. Each call to a procedure with an atomic contract has an associated ghost resource, the atomic update, which tracks the state of the atomic contract throughout the procedure's execution. These resources are uniquely identified by *atomic tokens*. The statement bindAU can be used to obtain a handle on the atomic token associated with the call to the current procedure (e.g. Line 43). Using this handle, ghost code can then manipulate the state of the atomic update. For example, if code needs access to a resource in the atomic precondition of the update, then this is achieved with the statement openAU (e.g. Line 19). The statement returns the current values of the logical variables $\overline{x}$ associated with the atomic update. After opening the atomic update and taking an atomic step, it needs to be closed again. This can be done in two ways. The statement abortAU (e.g. Line 29) checks that the atomic precondition P still holds for the same values $\overline{x}$ that were obtained when opening the atomic update and then relinquishes ownership of the associated resources back to the atomic update. In contrast, the statement commitAU is used at the linearization point to check that Q holds for the provided return values (e.g. Line 25). It then transfers ownership of Q to the atomic update and marks it as committed. Raven checks at each return point of an atomic procedure, that the associated atomic update has indeed been previously committed for the actual return values.

Implicit Predicate Parameters. Predicates and invariants also support implicit parameters. These are separated from the input parameters with a semicolon in the predicate definition, such as r:R and b:Bool in Line 1 of Fig. 3. This indicates that if a thread owns is_lock for some l, then the values of r and b can be inferred from the symbolic state of that predicate instance. For example, this allows us to omit these arguments when unfolding is_lock(l), since Raven can automatically compute the appropriate witness for the resulting existential quantifiers. Raven's witness computation feature is discussed in more detail below. The ghost resource associated with a predicate $p(\overline{x}; \overline{y})$ tracks exactly one valuation of the implicit parameters $\overline{y}$ for each valuation of the parameters $\overline{x}$. To guarantee soundness, Raven checks that it is impossible to *simultaneously* have ownership of the resources contained in $p(\overline{x}; \overline{y_1})$ and $p(\overline{x}; \overline{y_2})$ for any $\overline{y_1} \neq \overline{y_2}$.

Iterated Separating Conjunctions. Reasoning about unbounded memory regions in separation logic, e.g. to express ownership over array segments, requires support for *iterated separating conjunctions* (ISCs). Raven supports automated reasoning about ISCs using an SMT encoding that adapts the technique proposed in [36]. We extend this technique by generalizing it to resources over arbitrary RAs and by providing heuristic support for dealing with ∀∃ quantifier alternations.

For illustrative purposes, we present a simplified version of a predicate that we use in the Raven implementation of a case study discussed in more detail in §5.2:

```
pred cssR(r: Ref) {
  forall n: Ref :: n in nodeSet(r) ==>
    exists b: Bool, cn: Set[K] ::
      own(n.lock, b, 1.0) && (b ? true : nodePred(r, n, cn))
}
```

The predicate cssR(r: Ref; nodeSet: Set[Ref]) expresses ownership of the resource nodePred(r, n, cn) associated with each node n in the set nodeSet(r), provided m's lock bit is false (i.e., the node is unlocked). Intuitively, the nodes constitute a data structure associated with the given root node r. The existentially quantified cn is a set of keys that represents the logical state of node n.

Raven handles such assertions as follows. When an ISC is assumed to hold (e.g., if it occurs in a precondition), any nested existential quantifiers are skolemized. The remaining universal quantifiers are translated to universally quantified first-order formulas, which are sent to the SMT solver. Following [36], the supported ISCs must adhere to certain restrictions so that the quantifiers can be automatically annotated with appropriate triggers to ensure robust proof automation using E-matching.

When an ISC is asserted to hold, the outermost universal quantifier is skolemized and the inner existential quantifier turns into a universal quantifier. Rather than passing such quantifiers on to the SMT solver directly, Raven provides heuristic support for instantiating them upfront by computing appropriate witness terms, say b_wtns(n) and cn_wtns(n) in the example above.

Existential Witness Computation. The witness computation heuristic exploits the fact that the values of existential quantifiers in separation logic formulas are often uniquely determined by the underlying (ghost) heap state. In our example, the value of b is determined by n's lock location and the value of cn is determined by nodePred whose third parameter is implicit. This allows Raven to compute the following constraints on the witness terms, expressed in terms of the field and predicate heaps used for the SMT encoding of the resources:

```
n in nodeSet ==> b_wtns(n) == lock#Heap(n)#0
n in nodeSet && !b ==> cn_wtns(n) == (node#PredHeap[ (r, n) ])
```

In this example, the witness computation and ISC encoding together enables automated reasoning about the predicate cssR without requiring the proof author to manually instantiate universal quantifiers or provide witness terms.

5 Implementation and Evaluation

Raven is implemented in about 16K lines of OCaml code. The tool operates on source programs written in the Raven language. We additionally provide integration into Visual Studio Code via a rudimentary language server written in TypeScript. The current test and benchmark suite consists of over 9K lines of Raven code with the largest case study (discussed in §5.2) in the order of 1K lines (including specifications and proofs). The tool and benchmarks are made available with the artifact accompanying this paper [16].

After parsing and type checking, the input program is compiled into verification conditions expressed in SMT-LIB format. These are then dispatched with Z3 [33], utilizing the solver's incremental solving capability.

Evaluation. We evaluate Raven's effectiveness as a verification tool by comparing it with existing automation efforts for Iris. We focus our comparison on Diaframe [34,35], a proof search engine built for the Rocq mechanization of Iris that helps to automate linearizability proofs for fine-grained concurrent data structures. While there exist a number of other tools that automate proofs in concurrent separation logics, these tools make different trade-offs in terms of generality vs. degree of automation compared to

Raven. Moreover, none of these tools are based directly on Iris. We therefore focus on Diaframe for our experimental comparison and discuss other tools in §6.

In our first experiment (§5.1), we reimplement Diaframe's benchmark suite of data structures in Raven and compare the performance of the two tools on these benchmarks. While Diaframe is able to automatically construct foundational proofs of correctness when it works, its approach to automation comes with certain tradeoffs, particularly when dealing with proof-specific resource algebras, and when scaling to more complex developments. In order to examine how the tools perform in such cases, our second experiment (§5.2) reimplements the proof of one of the concurrent *template* algorithms of [27] (which was originally done in Iris) and its instantiation to B+ trees (which was originally done using the SMT-based verifier GRASShopper [42]).

To compare Raven's performance with other SMT-based tools, we conduct an experiment (§5.3) that compares Raven with Viper on examples that are supported by both tools. Finally, we conduct an additional experiment (§5.4) where we inject bugs in Raven programs to determine performance for failing programs.

5.1 Experiment 1: Comparison with Diaframe on Diaframe benchmarks

Diaframe implements a goal-directed proof search engine using ideas from linear logic programming and biabduction. It relies on a large library of hints, as well as custom user-provided hints to guide the proof search. Foundational tools like Rocq provide stronger correctness guarantees than SMT-based tools as they rely on a much smaller trusted computing base. However, they typically require a user to spell out proofs in much more detail. Diaframe aims to automate a lot of this low-level proof burden while still ensuring foundational correctness.

We reimplemented Diaframe's benchmark suite of 23 examples in Raven[3]. It consists of 19 concurrent data structures including different variants of locks, counters, sets, queues, and stacks, as well as four clients for some of these data structures. We additionally include the implementation of a *fractional token* resource algebra that is used in several of the benchmark examples.

We aimed to stay as close as possible to Diaframe's implementations and specifications. Some differences in the specifications arise due to Raven's more restricted support of higher-order features. For example, our lock implementations parameterize over the locked resources using abstract predicates and higher-order modules (as in Fig. 1a). In contrast, the Diaframe versions directly use higher-order quantification over Iris assertions. This makes the Diaframe specifications slightly more general than the Raven versions. So far we have not encountered situations where the more restrictive specification was a hindrance to verification of clients. However, one can easily construct artificial examples that cannot be verified using the Raven specifications.

The results of our comparison are summarized in Table 1. We list the size of each benchmark (measured in the number of program instructions and declarations in the Raven implementation). In addition, for each tool we measure the number of proof-related declarations "pf decl" (e.g., ghost fields, RA functor instantiations, Iris name

---

[3] We merge Diaframe's 'lclist' and 'lclist-extra' benchmarks, resulting in 23 examples instead of 24 in the original paper.

benchmark	Raven					Diaframe		
	size	pf decl	pf instr	pf ovrhd	runtime	pf decl	pf instr	runtime
arc	24	18	50	2.83x	0.36 s	15	0	9.48 s
bag stack (aka Treiber stack)	20	6	32	1.90x	0.40 s	24	19	16.89 s
barrier	44	31	90	2.75x	3.90 s	35	6	379.49 s
bounded counter	13	4	7	0.84x	0.16 s	18	6	12.59 s
cas counter	12	11	12	1.91x	0.20 s	19	0	8.51 s
clh lock	25	11	13	0.96x	0.34 s	26	0	18.84 s
fork join	11	11	7	1.63x	0.19 s	19	0	7.45 s
inc dec	16	4	16	1.25x	0.18 s	22	0	22.64 s
lclist	114	25	46	0.62x	0.63 s	51	21	126.57 s
mcs lock	32	16	36	1.62x	1.24 s	31	0	50.75 s
msc queue	34	13	29	1.23x	0.34 s	16	0	88.83 s
peterson	29	11	40	1.75x	1.23 s	32	26	-
queue	36	14	32	1.27x	0.25 s	20	0	49.46 s
spin lock	10	6	8	1.40x	0.20 s	23	0	7.22 s
rwlock duolock	45	14	23	0.82x	0.45 s	22	0	16.43 s
rwlock lockless faa	19	7	25	1.68x	0.37 s	18	0	21.10 s
rwlock ticket bounded	30	22	39	2.03x	0.83 s	30	3	39.00 s
rwlock ticket unbounded	31	14	38	1.67x	0.50 s	30	0	17.50 s
ticket lock	16	17	12	1.81x	0.72 s	28	0	19.80 s
barrier client	35	50	87	3.91x	0.74 s	32	24	-
cas counter client	12	6	4	0.83x	0.20 s	10	0	5.68 s
fork join client	10	6	3	0.90x	0.18 s	9	0	3.76 s
ticket lock client	15	5	6	0.73x	0.21 s	11	0	5.61 s
tokens ra	0	54	46	-	0.34 s	131	290	18.05 s
Average				1.65x	0.54 s			26.96 s

Table 1: Comparison of Raven and Diaframe on Diaframe's benchmark suite; runtimes averaged over 10 runs. size = number of program instructions; pf decl = number of proof-related declarations; pf instr = number of proof instructions; pf ovrhd = proof overhead defined as (pf decl+pf instr)/size.

space declarations), proof-related instructions "pf instr" (e.g., ghost commands, proofs and invocations of auxiliary lemmas, proof tactic invocations, Diaframe hints), the proof overhead "pf ovrhd" defined as the ratio between "size" and "pf decl"+"pf instr", and the tool's runtime for the verification. Runtimes are measured on an Apple M1 Pro (32 GB RAM, 10 cores) and are averaged over 10 runs. We are unable to report runtimes for "peterson" and "barrier client" due to compilation issues on Diaframe's master branch.

We find that Raven requires considerably fewer proof declarations than Diaframe. This can be attributed to Raven's restricted support of higher order features, which reduces the amount of required boilerplate code. Proof overhead for Raven implementations varies between 0.62x to 3.91x, with a mean of 1.65x.

As an illustrative example, if we examine the 'barrier client' benchmark closely we find that out of its 87 proof instructions, 46 instructions pertain to (un-)folding predicates and 23 pertain to (un-)folding invariants, while the remaining 18 instructions relate to lemma calls, frame-preserving updates, etc. This is typical for the other benchmarks as well. Certain heuristics can be applied automatically to infer some of these instructions, however it may lead to slowdowns and inconsistent behaviour for the user. The development of robust heuristics for further proof automation is a lucrative future direction of research.

Owing to its considerable hints library, Diaframe is able to construct many of these proofs in their entirety. However, the automation comes at the cost of flexibility. When the user wants to use a resource algebra that is not supported by Diaframe out of the box, they are required to supply such hints manually. This is reflected in the 'tokens ra' benchmark, which contains the definition of the *fractional tokens* resource algebra that is used in the proofs of several of the data structures including "barrier", "rwlock duolock", "arc", etc. While Raven's implementation required 54 proof declarations and 46 proof instructions, Diaframe required 131 and 290, respectively.

These hints, broadly speaking, serve a similar purpose as Raven's RA axioms for the subtraction operator ($\setminus$). Raven provides SMT-based automation for proving that these axioms are satisfied for a particular RA definition, while Diaframe requires users to define these hints directly in Rocq/Iris with little automation.

Comparing runtimes, we find that Raven is typically between one to two *orders of magnitude* faster. While Diaframe has to perform the much harder task of searching through the space of proof tactics, Raven directly encodes separation logic reasoning to first-order logic and dispatches it to Z3.

In our experience, Raven's flexibility in adapting to user-defined resource algebras, as well as significantly faster runtimes make a considerable difference during the process of developing correctness proofs, by enabling rapid prototyping and iteration.

5.2 Experiment 2: The GIVEUP Template Case Study

The goal of our second experiment is to evaluate the performance of Raven on more complex verification tasks. For this purpose, we chose to reimplement the proof of one of the algorithms for concurrent search structures from [27] in Raven. Specifically, we reimplemented the *give-up* algorithm.

The original proof consists of two parts. The first part is a proof of linearizability of a template algorithm for a concurrent set data structure. It was mechanized using Iris's Rocq proof mode without the help of Diaframe. The template proof abstracts from the memory representation of the data structure by assuming *helper functions* that perform the node-local operations like inserting a key into a node. This way, the linearizability proof can be instantiated for vastly different concrete concurrent set implementations. The second part of the proof concerns the verification of the concrete helper function implementations, which only involves sequential reasoning. This part of the proof was originally done in the SMT-based verifier GRASShopper [42] for two concrete data structures: B+ trees and hash tables. We focus on the B+ tree instantiation.

The case study is a compelling target for our experiment because it heavily exercises Raven's higher-order module system and support for ISCs. The proofs also use complex proof-specific RAs (e.g., *keysets* [27] and *flows* [28,29]) to achieve the desired parametricity in the low-level memory representation of the data structure. Finally, the

component	Raven				Iris			GRASShopper		
	size	pf decl	pf instr	runtime	pf decl	pf instr	runtime	pf decl	pf instr	runtime
ccm	0	25	4	0.13s	107	484	2.13s	14	5	0.12s
flows-ra	0	37	22	0.75s	83	1804	23.90s	32	258	6.03s
keyset-ra	0	23	0	0.26s	27	661	24.55s	-	-	-
give-up	38	57	120	7.60s	56	465	21.13s	-	-	-
b-plus-tree	47	33	42	2.10s	-	-	-	18	24	10.60s
array-utils	57	75	60	3.13s	-	-	-	21	51	10.18s

Table 2: Comparison of the GIVEUP template implementation in Raven vs Iris + GRASShopper; runtimes averaged over 10 runs. size = number of program instructions; pf decl = number of proof-related declarations; pf instr = number of proof instructions.

fact that the original proof used both Iris/Rocq and an SMT-based tool makes for an interesting comparison point.

Table 2 shows the comparison of proof effort and verification times for the old and new proofs of the case study, aggregated according to the top-level components of the implementation and proof. As can be observed, Raven significantly reduces the proof effort and verification time compared with the Iris/Rocq mechanization. While the components mechanized in Iris amounted to a total of 273 proof declarations and 3414 proof instructions, the same components in Raven added up to 142 proof declarations and 146 proof instructions, while still being between 5x and 90x faster on each individual component. For the sequential components, Raven's performance is at par with GRASShopper; Raven ended up with 170 proof declarations and 128 proof instructions as opposed to GRASShopper's 85 and 338 respectively. This is to be expected since both tools depend on an SMT backend and provide similar levels of automation for reasoning about sequential code. Raven also provides faster runtimes than GRASShopper. This can be attributed to the fact that GRASShopper deploys its own E-matching engine as a preprocessing step to the SMT solver in order to provide completeness guarantees for certain decidable SL fragments [40, 41].

Diaframe Comparison. For the purpose of comparing Raven with Diaframe on a complex verification task, we attempted reimplementing the give-up proof using Diaframe. In our (anecdotal) experience, Diaframe struggles with verification of recursive functions, requiring manual user input around proof steps that involve inductive reasoning. This resulted in us having to guess *magic* parameters such as the maximal number of steps to attempt in the proof search so that the inductive hypothesis can be applied correctly. Similar difficulties arise when Diaframe fails to apply user-provided hints automatically and the user needs to carefully guide the proof search.

To be able to use Diaframe to its fullest capacity, the user needs to have a deep understanding of the Rocq formalization of Iris. Diaframe generates side conditions from proof steps in the search strategy. The authors, who are familiar with Iris, report instances where the origin or the proof of such side conditions was not clear.

The proof of give-up relies on complex resource algebras (flows and keysets) as mentioned earlier. Diaframe provides no support for proving that flows and keysets form a resource algebra. In addition, the proofs require elaborate custom hints to infer facts that follow from the algebraic structure of the resource algebras. The overall result is an increased burden on the user.

In summary, we believe that at least for now, significant automation gains by using Diaframe do not materialize for large proof developments due to the above reasons. The unpredictability of the proof search can lead to a brittle user experience, in particular during development when the program and its specification is still in flux. Finally, Diaframe's lack of sufficient support for custom resource algebras may lead to users having to fall back on vanilla Iris. However, we do note that Diaframe can provide impressive automation gains on smaller examples and is designed to support full Iris rather than a restrictive fragment. Moreover, unlike Raven, it constructs proof objects in Iris/Rocq that provide foundational correctness guarantees.

5.3 Experiment 3: Comparison between Raven and Viper

To determine how Raven compares with other SMT-based separation logic verifiers, we conduct an experiment where we reimplement a subset of Viper's example set[4] in Raven and compare the runtimes. We compare Raven with Viper's verification-condition generation backend Carbon, as well as its symbolic execution backend Silicon.

Our results are summarized in Table 3a. The column 'size' refers to the number of program instructions in the Raven implementation. Examples marked with (*) are faulty examples which yield verification failure on all three tools. We modified the original proof of the 'tree delete' benchmark to avoid the use of magic wand. We also prove only memory safety for this example since Raven does not support sequence types. We translated the modified version of this benchmark back to Viper to obtain a fair comparison.

We note that Raven is using similar techniques as Viper's Carbon backend, but translates directly to SMT rather than going through Boogie. We believe that the difference in runtimes in cases where Raven outperforms Viper are likely attributed at least in part to the Java Virtual Machine (and Common Language Runtime) startup time. So the runtimes will likely be more closely matched in a practical scenario where Viper is used in a language server mode.

5.4 Experiment 4: Comparison of successful vs failing Raven examples

We also inject bugs in a subset of our benchmarks to assess Raven's performance on failing examples and give a more well-rounded picture. Our results are summarized in Table 3b. We find most failing runtimes to be comparable to the succeeding runtimes.

6 Related Work

Raven has been designed as an intermediate verification language and backend (IVL) that aims to serve (deductive) verification tools targeting concurrent programs. Its basic philosophy follows that of other IVLs like Why3 [13], Boogie [3], and Viper [37] in

---

[4] http://viper.ethz.ch/examples/

benchmark	size	Raven	Viper (Carbon)	Viper (Silicon)
adt*	3	0.1 s	2.1 s	3.4 s
array max	12	0.3 s	2.4 s	3.0 s
binary search	13	0.2 s	2.0 s	2.4 s
dutch flag	22	0.3 s	2.2 s	3.0 s
graph marking*	33	10.3 s	2.6 s	3.7 s
tree delete	23	0.5 s	4.5 s	3.6 s

(a) Comparison of Raven with Viper's backends Silicon and Carbon on a subset of Viper's examples.

benchmark	valid	buggy
adt	0.1 s	0.1 s
arc	0.4 s	0.3 s
barrier	7.5 s	12.6 s
graph marking	0.3 s	10.3 s
lclist	0.8 s	0.5 s
peterson	1.7 s	0.7 s
rwlock duolock	0.5 s	0.4 s

(b) Comparing Raven runtimes on valid vs. buggy benchmarks.

Table 3: Comparison of Raven with Viper and on faulty/buggy benchmarks.

that it automates a Hoare-based program logic using SMT solvers. Unlike Raven, none of the mentioned IVLs provide native support for reasoning about concurrency. Thus, concurrency verifiers that build on these IVLs require an additional layer of encoding and extra effort by the developers to ensure overall soundness.

Similar to Raven, Boogie is a language and verifier for imperative programs whose states are first-order structures (in some background theory). Boogie's underlying program logic does not provide direct support for compositional reasoning about (heap) resources or concurrency. However, there are several verification tools for concurrent programs that build on Boogie. Two notable examples are CIVL [25] and Chalice [31]. (The latter has also been re-implemented on top of Viper.) CIVL implements a conservative extension of Boogie for verifying concurrent programs using a notion of layered refinement. Its design differs substantially from Raven's in that CIVL uses classical first-order logic (extended with linear maps [30]) rather than separation logic, and relational structured programming rather than logically atomic specifications.

Viper [37] is an IVL for reasoning about mutable heap-allocated state. It is based on implicit dynamic frames (IDF) [45], a cousin of separation logic. Viper provides two verification backends based on symbolic execution and verification condition generation (via a translation to Boogie) [24]. Notable features include support for abstract predicates, iterated separating conjunctions [36], and magic wands [8]. Several frontends for Viper target concurrent programs, including Voila [49], a proof outline checker for the concurrent separation logic TaDa [43], VerCors [6], which targets Java, C, and OpenCL among others, as well as Prusti [2,4], a verifier for (concurrent) Rust programs.

Raven owes some debt to Viper's conceptual design. In fact, the sequential subset of Raven's core language is compatible with Viper's. However, there are also important differences. (Ghost) resources in Viper are restricted to fractional permissions whereas Raven supports user-definable resource algebras. In particular, non-cancellative RAs supported by Raven but not Viper are often useful for verifying intricate concurrent algorithms (e.g., they are used in the case study discussed in §5.2). Also, Viper has no module system. At a more technical level, Raven's SMT encoding of resource reasoning can be thought of as generalizing the approach taken in Viper's VC generation backend to arbitrary RAs. A key technical difference is that Raven adheres to separation logic rather than IDF to maintain compatibility with Iris. This creates interesting trade-offs. In separation logic, expression evaluation is not dependent on resources, which simplifies some of the concurrency reasoning compared to IDF. On the other hand, SL relies more heavily on existential quantifiers. We alleviate the problem of reasoning about existential quantifiers in Raven with a preprocessing step that computes witness terms from resources and implicit parameters of predicates. Recent efforts aim to put Viper on a foundational footing by formalizing and mechanizing its meta-theory [9] and by enabling formal validation of its SMT translation pipeline [39].

We note that VerCors, which builds on Viper may also be seen as an IVL for concurrent programming languages [1]. However, we consider Raven to be situated further down in the tool pipeline. In fact, VerCors may benefit from Raven's improved support for user-definable ghost resources and its other inbuilt concurrency reasoning features. For example, Raven's concurrency primitives are expressive enough to encode VerCors's parallel blocks directly: Raven supports spawning a thread that executes a call to a procedure p (which may contain the code of a parallel block). Thread spawning consumes the resources from p's precondition. In addition, a shared state invariant allows transferring resources from the spawned thread back to the current thread. The examples 'fork_join' and 'fork_join_client' in our benchmark suite demonstrate this.

Steel Core [47] is an IDF-based resource logic embedded in dependent type theory. Similar to Raven, it supports user-definable partially commutative monoids, dynamically allocated invariants, and ghost computations. However, presently it does not support iterated separating conjunctions or atomic specifications. Steel Core provides foundational guarantees via a shallow embedding into F* [46]. Proof automation is enabled via the tactic engine Steel [14]. It relies on symbolic execution with a frame inference engine based on AC matching [23] and uses an SMT solver for equality reasoning modulo theories. In contrast, Raven offloads the entire reasoning to the SMT solver. By augmenting RAs with a subtraction function ($\setminus$), frames are automatically computed using theory solvers or E-matching.

VeriFast [18] is a verifier for C and Java based on separation logic with fractional permissions. It does not support user-definable RAs but can reason about fine-grained concurrency using a form of higher-order ghost code [17]. Implicit parameters of predicates in Raven are similar to VeriFast's predicate output parameters. However, implicit parameters are strictly more general than output parameters. In particular, output parameters require predicate definitions to be *precise*. Here, precise means that in any given state, there exists a unique substate that satisfies the predicate for a fixed valuation of the input parameters and this substate uniquely determines the values of the output parameters. In contrast, Raven supports imprecise predicates with implicit parameters like the is_lock in Fig. 3. For example, on Line 24, both is_lock(l, r, false) as well as is_lock(l, r, true) hold. For this reason, the user needs to specify the value of b to fold the predicate. However, importantly, both of these predicate instances cannot hold simultaneously (because e.g. own(l.next, n) is not duplicable). This correctness condition is enforced by Raven and guarantees the uniqueness of the implicit parameter values, once one of the instances has been folded.

Raven builds on the concurrent separation logic Iris [20, 22]. Iris is a higher-order impredicative logic, which necessitates a step-indexed semantic model. This is reflected in a more complex notion of RA (so-called *cameras*) and, in the form of the *later* modality in assertions. Moreover, shared invariants and judgements in Iris are annotated with namespaces and masks to soundly deal with impredicative (nested) invariants. These features add complexity when learning the logic, and considerable proof burden even for simple examples. A Raven RA roughly corresponds to a discrete unital camera in Iris. To facilitate proof automation and accessibility, we restrict Iris to its first-order subset by disallowing higher-order quantification and impredicativity. The simplified setting avoids the need for explicit reasoning about Iris's step-indexed semantics. Also, invariants in Raven impose restrictions on the structure of namespaces so that they are not directly exposed to the user and mask annotations can be automatically inferred. To compensate for the resulting loss of expressivity, Raven provides a higher-order module system, which can be used, e.g., to quantify over abstract predicates (like resource in Fig. 1a). Iris provides tooling support via integration with the Rocq proof assistant [26]. Recent work has extended the Rocq plugin with a tactics-based proof search engine, called Diaframe [34, 35], which we discuss in more detail in §5.

Several earlier notable concurrent separation logics that informed the development of Iris have been used as the foundation for tool development efforts. For instance, CAP [11] has been implemented in Caper [12], the views framework [10] in Starling [48], and TaDa [43] in Voila. Proofs conducted with these tools are either restricted to using specific notions of resources or provide less automation than Raven.

7 Conclusions

We introduce Raven, an intermediate language and tool for deductive verification of concurrent programs. Raven is based on the concurrent separation logic Iris, but carefully restricts its expressivity to enable proof automation via SMT solvers. Our experimental comparison shows that Raven is significantly faster and provides a better user experience for larger proof efforts compared to other existing proof automation tools targeting Iris.

We also have a formalization of Raven's program logic for a core fragment of its programming language as well as a pencil and paper soundness proof of the verification condition generator for this fragment. A Rocq mechanization that embeds Raven's program logic into an Iris instance is underway. However, this is outside the scope of the present paper.

We plan to expand Raven's ecosystem by integrating it into front-end verification tools. Other future work includes the integration of prophecies [21] to reason about future-dependent linearization points and exploring techniques for further improving proof automation, e.g., by using ghost state morphisms [38] to automatically infer frame-preserving updates.

Acknowledgments. This work is supported in parts by the National Science Foundation under the grant agreement CCF-2304758.

Disclosure of Interests. The authors have no competing interests to declare that are relevant to the content of this article.

References

1. Armborst, L., Bos, P., van den Haak, L.B., Huisman, M., Rubbens, R., Sakar, Ö., Tasche, P.: The vercors verifier: A progress report. In: Gurfinkel, A., Ganesh, V. (eds.) Computer Aided Verification - 36th International Conference, CAV 2024, Montreal, QC, Canada, July 24-27, 2024, Proceedings, Part II. Lecture Notes in Computer Science, vol. 14682, pp. 3–18. Springer (2024). https://doi.org/10.1007/978-3-031-65630-9_1, https://doi.org/10.1007/978-3-031-65630-9_1
2. Astrauskas, V., Bílý, A., Fiala, J., Grannan, Z., Matheja, C., Müller, P., Poli, F., Summers, A.J.: The Prusti project: Formal verification for Rust. In: Deshmukh, J.V., Havelund, K., Perez, I. (eds.) NASA Formal Methods - 14th International Symposium, NFM 2022, Pasadena, CA, USA, May 24-27, 2022, Proceedings. Lecture Notes in Computer Science, vol. 13260, pp. 88–108. Springer (2022). https://doi.org/10.1007/978-3-031-06773-0_5, https://doi.org/10.1007/978-3-031-06773-0_5
3. Barnett, M., Chang, B.E., DeLine, R., Jacobs, B., Leino, K.R.M.: Boogie: A modular reusable verifier for object-oriented programs. In: de Boer, F.S., Bonsangue, M.M., Graf, S., de Roever, W.P. (eds.) Formal Methods for Components and Objects, 4th International Symposium, FMCO 2005, Amsterdam, The Netherlands, November 1-4, 2005, Revised Lectures. Lecture Notes in Computer Science, vol. 4111, pp. 364–387. Springer (2005). https://doi.org/10.1007/11804192_17, https://doi.org/10.1007/11804192_17
4. Bílý, A., Pereira, J.C., Schär, J., Müller, P.: Refinement proofs in Rust using ghost locks. CoRR **abs/2311.14452** (2023). https://doi.org/10.48550/ARXIV.2311.14452, https://doi.org/10.48550/arXiv.2311.14452
5. Bizjak, A., Gratzer, D., Krebbers, R., Birkedal, L.: Iron: Managing obligations in higher-order concurrent separation logic. Proc. ACM Program. Lang. **3**(POPL), 65:1–65:30 (2019). https://doi.org/10.1145/3290378, https://doi.org/10.1145/3290378
6. Blom, S., Darabi, S., Huisman, M., Oortwijn, W.: The vercors tool set: Verification of parallel and concurrent software. In: Polikarpova, N., Schneider, S. (eds.) Integrated Formal Methods. pp. 102–110. Springer International Publishing, Cham (2017)
7. Bornat, R., Calcagno, C., O'Hearn, P.W., Parkinson, M.J.: Permission accounting in separation logic. In: Palsberg, J., Abadi, M. (eds.) Proceedings of the 32nd ACM SIGPLAN-SIGACT Symposium on Principles of Programming Languages, POPL 2005, Long Beach, California, USA, January 12-14, 2005. pp. 259–270. ACM (2005). https://doi.org/10.1145/1040305.1040327, https://doi.org/10.1145/1040305.1040327
8. Dardinier, T., Parthasarathy, G., Weeks, N., Müller, P., Summers, A.J.: Sound automation of magic wands. In: Shoham, S., Vizel, Y. (eds.) Computer Aided Verification - 34th International Conference, CAV 2022, Haifa, Israel, August 7-10, 2022, Proceedings, Part II. Lecture Notes in Computer Science, vol. 13372, pp. 130–151. Springer (2022). https://doi.org/10.1007/978-3-031-13188-2_7, https://doi.org/10.1007/978-3-031-13188-2_7
9. Dardinier, T., Sammler, M., Parthasarathy, G., Summers, A.J., Müller, P.: Formal foundations for translational separation logic verifiers. Proc. ACM Program. Lang. **9**(POPL) (Jan 2025). https://doi.org/10.1145/3704856, https://doi.org/10.1145/3704856
10. Dinsdale-Young, T., Birkedal, L., Gardner, P., Parkinson, M.J., Yang, H.: Views: Compositional reasoning for concurrent programs. In: Giacobazzi, R., Cousot, R. (eds.) The 40th Annual ACM SIGPLAN-SIGACT Symposium on Principles of Programming Languages, POPL '13, Rome, Italy - January 23 - 25, 2013. pp. 287–300. ACM (2013). https://doi.org/10.1145/2429069.2429104, https://doi.org/10.1145/2429069.2429104
11. Dinsdale-Young, T., Dodds, M., Gardner, P., Parkinson, M.J., Vafeiadis, V.: Concurrent abstract predicates. In: D'Hondt, T. (ed.) ECOOP 2010 - Object-Oriented Programming, 24th

European Conference, Maribor, Slovenia, June 21-25, 2010. Proceedings. Lecture Notes in Computer Science, vol. 6183, pp. 504–528. Springer (2010). https://doi.org/10.1007/978-3-642-14107-2_24, https://doi.org/10.1007/978-3-642-14107-2_24

12. Dinsdale-Young, T., da Rocha Pinto, P., Andersen, K.J., Birkedal, L.: Caper - automatic verification for fine-grained concurrency. In: Yang, H. (ed.) Programming Languages and Systems - 26th European Symposium on Programming, ESOP 2017, Held as Part of the European Joint Conferences on Theory and Practice of Software, ETAPS 2017, Uppsala, Sweden, April 22-29, 2017, Proceedings. Lecture Notes in Computer Science, vol. 10201, pp. 420–447. Springer (2017). https://doi.org/10.1007/978-3-662-54434-1_16, https://doi.org/10.1007/978-3-662-54434-1_16

13. Filliâtre, J., Paskevich, A.: Why3 - where programs meet provers. In: Felleisen, M., Gardner, P. (eds.) Programming Languages and Systems - 22nd European Symposium on Programming, ESOP 2013, Held as Part of the European Joint Conferences on Theory and Practice of Software, ETAPS 2013, Rome, Italy, March 16-24, 2013. Proceedings. Lecture Notes in Computer Science, vol. 7792, pp. 125–128. Springer (2013). https://doi.org/10.1007/978-3-642-37036-6_8, https://doi.org/10.1007/978-3-642-37036-6_8

14. Fromherz, A., Rastogi, A., Swamy, N., Gibson, S., Martínez, G., Merigoux, D., Ramananandro, T.: Steel: Proof-oriented programming in a dependently typed concurrent separation logic. Proc. ACM Program. Lang. **5**(ICFP), 1–30 (2021). https://doi.org/10.1145/3473590, https://doi.org/10.1145/3473590

15. Gäher, L., Sammler, M., Jung, R., Krebbers, R., Dreyer, D.: RefinedRust: A type system for high-assurance verification of Rust programs. Proc. ACM Program. Lang. **8**(PLDI) (Jun 2024). https://doi.org/10.1145/3656422, https://doi.org/10.1145/3656422

16. Gupta, E., Nisarg, P., Wies, T.: Raven: An SMT-based concurrency verifier (May 2025). https://doi.org/10.5281/zenodo.15477369, https://doi.org/10.5281/zenodo.15477369

17. Jacobs, B., Piessens, F.: Expressive modular fine-grained concurrency specification. In: Ball, T., Sagiv, M. (eds.) Proceedings of the 38th ACM SIGPLAN-SIGACT Symposium on Principles of Programming Languages, POPL 2011, Austin, TX, USA, January 26-28, 2011. pp. 271–282. ACM (2011). https://doi.org/10.1145/1926385.1926417, https://doi.org/10.1145/1926385.1926417

18. Jacobs, B., Smans, J., Philippaerts, P., Vogels, F., Penninckx, W., Piessens, F.: VeriFast: A powerful, sound, predictable, fast verifier for C and Java. In: Bobaru, M.G., Havelund, K., Holzmann, G.J., Joshi, R. (eds.) NASA Formal Methods - Third International Symposium, NFM 2011, Pasadena, CA, USA, April 18-20, 2011. Proceedings. Lecture Notes in Computer Science, vol. 6617, pp. 41–55. Springer (2011). https://doi.org/10.1007/978-3-642-20398-5_4, https://doi.org/10.1007/978-3-642-20398-5_4

19. Jung, R., Jourdan, J.H., Krebbers, R., Dreyer, D.: RustBelt: Securing the foundations of the Rust programming language. Proceedings of the ACM on Programming Languages **2**(POPL), 1–34 (2017)

20. Jung, R., Krebbers, R., Jourdan, J., Bizjak, A., Birkedal, L., Dreyer, D.: Iris from the ground up: A modular foundation for higher-order concurrent separation logic. J. Funct. Program. **28**, e20 (2018). https://doi.org/10.1017/S0956796818000151, https://doi.org/10.1017/S0956796818000151

21. Jung, R., Lepigre, R., Parthasarathy, G., Rapoport, M., Timany, A., Dreyer, D., Jacobs, B.: The future is ours: Prophecy variables in separation logic. Proc. ACM Program. Lang. **4**(POPL), 45:1–45:32 (2020). https://doi.org/10.1145/3371113, https://doi.org/10.1145/3371113

22. Jung, R., Swasey, D., Sieczkowski, F., Svendsen, K., Turon, A., Birkedal, L., Dreyer, D.: Iris: Monoids and invariants as an orthogonal basis for concurrent reasoning. In: Rajamani, S.K., Walker, D. (eds.) Proceedings of the 42nd Annual ACM SIGPLAN-SIGACT

Symposium on Principles of Programming Languages, POPL 2015, Mumbai, India, January 15-17, 2015. pp. 637–650. ACM (2015). https://doi.org/10.1145/2676726.2676980, https://doi.org/10.1145/2676726.2676980

23. Kapur, D., Narendran, P.: Complexity of unification problems with associative-commutative operators. J. Autom. Reason. **9**(2), 261–288 (1992). https://doi.org/10.1007/BF00245463, https://doi.org/10.1007/BF00245463

24. Kassios, I.T., Müller, P., Schwerhoff, M.: Comparing verification condition generation with symbolic execution: An experience report. In: Joshi, R., Müller, P., Podelski, A. (eds.) Verified Software: Theories, Tools, Experiments - 4th International Conference, VSTTE 2012, Philadelphia, PA, USA, January 28-29, 2012. Proceedings. Lecture Notes in Computer Science, vol. 7152, pp. 196–208. Springer (2012). https://doi.org/10.1007/978-3-642-27705-4_16, https://doi.org/10.1007/978-3-642-27705-4_16

25. Kragl, B., Qadeer, S.: The Civl verifier. In: Formal Methods in Computer Aided Design, FMCAD 2021, New Haven, CT, USA, October 19-22, 2021. pp. 143–152. IEEE (2021). https://doi.org/10.34727/2021/ISBN.978-3-85448-046-4_23, https://doi.org/10.34727/2021/isbn.978-3-85448-046-4_23

26. Krebbers, R., Jourdan, J., Jung, R., Tassarotti, J., Kaiser, J., Timany, A., Charguéraud, A., Dreyer, D.: Mosel: A general, extensible modal framework for interactive proofs in separation logic. Proc. ACM Program. Lang. **2**(ICFP), 77:1–77:30 (2018). https://doi.org/10.1145/3236772, https://doi.org/10.1145/3236772

27. Krishna, S., Patel, N., Shasha, D.E., Wies, T.: Verifying concurrent search structure templates. In: Donaldson, A.F., Torlak, E. (eds.) Proceedings of the 41st ACM SIGPLAN International Conference on Programming Language Design and Implementation, PLDI 2020, London, UK, June 15-20, 2020. pp. 181–196. ACM (2020). https://doi.org/10.1145/3385412.3386029, https://doi.org/10.1145/3385412.3386029

28. Krishna, S., Shasha, D.E., Wies, T.: Go with the flow: Compositional abstractions for concurrent data structures. Proc. ACM Program. Lang. **2**(POPL), 37:1–37:31 (2018). https://doi.org/10.1145/3158125, https://doi.org/10.1145/3158125

29. Krishna, S., Summers, A.J., Wies, T.: Local reasoning for global graph properties. In: Müller, P. (ed.) Programming Languages and Systems - 29th European Symposium on Programming, ESOP 2020, Held as Part of the European Joint Conferences on Theory and Practice of Software, ETAPS 2020, Dublin, Ireland, April 25-30, 2020, Proceedings. Lecture Notes in Computer Science, vol. 12075, pp. 308–335. Springer (2020). https://doi.org/10.1007/978-3-030-44914-8_12, https://doi.org/10.1007/978-3-030-44914-8_12

30. Lahiri, S.K., Qadeer, S., Walker, D.: Linear maps. In: Jhala, R., Swierstra, W. (eds.) Proceedings of the 5th ACM Workshop Programming Languages meets Program Verification, PLPV 2011, Austin, TX, USA, January 29, 2011. pp. 3–14. ACM (2011). https://doi.org/10.1145/1929529.1929531, https://doi.org/10.1145/1929529.1929531

31. Leino, K.R.M., Müller, P., Smans, J.: Verification of concurrent programs with Chalice. In: Aldini, A., Barthe, G., Gorrieri, R. (eds.) Foundations of Security Analysis and Design V, FOSAD 2007/2008/2009 Tutorial Lectures. Lecture Notes in Computer Science, vol. 5705, pp. 195–222. Springer (2009). https://doi.org/10.1007/978-3-642-03829-7_7, https://doi.org/10.1007/978-3-642-03829-7_7

32. Mansky, W., Du, K.: An Iris instance for verifying CompCert C programs **8**(POPL) (Jan 2024). https://doi.org/10.1145/3632848, https://doi.org/10.1145/3632848

33. de Moura, L.M., Bjørner, N.S.: Z3: an efficient SMT solver. In: Ramakrishnan, C.R., Rehof, J. (eds.) Tools and Algorithms for the Construction and Analysis of Systems, 14th International Conference, TACAS 2008, Held as Part of the Joint European Conferences on Theory and Practice of Software, ETAPS 2008, Budapest, Hungary, March 29-April 6, 2008. Proceedings. Lecture Notes in Computer Science, vol. 4963, pp. 337–

340. Springer (2008). https://doi.org/10.1007/978-3-540-78800-3_24, https://doi.org/10.1007/978-3-540-78800-3_24
34. Mulder, I., Krebbers, R.: Proof automation for linearizability in separation logic. Proc. ACM Program. Lang. **7**(OOPSLA1), 462–491 (2023). https://doi.org/10.1145/3586043, https://doi.org/10.1145/3586043
35. Mulder, I., Krebbers, R., Geuvers, H.: Diaframe: Automated verification of fine-grained concurrent programs in Iris. In: Jhala, R., Dillig, I. (eds.) PLDI '22: 43rd ACM SIGPLAN International Conference on Programming Language Design and Implementation, San Diego, CA, USA, June 13 - 17, 2022. pp. 809–824. ACM (2022). https://doi.org/10.1145/3519939.3523432, https://doi.org/10.1145/3519939.3523432
36. Müller, P., Schwerhoff, M., Summers, A.J.: Automatic verification of iterated separating conjunctions using symbolic execution. In: Chaudhuri, S., Farzan, A. (eds.) Computer Aided Verification - 28th International Conference, CAV 2016, Toronto, ON, Canada, July 17-23, 2016, Proceedings, Part I. Lecture Notes in Computer Science, vol. 9779, pp. 405–425. Springer (2016). https://doi.org/10.1007/978-3-319-41528-4_22, https://doi.org/10.1007/978-3-319-41528-4_22
37. Müller, P., Schwerhoff, M., Summers, A.J.: Viper: A verification infrastructure for permission-based reasoning. In: Jobstmann, B., Leino, K.R.M. (eds.) Verification, Model Checking, and Abstract Interpretation - 17th International Conference, VMCAI 2016, St. Petersburg, FL, USA, January 17-19, 2016. Proceedings. Lecture Notes in Computer Science, vol. 9583, pp. 41–62. Springer (2016). https://doi.org/10.1007/978-3-662-49122-5_2, https://doi.org/10.1007/978-3-662-49122-5_2
38. Nanevski, A., Banerjee, A., Delbianco, G.A., Fábregas, I.: Specifying concurrent programs in separation logic: Morphisms and simulations. Proc. ACM Program. Lang. **3**(OOPSLA), 161:1–161:30 (2019). https://doi.org/10.1145/3360587, https://doi.org/10.1145/3360587
39. Parthasarathy, G., Müller, P., Summers, A.J.: Formally validating a practical verification condition generator. In: Silva, A., Leino, K.R.M. (eds.) Computer Aided Verification - 33rd International Conference, CAV 2021, Virtual Event, July 20-23, 2021, Proceedings, Part II. Lecture Notes in Computer Science, vol. 12760, pp. 704–727. Springer (2021). https://doi.org/10.1007/978-3-030-81688-9_33, https://doi.org/10.1007/978-3-030-81688-9_33
40. Piskac, R., Wies, T., Zufferey, D.: Automating separation logic using SMT. In: Sharygina, N., Veith, H. (eds.) Computer Aided Verification - 25th International Conference, CAV 2013, Saint Petersburg, Russia, July 13-19, 2013. Proceedings. Lecture Notes in Computer Science, vol. 8044, pp. 773–789. Springer (2013). https://doi.org/10.1007/978-3-642-39799-8_54, https://doi.org/10.1007/978-3-642-39799-8_54
41. Piskac, R., Wies, T., Zufferey, D.: Automating separation logic with trees and data. In: Biere, A., Bloem, R. (eds.) Computer Aided Verification - 26th International Conference, CAV 2014, Held as Part of the Vienna Summer of Logic, VSL 2014, Vienna, Austria, July 18-22, 2014. Proceedings. Lecture Notes in Computer Science, vol. 8559, pp. 711–728. Springer (2014). https://doi.org/10.1007/978-3-319-08867-9_47, https://doi.org/10.1007/978-3-319-08867-9_47
42. Piskac, R., Wies, T., Zufferey, D.: Grasshopper - complete heap verification with mixed specifications. In: Ábrahám, E., Havelund, K. (eds.) Tools and Algorithms for the Construction and Analysis of Systems - 20th International Conference, TACAS 2014, Held as Part of the European Joint Conferences on Theory and Practice of Software, ETAPS 2014, Grenoble, France, April 5-13, 2014. Proceedings. Lecture Notes in Computer Science, vol. 8413, pp. 124–139. Springer (2014). https://doi.org/10.1007/978-3-642-54862-8_9, https://doi.org/10.1007/978-3-642-54862-8_9

43. da Rocha Pinto, P., Dinsdale-Young, T., Gardner, P.: Tada: A logic for time and data abstraction. In: Jones, R.E. (ed.) ECOOP 2014 - Object-Oriented Programming - 28th European Conference, Uppsala, Sweden, July 28 - August 1, 2014. Proceedings. Lecture Notes in Computer Science, vol. 8586, pp. 207–231. Springer (2014). https://doi.org/10.1007/978-3-662-44202-9_9, https://doi.org/10.1007/978-3-662-44202-9_9
44. Schwerhoff, M.: Voila GitHub issue #33. https://github.com/viperproject/voila/issues/33, last accessed: April 15, 2025
45. Smans, J., Jacobs, B., Piessens, F.: Implicit dynamic frames. ACM Trans. Program. Lang. Syst. **34**(1), 2:1–2:58 (2012). https://doi.org/10.1145/2160910.2160911, https://doi.org/10.1145/2160910.2160911
46. Swamy, N., Hritcu, C., Keller, C., Rastogi, A., Delignat-Lavaud, A., Forest, S., Bhargavan, K., Fournet, C., Strub, P., Kohlweiss, M., Zinzindohoue, J.K., Zanella-Béguelin, S.: Dependent types and multi-monadic effects in F. In: Bodík, R., Majumdar, R. (eds.) Proceedings of the 43rd Annual ACM SIGPLAN-SIGACT Symposium on Principles of Programming Languages, POPL 2016, St. Petersburg, FL, USA, January 20 - 22, 2016. pp. 256–270. ACM (2016). https://doi.org/10.1145/2837614.2837655, https://doi.org/10.1145/2837614.2837655
47. Swamy, N., Rastogi, A., Fromherz, A., Merigoux, D., Ahman, D., Martínez, G.: SteelCore: an extensible concurrent separation logic for effectful dependently typed programs. Proc. ACM Program. Lang. **4**(ICFP), 121:1–121:30 (2020). https://doi.org/10.1145/3409003, https://doi.org/10.1145/3409003
48. Windsor, M., Dodds, M., Simner, B., Parkinson, M.J.: Starling: Lightweight concurrency verification with views. In: Majumdar, R., Kuncak, V. (eds.) Computer Aided Verification - 29th International Conference, CAV 2017, Heidelberg, Germany, July 24-28, 2017, Proceedings, Part I. Lecture Notes in Computer Science, vol. 10426, pp. 544–569. Springer (2017). https://doi.org/10.1007/978-3-319-63387-9_27, https://doi.org/10.1007/978-3-319-63387-9_27
49. Wolf, F.A., Schwerhoff, M., Müller, P.: Concise outlines for a complex logic: A proof outline checker for tada. Formal Methods Syst. Des. **61**(1), 110–136 (2022). https://doi.org/10.1007/S10703-023-00427-W, https://doi.org/10.1007/s10703-023-00427-w

Open Access. This chapter is licensed under the terms of the Creative Commons Attribution 4.0 International License (http://creativecommons.org/licenses/by/4.0/), which permits use, sharing, adaptation, distribution, and reproduction in any medium or format, as long as you give appropriate credit to the original author(s) and the source, provide a link to the Creative Commons license and indicate if changes were made.

The images or other third party material in this chapter are included in the chapter's Creative Commons license, unless indicated otherwise in a credit line to the material. If material is not included in the chapter's Creative Commons license and your intended use is not permitted by statutory regulation or exceeds the permitted use, you will need to obtain permission directly from the copyright holder.

Fifteen Years of Viper

Marco Eilers[1](✉)[iD], Malte Schwerhoff[1][iD], Alexander J. Summers[2][iD], and Peter Müller[1][iD]

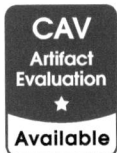

[1] Department of Computer Science, ETH Zurich, Zurich, Switzerland
{marco.eilers,malte.schwerhoff, peter.mueller}@inf.ethz.ch

[2] Department of Computer Science, University of British Columbia, Vancouver, Canada
alex.summers@ubc.ca

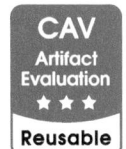

Abstract. Viper is a verification infrastructure that facilitates the development of automated verifiers based on separation logic. Viper consists of the Viper intermediate language and two backend verifiers based on symbolic execution and verification condition generation, respectively. It has been used to build over a dozen program verifiers that translate verification problems in Go, Java, Python, Rust, and many others, into the Viper language and automate verification using the Viper backends. In this paper, we describe the original design goals for Viper's language, verification logic, and tool architecture, summarize our experiences, and explain our principles for evolving the system.

Keywords: Intermediate verification language · separation logic · verification structure · automated reasoning

1 Introduction

Automated program verifiers are often organized into a frontend, which translates verification problems into an intermediate verification language (IVL), and a backend, which extracts proof obligations from the IVL program and uses an SMT solver to discharge them. For instance, Corral [33], Dafny [35], Spec# [6], and SymDiff [32] are based on the Boogie IVL [34], whereas Frama-C [12] and Creusot [17] use WhyML [27]. This architecture allows backends to be reused across many different verifiers, such that sophisticated proof search algorithms, inference, error reporting, etc. do not have to be re-implemented for each tool.

The main goal of the Viper [41] project is to bring these benefits to the realm of separation logic verifiers, for which Boogie and WhyML provide no dedicated support. Fifteen years after starting the Viper project, we have by and large achieved this goal; over a dozen frontends have been built on top of Viper [3,9,10,13,21,23,28,49,50,57,59–61], several complex verification projects apply Viper-based tools [2,47], and Viper has been used successfully in teaching.

To make Viper an attractive IVL for separation logic verifiers, we have prioritized the following three design goals:

- *Expressiveness:* Viper can capture a wide range of programs and properties, as well as the proof principles of a wide variety of different separation logics.
- *Soundness:* Viper is designed to be sound, that is, successful verification implies that the input program always satisfies its specifications. Viper does not aim to be complete in general (as is standard for SMT-based verifiers), but does aim for a clear definition of which questions it *should* be expected to answer automatically (and conversely, where annotations are expected).
- *Usability:* Viper aims to offer a smooth user experience, most importantly, by (1) effectively automating separation logic proofs with modest user annotations, (2) being user-friendly for humans who manipulate Viper code directly without going through a frontend, and (3) providing helpful error messages when verification fails.

In this paper, we describe how these design goals are reflected in Viper's language, verification logic, and tool architecture, summarize our experiences, and explain our principles for evolving the system. We believe our observations can be transferred to other formal methods tools and will be useful for developers and maintainers of such tools.

2 The Viper Language

In this section, we discuss how the three design goals from the introduction are reflected in Viper's language design, and we explain our principles for extending the language.

2.1 Language Design

Expressiveness. To support the translation of diverse source languages, the Viper language offers a very permissive type system, imperative statements with structured and unstructured control flow (e.g. to encode languages with abrupt termination), as well as features to encode language features not directly supported by Viper, such as arrays.

Viper's assertion language supports a rich first-order separation logic (see Sect. 3.1 for details) including universal and existential quantification. Moreover, it allows defining custom datatypes, either as algebraic datatypes or as (interpreted or uninterpreted) sorts and functions.

A core virtue of Viper is its ability to encode the proof rules of a wide range of separation logics. To this end, Viper offers `inhale` and `exhale` statements. Inhaling an assertion P adds the separation logic resources described by P to the current state and assumes the value constraints in P. Conversely, exhaling P checks that its resources are available in the current state and removes them; moreover it asserts all value constraints. `inhale` and `exhale` are separation logic's analogs of `assume` and `assert`, and equally versatile in encoding proof rules, as demonstrated by frontends for complex logics such as RSL [57] and TaDA [60].

Human-Friendliness. When designing an IVL, there is an inherent trade-off between keeping the language minimal (which simplifies both tool development and formalization) and adding richer language constructs to make the language more human-friendly. Following the examples of Boogie and WhyML, we designed Viper to be well-suited as both a target language for verification frontends *and* a language directly usable by humans. The latter has proven invaluable for prototyping new encoding schemes that a frontend might eventually automate, for debugging frontend-generated code, and for having raw access to Viper's features, for instance, in teaching and during verification competitions.

To support direct use, Viper's core language provides various constructs that do not increase expressiveness, but make the code more accessible. Examples include method calls (which, given Viper's modular verification could be encoded using `inhale` and `exhale`) as well as structured control flow with conditional statements and loops (which could be encoded using `goto`). Similarly, Viper's assertion language includes some technically-redundant connectives (e.g. includes disjunction as well as implication) to make formulas easier to understand. Moreover, macros greatly increase the readability of Viper code by providing concise notations for complex statements or assertions. These features not only improve usability, but also enable potential future Viper functionality, such as method inlining and specification inference techniques (e.g. for explicit loops). We have found that these benefits clearly outweigh their very modest development effort.

Error Reporting. Even though error reporting mostly concerns the verification logic and tool architecture, it also represents an important trade-off in terms of language design. In general, a tool that checks more properties (particularly well-definedness of expressions) by default is able to provide more-precise error messages, at the cost of increased verification effort. For instance, SMT solvers are based on a logic with total functions, where operations that are not meaningful, such as division by zero or out-of-bounds sequence access, yield unspecified results [7]. Even though Viper expressions and assertions are encoded into SMT, Viper instead uses a partial interpretation of these operations and imposes proof obligations to ensure that they are always applied within their domain. This choice enables more precise error reporting. For instance, for the assertion $x/y > 0$, Viper reports different error messages when y might be zero vs. when y is non-zero but the division might not yield a positive result. We have found that Viper's well-definedness checks for assertions have proven very useful both during the development of frontends and for direct uses of Viper, especially in teaching. However, they slightly increase verification time, and it would sometimes be useful to (selectively) disable well-definedness checks, for instance, when a frontend guarantees that they will always succeed.

2.2 Growing the Language

Increasing adoption of Viper as the IVL for diverse verifiers and as a teaching language continuously leads to new requirements. We add a new language feature only if it does not compromise our overarching goals (e.g. we know how to soundly automate verification) and at least one of the following criteria applies: (1) The new feature simplifies the development of multiple frontends, (2) it enhances the experience of manually writing Viper programs, or (3) it enables more efficient verification. Features in the first two categories are often implemented as plugins (cf. Sect. 4) that extend Viper's surface language but desugar into core Viper, so that backends need not be adapted. Features in the third category require changes to the backends to realize the intended performance improvement.

As an example for criterion (1), a common demand from frontends to support the verification of hyperproperties motivated us to implement a product program construction [24], initially needed by the Python frontend Nagini, in Viper [22]. It was subsequently used by other frontends [21,58]. However, there are also concepts that occur in many frontends, but are have not yet found their way into Viper. For instance, each occurrence of ghost code in a frontend has specific characteristics, and we were not yet able to devise unified support in the IVL.

As an example for criterion (2), we added (optional) support for proving termination. This feature is not required by frontends because termination checks can easily be encoded. However, such an encoding is tedious when using Viper directly because programmers not only have to insert the necessary assertions (which is error-prone) but also need to define appropriate well-founded orders. Built-in support for termination proofs is especially useful for teaching.

As an example for criterion (3), we added support for havocking parts of the heap, which can be handled much more efficiently than encodings that achieve the same result. This feature reduced the verification time of many Voila [60] examples by an order of magnitude.

When there has been tension between requirements for using Viper as an IVL and using it manually, we have tended to resolve it in favor of IVL usage. As a result, the Viper language does not directly offer some features (e.g. arrays, lemmas, and the aforementioned ghost code) that exist in verification languages for manual use, such as Dafny. In Viper, those features have to be encoded.

Possible future extensions include extended support for generic types, and modularization features that allow one to control dependencies between modules to improve verification time and facilitate the maintenance of verified code.

3 Verification Logic

As a deductive program verifier, Viper automates proof search in a program logic for the Viper language (by generating and checking logical conditions). In this section, we reflect on our choice of program logic, summarize our efforts to formalize it, and discuss our approach to increasing its expressiveness over time.

3.1 Implicit Dynamic Frames

The main application domain for Viper is the verification of imperative, concurrent programs, which makes separation logic [42,51] a fairly obvious choice for Viper's program logic. However, even at the time when the work on Viper started, there were dozens of different separation logics to choose from, with different trade-offs in expressiveness, simplicity, and potential for automation.

Based on our prior experience with Chalice [36,37], we decided to use Implicit Dynamic Frames (IDF) [56], a dialect of separation logic whose assertions express constraints on ownership and values separately. For instance, instead of separation logic's points-to predicate $x.f \mapsto v$, IDF uses an accessibility predicate `acc(x.f)` to express ownership of the heap location, and an expression `x.f == v` to express a constraint on the value stored in the location. This separation is lifted to entire data structures, where inductive predicates [44] abstract over permissions, and side-effect free functions over values; notably, these functions may read from heap locations [29]. For instance, the IDF assertion `list(l) && length(l) > 0` expresses that the data structure stored in `l` is a non-empty list. Suitable well-formedness checks ensure that assertions constrain the value of a heap location only in contexts where that location is owned.

Choosing IDF over a more standard separation logic has the potential drawback of being less known in the community, thus potentially making Viper more difficult for others to adopt. Overall, however, IDF proved to be an excellent foundation for an IVL such as Viper for the following main reasons: (1) Source programs typically contain deterministic, side-effect free methods such as getters, comparison functions, and other operations to inspect data structures. These can be encoded as Viper functions and used directly in specifications. For instance, in the verification of a large Go codebase [11], 324 out of 823 (non-ghost and ghost) source methods fell into this category (ca. 40%). (2) Separating permission specifications from value specifications facilitates incremental verification. Verification typically starts by proving memory safety, which requires mostly permission specifications. With IDF, functional specifications can later define various abstractions of data structures without modifying the predicates used for proving memory safety and, thus, without adjusting the features of the original proof. In contrast, standard separation logics must express data abstractions as part of the predicate, such that the abstractions need to be fixed upfront when the predicates are declared. For instance, a binomial heap implementation in Viper [39] uses three predicates to prove memory safety and then introduces ten functions to express various layers of invariants and functional properties. This separation of concerns greatly simplified its verification. (3) Separating permission from value constraints enables the development of tools that handle these two aspects differently. For instance, specification inference techniques may target only one kind of constraint [20]. Moreover, Viper frontends for languages with ownership type systems, most prominently Prusti for Rust [3], automatically extract permission specifications from type information and then simply conjoin user-provided value constraints. Finally, IDF proved to be useful for gradual verification [62], because it allows programmers to provide partial specifications that contain relevant value constraints, but to defer permission specifications.

In our experience, these advantages clearly outweigh the potential drawbacks of IDF in the context of an intermediate verification language.

3.2 Formalization and Soundness

Viper has been designed to be sound, that is, if verification succeeds for a Viper program then it is actually correct. However, like other SMT-based verifiers [27,34], Viper does not yet provide end-to-end formal soundness guarantees. Users have to trust the definition of Viper's program logic, the correctness of its implementation in the Viper backends, and the underlying SMT solver (plus the correctness of the Viper frontend). On the other hand, verification in interactive theorem provers typically focuses on formal soundness proofs first and considers automation as an afterthought.

A fundamental question is thus how best to design verification tools that provide good automation *and* formal soundness guarantees. In Viper, we have chosen to focus on practical applications first: Once a feature is sufficiently automated and has proved useful, we formalize its semantics and prove soundness. We found that this "practice drives theory" approach is a viable alternative to the prevalent theory-first approach and has led to alternative mathematical directions and the discovery and solution of interesting theoretical problems [14,15].

There have been recent efforts to provide a formal semantics for parts of the Viper language [16,45,62]. In particular, Dardinier et al. [16] formalize an operational and an axiomatic Viper semantics in Isabelle and prove soundness and completeness between them. Their supported subset contains core features such as fractional permissions and Viper's `exhale` and `inhale` statements. The formal treatment of other important features such as inductive predicates and abstraction functions are planned for future work. Dardinier et al. use their semantics to formally connect a frontend based on concurrent separation logic to two Viper backends. In contrast to this once-and-for-all soundness proof, Parthasarathy et al. [45] extended Viper's verification condition generator to produce a certificate for each successful verification. This certificate is a formal proof in Isabelle that shows that correctness of the Boogie program produced by Viper's verification condition generator implies correctness of the Viper program; this result can be combined with an existing certification for Boogie [46]. In contrast to a soundness proof for the logic, certification covers also the *implementation* of the logic in the backend. These works suggest avenues for obtaining foundational guarantees for an automated verifier such as Viper. Extending them to a larger Viper subset and combining them with certification techniques for SMT solvers to obtain end-to-end guarantees is promising future work.

3.3 Growing the Logic

Since the original design of Viper, the expressiveness of state-of-the-art separation logics has grown tremendously, for instance, by supporting higher-order programs and specifications, as well as various forms of concurrency reasoning. Viper's philosophy for growing its own supported logic has been rather conservative. We consider adding a feature if (1) an encoding into existing features is not possible or leads to bad performance, (2) there is a demand from several frontends for this feature, and (3) the feature can be automated reliably. The third criterion is especially important to preserve Viper's usability.

The two most significant extensions to Viper's logic have been magic wands [55] and iterated separating conjunctions [40]. Magic wands allow one to specify partial data structures and were initially added to express invariants for iterative traversals: in particular, the permissions to the part of the data structure already visited can be conveniently expressed with a wand. Later, magic wand support turned out to be essential for the encoding of borrowing in the Rust verifier Prusti [3]. Iterated separating conjunctions are especially useful for specifying random-access data structures such as arrays, as well as data structures with complex sharing such as arbitrary graphs. In the latter case, specifications can maintain a set of nodes and express ownership of all nodes in the graph by quantifying over the set members using an iterated separating conjunction. This use of a set results in specifications akin to those in Dafny [35], but with support for concurrent programs. Adding these features required developing novel verification algorithms and, for magic wands, also novel theoretical foundations [15].

A recent development has been to start fine tuning the degree of automation Viper provides, another key trade-off in verifier design: Verifiers can generally choose to require more user input for their proofs and thereby obtain simpler, fast proof automation, or alternatively provide more automation at the expense of a more complex proof search. Viper generally aims for a high degree of automation (higher than, for example, VeriFast); this choice increases usability, but can negatively impact verification performance for complex projects. Thus, we have started adding features that enable users to control the degree of automation (e.g. the automatic unfolding of function definitions); more such extensions are necessary to improve scalability further. Another avenue for future work is Viper's fixed permission model. It is able to encode many program logics, but such encodings can lack automation. Therefore, inspired by Gillian [53], we plan to add support for custom permission models and separation algebras.

4 Tool Architecture

Over the years, many new frontends have been added to Viper's ecosystem, but the core architecture (Fig. 1) has remained unchanged. Its central component is the Viper IVL, targeted by frontends for real-world programming languages [3, 9, 10, 23, 28, 49, 50, 59, 61] and specialized program logics [13, 21, 57, 60].

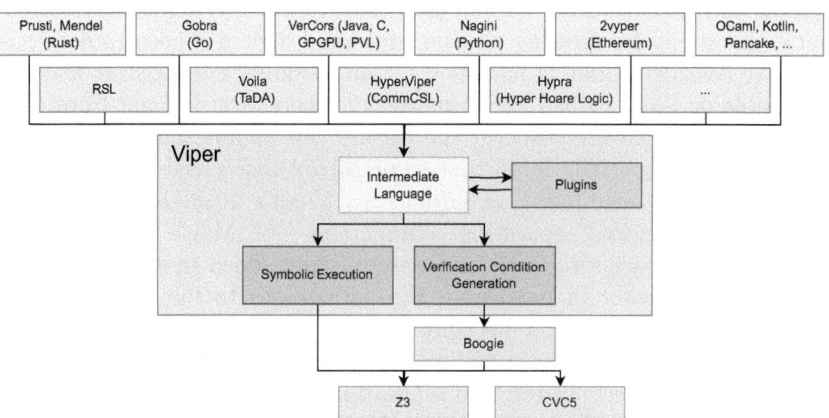

Fig. 1. Viper's architecture, with frontends (blue), backends (red), dependencies (green), and plugin infrastructure (purple). (Color figure online)

Viper programs, no matter whether they are generated by a frontend or written manually, are verified by one of Viper's two backends. The symbolic execution (SE) backend [54] operates in the style of Smallfoot [8] and VeriFast [30], but employs different algorithms for Viper's more advanced features. It maintains a symbolic heap to track separation logic resources and interacts directly with an SMT solver to discharge verification conditions. The verification condition generation (VCG) backend encodes Viper programs into Boogie [5], that is, it is based on another, lower-level IVL. Viper mainly uses the Z3 SMT solver [38], but also has support for others, e.g. CVC5 [4].

A core design principle behind Viper's architecture, which is essential for its overall usability, is to shield Viper users from the details of the backends and the underlying SMT solver. All interactions happen through the Viper language, and any kind of feedback from the tool can be understood at the level of the language. For instance, Viper's error messages and counterexamples do not refer to details of the backends, and it remains transparent whether a Viper feature is implemented natively or via a plugin. We successfully maintain this abstraction with very few exceptions; for instance, even though Viper offers trigger inference for the SMT solver's quantifier instantiation algorithm, users sometimes have to specify triggers manually (although nonetheless in terms of Viper-level features, not their SMT representations). Most Viper frontends provide a similar abstraction, that is, they in turn shield their users from Viper, such that they can work entirely on the level of the source language.

4.1 Project Management

Developing a tool infrastructure over 15 years in an academic research group is a major challenge because the development spans several generations of PhD students and postdocs, and because the incentives to implement features, fix bugs, and optimize performance are not aligned well with the realities of academia.

We have addressed the first challenge by having team members from several generations work on each Viper component, to ensure continuity and to retain expertise in the group as members graduate and leave. We were also fortunate that some key team members decided to stay at ETH Zurich beyond their graduation or to continue contributing to Viper in their next job.

We have addressed the second challenge by having an owner for each Viper component (including frontends and IDE), who is responsible for bug fixing and maintenance. This allows us to spread this effort over many people, making it bearable for each of them. Moreover, new PhD projects such as the development of frontends or major case studies are usually a good motivation for PhD students to extend Viper to better support their work.

Over the last 15 years, we usually had between 10 and 20 people working on Viper and its frontends. We coordinate them in monthly project meetings, and (since 2021) maintain a biannual release schedule to drive the project and ensure steady improvements. Finally, we have found occasional hackathons and regular participation in verification competitions to be great ways to obtain experience with our own tools, to find new areas for improvement and to boost team spirit.

4.2 Backends

A key feature that distinguishes Viper from many (intermediate) verification languages is its support for two different backend verifiers that implement two technically very different verification techniques. The decision to support multiple backends instead of a single one represents a major trade-off with far-reaching consequences.

The main advantages are the backends' varied performance and completeness characteristics for different classes of programs (as we explored previously [25]), which enabled frontends and verification efforts that would not have been possible with only one backend.

Another major advantage is that the two backends enable differential testing: any case where the two backends disagree signals either a bug, an incompleteness, or possibly unclear semantics of a Viper feature. Such testing has been one of the main ways to detect such issues, and also helps users triage their own issues.

On the other hand, supporting different backends limits extensions of the language and logic to features that can be automated well in both: e.g. SE-based verifiers can easily support pattern matching for separation-logic resources, whereas a VCG-based backend would have to produce verification conditions containing (both universal and) existential quantifiers, which are not supported well by SMT solvers. Hence, Viper does not have this feature (which is rarely needed with IDF). Similarly, since Viper's VCG backend goes through Boogie, it can only use SMT-level features (e.g. natively-supported types) that are exposed by Boogie. Finally, counterexamples returned by Viper must be generated from two substantially different sources, which limits the information that can be presented. Despite such individual cases, this limitation has not proved to be a major obstacle in practice. As a mitigation, we have recently introduced annotations to express backend-specific instructions in Viper programs, although we expect these to be used only rarely.

Moreover, maintaining two backends incurs substantial engineering costs: language or logic extensions have to be implemented for both backends, which can slow down development and lead to situations where a new language feature is temporarily supported by only one backend. To mitigate this issue, Viper uses plugins, which enable modular extensions of Viper's syntax that are desugared into the core IVL *before* reaching the backends. This allows us to extend the language and logic *without* impacting the backends. For example, user-defined

ADTs and termination checks are implemented as plugins. Facilitating extensions via plugins has substantially contributed to Viper's agility and expressiveness.

Overall, we have enjoyed significant benefits from Viper's two-backend strategy in terms of our ability to use Viper for challenging verification projects, and to advance the state of the art in SE- and VCG-based verification. However, the implementation and maintenance effort required to do this, especially in a research group, should not be underestimated.

4.3 Growing the Architecture

The most significant additions to the Viper ecosystem since its inception have been its frontends, particularly its four most mature frontends for real-world languages (Prusti for Rust, Gobra for Go, VerCors for Java and CUDA/OpenCL, and Nagini for Python). Each is able to verify realistic code; for instance, we have verified an entire system (of over 4,000 lines of production code) with Gobra [47]. VerCors has been used for multiple realistic Java and CUDA case studies [1,43,52]. Nagini targets statically-typed Python and has support for some of Python's more dynamic features (such as dynamic addition of fields). In addition to these main frontends, a substantial number of research prototypes for automating advanced program logics has been developed, and there is ongoing work on further frontends.

Each new frontend has significantly benefitted from the shared infrastructure built around the Viper language, but also challenged Viper and motivated improvements that ultimately benefit the whole ecosystem. An interesting special case is the gradual verification tool Gradual C0 [19], which is not implemented as a frontend, but as a fork of Viper and its SE backend.

Most changes to the Viper backends are triggered by extensions of the Viper language and logic (see Sect. 2.2 and Sect. 3.3). In addition to those, we have extended both backends to explore different core algorithms, combinations of heap models and proof search algorithms. These exhibit different performance and completeness tradeoffs [25], and users can choose the algorithm that best suits the verification problem domain at hand. As it has become difficult even for experts to predict which specific algorithm will perform best on a given example, automating this process is ongoing work.

Finally, one of the most important additions to the Viper architecture has been its IDE integration in the form of a mature plugin for VSCode, which significantly simplifies the process of installing and running Viper, and additionally enhances the user experience through features such as verification result caching, intuitive error reporting, and many standard IDE features. We are convinced that Viper's availability in VSCode has played a central role in its adoption for teaching at multiple universities.

5 Related Work

There are a number of other verification tools for separation logics, such as VeriFast [30], GRASShopper [48], SecC [26], the Gillian verifiers [53], and Caper [18], as well as other similar tools not based on separation logic, in particular, Dafny [35], which uses dynamic frames [31] to reason about heap-manipulating programs. Moreover, there are other intermediate verification languages (IVLs) with corresponding backends, most notably Boogie [34], Why3 [27], and GIL [53].

Compared to most other separation logic based tools, Viper supports a richer set of core features in its separation logic (offering, e.g., magic wands, iterated separating conjunction, and permission introspection), along with appropriate proof search algorithms, which facilitates the encoding of a wide range of verification problems. For example, SecC and Caper directly implement more specific logics (for information flow security and fine-grained concurrency, respectively), while those use cases can both be supported in Viper via a plugin and a frontend, respectively. Moreover, Viper supports specific assertions and statements (e.g., inhale and exhale) whose purpose is to *encode* separation logic proof rules in Viper; no other tool has those. Compared to VeriFast, Viper requires less user input and provides more automation at the cost of a more complex proof search that can potentially lead to worse performance.

Compared to Dafny, Viper's logical foundation allows one to encode verification problems for concurrent programs, whereas Dafny is limited to sequential code. On the other hand, Dafny offers advanced features for proof authoring and specification inference, whereas Viper leaves such tasks to frontends.

Compared to other IVLs, Viper supports a fixed heap model and logic (implicit dynamic frames), whereas GIL is parametric in its memory model, and Boogie and Why3 require frontends to encode the memory model. Viper's approach allows it to provide predictable automated proof search algorithms tailored to its heap model and logic.

Viper is also unique in that it is (to our knowledge) the only deductive verification framework supporting more than one independent verification backend.

6 Discussion

Revisiting our original design goals, we believe we have achieved the goal of *expressiveness*, as demonstrated by Viper's ability to verify a wide range of frontend languages, and advanced properties expressed in complex program logics. Making Viper parametric in its permission model and adding support for higher-order code and assertions would further increase expressiveness.

Viper is designed for *soundness* above all else; we leverage differential testing to effectively identify implementation bugs in the backends, and extensions such as termination checks help detect inconsistent encodings. Significant progress has been made in formalizing Viper's semantics and generating proof certificates, with ongoing efforts to enable independent proof validation.

As for *usability*, we find it very encouraging that Viper is increasingly used by people with little or no connection to the Viper team, for both teaching (e.g., in Copenhagen, Nancy, and Oldenburg) and tooling (e.g., frontends for Java, Kotlin, OCaml, Pancake; Gradual Viper). It has also won awards in several categories of the VerifyThis verification competition (best team, best student team, tool used by most teams), demonstrating its effectiveness. Ongoing work on specification inference and verification debugging will further increase usability.

Overall, we see the verification of a next-generation internet router [47] as evidence for Viper's usability and expressiveness. This is a substantial Go codebase under active development, not written with verification in mind, optimized for performance, and one of the largest verification efforts ever undertaken with automated separation logic verifiers.

Such ambitious projects demonstrate the capabilities of the Viper infrastructure, but also relentlessly expose aspects that need improving. In fact, many of the directions for future work mentioned throughout this paper are motivated by large case studies on correctness and security verification. They will fuel our research agenda for the next 15 years.

Acknowledgments. Numerous people have contributed to the development of the Viper infrastructure and its frontends, both in our team and elsewhere. We are very grateful for all of these contributions.

Disclosure of Interests. The authors have no competing interests to declare that are relevant to the content of this article.

References

1. Armborst, L., Huisman, M.: Permission-based verification of red-black trees and their merging. In: FormaliSE@ICSE, pp. 111–123. IEEE (2021)
2. Arquint, L., Schwerhoff, M., Mehta, V., Müller, P.: A generic methodology for the modular verification of security protocol implementations. In: CCS, pp. 1377–1391. ACM (2023)
3. Astrauskas, V., Müller, P., Poli, F., Summers, A.J.: Leveraging Rust types for modular specification and verification. Proc. ACM Program. Lang. **3**(OOPSLA), 147:1–147:30 (2019)

4. Barbosa, H., et al.: CVC5: a versatile and industrial-strength SMT solver. In: TACAS (1). LNCS, vol. 13243, pp. 415–442. Springer, Cham (2022)
5. Barnett, M., Chang, B.E., DeLine, R., Jacobs, B., Leino, K.R.M.: Boogie: A modular reusable verifier for object-oriented programs. In: FMCO. LNCS, vol. 4111, pp. 364–387. Springer, Cham (2005)
6. Barnett, M., Fähndrich, M., Leino, K., Müller, P., Schulte, W., Venter, H.: Specification and verification: the Spec# experience. Commun. ACM **54**(6), 81–91 (2011)
7. Barrett, C., Fontaine, P., Tinelli, C.: The SMT-LIB standard: version 2.6. Technical report, Department of Computer Science, The University of Iowa (2017). www.SMT-LIB.org
8. Berdine, J., Calcagno, C., O'Hearn, P.W.: Smallfoot: modular automatic assertion checking with separation logic. In: FMCO. LNCS, vol. 4111, pp. 115–137. Springer, Cham (2005)
9. Blom, S., Huisman, M.: The VerCors tool for verification of concurrent programs. In: FM. LNCS, vol. 8442, pp. 127–131. Springer, Cham (2014)
10. Bräm, C., Eilers, M., Müller, P., Sierra, R., Summers, A.J.: Rich specifications for Ethereum smart contract verification. Proc. ACM Program. Lang. **5**(OOPSLA), 1–30 (2021)
11. Chuat, L., et al.: The Complete Guide to SCION - From Design Principles to Formal Verification. Information Security and Cryptography. Springer, Cham (2022)
12. Cuoq, P., Kirchner, F., Kosmatov, N., Prevosto, V., Signoles, J., Yakobowski, B.: Frama-C – a software analysis perspective. In: SEFM. LNCS, vol. 7504, pp. 233–247. Springer, Cham (2012)
13. Dardinier, T., Li, A., Müller, P.: Hypra: a deductive program verifier for hyper hoare logic. Proc. ACM Program. Lang. **8**(OOPSLA2), 1279–1308 (2024). https://doi.org/10.1145/3689756
14. Dardinier, T., Müller, P., Summers, A.J.: Fractional resources in unbounded separation logic. Proc. ACM Program. Lang. **6**(OOPSLA2), 1066–1092 (2022). https://doi.org/10.1145/3563326
15. Dardinier, T., Parthasarathy, G., Weeks, N., Müller, P., Summers, A.J.: Sound automation of magic wands. In: CAV (2). LNCS, vol. 13372, pp. 130–151. Springer, Cham (2022)
16. Dardinier, T., Sammler, M., Parthasarathy, G., Summers, A.J., Müller, P.: Formal foundations for translational separation logic verifiers. Proc. ACM Program. Lang. **9**(POPL) (2025)
17. Denis, X., Jourdan, J., Marché, C.: Creusot: a foundry for the deductive verification of Rust programs. In: ICFEM. LNCS, vol. 13478, pp. 90–105. Springer, Cham (2022)
18. Dinsdale-Young, T., da Rocha Pinto, P., Andersen, K.J., Birkedal, L.: Caper - automatic verification for fine-grained concurrency. In: ESOP. LNCS, vol. 10201, pp. 420–447. Springer, Cham (2017)
19. DiVincenzo, J., et al.: Gradual C0: symbolic execution for gradual verification. ACM Trans. Program. Lang. Syst. **46**(4) (2025). https://doi.org/10.1145/3704808
20. Dohrau, J., Summers, A.J., Urban, C., Münger, S., Müller, P.: Permission inference for array programs. In: Chockler, H., Weissenbacher, G. (eds.) Computer Aided Verification - CAV 2018, Part II. LNCS, vol. 10982, pp. 55–74. Springer, Cham (2018). https://doi.org/10.1007/978-3-319-96142-2_7
21. Eilers, M., Dardinier, T., Müller, P.: CommCSL: proving information flow security for concurrent programs using abstract commutativity. Proc. ACM Program. Lang. **7**(PLDI), 1682–1707 (2023). https://doi.org/10.1145/3591289

22. Eilers, M., Meier, S., Müller, P.: Product programs in the wild: retrofitting program verifiers to check information flow security. In: CAV (1). LNCS, vol. 12759, pp. 718–741. Springer, Cham (2021)
23. Eilers, M., Müller, P.: Nagini: a static verifier for Python. In: CAV (1). LNCS, vol. 10981, pp. 596–603. Springer, Cham (2018)
24. Eilers, M., Müller, P., Hitz, S.: Modular product programs. ACM Trans. Program. Lang. Syst. **42**(1), 3:1–3:37 (2020)
25. Eilers, M., Schwerhoff, M., Müller, P.: Verification algorithms for automated separation logic verifiers. In: Gurfinkel, A., Ganesh, V. (eds.) Computer Aided Verification - CAV 2024, Part I. LNCS, vol. 14681, pp. 362–386. Springer, Cham (2024). https://doi.org/10.1007/978-3-031-65627-9_18
26. Ernst, G., Murray, T.: SecCSL: security concurrent separation logic. In: CAV (2). LNCS, vol. 11562, pp. 208–230. Springer, Cham (2019)
27. Filliâtre, J., Paskevich, A.: Why3 - where programs meet provers. In: ESOP. LNCS, vol. 7792, pp. 125–128. Springer, Cham (2013)
28. Gros, C., Pereira, M.: Le chameau et le serpent rentrent dans un bar : vérification quasi-automatique de code OCaml en logique de séparation (2024). https://arxiv.org/abs/2412.14894
29. Heule, S., Kassios, I.T., Müller, P., Summers, A.J.: Verification condition generation for permission logics with abstract predicates and abstraction functions. In: ECOOP. LNCS, vol. 7920, pp. 451–476. Springer, Cham (2013)
30. Jacobs, B., Smans, J., Philippaerts, P., Vogels, F., Penninckx, W., Piessens, F.: VeriFast: a powerful, sound, predictable, fast verifier for C and Java. In: NASA Formal Methods. LNCS, vol. 6617, pp. 41–55. Springer, Cham (2011)
31. Kassios, I.T.: Dynamic frames: support for framing, dependencies and sharing without restrictions. In: Misra, J., Nipkow, T., Sekerinski, E. (eds.) FM 2006. LNCS, vol. 4085, pp. 268–283. Springer, Cham (2006). https://doi.org/10.1007/11813040_19
32. Lahiri, S.K., Hawblitzel, C., Kawaguchi, M., Rebêlo, H.: SYMDIFF: a language-agnostic semantic diff tool for imperative programs. In: CAV. LNCS, vol. 7358, pp. 712–717. Springer, Cham (2012)
33. Lal, A., Qadeer, S., Lahiri, S.K.: A solver for reachability modulo theories. In: CAV. LNCS, vol. 7358, pp. 427–443. Springer, Cham (2012)
34. Leino, K.R.M.: This is Boogie 2 (2008). https://www.microsoft.com/en-us/research/publication/this-is-boogie-2-2/
35. Leino, K.R.M.: Dafny: an automatic program verifier for functional correctness. In: LPAR (Dakar). LNCS, vol. 6355, pp. 348–370. Springer, Cham (2010)
36. Leino, K.R.M., Müller, P.: A basis for verifying multi-threaded programs. In: ESOP. LNCS, vol. 5502, pp. 378–393. Springer, Cham (2009)
37. Leino, K.R.M., Müller, P., Smans, J.: Verification of concurrent programs with Chalice. In: FOSAD. LNCS, vol. 5705, pp. 195–222. Springer, Cham (2009)
38. de Moura, L.M., Bjørner, N.S.: Z3: an efficient SMT solver. In: TACAS. LNCS, vol. 4963, pp. 337–340. Springer, Cham (2008)
39. Müller, P.: The binomial heap verification challenge in Viper. In: Müller, P., Schaefer, I. (eds.) Principled Software Development - Essays Dedicated to Arnd Poetzsch-Heffter on the Occasion of his 60th Birthday, pp. 203–219. Springer (2018). https://doi.org/10.1007/978-3-319-98047-8_13
40. Müller, P., Schwerhoff, M., Summers, A.J.: Automatic verification of iterated separating conjunctions using symbolic execution. In: CAV (1). LNCS, vol. 9779, pp. 405–425. Springer, Cham (2016)

41. Müller, P., Schwerhoff, M., Summers, A.J.: Viper: a verification infrastructure for permission-based reasoning. In: VMCAI. LNCS, vol. 9583, pp. 41–62. Springer, Cham (2016)
42. O'Hearn, P.W.: Resources, concurrency and local reasoning. In: Gardner, P., Yoshida, N. (eds.) CONCUR 2004. LNCS, vol. 3170, pp. 49–67. Springer, Cham (2004). https://doi.org/10.1007/978-3-540-28644-8_4
43. Oortwijn, W., Huisman, M.: Formal verification of an industrial safety-critical traffic tunnel control system. In: Ahrendt, W., Tarifa, S.L.T. (eds.) Integrated Formal Methods - IFM 2019. LNCS, vol. 11918, pp. 418–436. Springer, Cham (2019). https://doi.org/10.1007/978-3-030-34968-4_23
44. Parkinson, M.J., Bierman, G.M.: Separation logic and abstraction. In: POPL, pp. 247–258. ACM (2005)
45. Parthasarathy, G., Dardinier, T., Bonneau, B., Müller, P., Summers, A.J.: Towards trustworthy automated program verifiers: formally validating translations into an intermediate verification language. Proc. ACM Program. Lang. **8**(PLDI), 1510–1534 (2024). https://doi.org/10.1145/3656438
46. Parthasarathy, G., Müller, P., Summers, A.J.: Formally validating a practical verification condition generator. In: Silva, A., Leino, K.R.M. (eds.) Computer Aided Verification , CAV 2021, Part II. LNCS, vol. 12760, pp. 704–727. Springer, Cham (2021). https://doi.org/10.1007/978-3-030-81688-9_33
47. Pereira, J.C., et al.: Protocols to code: formal verification of a next-generation internet router (2024). https://arxiv.org/abs/2405.06074
48. Piskac, R., Wies, T., Zufferey, D.: GRASShopper - complete heap verification with mixed specifications. In: TACAS. LNCS, vol. 8413, pp. 124–139. Springer, Cham (2014)
49. Poli, F., Denis, X., Müller, P., Summers, A.J.: Reasoning about interior mutability in Rust using library-defined capabilities (2024)
50. Protopapa, F.: Verifying Kotlin Code with Viper by Controlling Aliasing. Master's thesis, University of Padua (2024)
51. Reynolds, J.C.: Separation logic: a logic for shared mutable data structures. In: LICS, pp. 55–74. IEEE Computer Society (2002)
52. Safari, M., Huisman, M.: Formal verification of parallel prefix sum and stream compaction algorithms in CUDA. Theor. Comput. Sci. **912**, 81–98 (2022)
53. Santos, J.F., Maksimovic, P., Ayoun, S., Gardner, P.: Gillian, part I: a multi-language platform for symbolic execution. In: PLDI, pp. 927–942. ACM (2020)
54. Schwerhoff, M.: Advancing automated, permission-based program verification using symbolic execution. Ph.D. thesis, ETH Zurich, Zürich, Switzerland (2016)
55. Schwerhoff, M., Summers, A.J.: Lightweight support for magic wands in an automatic verifier. In: ECOOP. LIPIcs, vol. 37, pp. 614–638. Schloss Dagstuhl - Leibniz-Zentrum für Informatik (2015)
56. Smans, J., Jacobs, B., Piessens, F.: Implicit dynamic frames: Combining dynamic frames and separation logic. In: ECOOP. LNCS, vol. 5653, pp. 148–172. Springer, Cham (2009)
57. Summers, A.J., Müller, P.: Automating deductive verification for weak-memory programs. In: TACAS (1). LNCS, vol. 10805, pp. 190–209. Springer, Cham (2018)
58. Wolf, F.A., Müller, P.: Verifiable security policies for distributed systems. In: Computer and Communications Security (CCS). CCS '24, pp. 4–18. Association for Computing Machinery, New York, NY, USA (2024). https://doi.org/10.1145/3658644.3690303

59. Wolf, F.A., Arquint, L., Clochard, M., Oortwijn, W., Pereira, J.C., Müller, P.: Gobra: modular specification and verification of Go programs. In: CAV (1). LNCS, vol. 12759, pp. 367–379. Springer, Cham (2021)
60. Wolf, F.A., Schwerhoff, M., Müller, P.: Concise outlines for a complex logic: a proof outline checker for TaDA, **13047**, 407–426 (2021)
61. Zhao, J., et al.: Verifying device drivers with Pancake (2025). https://arxiv.org/abs/2501.08249
62. Zimmerman, C., DiVincenzo, J., Aldrich, J.: Sound gradual verification with symbolic execution. Proc. ACM Program. Lang. **8**(POPL), 2547–2576 (2024). https://doi.org/10.1145/3632927

Open Access This chapter is licensed under the terms of the Creative Commons Attribution 4.0 International License (http://creativecommons.org/licenses/by/4.0/), which permits use, sharing, adaptation, distribution and reproduction in any medium or format, as long as you give appropriate credit to the original author(s) and the source, provide a link to the Creative Commons license and indicate if changes were made.

The images or other third party material in this chapter are included in the chapter's Creative Commons license, unless indicated otherwise in a credit line to the material. If material is not included in the chapter's Creative Commons license and your intended use is not permitted by statutory regulation or exceeds the permitted use, you will need to obtain permission directly from the copyright holder.

Model Checking

Efficient Probabilistic Model Checking for Relational Reachability

Lina Gerlach[1], Tobias Winkler[1], Erika Ábrahám[1],
Borzoo Bonakdarpour[2], and Sebastian Junges[3](✉)

[1] RWTH Aachen University, Aachen, Germany
[2] Michigan State University, East Lansing, MI, USA
[3] Radboud University, Nijmegen, The Netherlands
sebastian.junges@ru.nl

Abstract. Markov decision processes model systems subject to nondeterministic and probabilistic uncertainty. A plethora of verification techniques addresses variations of reachability properties, such as: *Is there a scheduler resolving the nondeterminism such that the probability to reach an error state is above a threshold?* We consider an understudied extension that relates different reachability probabilities, such as: *Is there a scheduler such that two sets of states are reached with different probabilities?* These questions appear naturally in the design of randomized algorithms and in various security applications. We provide a tractable algorithm for many variations of this problem, while proving computational hardness of some others. An implementation of our algorithm beats solvers for more general probabilistic hyperlogics by orders of magnitude, on the subset of their benchmarks that are within our fragment.

1 Introduction

Markov decision processes (MDPs) are the ubiquitous model to describe system behavior subject to both nondeterminism and probabilistic uncertainty. During the execution of an MDP, a *scheduler* (aka *policy* or *strategy*) resolves the nondeterminism at every state by choosing one out of several available actions specifying the possible next states and their probabilities. A classic verification task in an MDP is to determine whether there is a scheduler such that, using this scheduler, the probability to reach an error state exceeds a threshold. To decide this, one can compute and evaluate the performance of the *maximizing* scheduler, as is well established both in theory and in practice [4]. Such *reachability properties* are the cornerstone to support, e.g., linear temporal logics [7].

However, evaluating the maximizing (or minimizing) scheduler as outlined above is only applicable to the most basic types of reachability properties. Indeed, for *relational reachability* properties like:

The original version of the chapter has been revised. A correction to this chapter can be found at https://doi.org/10.1007/978-3-031-98668-0_20

© The Author(s) 2025, corrected publication 2025
R. Piskac and Z. Rakamarić (Eds.): CAV 2025, LNCS 15931, pp. 127–147, 2025.
https://doi.org/10.1007/978-3-031-98668-0_6

"Is there a scheduler reaching state a with a *different* probability than state b?"

we are not necessarily interested in maximizing the probability of reaching either a or b—the two probabilities just have to be different. *This paper contributes practically efficient algorithms and complexity results for model checking relational reachability properties*, including the above example and many more (see below).

Relational reachability properties go beyond the queries considered in multi-objective model checking [5,6,12,25], while they can be expressed in (generally intractable) probabilistic hyperlogics [2,9,11]. We discuss the precise relation to these works in Sect. 7. Our algorithm solves some standard benchmarks for these hyperlogics orders of magnitude faster than the state of the art [3,10].

Motivating Example. We wish to simulate an unbiased, perfectly random coin flip using an infinite stream of possibly *biased* random bits, each of which is 0 with an unknown but fixed probability $0 < p < 1$ and otherwise 1. The following simple solution is due to von Neumann [29]: Extract the first two bits from the stream; if they are different, return the value of the first; otherwise try again. Now, consider a variation of the problem where the stream comprises random bits with *different*, unknown biases $p_0, p_1, \ldots$ which are, however, all known to lie in an interval $[\underline{p}, \overline{p}] \subset (0, 1)$. Is von Neumann's solution still applicable in this new situation? To address this question for a concrete interval $[\underline{p}, \overline{p}]$, say $[0.59, 0.61]$, we may model the situation as shown in Fig. 1 and formalize the property as

$$\forall \sigma.\ \Pr_{s_0}^\sigma(\Diamond\{01\}) \approx_\varepsilon \Pr_{s_0}^\sigma(\Diamond\{10\}) \quad (\dagger)$$

where σ is a universally quantified scheduler, s_0 is the initial state, and $\approx_\varepsilon$ means approximate equality up to absolute error $\varepsilon \geq 0$. Using the techniques presented in this paper, we can establish automatically that, as expected, $(\dagger)$ is false for $\varepsilon = 0$ (exact equality), but holds if we relax the constraint to $\varepsilon = 0.05$. In words, von Neumann's trick continues to work "approximately" in the new setting. Note that the universal quantification in $(\dagger)$ is over *general* policies that may use both unbounded memory and randomization. This is essential to model the problem properly: Without randomization, all biases would be either $\underline{p}$ or $\overline{p}$ and a bounded-memory policy would induce an ultimately periodic stream of biases.

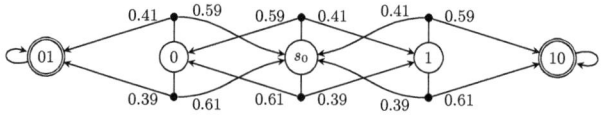

Fig. 1. MDP from illustrative example.

Table 1. Complexity of selected classes of simple relational reachability properties over MD schedulers, where $\varepsilon > 0$ and $\trianglerighteq \in \{\geq, >, \not\approx_{\varepsilon'} \mid \varepsilon' \geq 0\}$. Over general schedulers, all variants considered here are in PTIME (Theorem 3).

Property class	Complexity over MD schedulers
$\exists \sigma.\ \mathrm{Pr}_s^\sigma(\lozenge T_1) = \mathrm{Pr}_s^\sigma(\lozenge T_2)$	strongly NP-complete [Th. 4(a)]
$\exists \sigma.\ \mathrm{Pr}_s^\sigma(\lozenge T_1) \approx_\varepsilon \mathrm{Pr}_s^\sigma(\lozenge T_2)$	NP-complete [Th. 4(a)]
$\exists \sigma.\ \mathrm{Pr}_s^\sigma(\lozenge T_1) \trianglerighteq \mathrm{Pr}_s^\sigma(\lozenge T_2)$	in NP [Th. 4]; PTIME if T_1, T_2 absorb. [Th. 6(b)]
$\exists \sigma.\ \mathrm{Pr}_{s_1}^\sigma(\lozenge T_1) = \mathrm{Pr}_{s_2}^\sigma(\lozenge T_2)$	strongly NP-complete [Th. 4(a)]
$\exists \sigma.\ \mathrm{Pr}_{s_1}^\sigma(\lozenge T_1) \approx_\varepsilon \mathrm{Pr}_{s_2}^\sigma(\lozenge T_2)$	NP-complete [Th. 4(a)]
$\exists \sigma.\ \mathrm{Pr}_{s_1}^\sigma(\lozenge T_1) \trianglerighteq \mathrm{Pr}_{s_2}^\sigma(\lozenge T_2)$	in NP [Th. 4]
$\exists \sigma_1, \sigma_2.\ \mathrm{Pr}_{s_1}^{\sigma_1}(\lozenge T_1) = \mathrm{Pr}_{s_2}^{\sigma_2}(\lozenge T_2)$	strongly NP-complete [Th. 4(b)]
$\exists \sigma_1, \sigma_2.\ \mathrm{Pr}_{s_1}^{\sigma_1}(\lozenge T_1) \approx_\varepsilon \mathrm{Pr}_{s_2}^{\sigma_2}(\lozenge T_2)$	NP-complete [Th. 4(b)]
$\exists \sigma_1, \sigma_2.\ \mathrm{Pr}_{s_1}^{\sigma_1}(\lozenge T_1) \trianglerighteq \mathrm{Pr}_{s_2}^{\sigma_2}(\lozenge T_2)$	PTIME [Th. 3(c)]

A Zoo of Relational Properties. In this paper, we consider variations of relational reachability properties, like asking for a single scheduler ensuring that a set of states is reached with higher probability than a different set of states (inequality properties), or that these probabilities are approximately or exactly the same (equality properties). These probabilities can be evaluated from the same or from different initial states. Furthermore, one can consider two schedulers, which allows us to express, e.g., that any pair of schedulers induces roughly the same reachability probability. On top of these variations, we consider weighted sums of reachability probabilities. We formally introduce the properties in Sect. 3.

Verifying Relational Reachability Properties. Given an MDP and a relational reachability property, we provide an algorithm to decide satisfaction and construct, if possible, the corresponding witnessing scheduler(s). The key insight is that these (possibly randomized memoryful) schedulers can be constructed by translating the given property to *expected reward* computations in a series of mildly transformed MDPs. For inequality properties, it suffices to optimize the total expected reward. For (approximate) equality, the main idea is to construct a randomized memoryful scheduler from the schedulers witnessing the corresponding two inequality properties (Sect. 4). Our prototypical implementation of this approach on top of STORM [21] shows its practical feasibility (Sect. 6).

Computational Complexity. The algorithm outlined above is exponential *only* in the number of different target sets that occur in the property, i.e., the algorithm is *fixed-parameter tractable* (FPT) [18]. In Sect. 5, we study the computational complexity of the problem in greater detail. Besides the FPT result, we show that the problem is in general PSPACE-hard, but can be solved in PTIME under one of various (mild) assumptions. Furthermore, when restricting the schedulers to be *memoryless and deterministic* (MD), several types of equality properties are strongly NP-hard. We also list various fragments where we can compute MD schedulers in polynomial time. Table 1 gives an overview on the complexity of *selected* fragments that compare two probabilities, illustrating the border between PTIME and strong NP-hardness for MD schedulers.

Summary and Contributions. In summary, in this paper we present model checking for relational reachability properties, which go beyond standard reachability and multi-objective properties while remaining tractable (see Sect. 7 for a discussion of related work). The tractability is in sharp contrast with the more general probabilistic hyperlogics. The key contributions are the efficient algorithm (Sect. 4), a prototypical implementation thereof (Sect. 6), and a study of the complexity landscape for relational reachability properties (Sect. 5). For details on the algorithms, proofs and benchmarks we refer to the extended version [17].

2 Preliminaries

We use $\mathbb{N}, \mathbb{Q}, \mathbb{Q}_{\geq 0}$, and $\mathbb{R}$ to denote the sets of natural, rational, non-negative rational and real numbers, respectively. For $r, r', \varepsilon \in \mathbb{R}$ with $\varepsilon \geq 0$, we write $r \approx_\varepsilon r'$ iff $|r-r'| \leq \varepsilon$, and $r \not\approx_\varepsilon r'$ iff $|r - r'| > \varepsilon$. The set $Distr(V)$ of *probability distributions* over a finite set V contains all $\mu \colon V \to [0,1]$ s.t. $\sum_{v \in V} \mu(v) = 1$.

Definition 1. *A* Markov decision process (MDP) *is a triple* $\mathcal{M} = (S, Act, \mathbf{P})$ *s.t. S is a non-empty finite set of* states, *Act is a non-empty finite set of* actions, *and* $\mathbf{P} \colon S \times Act \times S \to [0,1]$ *is a* transition probability function *s.t. for all $s \in S$ the set of its* enabled actions $Act(s) = \{\alpha \in Act \mid \sum_{s' \in S} \mathbf{P}(s, \alpha s') = 1\}$ *is non-empty and* $\sum_{s' \in S} \mathbf{P}(s, \alpha s') = 0$ *for all $\alpha \in Act \setminus Act(s)$.*

A state $s \in S$ is *absorbing* if $\mathbf{P}(s, \alpha s) = 1$ for all $\alpha \in Act(s)$. A set of states $S' \subseteq S$ is absorbing if all $s \in S'$ are absorbing.

An *(infinite) path* of an MDP $\mathcal{M}$ is an infinite sequence of states and actions $\pi = s_0 \alpha_0 s_1 \alpha_1 \ldots$ such that for all i we have $\mathbf{P}(s_i, \alpha_i, s_{i+1}) > 0$. A *finite path* is a finite prefix of an infinite path ending in a state. We use $Paths^\mathcal{M}$ (respectively, $Paths_{fin}^\mathcal{M}$) to denote the set of all infinite (respectively, finite) paths of $\mathcal{M}$, and for some state $s \in S$ we use $Paths_{fin}^\mathcal{M}$ (respectively, $Paths_{fin}^\mathcal{M}(s)$) to denote the set of all infinite (respectively, finite) paths of $\mathcal{M}$ starting at s. For a finite or infinite path π we use $\pi(i) := s_i$ to denote the ith state of π. For a finite path $\pi = s_0 \alpha_0 \ldots \alpha_{n-1} s_n$, we define $last(\pi) := s_n$ and $|\pi| := n$.

A *scheduler* resolves the nondeterminism in an MDP.

Definition 2. *A* scheduler *for an MDP* $\mathcal{M} = (S, Act, \mathbf{P})$ *is a function* $\sigma \colon Paths_{fin}^\mathcal{M} \to Distr(Act)$ *with* $\sigma(\pi)(\alpha) = 0$ *for all* $\pi \in Paths_{fin}^\mathcal{M}$ *and* $\alpha \in Act \setminus Act(last(\pi))$.

A scheduler is *memoryless* if it can be defined as a function $\sigma \colon S \to Distr(Act)$, and *memoryful* (oder history-dependent) otherwise. A scheduler is *deterministic* if $\sigma(\pi) \in \{0,1\}$ for all $\pi \in Paths_{fin}^\mathcal{M}$, and *randomized* otherwise. The set of all general (i.e., history-dependent randomized (HR)) schedulers for an MDP $\mathcal{M}$ is denoted by $\Sigma^\mathcal{M}$, the set of all memoryless deterministic (MD) ones by $\Sigma_{MD}^\mathcal{M}$.

Applying a scheduler to an MDP induces a *discrete-time Markov chain (DTMC)*, which is an MDP where the set of actions is a singleton. We usually omit the actions and define a DTMC as a tuple $\mathcal{D} = (S, \mathbf{P})$.

Definition 3. *For an MDP $\mathcal{M} = (S, Act, \mathbf{P})$ and a scheduler $\sigma \in \Sigma^{\mathcal{M}}$, the DTMC induced by $\mathcal{M}$ and σ is defined as $\mathcal{M}^\sigma = (S^\sigma, \mathbf{P}^\sigma)$ with $S^\sigma = Paths_{fin}^{\mathcal{M}}$,*

$$\mathbf{P}(\pi, \pi') = \begin{cases} \mathbf{P}(last(\pi), \alpha, s') \cdot \sigma(\pi)(\alpha) & \text{if } \pi' = \pi \alpha s' \\ 0 & \text{otherwise .} \end{cases}$$

For an MDP $\mathcal{M}$, a scheduler σ and a state $s \in S^\sigma$ in the induced DTMC $\mathcal{M}^\sigma$, we use $\Pr_s^{\mathcal{M},\sigma}$ or simply $\Pr_s^\sigma$ to denote the associated probability measure. For a target set $T \subseteq S$, we further use $\Pr_s^\sigma(\Diamond T)$ to denote the probability of reaching T from s in $\mathcal{M}^\sigma$. We refer to [4] for details.

3 Problem Statement

The problem we study in this paper is formally defined as follows:

Problem RelReach: Given an MDP $\mathcal{M}$ with states S, decide whether

$$\exists \sigma_1, \ldots, \sigma_n \in \Sigma^{\mathcal{M}}. \sum_{i=1}^{m} q_i \cdot \Pr_{s_i}^{\sigma_{k_i}}(\Diamond T_i) \bowtie q_{m+1}, \qquad \text{where}$$

- m, n are natural numbers with $m \geq n$,
- $q_1, \ldots, q_{m+1}$ are rational coefficients,
- $s_1, \ldots s_m \in S$ are (not necessarily distinct) initial states,
- $\{k_1, \ldots, k_m\} = \{1, \ldots, n\}$ is a set of indices,
- $T_1, \ldots, T_m \subseteq S$ are (not necessarily distinct) target sets, and
- $\bowtie \; \in \{>, \geq, \approx_\varepsilon, \not\approx_\varepsilon | \; \varepsilon \in \mathbb{Q}_{\geq 0}\}$ is a comparison operator.

The comparison operators $=$ and $\neq$ are supported via $\approx_0$ and $\not\approx_0$, respectively, while properties with $\bowtie \; \in \{<, \leq\}$ can be reduced to the above form by multiplying coefficients with -1. Purely universally quantified properties (e.g. (†) on page 2) are readily reducible to RelReach via negation. We do not consider properties with quantifier alternations. Throughout the paper, the universally quantified variant is loosely referred to as "relational reachability" as well, but "RelReach" is reserved for the existential variant defined above (this distinction is relevant for the complexity results). Note that properties like $\exists \sigma. \Pr_s^\sigma(\Diamond T) = \Pr_s^\sigma(\Diamond T)$ can be brought into the above form by subtracting the right-hand-side on both sides of the equality, since we allow positive and negative coefficients. Below, we provide some further examples properties:

(1) *The probability of reaching T from s is "approximately scheduler-independent":*

$$\forall \sigma_1 \forall \sigma_2. \Pr_s^{\sigma_1}(\Diamond T) \approx_\varepsilon \Pr_s^{\sigma_2}(\Diamond T) .$$

(2) *The probability to reach T from s_1 is at least twice / 10% higher than the probability of reaching T from s_2, no matter the scheduler:*

$$\forall \sigma. \Pr_{s_1}^\sigma(\Diamond T) \geq 2 \cdot \Pr_{s_2}^\sigma(\Diamond T) \quad / \quad \forall \sigma. \Pr_{s_1}^\sigma(\Diamond T) \geq \Pr_{s_2}^\sigma(\Diamond T) + 0.1 .$$

(3) *There is a scheduler that, in expectation, visits more (different) targets from $\{T_1, \ldots, T_k\}$ than from $\{U_1, \ldots, U_\ell\}$:*

$$\exists \sigma. \Pr_s^\sigma(\Diamond T_1) + \ldots + \Pr_s^\sigma(\Diamond T_k) > \Pr_s^\sigma(\Diamond U_1) + \ldots + \Pr_s^\sigma(\Diamond U_\ell) .$$

4 Verifying Relational Reachability Properties Efficiently

Assume an arbitrary MDP $\mathcal{M} = (S, Act, \mathbf{P})$ and a RelReach property

$$\exists \sigma_1, \ldots, \sigma_n \in \Sigma^{\mathcal{M}}. \sum_{i=1}^{m} q_i \cdot \Pr_{s_i}^{\sigma_{k_i}}(\Diamond T_i) \bowtie q_{m+1} \, . \qquad (\star)$$

In the following, we outline a four-step procedure that checks whether property $(\star)$ holds and, if yes, constructs (possibly memoryful randomized) witness schedulers. The procedure is summarized in Algorithm 1 for the comparison relation $\approx_\varepsilon$.

Example 1. The MDP in Fig. 2 (left) together with the property

$$\exists \sigma. \; \Pr_{s_1}^{\sigma}(\Diamond T_1) - 1/2 \cdot \Pr_{s_1}^{\sigma}(\Diamond T_2) - 1/2 \cdot \Pr_{s_2}^{\sigma}(\Diamond T_2) \approx_\varepsilon 0 \, ,$$

(Does there exist a scheduler such that the probability of reaching T_1 from s_1 is approximately equal to the mean of the probabilities of reaching T_2 from s_1 and T_2 from s_2?) will serve as a running example throughout the section.

Step 1: Collect Combinations of Initial States and Schedulers. We start by analyzing the relationship of schedulers and states in the property.

Definition 4 (State-scheduler combinations). *We define* $\mathsf{Comb} = \{(s_i, \sigma_{k_i}) \mid i = 1, \ldots, m\}$, *the set of all different combinations of initial states and schedulers that occur in the property $\star$. Furthermore, for every $c = (s, \sigma) \in \mathsf{Comb}$, we define $ind(c)$ as the set of indices i such that $(s_i, \sigma_{k_i}) = c$.*

Example 2. In the property from Example 1 we have $\mathsf{Comb} = \{c_1 = (s_1, \sigma), c_2 = (s_2, \sigma)\}$. Furthermore, $ind(c_1) = \{1, 2\}$ and $ind(c_2) = \{3\}$.

Notice that $n \leq |\mathsf{Comb}| \leq m$. State-scheduler combinations allow introducing fresh scheduler variables, one per combination:

Lemma 1. *Let* $\mathsf{Comb} = \{c_1, \ldots, c_k\}$. *Then property $\star$ is equivalent to*

$$\exists \sigma_{c_1}, \ldots, \sigma_{c_k}. \sum_{i=1}^{k} \left[\sum_{j \in ind(c_i)} q_j \cdot \Pr_{s_j}^{\sigma_{c_i}}(\Diamond T_j) \right] \bowtie q_{m+1} \, .$$

Proof (Sketch). Quantifying over each state-scheduler combination individually is justified because schedulers may use memory and thus remember the initial state, see [17] for details. □

Example 3. Applying Lemma 1 to the property from Example 1 yields the following equivalent property (over general, memoryful schedulers):

$$\exists \sigma_{c_1}, \sigma_{c_2}. \; \underbrace{\left[1 \cdot \Pr_{s_1}^{\sigma_{c_1}}(\Diamond T_1) - \tfrac{1}{2} \cdot \Pr_{s_1}^{\sigma_{c_1}}(\Diamond T_2)\right]}_{\text{combination } c_1 = (s_1, \sigma)} + \underbrace{\left[-\tfrac{1}{2} \cdot \Pr_{s_2}^{\sigma_{c_2}}(\Diamond T_2)\right]}_{\text{combination } c_2 = (s_2, \sigma)} \approx_\varepsilon 0 \, .$$

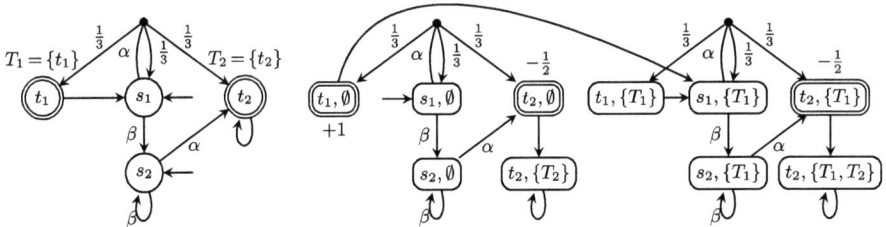

Fig. 2. An MDP (left) and its goal unfolding with rewards (right).

Step 2: Unfold Targets and Set up Reward Structures. Next we process each combination $c \in \mathsf{Comb}$ individually. We rely on two established techniques from the literature: Including reachability information in the state space [14, 25] and encoding reachability probabilities as *expected rewards* (e.g., [25, pp. 51 ff.]). For the sake of completeness, we detail these steps nonetheless:

Definition 5 (Goal unfolding). *Let $c \in \mathsf{Comb}$. The goal unfolding of $\mathcal{M}$ w.r.t. c is the MDP $\mathcal{M}_c = (S_c, \mathrm{Act}, \mathbf{P}_c)$ where $S_c = S \times 2^{\mathcal{T}_c}$ for $\mathcal{T}_c = \{T_i \mid i \in \mathrm{ind}(c)\} \neq \emptyset$ the target sets corresponding to c, and $\mathbf{P}_c$ is defined as follows: For $ss' \in S$, $\mathcal{T}, \mathcal{T}' \subseteq \mathcal{T}_c$, and $\alpha \in \mathrm{Act}$,*

$$\mathbf{P}_c\big((s, \mathcal{T}), \alpha, (s', \mathcal{T}')\big) = \begin{cases} \mathbf{P}(s, \alpha s') & \text{if } \mathcal{T}' = \mathcal{T} \cup \{T \in \mathcal{T}_c \mid s \in T\} \\ 0 & \text{else} \end{cases}.$$

For a combination $c = (s, \sigma)$ we use s_c to denote the state $(s, \emptyset)$ in $\mathcal{M}_c$.

Example 4. The goal unfolding of the MDP in Fig. 2 (left) w.r.t. combination $c_1 = (s_1, \sigma)$, for which we have $\mathcal{T}_{c_1} = \{T_1, T_2\}$, is depicted in Fig. 2 (right).

Definition 6 (Reward structure for state-scheduler combination). *Let $c \in \mathsf{Comb}$. We define the reward structure $\mathcal{R}_c \colon S_c \to \mathbb{Q}$ on the goal unfolding $\mathcal{M}_c$ by $\mathcal{R}_c = \sum_{T \in \mathcal{T}_c} q_T \cdot \mathcal{R}_T$, where $q_T = \sum_{i \in \{\mathrm{ind}(c) \mid T = T_i\}} q_i$ and*

$$\mathcal{R}_T \colon S_c \to \mathbb{Q}, \ (s, \mathcal{T}) \mapsto \begin{cases} 1 & \text{if } s \in T \wedge T \notin \mathcal{T} \\ 0 & \text{else} \end{cases}.$$

Intuitively, we collect reward equal to the sum of the coefficients occurring together with a target $T \in \mathcal{T}_c$ when we visit T *for the first time*. For any $\sigma \in \Sigma^{\mathcal{M}_c}$, the reward function $\mathcal{R}_c$ can be naturally lifted to $\mathcal{M}_c^\sigma$ and further to infinite paths of $\mathcal{M}_c^\sigma$ by letting $\mathcal{R}_c(\pi) = \sum_{i=0}^{\infty} \mathcal{R}_c(\pi(i))$ for $\pi \in \mathrm{Paths}^{\mathcal{M}} \mathcal{M}_c$; this is well-defined because we collect reward only finitely often on any path. The *Expected reward* of $\mathcal{R}_c$ on $\mathcal{M}_c$ from s_c under some $\sigma \in \Sigma^{\mathcal{M}_c}$ is then defined as the expectation of the function $\mathcal{R}_c(\pi) = \sum_{i=0}^{\infty} \mathcal{R}_c(\pi(i))$. Then, we can reduce our query to a number of expected reward queries (see [17] for the proof):

Lemma 2. *For every combination $c = (s, \sigma) \in \mathsf{Comb}$ and $\mathrm{opt} \in \{\min, \max\}$:*

$$\mathrm{opt}_{\sigma \in \Sigma^{\mathcal{M}}} \sum_{j \in \mathrm{ind}(c)} q_j \cdot \mathrm{Pr}_s^{\mathcal{M}, \sigma}(\lozenge T_j) = \mathrm{opt}_{\sigma \in \Sigma^{\mathcal{M}_c}} \mathbb{E}_{S_c}^{\mathcal{M}_c, \sigma}(\mathcal{R}_c).$$

Example 5. Following Example 4, the (non-zero) rewards $\mathcal{R}_c$ for $c = (s_1, \sigma)$ are given in red next to the states in Fig. 2 (right).

Step 3: Compute Expected Rewards. The next step is to compute, for each individual scheduler-state combination c, the maximal and minimal rewards occurring in Lemma 2. Again, we rely on existing techniques from the literature [22,24,25].[1] We refer to [17] for the proof.

Lemma 3. *Let $c \in$ Comb and opt $\in \{\max, \min\}$. The optimal expected reward $\text{opt}_{\sigma \in \Sigma^{\mathcal{M}_c}} \mathbb{E}^{\mathcal{M}_c,\sigma}_{S_c}(\mathcal{R}_c) \in \mathbb{Q}$ is computable in time polynomial in the size of $\mathcal{M}_c$. Moreover, the optimum is attained by an MD scheduler $\sigma \in \Sigma^{\mathcal{M}_c}_{MD}$.*

Example 6. Reconsider the MDP in Fig. 2 (right). The maximal expected reward from initial state $(s_1, \emptyset)$ is $\frac{1}{4}$ and is attained by the MD strategy that always chooses α in $(s_1, \emptyset)$ and thus eventually reaches either $(t_2, \emptyset)$ or $(t_1, \emptyset)$ with probability $\frac{1}{2}$ each. In the latter case, the strategy then selects β in $(s_1, \{T_1\})$ to reach $(s_2, \{T_1\})$ and remain there forever, not collecting any further reward. Overall, this strategy collects a total expected reward of $\frac{1}{2} \cdot 1 + \frac{1}{2} \cdot (-\frac{1}{2}) = \frac{1}{4}$. The minimal expected reward is easily seen to be $-\frac{1}{2}$.

Remark 1 (Approximate vs exact). In practice, *exact* computation of the optimal expected reward via LP as suggested by Lemma 3 (and its proof) may be significantly slower than approximation [19]. Fortunately, it is possible to amend our algorithm to *approximate* expected reward computation. To retain soundness, it is crucial to employ a procedure such as *Sound Value Iteration* [27] that yields guaranteed *under-* and *over-approximations* of the true result. Appropriate handling of such approximations is detailed in [17]. Note that approximation inherently leads to incompleteness, i.e., the algorithm may return "inconclusive" in some cases. Further, for each $c \in$ Comb with $|ind(c)| > 1$ we can view $\text{opt}_{\sigma \in \Sigma^{\mathcal{M}}} \sum_{j \in ind(c)} q_j \cdot \Pr_s^{\mathcal{M},\sigma}(\Diamond T_j)$ as a *weighted-sum optimization problem* and employ multi-objective model-checking techniques [25]. (For $|ind(c)| = 1$ this is a single-objective model-checking query.)

Step 4: Aggregate Results and Check Relational Property. We now combine the optimal expected rewards $\text{opt}_{\sigma \in \Sigma^{\mathcal{M}_c}} \mathbb{E}^{\mathcal{M}_c,\sigma}_{S_c}(\mathcal{R}_c)$ for each state-scheduler combination $c \in$ Comb obtained via the previous two steps. We exemplify this for the comparison relation $\approx_\varepsilon$, the other relations are handled similarly (see [17]).

Lemma 4. *For each $c \in$ Comb and opt $\in \{\max, \min\}$ let*

$$v_c^{\text{opt}} = \underset{\sigma \in \Sigma^{\mathcal{M}_c}}{\text{opt}} \ \mathbb{E}^{\mathcal{M}_c,\sigma}_{S_c}(\mathcal{R}_c) \ .$$

Furthermore, let $v^{\text{opt}} = \sum_{c \in \text{Comb}} v_c^{\text{opt}}$. Then, assuming that the comparison operator $\bowtie$ in the property $\star$ is $\approx_\varepsilon$ for some $\varepsilon \geq 0$:

$$q_{m+1} \in [v^{\min} - \varepsilon, v^{\max} + \varepsilon] \iff \textit{Property } \star \textit{ holds} \ .$$

Lemma 4 relies on the fact that any value in the interval of achievable probabilities $[v_c^{\min}, v_c^{\max}]$ can be achieved by constructing the *convex combination* (e.g., [25, p. 71]) of the minimizing and the maximizing scheduler.

---

[1] Note that we (must) rely on results supporting positive and negative reward, since we allow positive and negative coefficients.

Proof (of Lemma 4; sketch). The interesting direction is "⇒": By Lemmas 1 and 2 there exist schedulers $\sigma_1^\geq, \ldots, \sigma_n^\geq$ and $\sigma_1^\leq, \ldots, \sigma_n^\leq$ for $\mathcal{M}$ such that

$$\bar{v} := \sum_{i=1}^m q_i \cdot \mathrm{Pr}_{s_i}^{\sigma_{k_i}^\geq}(\Diamond T_i) \geq q_{m+1} - \varepsilon \;, \quad \underline{v} := \sum_{i=1}^m q_i \cdot \mathrm{Pr}_{s_i}^{\sigma_{k_i}^\leq}(\Diamond T_i) \leq q_{m+1} + \varepsilon \;.$$

If $\bar{v} \leq q_{m+1}+\varepsilon$ or $\underline{v} \geq q_{m+1}-\varepsilon$, then $\sigma_1^\geq, \ldots, \sigma_n^\geq$ or $\sigma_1^\leq, \ldots, \sigma_n^\leq$ are already witnessing schedulers and there is nothing else to show. Otherwise, $\bar{v} > q_{m+1}+\varepsilon$ and $\underline{v} < q_{m+1}-\varepsilon$. Thus there exists $\lambda \in (0,1)$ such that $q_{m+1} = \lambda \underline{v} + (1-\lambda) \bar{v}$. The schedulers $\sigma_i^\lambda = [\sigma_i^\leq \oplus_\lambda \sigma_i^\geq]$, $i=1,\ldots,n$ [25, p. 71] then witness satisfaction of property $\star$ with *exact* equality ($\approx_0$). See [17] for more details. □

Example 7. We wrap up our running example by proving that the property from Example 1 indeed holds in the MDP in Fig. 2 (left). For combination $c_1 = (s_1, \sigma)$ we have already established in Example 6 that $v_{c_1}^{\max} = \frac{1}{4}$ and $v_{c_1}^{\min} = -\frac{1}{2}$. For the other combination c_2 one easily finds $v_{c_2}^{\max} = 0$ and $v_{c_2}^{\min} = -\frac{1}{2}$. Summing up these values yields $v^{\min} = -1$ and $v^{\max} = \frac{1}{4}$. Since $0 \in [v^{\min}, v^{\max}]$, the property is satisfiable, even with exact equality $\approx_0$.

We remark that for $\bowtie \,\in \{\geq, >\}$, it actually suffices to compute *only* $v^{\max}$ rather than both $v^{\max}$ and $v^{\min}$ as in Lemma 4.

Overall Algorithm. The algorithm resulting from Steps 1–4 is stated explicitly as Algorithm 1 for $\approx_\varepsilon$ and in full generality in [17].

Algorithm 1: Solving RelReach with $\approx_\varepsilon$

Input: MDP $\mathcal{M} = (S, Act, \mathbf{P})$ and a RelReach property

$$\text{``}\exists \sigma_1, \ldots, \sigma_n \in \Sigma^\mathcal{M}. \; \sum_{i=1}^m q_i \cdot \mathrm{Pr}_{s_i}^{\sigma_{k_i}}(\Diamond T_i) \approx_\varepsilon q_{m+1}\text{''}$$

Output: Whether the property is true in $\mathcal{M}$

// Step 1: Loop over all state-scheduler combinations:

1 **for** $c = (s, \sigma) \in \mathsf{Comb} = \{(s_i, \sigma_{k_i}) \mid i = 1, \ldots, m\}$ **do**

 // Step 2: Unfold and define reward structures:

2     $\mathcal{M}_c \leftarrow$ goal unfolding of $\mathcal{M}$ w.r.t. target sets for c // See Definition 5

3     $\mathcal{R}_c \leftarrow$ reward structure on $\mathcal{M}_c$ for c // See Definition 6

 // Step 3: Compute (or approximate) expected rewards:

4     $v_c^{\max} \leftarrow \max_{\sigma \in \Sigma^{\mathcal{M}_c}} \mathbb{E}_{s_c}^{\mathcal{M}_c, \sigma}(\mathcal{R}_c) \;;\; v_c^{\min} \leftarrow \min_{\sigma \in \Sigma^{\mathcal{M}_c}} \mathbb{E}_{s_c}^{\mathcal{M}_c, \sigma}(\mathcal{R}_c)$

// Step 4: Aggregate results from state-scheduler combinations and check:

5 $v^{\max} \leftarrow \sum_{c \in \mathsf{Comb}} v_c^{\max} \;;\; v^{\min} \leftarrow \sum_{c \in \mathsf{Comb}} v_c^{\min}$

6 **return** $q_{m+1} \in [v^{\min} - \varepsilon, v^{\max} + \varepsilon]$

Theorem 1 (Correctness and time complexity). *Algorithm 1 adheres to its input-output specification. It can be implemented with worst-case running time of $\mathcal{O}(m \cdot \mathrm{poly}(2^m \cdot |\mathcal{M}|))$, where $|\mathcal{M}|$ is the size of (an explicit encoding of) $\mathcal{M}$ and m is the number of probability operators in the property.*

Proof. Lemma 4 establishes correctness. Regarding time complexity, notice that for each $c \in \mathsf{Comb}$, the size of the goal unfolding $\mathcal{M}_c$ is bounded by $2^m \cdot |\mathcal{M}|$ (Step 2). Exact computation of expected rewards is possible in time polynomial in the size of the MDP $\mathcal{M}_c$ (Step 3). Steps 2 and 3 have to be executed for at most $|\mathsf{Comb}| \leq m$ state-scheduler combinations. □

5 Complexity of Relational Reachability

In this section, we analyze the computational complexity of the RelReach problem over general and over memoryless deterministic schedulers, respectively. We also identify restricted variants of RelReach that are decidable in polynomial time.

5.1 General Schedulers

The runtime analysis from Theorem 1 yields an EXPTIME upper bound for the complexity of the RelReach problem.

Theorem 2. *Problem RelReach is PSPACE-hard and decidable in EXPTIME.*

Proof. For PSPACE-hardness observe that *simultaneous almost-sure reachability* of m target sets $T_1, \ldots, T_m$ (which is known to be PSPACE-complete [28, Theorem 2]) is expressible as the RelReach property "$\exists \sigma. \Pr_s^\sigma(\Diamond T_1) + \ldots \Pr_s^\sigma(\Diamond T_m) \geq m$".

Membership in EXPTIME follows from Theorem 1. □

Tighter bounds are ongoing work. Taking a closer look, we however observe that RelReach can be solved in PTIME if the number of probability operators m is fixed. Hence, RelReach is *fixed-parameter tractable* [18] with parameter m. The following theorem generalizes this observation and further states that the exponential blow-up of the goal unfolding can be avoided if all target states are absorbing, or if each probability operator is evaluated under a different scheduler (i.e., if $n = m$). We refer to [17] for the proof.

Theorem 3. *The following special cases of RelReach are in PTIME:*

(a) The number of different target sets $|\{T_1, \ldots, T_m\}|$ is at most a constant.
(b) The target sets $T_1, \ldots, T_m$ are all absorbing.
(c) $n = m$, i.e., each probability operator in the property has its own quantifier.

5.2 Memoryless Deterministic Schedulers

We now consider RelReach$_{\text{MD}}$, the RelReach problem over MD schedulers. RelReach$_{\text{MD}}$ is in NP because we can non-deterministically guess schedulers and verify whether they are witnesses in polynomial time by computing the (exact) reachability probabilities in the induced DTMC [4, Ch. 10]. Further, RelReach is *strongly* NP-hard[2] [16] over MD schedulers already for simple variants with equality.

Theorem 4. *RelReach$_{\text{MD}}$ is strongly NP-complete. Strong NP-hardness already holds for the following special cases: For a given MDP $\mathcal{M}$, initial states $s_1, s_2 \in S$, target sets $T_1, T_2 \subseteq S$, decide if*

(a) $\exists \sigma \in \Sigma_{\text{MD}}^{\mathcal{M}}. \ Pr_{s_1}^\sigma(\Diamond T_1) - Pr_{s_2}^\sigma(\Diamond T_2) = 0$.
(b) $\exists \sigma_1, \sigma_2 \in \Sigma_{\text{MD}}^{\mathcal{M}}. \ Pr_{s_1}^{\sigma_1}(\Diamond T_1) - Pr_{s_2}^{\sigma_2}(\Diamond T_2) = 0$.

Strong NP-hardness of (a) and (b) holds irrespective of whether $s_1 = s_2$ and whether T_1 and/or T_2 are absorbing. Moreover, (a) and (b) with relation $\approx_\varepsilon$, $\varepsilon > 0$, are NP-hard.

---

[2] A problem is strongly NP-hard if it is NP-hard even if all numerical quantities (here: rational transition probabilities) in a given input instance are encoded in unary.

Proof (Sketch). We show strong NP-hardness by giving a pseudo-polynomial transformation from the *Hamiltonian path* problem, which is known to be strongly NP-hard [16], inspired by [13]. NP-hardness of the cases for approximate equality follows by an analogous transformation, but for ε the transformation is only polynomial, not pseudo-polynomial, hence establishing NP-hardness but not strong NP-hardness. We refer to [17] for the full proof. □

Note that the hardness of the problem does not rely on whether all probability operators are evaluated under the same scheduler and from the same initial state.

We observe that Steps 1–4 detailed in Sect. 4 construct memoryful randomized witness schedulers in case of approximate equality, if they exist. Memory and/or randomization are necessary for constructing a scheduler that exactly achieves some specified reachability probability, in general (see [17] for details).

Theorem 5. *Memory and randomization are necessary for* RelReach *with approximate equality.*

Note that Theorems 4 and 5 only make statements about properties with (approximate) equality. Let us now consider RelReach with inequality or disequality ($\bowtie \in \{\geq, >, \neq_\varepsilon | \varepsilon \geq 0\}$). Recall that, for inequality, we only have to check the maximizing (or, for $\neq_\varepsilon$, possibly also the minimizing) schedulers for the goal unfoldings and transform them back to schedulers for the original MDP. This transformation introduces memory in general: If several probability operators are associated with the same scheduler but different initial states, then, intuitively, it might be necessary to switch behavior depending on the initial state. Further, if several probability operators are evaluated under the same scheduler but for different target sets, then it might be necessary to switch behavior depending on which target sets were already visited.

The next example illustrates that memory may be necessary for relational reachability properties with disequality even for just a single, absorbing target.

Example 8. Consider the MDP depicted below and the property

$$\exists \sigma \in \Sigma^{\mathcal{M}}. \ \Pr^\sigma_{s_2}(\Diamond\{t\}) < \Pr^\sigma_{s_1}(\Diamond\{t\}) \ .$$

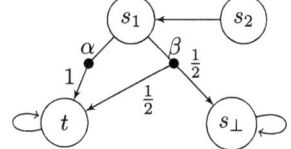

Here, both probability operators are evaluated under the *same scheduler* but *different initial states*, and have the same, absorbing target set. Over MD schedulers this property cannot be satisfied: For all MD schedulers it holds that $\Pr^\sigma_{s_1}(\Diamond\{t\}) = \Pr^\sigma_{s_2}(\Diamond\{t\})$.

In contrast, there does exist a memoryful scheduler such that the probability of reaching t from s_1 exceeds the probability of reaching t from s_2, namely the scheduler that chooses α at s_1 if the execution was started at s_1, and β otherwise. This also implies that

$$\exists \sigma \in \Sigma^{\mathcal{M}}. \ \Pr^\sigma_{s_1}(\Diamond\{t\}) \neq \Pr^\sigma_{s_2}(\Diamond\{t\}) eUnALT$$

can be satisfied over general schedulers but not over MD schedulers.

However, under some mild restrictions on the target sets and/or the structure of the state-scheduler combinations, the procedure detailed in Sect. 4 returns MD schedulers in PTIME, if they exist. Correctness (Theorem 1) then directly implies that MD schedulers suffice in these cases. It remains future work to determine whether there are variants of RelReach$_{MD}$ with disequality that are NP-hard.

Theorem 6. *For the following special cases of RelReach with* $\bowtie \ \in \{\geq, >, \not\approx_\varepsilon | \ \varepsilon \geq 0\}$, *the procedure detailed in Sect. 4 runs in polynomial time and returns MD schedulers, if they exist:*

(a) $n = m$.
(b) *Probability operators with the same scheduler variable have the same initial state (formally, $\forall i, i'$. $\sigma_{k_i} = \sigma_{k_{i'}} \Rightarrow s_i = s_{i'}$) and all target sets are absorbing.*
(c) *Probability operators with the same scheduler variable have equally signed coefficients and the same target sets (formally, $\forall i, i'$. $\sigma_{k_i} = \sigma_{k_{i'}} \Rightarrow ((q_i \geq 0 \Leftrightarrow q_{i'} \geq 0) \wedge T_i = T_{i'}))$.*

Corollary 1. *For the RelReach variants from Theorem 6, MD schedulers suffice.*

The proof of Theorem 6 can be found in [17]. We focus here on the intuition. Firstly, if $n = m$ ((a)), then all probability operators are independent in the sense that we only need to solve $n = m$ independent single-objective queries, for which there exist optimal MD schedulers [24].[3]

For (b), we consider the statement for $n = 1$. If all probability operators are associated with the same scheduler and initial state and all target states are sinks, then MD schedulers suffice as there is nothing to remember: We know which state we started from (since there is only a single initial state), and we know which target sets have already been visited (since all targets are sinks).

Lastly, consider (c) for $n = 1$ and non-negative coefficients. In this case, since all target sets are the same, there must exist a MD scheduler maximizing all reachability probabilities $\Pr^\sigma_{s_i}(\Diamond T)$ at the same time [24]. Since all coefficients are non-negative, this scheduler also maximizes the weighted sum over the probabilities. We can analogously reason about minimizing the weighted sum.

6 Implementation and Evaluation

We have implemented a model checking algorithm based on the procedure described in Sect. 4, which we use to investigate what model sizes our approach can handle, and how it performs compared to existing tools that can check relational reachability properties.

6.1 Setup

Our prototype[4] is implemented on top of (the python bindings of) the probabilistic model checker STORM [21] and supports an expressive fragment of relational reachability properties. It takes as input an MDP (in the form of a PRISM file [23]) with m (not

---
[3] Note that this reasoning does not work for $\approx_\varepsilon$, because there we may need to combine the optimal MD schedulers into memoryful randomized schedulers to obtain a witness.
[4] Source code and benchmarks: https://github.com/carolinager/RelReach, artifact: https://doi.org/10.5281/zenodo.15209574.

necessarily distinct) initial states and m (not necessarily distinct) target sets, as well as a *universally quantified* relational reachability property. Most available case studies for relational reachability properties are universally quantified. Recall that, while the previous sections addressed existentially quantified relational reachability properties, we can transfer our results to universally quantified relational reachability properties by considering their negation. If we conclude that the given (universal) property does not hold, out implementation can return witnesses in the form of schedulers returned by STORM for the expected rewards computed in Step 3, plus a solution for λ as defined in the proof of Lemma 4 in case of (universal quantification with) $\not\approx$. Scheduler export is disabled by default and also in our experiments.

Note that the tool's output ('Yes'/'No') depends only on comparing an expected reward to a threshold (Algorithm 1, Line 6). Since the same calculations are performed regardless of the comparison's outcome, performance is generally unaffected by an instance's falsifiability.

We use STORM's internal single- and multi-objective model checking capabilities for the computation of expected rewards (Step 3 in Sect. 4), where single-objective model checking employs *Optimistic Value Iteration* [20] for approximate expected reward computation with a default tolerance of 10^{-6}.[5] The multi-objective model checking employs *Sound Value Iteration* [27] with the same tolerance.[6] We note that the implementation also supports *exact* solving. Here, we report results for approximate computation of expected rewards with tolerance 10^{-6}. Our experiments were performed on a laptop with a single core of a 1.80GHz Intel i7 CPU and 16GB RAM under Linux Ubuntu 24.04.1 LTS.

We compare our tool against two baselines: HYPERPROB[7] and HYPERPAYNT[8] [3]. These tools handle (fragments of much more expressive) probabilistic hyperproperties that partially overlap with relational reachability properties. HYPERPROB encodes the HyperPCTL model-checking problem in SMT with an exponential number of variables. HYPERPAYNT uses abstraction refinement to model-check a fragment of HyperPCTL, potentially exploring an exponential number of schedulers. To the best of our knowledge, no other tools support a (nontrivial) fragment of relational reachability properties. HYPERPROB and HYPERPAYNT support approximate comparison operators via an equivalent conjunction or disjunction of two inequalities.[9]

Both HYPERPROB and HYPERPAYNT search for policies and restrict themselves to MD schedulers. Solving a property over MD schedulers is not always equivalent to checking it over general schedulers (see, e.g., Theorem 5, Example 8), but it coincides sometimes (Corollary 1). Further, HYPERPROB supports only properties with a single scheduler quantifier (i.e., all probability operators are evaluated over the same MD scheduler). HYPERPAYNT, on the other hand, supports an arbitrary number of

---

[5] Note that STORM returns a single value x with relative difference at most 10^{-6} to the exact result instead of sound lower and upper bounds here. We ensure soundness by computing conservative lower and upper bounds as $\frac{x}{1+10^{-6}}$ and $\frac{x}{1-10^{-6}}$.

[6] STORM (currently) returns a single value with relative difference at most 10^{-6} to the exact result as both lower and upper bound and we again ensure soundness manually.

[7] https://github.com/TART-MSU/HyperProb.

[8] https://github.com/probing-lab/HyperPAYNT, we used this docker container: https://zenodo.org/records/8116528. Also referred to as "AR loop" in [3].

[9] While not covered in [3], HYPERPAYNT also allows to add a constant to one side of the (in)equality.

scheduler quantifiers.[10] To account for the different scheduler classes considered by the tools, we will in the following denote the validity of a property over general as well as over MD schedulers as *HR result* and *MD result*, respectively, when comparing the tools.[11] We will also denote for each benchmark family whether the considered property belongs to a fragment for which checking MD schedulers is equivalent to checking general schedulers.

Our tool's core procedure consists of polynomially many calls to well-established, practically efficient subroutines based on value iteration [26]. In contrast, HYPERPROB and HYPERPAYNT use exponential algorithms to solve the NP-hard RelReach problems over MD schedulers and do not optimize for the PTIME special cases (Theorem 3). Further, to optimize a linear combination of expected rewards over different schedulers, we can treat the different state-scheduler combinations independently and then aggregate them in Step 4.

6.2 Case Studies

Let us first illustrate that RelReach covers interesting problems.

Generalization of Von Neumann's trick (VN). We generalize Von Neumann's trick from the motivating example of Sect. 1 to $2N$ bits. The idea is as follows: Extract the first $2N$ bits from the stream; if the number of zeros equals the number of ones, return the value of the first bit; otherwise try again. We check whether

$$\forall \sigma.\ \Pr_{s_0}^\sigma(\Diamond\{\texttt{return 0}\}) \approx_\varepsilon \Pr_{s_0}^\sigma(\Diamond\{\texttt{return 1}\})$$

for $\varepsilon = 0$ and $\varepsilon = 0.1$ and varying values for N. By Corollary 1(b), checking this property over MD schedulers is equivalent to checking it over general schedulers since all target sets are absorbing. Therefore, HYPERPROB and HYPERPAYNT can also check the general problem in this case even though they restrict to MD schedulers.

Robot tag (RT). Consider a $N \times N$ grid world with a robot and a janitor, where both move in turns, starting with the robot.[12] The robot starts in the lower left corner, the janitor in the upper right corner. The robot has fixed the following strategy: It moves right until it reaches the lower right corner, then moves up until it reaches the upper right corner, its target. The janitor can hinder the robot from reaching its target by occupying a cell that the robot wants to move to. We now want to check whether this strategy is approximately robust against adversarial behavior by the janitor, in the sense that the probability of reaching the target should be approximately independent of the janitor strategy. Formally,

$$\forall \sigma_1, \sigma_2.\ \Pr_s^{\sigma_1}(\Diamond\{t\}) \approx_{10^{-5}} \Pr_s^{\sigma_2}(\Diamond\{t\}) ,$$

---

[10] For both HYPERPROB and HYPERPAYNT, one could alternatively consider a single scheduler on a manually created self-composition to simulate multiple schedulers (from the same initial state). Based on the large performance gap with HYPERPROB and HYPERPAYNT seen below, we did not consider such tweaks.

[11] Note that HYPERPAYNT expects existentially quantified properties, but we report the validity w.r.t. the universally quantified property, so the MD result stated here is the opposite of the result reported by HYPERPAYNT.

[12] Our model is based on a PRISM model and a Gridworld-By-Storm model.

Table 2. Experimental results. *HR res./MD res.*: Does the universally quantified property hold over general (HR)/MD schedulers? ≡?: Is checking the property over general scheduler equivalent to checking over MD schedulers? *Time* is rounded to the nearest second, with the exception of values <1s which are denoted as such. For every tool, we give the total time and, in brackets, (1) for our tool: the total time excluding model building, (2) for HYPERPROB: z3 solving time, (3) for HYPERPAYNT: the reported 'synthesis time'. **TO**: Timeout (1 h). **OOM**: Out of memory.

	Case study Variant	$|S|$	Our tool HR res.	Our tool Time	≡?	Comparison over MD sched. MD res.	HYPERPROB	HYPERPAYNT
VN	$N=1$ $\varepsilon=0$	5	No	<1s (<1s)		No	<1s (<1s)	<1s (<1s)
	$N=1$ $\varepsilon=0.1$	5	Yes	<1s (<1s)		Yes	<1s (<1s)	<1s (<1s)
	$N=10$ $\varepsilon=0$	383	No	<1s (<1s)		No	TO	<1s (<1s)
	$N=10$ $\varepsilon=0.1$	383	No	<1s (<1s)		No	TO	<1s (<1s)
	$N=100\,\varepsilon=0$	39 803	No	3s (3s)		-	TO	TO
	$N=100\,\varepsilon=0.1$	39 803	No	3s (3s)	≡	-	TO	TO
	$N=200\,\varepsilon=0$	159 603	No	218s (217s)	Cor. 1	-	OOM	TO
	$N=200\,\varepsilon=0.1$	159 603	No	209s (209s)		-	OOM	TO
	$N=250\,\varepsilon=0$	249 503	No	1 358s (1 357s)		-	OOM	TO
	$N=250\,\varepsilon=0.1$	249 503	No	1 323s (1 322s)		-	OOM	TO
	$N=300\,\varepsilon=0$	359 403	-	TO		-	OOM	TO
	$N=300\,\varepsilon=0.1$	359 403	-	TO		-	OOM	TO
RT	$N=10$ (N,N)	933	Yes	<1s (<1s)		Yes		<1s (<1s)
	$N=10$ $(N,N{-}1)$	1 021	No	<1s (<1s)		No		<1s (<1s)
	$N=100\,(N,N)$	994 803	Yes	6s (<1s)		-		TO
	$N=100\,(N,N{-}1)$	1 004 701	No	5s (<1s)	≡	-	n/a	TO
	$N=200\,(N,N)$	7 979 603	Yes	48s (10s)	Cor. 1	-		TO
	$N=200\,(N,N{-}1)$	8 019 401	No	44s (6s)		-		TO
	$N=300\,(N,N)$	26 954 403	-	OOM		-		OOM
	$N=300\,(N,N{-}1)$	27 044 101	-	OOM		-		OOM

where s represents the initial state with robot and janitor in their initial locations, and t represents that the robot has reached its target. We check this property for different grid sizes N and different starting positions for the janitor: If the janitor starts in the upper right corner, they cannot hinder the robot, but if they start in location $(N, N{-}1)$, then they can always stop the robot.

By Corollary 1(c), MD schedulers suffice here. However, HYPERPROB does not natively support this problem as it only allows a single scheduler quantifier and the property is trivially satisfied if we use a single scheduler quantifier for both probability operators.

Results. The results for both case studies are presented in Table 2. Firstly, we observe that the quality of the coin simulation decreases with a growing number of bits N: While approximate equality with $\varepsilon = 0.1$ holds for $N = 10$, it does not hold anymore for $N = 100$. Further, our tool handles 1 million states in 5–6 s for **RT** but times out for the **VN** instances of comparable size. Besides the size of the state space, the computation time of expected rewards also depends on structural aspects, e.g. many cycles (as in

VN) cause slower convergence of the approximation algorithm for expected rewards. On problem instances that are also supported by HYPERPROB or HYPERPAYNT, our tool performs drastically better: HYPERPROB times out already for **VN** with $N = 10$, and HYPERPAYNT for **VN** with $N = 100$ while our tool solves these instances in a matter of seconds.

Table 3. Comparison on benchmarks for probabilistic hyperproperties. The meaning of columns and abbreviations is the same as in Table 2.

Case study	Variant	$|S|$	Our tool HR res.	Our tool Time	$\equiv$?	Comparison over MD sched. MD res.	HYPERPROB	HYPERPAYNT
TA(1)	$M = 8$	423	No	$<1s\,(<1s)$		No	$3055s\,(2858s)$	$<1s\,(<1s)$
	$M = 16$	13 039	No	$<1s\,(<1s)$		No	OOM	$21s\,(1s)$
	$M = 24$	307 175	No	$20s\,(<1s)$	$\not\equiv$ Ex 8	-	OOM	TO -
	$M = 28$	1 425 379	No	$490s\,(<1s)$		-	OOM	TO -
	$M = 32$	6 488 031	-	TO -		-	TO	TO -
TA(2)	$M = 8$	423	No	$<1s\,(<1s)$		No		$<1s\,(<1s)$
	$M = 16$	13 039	No	$<1s\,(<1s)$		No		$115s\,(2s)$
	$M = 24$	307 175	No	$20s\,(<1s)$	$\equiv$ Cor. 1	-	n/a	TO -
	$M = 28$	1 425 379	No	$493s\,(<1s)$		-		TO -
	$M = 32$	6 488 031	-	TO -		-		TO -
PW(1)	$M = 2$	2 307	No	$<1s\,(<1s)$	$\not\equiv$ Ex 8	No	OOM	$<1s\,(<1s)$
	$M = 4$	985 605	-	TO -		-	TO	TO -
PW(2)	$M = 2$	2 307	No	$<1s\,(<1s)$	$\equiv$ Cor. 1	No	n/a	$5s\,(<1s)$
	$M = 4$	985 605	-	TO -		-		TO -
TS	$h = (10, 20)$	252	No	$<1s\,(<1s)$		No	$112s\,(38s)$	$<1s\,(<1s)$
	$h = (20, 200)$	2 412	No	$<1s\,(<1s)$		No	OOM	$2s\,(<1s)$
	$h = (20, 5\,000)$	60 012	No	$<1s\,(<1s)$	$\not\equiv$ Ex 8	No	OOM	$1076s\,(20s)$
	$h = (50, 10\,000)$	120 012	No	$<1s\,(<1s)$		-	OOM	TO -
	$h = (50, 20\,000)$	240 012	No	$<1s\,(<1s)$			OOM	TO -
SD	simple	10	No	$<1s\,(<1s)$		Yes	$3s\,(<1s)$	$2s\,(2s)$
	splash-1	16	No	$<1s\,(<1s)$		No	$1184s\,(1183s)$	$<1s\,(<1s)$
	splash-2	25	No	$<1s\,(<1s)$		Yes	TO -	$2487s\,(2485s)$
	larger-1	25	No	$<1s\,(<1s)$	$\not\equiv$ Ex 8	No	TO -	$310s\,(310s)$
	larger-2	25	No	$<1s\,(<1s)$		Yes	TO -	$925s\,(<1s)$
	larger-3	25	No	$<1s\,(<1s)$		No	TO -	$<1s\,(<1s)$
	train	48	No	$<1s\,(<1s)$		Yes	TO -	$14s\,(14s)$

6.3 Benchmarks for Probabilistic Hyperproperties

Next, we investigate the scalability of our tool on benchmarks from the literature on probabilistic hyperproperties that are relational reachability properties. These benchmarks are typically motivated by security use cases. In particular, three out of four HyperPCTL case studies for MDPs presented in [1] are covered by our approach: We consider (mild variations of) **TA**, **PW**, **TS** from [1]. **TA** and **PW** check properties of the form

$$\bigwedge_{s_1,s_2 \in \mathit{Init}} \bigwedge_{i=0}^{M} \forall \sigma_1, \sigma_2.\ \Pr_{s_1}^{\sigma_1}(\Diamond T_i) = \Pr_{s_2}^{\sigma_2}(\Diamond T_i) \ ,$$

where *Init* is a set of initial states. Here, we benchmark only the first conjunct (which can be falsified) for all tools. We consider two variations of **TA** and **PW**: **TA(1)** and **PW(1)** use only a single scheduler quantifier for both probability operators while **TA(2)** and **PW(2)** use two scheduler quantifiers, as in the original formulation [1].[13] The property for **TS** is analogous, but with only a single scheduler quantifier and we fix a different pair of initial states for each instance. Further, we consider **SD** from [3], which checks

$$\forall \sigma.\ \Pr_{s_1}^{\sigma}(\Diamond T) \geq \Pr_{s_2}^{\sigma}(\Diamond T) \ .$$

Details on all four benchmarks can be found in [17], including the differences in our models to the models from [1,3].

Results. Table 3 presents our experimental results on these four case studies and provides a comparison with HYPERPROB and HYPERPAYNT. We observe that for all benchmarks in Table 3, the running time of our tool consists almost entirely of building the model.

For the benchmarks with a single scheduler quantifier (**TA(1)**, **PW(1)**, **TS**, **SD**), checking over general schedulers is, in general, not equivalent to checking over MD schedulers (see Example 8). Notably, already instances with 100 000 states prove to be challenging over MD schedulers for HYPERPROB and HYPERPAYNT, while our tool solves these instances over general schedulers in over a minute and can handle instances of **TA(1)** with 1 million states in less than 10 min.

For the benchmarks with two scheduler quantifiers (**TA(2)** and **PW(2)**), checking over MD schedulers is equivalent to checking over general schedulers since both probability operators are independent (Corollary 1).[14] Notably, our tool solves the instance for $M = 24$ in over a minute while HYPERPAYNT times out. Our tool can solve instances of **TA(2)** with more than 1 million states, but times out for the instance of **PW(2)** with almost 1 million states.

In summary, our tool is orders of magnitude faster than existing tools, which restrict to MD schedulers but nevertheless solve an equivalent problem in some cases (**TA(2)**, **PW(2)**). For problem instances belonging to fragments whose decision problems are NP-hard over MD schedulers but in PTIME over general schedulers, we show that solving the NP-hard problem via SMT solving (HYPERPROB) or an abstraction-refinement approach (HYPERPAYNT) is also much harder in practice than solving the PTIME problem.

7 Related Work

We discuss two main areas of related work: *multi-objective MDP model checking* and *probabilistic hyperlogics*.

---

[13] Note that both variants are equivalent over general schedulers.
[14] Checking for two scheduler quantifiers on a manually created self-composition of the MDP with HYPERPROB already exceeds memory bounds for **TA** with $m = 8$.

Multi-objective Model Checking. The techniques and results of this paper are strongly related to multi-objective model checking (MOMC) for MDPs [5,6,12,25]. In MOMC, the key question is: *Is there a scheduler such that target set A is reached with probability at least λ_A and target set B is reached with probability at least λ_B?* With appropriate preprocessing, MOMC can moreover ask whether a set of states is reached with probability *exactly*, say, 0.5—but not whether there exists a scheduler such that A and B are reached with equal (or approximately equal) probability. Indeed, MOMC and the relational properties we study are incomparable in the sense that they are disjoint up to single-objective queries: MOMC focuses on *conjuctive* queries but each conjunct can only compare a probability to a *constant*. In contrast, our relational properties are single constraints involving multiple probability operators; they do not support conjunctions but allow *comparing* probabilities. Similar to our results, however, MOMC with a fixed number of targets is NP-complete over MD schedulers [25], and solvable in PTIME over general schedulers. Moreover, prominent algorithms [15] for MOMC also rely on optimizing weighted sums of probabilities just like we do. MOMC is supported in probabilistic model checkers like PRISM [23] and STORM [21]. Due to the similarities outlined above, we were able to reuse some of STORM's MOMC capabilities in our implementation.

Probabilistic Hyperlogics. Our paper was motivated by recent emerging interest in algorithms for probabilistic hyperlogics, like HyperPCTL [1,2] and PHL [9]. Relational reachability properties are a strict fragment of HyperPCTL. While PHL cannot naturally compare probabilities from different initial states, every MDP $\mathcal{M}$ and RelReach property φ can be transformed to an MDP $\mathcal{M}'$ and PHL formula φ' s.t. $\mathcal{M}$ satisfies φ iff $\mathcal{M}'$ satisfies φ' over general schedulers (by making a copy of the MDP for every state-scheduler combination). HyperPCTL and PHL both can express properties like *Does there exist a scheduler such that all paths are trace-equivalent almost-surely?*, which RelReach does not cover. Due to their high expressiveness, the corresponding model-checking problems are undecidable. This paper contributes two main points to the study of probabilistic hyperlogics. First, searching for randomized and memoryful schedulers may be beneficial complexity-wise, both in theory and in practice. Second, many of the motivating case studies for probabilistic hyperlogics can also be treated by dedicated and therefore much more efficient routines, which also motivated the use of an AR-loop in [3]. However, in [3] a *search* over a finite amount of (MD) schedulers is suggested, while we study the computational complexity and consider an algorithm for general (and thus uncountably many) schedulers. While UPPAAL-SMC is not a tool for probabilistic hyperproperties, it also supports *statistical* model-checking for comparison of two cost-bounded reachability probabilities *on DTMCs* [8].

8 Conclusion

In this paper, we investigated probabilistic model checking for relational reachability properties in MDPs. We presented a practically and theoretically efficient algorithm for these properties and demonstrated the hardness of some other fragments. Relational reachability properties are a sub-class of probabilistic hyperproperties and we showed that, compared to existing approaches for model checking probabilistic hyperproperties, our approach does not (need to) restrict itself to only memoryless deterministic schedulers. In addition, it scales orders of magnitudes better on various benchmarks used to motivate probabilistic hyperproperties.

For future work, we aim to study more expressive fragments. In particular, we would like to consider Boolean combinations (generalizing to multi-objective model checking), relate ω-regular properties or properties that require trace equivalence, and consider models like POMDPs with restricted scheduler classes.

Acknowledgements. We thank Oyendrila Dobe for fruitful discussions on earlier versions of this work. We are grateful to Tim Quatmann for his continuous and reliable STORM support. Lina Gerlach and Tobias Winkler are supported by the DFG RTG 2236/2 *UnRAVeL*. Sebastian Junges is supported by the NWO VENI Grant ProMiSe (222.147). This work is partially sponsored by the United States National Science Foundation (NSF) Award SaTC 2245114.

Disclosure of Interests. The authors have no competing interests to declare that are relevant to the content of this article.

References

1. Ábrahám, E., Bartocci, E., Bonakdarpour, B., Dobe, O.: Probabilistic hyperproperties with nondeterminism. In: Proceedings of the 18th Symposium on Automated Technology for Verification and Analysis (ATVA'20), pp. 518–534 (2020)
2. Ábrahám, E., Bonakdarpour, B.: HyperPCTL: A temporal logic for probabilistic hyperproperties. In: Proceedings of the 15th International Conference on Quantitative Evaluation of Systems (QEST'18), pp. 20–35 (2018)
3. Andriushchenko, R., Bartocci, E., Češk, M., Pontiggia, F., Sallinger, S.: Deductive controller synthesis for probabilistic hyperproperties. In: Proceedings of the 20th International Conference on Quantitative Evaluation of Systems (QEST'23), pp. 288–306 (2023)
4. Baier, C., Katoen, J.P.: Principles of Model Checking. The MIT Press, Cham (2008)
5. Chatterjee, K.: Markov decision processes with multiple long-run average objectives. In: Proceedings of the 27th International Conference on Foundations of Software Technology and Theoretical Computer Science (FSTTCS'07), pp. 473–484 (2007)
6. Chatterjee, K., Majumdar, R., Henzinger, T.A.: Markov decision processes with multiple objectives. In: Proceedings of the 23rd Annual Symposium on Theoretical Aspects of Computer Science (STACS'06), pp. 325–336 (2006)
7. Courcoubetis, C., Yannakakis, M.: Verifying temporal properties of finite-state probabilistic programs. In: Proceedings of the 29th Annual Symposium on Foundations of Computer Science (SFCS'88), pp. 338–345 (1988)
8. David, A., Larsen, K.G., Legay, A., Mikucionis, M., Wang, Z.: Time for statistical model checking of real-time systems. In: Proceedings of the 23rd International Conference on Computer Aided Verification (CAV'11), pp. 349–355 (2011)
9. Dimitrova, R., Finkbeiner, B., Torfah, H.: Probabilistic hyperproperties of Markov decision processes. In: Proceedings of the 18th International Symposium on Automated Technology for Verification and Analysis (ATVA'20), pp. 484–500 (2020)
10. Dobe, O., Ábrahám, E., Bartocci, E., Bonakdarpour, B.: HyperProb: a model checker for probabilistic hyperproperties. In: Proceedings of the 24th International Symposium on Formal Methods (FM'21), pp. 657–666 (2021)

11. Dobe, O., Ábrahám, E., Bartocci, E., Bonakdarpour, B.: Model checking hyperproperties for Markov decision processes. Inf. Comput. **289**(Part), 104978 (2022)
12. Etessami, K., Kwiatkowska, M.Z., Vardi, M.Y., Yannakakis, M.: Multi-objective model checking of Markov decision processes. Log. Methods Comput. Sci. **4**(4) (2008)
13. Foote, D., Chu, B.: Polynomial time approximate solutions to Markov decision processes with many objectives. https://edge.edx.org/assets/courseware/2b2f9dc7f70eb9b709c3b64b452f6263/asset-v1:BerkeleyX+CS188-SU16+SU16+type@asset+block/approx_momdp.pdf. Accessed 13 Jan 2025
14. Forejt, V., Kwiatkowska, M.Z., Norman, G., Parker, D., Qu, H.: Quantitative multi-objective verification for probabilistic systems. In: Proceedings of the 17th International Conference on Tools and Algorithms for the Construction and Analysis of Systems (TACAS'11), pp. 112–127 (2011)
15. Forejt, V., Kwiatkowska, M.Z., Parker, D.: Pareto curves for probabilistic model checking. In: Proceedings of the 10th International Symposium om Automated Technology for Verification and Analysis (ATVA'12), pp. 317–332 (2012)
16. Garey, M.R., Johnson, D.S.: "Strong" NP-completeness results: motivation, examples, and implications. J. ACM **25**(3), 499–508 (1978)
17. Gerlach, L., Winkler, T., Ábrahám, E., Bonakdarpour, B., Junges, S.: Efficient probabilistic model checking for relational reachability (extended version) (2025). https://arxiv.org/abs/2505.16357
18. Grohe, M.: Descriptive and parameterized complexity. In: Proceedings of the 8th International Workshop on Computer Science Logic (CSL'99), pp. 14–31 (1999)
19. Hartmanns, A., Junges, S., Quatmann, T., Weininger, M.: A practitioner's guide to MDP model checking algorithms. In: Proceedings of the 29th International Conference on Tools and Algorithms for the Construction and Analysis of Systems (TACAS'23), pp. 469–488 (2023)
20. Hartmanns, A., Kaminski, B.L.: Optimistic value iteration. In: Proceedings of the 32nd International Conference on Computer Aided Verification (CAV'20), pp. 488–511 (2020)
21. Hensel, C., Junges, S., Katoen, J.P., Quatmann, T., Volk, M.: The probabilistic model checker Storm. Int. J. Softw. Tools Technol. Transf. **24**(4), 589–610 (2022)
22. Karmarkar, N.: A new polynomial-time algorithm for linear programming. In: Proceedings of the 16th Annual ACM Symposium on Theory of Computing (STOC'84), pp. 302–311 (1984)
23. Kwiatkowska, M.Z., Norman, G., Parker, D.: PRISM 4.0: verification of probabilistic real-time systems. In: Proceedings of the 23rd International Conference on Computer Aided Verification (CAV'11), pp. 585–591 (2011)
24. Puterman, M.L.: Markov Decision Processes: Discrete Stochastic Dynamic Programming. Wiley, New York (1994)
25. Quatmann, T.: Verification of multi-objective markov models. Ph.D. thesis, RWTH Aachen University (2023)
26. Quatmann, T., Dehnert, C., Jansen, N., Junges, S., Katoen, J.: Parameter synthesis for Markov models: faster than ever. In: Proceedings of ATVA 2016. LNCS, vol. 9938, pp. 50–67 (2016). https://doi.org/10.1007/978-3-319-46520-3_4
27. Quatmann, T., Katoen, J.: Sound value iteration. In: Proceedings of the 30th International Conference on Computer Aided Verification (CAV'18), pp. 643–661 (2018)
28. Randour, M., Raskin, J., Sankur, O.: Percentile queries in multi-dimensional Markov decision processes. In: Proceedings of the 27th International Conference on Computer Aided Verification (CAV'15), pp. 123–139 (2015)

29. Von Neumann, J.: Various techniques used in connection with random digits. Appl. Math. Ser. **12**(36–38), 5 (1951)

Open Access This chapter is licensed under the terms of the Creative Commons Attribution 4.0 International License (http://creativecommons.org/licenses/by/4.0/), which permits use, sharing, adaptation, distribution and reproduction in any medium or format, as long as you give appropriate credit to the original author(s) and the source, provide a link to the Creative Commons license and indicate if changes were made.

The images or other third party material in this chapter are included in the chapter's Creative Commons license, unless indicated otherwise in a credit line to the material. If material is not included in the chapter's Creative Commons license and your intended use is not permitted by statutory regulation or exceeds the permitted use, you will need to obtain permission directly from the copyright holder.

Verifying PETSc Vector Components Using CIVL

Venkata Dhavala[1](✉), Jan Hückelheim[2], Paul D. Hovland[2], and Stephen F. Siegel[1]

[1] University of Delaware, Newark, DE 19716, USA
{dhavala,siegel}@udel.edu
[2] Argonne National Laboratory, Lemont, IL 60439, USA
{jhueckelheim,hovland}@anl.gov

Abstract. This paper presents a modular approach to verifying the vector module of PETSc, a widely used library in scientific computing, using the CIVL model checker. Our approach relies on the creation of stub functions, which serve a dual purpose of specifying the intended behavior of individual PETSc functions and providing an abstraction for called functions to allow efficient verification of callers. This facilitates the use of symbolic execution and model checking to establish the correctness of isolated functions. Our work contributes to the ongoing effort to enhance the reliability of high-performance computing libraries and proposes an effective verification strategy for complex scientific software.

Keywords: Verification · Symbolic execution · High-performance computing · Linear algebra · PETSc

1 Introduction

Modern computational science applications rely on numerical libraries for portable and efficient implementations of numerical algorithms and data structures. One widely used example is the Portable, Extensible Toolkit for Scientific Computation (PETSc) [1–3]. PETSc provides a suite of parallel linear and nonlinear solvers, ordinary differential equation (ODE) integrators, and numerical optimization solvers, along with supporting mathematical objects including vectors, matrices, structured grids, and graphs, with associated abstractions and data structures for managing parallel domain decomposition and communication.

PETSc and its development team have received numerous accolades, including the 2015 SIAM/ACM Prize in Computational Science and Engineering and inclusion as one of the Top Ten Advances in Computational Science Accomplishments of the U.S. Department of Energy in 2008. An incomplete list of application domains using PETSc includes acoustics, aerodynamics, air pollution, bone fractures, cancer treatment, cardiology, combustion, earthquake modeling, economics, fission and fusion modeling, magnetics, ocean dynamics, polymeric membranes, and subsurface modeling. The users manual [1] and primary paper [3] have been cited almost 6,000 times and almost 3,000 times, respectively.

Because PETSc is used by so many and such important applications, any defect could have wide-ranging and potentially devastating consequences. For this reason, PETSc, like most high-consequence software, undergoes extensive testing. PETSc uses GitLab pipelines for testing during continuous integration, and the PETSc test suite executes over 13,000 tests. Nonetheless, even test suites with excellent (path) coverage can miss defects, especially subtle ones such as data races that may result in incorrect behavior only occasionally and under particular circumstances. We are therefore engaged in an effort, in collaboration with the PETSc developers, to verify PETSc's functional correctness using a combination of symbolic execution [11] and model checking [8], starting with the most fundamental mathematical object in PETSc: vectors.

The rest of this paper is organized as follows. In the remainder of this section, we introduce the CIVL model checker [17] and provide an overview of PETSc's vector module. In Sect. 2, we describe how we created an abstract vector library. In Sect. 3, we introduce our modular verification approach that leverages this library and specification stubs. We summarize our results in Sect. 4 and conclude with lessons learned and future plans in Sect. 5.

1.1 Background on the CIVL Model Checker

The CIVL model checker [7,15] is a verification tool for sequential or parallel C and Fortran programs. It uses an intermediate verification language, CIVL-C, which adds primitives for verification and concurrency to standard sequential C. The additional primitives begin with $ to clearly distinguish them from standard C keywords. One of these is the type modifier `$input`, which specifies that a global variable should be read-only and assigned an unconstrained value of its type in the initial state. Another is the `$assert` statement, which is similar to C's `assert` but accepts a richer assertion language, including universal and existential quantifiers (`$forall` and `$exists`). The `$assume` statement indicates that an execution should be ignored if its Boolean argument evaluates to *false*.

The CIVL front end consumes a source program in C or Fortran—possibly with MPI [12] and/or OpenMP [14]—and converts it to a "pure" CIVL-C program. The back end uses symbolic execution [11] and model checking [8] to explore all possible program executions for all possible inputs. The program must define a finite state space, which in practice requires small bounds on parameters such as the number of processes or threads, input array sizes, and any parameter controlling the number of loop iterations. CIVL uses a built-in model checker as well as calls to Z3 [9] and CVC4 [4] to enumerate reachable symbolic states and verify the absence of assertion violations, deadlocks, out-of-bound indexes, illegal pointer operations, memory leaks, and other types of faults. If a violation is detected, diagnostic information is printed and a trace for replay is saved.

We chose CIVL for this project because of its ability to handle C and MPI, as well as its ability to reason precisely about formulas in real arithmetic, including nonlinear arithmetic—all essential requirements for verification of PETSc.

```
#define PetscUseTypeMethod(obj, ...)                                    \
  do {                                                                  \
    PetscCheck((obj)->ops->PETSC_FIRST_ARG((__VA_ARGS__, unused)),      \
    PetscObjectComm((PetscObject)obj), PETSC_ERR_SUP,                   \
    "No method %s for %s of type %s",                                   \
    PetscStringize(PETSC_FIRST_ARG((__VA_ARGS__, unused))),             \
    ((PetscObject)obj)->class_name, ((PetscObject)obj)->type_name);     \
    PetscCall(((obj)->ops->PETSC_FIRST_ARG((__VA_ARGS__, unused)))      \
              (obj PETSC_REST_ARG(__VA_ARGS__)));                       \
  } while (0)
```

Fig. 1. Macro definition for `PetscUseTypeMethod`.

1.2 Overview of PETSc's Vector Class

Although PETSc is written primarily in standard C, it follows a highly object-oriented design, implementing its own mechanisms for inheritance, dynamic dispatch, and so on. The library is organized as a collection of several classes, with each class providing an abstract interface (a set of calling sequences similar to an abstract base class in C++) and one or more *implementations* that provide specific solver algorithms or target a particular execution resource. The collection of classes in PETSc can be viewed as a hierarchy of mathematical abstractions. At the lowest level of this hierarchy sits the `Vec` vector class, which provides the abstract interfaces for creation and manipulation of vectors, along with several high-performance implementations: the "sequential" (`_Seq`) implementation that targets execution on a single MPI rank on a CPU, the "MPI" (`_MPI`) implementation targeting distributed-memory parallel execution, and several implementations targeting different GPU programming models.

PETSc employs numerous preprocessor macros to improve portability and maintainability, but these can complicate both manual comprehension and automated analysis. Consider the `PetscUseTypeMethod` macro in Fig. 1, which is used by `VecMethodDispatch`, itself a macro. First, `PETSC_FIRST_ARG` extracts the name of the function to call and `PETSC_REST_ARG` expands the remainder of the arguments. Then, `PetscCheck` uses stringification (`PetscStringize`) to generate the function name by concatenating parts of the object class and type names. Next, after confirming that the function pointer is valid, `PetscCall` uses the expanded parameters to invoke the appropriate function, using the table of function pointers associated with object `obj`, created at runtime. This use of macro-expansions underscores the complexity of string manipulations, argument extraction, and dynamic method dispatch in PETSc.

2 Abstraction

We developed two new CIVL-C libraries to help specify the intended behavior of PETSc's vector functions: one for *complex numbers* and one for *abstract vectors*.

In PETSc, scalar values can have either a real or complex floating point type. The choice is specified when PETSc is compiled. The library defines a preprocessor macro `PetscScalar` to be this scalar type, and `PetscReal` to be the corresponding real type. PETSc functions are written in a generic way using these symbols so that the same code works for both real and complex configurations.

While CIVL has a built-in real type `$real`, there is no support for complex numbers. Thus we developed a simple implementation that provides a type `$complex` and functions such as complex addition:

```
typedef struct $complex { RTYPE real; RTYPE imag; } $complex;
$complex $cadd($complex x, $complex y) {
  return ($complex){x.real + y.real, x.imag + y.imag};
}
```

Here, `RTYPE` is the real type. Complex multiplication, division, conjugation, and absolute value are also supported.

We also created a header file that defines a macro `STYPE`, which is either `$complex` or `$real`. Similar to PETSc, we use a preprocessor object macro provided at verification time (`-DCIVL_COMPLEX`) to specify whether scalars are complex or real. Additionally, the header file defines generic functions such as `scalar_add`, `scalar_mul`, etc., to be either the real or complex operation, as the case may be, enabling CIVL-C functions to be written in a generic way.

The vector library provides an abstract vector type, `$vec`. Objects of this type are immutable and do not require memory allocation or deallocation. Thus this library provides a simple functional interface which can be used to formulate complex assertions. Functions include the following:

```
$vec $vec_make_from_dense(int len, STYPE *vals);
int $vec_len($vec vec);
bool $vec_eq($vec vec1, $vec vec2);
STYPE $vec_ith($vec vec, int i);
$vec $vec_add($vec vec1, $vec vec2);
$vec $vec_scalar_mul(STYPE a, $vec vec);
RTYPE $vec_norm($vec vec, int p); // the L_p norm of vec
$vec $vec_set($vec vec, int i, STYPE x);
```

The type `$vec` is a struct with two fields: `len` (type `int`) and `data` (type `STYPE[]`). The latter can hold a sequence of any length and can be initialized using a `$lambda` expression. The function definitions are short; for example:

```
$vec $vec_set($vec vec, int i, STYPE x) {
  $assert(i >= 0 && i < vec.len, "Index out of bounds");
  $vec res;
  res.len = vec.len;
  res.data = (STYPE[vec.len])$lambda(int j) j == i ? x : vec.data[j];
  return res;
}
```

The entire library implementation comprises less than two hundred lines of CIVL-C code.

```
$vec CIVL_PetscToCivlVec(Vec petscVec) {
  int N = petscVec->map->N;
  PetscScalar *data = petscVec->data;
  MPI_Comm comm = petscVec->comm;
  int rank, nproc, n = petscVec->map->n;
  MPI_Comm_rank(comm, &rank); MPI_Comm_size(comm, &nproc);
  int *recvcounts = rank == 0 ? (int*)malloc(nproc * sizeof(int)) : NULL;
  int *displs = rank == 0 ? (int*)malloc(nproc * sizeof(int)) : NULL;
  MPI_Gather(&n, 1, MPI_INT, recvcounts, 1, MPI_INT, 0, comm);
  if (rank == 0) {
    displs[0] = 0;
    for (int i = 1; i < nproc; i++)
      displs[i] = displs[i - 1] + recvcounts[i - 1];
  }
  PetscReal *globalData =
      rank == 0 ? (PetscReal *)malloc(N * sizeof(PetscReal)) : NULL;
  MPI_Gatherv(data, n, PETSC_REAL, globalData, recvcounts, displs,
              PETSC_REAL, 0, comm);
  $vec result =
      rank == 0 ? $vec_make_from_dense(N, globalData) : $vec_zero(0);
  if (rank == 0) { free(recvcounts); free(displs); free(globalData); }
  return result;
}
```

Fig. 2. The CIVL_PetscToCivlVec representation function (excerpt).

As described in Sect. 1.2, the PETSc vector type Vec supports different architectures and manages the storage of values across distributed memory machines, as well as caches to improve performance. At any state, a PETSc Vec nevertheless represents a unique abstract vector, which allows us to define a function from Vec to $vec, which we call a *representation function*, similar to the *representation relation* used in certain declarative deductive verification approaches [10]. We implemented this representation function in the CIVL-C function CIVL_PetscToCivlVec, allowing us to convert PETSc vectors to abstract vectors as needed, for example to more easily express assertions.

Figure 2 shows a simplified version of the CIVL_PetscToCivlVec representation function, specialized for distributed vectors with real-valued elements. (The actual implementation also handles sequential vectors and vectors with complex-valued elements.) This function uses MPI communication to gather all vector entries into a contiguous buffer on process 0. On process 0, this data is used to create a CIVL $vec.

It is sometimes necessary to convert an abstract vector to a new PETSc vector, which is implemented in CIVL_CivlToPetscVec and requires additional arguments, e.g., to specify the data distribution. CIVL_CivlToPetscVecCopy is a variant that modifies an existing Vec to reflect the data in a given $vec.

3 Modular Verification Approach

As explained in Sect. 1, we follow a modular verification approach in which each function is specified and verified independently of other functions. We begin by identifying the functions targeted for verification. The function definition of a *target* `f` is copied into its own file, `f.c`. To verify `f.c`, two issues arise. The first is that `f` may call other functions. Pulling in the definitions of the functions called by `f` would defeat the goal of modularity. The second is that each function has specific (and sometimes elaborate) preconditions and postconditions. The two technical components addressing these issues are *spec stubs* and *drivers*. We now describe these techniques in detail.

3.1 Verification Targets

In many cases, we observed that a public PETSc function is implemented using a small number of (typically one or two) auxiliary functions that do most of the "work." These auxiliary functions have internal linkage (declared with `static`) and exist primarily to support the public function. In such cases, we relax our strict definition of *modular* and include the auxiliary functions with the public function in the target file. This seems an appropriate level of granularity for modular verification.

Ideally, the target code would be extracted from the PETSc source without modification. However, we found it necessary to make some manual modifications to overcome current limitations in CIVL. Most of the issues relate to the use of complex arithmetic. Standard C allows the usual arithmetic operators (+, -, etc.) to apply to complex as well as real floating point types. We replaced these with calls to our generic functions, such as `scalar_add` (Sect. 2), which operate correctly in both the real and complex context. In the future, we plan to either automate this transformation or add support for C's complex arithmetic to CIVL.

Figure 3 shows the target code for PETSc's implementation of `VecAXPY`, after modification. This function computes $y := \alpha x + y$ for vectors x and y and scalar α. Note it calls functions such as `VecScale`, `VecLockReadPush`, and `VecLockReadPop`. These calls will be directed to the spec stub definitions during verification. This implementation is more complicated than the abstract mathematical definition. For example, it includes performance optimizations for the case where $\alpha = 0$ or $x = y$. One reason for verification is to ensure that these performance optimizations preserve the mathematical semantics.

3.2 Specification Stubs

We developed *specification stubs* (or *spec stubs*) for all target functions and functions called by targets. The CIVL source file `petscvec.cvl` contains all spec stub definitions, while the header file `petscvec.h` contains the function prototypes, and macro and type definitions.

```
PetscErrorCode VecAXPY(Vec y, PetscScalar alpha, Vec x) {
  // PETSc preamble and preconditions omitted for brevity
  if (scalar_eq(scalar_of(0.0), alpha))
    PetscFunctionReturn(PETSC_SUCCESS);
  if (x == y) {
    PetscCall(VecScale(y, scalar_add(alpha, scalar_of(1))));
    PetscFunctionReturn(PETSC_SUCCESS);
  }
  PetscCall(VecLockReadPush(x));
  PetscCall(PetscLogEventBegin(VEC_AXPY, x, y, 0, 0));
  VecMethodDispatch(y, NULL, VecAsyncFnName(AXPY), axpy,
    (Vec, PetscScalar, Vec, PetscDeviceContext), alpha, x);
  PetscCall(PetscLogEventEnd(VEC_AXPY, x, y, 0, 0));
  PetscCall(VecLockReadPop(x));
  PetscCall(PetscObjectStateIncrease((PetscObject)y));
  PetscFunctionReturn(PETSC_SUCCESS);
}
```

Fig. 3. A verification target: PETSc implementation of `VecAXPY` (after modifications to use scalar functions).

```
PetscErrorCode VecAXPY(Vec y, PetscScalar alpha, Vec x) {
  $assert(y->read_lock_count == 0,
    "VecAXPY: Cannot modify vector y because it is locked for reading.");
  $assert(x->map->n == y->map->n,
    "VecAXPY: Input vectors x and y must have the same local size.");
  $vec c_x = CIVL_PetscToCivlVec(x), c_y = CIVL_PetscToCivlVec(y),
       c_z = $vec_add($vec_scalar_mul(alpha, c_x), c_y);
  CIVL_CivlToPetscVecCopy(c_z, y);
  return 0;
}
```

Fig. 4. Spec stub for the `VecAXPY` function.

For each function f, the spec stub f' provides a succinct, high-level implementation of f, based on the mathematical description in the PETSc documentation. This is considered the trusted, authoritative encoding of the intended behavior of f. The implementation of f' may use CIVL-C constructs and libraries, including the vector library described in Sect. 2.

A spec stub plays two roles in our framework. As mentioned above, when verifying a target function that calls f, the verifier will use the spec stub definition f' instead of the actual PETSc definition of f. This is the "stub" aspect which enables modular verification. The second role is the specification of correct behavior of f: when f itself is a verification target, the driver will call f and f' and assert that the results are equivalent.

Figure 4 shows the spec stub for `VecAXPY`. Note that this specification uses the abstract vector library to concisely capture the mathematics. It also uses the functions `CIVL_PetscToCivlVec` and `CIVL_CivlToPetscVecCopy` discussed in Sect. 2 to create abstract vectors c_x and c_y from PETSc vectors x and y and to copy the result c_z back to the PETSc vector y. Note also that the return value is always 0, since any condition that would result in a nonzero error code is captured by one of the assertions.

3.3 Driver

For a target function f, we now have (1) the actual PETSc implementation of f, (2) a spec stub f' for f, and (3) a spec stub for every function called by f. We next create a custom driver, f_driver.cvl. This translation unit has a main function which creates appropriate symbolic inputs and verifies that the outputs of f and f' agree. Together with the complex and abstract vector libraries, the spec stub file petscvec.cvl, target file f.c, and driver f_driver.cvl form a complete CIVL-C program which can be verified with the CIVL model checker.

CIVL is invoked with the command-line flag -DVecAXPY=VecAXPY_spec, directing the preprocessor to replace instances of VecAXPY with VecAXPY_spec. Hence in petscvec.cvl and petscvec.h, the definition of spec stub VecAXPY is renamed to a definition of VecAXPY_spec. The driver and target files, however, contain the directive #undef VecAXPY, which cancels the command-line instruction. Hence both versions of the function—the original PETSc implementation (VecAXPY) and the spec stub (VecAXPY_spec)—are available to the driver. Function calls to all other PETSc functions refer to the spec stub versions.

Figure 5 shows the custom driver for VecAXPY. This driver defines the vector size (N), real and imaginary parts of the vector elements, and the scalar alpha (real and imaginary parts) as symbolic inputs using the $input keyword in lines 5–10. In addition, the driver: uses the macro scalar_make to drop the imaginary parts when working with real-valued vectors in lines 18, 21, and 22; creates PETSc vector objects from CIVL's symbolic data in lines 19–31; calls the actual VecAXPY and the spec stub version (VecAXPY_spec), and asserts the return code of the actual is 0 on line 34; and uses VecEqual to confirm that the modified actual and expected vectors match exactly at lines 39–41.

When invoking the CIVL model checker on this program, the command-line is also used to specify concrete upper and lower bounds on N by specifying values for N_MIN and N_MAX. Concrete bounds are also specified for the number of MPI processes. Within these bounds, the model checker explores all reachable symbolic states of the program. This entails the exploration of different branch choices as well as process interleavings. During the search, automated theorem provers are invoked to determine whether the path condition has become unsatisfiable (in which case the current path is pruned) and to validate the assertions. If the search completes with no violations found, the assertions have been proved to hold for all inputs and for all executions within the given bounds.

```
1  #include "petscvec.h"
2  #undef VecAXPY
3  PetscErrorCode VecAXPY(Vec y, PetscScalar alpha, Vec x);
4
5  $input int N_MIN, N_MAX, N;
6  $assume(N_MIN <= N && N <= N_MAX);
7  $input CIVL_RTYPE X_Real[N], Y_Real[N], alpha_Real;
8  #ifdef USE_COMPLEX
9  $input CIVL_RTYPE X_Imag[N], Y_Imag[N], alpha_Imag;
10 #endif
11
12 int main(void) {
13   MPI_Init(NULL, NULL);
14   int rank, size;
15   MPI_Comm_size(MPI_COMM_WORLD, &size);
16   MPI_Comm_rank(MPI_COMM_WORLD, &rank);
17   $vec x = $vec_zero(0), y = $vec_zero(0), z = $vec_zero(0);
18   STYPE x_values[N], y_values[N], alpha = scalar_make(alpha_Real,
         alpha_Imag);
19   if (rank == 0) {
20     for (int i = 0; i < N; i++) {
21       x_values[i] = scalar_make(X_Real[i], X_Imag[i]);
22       y_values[i] = scalar_make(Y_Real[i], Y_Imag[i]);
23     }
24     x = $vec_make_from_dense(N, x_values);
25     y = $vec_make_from_dense(N, y_values);
26     $print("\nVecAXPY_driver: nprocs = ", size, ", N = ", N,
27            ", Alpha = ", alpha, " ...");
28   }
29   Vec p_x = CIVL_CivlToPetscVec(x, PETSC_DECIDE, MPI_COMM_WORLD);
30   Vec p_y = CIVL_CivlToPetscVec(y, PETSC_DECIDE, MPI_COMM_WORLD);
31   Vec expected = CIVL_CivlToPetscVec(y, PETSC_DECIDE, MPI_COMM_WORLD);
32   VecAXPY_spec(expected, alpha, p_x);
33   PetscErrorCode err_actual = VecAXPY(p_y, alpha, p_x);
34   $assert(err_actual == 0);
35 #ifdef DEBUG
36   CIVL_PrintVec("Actual   AXPY", p_y);
37   CIVL_PrintVec("Expected AXPY", expected);
38 #endif
39   bool flg;
40   VecEqual(p_y, expected, &flg);
41   $assert(flg, "VecAXPY mismatch between actual and expected results.");
42   VecDestroy(&p_x); VecDestroy(&p_y); VecDestroy(&expected);
43   MPI_Finalize();
44 }
```

Fig. 5. The VecAXPY driver VecAXPY_driver.cvl.

4 Experiment Setup and Results

Having explained the general verification methodology, we now describe specific experiments applying that methodology to functions in the PETSc vector module. We first describe the set of targeted functions and the verification configurations and hardware used. We then summarize the verification results. Finally, we discuss several issues that arose and how we dealt with them. All experimental artifacts can be found on the GitHub repository for this project.[1]

4.1 Experimental Framework

PETSc's vector module comprises approximately six hundred C functions. Over one hundred of them are static helper functions that are only used internally, leaving well over four hundred functions that have a documented interface. We formally verified 61 of those, in the order they appear in `rvector.c` and `bvec2.c`. This choice was motivated by the fact that most of these functions are listed as Basic Vector Operations in the PETSc manual and are likely to be among the most commonly used functions. As discussed in Sect. 3.2, we developed the spec stubs using the function descriptions in the PETSc manual. Occasionally, the documentation did not precisely specify the semantics, and we relied on the PETSc developers for clarification.

The driver for each function enables us to specify the maximum vector length and, where applicable, the maximum number of vectors—for example for `VecMAXPY`, which accepts multiple input vectors. The corresponding makefile specifies a "small" and a "big" configuration. In all cases, the small configuration uses 3 as both the maximum vector length and the maximum number of vectors and is verified for 1 or 2 MPI processes. In most cases, the big configuration uses a maximum vector length of 5 and a maximum number of vectors of 3 and is verified for 1 through 5 MPI processes. For 16 functions susceptible to state space explosion, the big configuration uses a maximum vector length of 4 and is verified for up to 4 processes. For the experiments reported in Sect. 4.2, we used CIVL revision 5965 on a Macbook Pro with a 14-core M3 Max processor and 96 GB memory.

4.2 Summary of Results

Within the 61 functions verified, we identified 2 previously undiscovered defects:

1. **VecMaxPointwiseDivide: missing global reduction.** The MPI `_VecOps` struct mistakenly dispatched `maxpointwisedivide` to the sequential implementation, so each process only computed its local maximum. After reporting this defect, the PETSc developers added `VecMaxPointwiseDivide_MPI`, which invokes the sequential routine on each rank and then performs an `MPI_Allreduce` with operator `MPI_MAX`. The pointer in `_VecOps` was updated accordingly[2]. CIVL successfully verifies the corrected code.

---
[1] https://github.com/verified-software-lab/civl-petsc/.
[2] https://gitlab.com/petsc/petsc/-/merge_requests/8339.

2. **VecNorm_MPI: incorrect NORM_FROBENIUS fall-through.** In the MPI implementation's switch case, the NORM_FROBENIUS label was misplaced, so the required squaring step z[0]*=z[0] was never executed. CIVL flagged the assertion violation in the driver. The PETSc developers accepted our report and repaired the code[3]; Again, CIVL successfully verifies the fix.

We measured the time required to verify all 61 functions, including the original and corrected version for the two cases where a defect was discovered, for a total of 63 functions. Verification using the small configurations took a total of 17 min and 49 s, with the time to verify individual functions ranging from 6 s to 46 s. Verification using the big configurations took a total of 4 h and 35 min, with the time to verify individual functions ranging from 6 s to 11 min and 49 s.

4.3 Issues and Limitations

Path explosion was the biggest challenge to scaling this verification approach, especially for functions containing loops with branches in the loop body. There is often a trade-off between path explosion and complexity of assertions. CIVL provides some ways to control this tradeoff. For example, to compute the maximum of a and b, and store the result in c, one could write either c=a>b?a:b; or if (a>b) c=a; else c=b;. The result of evaluating the ternary expression is a single symbolic expression, using the "ite" operator supported by most provers. Hence the first approach results in fewer paths but more complex path conditions, which can challenge the automated provers. The second results in more paths but simpler path conditions. We found in most cases the use of the ternary operator reduced verification time, but in a few cases the path conditions exploded and the provers started returning "unknown" results. The best option is hard to predict and we proceeded by trial and error as we developed each spec stub.

Perhaps surprisingly, concurrency interleaving was not a major source of state explosion. We attribute this to the fact that all MPI usage in our verification targets is deterministic. In particular, only blocking point-to-point and collective operations are used, and MPI_ANY_SOURCE is not used. Because of this, CIVL's partial order reduction algorithm is able to deduce that only a single interleaving needs to be explored. Nevertheless, increasing the process count introduces overhead and sometimes increases the number of branches, so there is some cost.

One limitation of our approach is that we only considered vectors that use PETSc's default distribution, a standard block distribution into chunks whose sizes can differ by at most 1. However, PETSc also allows the user to specify an arbitrary distribution, and there may be defects that are revealed only by nonstandard distributions. Enumerating all possible distributions would lead to an enormous combinatorial explosion, so this is a very challenging problem. We have also not yet verified any multithreaded (shared-memory concurrency) executions of PETSc.

---

[3] https://gitlab.com/petsc/petsc/-/merge_requests/8172.

5 Conclusions and Future Work

This work demonstrates the feasibility of computer-aided verification for large scientific libraries such as PETSc [1], using symbolic execution and model checking techniques [11,16] to verify individual functions. Using this approach, we were able to verify 61 functions from PETSc's vector module, within small but nontrivial bounds (4 or 5) on the number of MPI processes and vector length. We also found two previously undiscovered defects that were accepted and corrected by the developers, and we verified the fixes.

The key insight enabling this modularity is the use of *specification stubs* that act as surrogates for lower-level functions—ensuring modular analysis of the function under test—and provide a separate "gold standard" version of the function under test. This design has enabled flexible, focused verification runs that detect subtle logic errors more easily than conventional testing.

We also observe that the use of executable driver code to formulate the specification is intuitive to developers who are not experts in formal verification, as it is similar to unit testing. The same observation has been made in other contexts [6]. This approach also enables familiar "printf" debugging, which allowed us to "see" the symbolic values in the state at various points. Output from the VecAXPY driver in Fig. 5, for example, includes the text

```
Actual   AXPY: { (X_X_Real[0]*X_alpha_Real)+X_Y_Real[0] }
Expected AXPY: { (X_X_Real[0]*X_alpha_Real)+X_Y_Real[0] }.
```

This proved invaluable in tracking down bugs in our spec stubs and drivers, especially when the error messages from CIVL were difficult to decipher. Function contracts [13] offer an alternative approach, with advantages and disadvantages: drivers are more flexible, allowing arbitrary executable statements, but contracts are more concise and can be placed next to the functions they specify. We plan to explore ways to use or extend existing contract languages, such as ACSL [5], for PETSc.

The results presented in this paper are part of an ongoing project to verify larger parts of PETSc, starting with full coverage of the vector module, and subsequently, higher-level PETSc features that use PETSc vectors. In particular, we plan to extend our spec stub approach to handle PETSc's matrix classes and routines, which introduce further complexity in data structures and parallel communication. We also plan to continue our close collaboration with the PETSc developer community to incorporate computer-aided verification into PETSc's code base by integrating CIVL checks with continuous integration, with the ultimate goal that every new commit is symbolically verified.

Acknowledgements. This material is based upon work by the RAPIDS Institute, supported by the U.S. Department of Energy, Office of Science, Office of Advanced Scientific Computing Research, Scientific Discovery through Advanced Computing (SciDAC) program, under contract DE-AC02-06CH11357.

Disclosure of Interests. The authors have no competing interests to declare that are relevant to the content of this article.

References

1. Balay, S., et al.: PETSc/TAO users manual. Technical report, ANL-21/39 - Revision 3.21, Argonne National Laboratory (2024). https://doi.org/10.2172/2205494
2. Balay, S., et al.: PETSc Web page (2024). https://petsc.org/
3. Balay, S., Gropp, W.D., McInnes, L.C., Smith, B.F.: Efficient management of parallelism in object-oriented numerical software libraries. In: Modern Software Tools for Scientific Computing, pp. 163–202. Springer, Cham (1997). https://doi.org/10.1007/978-1-4612-1986-6_8
4. Barrett, C., et al.: CVC4. In: Computer Aided Verification: 23rd International Conference (CAV 2011). Lecture Notes in Computer Science, vol. 6806, pp. 171–177. Springer, Cham (2011). https://doi.org/10.1007/978-3-642-22110-1_14
5. Baudin, P., et al.: ACSL: ANSI/ISO C Specification Language, version 1.16 (2020). http://frama-c.com/download/acsl-1.16.pdf
6. Chong, N., et al.: Code-level model checking in the software development workflow. In: Proceedings of the ACM/IEEE 42nd International Conference on Software Engineering: Software Engineering in Practice. ICSE-SEIP '20, pp. 11–20. Association for Computing Machinery, New York, NY, USA (2020). https://doi.org/10.1145/3377813.3381347
7. CIVL: The Concurrency Intermediate Verification Language. https://civl.dev. Accessed 20 May 2024
8. Clarke Jr., E.M., Grumberg, O., Kroening, D., Peled, D., Veith, H.: Model Checking. MIT Press, Cambridge, MA, USA, 2 edn (2018). https://mitpress.mit.edu/books/model-checking-second-edition
9. De Moura, L., Bjørner, N.: Z3: an efficient SMT solver. In: International conference on Tools and Algorithms for the Construction and Analysis of Systems (TACAS 2008). Lecture Notes in Computer Science, vol. 4963, pp. 337–340. Springer, Cham (2008). https://doi.org/10.1007/978-3-540-78800-3_24
10. Kellison, A.E., Appel, A.W., Tekriwal, M., Bindel, D.: LAProof: a library of formal proofs of accuracy and correctness for linear algebra programs. In: 2023 IEEE 30th Symposium on Computer Arithmetic (ARITH), pp. 36–43. IEEE (2023). https://doi.org/10.1109/ARITH58626.2023.00021
11. King, J.C.: Symbolic execution and program testing. Commun. ACM **19**(7), 385–394 (1976). https://doi.org/10.1145/360248.360252
12. Message Passing Interface Forum: MPI: A Message-Passing Interface Standard Version 4.1 (2023). https://www.mpi-forum.org/docs/mpi-4.1/mpi41-report.pdf
13. Meyer, B.: Applying "design by contract." IEEE Comput. **25**(10), 40–51 (1992). https://doi.org/10.1109/2.161279
14. OpenMP Architecture Review Board: OpenMP Application Programming Interface, version 6.0 (2024). https://www.openmp.org/wp-content/uploads/OpenMP-API-Specification-6-0.pdf
15. Siegel, S.F., et al.: CIVL: the concurrency intermediate verification language. In: SC15: Proceedings of the International Conference for High Performance Computing, Networking, Storage and Analysis. ACM, New York (2015). https://doi.org/10.1145/2807591.2807635, Article No. 61, pp. 1–12
16. Siegel, S.F., Zirkel, T.K.: TASS: the toolkit for accurate scientific software. Math. Comput. Sci. **5**(4), 395–426 (2011). https://doi.org/10.1007/s11786-011-0100-7
17. Zheng, M., Rogers, M.S., Luo, Z., Dwyer, M.B., Siegel, S.F.: CIVL: formal verification of parallel programs. In: Proceedings of the 30th ACM/IEEE International Conference on Automated Software Engineering (ASE'15), pp. 830–835. ACM, New York, NY, USA (2015). https://doi.org/10.1109/ASE.2015.99

Open Access This chapter is licensed under the terms of the Creative Commons Attribution 4.0 International License (http://creativecommons.org/licenses/by/4.0/), which permits use, sharing, adaptation, distribution and reproduction in any medium or format, as long as you give appropriate credit to the original author(s) and the source, provide a link to the Creative Commons license and indicate if changes were made.

The images or other third party material in this chapter are included in the chapter's Creative Commons license, unless indicated otherwise in a credit line to the material. If material is not included in the chapter's Creative Commons license and your intended use is not permitted by statutory regulation or exceeds the permitted use, you will need to obtain permission directly from the copyright holder.

Compositional Abstraction for Timed Systems with Broadcast Synchronization

Hanyue Chen[1], Miaomiao Zhang[1(✉)], and Frits Vaandrager[2]

[1] Tongji University, Shanghai, China
{2111285,miaomiao}@tongji.edu.cn
[2] Radboud University, Nijmegen, The Netherlands
f.vaandrager@cs.ru.nl

Abstract. Simulation-based compositional abstraction effectively mitigates state space explosion in model checking, particularly for timed systems. However, existing approaches do not support broadcast synchronization, an important mechanism for modeling non-blocking one-to-many communication in multi-component systems. Consequently, they also lack a parallel composition operator that simultaneously supports broadcast synchronization, binary synchronization, shared variables, and committed locations. To address this, we propose a simulation-based compositional abstraction framework for timed systems, which supports these modeling concepts and is compatible with the popular UPPAAL model checker. Our framework is general, with the only additional restriction being that the timed automata are prohibited from updating shared variables when receiving broadcast signals. Through two case studies, our framework demonstrates superior verification efficiency compared to traditional monolithic methods.

1 Introduction

Model checking [4,16,35,39] is a widely used technique for automatically verifying whether a system meets specified properties by exploring its state space. However, in real-world systems, especially timed systems, the state space size grows exponentially with the number of components [17]. This leads to the state space explosion problem, making exploring and storing the states harder for verification. *Simulation-based compositional abstraction* [37] is a recognized method to address this issue [9], which simplifies systems by replacing complex components with abstractions that preserve essential behavior, reducing the state space and improving verification efficiency.

Models of the systems have different communication mechanisms, such as reading and writing *shared variables* in TLA and TLA+ [30], *binary synchronization* through paired input/output actions in CCS [36] and Pi-Calculus [38], etc. Among them, *broadcast synchronization* is also important, where a sender emits a synchronization signal in a non-blocking manner to multiple receivers, each deciding independently whether to accept the signal. The non-blocking nature allows for unified and concise modeling of synchronization among multiple components, as it imposes no limit on the number of actual receivers. For the widely used model-checking tool UPPAAL [6,31], it supports broadcast synchronization and has been applied successfully in various industrial cases [7,13,23,24,27–29].

Several simulation-based compositional abstraction frameworks address synchronization involving multiple participants. For instance, the framework in [1] prohibits receivers from updating shared variables to support one-to-one, one-to-many, and many-to-many synchronization. However, this framework is designed for untimed systems, and its compositional rules are not associative [10]. The frameworks in [5,40] integrate shared variables with *multi-cast synchronization* in timed systems. They achieve associative compositional rules by requiring synchronized transitions to update shared variables simultaneously, ensuring consistent valuations before and after synchronization. Nevertheless, this kind of synchronization needs all components with synchronized actions to participate, which conflicts with the non-blocking nature of broadcast synchronization. A specification framework for real-time systems based on timed input/output automata (TIOAs) is developed in [26], but the synchronization between TIOAs is also a kind of multicast synchronization. To our knowledge, no simulation-based compositional abstraction framework currently exists to handle timed models with broadcast synchronization. Although it is possible to emulate broadcast synchronization in terms of other communication mechanisms, e.g., binary synchronization, this often introduces additional states, reducing the naturalness and readability of the models [12], and bringing difficulty to verification.

Furthermore, designing a simulation-based compositional abstraction framework that supports multiple communication mechanisms for timed systems is necessary. Several efforts have been made on compositional verification for the composed models with shared variables and binary synchronization. For example, the framework in [32] restricts that a shared variable can only be updated in the same automaton. The work in [21] relaxes the restriction by allowing the update of shared variables in multiple automata through internal transitions, whereas it still does not support the update during synchronization. The framework proposed by Berendsen and Vaandrager removes this restriction, supporting binary synchronization, shared variables, and *committed locations* [9], which is one of the key features of UPPAAL, ensuring atomic transitions and significantly reducing the state space by excluding irrelevant behavior [11]. As known, if a system component is in a committed location, time cannot progress, and the next system transition must start from that location. This framework has been successfully used to verify the Zeroconf protocol for any number of hosts [7] but lacks support for compositional abstraction with broadcast synchronization.

Hence, we aim to develop a simulation-based compositional abstraction framework for timed systems with broadcast synchronization. Given that UPPAAL offers a rich syntax for modeling complex systems as *networks of timed automata* (NTAs) [2,3], this framework is also designed to support binary synchronization, shared variables, and committed locations.

To achieve this, first inspired by the definition of *timed transition systems* (TTSs) in [9], we introduce the *timed transition systems with broadcast actions* (TTSBs), which extend *labeled transition systems* (LTSs) with state variables, transition commitments, and time-related behavior. When combining broadcast synchronization with shared variables, the order in which these variables are updated by the transitions involved in the synchronization can lead to different system states. Therefore, we prohibit TTSBs from updating shared variables when receiving broadcast signals, which is crucial for proving the theorem that the parallel composition we designed for TTSBs is both commutative and associative. Next, we introduce a CCS-style restriction operator to internalize a set of synchronized actions and shared variables so that no further TTSBs may communicate via them. This restriction is useful, as multiple component models might be abstracted into a single model, and these actions and variables should be considered as internal in the abstraction.

Secondly, considering that timed systems are often modeled as NTAs, we give two kinds of semantics of NTAs for subsequent compositional abstraction. The first one strictly follows the UPPAAL semantics, which directly transforms an entire NTA of a timed system into an LTS. However, this semantics lacks compositionality, making it impossible to abstract parts of the system model, that is, to replace several components with a simpler one. We refer to it as non-compositional semantics. So we define the second one, compositional semantics for NTAs, achieved by converting each *timed automaton* (TA) into its corresponding TTSB, composing them in parallel, applying restriction operations, and extracting the underlying LTS. We further prove the theorem that these two semantics are equivalent, laying the foundation for subsequent compositional abstraction.

Thirdly, since the compositional semantics of an NTA are derived based on a TTSB, the abstraction relations between NTAs can be defined in terms of the relation between TTSBs. We describe a timed step simulation relation of TTSBs and prove the theorem that this relation is a precongruence for parallel composition. This allows a system to be abstracted by replacing several components with a simpler model that preserves essential behavior. For example, abstracting multiple consumers in a producer-consumer system into a single model.

Finally, based on the previous theorems we prove that if the abstraction of an NTA with broadcast synchronization satisfies a safety property, then the original NTA also satisfies it. We apply our compositional abstraction framework to the case studies of a producer-consumer system and the clock synchronization protocol in [28], improving verification efficiency compared to the traditional monolithic method.

The rest of the paper is organized as follows. Section 2 introduces necessary background knowledge. Section 3 introduces the TTSB and corresponding operations of parallel composition and restriction. Section 4 introduces the non-compositional and compositional semantics of NTA with broadcast synchronization and proves their equivalence. Section 5 proposes the timed step simulation for TTSBs and demonstrates the compositionality of the resulting preorder. In

2 Preliminaries

We use $\mathbb{N}$ to denote the set of natural numbers, $\mathbb{R}_{\geq 0}$ the set of non-negative reals, and let $\mathbb{B} = \{1, 0\}$, where 1 stands for true and 0 stands for false.

2.1 Notations for Functions

The domain of function f is represented as $dom(f)$. If X is a set, then $f \lceil X$ denotes the restriction of f to X, forming function g with $dom(g) = dom(f) \cap X$ and $g(z) = f(z)$ for each $z \in dom(g)$. The *override* operators [8] on functions are $\triangleright$ and $\triangleleft$. For arbitrary functions f and g, $f \triangleright g$ denotes the function with $dom(f \triangleright g) = dom(f) \cup dom(g)$ such that for all $z \in dom(f \triangleright g)$,

$$(f \triangleright g)(z) \triangleq \begin{cases} f(z) & \text{if } z \in dom(f) \\ g(z) & \text{if } z \in dom(g) - dom(f) \end{cases}$$

and $f \triangleleft g \triangleq g \triangleright f$. Functions f and g are compatible, denoted as $f \heartsuit g$, if $f(z) = g(z)$ for all $z \in dom(f) \cap dom(g)$. For compatible functions f and g, their merge is $f \| g \triangleq f \triangleright g$. Clearly, $\|$ and $\heartsuit$ are commutative and associative. When we use $f \| g$, it is implicit that $f \heartsuit g$. The notation $f[g]$ represents the *update* of function f according to g, defined as $f[g] \triangleq (f \triangleleft g) \lceil dom(f)$.

Below are some fundamental properties of functions necessary for the subsequent content of this paper.

Lemma 1. *For any functions f, g, and h, and set X the following formulas always hold:*

$$f \heartsuit g[f] \tag{1}$$
$$f \heartsuit g \wedge (f \| g) \heartsuit h \Leftrightarrow f \heartsuit g \wedge f \heartsuit h \wedge g \heartsuit h \tag{2}$$
$$f \triangleright g = f \| g[f] \tag{3}$$
$$f[g][h] = f[h \triangleright g] \tag{4}$$
$$(f \triangleright g)[h] = f[h] \triangleright g[h] \tag{5}$$
$$f \heartsuit g \Rightarrow f \lceil X \heartsuit g \tag{6}$$
$$f \heartsuit g, f \heartsuit h \Rightarrow f \heartsuit (g \triangleright h) \tag{7}$$

Proof. Among the formulas above, (1)–(5) are proved in [9] and the proofs are straightforward from the definitions. The formulas (6) and (7) are newly introduced. Their proof is provided below.

(6) Since $dom(f \lceil X) \subseteq dom(f)$ and $f \heartsuit g$, for any $z \in dom(f \lceil X) \cap dom(g)$, $(f \lceil X)(z) = g(z)$, that is, $f \lceil (X) \heartsuit g$.
(7) For any $z \in dom(f) \cap dom(g)$, since $f \heartsuit g$, $f(z) = g(z)$. For any $z \in dom(f) \cap (dom(h) - dom(g))$, since $f \heartsuit h$, $f(z) = h(z)$. Hence, we have $f \heartsuit (g \triangleright h)$. □

2.2 Labeled Transition Systems

We consider two types of *channels*, i.e., *broadcast channels* and *binary channels*. The former allows non-blocking one-to-many synchronization while the latter is used for *binary synchronization* where one side sends, and the other receives. We use Δ and $\mathcal{C}$ to represent their respective sets. The set of *broadcast actions* is $\mathcal{E}_\Delta \triangleq \{\delta!, \delta? \mid \delta \in \Delta\}$ and the set of *binary actions* is $\mathcal{E}_\mathcal{C} \triangleq \{c!, c? \mid c \in \mathcal{C}\}$. The action marked with ! or ? is called *output action* or *input action*, respectively. We assume that there is a special *internal action* represented as τ and *time-passage actions* represented as non-negative real numbers in $\mathbb{R}_{\geq 0}$. We consider *labeled transition systems* associated with the action set $Act \triangleq \mathcal{E}_\Delta \cup \mathcal{E}_\mathcal{C} \cup \{\tau\} \cup \mathbb{R}_{\geq 0}$.

Definition 1 (LTS). *A labeled transition system (LTS) is a tuple*

$$\mathcal{L} = \langle S, s^0, Act, \rightarrow \rangle,$$

where S is a set of states, $s^0 \in S$ is the initial state, Act is the action set, and $\rightarrow \subseteq S \times Act \times S$ is the transition relation. We use $r, s, t, \ldots$ to range over S, and write $s \xrightarrow{a} t$ if $(s, a, t) \in \rightarrow$. Here, s is the transition source, and t is the target. An a-transition is enabled in s, denoted as $s \xrightarrow{a}$, if a state t exists such that $s \xrightarrow{a} t$. A state s is reachable iff there exists a sequence of states $s_1, \ldots, s_n$ where $s_1 = s^0$, $s_n = s$ and for all $i < n$ there exists an action a such that $s_i \xrightarrow{a} s_{i+1}$.

2.3 Networks of Timed Automata

Let $\mathcal{V}$ be a universal set of typed *variables*, with a subset $\mathcal{X} \subseteq \mathcal{V}$ of *clocks* having domain $\mathbb{R}_{\geq 0}$. A *valuation* for a set $V \subseteq \mathcal{V}$ is a function that maps each variable in V to an element in its domain. We write $\{y_i \mapsto z_i, \ldots, y_n \mapsto z_n\}$ for the valuation that assigns value z_i to variable y_i, for $i = 1, \ldots, n$. We use $Val(V)$ to denote the valuations set for V. For valuation $v \in Val(V)$ and time-passage action $d \in \mathbb{R}_{\geq 0}$, $v \oplus d$ is the valuation for V that increases the clocks by d and leaves the other variables unchanged, that is, for all $y \in V$,

$$(v \oplus d)(y) \triangleq \begin{cases} v(y) + d & \text{if } y \in \mathcal{X} \\ v(y) & \text{otherwise} \end{cases}$$

A *property* P over V is a subset of $Val(V)$. Given $W \supseteq V$ and $v \in Val(W)$, we say that P holds in v, denoted as $v \models P$, if $v\lceil V \in P$. A property P over V is *left-closed* w.r.t for all $v \in Val(V)$ and $d \in \mathbb{R}_{\geq 0}$, $v \oplus d \models P \Rightarrow v \models P$ holds. A property P over V is said *not depend on* a set of variables $W \subseteq V$ if for every $v \in Val(V)$ and $u \in Val(W)$, $v \models P$ holds iff $v[u] \models P$ holds.

A network of timed automata is a finite set of timed automata *compatible* with each other and communicating through broadcast and binary channels and shared *external variables*. The state variables of a timed automaton are divided into external and *internal variables*. Internal variables are private to the TA and cannot be accessed by other TAs, while external variables are shared among multiple TAs and can both be read and updated by them. In UPPAAL, internal variables are declared locally within a template, and external variables are declared in global declarations.

Definition 2 (TA). *A timed automaton is a tuple* $\mathcal{A} = \langle L, K, l^0, E, H, v^0, I, \rightarrow, \rightarrow^u \rangle$, *where L represents the set of locations, $K \subseteq L$ denotes the set of committed locations, $l^0 \in L$ is the initial location, E and H are disjoint sets of external and internal variables, respectively. $V = E \cup H$, $v^0 \in \mathit{Val}(V)$ signifies the initial valuation, and $I : L \rightarrow 2^{\mathit{Val}(V)}$ assigns a left-closed invariant property to each location, ensuring that $v^0 \models I(l^0)$,*

$$\rightarrow \subseteq L \times 2^{\mathit{Val}(V)} \times \mathcal{E}_\Delta \cup \mathcal{E}_\mathcal{C} \cup \{\tau\} \times (\mathit{Val}(V) \rightarrow \mathit{Val}(V)) \times L$$

is the set of transitions, and $\rightarrow^u \subseteq \rightarrow$ is the set of urgent transitions. We write $l \xrightarrow{g,a,\rho} l'$ if $(l, g, a, \rho, l') \in \rightarrow$, where l and l' are the source and the target, a is the action, g is the guard, and ρ is the update function. The guard g must be a conjunction of simple conditions on clocks, differences between clocks, and boolean expressions that do not involve clocks.

Notably, a location invariant is a left-closed property, meaning that lower bounds on clocks, such as $x \geq 5$ for $x \in V \cap \mathcal{X}$, are disallowed, as required by UPPAAL. Our restriction on transition guards is consistent with that of UPPAAL. For example, convex guards such as $x - y < 5 \wedge x > 3$ are allowed, while expressions like $x < 2 \vee x > 5$ are not permitted, where $x, y \in V \cap \mathcal{X}$. Certainly, the transition guarded by $x < 2 \vee x > 5$ can be replaced by two transitions guarded by $x < 2$ and $x > 5$, respectively. Compared to the TA considered in [9], the TA considered here additionally includes broadcast actions in $\mathcal{E}_\Delta$.

Throughout this paper, we employ indices to denote individual system components when dealing with multiple indexed systems. For instance, H_i represents the internal variable set of TA $\mathcal{A}_i$.

Definition 3 (NTA). *Two timed automata $\mathcal{A}_1$ and $\mathcal{A}_2$ are compatible if $H_1 \cap V_2 = H_2 \cap V_1 = \emptyset$ and $v_1^0 \heartsuit v_2^0$. A network of timed automata (NTA) consists of a finite tuple $\mathcal{N} = \langle \mathcal{A}_1, \ldots, \mathcal{A}_n \rangle$ of pairwise compatible timed automata.*

3 Timed Transition Systems with Broadcast Actions

The timed transition systems considered in [9] support shared variables, binary actions, and committed locations but exclude broadcast actions. To perform compositional abstraction on the NTAs with broadcast channels, in this section, we introduce the timed transition systems with broadcast actions and corresponding operations of parallel composition and restriction.

3.1 Definition of TTSB

TTSBs extend LTSs with state variables, transition commitments, and time-related behavior. We follow the approach in [9], treating committedness as an attribute of transitions rather than an attribute of locations as in UPPAAL to obtain compositional semantics. Therefore, when interpreting the semantics of TAs using TTSB, transitions starting from committed locations in the TA are interpreted as committed transitions in the corresponding TTSB. Obviously, committed transitions have higher priority over uncommitted transitions.

Definition 4 (TTSB). *A timed transition system with broadcast actions is a tuple*

$$\mathcal{T} = \langle E, H, S, s^0, Act, \rightarrow^1, \rightarrow^0 \rangle$$

where $E, H \subseteq \mathcal{V}$ are disjoint sets of external and internal variables, respectively. $S \subseteq Val(V)$ is the set of states, where $V = E \cup H$, and $s^0 \in S$ is the initial state. Act is the action set which includes broadcast actions. $\rightarrow^1, \rightarrow^0$ are disjoint sets of committed and uncommitted transitions, respectively. A transition $(s, a, t) \in \rightarrow^b$ can also be denoted as $s \xrightarrow{a,b} t$, where $b \in \mathbb{B}$. A state s is considered as a committed state, denoted as $Comm(s)$, iff there is at least one committed transition starting from it, i.e., $s \xrightarrow{a,1}$ for some $a \in Act$. The underlying LTS of $\mathcal{T}$ is $\langle S, s^0, Act, \rightarrow^1 \cup \rightarrow^0 \rangle$, denoted as $\mathsf{LTS}(\mathcal{T})$.

We require the following axioms to hold, for all $s, t \in S$, $a, a' \in Act$, $\sigma \in \mathcal{C} \cup \mathcal{A}$, $\delta \in \Delta$, $b \in \mathbb{B}$, $d \in \mathbb{R}_{\geq 0}$ and $u \in Val(E)$,

$$s \xrightarrow{a,1} \land s \xrightarrow{a',b} \Rightarrow a' \in \mathcal{E}_\mathcal{C} \cup \mathcal{E}_\Delta \lor (a' = \tau \land b) \quad \text{(Axiom I)}$$

$$s[u] \in S \quad \text{(Axiom II)}$$

$$s \xrightarrow{\sigma?,b} \Rightarrow s[u] \xrightarrow{\sigma?,b} \quad \text{(Axiom III)}$$

$$s \xrightarrow{d,0} t \Rightarrow t = s \oplus d \quad \text{(Axiom IV)}$$

$$s \xrightarrow{\delta?,b} \quad \text{(Axiom V)}$$

$$s \xrightarrow{\delta?,b} t \Rightarrow s \lceil E = t \lceil E \quad \text{(Axiom VI)}$$

Note that in a TTSB, from a committed state, the outgoing transitions might be uncommitted. Axiom I stipulates that neither time passage nor uncommitted τ-transitions can occur in a committed state. In contrast, uncommitted transitions labeled with broadcast or binary actions can occur in this state since they may synchronize with committed transitions of other TTSBs. Axiom II asserts that by updating the values of external variables of a state, the result is still a state. Axiom III affirms that updating external variables does not affect the enabledness of transitions labeled with input actions, whether binary or broadcast, which is crucial for compositionality. Axiom IV asserts that if time advances with d units, all the clocks advance by d, while other variables remain unchanged.

Axiom V stipulates that for any broadcast channel δ, all the states in TTSB have the corresponding outgoing $\delta?$-transition, that is, TTSB is *input-enabled* for broadcast actions. This axiom aligns with the constraint in *broadcast protocols* definition [19,22,25] and fundamental assumptions of input actions for each state in TIOA work [26,34]. As elaborated in Sect. 3.2 about the parallel composition of TTSBs, this axiom reduces broadcast synchronization to two scenarios, enabling a concise design of our parallel composition operator that also guarantees the non-blocking nature of UPPAAL broadcast synchronization. Notably, this axiom does not restrict TTSB to interpreting a limited TA that can execute $\delta?$-transition in any state, i.e., there is no requirement for each location of the TA to have an outgoing $\delta?$-transition, which avoids the cumbersome construction of such TA from a general one. Later in Sect. 4.2 focusing on the compositional semantics of NTAs, we will define the TTSB semantics for a general TA. In terms of the designed rule that introduces suitable self-loop transitions in the TTSB associated with a TA, the semantic conforms with this axiom without any preprocessing of the TA model. Correctness of the rule design is guaranteed by the equivalence between the non-compositional semantics and the compositional semantics of an NTA, which is also proved in Sect. 4.2.

Axiom VI is introduced to address the problem caused by a kind of transitions involving broadcast actions and updates of shared variables. According to the UPPAAL help menu, in broadcast synchronization, the update on the $\delta!$-transition is executed first, then those on the $\delta?$-transitions are executed left-to-right in the order of the TAs given in the system definition. This means that the order of the components affects the final composition, as illustrated in Example 1.

Example 1. As shown in Fig. 1, when defining the system, if TA $\mathcal{A}_2$ is to the left of $\mathcal{A}_3$, i.e., $\mathcal{N} = \langle \mathcal{A}_1, \mathcal{A}_2, \mathcal{A}_3 \rangle$, then after executing the broadcast synchronization via δ, the value of the external variable n is 2. In contrast, if $\mathcal{N} = \langle \mathcal{A}_1, \mathcal{A}_3, \mathcal{A}_2 \rangle$, the value of n becomes 1.

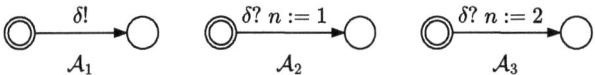

Fig. 1. Updates in broadcast synchronization

Therefore, to make our compositional framework compatible with UPPAAL semantics while avoiding the occurrence of this scenario, we allow value updates of variables in $\delta!$-transition but introduce Axiom VI to forbid the value updates of the external variables in $\delta?$-transition. Although this results in some loss of modeling capability for TTSB, ensuring the associativity of TTSB's parallel composition rules introduced in Sect. 3.2 is crucial.

3.2 Parallel Composition

We now introduce the parallel composition operation on TTSBs. It is a partial operation, defined only when TTSBs are compatible: the internal variable set of one TTSB must not overlap with the variable set of the other, and their initial states must be compatible. Recall that E_i (resp. H_i) represents the external (resp. internal) variable set of TTSB $\mathcal{T}_i$, $V_i = E_i \cup H_i$, Δ (resp. $\mathcal{C}$) is the broadcast (resp. binary) channel set, and $\mathcal{E}_\mathcal{C}$ is the set of binary actions.

Definition 5 (Parallel Composition). *Two TTSBs $\mathcal{T}_1$ and $\mathcal{T}_2$ are compatible if $H_1 \cap V_2 = H_2 \cap V_1 = \emptyset$ and $s_1^0 \heartsuit s_2^0$. Their parallel composition $\mathcal{T}_1 \| \mathcal{T}_2$ is denoted as $\mathcal{T} = \langle E, H, S, s^0, Act, \rightarrow^1, \rightarrow^0 \rangle$, where $E = E_1 \cup E_2$, $H = H_1 \cup H_2$, $S = \{r\|s \mid r \in S_1 \land s \in S_2 \land r \heartsuit s\}$, $s^0 = s_1^0 \| s_2^0$, and $\rightarrow^1, \rightarrow^0$ are the least relations satisfying the rules in Fig. 2. Here, $i,j \in \{1,2\}$, $r, r' \in S_i$, $s, s' \in S_j$, $b, b' \in \mathbb{B}$, $\delta \in \Delta$, $c \in \mathcal{C}$, $a \in \mathcal{E}_\mathcal{C}$ and $d \in \mathbb{R}_{\geq 0}$.*

$$\frac{r \xrightarrow{a,b}_i r'}{r\|s \xrightarrow{a,b} r' \triangleright s} \text{ EXT} \qquad \frac{r \xrightarrow{\tau,b}_i r' \quad Comm(s) \Rightarrow b}{r\|s \xrightarrow{\tau,b} r' \triangleright s} \text{ TAU}$$

$$\frac{r \xrightarrow{c!,b}_i r' \quad s[r'] \xrightarrow{c?,b'}_j s' \quad i \neq j \quad Comm(r) \lor Comm(s) \Rightarrow b \lor b'}{r\|s \xrightarrow{\tau,b \lor b'} r' \triangleleft s'} \text{ SYNC} \qquad \frac{r \xrightarrow{d,0}_i r' \quad s \xrightarrow{d,0}_j s' \quad i \neq j}{r\|s \xrightarrow{d,0} r'\|s'} \text{ TIME}$$

$$\frac{r \xrightarrow{\delta!,b}_i r' \quad s[r'] \xrightarrow{\delta?,b'}_j s' \quad i \neq j}{r\|s \xrightarrow{\delta!,b \lor b'} r'\|s'} \text{ SND} \qquad \frac{r \xrightarrow{\delta?,b}_i r' \quad s \xrightarrow{\delta?,b'}_j s' \quad i \neq j}{r\|s \xrightarrow{\delta?,b \lor b'} r'\|s'} \text{ RCV}$$

Fig. 2. Rules for parallel composition of TTSBs

Since broadcast transitions do not interact with binary transitions, internal transitions, or time passage, the parallel composition rules for these transitions are consistent with those in TTSs, as shown in rules **EXT**, **TAU**, **SYNC**, and **TIME** in Fig. 2. Rule **EXT** specifies that a transition labeled with binary action a in component $\mathcal{T}_i$ from state r leads to a corresponding transition in the composition $\mathcal{T}$. Occurrence of the a-transition may override some of the shared variables, and $r' \triangleright s$ is again a state of $\mathcal{T}$. Rule **TAU** states that a τ-transition from r in $\mathcal{T}_i$ induces a corresponding transition in $\mathcal{T}$, except for the case where the τ-transition is uncommitted and $\mathcal{T}_j$ is in a committed state. Rule **SYNC** describes the binary synchronization between components. If $\mathcal{T}_i$ has a $c!$-transition from r to r', and $\mathcal{T}_j$ has a corresponding $c?$-transition from $s[r']$, i.e. state s updated by r', to s', then the composition will have a τ-transition to from $r\|s$ to $r' \triangleleft s'$. We say a binary synchronization is committed if at least one involved transition is committed, that is, $b \lor b' = 1$. The condition $Comm(r) \lor Comm(s) \Rightarrow b \lor b'$ implies that a committed binary synchronization can always occur, and an uncommitted binary synchronization can only occur when neither of the components is in a committed state. Rule **TIME** states that time progresses at the same rate in both components.

For the composition of broadcast transitions, generally, there are four scenarios, $(\delta!,\delta?)$, $(\delta?,\delta?)$, $(\delta!,\cdot)$ and $(\delta?,\cdot)$ in two components. By Axiom V that each TTSB is input-enabled for broadcast actions, we only need to tackle the composition for the first two scenarios. We first consider the designed rule **SND** for $(\delta!,\delta?)$ transitions. Different from rule **SYNC** that generates a τ-transition in $\mathcal{T}$, rule **SND** states that if $\mathcal{T}_i$ has a $\delta!$-transition from r to r', and $\mathcal{T}_j$ has $\delta?$-transition from $s[r']$ to s', the composition will have a transition from $r\|s$ to $r'\|s'$, which is still labeled with $\delta!$. Intuitively, this rule allows a $\delta!$-transition, after synchronizing with a $\delta?$-transition, to synchronize with $\delta?$-transitions in other components. By Axiom VI, since the shared variable is not updated in the $\delta?$-transition, we have $r'\|s' = r' \triangleleft s'$. As the compositional framework also addresses scenarios combining broadcast synchronization and committed locations in NTAs, we must consider committedness for the rule **SND** in two aspects. For the first one, whether the composed $\delta!$-transition is committed is decided by the value of $b \vee b'$. For the second aspect, it should be noted that unlike rule **SYNC**, rule **SND** does not have the condition $Comm(r) \vee Comm(s) \Rightarrow b \vee b'$. This is because having this condition would cause the associativity violation of the parallel composition operation of TTSBs, which is illustrated by Example 2.

Example 2. Consider the three TTSBs shown in Fig. 3, where r and t are committed states. Suppose we add the condition $Comm(r) \vee Comm(s) \Rightarrow b \vee b'$ to rule **SND**. If we compose $\mathcal{T}_1$ and $\mathcal{T}_2$ first, since $r \xrightarrow{\delta?,0} r$ and $s \xrightarrow{\delta!,0} s'$ are both uncommitted, then $Comm(r) \vee Comm(s) \Rightarrow b \vee b'$ values false. So $\mathcal{T}_1\|\mathcal{T}_2$ does not have $\delta!$-transitions, resulting in the absence of $\delta!$-transition in the composition of $\mathcal{T}_1\|\mathcal{T}_2$ and $\mathcal{T}_3$, i.e. $\mathcal{T}_1\|\mathcal{T}_2\|\mathcal{T}_3$. However, if we compose $\mathcal{T}_2$ and $\mathcal{T}_3$ first, the final composition $\mathcal{T}_1\|(\mathcal{T}_2\|\mathcal{T}_3)$ will contain a committed $\delta!$-transition. Obviously, this violates the associative requirement.

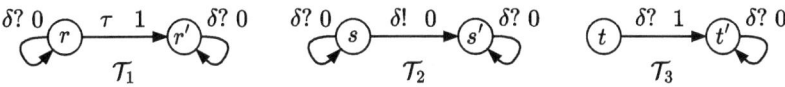

Fig. 3. Composition of three TTSBs

In contrast, our current design of rule **SND** ensures the parallel composition operator associative, which will be shown by Theorem 1 at the end of this section. We now prove that the target states of the transitions generated by rule **SND** are always states of $\mathcal{T}$. By Axiom II for $\mathcal{T}_j$, it follows that $s[r']$ is a state of $\mathcal{T}_j$. Further by Lemma 1(1), we have $r' \heartsuit s[r']$, then by Lemma 1(6), $r' \heartsuit s[r'] \lceil E_j$. By Axiom VI, $s[r']\lceil E_j = s'\lceil E_j$, which means $r' \heartsuit s'\lceil E_j$. Since $V_i \cap H_j = \emptyset$, $r' \heartsuit s'\lceil H_j$ holds. Finally by Lemma 1(7), we obtain $r' \heartsuit s'$. Hence, $r'\|s'$ is a state of $\mathcal{T}$.

We now consider the designed rule **RCV** for ($\delta?, \delta?$) transitions, which states that if $\mathcal{T}_i$ has a $\delta?$-transition from r to r' and $\mathcal{T}_j$ has a $\delta?$-transition from s to s', the composition will have a $\delta?$-transition from $r\|s$ to $r'\|s'$. Like the composed $\delta!$-transition in rule **SND**, the composed $\delta?$-transition in rule **RCV** has the committedness $b \vee b'$. Still, to guarantee associativity, rule **RCV** does not have the condition $Comm(r) \vee Comm(s) \Rightarrow b \vee b'$. The target state of the generated $\delta?$-transition also remains a state of $\mathcal{T}$. Since $r\|s$ is a state of $\mathcal{T}$, we have $r \heartsuit s$, which implies $r \lceil E_i \heartsuit s \lceil E_j$ by Lemma 1(6). Further by Axiom VI, neither $r \xrightarrow{\delta?,b}_i r'$ nor $s \xrightarrow{\delta?,b'}_j s'$ modifies the value of external variables, i.e. $r \lceil E_i = r' \lceil E_i, s \lceil E_j = s' \lceil E_j$. Based on this and $r \lceil E_i \heartsuit s \lceil E_j$, we have $r' \lceil E_i \heartsuit s' \lceil E_j$. Finally, since $H_i \cap V_j = H_j \cap V_i = \emptyset$, by Lemma 1(7), we get $r' \heartsuit s'$, following that $r'\|s' \in S$.

The parallel composition operation on TTSBs is well-defined, that is, the composition of two TTSBs remains a TTSB. The proof is in Appendix A of the extended version of this paper [15].

Lemma 2 (Composition Well-Defined). *Let $\mathcal{T}_1$ and $\mathcal{T}_2$ be compatible TTSBs. Then $\mathcal{T}_1 \| \mathcal{T}_2$ is a TTSB.*

Notably, the parallel composition operator defined in this paper satisfies two crucial properties for compositional abstraction: commutativity and associativity. This is a main theorem in this paper, and the proof is in Appendix B of [15].

Theorem 1 (Commutativity and Associativity). *The parallel composition operation on TTSBs is commutative and associative.*

3.3 Restriction

The designed parallel composition rules allow three types of component communication through broadcast channels, binary channels, and shared variables. For the first two types, when no matching component is available, a broadcast or binary transition can be removed or replaced with a τ-transition. For the third type, if an external variable is no longer used in other components, it can be converted to an internal one. Therefore, we introduce the restriction operation to handle these channels and variables. This operation not only enables simpler abstractions but is also crucial for establishing the correct compositional semantics of NTAs in Sect. 4.2.

Definition 6 (Restriction for TTSB). *Given a TTSB $\mathcal{T}$ and a set $C \subseteq \Delta \cup \mathcal{C} \cup E$ of broadcast, binary channels, and external variables, we denote the $\mathcal{T}$ restricted by C as $\mathcal{T} \backslash C$. The TTSB $\mathcal{T} \backslash C$ is identical to $\mathcal{T}$, except that for any transition $s \xrightarrow{a,b} s'$ of $\mathcal{T}$:*

1. *If $a \in \{\delta?, c!, c? \mid \delta \in C \cap \Delta, c \in C \cap \mathcal{C}\}$, it will be removed from $\mathcal{T} \backslash C$.*
2. *If $a \in \{\delta! \mid \delta \in C \cap \Delta\}$ and $Comm(s) \wedge \neg b$, it will be removed from $\mathcal{T} \backslash C$.*
3. *If $a \in \{\delta! \mid \delta \in C \cap \Delta\}$ and $Comm(s) \Rightarrow b$, it will be replaced by $s \xrightarrow{\tau,b} s'$ in $\mathcal{T} \backslash C$.*

and the external and internal variable sets of $\mathcal{T}\backslash C$ are $E - C$ and $H \cup (E \cap C)$, respectively.

The first type of transitions labeled with input broadcast actions or binary actions is removed because they cannot occur independently. For the output broadcast transitions, i.e., $\delta!$-transitions, due to the non-blocking nature of broadcast synchronization, they can occur independently but with consideration of their committedness and that of their source states. Recall that a committed state can have uncommitted outgoing transitions. So, a $\delta!$-transition can be uncommitted while its source state is committed. This also implies that the source state has another outgoing committed transition. In this case, this $\delta!$-transition should be removed because it cannot occur due to its low priority. Otherwise, for the cases where the sourcing state is not committed or the $\delta!$-transition itself is committed, the $\delta!$-transition can occur and should be replaced with a τ-transition, since no other transitions can synchronize with it. Obviously, the treatment of these output broadcast transitions depends both on their own committedness and that of their source states. A more general priority relation over transitions is meaningful and will be considered in the future.

Obviously, $\mathsf{LTS}(\mathcal{T}) = \mathsf{LTS}(\mathcal{T}\backslash C)$, if $C \subseteq E$. We write $\Sigma(\mathcal{T})$ for the set of channels that are enabled in the transitions of $\mathcal{T}$. Using this notation, we can formulate some restriction laws, such as $\mathcal{T}\backslash C = \mathcal{T}$ if $\Sigma(\mathcal{T}) \cap C = E \cap C = \emptyset$.

4 Two Definitions of NTA Semantics

This section introduces two definitions of the semantics of NTA with broadcast channels. One strictly follows UPPAAL semantics by constructing an LTS directly, but is not compositional, therefore called non-compositional semantics in this paper. The other is compositional, which is achieved by associating TTSBs to each TA, applying parallel composition and restriction operations, and finally extracting the underlying LTS. We prove that these two semantics are equivalent, which is also a main theorem to implement compositional abstraction for timed systems with broadcast synchronization.

For the compositional semantics of NTA, we first impose some axioms that UPPAAL does not require on timed automata to obtain compositionality. For any TA $\mathcal{A} = \langle L, K, l^0, E, H, v^0, I, \rightarrow \rangle$, we require:

$$I(l) \text{ does not depend on } E \qquad \text{(Axiom VII)}$$

$$l \xrightarrow{g,\sigma?,\rho} l' \;\Rightarrow\; g \text{ does not depend on } E \qquad \text{(Axiom VIII)}$$

$$\forall l \in K \; \forall v \in I(l) \; \exists (l \xrightarrow{g,a,\rho} l') : v \models g \wedge \rho(v) \models I(l') \qquad \text{(Axiom IX)}$$

$$l \xrightarrow{g,a,\rho}^u l' \;\Rightarrow\; a = \tau \wedge g \text{ does not depend on } \mathcal{X} \qquad \text{(Axiom X)}$$

$$l \xrightarrow{g,\delta?,\rho} l' \;\Rightarrow\; \rho \text{ does not update } Val(E) \qquad\qquad \text{(Axiom XI)}$$

Axioms VII-X are similar to the corresponding axioms of TTS in [9], with the new constraints with regard to broadcast synchronization. Axiom VII is introduced to avoid runtime errors in the scenario: modification of external variables in one automaton causes the violation of location invariant in another, which makes the NTA reach a state undefined in UPPAAL. Axiom VIII ensures that the update function ρ of σ!-transition does not affect satisfaction of the guard g in the corresponding σ?-transitions, where σ could be either a broadcast or a binary channel. As shown in [9], real-world models rarely violate this axiom. Axiom IX requires that for any committed location l, a transition must exist starting from it. This axiom excludes some "bad" models that may leads to deadlock and ensures that when associating a TTSB to a TA, the states corresponding to the committed location l must be committed ones. Axiom X says that an urgent transition should be internal and not have clock guards. This excludes most TAs with urgent transitions, as totally supporting this feature is beyond the scope of this work. Axiom XI, newly introduced in this paper, corresponds to Axiom VI for TTSB. It prohibits the values of external variables from being updated in the update function ρ for a δ?-transition, thus guaranteeing the associativity of parallel composition operation. Empirically, real-world models violating this axiom are uncommon. Overall, these axioms impose acceptable restrictions on TAs while ensuring their applicability to modeling the majority of timed systems.

4.1 Non-Compositional Semantics

Strictly following the UPPAAL help menu, we give the non-compositional LTS semantics of an NTA, in which all the TAs satisfy Axiom VII–XI. It can be viewed as a further formalization of the UPPAAL official semantics and is essential for the subsequent proof of semantics equivalence.

Definition 7 (LTS semantics of NTA). Let $\mathcal{N} = \langle \mathcal{A}_1, \ldots, \mathcal{A}_n \rangle$ be an NTA. Let $V = \bigcup_{i=1}^n (V_i \cup \mathsf{loc}_i)$, where loc_i is a fresh variable with type L_i. The LTS semantics of $\mathcal{N}$, denoted as $\mathsf{LTS}(\mathcal{N})$, is the LTS $\langle S, s^0, \to \rangle$, where

$$S = \{v \in Val(V) \mid \forall i : v \models I_i(v(\mathsf{loc}_i))\},$$
$$s^0 = v_1^0 \| \cdots \| v_n^0 \| \{\mathsf{loc}_1 \mapsto l_1^0, \ldots, \mathsf{loc}_n \mapsto l_n^0\},$$

and $\to$ is defined by the rules in Fig. 4.

Rule **TAU**, **SYNC**, and **TIME** respectively describe the internal transitions of each TA in the NTA, the binary synchronization between TAs, and the passage of time. We refer to [9] for the detailed description of these rules. Rule **BCST** describes broadcast synchronization among TAs. According to the UPPAAL help menu, when the NTA $\mathcal{N}$ is in a certain state s and a δ!-transition in a certain $\mathcal{A}_i$ is activated, all other TAs in $\mathcal{N}$ with executable δ?-transitions must select one to

$$\dfrac{l \xrightarrow{g,\tau,\rho}_i l' \quad s(\mathsf{loc}_i) = l \quad s' = \rho(s)[\{\mathsf{loc}_i \mapsto l'\}]}{s \xrightarrow{\tau} s'} \quad \text{TAU}$$

$$\dfrac{l_i \xrightarrow{g_i,c!,\rho_i}_i l'_i \quad l_j \xrightarrow{g_j,c?,\rho_j}_j l'_j \quad s' = \rho_j(\rho_i(s))[\{\mathsf{loc}_i \mapsto l'_i, \mathsf{loc}_j \mapsto l'_j\}]}{s \xrightarrow{\tau} s'} \quad \text{SYNC}$$

with side conditions: $s(\mathsf{loc}_i) = l_i$, $s(\mathsf{loc}_j) = l_j$, $s \models g_i$, $s \models g_j$, $(\forall q : s(\mathsf{loc}_q) \notin K_q) \vee l_i \in K_i \vee l_j \in K_j$, $i \neq j$.

$$\dfrac{s' = s \oplus d \quad \forall k : s(\mathsf{loc}_k) \notin K_k \quad \nexists(l \xrightarrow{g,\tau,\rho\ u}_i l') : s(\mathsf{loc}_i) = l \vee s \models g}{s \xrightarrow{d} s'} \quad \text{TIME}$$

$$\dfrac{l_i \xrightarrow{g_i,\delta!,\rho_i}_i l'_i \quad s(\mathsf{loc}_i) = l_i \quad s \models g_i \quad \cdots}{s \xrightarrow{\tau} s'} \quad \text{BCST}$$

with $\forall j \in RS(\delta, i, s) : l_j \xrightarrow{g_j, \delta?, \rho_j} l'_j, s(\mathsf{loc}_j) = l_j, s \models g_j$, $(\forall q : s(\mathsf{loc}_q) \notin K_q) \vee l_i \in K_i \vee (\exists j \in RS(\delta, i, s) : l_j \in K_j)$, $s' = \rho_{j_m}(\cdots \rho_{j_1}(\rho_i(s)))[\{\mathsf{loc}_i \mapsto l'_i, \mathsf{loc}_{j_1} \mapsto l'_{j_1}, \ldots, \mathsf{loc}_{j_m} \mapsto l'_{j_m}\}]$.

Fig. 4. LTS semantics of an NTA in UPPAAL

synchronize with it. This is described in the first two lines of rule **BCST**, where the set $RS(\delta, i, s)$, defined as the set of indices of all the TAs with executable δ?-transitions[1], is $\{j \mid i \neq j, s(\mathsf{loc}_j) = l_j, \exists(l_j \xrightarrow{g_j, \delta?, \rho_j} l'_j) : s \models g_j\}$. Considering that in the current state s, some TAs can be in committed locations, the third line is imposed to clarify that the broadcast synchronization can only occur under two conditions: 1) no TA is in a committed location, 2) at least one of the TAs participating in the synchronization is in a committed location. In the last line, $\rho_i(s)$ is defined as $v[\rho_i(v\lceil V_i)]$, meaning that if an update function $\rho_i : Val(V_i) \to Val(V_i)$ is applied to state s, it only modifies the variables in V_i. This line provides the update rule: ρ_i in the δ!-transition is executed first, then $\rho_{j_1}, \ldots, \rho_{j_m}$ in the δ?-transitions, where $j_1, \ldots, j_m$ are the indices in $RS(\delta, i, s)$. Notably, due to Axiom XI, arbitrary execution of $\rho_{j_1}, \ldots, \rho_{j_m}$ will result in the same target state s', i.e., the result is deterministic.

4.2 Compositional Semantics

To derive the compositional semantics of an NTA, we first obtain the TTSB semantics for each TA in the NTA, then compose them into a single TTSB, apply restrictions, and finally extract the underlying LTS.

---

[1] For the guard g_j in the input broadcast transition $l_j \xrightarrow{g_j, \delta?, \rho_j} l'_j$, although the current UPPAAL help menu states that it can not have clock constraints, the UPPAAL change log states that it can have clock constraints since version 4.1.3, and our framework also supports clock constraints in broadcast transitions.

Definition 8 (TTSB Semantics of TA). Let $\mathcal{A} = \langle L, K, l^0, E, H, v^0, I, \rightarrow \rangle$ be a TA. The TTSB associated to $\mathcal{A}$, denoted as $\mathsf{TTSB}(\mathcal{A})$, is the tuple

$$\langle E, H \cup \{\mathsf{loc}\}, S, s^0, \rightarrow^1, \rightarrow^0 \rangle,$$

where loc is a fresh variable with type L. Let $W = E \cup H \cup \{\mathsf{loc}\}$, $S = \{v \in Val(W) \mid v \in I(v(\mathsf{loc}))\}$, $s^0 = v^0 \| \{\mathsf{loc} \mapsto l^0\}$. The transitions are defined by the rules in Fig. 5.

$$\frac{l \xrightarrow{g,a,\rho} l' \quad s(\mathsf{loc}) = l \quad s \models g \quad s' = \rho(s)[\{\mathsf{loc} \mapsto l'\}] \quad b \Leftrightarrow (l \in K)}{s \xrightarrow{a,b} s'} \; \textbf{ACT}$$

$$\frac{s' = s \oplus d \quad s(\mathsf{loc}) \notin K \quad \nexists (l \xrightarrow{g,\tau,\rho}{}^u l') : s(\mathsf{loc}) = l \wedge s \models g}{s \xrightarrow{d,0} s'} \; \textbf{TIME}$$

$$\frac{s(\mathsf{loc}) = l \quad \exists \delta \forall l \xrightarrow{g,\delta?,\rho} l' : s \not\models g}{s \xrightarrow{\delta?,0} s} \; \textbf{VIRT}$$

Fig. 5. TTSB semantics of a TA

Rule **ACT** describes state transitions in $\mathcal{A}$ caused by broadcast, binary, and internal actions, where the action $a \in \mathcal{E}_\Delta \cup \mathcal{E}_\mathcal{C} \cup \{\tau\}$. Rule **TIME** describes delay transitions, where $d \in \mathbb{R}_{\geq 0}$. Given a broadcast channel δ, if state s (with $s(\mathsf{loc}) = l$) does not have outgoing δ?-transition, then Rule **VIRT** will generate an additional self-loop δ?-transition for s, which ensures the satisfaction of Axiom V discussed in Sect. 3.1. In what follows, Theorem 2, stating the equivalence between the compositional and the non-compositional semantics, implies that the additional transitions will not affect the correctness of final NTA semantics. Note that the generated self-loop δ?-transition must be non-committed, even when l is a committed location. This is consistent with the definition of $Comm(s)$ that allows for non-committed outgoing transitions from s, further avoids the committedness change of the transitions generated by the subsequent parallel composition. Without this requirement, the additional self-loop δ?-transition is designed to be committed. If there is an uncommitted transition labeled with δ! or δ? in another component, then the composed transition will be incorrectly turned into a committed one. We can prove that the structure obtained from $\mathcal{A}$ by this definition is indeed a TTSB, and Appendix C of [15] shows the details.

Lemma 3. $\mathsf{TTSB}(\mathcal{A})$ is a TTSB.

Based on the TTSB semantics of TA, the LTS semantics of a given NTA $\mathcal{N} = \langle \mathcal{A}_1, \ldots, \mathcal{A}_n \rangle$, can be represented by the following expression:

$$\mathsf{LTS}((\mathsf{TTSB}(\mathcal{A}_1) \| \cdots \| \mathsf{TTSB}(\mathcal{A}_n) \setminus (\Delta \cup \mathcal{C}))$$

The following theorem, which is proven in Appendix D of [15] in detail, states that the compositional semantics of NTAs with broadcast channels, defined in terms of TTSBs, is equivalent (modulo isomorphism) to the non-compositional semantics defined Definition 7. This implies that our design of the compositional semantics of NTAs with broadcast channels is correct.

Theorem 2. *Let $\mathcal{N} = \langle \mathcal{A}_1, \ldots, \mathcal{A}_n \rangle$ be an NTA. Then*

$$\mathsf{LTS}(\mathcal{N}) \cong \mathsf{LTS}((\mathsf{TTSB}(\mathcal{A}_1) \| \cdots \| \mathsf{TTSB}(\mathcal{A}_n)) \backslash (\Delta \cup \mathcal{C})).$$

5 Compositional Abstraction

This section introduces the timed step simulation for TTSBs. It demonstrates the compositionality of the induced preorder, providing formal support for the compositional abstraction of timed systems with broadcast synchronization.

Definition 9 (Timed step simulation for TTSBs). *Two TTSBs $\mathcal{T}_1$ and $\mathcal{T}_2$ are comparable if $E_1 = E_2$. Given comparable TTSBs $\mathcal{T}_1$ and $\mathcal{T}_2$, we say that a relation $R \subseteq S_1 \times S_2$ is a timed step simulation from $\mathcal{T}_1$ to $\mathcal{T}_2$, provided that $s_1^0 \ R \ s_2^0$ and if $r \ R \ s$, then*

1. *$r \lceil E_1 = s \lceil E_2$,*
2. *$\forall u \in Val(E_1) : r[u] \ R \ s[u]$,*
3. *if $Comm(s)$ then $Comm(r)$,*
4. *if $r \xrightarrow{a,b} r'$ then either there exists an s' such that $s \xrightarrow{a,b} s'$ and $r' \ R \ s'$, or $a = \tau$ and $r' \ R \ s$.*

We denote $\mathcal{T}_1 \preceq \mathcal{T}_2$ when there exists a timed step simulation from $\mathcal{T}_1$ to $\mathcal{T}_2$. If $\mathcal{T}_1 \preceq \mathcal{T}_2$, then $\mathcal{T}_2$ can either simulate the transitions of $\mathcal{T}_1$ or remain idle if the transition is internal. However, $\mathcal{T}_2$ is not allowed to introduce internal transitions absent in $\mathcal{T}_1$. Thus, the partial order $\preceq$ defined by timed step simulation characterizes a behavioral relation between timed systems. It requires $\mathcal{T}_2$ to preserve all external behavior of $\mathcal{T}_1$, while allowing it to abstract away some internal behavior. This property is essential for constructing compositional abstractions, as discussed in Sect. 6.

Based on the definition, it is straightforward to establish that $\preceq$ is reflexive and transitive. Furthermore, we demonstrate that $\preceq$ is a precongruence for parallel composition, which is another main theorem in this paper. The corresponding proof is in Appendix E of [15].

Theorem 3. *Let $\mathcal{T}_1, \mathcal{T}_2, \mathcal{T}_3$ be TTSBs with $\mathcal{T}_1$ and $\mathcal{T}_2$ comparable, $\mathcal{T}_1 \preceq \mathcal{T}_2$, and both $\mathcal{T}_1$ and $\mathcal{T}_2$ compatible with $\mathcal{T}_3$. Then $\mathcal{T}_1 \| \mathcal{T}_3 \preceq \mathcal{T}_2 \| \mathcal{T}_3$.*

The timed step simulation preorder $\preceq$ is typically not a precongruence for restriction because a committed state will be turned into an uncommitted one if all its outgoing committed transitions are removed during the restriction process, which may violate the third condition of the timed step simulation. To address this, we provide the following theorem to guarantee that the timed step simulation preorder is a precongruence for restriction. The corresponding proof is provided in Appendix F of [15].

Theorem 4. *Let $\mathcal{T}_1$ and $\mathcal{T}_2$ be comparable TTSBs such that $\mathcal{T}_1 \preceq \mathcal{T}_2$. Let $C \subseteq \Delta \cup \mathcal{C} \cup E_1$. If for any committed state r of $\mathcal{T}_1$, there exists $a \in Act - \{\delta?, c!, c? \mid \delta \in C \cap \Delta, c \in C \cap \mathcal{C}\}$ such that $r \xrightarrow{a,1} {}_1$, then $\mathcal{T}_1 \backslash C \preceq \mathcal{T}_2 \backslash C$.*

Intuitively, the side condition of Theorem 4 ensures that a committed state in $\mathcal{T}_1$ is still committed in $\mathcal{T}_1 \backslash C$. This condition is not problematic in practice, as a well-defined timed system model should ensure that from any committed state, there is always an executable transition, which could be labeled with an input broadcast action $\delta!$ or internal action τ, thereby satisfying the side condition.

6 Compositional Verification

This section shows how our theorems help reduce the state space in verifying timed systems with broadcast synchronization. To the best of our knowledge, UPPAAL is the only existing model checker for timed automata that supports non-blocking broadcast; however, there is currently no dedicated benchmark for evaluating such features. In our experiments, we apply the framework to two case studies: a producer-consumer system and the clock synchronization protocol from [28] and compare the time cost with that of UPPAAL. All the experiments[2] in this paper were conducted using the UPPAAL 5.0 tool on a 4.0 GHz AMD Ryzen 5 2600X processor with 32 GB of RAM, running 64-bit Windows 10, with a timeout of 3,600 s.

6.1 Verification Framework for Safety Properties

This paper focuses on verifying safety properties, which asserts that "something bad never happens".

Definition 10 (Safety Properties of NTA). *Let $\mathcal{N} = \langle \mathcal{A}_1, \ldots, \mathcal{A}_n \rangle$ be an NTA, and P be a property over a subset of $V = \bigcup_{i=1}^{n}(V_i \cup \text{loc}_i)$. We say that P is a safety property of $\mathcal{N}$, notation $\mathcal{N} \models \forall \Box P$, iff for all reachable states s of $\text{LTS}(\mathcal{N})$, $s \models P$.*

The following theorem states that, given a timed system and a property, we can replace some system components with their corresponding abstractions to obtain an abstract version of the original system. If the property is proven to be a safety property of the abstraction, it must also be a safety property of the original system. Naturally, the property should not depend on the internal variables or locations of the components to be abstracted, as they may be merged or even deleted during the abstraction process.

---

[2] All the UPPAAL models and raw experiment data for this paper are available at https://github.com/zeno-98/CAV-2025-333.

Theorem 5. *Let $\mathcal{N} = \langle \mathcal{A}_1, \ldots, \mathcal{A}_i, \mathcal{A}_{i+1}, \ldots, \mathcal{A}_n \rangle$ and $\mathcal{N}' = \langle \mathcal{B}_1, \ldots, \mathcal{B}_j, \mathcal{A}_{i+1}, \ldots, \mathcal{A}_n \rangle$ be two NTAs and P be a property over $\hat{V} = \bigcup_{k=i+1}^{n}(V_k \cup \mathsf{loc}_k)$. Let $\hat{E} = \bigcup_{k=1}^{i} E_k - \hat{V}$, $\mathcal{T}_a = (\mathsf{TTSB}(\mathcal{A}_1)\|\ldots\|\mathsf{TTSB}(\mathcal{A}_i))\backslash(\Delta \cup \mathcal{C} \cup \hat{E} - \Sigma(\mathcal{T}_c))$, $\mathcal{T}_b = (\mathsf{TTSB}(\mathcal{B}_1)\|\ldots\|\mathsf{TTSB}(\mathcal{B}_j))\backslash(\Delta \cup \mathcal{C} \cup \hat{E} - \Sigma(\mathcal{T}_c))$, and $\mathcal{T}_c = \mathsf{TTSB}(\mathcal{A}_{i+1})\|\ldots\|\mathsf{TTSB}(\mathcal{A}_n)$. If P is a safety property of $\mathcal{N}'$, $\mathcal{T}_a$ and $\mathcal{T}_b$ are comparable with $\mathcal{T}_a \preceq \mathcal{T}_b$, and $\mathcal{T}_a\|\mathcal{T}_c$ satisfies the side condition of Theorem 4 with $C = \Delta \cup \mathcal{C}$, then P is also a safety property of $\mathcal{N}_1$.*

The proof of Theorem 5 is in Appendix G of [15]. By this theorem, we can check property P is a safety property of NTA $\mathcal{N} = \langle \mathcal{A}_1, \ldots, \mathcal{A}_n \rangle$ in a compositional way using the following steps:

1. Partition $\mathcal{N}$ appropriately into two parts $\mathcal{A}_1, \ldots, \mathcal{A}_i$ and $\mathcal{A}_{i+1}, \ldots, \mathcal{A}_n$, such that P does not depend on the internal variables and locations of $\mathcal{A}_1, \ldots, \mathcal{A}_i$.
2. Construct suitable TAs $\mathcal{B}_1, \ldots, \mathcal{B}_j$, such that $(\mathsf{TTSB}(\mathcal{A}_1)\|\ldots\|\mathsf{TTSB}(\mathcal{A}_i))\backslash C \preceq (\mathsf{TTSB}(\mathcal{B}_1)\|\ldots\|\mathsf{TTSB}(\mathcal{B}_j))\backslash C$, where C is the set of broadcast channels, binary channels and external variables unused in $\mathcal{A}_{i+1}, \ldots, \mathcal{A}_n$.
3. Use model-checking tool UPPAAL to verify if $\mathcal{N}' \models \forall \Box P$, where $\mathcal{N}' = \langle \mathcal{B}_1, \ldots, \mathcal{B}_j, \mathcal{A}_{i+1}, \ldots, \mathcal{A}_n \rangle$. If it does, then by Theorem 5, P is a safety property of $\mathcal{N}$. Otherwise, return to step 1 or 2 to try alternative partitioning methods or construct another suitable group of abstract automata.

6.2 Case Study I: Producer-Consumer System

We first apply our framework to a producer-consumer system, which includes one producer, N consumers, and a coordinator. The producer generates data packets at fixed time intervals and stores the packets in a buffer for consumers to consume later. Each consumer obtains an exclusive right to consume a data packet. Once obtained, the consumer will either consume a packet and release the right or defer the consumption. The coordinator ensures that once a consumer obtains the right, it should consume a packet within a required interval. These components communicate via broadcast channels, binary channels, and a shared variable. In addition, the system model also has several committed locations. Because of the limited buffer size of the producer, given a certain valuation of parameter N, we expect there will be no overflow during system operation.

Since the target property is directly associated with the producer model, we manually construct the abstraction $\mathcal{A}$ for the coordinator and all consumers, with the producer excluded. Additionally, as the satisfaction of the safety property depends on whether the consumers can consume data packets in time, this abstraction must capture all possible time intervals between two consecutive data packet consumptions while omitting other operational details. It should be noted that $\mathcal{A}$ is independent of the parameter N, implying that it can simulate the coordinator and any number of consumers. Due to the page limit, the NTA model, the abstracted model, and the corresponding proof are given in Appendix H of [15].

We apply both the traditional monolithic verification (MV), which directly uses the UPPAAL tool to checks the property of the original model and the compositional verification (CV) described in Sect. 6.1. The experimental results confirm that no overflow occurs, and Table 1 presents the average verification time in seconds over five runs for different values of N with MV and CV.

Table 1. Verification time of no overflow

N	9	10	11	12	13	14	15
MV	3.769	11.778	36.767	109.843	412.710	1656.301	timeout
CV	0.005	0.005	0.005	0.005	0.005	0.005	0.005

The MV row shows that the verification time required by the traditional monolithic method grows exponentially as n increases and exceeds $3,600$ seconds when N = 15. The CV row presents the verification time by our compositional verification method, which implies that CV outperforms MV significantly. Since the abstraction we built simulates the compositional behavior of the coordinator and all the consumers for any N $\geq$ 1, we obtain the verification results for the system with an arbitrary number of consumers in 5 ms.

6.3 Case Study II: Clock Synchronization Protocol

Secondly, we consider the clock synchronization protocol presented in [28] as a case study. This protocol, developed by the Dutch company Chess, addresses a key challenge in designing *wireless sensor networks*: the potential drift of hardware clocks across sensor nodes. It aims to ensure that, under a given parameter setting, the hardware clocks of all nodes remain synchronized throughout network operation, thereby enabling reliable communication.

The NTA model of this protocol consists of N nodes, named $0, \ldots, N-1$. In turn, these nodes broadcast messages to the others in a fixed order to perform clock synchronization, with a time interval between each pair of successive transmissions. Each node internally contains three TAs: **Clock**, **WSN**, and **Synchronizer**, which communicate with each other through broadcast channels and shared variables. Automaton **Clock** models the node's hardware clock, which may drift, automaton **WSN** takes care of broadcasting messages, and automaton **Synchronizer** resynchronizes the hardware clock upon receipt of a message. As can be seen, in the designed model, two types of broadcast synchronization should exist: the internal type in each node and the external type among the nodes. The NTA model is provided in Appendix I of [15].

Obviously, the safety property can be formulated as the requirement that the hardware clocks of any two nodes in the network remain synchronized throughout network operation. Therefore, for property checking via CV, we can select two nodes a and b from the N nodes (where $0 \leq a < b \leq N-1$), and manually abstract the remaining $N-2$ nodes into a single timed automaton $\mathcal{A}$, provided in Appendix I of [15]. This abstraction over-approximates the clock drift of the $N-2$ nodes and maintains the timing constraints for message broadcasting while omitting other behavioral details. Clearly, if for all the choices of a and b, their hardware clock remains synchronized, we can conclude that the original system satisfies the target property. Note that the system is not strictly symmetric, as nodes broadcast messages periodically in a fixed order, and different choices of a and b result in different time intervals between their broadcast actions. Therefore, we must enumerate all possible pairs of a and b, and the total verification time of our compositional method is the sum of the checking times for all these cases. For instance, when $N = 6$, we need to verify $C_6^2 = \frac{(6\times 5)}{2} = 15$ different cases.

The experimental results show that the target property is satisfied, and Table 2 presents the average verification time in seconds over five runs for different values of N with MV and CV.

Table 2. Verification time of hardware clocks synchronization

N	3	4	5	6	7
MV	0.070	2.256	185.641	timeout	timeout
CV	0.303	0.936	2.230	4.309	7.629

The MV row shows that the verification time required by the traditional monolithic method grows significantly as N increases. The CV row demonstrates the total verification time required by our compositional verification method for each N. Although in the case of $N = 3$, our method takes a slightly longer time since $\mathcal{A}$ has more behavior than a single node, it demonstrates significant efficiency advantages when $N \geq 5$.

7 Conclusion

This paper proposes the first compositional abstraction framework for timed systems with broadcast synchronization, providing a method to reduce state space in model checking. Specifically, this framework focuses on timed systems modeled as NTAs in UPPAAL, and also supports binary synchronization, shared variables, and committed locations. For this purpose, we first define TTSB, which extends LTSs with state variables, transition commitments, and time-related behavior, along with corresponding parallel composition and restriction operations. We prove that the parallel composition operator is both commutative and associative. Secondly, we provide compositional and non-compositional semantics for NTAs with broadcast synchronization in UPPAAL and prove their equivalence. Thirdly, we define the timed step simulation relation for TTSBs and prove it is a precongruence for parallel composition. Finally, we demonstrate that safety properties verified on abstractions are preserved in the original models and validate the efficiency of our framework through two case studies. Future work includes extending the framework to support other UPPAAL features, such as urgent channels and general priorities. We also plan to integrate abstraction refinement methods [18] to develop an automated compositional verification workflow similar to those in [14,20]. This would enable the application of our compositional abstraction framework to a broader range of real-world cases, such as the timing-based broadcast algorithms discussed in [33].

Acknowledgements. This work was supported by the National Natural Science Foundation of China (No. 62472316), Shanghai 2023 "Science and Technology Innovation Action Plan": Special Project for Key Technical Breakthrough of Blockchain (No. 23511100800) and the National Natural Science Foundation of China (No. 62032019).

References

1. de Alfaro, L., da Silva, L.D., Faella, M., Legay, A., Roy, P., Sorea, M.: Sociable interfaces. In: Frontiers of Combining Systems, pp. 81–105. Springer, Heidelberg (2005)
2. Alur, R.: Timed automata. In: Proceeding of the 11th International Conference on Computer Aided Verification, pp. 8–22. Springer (1999)
3. Alur, R., Dill, D.L.: A theory of timed automata. Theoret. Comput. Sci. **126**(2), 183–235 (1994)
4. Baier, C., Katoen, J.P.: Principles of Model Checking. MIT Press (2008)
5. van Beek, D.A., Reniers, M.A., Schiffelers, R.R.H., Rooda, J.E.: Foundations of a compositional interchange format for hybrid systems. In: Hybrid Systems: Computation and Control, pp. 587–600. Springer, Heidelberg (2007)
6. Behrmann, G., David, A., Larsen, K.G.: A Tutorial on UPPAAL. In: Bernardo, M., Corradini, F. (eds.) SFM-RT 2004. LNCS, vol. 3185, pp. 200–236. Springer, Heidelberg (2004). https://doi.org/10.1007/978-3-540-30080-9_7
7. Berendsen, J., Gebremichael, B., Vaandrager, F.W., Zhang, M.: Formal specification and analysis of zeroconf using uppaalS **10**(3) (2011)
8. Berendsen, J., Jansen, D.N., Schmaltz, J., Vaandrager, F.W.: The axiomatization of override and update. J. Appl. Log. **8**(1), 141–150 (2010)
9. Berendsen, J., Vaandrager, F.: Compositional abstraction in real-time model checking. In: Formal Modeling and Analysis of Timed Systems, pp. 233–249. Springer, Heidelberg (2008)
10. Berendsen, J., Vaandrager, F.: Parallel composition in a paper of Jensen, Larsen and Skou is not associative. Technical report, technical note (2007)
11. Bhat, G., Cleaveland, R., Lüttgen, G.: Dynamic priorities for modeling real-time, pp. 321–336. Springer (1997)
12. Brockway, M.J.: A Compositional Analysis of Broadcasting Embedded Systems. Ph.D. thesis (2010)
13. Cao, Y., Duan, Z., Wang, Y.: Uninterrupted automatic broadcasting based on timed automata. In: 2015 3rd International Conference on Applied Computing and Information Technology/2nd International Conference on Computational Science and Intelligence, pp. 489–494 (2015)
14. Chen, H., Su, Y., Zhang, M., Liu, Z., Mi, J.: Learning assumptions for compositional verification of timed automata. In: Proceeding of the 35th International Conference on Computer Aided Verification, pp. 40–61. Springer, Cham (2023)

15. Chen, H., Zhang, M., Vaandrager, F.: Compositional abstraction for timed systems with broadcast synchronization (2025). https://arxiv.org/abs/2505.12436
16. Clarke, E.M., Grumberg, O., Peled, D.: Model checking. Springer, Heidelberg (1997)
17. Clarke, E.M., Emerson, E.A.: Design and synthesis of synchronization skeletons using branching time temporal logic. In: Workshop on Logic of Programs, pp. 52–71. Springer (1981)
18. Clarke, E.M., Grumberg, O., Long, D.E.: Model checking and abstraction. In: ACM-SIGACT Symposium on Principles of Programming Languages (1992)
19. Delzanno, G., Podelski, A., Esparza, J.: Constraint-based analysis of broadcast protocols. In: Computer Science Logic, pp. 50–66. Springer, Heidelberg (1999)
20. Dierks, H., Kupferschmid, S., Larsen, K.G.: Automatic abstraction refinement for timed automata. In: Formal Modeling and Analysis of Timed Systems, pp. 114–129. Springer, Heidelberg (2007)
21. Ejersbo Jensen, H., Guldstrand Larsen, K., Skou, A.: Scaling up uppaal. In: Formal Techniques in Real-Time and Fault-Tolerant Systems, pp. 19–30. Springer, Heidelberg (2000)
22. Esparza, J., Finkel, A., Mayr, R.: On the verification of broadcast protocols. In: Proceedings of the 14th Symposium on Logic in Computer Science (Cat. No. PR00158), pp. 352–359 (1999)
23. Fehnker, A., van Glabbeek, R., Höfner, P., McIver, A., Portmann, M., Tan, W.L.: Automated analysis of AODV using UPPAAL. In: Tools and Algorithms for the Construction and Analysis of Systems, pp. 173–187. Springer, Heidelberg (2012)
24. Fei, Y., Zhu, H., Li, X.: Modeling and verification of NLSR protocol using UPPAAL. In: 2018 International Symposium on Theoretical Aspects of Software Engineering, pp. 108–115 (2018)
25. Fisman, D., Izsak, N., Jacobs, S.: Learning broadcast protocols. In: Proceedings of the AAAI Conference on Artificial Intelligence, vol. 38, no. 11, pp. 12016–12023 (2024)
26. Goorden, M.A., Larsen, K.G., Legay, A., Lorber, F., Nyman, U., Wasowski, A.: Timed I/O automata: it is never too late to complete your timed specification theory. CoRR **abs/2302.04529** (2023). https://doi.org/10.48550/arXiv.2302.04529
27. Hanssen, F., Mader, A., Jansen, P.: Verifying the distributed real-time network protocol RTnet using Uppaal. In: 14th IEEE International Symposium on Modeling, Analysis, and Simulation, pp. 239–246 (2006)
28. Heidarian, F., Schmaltz, J., Vaandrager, F.: Analysis of a clock synchronization protocol for wireless sensor networks. Theoret. Comput. Sci. **413**(1), 87–105 (2012)
29. Henderson, W.D., Tron, S.: Verification of the minimum cost forwarding protocol for wireless sensor networks. In: 2006 IEEE Conference on Emerging Technologies and Factory Automation, pp. 194–201 (2006)
30. Lamport, L.: The temporal logic of actions. ACM Trans. Program. Lang. Syst. **16**, 872–923 (1994)
31. Larsen, K.G., Schilling, C., Srba, J.: Simulation Relations and Applications in Formal Methods, pp. 272–291. Springer, Cham (2022)
32. Lynch, N., Segala, R., Vaandrager, F.: Hybrid I/O automata. Inf. Comput. **185**(1), 105–157 (2003)
33. Lynch, N.A.: Distributed Algorithms. Morgan Kaufmann Publishers Inc., San Francisco (1996)
34. Lynch, N.A., Tuttle, M.R.: An introduction to input/output automata. CWI Q. **2**, 219–246 (1989)

35. Merz, S.: Model checking: a tutorial overview. In: Modeling and Verification of Parallel Processes, vol. 2067, pp. 3–38. Springer (2000)
36. Milner, R.: Communication and Concurrency. Prentice-Hall, Inc (1989)
37. Milner, R.: An algebraic definition of simulation between programs. In: Proceedings of the 2nd International Joint Conference on Artificial Intelligence, IJCAI 1971, pp. 481–489. Morgan Kaufmann Publishers Inc. (1971)
38. Milner, R., Parrow, J., Walker, D.: A calculus of mobile processes. I. Inf. Comput. **100**(1), 1–40 (1992)
39. Queille, J.P., Sifakis, J.: Specification and verification of concurrent systems in CESAR. In: Dezani-Ciancaglini, M., Montanari, U. (eds.) Programming 1982. LNCS, vol. 137, pp. 337–351. Springer, Heidelberg (1982). https://doi.org/10.1007/3-540-11494-7_22
40. Szpak, R., de Queiroz, M.H., Ribeiro Cury, J.E.: Synthesis and implementation of supervisory control for manufacturing systems under processing uncertainties and time constraints. IFAC-PapersOnLine **53**(4), 229–234 (2020)

Open Access This chapter is licensed under the terms of the Creative Commons Attribution 4.0 International License (http://creativecommons.org/licenses/by/4.0/), which permits use, sharing, adaptation, distribution and reproduction in any medium or format, as long as you give appropriate credit to the original author(s) and the source, provide a link to the Creative Commons license and indicate if changes were made.

The images or other third party material in this chapter are included in the chapter's Creative Commons license, unless indicated otherwise in a credit line to the material. If material is not included in the chapter's Creative Commons license and your intended use is not permitted by statutory regulation or exceeds the permitted use, you will need to obtain permission directly from the copyright holder.

The rIC3 Hardware Model Checker

Yuheng Su[1,2], Qiusong Yang[1,3(✉)], Yiwei Ci[1], Tianjun Bu[1,2], and Ziyu Huang[4]

[1] Institute of Software, Chinese Academy of Sciences, Beijing, China
gipsyh.icu@gmail.com, yiwei@iscas.ac.cn, butianjun24@mails.ucas.ac.cn
[2] University of Chinese Academy of Sciences, Beijing, China
[3] Advanced Computing and Intelligence Engineering, Wuxi, China
qiusong@iscas.ac.cn
[4] Beijing Forestry University, Beijing, China
fyy0007@bjfu.edu.cn

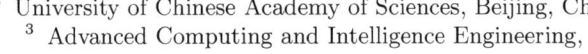

Abstract. In this paper, we present rIC3, an efficient bit-level hardware model checker primarily based on the IC3 algorithm. It boasts a highly efficient implementation and integrates several recently proposed optimizations, such as the specifically optimized SAT solver, dynamically adjustment of generalization strategies, and the use of predicates with internal signals, among others. As a first-time participant in the Hardware Model Checking Competition, rIC3 was independently evaluated as the best-performing tool, not only in the bit-level track but also in the word-level bit-vector track through bit-blasting. Our experiments further demonstrate significant advancements in both efficiency and scalability. rIC3 can also serve as a backend for verifying industrial RTL designs using SymbiYosys. Additionally, the source code of rIC3 is highly modular, with the IC3 algorithm module being particularly concise, making it an academic platform that is easy to modify and extend.

Keywords: Formal Verification · Model Checking · IC3/PDR

1 Introduction

Model checking [19,20] is a powerful formal verification technique widely used in modern system design. Given a transition system and a property that describes the desired system behavior, it can efficiently and automatically detect bugs (violations of the property) or prove that the property holds.

IC3 [14], also known as PDR [22], is a prominent SAT-based model checking algorithm widely used in hardware formal verification. It efficiently searches for inductive invariants without unrolling the model. IC3 is distinguished by its completeness in comparison to BMC [10], its scalability compared to IMC [33] and K-Induction [38]. Recognized as a state-of-the-art algorithm, IC3 serves as the primary engine for numerous efficient model checkers [16,17,25,32].

IC3 has been successfully applied to the verification of industrial designs [23]. However, it still faces significant challenges due to the state space explosion problem. Therefore, improving the IC3 algorithm and developing more efficient tools to enhance scalability for verifying larger-scale hardware models remains a critical research direction. IC3ref [4], the reference implementation of the IC3 algorithm developed by its inventor, serves as a baseline in many IC3-related studies [28,37,39,44] due to its efficiency and relatively simple codebase. However, it has not been updated in years, and its lack of recent advancements has led to a performance gap. ABC [16] provides a highly efficient implementation of the PDR algorithm. However, it is implemented in C and heavily relies on custom data structures, macros, and extensive use of raw pointers, which complicates modification and extension. Similarly, the IC3 implementation in nuXmv [17] delivers outstanding performance, but its source code is not open-sourced.

In this paper, we introduce rIC3, an bit-level model checker primarily based on the IC3 algorithm. It integrates several optimizations proposed recently. The SAT solver within the IC3 engine is deeply optimized by reducing the number of variables decided through Cone of Influence (COI) analysis [41]. Furthermore, a more efficient data structure in VSIDS has been implemented to further reduce the solving time for IC3 queries. The tool also leverages CTG [26] and EXCTG [40] to achieve better generalization. Moreover, it employs a heuristic method that dynamically adjusts generalization strategies [40] to balance the trade-off between generalization quality and computational overhead. Furthermore, the use of internal signals [21] enables the derivation of more compact invariants.

rIC3 was independently evaluated as the top-performing tool in both the bit-level track and the word-level bit-vector track (via bit-blasting) at the 2024 Hardware Model Checking Competition (HWMCC'24) [3]. Our experiments further highlight significant advancements in both efficiency and scalability. Additionally, rIC3 can be utilized as a backend for verifying industrial RTL designs with SymbiYosys. The source code of rIC3 is designed with high modularity, and its IC3 algorithm module is remarkably compact, comprising only around 1,700 lines of code. This makes rIC3 an excellent academic platform that is both easy to modify and extend.

2 Architecture

rIC3 is an efficient bit-level model checker primarily based on the IC3 algorithm, and it also incorporates a portfolio approach with the BMC and K-Induction algorithms. Figure 1 shows the architecture and verification flow of rIC3.

- Users provide the model to be verified and the desired properties to the rIC3 frontend, which then obtains the final result certificate from the checker. The certificate is either a proof that the model is safe or a concrete counterexample demonstrating that the model is unsafe.
- The frontends in rIC3 support two widely used formats: AIGER [13], which provides a bit-level representation of hardware, and Btor2 [35], which uses a word-level bit-vector representation. Since rIC3 operates at the bit level, Btor2 models are bit-blasted into AIGER models using btor2aiger [2].

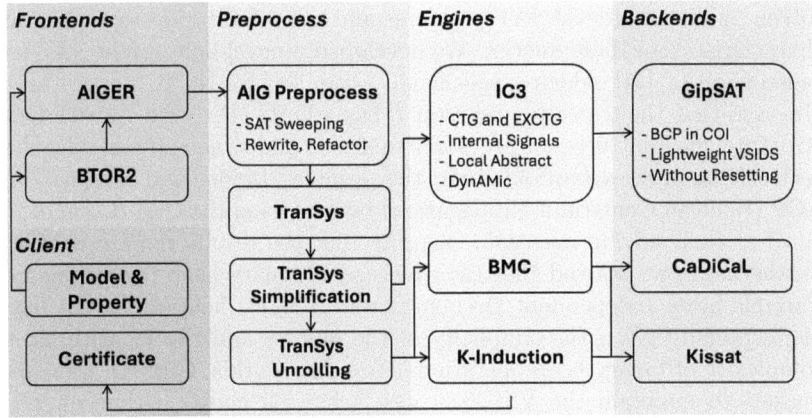

Fig. 1. rIC3 Architecture and Verification Flow

- The AIGER model is first preprocessed to obtain a more compact representation, which involves SAT sweeping [29], rewriting [36] and refactoring [34]. This step is performed using ABC [16]. Subsequently, the model is transformed into TranSys, an intermediate representation of the Transition System, primarily involving CNF encoding. The CNF of TranSys is then further simplified using a SAT solver. Depending on the engine in use, an additional unrolling step may be required.
- The engine in rIC3 integrates the IC3, BMC, and K-Induction algorithms, which can also operate in a portfolio mode. These engines formulate SAT problems and delegate them to backend SAT solvers, driving the model checking process based on the results returned. Once a final result is obtained, it is provided to the user along with the corresponding certificate.
- The backend supports various SAT solvers, including GipSAT, which excels at solving the relatively simpler SAT problems generated by IC3, as well as CaDiCaL [11] and Kissat [12], which are more suited for addressing the comparatively complex problems formulated by BMC and K-Induction.

3 Techniques

Since the BMC and K-Induction are relatively consistent across different model checkers, we focus on introducing the techniques used in the IC3 engine.

- **Specifically optimized SAT solver.** The SAT solver in IC3 primarily focuses on solving the relative induction query $F \wedge c \wedge T \wedge \neg c'$, where F represents the frame, c is a clause, and T denotes the transition relation. We observed that these queries are relatively simple and are typically solved within milliseconds, exhibiting unique characteristics. Current IC3 implementations mainly rely on modern general-purpose SAT solvers, which offer excellent scalability. However, these solvers may not always be efficient for solving millisecond-level SAT problems and often fail to leverage the unique characteristics of these queries. We developed a novel lightweight SAT solver called GipSAT [41], which is specifically optimized for the IC3 algorithm. We observed that the transition relation T has a DAG (Directed Acyclic Graph) structure, meaning it is not necessary to decide and assign all variables during each solving process. GipSAT limits the variables decided and assigned during BCP (Boolean Constraint Propagation) by analyzing the COI (Cone of Influence) at each solving iteration, ensuring that the results remain unaffected. Furthermore, we noticed that the overhead of binary heap operations in the Variable State Independent Decaying Sum (VSIDS) heuristic is not negligible, especially given the simplicity of the queries and the logarithmic time complexity of binary heap operations. To mitigate this, GipSAT uses several buckets to maintain the VSIDS scores, achieving constant-time operations and reducing overhead. Additionally, GipSAT supports temporary clauses, eliminating the need for resetting the SAT solver between queries.

- **Better generalization with CTG and extended CTG.** In IC3, the generalization process aims to expand a bad state to include additional unreachable states, thereby reducing the number of iterations. Standard generalization [15] achieves this by removing literals from a cube, effectively encompassing more unreachable states. CTG generalization [26] improves upon this approach by blocking counterexamples to generalization (CTG) when dropping literals fails to yield better generalization results. However, the results of CTG may sometimes still be suboptimal. This is because CTG only considers blocking the predecessors of the literal-dropped clause. If blocking these predecessors fails, it abandons further attempts to block the clause, even though the predecessors of the clause's predecessors might still be blockable. To address this limitation, we propose EXCTG [40], an extension of CTG. Similar to CTG, EXCTG attempts to block the predecessors when literal dropping fails. However, if blocking the predecessors also fails, EXCTG goes further by recursively attempting to block the predecessors of the predecessors, and so on. This iterative approach enables EXCTG to achieve improved generalization results.
- **Dynamic adjustment of generalization strategies.** While CTG and EXCTG offer better generalization results, they also incur higher computational costs. The generalization strategies: Standard, CTG, and EXCTG, produce progressively better results but also come with increased computational overhead. Finding an appropriate balance between generalization quality and computational overhead is challenging with a static strategy. To address this, we introduce DynAMic (Dynamic Adjustment of MIC Strategies) [40], which dynamically adjusts generalization strategies based on the difficulty of blocking bad states, as indicated by the number of failed attempts to block them. The more difficult a bad state is to block, the more effort is devoted to generalization. For states that are easy to block, it uses the lightweight standard strategy to reduce overhead. For more challenging states, it applies more effective generalization strategies, such as CTG or EXCTG, depending on the difficulty. This approach enhances scalability without sacrificing efficiency.

- **Predicate with internal signals.** IC3 incrementally learns inductive invariants that over-approximate the set of reachable states. These invariants are represented in CNF as predicates over state variables. However, IC3 struggles with designs that lack a concise CNF invariant over state variables. To address this limitation, IC3-INN [21] extends the traditional IC3 approach by learning invariants based not only on state variables but also on internal signals within the design. This enhancement enables the derivation of significantly more compact invariants while maintaining the efficiency of the CNF representation.
- **Localization abstraction with constraints.** Localization abstraction [43] is a method aimed at reducing the complexity of a verification instance by removing certain logic. Previous work [27] that utilized this method abstracts the transition relation by treating some registers as primary inputs and then refines the abstraction using counterexamples found by IC3. Similarly, rIC3 also takes this approach, but instead of the transition relation, it only focuses on constraints. Initially, it abstracts away all constraints to reduce the complexity. Then, it gradually adds back the constraints that cannot be ignored, based on the counterexamples.

4 Portfolio

Certain optimizations can significantly improve the solving efficiency of specific model-checking problems. However, achieving consistent performance improvements across all problems remains challenging, as some optimizations may even degrade performance for some other cases. For example, IC3-INN [21] excels at solving many previously intractable problems, especially SEC problems. However, its overall performance across the entire benchmark set decreases due to treating more variables as latches. Consequently, using a portfolio of configurations in parallel has emerged as a viable strategy to improve scalability. rIC3 includes a 16-thread parallel portfolio combining IC3, BMC, and K-Induction configurations, which is also the competition version. Specifically, it uses 11 threads for IC3 with different combinations of the techniques mentioned above, 4 threads for BMC with varying steps, and 1 thread for K-Induction.

5 Implementation

All algorithms in rIC3 are implemented in Rust, a modern programming language renowned for its emphasis on performance and security. We have open-sourced rIC3 at [7]. The implementation is designed to be concise while preserving the algorithm's efficiency, and the codebase is highly modular. Table 1 provides statistics on the number of lines of code for various modules in rIC3.

Table 1. Lines of Code (LOC) for Modules in rIC3

Modules	IC3	BMC	K-Induction	TranSys	GipSAT	AIG-rs	logic-form	Total
LOC	1686	115	244	739	2293	1654	1297	10571

AIG-rs, a self-maintained AIG library, supports AIGER parsing, AIG simulation, and related functionalities. The logic-form library offers data structures for representing basic propositional logic expressions, such as Literal and Cube. Other modules have been introduced earlier. Notably, the IC3 engine demonstrates excellent performance, with its implementation being remarkably simple—comprising only about 1700 lines of code. This simplicity makes it an academic research platform for experimentation and enhancement.

Furthermore, rIC3 is integrated as a backend for SymbiYosys (sby)[1], a frontend driver program for Yosys formal hardware verification flows. This integration enables rIC3 to serve as a backend for verifying industrial RTL designs.

6 Related Work

IC3 was originally introduced as a SAT-based bit-level model checking algorithm. Since its inception, numerous tools have been developed based on this foundational approach. **IC3ref** [4], created by the algorithm's inventor, stands out for its efficiency and relatively simple implementation, making it a baseline for many IC3-related studies [28,37,39,44]. The **ABC** framework [16] includes an implementation of the PDR algorithm [22], while the **nuXmv** model checker [17] also integrates IC3. Additionally, **SimpleCAR** [30] implements the CAR algorithm [31], which excels at bug detection, and **Avy** [42] combines sequence interpolants with IC3.

The IC3 algorithm has also been extended to address word-level problems by leveraging SMT solvers. **AVR** [25] implements IC3sa [24], combining IC3 with syntax-guided abstraction to enable scalable word-level model checking. Furthermore, **Pono** [32] supports both IC3sa and IC3ia [18], which extends IC3 to modulo theories through implicit predicate abstraction.

The Hardware Model Checking Competition (HWMCC) [3] has been instrumental in driving advancements in hardware model checkers. Submissions to the competition are typically executed in a 16-thread portfolio mode, prompting many model checkers to develop portfolio versions that integrate various configurations of IC3, BMC, and K-Induction engines. Examples include **Superprove** [9] for ABC, **SuperCAR** [8] for SimpleCAR, and **Pavy** [6] for Avy. AVR and Pono also have their own portfolio versions.

rIC3, like these tools, is used for hardware model checking. It incorporates several optimization techniques proposed in recent years to achieve better scalability, delivering superior performance compared to existing tools. It can also

---
[1] https://github.com/YosysHQ/sby/pull/313

be used to verify industrial models through SymbiYosys. Moreover, it is implemented in the modern programming language Rust, featuring a modular and concise codebase, making it an excellent platform for academic research as well.

7 Evaluation

7.1 Setup

We evaluated the following tools, all of which are the latest versions or the HWMCC'24 submission versions. The specific versions and configurations are detailed in our artifact [1].

- **rIC3** [7]: rIC3-ic3 is a single-thread IC3 engine that utilizes the DynAMic heuristic method and the specifically optimized SAT solver. Internal signals and localization abstraction are excluded, as they do not enhance overall performance. rIC3-portfolio is the portfolio version of rIC3.
- **IC3ref** [4]: A single-thread IC3 engine with CTG generalization.
- **ABC** [16]: ABC-superprove [9] is the portfolio engine of ABC. ABC-pdr is the PDR engine using the configuration from ABC-superprove, which includes CTG and localization abstraction.
- **nuXmv** [17]: We evaluated the IC3 engine in nuXmv, enhanced by a recently proposed heuristic optimization [44], available at [5]. We refer to this as nuXmv-cav23.
- **AVR** [25]: AVR-ic3sa is the IC3sa engine using the default configuration, and AVR-portfolio is the portfolio engine of AVR.
- **Pono** [32]: Pono-portfolio is the portfolio engine submitted in HWMCC'24. Pono-ic3ia and Pono-ic3sa are engines implementing IC3ia and IC3sa, respectively, using the same configurations as in the HWMCC'24 submission.
- **Avy** [42]: Avy is the IC3 engine integrated with interpolants, while Pavy [6] is the portfolio engine that combines Avy, PDR, and BMC.

For the evaluation of single-thread engines, we utilized the complete benchmark suites from the bit-level track (AIGER format) and the word-level bit-vector track (Btor2 format) of the three most recent Hardware Model Checking Competitions (HWMCC'19, HWMCC'20, and HWMCC'24) [3]. The bit-level benchmarks were derived by bit-blasting the word-level bit-vector benchmarks. After removing duplicates, the combined suite comprised 840 unique cases, each available in both AIGER and Btor2 formats. For portfolio engines, due to limited computational resources, we restricted our evaluation to the HWMCC'24 benchmark, which included 319 cases.

All single-thread configurations were tested under consistent resource constraints: 32 GB of RAM and a 3600-second time limit. For the portfolio engine, we followed the HWMCC resource limits, which provided 16 cores, 128 GB of RAM, and the same 3600-s time limit. The experiments were conducted on an AMD EPYC 7532 processor (2.4 GHz) running Ubuntu 24.10. To ensure reproducibility, we have made the source code and binary releases of all evaluated

Table 2. Number of solved, timed-out, and memory-out cases, PAR-2 score, number of uniquely solved cases, and fastest solved cases for various IC3 engines. The upper part shows the bit-level engines, and the lower part shows the word-level engines.

Tools	Solved(840)	TO	MO	PAR-2	Unique	Best
rIC3-ic3	606	225	9	2147.70	61	398
nuXmv-cav23	533	302	5	2777.30	8	41
ABC-pdr	516	320	4	2900.99	1	80
Avy	488	350	2	3142.87	29	38
IC3ref	486	353	1	3169.29	1	59
AVR-ic3sa	353	481	6	4305.24	22	53
Pono-ic3ia	311	518	11	4652.29	1	7
Pono-ic3sa	212	614	14	5459.96	0	5

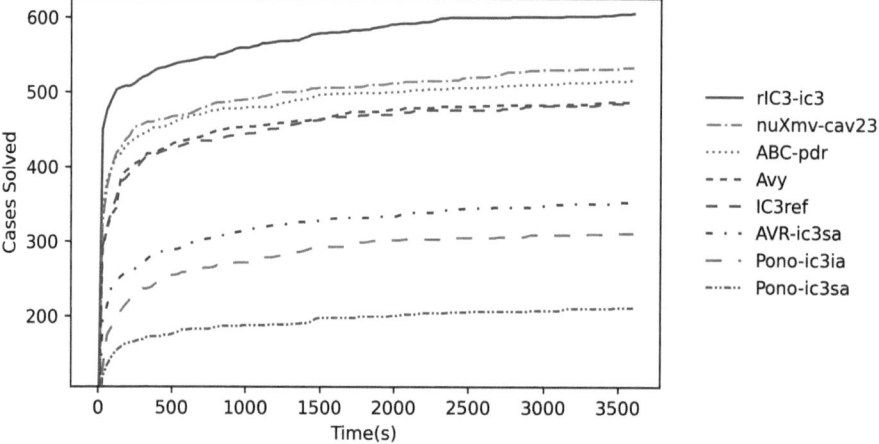

Fig. 2. The number of cases solved over time by various single-thread IC3 engines.

tools available, along with detailed experimental results in [1]. Additionally, to enhance confidence in the correctness of the results, all outputs from rIC3 were certified using Certifaiger [45].

7.2 Results

Table 2, Fig. 2, and Fig. 3 present the results of various IC3 engines. The data clearly demonstrate that rIC3 significantly outperforms other engines in terms of scalability. Specifically, rIC3 solves 73 more cases than nuXmv-cav23 and 90 more cases than ABC-pdr. Additionally, rIC3 uniquely solves 61 cases. Both the scatter plot and the PAR-2 score further highlight rIC3's efficiency, as it solves the vast majority of cases faster than the other engines and achieves the best performance in 398 cases. The results for the portfolio engines are presented in

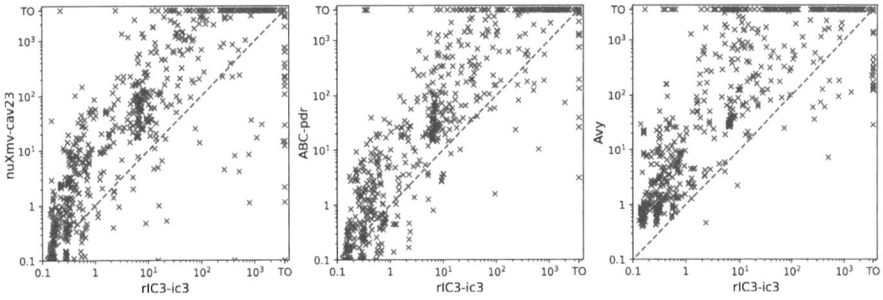

Fig. 3. The solving times (in seconds) comparisons between various IC3 engines.

Table 3. The number of solved, timeout, and memory-out cases, the PAR-2 score, the number of uniquely solved cases, and the fastest solved cases for portfolio engines.

Tools	Solved(319)	TO	MO	PAR-2	Unique	Best
rIC3-portfolio	245	73	1	1809.74	16	171
ABC-superprove	226	92	1	2197.01	2	43
Pavy^2	202	116	1	2801.99	0	1
AVR-portfolio	181	137	1	3220.23	3	22
Pono-portfolio	156	163	0	3780.85	1	19

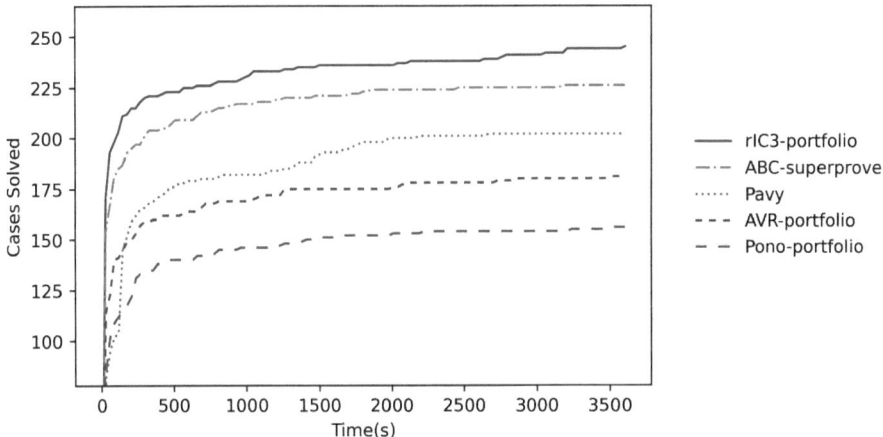

Fig. 4. The number of cases solved over time by various portfolio engines.

Table 3, Fig. 4, and Fig. 5. It is also evident that the portfolio engine of rIC3 maintains a competitive advantage over the other engines.[1]

To evaluate the effectiveness of the techniques employed, we conducted ablation experiments, as detailed in Table 4. The default configuration, referred to

---

[1] Pavy results differ slightly from HWMCC'24, possibly the version we found [6] differs from the final submitted version.

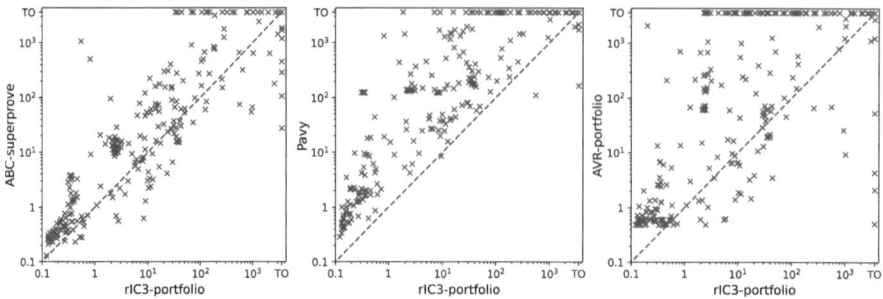

Fig. 5. The solving times (in seconds) comparisons between various portfolio engines.

Table 4. The number of solved, timeout, and memory-out cases, the PAR-2 score, and the number of uniquely solved cases for various configurations.

Tools	Solved(840)	TO	MO	PAR-2	Unique
rIC3-ic3	606	225	9	2147.70	13
rIC3-ic3-ms	564	275	1	2492.34	1
rIC3-ic3-ctg	590	242	8	2254.30	6
rIC3-ic3-inn	564	274	2	2447.95	12
rIC3-ic3-la	605	226	9	2173.03	25

as rIC3-ic3, incorporates DynAMic and GipSAT but does not utilize internal signals or localization abstraction. To assess the impact of each optimization, we experimented with several variations: replacing GipSAT with Minisat (rIC3-ic3-ms), disabling DynAMic and using CTG (rIC3-ic3-ctg), and enabling internal signals (rIC3-ic3-inn) and localization abstraction (rIC3-ic3-la). The results indicate that disabling either DynAMic or GipSAT led to a reduction in the number of solved cases. Moreover, while enabling internal signals or localization abstraction caused some performance degradation, these configurations uniquely solved certain cases that other setups could not address.

8 Strengths and Limitations

As a bit-level model checker, rIC3 demonstrates significant performance advancements, outperforming not only other bit-level checkers but also those leveraging word-level information. Its implementation is highly modular, with the IC3 algorithm module being particularly concise. However, due to its lack of utilization of word-level information, rIC3 is relatively inefficient in handling cases involving arithmetic logic. Moreover, it currently cannot solve bit-vector problems involving arrays, as bit-blasting an array model can lead to an explosion. Additionally, as shown in Table 2, AVR and Avy uniquely solved many cases that rIC3 could not, as their algorithms differ substantially from the original IC3 algorithm.

Therefore, incorporating more algorithm variants into rIC3's portfolio engine could further enhance its performance.

9 Conclusion

In this paper, we introduce rIC3, a novel hardware model checker. Both the HWMCC'24 results and our experimental evaluations highlight its significant advancements over existing tools. rIC3 can also function as a backend for verifying industrial RTL designs using SymbiYosys. Furthermore, the source code of its IC3 algorithm module is highly concise, making rIC3 an ideal academic platform that is easy to modify and extend. Looking ahead, we plan to enhance rIC3 by incorporating word-level information to further boost its performance and to enable support for solving word-level problems involving arrays.

Acknowledgement. This work was supported by the Beijing Municipal Natural Science Foundation (Grant No. 4252024), the Foundation of Laboratory for Advanced Computing and Intelligence Engineering (Grant No. 2023-LYJJ-01-013), the Basic Research Projects from the Institute of Software, Chinese Academy of Sciences (Grant No. ISCAS-JCZD-202307) and the National Natural Science Foundation of China (Grant No. 62372438).

Disclosure of Interests. The authors have no competing interests to declare that are relevant to the content of this article.

References

1. Artifact. https://github.com/gipsyh/rIC3-CAV25
2. btor2aiger tool. https://github.com/hwmcc/btor2tools
3. Hardware model checking competition. https://hwmcc.github.io
4. Ic3ref. https://github.com/arbrad/IC3ref
5. nuxmv artifact. https://github.com/youyusama/i-Good_Lemmas_MC.git
6. Pavy. https://github.com/TechnionFV/hwmcc24_submission
7. ric3. https://github.com/gipsyh/rIC3
8. Supercar. https://github.com/lijwen2748/hwmcc24
9. Superprove. https://github.com/sterin/super-prove-build
10. Biere, A., Cimatti, A., Clarke, E.M., Fujita, M., Zhu, Y.: Symbolic model checking using SAT procedures instead of BDDs. In: Irwin, M.J. (ed.) Proceedings of the 36th Conference on Design Automation, New Orleans, LA, USA, 21–25 June 1999, pp. 317–320. ACM Press (1999). https://doi.org/10.1145/309847.309942
11. Biere, A., Faller, T., Fazekas, K., Fleury, M., Froleyks, N., Pollitt, F.: Cadical 2.0. In: Gurfinkel, A., Ganesh, V. (eds.) Computer Aided Verification - 36th International Conference, CAV 2024, Montreal, QC, Canada, 24–27 July 2024, Proceedings, Part I. LNCS, vol. 14681, pp. 133–152. Springer (2024). https://doi.org/10.1007/978-3-031-65627-9_7
12. Biere, A., Faller, T., Fazekas, K., Fleury, M., Froleyks, N., Pollitt, F.: CaDiCaL, Gimsatul, IsaSAT and Kissat entering the SAT competition 2024. In: Heule, M., Iser, M., Järvisalo, M., Suda, M. (eds.) Proceedings of SAT Competition 2024 – Solver, Benchmark and Proof Checker Descriptions. Department of Computer Science Report Series B, vol. B-2024-1, pp. 8–10. University of Helsinki (2024)

13. Biere, A., Heljanko, K., Wieringa, S.: AIGER 1.9 and beyond. Technical report 11/2, Institute for Formal Models and Verification, Johannes Kepler University, Altenbergerstr. 69, 4040 Linz, Austria (2011). https://fmv.jku.at/papers/BiereHeljankoWieringa-FMV-TR-11-2.pdf
14. Bradley, A.R.: SAT-based model checking without unrolling. In: Jhala, R., Schmidt, D. (eds.) VMCAI 2011. LNCS, vol. 6538, pp. 70–87. Springer, Heidelberg (2011). https://doi.org/10.1007/978-3-642-18275-4_7
15. Bradley, A.R., Manna, Z.: Checking safety by inductive generalization of counterexamples to induction. In: Formal Methods in Computer-Aided Design, 7th International Conference, FMCAD 2007, Austin, Texas, USA, 11–14 November 2007, Proceedings, pp. 173–180. IEEE Computer Society (2007). https://doi.org/10.1109/FAMCAD.2007.15
16. Brayton, R., Mishchenko, A.: ABC: an academic industrial-strength verification tool. In: Touili, T., Cook, B., Jackson, P. (eds.) CAV 2010. LNCS, vol. 6174, pp. 24–40. Springer, Heidelberg (2010). https://doi.org/10.1007/978-3-642-14295-6_5
17. Cavada, R., et al.: The nuXmv symbolic model checker. In: Biere, A., Bloem, R. (eds.) Computer Aided Verification - 26th International Conference, CAV 2014, Held as Part of the Vienna Summer of Logic, VSL 2014, Vienna, Austria, 18–22 July 2014. Proceedings. LNCS, vol. 8559, pp. 334–342. Springer (2014). https://doi.org/10.1007/978-3-319-08867-9_22
18. Cimatti, A., Griggio, A., Mover, S., Tonetta, S.: IC3 modulo theories via implicit predicate abstraction. In: Ábrahám, E., Havelund, K. (eds.) Tools and Algorithms for the Construction and Analysis of Systems - 20th International Conference, TACAS 2014, Held as Part of the European Joint Conferences on Theory and Practice of Software, ETAPS 2014, Grenoble, France, 5–13 April 2014. Proceedings. LNCS, vol. 8413, pp. 46–61. Springer (2014). https://doi.org/10.1007/978-3-642-54862-8_4
19. Clarke, E.M., Grumberg, O., Kroening, D., Peled, D.A., Veith, H.: Model Checking, 2nd edn. MIT Press (2018). https://mitpress.mit.edu/books/model-checking-second-edition
20. Clarke, E.M., Henzinger, T.A., Veith, H., Bloem, R.: Handbook of Model Checking, 1st edn. Springer (2018). https://doi.org/10.1007/978-3-319-10575-8
21. Dureja, R., Gurfinkel, A., Ivrii, A., Vizel, Y.: IC3 with internal signals. In: Formal Methods in Computer Aided Design, FMCAD 2021, New Haven, CT, USA, 19–22 October 2021, pp. 63–71. IEEE (2021). https://doi.org/10.34727/2021/ISBN.978-3-85448-046-4_14
22. Eén, N., Mishchenko, A., Brayton, R.K.: Efficient implementation of property directed reachability. In: Bjesse, P., Slobodová, A. (eds.) International Conference on Formal Methods in Computer-Aided Design, FMCAD 2011, Austin, TX, USA, October 30 - November 02, 2011, pp. 125–134. FMCAD Inc. (2011). http://dl.acm.org/citation.cfm?id=2157675
23. Goel, A., Sakallah, K.A.: Empirical evaluation of IC3-based model checking techniques on verilog RTL designs. In: Teich, J., Fummi, F. (eds.) Design, Automation & Test in Europe Conference & Exhibition, DATE 2019, Florence, Italy, 25–29 March 2019, pp. 618–621. IEEE (2019). https://doi.org/10.23919/DATE.2019.8715289
24. Goel, A., Sakallah, K.: Model checking of verilog RTL Using IC3 with syntax-guided abstraction. In: Badger, J.M., Rozier, K.Y. (eds.) NFM 2019. LNCS, vol. 11460, pp. 166–185. Springer, Cham (2019). https://doi.org/10.1007/978-3-030-20652-9_11

25. Goel, A., Sakallah, K.A.: AVR: abstractly verifying reachability. In: Biere, A., Parker, D. (eds.) Tools and Algorithms for the Construction and Analysis of Systems - 26th International Conference, TACAS 2020, Held as Part of the European Joint Conferences on Theory and Practice of Software, ETAPS 2020, Dublin, Ireland, 25–30 April 2020, Proceedings, Part I. LNCS, vol. 12078, pp. 413–422. Springer (2020). https://doi.org/10.1007/978-3-030-45190-5_23
26. Hassan, Z., Bradley, A.R., Somenzi, F.: Better generalization in IC3. In: Formal Methods in Computer-Aided Design, FMCAD 2013, Portland, OR, USA, 20–23 October 2013. pp. 157–164. IEEE (2013). https://ieeexplore.ieee.org/document/6679405/
27. Ho, Y.S., Mishchenko, A., Brayton, R., Een, N.: Enhancing PDR/IC3 with localization abstraction. In: Proceedings of the 26th International Workshop on Logic and Synthesis (IWLS) (2017). https://people.eecs.berkeley.edu/~alanmi/publications/2017/iwls17_pdr.pdf
28. Hu, G., Tang, J., Yu, C., Zhang, W., Zhang, H.: DeepIC3: guiding IC3 algorithms by graph neural network clause prediction. In: Proceedings of the 29th Asia and South Pacific Design Automation Conference, ASPDAC 2024, Incheon, Korea, 22–25 January 2024, pp. 262–268. IEEE (2024). https://doi.org/10.1109/ASP-DAC58780.2024.10473807
29. Kuehlmann, A., Paruthi, V., Krohm, F., Ganai, M.K.: Robust Boolean reasoning for equivalence checking and functional property verification. IEEE Trans. Comput. Aided Des. Integr. Circuits Syst. **21**(12), 1377–1394 (2002). https://doi.org/10.1109/TCAD.2002.804386
30. Li, J., Dureja, R., Pu, G., Rozier, K.Y., Vardi, M.Y.: SimpleCAR: an efficient bug-finding tool based on approximate reachability. In: Chockler, H., Weissenbacher, G. (eds.) Computer Aided Verification - 30th International Conference, CAV 2018, Held as Part of the Federated Logic Conference, FloC 2018, Oxford, UK, 14–17 July 2018, Proceedings, Part II. LNCS, vol. 10982, pp. 37–44. Springer (2018).https://doi.org/10.1007/978-3-319-96142-2_5
31. Li, J., Zhu, S., Zhang, Y., Pu, G., Vardi, M.Y.: Safety model checking with complementary approximations. In: Parameswaran, S. (ed.) 2017 IEEE/ACM International Conference on Computer-Aided Design, ICCAD 2017, Irvine, CA, USA, 13–16 November 2017, pp. 95–100. IEEE (2017). https://doi.org/10.1109/ICCAD.2017.8203765
32. Mann, M., et al.: **Pono**: a flexible and extensible SMT-based model checker. In: Silva, A., Leino, K. (eds.) CAV 2021, Part II. LNCS, vol. 12760, pp. 461–474. Springer, Cham (2021). https://doi.org/10.1007/978-3-030-81688-9_22
33. McMillan, K.L.: Interpolation and sat-based model checking. In: Jr., W.A.H., Somenzi, F. (eds.) Computer Aided Verification, 15th International Conference, CAV 2003, Boulder, CO, USA, 8–12 July 2003, Proceedings. LNCS, vol. 2725, pp. 1–13. Springer (2003). https://doi.org/10.1007/978-3-540-45069-6_1
34. Mishchenko, A., Chatterjee, S., Brayton, R.K.: DAG-aware AIG rewriting a fresh look at combinational logic synthesis. In: Sentovich, E. (ed.) Proceedings of the 43rd Design Automation Conference, DAC 2006, San Francisco, CA, USA, 24–28 July 2006, pp. 532–535. ACM (2006). https://doi.org/10.1145/1146909.1147048
35. Niemetz, A., Preiner, M., Wolf, C., Biere, A.: Btor2 , BtorMC and Boolector 3.0. In: Chockler, H., Weissenbacher, G. (eds.) Computer Aided Verification - 30th International Conference, CAV 2018, Held as Part of the Federated Logic Conference, FloC 2018, Oxford, UK, 14–17 July 2018, Proceedings, Part I. LNCS, vol. 10981, pp. 587–595. Springer (2018). https://doi.org/10.1007/978-3-319-96145-3_32

36. Riener, H., Lee, S., Mishchenko, A., Micheli, G.D.: Boolean rewriting strikes back: reconvergence-driven windowing meets resynthesis. In: 27th Asia and South Pacific Design Automation Conference, ASP-DAC 2022, Taipei, Taiwan, 17–20 January 2022, pp. 395–402. IEEE (2022). https://doi.org/10.1109/ASP-DAC52403.2022.9712526
37. Seufert, T., Scholl, C., Chandrasekharan, A., Reimer, S., Welp, T.: Making PROGRESS in property directed reachability. In: Methods and Description Languages for Modelling and Verification of Circuits and Systems, MBMV 2022, 25th Workshop, Virtual Event, Germany, 17–18 February 2022, pp. 1–2. VDE/IEEE (2022). https://ieeexplore.ieee.org/document/9788579
38. Sheeran, M., Singh, S., Stålmarck, G.: Checking safety properties using induction and a sat-solver. In: Jr., W.A.H., Johnson, S.D. (eds.) Formal Methods in Computer-Aided Design, Third International Conference, FMCAD 2000, Austin, Texas, USA, 1–3 November 2000, Proceedings. LNCS, vol. 1954, pp. 108–125. Springer (2000). https://doi.org/10.1007/3-540-40922-X_8
39. Su, Y., Yang, Q., Ci, Y.: Predicting lemmas in generalization of IC3. In: De, V. (ed.) Proceedings of the 61st ACM/IEEE Design Automation Conference, DAC 2024, San Francisco, CA, USA, 23–27 June 2024, pp. 208:1–208:6. ACM (2024). https://doi.org/10.1145/3649329.3655970
40. Su, Y., Yang, Q., Ci, Y., Huang, Z.: Extended CTG generalization and dynamic adjustment of generalization strategies in IC3 (2025). https://arxiv.org/abs/2501.02480
41. Su, Y., Yang, Q., Ci, Y., Li, Y., Bu, T., Huang, Z.: Deeply optimizing the sat solver for the IC3 algorithm (2025). https://arxiv.org/abs/2501.18612
42. Vizel, Y., Gurfinkel, A.: Interpolating property directed reachability. In: Biere, A., Bloem, R. (eds.) Computer Aided Verification - 26th International Conference, CAV 2014, Held as Part of the Vienna Summer of Logic, VSL 2014, Vienna, Austria, 18–22 July 2014. Proceedings. LNCS, vol. 8559, pp. 260–276. Springer (2014). https://doi.org/10.1007/978-3-319-08867-9_17
43. Wang, D., et al.: Formal property verification by abstraction refinement with formal, simulation and hybrid engines. In: Proceedings of the 38th Design Automation Conference, DAC 2001, Las Vegas, NV, USA, 18–22 June 2001, pp. 35–40. ACM (2001). https://doi.org/10.1145/378239.378260
44. Xia, Y., Becchi, A., Cimatti, A., Griggio, A., Li, J., Pu, G.: Searching for i-good lemmas to accelerate safety model checking. In: Enea, C., Lal, A. (eds.) Computer Aided Verification - 35th International Conference, CAV 2023, Paris, France, 17–22 July 2023, Proceedings, Part II. LNCS, vol. 13965, pp. 288–308. Springer (2023). https://doi.org/10.1007/978-3-031-37703-7_14
45. Yu, E., Froleyks, N., Biere, A., Heljanko, K.: Towards compositional hardware model checking certification. In: Nadel, A., Rozier, K.Y. (eds.) Formal Methods in Computer-Aided Design, FMCAD 2023, Ames, IA, USA, 24–27 October 2023, pp. 1–11. IEEE (2023). https://doi.org/10.34727/2023/ISBN.978-3-85448-060-0_12

Open Access This chapter is licensed under the terms of the Creative Commons Attribution 4.0 International License (http://creativecommons.org/licenses/by/4.0/), which permits use, sharing, adaptation, distribution and reproduction in any medium or format, as long as you give appropriate credit to the original author(s) and the source, provide a link to the Creative Commons license and indicate if changes were made.

The images or other third party material in this chapter are included in the chapter's Creative Commons license, unless indicated otherwise in a credit line to the material. If material is not included in the chapter's Creative Commons license and your intended use is not permitted by statutory regulation or exceeds the permitted use, you will need to obtain permission directly from the copyright holder.

HornStr: Invariant Synthesis for Regular Model Checking as Constrained Horn Clauses

Hongjian Jiang[1]✉ , Anthony W. Lin[1,2] , Oliver Markgraf[1] ,
Philipp Rümmer[3,4] , and Daniel Stan[5,6]

[1] University of Kaiserslautern-Landau,
Kaiserslautern, Germany
hongjian.jiang@mpi-inf.mpg.de
[2] Max Planck Institute for Software Systems,
Kaiserslautern, Germany
[3] University of Regensburg, Regensburg, Germany
[4] Uppsala University, Uppsala, Sweden
[5] EPITA, Laboratoire de Recherche de l'EPITA (LRE),
14-16 Rue Voltaire, 94270 Le Kremlin Bicêtre, France
[6] Université de Strasbourg, CNRS, ICube UMR7357, 67000 Strasbourg, France

Abstract. We present HornStr, the first solver for invariant synthesis for Regular Model Checking (RMC) with the specification provided in the SMT-LIB 2.6 theory of strings. It is well-known that invariant synthesis for RMC subsumes various important verification problems, including safety verification for parameterized systems. To achieve a simple and standardized file format, we treat the invariant synthesis problem as a problem of solving Constrained Horn Clauses (CHCs) over strings. Two strategies for synthesizing invariants in terms of regular constraints are supported: (1) L* automata learning, and (2) SAT-based automata learning. HornStr implements these strategies with the help of existing SMT solvers for strings, which are interfaced through SMT-LIB. HornStr provides an easy-to-use interface for string solver developers to apply their techniques to verification. At the same time, it allows verification researchers to painlessly tap into the wealth of modern string solving techniques. To assess the effectiveness of HornStr, we conducted a comprehensive evaluation using benchmarks derived from applications including parameterized verification and string rewriting tasks. Our experiments highlight HornStr's capacity to effectively handle these benchmarks, e.g., as the first solver to verify the challenging MU puzzle automatically. Finally, HornStr can be used to automatically generate a new class of interesting SMT-LIB 2.6 string constraint benchmarks, which might in the future be used in the SMT-COMP strings track. In particular, our experiments on the above invariant synthesis benchmarks produce more than 30000 new QF_S constraints. We also detail the performance of various integrated string solvers, providing insights into their effectiveness on our new benchmarks.

1 Introduction

Regular Model Checking (RMC) [1,10,33,40,54] is a prominent framework for modeling an infinite-state transition system as a string rewrite system. Classically, the transition relation is specified as a length-preserving transducer. It is well-known that RMC can be used to model a variety of systems, most notably *parameterized systems*, i.e., distributed protocols with an arbitrary number of processes. Many RMC tools have been developed, focusing on safety verification, e.g., [1,3,4,9,10,15,36,44,46,53,54], to name a few.

Despite the amount of work on RMC in the past decades and the potential of RMC in addressing highly impactful verification problems, RMC tools are typically cumbersome to use. The first problem is the need for the user to specify the model in a low-level language, usually in terms of transducers. The second problem is the absence of a standard file format agreed upon by RMC tool developers. Perhaps this is one main reason that most RMC tools attracted very few users and are mostly no longer maintained today.

SMT-LIB 2.6 Theory of Strings. String constraints have been standardized as part of SMT-LIB 2.6 since 2020, enabling the organization of a track for string solvers at the annual SMT-COMP. The theory over strings has since attracted significant interest in academia [12,22,29] and industry [6,41,48]. The theory provides rich support for string operators (concatenation, replace-all, regular constraints, length constraints, etc.), allowing one to conveniently express operations performed in string-manipulating programs in a high-level language like JavaScript. Out of the many existing string solvers [2,32,34,45,49,51,52,55], at least five solvers (Z3 [16], Z3-alpha [42], Z3-noodler [14], cvc5 [7], and OSTRICH [13]) now support the SMT-LIB 2.6 format.

RMC Meets String Solvers. In this paper, we propose to connect RMC with string solvers. Our goal is to provide an easy-to-use and *unified* interface: (i) for string solver developers to apply their techniques to verification, and (ii) for verification researchers/users who could benefit from RMC and parameterized verification to easily tap into the wealth of modern string-solving techniques. To this end, we propose to *treat invariant synthesis for RMC as a sub-problem of Constrained Horn Clauses (CHCs) over the theory of strings*. CHCs [8,20] form a fragment of first-order logic over background theories that serves as an intermediate language for expressing safety verification problems. A CHC formulation of RMC benefits from the *standard and familiar SMT-LIB specification language*. Before our work, no existing CHC solvers directly supported the theory of strings.

Our **first contribution** is, therefore, to develop the first solver HornStr for invariant synthesis for RMC expressed as a CHC problem over strings. Our solver HornStr supports two strategies for synthesizing invariants in terms of regular constraints: (1) L* automata learning [5], and (2) SAT-based automata learning [23]. Both solvers interact with a string solver via *equivalence queries*, which ask the string solver to verify whether an invariant candidate is correct. The first strategy also interacts with the string solver via *membership queries*, which check whether a guessed string is contained in all invariants. To handle both kinds of queries, HornStr uses other string solvers as backends through the SMT-LIB 2.6 interface. Note that similar strategies were already used in other RMC tools [15,46], where these queries were answered by interacting with an *ad-hoc* automata implementation, in contrast to string solvers, which are continuously being improved. To assess the effectiveness of HornStr, we conducted a comprehensive evaluation using benchmarks derived from applications, including parameterized verification and string rewriting tasks, integrating the available string solvers individually and in combination. Our experiments highlight HornStr's ability to effectively handle these benchmarks, e.g., as the first solver to verify the challenging MU puzzle automatically.

As a by-product of our tool development, our **second contribution** is the generation of a new class of QF_S constraints, which could be used in future SMT-COMP competitions for string solvers. These constraints differ from most benchmarks currently available in SMT-LIB, as they are derived from an invariant synthesis problem. In contrast, the majority of existing benchmarks stem from symbolic execution (like, e.g., the PyEx family). We have evaluated available string solvers on these benchmarks and report the results in this paper.

For the full version, we refer the reader to the technical report [30], and for implementation and benchmark details, to the artifact [31].

2 Constraint Horn Clauses

We describe in this section the CHC formalism used as input format by HornStr, as well as examples of applications, illustrating the relationship with RMC and string-rewrite systems.

Definition 1. *A Constrained Horn Clause (CHC) is a first-order logic formula of the form*

$$\forall \mathcal{X}. \varphi \land p_1(T_1) \land \cdots \land p_k(T_k) \rightarrow \psi, \ (k \geq 0),$$

in which the term ψ is either an uninterpreted predicate $h(T)$ or $\bot$, and $p_1, \ldots, p_k$ are uninterpreted predicates. The set of variables $\mathcal{X}$ contains all variables from $T \cup \bigcup_{i=1}^{k} T_i$. The formula φ represents a constraint in the background theory, such as linear arithmetic or strings.

A *CHC system* is a conjunction of constrained Horn clauses. To solve a CHC system, it is necessary to find interpretations of the uninterpreted predicates that satisfy all clauses. We focus in the following on CHC systems over the theory of strings, with one unary uninterpreted predicate. Finding a valuation for this predicate p amounts to finding a set of words w for which $p(w)$ holds, so that all clauses are satisfied. As a finite representation is needed, HornStr will focus on regular language solutions.

2.1 Regular Model Checking

Example 1. Consider the token passing protocol on a ring topology, with two initial tokens, red and blue, at first and last position respectively, moving synchronously in opposite directions, without possibly colliding. A configuration can be seen as a word over $\Sigma = \{r, b, n\}$ where n denotes the absence of a token. Assume we are interested in the safety property "the two tokens never reach the other end", invalidated by a word in the language $\mathcal{L}(b \cdot n^* \cdot r)$. One can observe that an initial odd distance between the two tokens is a necessary and sufficient condition for avoiding these configurations.

Checking the safety of this protocol can therefore be specified with the following CHC System:

$$V_i \in \mathcal{L}(rn(nn)^*b) \to p(V_i) \quad (1)$$

$$p(V_i) \land V_i \in \mathcal{L}(bn^*r) \to \bot \quad (2)$$

$$p(V_i) \land V_i = A \cdot (rn) \cdot B \cdot (nb) \cdot C \land V_o = A \cdot (nr) \cdot B \cdot (bn) \cdot C \to p(V_o) \quad (3)$$

$$p(V_i) \land V_i = A \cdot (nb) \cdot B \cdot (rn) \cdot C \land V_o = A \cdot (bn) \cdot B \cdot (nr) \cdot C \to p(V_o) \quad (4)$$

$$p(V_i) \land V_i = A \cdot (rb) \cdot B \land V_o = A \cdot (br) \cdot B \to p(V_o) \quad (5)$$

The variables V_i, V_o, A, B, C in the clauses are implicitly universally quantified. The clauses can be partitioned into three categories: $Init = \{(1)\}$ expresses membership of an initial configuration, while $Bad = \{(2)\}$ expresses undesired configurations. The rest of the clauses, $Tr = \{(3), (4), (5)\}$, model the different transitions where tokens move synchronously, possibly changing their order in (5). Note that arbitrarily many extra string variables may be used as long as they are universally quantified. The different constraints involve string constraints either in the form of regular expression constraints ((1) and (2)) or in terms of string equality with concatenation operations ((3) – (5)).

Example 1 is a rather usual instance of RMC problem, where one asks whether a system is safe by finding an *inductive invariant*, that is, a set of states or words containing all initial states (1), no bad state (2), and that is closed under the transitions (3) – (5).

Several candidate sets can be considered, such as the set of all reachable words from an initial clause (the strongest possible invariant), or the set of words from which no bad state can be reached (the weakest possible invariant). Recall, however, that we need to compute finite representations of the considered invariants; in our case, as regular languages. The previously mentioned sets are therefore less useful: any reachable and any unsafe configuration must have tokens at equal distance for the word borders, making the language irregular. However, a suitable regular inductive invariant does exist, for example $\mathcal{L}(n^*\Sigma(n(nn)^*)\Sigma n^*)$, which translates to "an odd distance between two tokens".

2.2 String-Rewrite System: The MU Puzzle

The previous CHC system provided an example of a Regular Model Checking problem for a system with an initial state of arbitrary length, but where transitions preserve the length of the word. Such transitions can usually be represented by length-preserving transducers. HornStr's input formalism is, however, not restricted to this setting, and can, for example, be applied to string-rewrite systems:

Example 2. The MU puzzle [25] is a string-rewrite system over the alphabet $\Sigma = \{M, I, U\}$: Its objective is to determine whether the string MU can be derived from the Initial string MI by applying the given rewriting rules: $R = \{(xI \to xIU), (Mx \to Mxx), (xIIIy \to xUy), (xUUy \to xy) \mid x, y \in \Sigma^*\}$. For example, using the first rule, the string MI is transformed to MIU in one step.

We can model the puzzle using the following CHCs, where all variables $V_i, V_o, x, y \in \Sigma^*$ are universally quantified:

$$V_i = MI \to p(V_i) \tag{1}$$
$$p(V_i) \wedge V_i = xI \wedge V_o = xIU \to p(V_o) \tag{2}$$
$$p(V_i) \wedge V_i = Mx \wedge V_o = Mxx \to p(V_o) \tag{3}$$
$$p(V_i) \wedge V_i = xIIIy \wedge V_o = xUy \to p(V_o) \tag{4}$$
$$p(V_i) \wedge V_i = xUUy \wedge V_o = xy \to p(V_o) \tag{5}$$
$$p(V_i) \wedge V_i = MU \to \bot \tag{6}$$

This CHC system is satisfiable, proving that the MU puzzle cannot be solved.

3 Architecture of HornStr

The HornStr framework integrates CHC and string constraints, leveraging automata learning techniques in combination with string solvers. This integration addresses complex problems expressed in SMT-LIB files, and modeling, e.g., parameterized systems or string-rewrite systems. Figure 1 illustrates the overall architecture of HornStr.

The framework commences with an SMT-LIB formatted file as its input, a format prevalent in the SMT community for describing problems that require solutions to satisfy constraints involving complex data types and operations. The *Learners* play a crucial role in synthesizing predicates based on regular constraints. They employ two different strategies:

1. *SAT-based Enumeration* utilizes SAT solvers to generate potential solutions, as well as string solvers to assess whether the solution satisfies given CHCs. In case of violated CHCs, the string solvers can provide a counterexample. Initially, the set of counterexamples is empty. The learner constructs a Deterministic Finite-state Automaton (DFA) as a hypothesis solution that accepts every word. This DFA is transformed into a regular expression via an intermediate translator, implemented by Brzozowski and McCluskey's state elimination method [11]. The translator then sends an SMT-LIB query to the *String Solvers* to check for consistency with the CHCs. Upon receiving the query, the string solvers check the solution behind the scenes, returning either *unsat* or a counterexample to the learner.
2. *Active Learner* directly interacts with the learning model through queries. This learner constructs both equivalence queries and membership queries to verify if a string or sequence belongs to the model's language or reachability

queries to determine if a certain state or condition is achievable. It maintains an observation table [5] in its cache, from which it constructs a DFA. The *Reachability* module is responsible for communicating with the string solvers to ascertain whether the queried word is within the language: this involves several string queries, enumerating initial words ($Init$), then using all applicable transitions (Tr) to find all reachable words iteratively. The membership query is answered positively when the desired word is found in the reachable fragment, or negatively if all the words of the same length, or up to a fixed constant, have been explored. The latter rule constitutes a heuristic inspired by the length-preserving transition models.

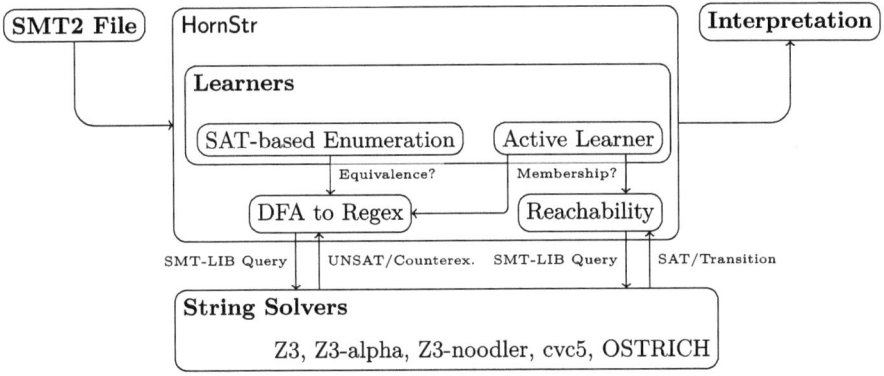

Fig. 1. The overall framework of HornStr.

Furthermore, String Solvers respond to queries from the Learners by resolving a series of string constraints. To enhance the efficiency of answering equivalence and membership queries, the framework has integrated an incremental solving technique. Each CHC is assigned to a dedicated solver thread, for precomputation purposes. For each word or automata query, the system saves the current constraints (push), inserts the new query constraint, computes the result, and upon obtaining the result, it restores the saved constraints (pop), provides the response, and prepares for the next query. Through a command line argument, the user can also instruct HornStr to handle all CHCs using a single solver, as this may save processing time for larger equivalence queries. On the contrary, word queries involve small input values, so they usually benefit from specific String Solver optimizations, one for each clause. HornStr employs a variety of state-of-the-art solvers, such as Z3, Z3-alpha, Z3-noodler, cvc5, and OSTRICH. Each of these solvers brings unique capabilities that range from basic string manipulations to more complex pattern matching and replacement operations. These specialized tools are adept at managing string operations within the constraints specified in SMT-LIB queries. Additionally, the framework offers a configuration file for users to specify their own string solver, as an external implementation of the interactive mode of the SMT-LIB 2.6 standard.

The execution of HornStr progresses through the following phases:

1. **Initialization**: The procedure begins with the selection of a suitable learning strategy and a string solver. Subsequently, an SMT-LIB file containing the uninterpreted predicate declaration, followed by constraint Horn clauses, is loaded, and the designated solver is instantiated together with the necessary oracles.
2. **Query Processing and Model Refinement**: When employing the SAT-based enumeration approach [46], the learner initially constructs a DFA with a single state and an empty counterexample set using a SAT solver. Once an appropriate DFA is generated that integrates the counterexample set, an equivalence check is conducted against the hypothesis using the string solver. If a new counterexample is detected, the hypothesis undergoes refinement and reconstruction. If the SAT solver returns an unsatisfiable outcome, the automaton's state space is incrementally expanded, and the process iterates until the string solver fails to find further counterexamples and accepts the hypothesis.

    Alternatively, if the active learner is selected [15], membership queries are issued to verify whether a given word w belongs to the target language L, leveraging the reachability module. This initiates an iterative process in which membership queries facilitate hypothesis generation, which is subsequently validated via equivalence queries.
3. **Solution Generation**: Based on the preliminary results and constructed queries, the string solver is employed to analyze and resolve regular constraints. Within this framework, the solver integrates the $Init$ and Tr components to determine whether a word w is accepted. Conversely, if the word is rejected, the decision is justified through the Bad and Tr components.

    For equivalence queries, all Horn clauses are evaluated by testing them with two free variables, var_{in} and var_{out}. For example, if var_{out} appears as part of a word in the hypothesis and satisfies the Bad clause, it is classified as a negative counterexample. Similarly, positive and inductive counterexamples can be identified using the $Init$ and Tr components, respectively. If unsupported by the learner, inductive counterexamples are converted into positive and negative counterexamples thanks to reachability analysis, following the *strict but generous teacher* [15] concept.

4 Evaluation

In this section, we evaluate the performance and capabilities of HornStr[1] on a set of benchmarks derived from the verification of distributed systems and string rewriting systems. HornStr uses string solvers as oracles for membership and equivalence queries, the choice of the solvers in use is an important aspect of its performance.

---

[1] https://arg-git.informatik.uni-kl.de/pub/string-chc-lib.

Our evaluation is divided into two parts. First, we examine how the different string solvers can handle the string formulas generated as queries during the CHC-solving process. As described in Sect. 3, HornStr supports incremental solving, which can improve efficiency by reusing information across related queries. We compare the performance of string solvers on both incremental and non-incremental queries.

Second, we evaluate HornStr's overall performance using the string solvers that performed best in the first part of the evaluation. Experiments were conducted on an Intel Core i7-10510U CPU at 1.8 GHz with 16 GB of RAM running on Windows 11.

Our benchmarks are derived from two distinct domains:

- **Verification of Distributed Systems:** We transform Regular Model Checking protocols [15,18] into Constrained Horn Clause (CHC) programs using automatic translations: Bakery [35], Szymanski [21,50], Dijkstra [43], Burns [43], Dining Philosopher Protocol [24], Israeli-Jalfon's self-stabilising protocol [28], Resource-allocator protocol [17], David Gries's coffee can problem [38], german protocol [3] and Kanban production system [19].
- **String Rewriting Systems:** We also manually model the MU puzzle and EqDist protocols as CHC programs, demonstrating the versatility of the approach.

4.1 Results of the String Solver Experiments

Table 1 provides a comparison of the string solvers Z3, cvc5, Z3-noodler, Z3-alpha, and OSTRICH. The benchmarks are categorized into incremental and non-incremental queries, further divided by the query type: membership or equivalence. Our primary metric of interest is the number of benchmarks solved, as failing to resolve even a single query can prevent the CHC solver from terminating. The timeout for each benchmark is set to 30 s.

Equivalence queries predominantly involve reasoning over regular expressions but may also include word equations when these are part of the Horn clause. Membership queries, while also involving regular expressions, tend to emphasize disequalities ($x \neq c$, where x is a string variable and c is a string constant).

In the incremental setting, the membership results are relatively similar, with all solvers processing over 514 benchmarks. Notably, Z3-Noodler leads by solving all 523 benchmarks in an average of 109.7 s, whereas OSTRICH, cvc5, Z3, and Z3-alpha solve between 514 and 518 benchmarks in slightly higher runtimes.

For the incremental equivalence queries, we see different behaviors among the solvers. Z3-noodler solves all 396 queries in just 15.5 s, while OSTRICH manages 378. On the other hand, cvc5, Z3, and Z3-alpha only solve between 109 and 126 queries. A similar pattern shows up in the non-incremental equivalence queries: Z3-noodler handles all 848 queries, with OSTRICH coming in close with 784, whereas cvc5, Z3, and Z3-alpha solve between 403 and 457 queries. In the case of membership queries, every solver covers nearly all of the 30,902 benchmarks, with only cvc5 and OSTRICH missing about 1%, while Z3-noodler and Z3 turn out to be the fastest to solve them all.

Across both incremental and non-incremental benchmarks, the results demonstrate a consistent pattern: membership queries are generally handled well by most solvers, while equivalence queries involving regular expressions remain a challenge for many. Notably, automata-based solvers such as Z3-noodler and OSTRICH consistently show superior performance on equivalence queries, likely due to their design being well-suited for reasoning over regular expressions. These results also highlight the high incrementality of our approach, as seen when comparing the total time spent on all incremental vs. non-incremental queries. Note that OSTRICH's overall runtime is a bit higher partly due to the JVM startup time incurred for each benchmark.

To address the challenges faced by solvers struggling with equivalence queries, we experimented with different settings and flags for those solvers and implemented a regular expression simplifier on our end before sending the queries. The simplifier aimed to reduce the nesting of Kleene stars using algebraic transformations on regular expressions. While this led to marginal improvements for some poorly performing solvers, it had little impact overall and even worsened performance for solvers already handling regular expressions effectively.

Table 1. Comparison of state-of-the-art string solvers. Benchmarks are divided into incremental and non-incremental membership and equivalence queries. The timeout is 30 s. Timeouts are excluded from solved time.

Solver	Incremental				Non-Incremental			
	Mem	Time (s)	Equiv	Time (s)	Mem	Time (s)	Equiv	Time (s)
OSTRICH	514	453.2	378	410.8	30773	16504.9	784	980.8
cvc5	517	97.8	126	7948.4	30652	610.5	457	270.7
Z3	517	33.7	109	506.7	30902	1511.7	403	102.1
Z3-noodler	523	109.7	396	15.5	30902	806.3	848	17.9
Z3-alpha	518	86.4	109	516.6	30902	3839.1	404	162.7

4.2 Results of the HornStr Experiments

After evaluating the performance of various string solvers as membership and equivalence oracles in our preliminary experiments, we now assess HornStr for CHC solving. Based on the incremental benchmark results (Table 1), we chose Z3 for membership queries and Z3-noodler for equivalence queries.

We developed an automatic parser that transforms length-preserving RMC protocols into CHC SMT2 format, incorporating word equations and regular membership constraints. Next, we evaluate the efficiency of HornStr using both SAT-based Enumeration and the Active Learner, as described in Sect. 3. In our evaluation, we record whether HornStr produces a deterministic finite automaton for the uninterpreted invariant within a predefined time limit or identifies an unsafe trace during the benchmark evaluation.

Our evaluation demonstrates that our tool solved most benchmarks in under a second using either SAT-based enumeration or the active learner. Notably, SAT-based enumeration solved every protocol listed in Table 2, whereas the active learner failed to find solutions for some benchmarks. However, certain protocols—such as *Kanban* and *German*—exceeded the 60-s timeout due to the complexity of transitions in their CHC representations. Detailed evaluation results are presented in Table 2.

Table 2. Comparison of protocols: automaton size and learning time across SAT-Based and active Learner

Protocol	SAT-based Enumeration		Active Learner	
	Size	Time(s)	Size	Time(s)
Token Pass	3	0.41	3	0.10
2 Tokens Pass	3	0.78	6	0.57
3 Tokens Pass	2	0.30	2	0.17
Power-Binary	1	0.2	1	0.01
Bakery	2	0.15	3	0.37
Burns	2	2.09	✗	TO
Coffee-Can	2	0.52	5	9.66
Coffee-Can-v2	3	0.31	4	23.45
Herman-Linear	2	0.11	2	0.08
Herman-Ring	2	0.51	2	0.33
Israeli-Jalfon	3	0.35	4	0.46
LR-Philo	2	0.80	3	2.84
Mux-Array	2	0.49	✗	TO
Resource-Allocator	2	0.14	4	25.19
Eqdist	3	1.45	✗	TO
MU Puzzle	3	11.01	✗	TO
Water-Jug	2	2.05	✗	TO
Dining-Crypt	2	10.02	✗	TO

5 Conclusions

We introduced HornStr, the first solver for invariant synthesis in RMC that leverages the SMT-LIB 2.6 Theory over Strings. By formulating invariant synthesis as a problem of solving CHCs over strings, HornStr provides a standardized, scalable, and automated approach to verification. Our approach enables seamless integration of modern SMT solvers into RMC verification, bridging parameterized verification and string solving in a novel way.

Our evaluation demonstrated HornStr's effectiveness in handling complex verification tasks, including parameterized systems and string rewriting problems (e.g., the MU puzzle). By integrating incremental solving techniques, HornStr significantly improves the performance of string solvers, reducing computational overhead and enhancing scalability. Additionally, our work contributes more than 10,000 new `QF_S` constraints, providing a valuable benchmark suite for SMT solver evaluations.

We mention several future research avenues. The first is to extend HornStr by handling general CHCs over strings, i.e., non-linear and monadic CHCs that permit *symbolic alphabets*. This would allow one to model certain protocols, wherein process IDs are passed around (e.g. Chang-Roberts protocol; see [26, 47]). Second, one could extend our CHC framework to other types of RMC verification including liveness [37,39] and bisimulation [27,38].

Acknowledgement. Jiang, Lin and Markgraf are supported by the European Research Council under the European Union's Horizon 2020 research and innovation programme under number 101089343. Rümmer is supported by the Swedish Research Council through grant 2021–06327. The authors thank the CAV reviewers and all of the OSTRICH, cvc5, Z3, Z3-noodler, and the Z3-alpha team developers.

References

1. Abdulla, P.A.: Regular model checking. STTT **14**(2), 109–118 (2012). https://doi.org/10.1007/s10009-011-0216-8
2. Abdulla, P.A., et al.: Norn: an SMT solver for string constraints. In: International Conference on Computer Aided Verification, pp. 462–469. Springer (2015)
3. Abdulla, P.A., Delzanno, G., Henda, N.B., Rezine, A.: Regular model checking without transducers (on efficient verification of parameterized systems). In: Tools and Algorithms for the Construction and Analysis of Systems: 13th International Conference, TACAS 2007, Held as Part of the Joint European Conferences on Theory and Practice of Software, ETAPS 2007 Braga, Portugal, March 24-April 1 2007. Proceedings 13, pp. 721–736. Springer (2007)
4. Abdulla, P.A., Haziza, F., Holík, L.: All for the price of few. In: Giacobazzi, R., Berdine, J., Mastroeni, I. (eds.) VMCAI 2013. LNCS, vol. 7737, pp. 476–495. Springer, Heidelberg (2013). https://doi.org/10.1007/978-3-642-35873-9_28
5. Angluin, D.: Learning regular sets from queries and counterexamples. Inf. Comput. **75**(2), 87–106 (1987)
6. Backes, J., Bolignano, P., et al.: Semantic-based automated reasoning for AWS access policies using SMT. In: Bjørner, N.S., Gurfinkel, A. (eds.) 2018 Formal Methods in Computer Aided Design, FMCAD 2018, Austin, TX, USA, October 30 - November 2 2018, pp. 1–9. IEEE (2018). https://doi.org/10.23919/FMCAD.2018.8602994

7. Barbosa, H., et al.: CVC5: a versatile and industrial-strength SMT solver. In: Fisman, D., Rosu, G. (eds.) Tools and Algorithms for the Construction and Analysis of Systems, pp. 415–442. Springer, Cham (2022)
8. Bjørner, N., Gurfinkel, A., McMillan, K., Rybalchenko, A.: Horn clause solvers for program verification. In: Fields of Logic and Computation II: Essays Dedicated to Yuri Gurevich on the Occasion of His 75th Birthday, pp. 24–51. Springer (2015)
9. Bouajjani, A., Habermehl, P., Rogalewicz, A., Vojnar, T.: Abstract regular (tree) model checking. STTT **14**(2), 167–191 (2012). https://doi.org/10.1007/s10009-011-0205-y. http://dx.doi.org/10.1007/s10009-011-0205-y
10. Bouajjani, A., Jonsson, B., Nilsson, M., Touili, T.: Regular model checking. In: CAV, pp. 403–418 (2000)
11. Brzozowski, J.A., McCluskey, E.J.: Signal flow graph techniques for sequential circuit state diagrams. IEEE Trans. Electron. Comput. **2**, 67–76 (1963)
12. Chen, T., et al.: Solving string constraints with regex-dependent functions through transducers with priorities and variables. Proc. ACM Program. Lang. **6**(POPL), 1–31 (2022). https://doi.org/10.1145/3498707
13. Chen, T., Hague, M., Lin, A., Ruemmer, P., Wu, Z.: Decision procedures for path feasibility of string-manipulating programs with complex operations. Proc. ACM Program. Lang. **3**, 1–30 (2019)
14. Chen, Y.F., Chocholatý, D., Havlena, V., Holík, L., Lengál, O., Síč, J.: Z3-noodler: an automata-based string solver. In: Finkbeiner, B., Kovács, L. (eds.) Tools and Algorithms for the Construction and Analysis of Systems, pp. 24–33. Springer, Cham (2024)
15. Chen, Y., Hong, C., Lin, A.W., Rümmer, P.: Learning to prove safety over parameterised concurrent systems. In: Stewart, D., Weissenbacher, G. (eds.) 2017 Formal Methods in Computer Aided Design, FMCAD 2017, Vienna, Austria, 2–6 October 2017, pp. 76–83. IEEE (2017). https://doi.org/10.23919/FMCAD.2017.8102244
16. De Moura, L., Bjørner, N.: Z3: an efficient SMT solver. In: Proceedings of the Theory and Practice of Software, 14th International Conference on Tools and Algorithms for the Construction and Analysis of Systems, TACAS 2008/ETAPS 2008, pp. 337–340. Springer, Heidelberg (2008)
17. Donaldson, A.F.: Automatic techniques for detecting and exploiting symmetry in model checking. Ph.D. thesis, University of Glasgow (2007)
18. Esparza, J., Raskin, M., Welzel, C.: Regular model checking upside-down: an invariant-based approach. In: Klin, B., Lasota, S., Muscholl, A. (eds.) 33rd International Conference on Concurrency Theory (CONCUR 2022). Leibniz International Proceedings in Informatics (LIPIcs), vol. 243, pp. 23:1–23:19. Schloss Dagstuhl – Leibniz-Zentrum für Informatik, Dagstuhl, Germany (2022). https://doi.org/10.4230/LIPIcs.CONCUR.2022.23. https://drops.dagstuhl.de/entities/document/10.4230/LIPIcs.CONCUR.2022.23
19. Geeraerts, G., Raskin, J.F., Van Begin, L.: Expand, enlarge and check: new algorithms for the coverability problem of WSTS. J. Comput. Syst. Sci. **72**(1), 180–203 (2006)
20. Grebenshchikov, S., Lopes, N.P., Popeea, C., Rybalchenko, A.: Synthesizing software verifiers from proof rules. ACM SIGPLAN Not. **47**(6), 405–416 (2012)
21. Gribomont, E.P., Zenner, G.: Automated verification of Szymanski's algorithm. In: International Conference on Tools and Algorithms for the Construction and Analysis of Systems, pp. 424–438. Springer (1998)
22. Gutiérrez, C.: Solving equations in strings: on Makanin's algorithm. In: Latin American Symposium on Theoretical Informatics, pp. 358–373. Springer (1998)

23. Heule, M., Verwer, S.: Exact DFA identification using SAT solvers. In: Sempere, J.M., García, P. (eds.) ICGI 2010. LNCS (LNAI), vol. 6339, pp. 66–79. Springer, Heidelberg (2010). https://doi.org/10.1007/978-3-642-15488-1_7
24. Hoare, C.: Communicating sequential processes. Commun. ACM **21**(8), 666–677 (1978)
25. Hofstadter, D.R.: Gödel, Escher, Bach: An Eternal Golden Braid. Basic Books, Inc. (1979)
26. Hong, C., Lin, A.W.: Regular abstractions for array systems. Proc. ACM Program. Lang. **8**(POPL), 638–666 (2024)
27. Hong, C.-D., Lin, A.W., Majumdar, R., Rümmer, P.: Probabilistic bisimulation for parameterized systems. In: Dillig, I., Tasiran, S. (eds.) CAV 2019. LNCS, vol. 11561, pp. 455–474. Springer, Cham (2019). https://doi.org/10.1007/978-3-030-25540-4_27
28. Israeli, A., Jalfon, M.: Uniform self-stabilizing ring orientation. Inf. Comput. **104**(2), 175–196 (1993)
29. Jeż, A.: Recompression: a simple and powerful technique for word equations. J. ACM **63**(1) (2016). https://doi.org/10.1145/2743014
30. Jiang, H., Lin, A.W., Markgraf, O., Rümmer, P., Stan, D.: HornStr: a string theory solver for constrained horn clauses (technique report) (2025). https://arxiv.org/abs/2505.15959
31. Jiang, H., Lin, A.W., Markgraf, O., Rümmer, P., Stan, D.: HornStr: invariant synthesis for regular model checking as constrained horn clauses (2025). https://doi.org/10.5281/zenodo.15195124
32. Kan, S., Lin, A.W., Rümmer, P., Schrader, M.: CertiStr: a certified string solver. In: CPP, pp. 210–224. ACM (2022)
33. Kesten, Y., Maler, O., Marcus, M., Pnueli, A., Shahar, E.: Symbolic model checking with rich assertional languages. Theor. Comput. Sci. **256**(1-2), 93–112 (2001). https://doi.org/10.1016/S0304-3975(00)00103-1
34. Kiezun, A., Ganesh, V., Guo, P.J., Hooimeijer, P., Ernst, M.D.: HAMPI: a solver for string constraints. In: Proceedings of the Eighteenth International Symposium on Software Testing and Analysis, pp. 105–116 (2009)
35. Lamport, L.: A new solution of Dijkstra's concurrent programming problem. In: Concurrency: The Works of Leslie Lamport, pp. 171–178 (2019)
36. Legay, A.: T(O)RMC: a tool for (omega)-regular model checking. In: CAV, pp. 548–551 (2008)
37. Lengál, O., Lin, A.W., Majumdar, R., Rümmer, P.: Fair termination for parameterized probabilistic concurrent systems. In: Legay, A., Margaria, T. (eds.) TACAS 2017. LNCS, vol. 10205, pp. 499–517. Springer, Heidelberg (2017). https://doi.org/10.1007/978-3-662-54577-5_29
38. Lin, A.W., Nguyen, T.K., Rümmer, P., Sun, J.: Regular symmetry patterns. In: Jobstmann, B., Leino, K. (eds.) VMCAI 2016. LNCS, vol. 9583, pp. 455–475. Springer, Heidelberg (2016). https://doi.org/10.1007/978-3-662-49122-5_22
39. Lin, A.W., Rümmer, P.: Liveness of randomised parameterised systems under arbitrary schedulers. In: Chaudhuri, S., Farzan, A. (eds.) CAV 2016. LNCS, vol. 9780, pp. 112–133. Springer, Cham (2016). https://doi.org/10.1007/978-3-319-41540-6_7
40. Lin, A.W., Rümmer, P.: Regular model checking revisited. In: Model Checking, Synthesis, and Learning. LNCS, vol. 13030, pp. 97–114. Springer (2021)

41. Lotz, K., et al.: Solving string constraints using SAT. In: Enea, C., Lal, A. (eds.) Computer Aided Verification - 35th International Conference, CAV 2023, Paris, France, July 17-22, 2023, Proceedings, Part II. LNCS, vol. 13965, pp. 187–208. Springer (2023). https://doi.org/10.1007/978-3-031-37703-7_9
42. Lu, Z., Siemer, S., Jha, P., Day, J., Manea, F., Ganesh, V.: Layered and staged Monte Carlo tree search for SMT strategy synthesis. In: Larson, K. (ed.) Proceedings of the Thirty-Third International Joint Conference on Artificial Intelligence, IJCAI 2024. International Joint Conferences on Artificial Intelligence Organization, pp. 1907–1915 (2024). https://doi.org/10.24963/ijcai.2024/211, main Track
43. Lynch, N.: Distributed Algorithms. Morgan Kaufmann Publishers (1996)
44. Markgraf, O., Hong, C.-D., Lin, A.W., Najib, M., Neider, D.: Parameterized synthesis with safety properties. In: Oliveira, B. (ed.) APLAS 2020. LNCS, vol. 12470, pp. 273–292. Springer, Cham (2020). https://doi.org/10.1007/978-3-030-64437-6_14
45. Mora, F., Berzish, M., Kulczynski, M., Nowotka, D., Ganesh, V.: Z3str4: a multi-armed string solver. In: Huisman, M., Păsăreanu, C., Zhan, N. (eds.) FM 2021. LNCS, vol. 13047, pp. 389–406. Springer, Cham (2021). https://doi.org/10.1007/978-3-030-90870-6_21
46. Neider, D., Jansen, N.: Regular model checking using solver technologies and automata learning. In: Brat, G., Rungta, N., Venet, A. (eds.) NFM 2013. LNCS, vol. 7871, pp. 16–31. Springer, Heidelberg (2013). https://doi.org/10.1007/978-3-642-38088-4_2
47. Padon, O., McMillan, K.L., Panda, A., Sagiv, M., Shoham, S.: Ivy: safety verification by interactive generalization. In: Krintz, C., Berger, E.D. (eds.) Proceedings of the 37th ACM SIGPLAN Conference on Programming Language Design and Implementation, PLDI 2016, Santa Barbara, CA, USA, 13–17 June 2016, pp. 614–630. ACM (2016). https://doi.org/10.1145/2908080.2908118
48. Rungta, N.: A billion SMT queries a day (invited paper). In: Shoham, S., Vizel, Y. (eds.) Computer Aided Verification - 34th International Conference, CAV 2022, Haifa, Israel, 7–10 August 2022, Proceedings, Part I. LNCS, vol. 13371, pp. 3–18. Springer (2022). https://doi.org/10.1007/978-3-031-13185-1_1
49. Saxena, P., Akhawe, D., Hanna, S., Mao, F., McCamant, S., Song, D.: A symbolic execution framework for Javascript. In: 2010 IEEE Symposium on Security and Privacy, pp. 513–528. IEEE (2010)
50. Szymanski, B.K.: Mutual exclusion revisited. In: Proceedings of the 5th Jerusalem Conference on Information Technology, 1990. 'Next Decade in Information Technology', pp. 110–117. IEEE (1990)
51. Tateishi, T., Pistoia, M., Tripp, O.: Path-and index-sensitive string analysis based on monadic second-order logic. ACM Trans. Softw. Eng. Methodol. (TOSEM) **22**(4), 1–33 (2013)
52. Trinh, M.T., Chu, D.H., Jaffar, J.: Progressive reasoning over recursively-defined strings. In: Chaudhuri, S., Farzan, A. (eds.) Computer Aided Verification, pp. 218–240. Springer, Cham (2016)
53. Vardhan, A., Viswanathan, M.: LEVER: a tool for learning based verification. In: CAV, pp. 471–474 (2006). https://doi.org/10.1007/11817963_43
54. Wolper, P., Boigelot, B.: Verifying systems with infinite but regular state spaces. In: CAV, pp. 88–97 (1998). https://doi.org/10.1007/BFb0028736
55. Yu, F., Alkhalaf, M., Bultan, T.: Stranger: an automata-based string analysis tool for PHP. In: International Conference on Tools and Algorithms for the Construction and Analysis of Systems, pp. 154–157. Springer (2010)

Open Access This chapter is licensed under the terms of the Creative Commons Attribution 4.0 International License (http://creativecommons.org/licenses/by/4.0/), which permits use, sharing, adaptation, distribution and reproduction in any medium or format, as long as you give appropriate credit to the original author(s) and the source, provide a link to the Creative Commons license and indicate if changes were made.

The images or other third party material in this chapter are included in the chapter's Creative Commons license, unless indicated otherwise in a credit line to the material. If material is not included in the chapter's Creative Commons license and your intended use is not permitted by statutory regulation or exceeds the permitted use, you will need to obtain permission directly from the copyright holder.

Infinite-State Liveness Checking with rlive

Alessandro Cimatti[1], Alberto Griggio[1], Christopher Johannsen[2(✉)], Kristin Yvonne Rozier[2], and Stefano Tonetta[1]

[1] Fondazione Bruno Kessler, Trento, Italy
[2] Iowa State University, Ames, USA
cgjohann@iastate.edu

Abstract. rlive is a recently-proposed SAT-based liveness model checking algorithm that showed remarkable performance compared to other state-of-the-art approaches, both in absolute terms (solving more problems overall than other engines on standard benchmark sets) as well as in relative terms (solving several problems that none of the other engines could solve). rlive proves or disproves properties of the form FGq, by trying to show that $\neg q$ can be visited only a finite number of times via an incremental reduction to a sequence of reachability queries. A key factor in the good performance of rlive is the extraction of "shoals" from the inductive invariants of the reachability queries to block states that can reach $\neg q$ a bounded number of times.

In this paper, we generalize rlive to handle infinite-state systems, using the Verification Modulo Theories paradigm. In contrast to the finite-state case, liveness cannot be simply reduced to finding a bound on the number of occurrences of $\neg q$ on paths. We propose therefore a solution leveraging predicate abstraction and termination techniques based on well-founded relations. In particular, we show how we can extract shoals that take into account the well-founded relations. We implemented the technique on top of the open source VMT engine IC3ia and we experimentally demonstrate how the new extension maintains the performance advantages (both absolute and relative) of the original rlive, thus significantly contributing to advancing the state of the art of infinite-state liveness verification.

1 Introduction

Liveness checking is the problem of proving (or disproving) that a property of the form $\mathbf{FG}q$ holds in a given transition system S. When $S \models \mathbf{FG}q$, all the traces of S are such that q eventually stabilizes, i.e., it holds indefinitely from a certain state on (equivalently, $\neg q$ is visited only a finite number of times). Dually, when $S \not\models \mathbf{FG}q$, there exists an infinite path π satisfying $\mathbf{GF}\neg q$ that hits condition $\neg q$ (usually called a fairness condition) an infinite number of times. Liveness checking is a fundamental enabler for verification, since LTL model checking can be reduced to liveness checking thanks to standard techniques [17].

In this paper, we tackle the problem of liveness checking for infinite-state systems. In contrast to the finite-state case, the problem cannot be simply reduced to the search for lasso-shaped fair paths, as an infinite-state transition system may only admit violations that cannot be presented as lasso-shaped paths. Dually, even if the property holds, there may be no upper bound on the number of times the fairness condition is satisfied along any path.

Our starting point is rlive, a recently-proposed SAT-based liveness checking algorithm for the finite state case, that demonstrated remarkable performance compared to other state-of-the-art approaches [47]. The rlive algorithm proves or disproves properties of the form $\mathbf{FG}q$, by trying to show that $\neg q$ can be visited only a finite number of times via an incremental reduction to a sequence of reachability queries. A distinguishing feature of rlive is the extraction of "shoals" from the inductive invariants of the reachability queries, to block states that can reach $\neg q$ only a bounded number of times.

We generalize rlive to handle infinite-state systems, using the Verification Modulo Theories (VMT) paradigm [11]. In contrast to the finite-state case, liveness cannot be reduced to finding a bound on the number of occurrences of $\neg q$ that is global for all the paths. We propose therefore a solution integrating predicate abstraction and termination techniques based on well-founded relations.

At the top level, our new algorithm, which we call rlive-inf, can be seen as a counterexample-guided abstraction refinement loop (CEGAR) [29] that maintains a set of predicates inducing an abstract state space and a set of well-founded relations. The procedure enumerates *abstract lassos*, which are candidate counterexample traces containing a repeated abstract state satisfying the fairness condition $\neg q$. Well-founded relations are used to avoid discovering candidate loops that can be proved to be terminating. If an abstract lasso is returned, rlive-inf attempts to concretize it and, in case of failure, it refines the abstraction by finding more predicates and/or well-founded relations. A key non-trivial step in the generalization of rlive to the infinite-state case is the construction of shoals that take into account the well-founded relations to block states that can reach $\neg q$ a finite but potentially unbounded number of times.

We implemented rlive-inf on top of the open-source VMT engine ic3ia [34], hence obtaining a fully-symbolic LTL model checker for infinite-state transition systems. We evaluated our implementation on a wide set of benchmarks from the literature, and compared it with αL2S [23], the state-of-the-art technique based on abstract liveness-to-safety, which is also implemented in ic3ia. Our experimental evaluation clearly demonstrates the value of rlive-inf. First, rlive-inf solves more benchmarks than αL2S, both safe and unsafe. Second, rlive-inf is on average significantly faster than αL2S. Interestingly, the two approaches are quite complementary, in the sense that the virtual best solver is significantly more effective than both procedures alone.

Structure of the Paper. In Sect. 2 we present some background, and in Sect. 3 we discuss the liveness checking problem. We present the rlive-inf algorithm in Sect. 4, and we prove its correctness in Sect. 5. In Sect. 6 we discuss its limitations, and in Sect. 7 we compare it to other approaches for liveness checking. In Sect. 8 we present our experimental evaluation, and in Sect. 9 we draw conclusions and present some directions for future work.

2 Preliminaries

We focus on model checking of infinite state systems described with symbolic formulas. We work in the setting of SMT [2] to interpret formulas modulo a given background theory and of VMT [11] to describe states and transitions with SMT formulas.

A symbolic transition system is defined as $S := \langle X, I, T \rangle$ where X is a set of variables, $I(X)$ is a one-state formula defining the initial condition and $T(X, X')$ is a two-state formula defining the transition relation, where $X' = \{x' \mid x \in X\}$ is the set of next-state variables. For a formula ϕ, we denote ϕ' the formula obtained by replacing each $x \in X$ with its next-state variant $x' \in X'$ in ϕ. A state is an assignment to the variables of X. A finite path π of S is a finite sequence of states $s_0, s_1 \ldots, s_n$ such that $s_0 \models I$ and $s_i, s'_{i+1} \models T$ (and similarly for an infinite path $s_0, s_1, \ldots$). If π is a finite path of the form $s_0, \ldots, s_n$, we refer to s_0 as π_{first} and to s_n as π_{last}. A state is reachable in S if it occurs in a finite path of S. An infinite path is lasso-shaped if it can be expressed as $\alpha \cdot \beta^\omega$, where the stem $\alpha := s_0, s_2, \ldots, s_l$ and the loop $\beta := s_{l+1}, \ldots, s_k$ are finite sequences of states in S such that $s_0, \ldots, s_k$ is a finite path of S and $s_k = s_{l+1}$.

Invariant Checking. The invariant checking problem asks whether a state property $P(X)$ holds in all reachable states of a system $S = \langle X, I, T \rangle$. An invariant checking procedure check-inv(X, I, T, P) returns a finite trace $\pi := s_0, s_1, \ldots, s_n$ of S where $s_i \models \neg P$ for some $0 \leq i \leq n$, or an inductive invariant inv such that $inv \models P$, $I \models inv$, and $inv \wedge T \models inv'$. See [13] for details. Many techniques exist to perform invariant checking of infinite-state systems, e.g. [4,5,13,33,36–38,43]. In the following, we assume a symbolic transition system $S = \langle X, I(X), T(X, X') \rangle$ is given.

Predicate Abstraction. Predicate abstraction is defined over a set of predicates $\mathbb{P} = \{\gamma_1(X), \ldots, \gamma_n(X)\}$ [15,28]. For each predicate $\gamma_i(X)$ we assume a corresponding a Boolean variable $\widehat{\gamma_i}$. With an abuse of notation, we may also denote $\{\widehat{\gamma_1}, \ldots, \widehat{\gamma_n}\}$ with $\mathbb{P}$. We relate each predicate to its abstracted Boolean variable with the following formula:

$$\textsc{PrDef}(X, \mathbb{P}) = \bigwedge_i \widehat{\gamma_i} \leftrightarrow \gamma_i(X)$$

The predicate abstraction of S, denoted $\widehat{S} := \langle \widehat{X}, \widehat{I}, \widehat{T} \rangle$, is defined as:

$$\widehat{X} := \mathbb{P} \quad \widehat{I} := \exists X.(I(X) \wedge \textsc{PrDef}(X, \mathbb{P}))$$
$$\widehat{T} := \exists X.(T(X, X') \wedge \textsc{PrDef}(X, \mathbb{P}) \wedge \textsc{PrDef}(X', \mathbb{P}'))$$

Given a state s, its abstraction $\widehat{s}$ with respect to $\mathbb{P}$, referred to as $\mathbb{P}$-abstraction, is defined as $\{\widehat{\gamma_i} \mid s \models \gamma_i\} \cup \{\neg\widehat{\gamma_j} \mid s \not\models \gamma_j\}$. Given an abstract state $\widehat{s}$, its set of corresponding concrete states is denoted $[\![\widehat{s}]\!]$: these are all the states that satisfy the formula $\bigwedge_{\widehat{\gamma_i} \in \widehat{s}} \gamma_i \wedge \bigwedge_{\neg\widehat{\gamma_j} \in \widehat{s}} \neg\gamma_j$.

Disjunctive Well-Founded Relations. A *well-founded relation* $\rho \subseteq Q \times Q$ is a binary relation such that every non-empty subset $U \subseteq Q$ has a minimal element with respect to ρ, that is, there is some $m \in U$ such that no $u \in U$ satisfies $\rho(u, m)$. A *disjunctive* well-founded relation is defined as a finite union of well-founded relations.

Termination of a program can be proven by finding a well-founded relation for the program's states. In order to reason about general transition relations (including those with disjunctions) we use disjunctive well-founded relations. One way to obtain a well-founded relation for a program with non-disjunctive transition relation T is via a ranking function $r(X)$ that assigns a natural number to each program state such that the relation $\{(r(s_0), r(s_1)) \mid s_0, s_1' \models T\}$ is well-founded. Various techniques exist to synthesize ranking functions, e.g. [22,30,40,45].

3 Liveness Checking

The problem of model checking general LTL properties [17] can be reduced, following standard techniques (e.g., [7,17,46]), to the problem of model checking a property of the form **FG**q, where q is a state formula over X. The problem of checking whether **FG**q holds in S, denoted $S \models \mathbf{FG}q$, amounts to checking if q eventually stabilizes on every path of S, i.e., for all $\pi \in S.\exists i.\forall j \geq i.\pi[j] \models q$. The dual problem is checking the existence of an infinite path $\pi \in S$ satisfying **GF**$\neg q$, that is, visits $\neg q$ an infinite number of times. $\neg q$ may be referred to as the fairness condition, and π as a fair path. In the following, we assume the **FG**q property as given. Several algorithms for liveness checking have been proposed in the past, including Liveness-to-safety (L2S) [3], FAIR [8], k-liveness [16], k-FAIR [35], rlive [47]. We provide details on the algorithms most relevant to our contributions here.

rlive. The rlive algorithm [47] performs a depth-first search for a loop violating **FG**q, i.e., a fair path π satisfying **GF**$\neg q$, hitting $\neg q$ an infinite number of times. rlive (see Algorithm 1) incrementally performs a series of invariant model checking queries. If the algorithm determines that $\neg q$ is unreachable from the current state in the search, rlive adds the newly-found inductive invariant to a set of states known as *shoals*, otherwise it reaches another state s that satisfies $\neg q$. A *shoal* is a set of states that can only reach $\neg q$ a finite number of times. If s is already on the search stack B, then rlive has found a loop satisfying **GF**$\neg q$, so the algorithm terminates with *Unsafe*. Otherwise rlive adds this state to the stack B and continues the search. The algorithm terminates with *Safe* once it shows that the initial set of states is contained in the shoals.

Liveness to Safety. When S is finite, $S \not\models \mathbf{FG}q$ if and only if there exists a *lasso-shaped* path $\alpha \cdot \beta^\omega$ in S where some state $b \in \beta$ is such that $b \models \neg q$. The L2S transformation [3] is an approach for reducing the problem of checking for the existence of a lasso-shaped path violating q to that of checking an invariant property. The idea is to record the first state of a loop satisfying **GF**$\neg q$ by

Algorithm 1: rlive algorithm for finite-state systems for the property $\mathbf{FG}q$ with variable set X, initial condition I, and transition relation T.

```
1  Procedure rlive(X, I, T, FGq) begin
2      C := ⊥
3      B := empty stack of states
4      while check-inv(X, I, T ∧ (¬C ∧ ¬C'), T⁻¹(¬C) → q) is Unsafe do
5          s := final state of get-mc-cex()
6          B.push(s)
7          while B is not empty do
8              s := B.top()
9              if check-inv(X, T(s), T ∧ (¬C ∧ ¬C'), T⁻¹(¬C) → q) is Unsafe
                 then
10                 t := final state of get-mc-cex()
11                 if t ∈ B then
12                     return Unsafe
13                 B.push(t)
14             else
15                 inv := get-mc-inv()
16                 C := C ∨ inv
17                 B.pop()
18     return Safe
```

introducing a copy X_c of the state variables X of S and a fresh variable SVD (saved) to record that the loop has started. X_c is nondeterministically assigned a state violating q (the start of the loop) and never changed after that, and the search tries to reach a state where each state variable has the same value as its copy and SVD is true, which implies that a violating lasso is detected.

Abstract Liveness to Safety. If S is infinite, the existence of a loop $\alpha \cdot \beta^\omega$ proves that $S \not\models \mathbf{FG}q$, but there may be other non lasso-shaped counterexamples. This makes the L2S construction incomplete, in the sense that it is no longer guaranteed to find a counterexample to $S \models \mathbf{FG}q$ if one exists, and unsound, in that $S \models \mathbf{FG}q$ does not follow from proving the absence of lasso-shaped violations. One possibility for restoring soundness is to prove the absence of lasso-shaped counterexamples in a finite abstraction of the input system, e.g., one induced by a finite set of predicates $\mathbb{P}$.

Given $\mathbb{P}$, the abstract liveness-to-safety (αL2S) encoding [23] consists of storing only the truth assignments to the predicates non-deterministically, and detecting a loop if the system visits again the same abstract state violating q. Predicate abstraction is however not complete in general for proving liveness properties of infinite-state systems in the sense that, even if the property is satisfied by the concrete system, there may be no finite set of predicates such that the abstraction does not contain counterexamples. In [23], predicate abstraction was combined with arguments based on well-founded relations to strengthen the proof power of the abstraction, and integrated in a CEGAR loop [18] to

---
Algorithm 2: rlive-inf algorithm for infinite-state liveness checking of the property **FG**q with variable set X, initial condition I, transition relation T.
---
1 Procedure rlive-inf(X, I, T, **FG**q) begin
2     $\mathbb{P} :=$ predicate symbols in I, q
3     $\mathbb{W} := \emptyset$ // set of well-founded relations
4   while abs-rlive-wfr($X, I, T, q, \mathbb{P}, \mathbb{W}$) is Unsafe do
5        $\widehat{\pi} :=$ get-abs-cex()
6   if feasible($I, T, \mathbb{P}, \widehat{\pi}$) then
7   return Unsafe
8        $\mathbb{W}, \mathbb{P} :=$ refine($I, T, \mathbb{P}, \widehat{\pi}$)
9   return Safe
---

improve the precision of the abstraction (by discovering either new predicates or new well-founded relations) upon discovery of spurious counterexamples. The resulting algorithm performs very well in practice, outperforming alternative approaches on several benchmarks.

4 Infinite State rlive

In this section we present our generalization of rlive to the infinite-state case, obtained by leveraging predicate abstraction and well-founded relations. We use predicate abstraction to address the infiniteness of the state space and well-founded relations to address abstract paths of the form $\widehat{\alpha} \cdot \widehat{\beta}^\omega$ that are not feasible in S, even though every finite unrolling $\widehat{\alpha} \cdot \widehat{\beta} \ldots \widehat{\beta}$ is feasible.

4.1 High-Level CEGAR Loop

At the high level, rlive-inf implements a CEGAR loop that at each iteration generates and solves an *abstract liveness checking* problem using abs-rlive-wfr, refining the precision of the abstraction upon detection of spurious counterexamples. The pseudocode for the main rlive-inf procedure is shown in Algorithm 2. The algorithm consists of the following main ingredients:

Abstraction Precision. The *precision* for the abstraction consists of a finite set of predicates $\mathbb{P}$ and a finite set of well-founded relations $\mathbb{W}$. Initially, $\mathbb{P}$ contains all predicate symbols in I and q, and $\mathbb{W}$ is empty.

Problem Definition. At each iteration of the main loop of line 4, the procedure abs-rlive-wfr is called to solve the following problem.

Definition 1 (Abstract Liveness Checking Problem). *Given a variable set X, initial condition I, transition relation T, system $S := \langle X, I, T \rangle$, property $P := \boldsymbol{FG}q$, predicates $\mathbb{P}$, and set of well-founded relations $\mathbb{W}$, we call* abstract liveness checking *the problem of checking whether there exists a finite sequence $\pi^0, \ldots, \pi^l$ of finite paths (called segments) of S such that:*

- $\pi^0_{\text{first}} \models I$, $\pi^l_{\text{last}} \models \neg q$, and the segments can be concatenated to form an abstract path π, that is, for all $0 \leq m < l$, $\widehat{\pi^m_{\text{last}}} = \widehat{\pi^{m+1}_{\text{first}}}$;
- the path π contains four states s_i, $s_j \equiv \pi^l_{\text{last}}$, s_h, and s_k (with $i \leq h < k \leq j$) such that:
  1. $s_i \models \neg q$, $s_j \models \neg q$, $s_h \models \neg q$, $s_k \models \neg q$;
  2. $\widehat{s_i} = \widehat{s_j}$; and
  3. for all $W \in \mathbb{W}$, $(s_h, s_k) \notin W$.

If such paths $\pi^0, \ldots, \pi^l$ exist, we say that the abstract liveness checking problem is unsafe, and call the path π an abstract lasso.

If abs-rlive-wfr cannot find an abstract lasso, then the property holds, and rlive-inf returns $Safe^1$. Otherwise, the feasible procedure of line 6 checks whether the abstract lasso corresponds to at least one concrete lasso-shaped path in S in which $\neg q$ holds at least once in the loop; if this is the case, rlive-inf finds a counterexample to $\mathbf{FG}q$, and $Unsafe$ is returned.

Refinement. If the abstract lasso is infeasible, the refine procedure is invoked at line 8 to try to improve the precision of the abstraction, by discovering new predicates and/or new well-founded relations. The method is the same as that used in [23]. Specifically, the abstract lasso can be spurious for two reasons:

1. either there exists a finite unrolling of the abstract lasso that is infeasible in the concrete system S; or
2. the looping part of the abstract lasso cannot be executed infinitely often even though all its finite unrollings are feasible.

In the first case, refine generates new predicates to add to $\mathbb{P}$ using Craig interpolation [32], whereas in the second case, refine tries to generate both new predicates and new well-founded relations using ranking function synthesis techniques from termination analysis [30]. Since the approach in [30] only admits transition relations without disjunctions that represent "simple lassos" of the form $\varphi_{stem} \wedge \varphi_{loop}$, we enumerate all simple lassos symbolically represented by the candidate counterexample using [39] and synthesize a ranking function for each. See Sect. 4.2 of [23] for details. Note that, in general, refinement might fail (because both Craig interpolation and ranking function synthesis techniques are incomplete for some theories); in such cases, rlive-inf will diverge.

4.2 Abstract Liveness Checking

We now describe the core of rlive-inf: abstract liveness checking with the abs-rlive-wfr procedure. Algorithm 3 provides the pseudocode of the abs-rlive-wfr procedure, solving the abstract liveness checking problem in Definition 1. Conceptually, the procedure consists of two main blocks:

---

[1] Essentially, Definition 1 ensures that the absence of abstract lassos implies the disjunctive well-foundedness of the transitive closure of the transition relation of S [19].

Algorithm 3: abs-rlive-wfr procedure for fairness conditions q with variable set X, initial condition I, transition relation T, predicate set $\mathbb{P}$, and well-founded relation set $\mathbb{W}$.

```
 1  C := ⊥ // global persistent cache of blocked states (shoals)
 2  Procedure abs-rlive-wfr (X, I, T, q, P, W) begin
 3      B̂ := empty stack of abstract states
 4      while check-inv(X, I, T ∧ (¬C ∧ ¬C'), T⁻¹(¬C) → q) is Unsafe do
 5          ŝ := P-abstraction of final state of get-mc-cex()
 6          B̂.push(ŝ)
 7          while B̂ is not empty do
 8              ŝ := B̂.top()
 9              Xc := {xc | x ∈ X}, SVD := fresh-bool-var()
10              X̄ := X ∪ Xc ∪ {SVD}
11              T̄ := T ∧ ((¬SVD ∧ SVD') → ((X = Xc) ∧ ¬q)) ∧ (X'c = Xc) ∧
                   (SVD → SVD')
12              P̄ := (T̄⁻¹(¬C) ∧ SVD ∧ ¬W(Xc, X)) → q
13              if check-inv(X̄, ⟦ŝ⟧ ∧ ¬SVD, T̄ ∧ (¬C ∧ ¬C'), P̄) is Unsafe then
14                  t̂ := P-abstraction final state of get-mc-cex()
15                  if t̂ ∈ B̂ then
16                      return Unsafe
17                  B̂.push(t̂)
18              else
19                  B̂.pop()
20                  inv := get-mc-inv() // includes predicates over Xc, SVD
21                  Cnew := (∃Xc, SVD. (inv ∧ ¬SVD))
22                  C := C ∨ Cnew
23      return Safe
```

Segmented Search. abs-rlive-wfr translates the abstract liveness checking problem of Definition 1 into a *sequence* of invariant checking problems, in which candidate abstract lassos are constructed incrementally (segment-by-segment), with a depth-first search for successor $\neg q$-states from the current $\neg q$-state, analogously to how the original rlive works in the finite-state case.

Caching. abs-rlive-wfr maintains a (symbolic) *cache* of states that cannot be part of any counterexample, i.e., that cannot be part of any path of S satisfying $\neg q$ infinitely often. Such cache (made of states belonging to shoals [47]), is global and persistent across different calls of abs-rlive-wfr at different iterations of the main CEGAR loop of Algorithm 2, ensuring that once a set of states is blocked by rlive-inf, it is never considered again in the future when searching for abstract lassos.

As compared to finite-state rlive (Algorithm 1), the high-level structure is largely the same with the following key differences:

Abstract Search Stack. The search stack $\widehat{B}$ is a stack of $\mathbb{P}$-abstract states.

Well-founded Relation Reasoning. When searching for an abstract lasso, the algorithm checks for path segments that include a pair of $\neg q$-states not in any relation in $\mathbb{W}$. It does so with an extended system encoding (lines 10, 11) and modified property (line 12), explained in detail below.

Shoal Construction. When constructing shoals, the extra variables introduced by the extended system encoding are removed from the returned inductive invariant, by first forcing SVD to false and then by existentially eliminating them (line 21).

The algorithm returns *Unsafe* if it finds an abstract $\neg q$-state $\widehat{t}$ already in the search stack $\widehat{B}$, implying the existence of an abstract lasso. Crucially, the check of $\overline{P}$ on line 13 also implies the existence of at least one pair of $\neg q$-states within that abstract lasso not in any relation in $\mathbb{W}$. The resulting counterexample will then be checked for feasibility either due to the imprecision of the $\mathbb{P}$-abstraction or the existence of a well-founded relation proving the counterexample's finiteness by the outer CEGAR procedure.

Otherwise, if no $\neg q$-state pair not in any relation in $\mathbb{W}$ is reachable from the current top element of $\widehat{B}$, the inductive invariant from the corresponding model-checking call is added to the shoals C (lines 21-22). The algorithm returns *Safe* if there are no more $\neg q$-states outside the shoals that are reachable from the initial states.

Extended System Encoding. The encoding used to find path segments with pairs of states not in any well-founded relation in $\mathbb{W}$ is inspired by the L2S encoding. Specifically, it introduces a new variable SVD and a copy of the state variables X_c, with SVD initially set to false. The transition relation then enforces:

1. SVD is non-deterministically set to true in a state where $\neg q$ holds and X_c takes on the value of X: $((\text{SVD}' \wedge \neg\text{SVD}) \to ((X = X_c) \wedge \neg q))$.
2. Once SVD is true, it stays true: $(\text{SVD} \to \text{SVD}')$.
3. The variables in X_c are frozen: $(X_c' = X_c)$.

Putting this all together, the *extended system* $\overline{S} := \langle \overline{X}, \overline{I}, \overline{T} \rangle$ is defined as:

$$\overline{X} := X \cup \{\text{SVD}\} \cup X_c$$
$$\overline{I} := I \wedge \neg\text{SVD}$$
$$\overline{T} := T \wedge ((\text{SVD}' \wedge \neg\text{SVD}) \to ((X = X_c) \wedge \neg q)) \wedge$$
$$(X_c' = X_c) \wedge (\text{SVD} \to \text{SVD}')$$

We also modify the property to check instead for a pair of $\neg q$-states not in any well-founded relation in $\mathbb{W}$:

$$\overline{P} := \left(T^{-1}(\neg C) \wedge \text{SVD} \wedge \neg\mathbb{W}(X_c, X)\right) \to q$$

Model checking $\overline{S}$ for the property $\overline{P}$ will return *Unsafe* if there is a path $\pi := s_0, \ldots, s_c, s_c' \ldots, s$ where:

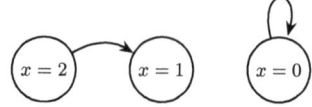

Fig. 1. Visualization of the transition system S of Example 1.

1. SVD is set after s_c: $s_c \not\models$ SVD, $s'_c \models$ SVD, $s \models$ SVD.
2. s and s_c are $\neg q$-states: $s \models \neg q$, $s_c \models \neg q$.
3. (s_c, s) are not part of any relation in $\mathbb{W}$: for all $W \in \mathbb{W}$, $\neg W(s_c, s)$.
4. s is not a predecessor of a shoal: $s \models T^{-1}(\neg C)$

As a result, the algorithm constructs a candidate counterexample segment-by-segment, where each segment has at least one pair of non-well-founded $\neg q$-states. Conversely, the algorithm learns states that cannot be part of any counterexample (i.e., shoals) if all pairs of $\neg q$-states are in some well-founded relation or no reachable $\neg q$-state pair exists.

Shoal Maintenance. In general, inductive invariants produced by the check-inv call on line 13 might contain the extended variables SVD and X_c. Such variables are not part of the original system, and should therefore be removed from the invariants in order to produce shoals. Note however that simply applying existential quantifier elimination for this would not work, as the resulting formula could be too general. Before applying existential elimination, it is necessary to force SVD to be false, as done on line 21. The following example illustrates the situation.

Example 1. Consider the following transition system $S := \langle X, I, T \rangle$:

$$X := \{x\} \qquad I := \top \qquad T := ((x = 2) \land (x' = 1)) \lor ((x = 0) \land (x' = 0)).$$

A graphical illustration of S is shown in Fig. 1. Suppose we are trying to prove **FG**q, where $q := (x < 0) \lor (x > 2)$, and that $\mathbb{P} := \{(x = 0), (x = 1), (x = 2)\}$ and $\mathbb{W} := \{W\}$, where $W(y, z) := (y > z) \land (z \geq 0)$. Note that $S \not\models$ **FG**q, since the path in which x is always set to 0 is a counterexample for the property. However, suppose that rlive-inf picks $\widehat{s} := (x = 2)$ as the $\neg q$-state on line 5. Then, the check on line 13 will return *Safe*, and suppose now that check-inv returns the following inductive invariant:

$$\overline{inv} := ((x = 2) \land \neg\text{SVD}) \lor ((x = 1) \land (\text{SVD} \to (x_c \geq 2))) \lor \\ (\text{SVD} \land (x_c = 1) \land (x = 0)).$$

Since $\overline{inv}$ contains the auxiliary variables x_c and SVD, we cannot take it directly as a shoal, because otherwise the check-inv call on line 4 could still return the same abstract state $\widehat{s}$, since $\widehat{s} \land \overline{T}^{-1}(\neg \overline{inv}) \not\models \bot$. However, simply projecting away the auxiliary variables via existential quantifier elimination would be unsound, as it would generalize $\overline{inv}$ too much: since $\exists (x_c, \text{SVD}).\overline{inv}$ is equivalent to $(x = 0) \vee (x = 1) \vee (x = 2)$, adding it as a shoal would block also the state $(x = 0)$, thus preventing rlive-inf to discover the counterexample and making it wrongly conclude that the property holds. By forcing SVD to false before applying existential elimination, instead, we obtain the formula $(x = 2) \vee (x = 1)$, which is a valid shoal. ◇

Finally, we would like to remark that in a practical implementation, quantifier elimination is typically not necessary. For example, if check-inv is based on some variant of IC3 such as [13], it is possible to prove that the inductive invariants produced on line 20 are of the form $\phi(X) \wedge \bigwedge_i (\text{SVD} \to \psi_i(X, X_c))$. In such cases, the transformation of line 21 to obtain shoals amounts to simply taking $\phi(X)$.

Example 2. We conclude the section with an example illustrating the behaviour of rlive-inf. Consider the following symbolic transition system $S := \langle X, I, T \rangle$, where:

$$X := \{l_0, l_1, x, y\}$$
$$I := L_A$$
$$T := (L_A \wedge L'_B) \vee$$
$$ (L_B \wedge L'_B \wedge (x > 0) \wedge (x' < x)) \vee$$
$$ (L_B \wedge L'_C) \vee (L_A \wedge L'_C) \vee$$
$$ (L_C \wedge L'_C \wedge (y < 2) \wedge (y < y')) \vee$$
$$ (L_C \wedge L'_D) \vee (L_B \wedge L'_D) \vee (L_D \wedge L'_D)$$

where $L_A := \neg l_0 \wedge \neg l_1$, $L_B := l_0 \wedge \neg l_1$, $L_C := \neg l_0 \wedge l_1$, $L_D := l_0 \wedge l_1$, and $x, y \in \mathbb{Z}$. We call out specifically that self-loop transitions on L_B and L_C cannot be taken forever—no matter the value of x and y initially, the self-loop guard conditions will eventually fail since at each transition x decreases in L_B and y increases in L_C. A visualization of the example is shown in Fig. 2. We now outline how rlive-inf proves that $S \models \mathbf{FG} L_D$ (thus, in this example, $q = L_D$).

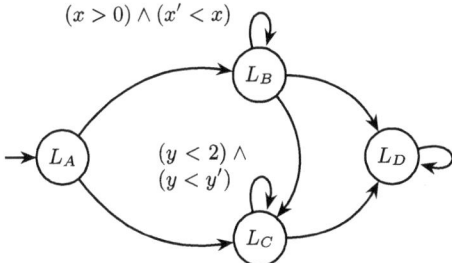

Fig. 2. Visualization of the transition system S of Example 2 with edges labeled with constraints placed on x and y wrt L_A, L_B, L_C, and L_D.

Initially, $\mathbb{P} := \{l_0, l_1\}$, $\mathbb{W} := \emptyset$, and $C := \bot$. The first check-inv call (line 4) will cause the abstract $\neg q$-state $\widehat{s_0} := \{\neg l_0, \neg l_1\}$ to be added to the stack $\widehat{B}$.

The subsequent call to check-inv on line 13 will reach a new abstract $\neg q$-state $\widehat{s_1} := \{l_0, \neg l_1\}$, which can also be reached again in the subsequent iteration of the inner loop of line 7, resulting in the abstract lasso $\widehat{s_0}, \widehat{s_1}, \widehat{s_1}$. The counterexample is spurious, however, and by analyzing the concretization of the looping part of the abstract lasso, refinement finds the well-founded relation $W_1(x_c, x) := (x_c > x) \land (x \geq 1)$, together with a new predicate $(x \geq 1)$, in order to improve the precision of the abstraction.[2]

The CEGAR loop then executes a new iteration with an updated precision $\mathbb{P} := \{l_0, l_1, (x \geq 1)\}$ and $\mathbb{W} := \{W_1\}$. abs-rlive-wfr will then produce another abstract lasso, namely: $\{\neg l_0, \neg l_1, (x \geq 1)\}, \{\neg l_0, l_1, (x \geq 1)\}, \{\neg l_0, l_1, (x \geq 1)\}$. Also this counterexample is spurious, and the abstraction in this case can be refined by adding the relation $W_2(y_c, y) := (y > y_c) \land (y \leq 1)$ to $\mathbb{W}$ and the predicate $(y \leq 1)$ to $\mathbb{P}$. At this point, the abstraction is sufficiently precise to make abs-rlive-wfr return *Safe*. More specifically:

- The check-inv call on line 4 adds the abstract state $\widehat{s_0} := \{l_0, \neg l_1, \neg(x \geq 1), \neg(y \leq 1)\}$ to the stack $\widehat{B}$;
- The check-inv call on line 13 finds a segment starting from $\widehat{s_0}$ to the abstract state $\widehat{s_1} := \{\neg l_0, l_1, \neg(x \geq 1), (y \leq 1)\}$, which is then added to $\widehat{B}$;
- The next check-inv call, to find another segment starting from $\widehat{s_1}$ and reaching the next $\neg q$-state, finds $\widehat{s_2} := \{\neg l_0, l_1, \neg(x \geq 1), \neg(y \leq 1)\}$ and adds it to $\widehat{B}$;
- At this point, the search for another segment starting from $\widehat{s_2}$ is unsuccessful, since all its successors are q-states. Therefore, the check-inv call on the extended system $\langle \overline{X}, [\![s_2]\!] \land \neg \text{SVD}, \overline{T} \rangle$ and invariant property $\overline{P}$ returns *Safe* and produces the inductive invariant $l_1 \land (l_0 \lor \neg(y \leq 1)) \land (\text{SVD} \to l_0)$, from which the shoal $l_1 \land (l_0 \lor \neg(y \leq 1))$ is extracted on line 21 and added to C.
- $\widehat{s_2}$ is then removed from $\widehat{B}$, and another call to check-inv is performed to find another abstract lasso segment starting from $\widehat{s_1}$. Also in this case, however, the search is not successful. This is because all successors of $\widehat{s_2}$ in S that satisfy $\neg q$ are either satisfying W_2, or contained in C; therefore, check-inv returns *Safe* and generates the invariant $l_1 \land \neg l_0 \land (\text{SVD} \to (y < y_c))$, resulting in the new shoal $l_1 \land \neg l_0$. C is then updated to $(l_1 \land (l_0 \lor \neg(y \leq 1))) \lor (l_1 \land \neg l_0)$.
- $\widehat{s_1}$ then is removed from $\widehat{B}$, and check-inv is called again on line 13 to find a segment starting from $\widehat{s_0}$. The search is again unsuccessful, with check-inv returning *Safe* with the invariant $l_0 \land (\text{SVD} \to (x_c > x))$, resulting in the shoal l_0, thus updating C to $(l_1 \land (l_0 \lor \neg(y \leq 1))) \lor (l_1 \land \neg l_0) \lor l_0$. In this case, the use of W_1 is crucial for excluding $\neg q$-successors.
- $\widehat{s_0}$ is removed from $\widehat{B}$, which becomes empty. A new iteration of the outer loop calls check-inv on line 4, finding no more $\neg q$-states outside the shoals, and rlive-inf returns *Safe*. ◇

---

[2] Our refinement procedure is discussed in Sect. 4.1. We refer to Sect. 4.2 of [23] for additional details.

5 Correctness

In this section, we prove that rlive-inf does not produce wrong results. We begin by proving the correctness of Algorithm 3, namely that it either proves that $S \models \mathbf{FG}q$ or it finds an abstract lasso. Note that if there is there is no abstract lasso, then $S \models \mathbf{FG}q$. This follows immediately from the following lemma proved in [23].

Lemma 1 (Lemma 1 of [23]). *Let π be a path satisfying $\mathbf{GF}\neg q$ and $\mathbb{W}$ be a finite set of well-founded relations. Then, any infinite suffix π' of π contains two states s_1, s_2, each satisfying $\neg q$, such that (s_1, s_2) is not in any relation in $\mathbb{W}$.*

Corollary 1. *If S has a path π satisfying $\mathbf{GF}\neg q$, then π is an abstract lasso for any sets $\mathbb{P}$ and $\mathbb{W}$.*

The main non-trivial point for proving the correctness of Algorithm 3 is the shoal construction defined at line 21. In the following lemma, we prove that there is no abstract lasso starting from any state in $C = \exists X_c, \text{SVD}. \left(\overline{inv} \land \neg \text{SVD}\right)$.

Lemma 2 (Shoal Correctness). *Let a variable set X, initial condition I, transition relation T, transition system $S := \langle X, I, T \rangle$, and a formula $C(X)$ such that there is no abstract lasso starting from C in S be given. Let $\overline{S} := \langle \overline{X}, [\![\hat{s}]\!] \land \neg \text{SVD}, \overline{T} \land (\neg C \land \neg C') \rangle$ where $\hat{s}$, $\overline{X}$ and $\overline{T}$ are defined as in lines 8, 10 and 11 of Algorithm 3. Let $\overline{inv}$ be an inductive invariant entailing $\neg \overline{P}$ as defined in line 12. Then there is no abstract lasso starting from $C_{new} = \exists X_c, \text{SVD}. \left(\overline{inv} \land \neg \text{SVD}\right)$.*

Proof. Suppose by contradiction that there is an abstract lasso $\pi := s_0, s_1, \ldots$ starting from a state s_0 in C_{new}. By definition, there exist s_i, s_j, s_h, and s_k (with $i \leq h < k \leq j$) such that:

1. $s_i \models \neg q$, $s_j \models \neg q$, $s_h \models \neg q$, $s_k \models \neg q$;
2. for all $w \in \mathbb{W}$, $(s_h, s_k) \notin w$.

We can extend π to a path $\overline{\pi}$ over $\overline{X}$ by setting SVD to false in $\overline{s}_0, \ldots, \overline{s}_h$, and true elsewhere, and by setting X_c to the value of X in s_h everywhere. In this way, for all $l \geq 0$, $\overline{s}_l, \overline{s}_{l+1} \models \overline{T}$. Since $\overline{inv}$ is inductive, then for all $l \geq 0$, $\overline{s}_l \models \overline{inv}$. However, $\overline{s}_k \models \neg q$ as mentioned before, $\overline{s}_k \models \text{SVD}$ by construction, $\overline{s}_k \models \neg \mathbb{W}(X, X_c)$ because $s_h, s_k \models \neg \mathbb{W}$. Finally, note that s_{h+1} cannot be in C. Thus, we reach a contradiction with the fact that $\overline{inv}$ entails $\neg \overline{P}$. □

Theorem 1 (abs-rlive-wfr Soundness). *Assuming that check-inv is correct, if Algorithm 3 returns Safe, then $S \models \mathbf{FG}q$; if Algorithm 3 returns Unsafe, then S has an abstract lasso.*

Proof The algorithm returns *Safe* when check-inv$(X, I, T \land (\neg C \land \neg C'), \neg q \land T^{-1}(\neg C))$ returns *Safe*. Thus no state in $\neg C$ can reach $\neg q$. Note that C is updated only at Line 21 and by Lemma 2, the algorithm maintains as invariant that C always contains states that cannot be the starting point of an abstract lasso. Thus, by Lemma 1, $S \models \mathbf{FG}q$.

The algorithm returns *Unsafe* when a new state $\widehat{t}$ is found as the last state of a counterexample by check-inv($\overline{X}, [\![\widehat{s}]\!] \wedge \neg\text{SVD}, \overline{T} \wedge (\neg C \wedge \neg C'), \overline{P}$) and $\widehat{t}$ is already on the stack of abstract states. For every pair of abstract states $\widehat{s}$ and $\widehat{t}$ that are consecutive on the stack, there exist a path $\pi := s_0, s_1, \ldots, s_k$ such that $s_0 \in [\![\widehat{s}]\!]$ and $s_k \in [\![\widehat{t}]\!]$; and for some h, for all $W \in \mathbb{W}$, $(s_h, s_k) \notin W$. Moreover there exists a path $\pi := s_0, s_1, \ldots, s_k$ where $s_0 \models I$ and the abstract state of s_k is the first on the stack. Finally, all abstract states on the stack satisfy $\neg q$. Therefore, there exists an abstract lasso. □

Theorem 1 allows us to prove the correctness of rlive-inf, provided that the procedures feasible and refine of Algorithm 2 satisfy some basic soundness assumptions. Specifically, we require feasible to return true only if there exists an infinite path in S in which $\neg q$ is true infinitely often (and that is consistent with the abstract lasso), and refine to only produce relations that are well-founded. We can then state the following.

Theorem 2 (rlive-inf Soundness). *Assuming that feasible and refine are correct, if Algorithm 2 returns Safe, then $S \models \boldsymbol{FG}q$, and if it returns Unsafe, then $S \not\models \boldsymbol{FG}q$.*

6 Limitations

Theorem 2 ensures that rlive-inf is sound, i.e. that a *Safe* result returned by Algorithm 2 implies that $S \models \boldsymbol{FG}q$, and an *Unsafe* one implies that $S \not\models \boldsymbol{FG}q$. However, since liveness checking for infinite-state systems is in general an undecidable problem, rlive-inf is necessarily incomplete.

A first source of incompleteness lies in the fact that rlive-inf currently only returns *Unsafe* if it finds a lasso-shaped counterexample, and therefore it will diverge (i.e., not terminate) for even simple systems whose only counterexamples are not lasso-shaped. This limitation can however be addressed by integrating techniques for LTL falsification in infinite-state systems such as [10]. A second source of incompleteness is that the calls to check-inv in abs-rlive-wfr are in general undecidable. Third, both interpolation-based refinement and ranking function synthesis procedures used for abstraction refinement are incomplete and might either fail to refine the precision of the abstraction, or produce an infinite sequence of refinements.

Finally, and perhaps more interestingly, another source of incompleteness is inherent to the way well-founded relations are integrated in the rlive search. The extended system encoding presented in Sect. 4.2, justified by Lemma 1, implies that abs-rlive-wfr returns an abstract lasso as soon as it finds *any* pair of $\neg q$-states that are not in any relation in $\mathbb{W}$. However, if that pair is part of a path that necessarily visits a different pair of abstract states such that all their concretizations are in some relation already in $\mathbb{W}$, then the entire abstract lasso is spurious. The following is an example illustrating such situation. Addressing such limitation of rlive-inf (as well as assessing its impact in practice) is part of our plans for future work.

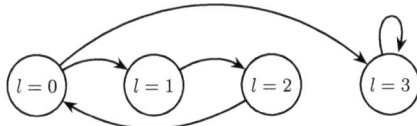

Fig. 3. Visualization of the transition system S of Example 3.

Example 3. Consider the following system $S := \langle X, I, T \rangle$ where:

$$X := \{l, x, q\}$$
$$I := (l = 0) \wedge (x > 0) \wedge q$$
$$T := \big((l = 0) \wedge (l' = 1) \wedge (x > 0) \wedge (x' = x - 1) \wedge \neg q'\big) \vee$$
$$\big((l = 1) \wedge (l' = 2) \wedge (x' = x + 1) \wedge \neg q'\big) \vee$$
$$\big((l = 2) \wedge (l' = 0) \wedge (x' = x - 1) \wedge \neg q'\big) \vee$$
$$\big((l = 0) \wedge (l' = 3) \wedge (x \leq 0) \wedge q'\big) \vee$$
$$\big((l = 3) \wedge (l' = 3) \wedge q'\big)$$

shown graphically in Fig. 3. The system satisfies the property **FG**q, because every loop from $l = 0$ to $l = 2$ (in which $\neg q$ holds) can only be executed a finite number of times, since the transition from $l = 0$ to $l = 1$ is guarded by a condition $(x > 0)$, and inside the loop x is decremented twice and only incremented once. Therefore, a suitable well-founded relation that proves that the loop cannot be executed infinitely often is $W(x_c, x) := (x_c > x) \wedge (x \geq 0)$. However, since the transition from $l = 1$ to $l = 2$ violates W, abs-rlive-wfr will find an abstract lasso and rlive-inf won't be able to prove the property. ◇

7 Related Work

Modern symbolic LTL model checking algorithms predominantly rely on SAT-based methods. Some of them can be trivially extended to infinite-state systems replacing SAT with SMT solvers.

For example, rlive and k-liveness [16] remain sound also for infinite-state systems, as they are based on proving **FG**q properties by showing that $\neg q$ can be visited only a finite number of times. k-liveness focuses on counting the number of times $\neg q$ can be visited, while rlive looks for counterexamples by state enumeration, while blocking states that can reach $\neg q$ only a bounded number of times (the "shoals").

Both rlive and k-liveness rely on invariant model checking with a series of reachability checks trying to reach $\neg q$. These subproblems can be addressed with implicit predicate abstraction [44] as done for example in [12] for k-liveness. However, they focus on finite paths, and are not amenable to include proofs based on well-founded relations. We here addressed this challenge in the case of rlive, but the same idea can be in principle extended to k-liveness.

FAIR [8] and liveness-to-safety [3] search only for lassos and are therefore unsound when extending to the infinite-state case by just replacing the SAT solver with an SMT one. The liveness-to-safety transformation was adapted for infinite-state systems in [23] with implicit predicate abstraction and well-founded relations. This approach was shown to be also more effective than algorithms focused on termination, also employing well-founded relations (cfr.,e.g., [24,42]). The extension of rlive is similar to the one presented in [23]. As we discussed above, it uses the same high-level CEGAR loop and the same refinement of predicates and well-founded relations. αL2S also shares the same limitations described in Sect. 6 and in particular cannot prove Example 3. However, the details of rlive-inf are quite different from αL2S. In particular, αL2S uses a monolithic encoding to find candidate counterexamples, using a single invariant model-checking call wrt. the current level of abstraction, whereas rlive-inf builds counterexamples iteratively with local searches that do not consider loop conditions. Further, rlive-inf explicitly caches states known to visit the fairness condition a finite number of times in shoals. While the formulation of αL2S does not do any caching, in practice the implementation of [23] uses certain invariants found from previous calls to the underlying ic3-based model checker.

Other techniques such as [22,27,30,41,45] focus specifically on proving termination of programs, sometimes under fairness conditions [19]. Extensions of these techniques to proving temporal properties of systems include [20,21], though they do not focus on liveness checking of general symbolic transition systems.

Another recent approach to LTL model checking uses neural networks to search for ranking functions that prove that there is no fair trace in the system satisfying the property [26]. The technique is based on generating candidate fair termination certificates by training a neural network on random traces of the system, and then checking the certificates with an SMT solver. When the check fails, the SMT counterexample is used for retraining and generate another candidate certificate. The approach is aimed at hardware designs, although in principle it could be generalised to infinite-state systems as well.

The model checking approach presented in [25] provides a BMC encoding for checking general LTL properties on infinite-state systems. The technique provides certain completeness guarantees given a finite domain and considers a variety of trace semantics beyond just infinite traces, though the BMC encoding especially limits its ability to prove properties and will diverge on many problem instances with infinite domains. Our technique uses implicit abstraction to deal with the challenges of infinite domains.

8 Experimental Evaluation

In this section, we experimentally evaluate the performance of rlive-inf. We have implemented the algorithm on top of ic3ia [34], an open source model checker based on IC3 with implicit abstraction [13], written in C++.[3] Although the rlive-inf procedure is independent from the underlying theory used to specify

---

[3] An artifact enabling full reproducibility, including also the source code of our implementation and log files of our experiments, is available at https://doi.org/10.5281/zenodo.15310253.

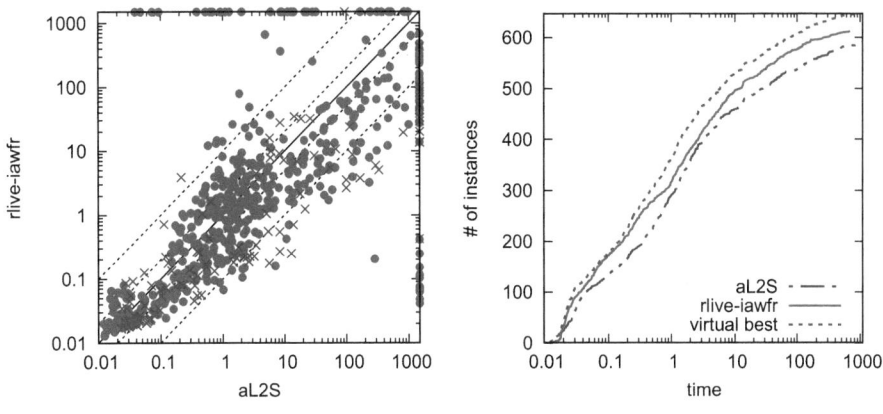

Algorithm	# Solved	Safe	Unsafe	$\Delta_{\text{rlive-inf}}$	Gained	Lost	Cumulative time (sec)
Virtual best	647	513	134	34	34	0	15164
rlive-inf	613	480	133	–	–	–	13110
αL2S	591	470	121	-22	34	56	22115

Fig. 4. Experimental results.

the input system, our implementation currently targets systems expressed using Boolean and linear arithmetic constraints.

Experimental Set Up. We compare rlive-inf to αL2S, which was shown in [23] to outperform other approaches to LTL verification for infinite-state symbolic transition systems, and which to the best of our knowledge still represents the state of the art in this context. Moreover, since αL2S was also implemented on top of ic3ia, we reused the same basic components (namely, invariant verification engine [13], SMT solver [14], predicate refinement procedure [32] and generation of well-founded relations via ranking function synthesis techniques [31]) for implementing rlive-inf. This ensures that the comparison between the two approaches is fair, and any differences in performance is due to the different features and search strategies employed by the two techniques, rather than to the different performance of the underlying engines.

Benchmarks. We use the benchmark set of the αL2S article [23] for our comparison. The set consists of 835 liveness verification problems expressed as symbolic transition systems in the VMT format [15], coming from multiple sources (including BIP models from [6], examples derived from the real-time domain [1], imperative programs from [24], and termination benchmarks from [9]).

Results. We ran our experimental evaluation on a cluster of machines with AMD EPYC 7413 CPUs and 500 Gb of RAM, running Ubuntu Linux 20.04. We used a timeout of 1200 s and a memory limit of 8 Gb per instance.

The results of the evaluation are summarized in Fig. 4. The scatter plot on the left shows a direct comparison of the run times of rlive-inf and αL2S on each individual instance (where safe ones are shown as blue dots and unsafe ones as red crosses), whereas the plot on the right shows, for each tool, the number of solved instances (y-axis) in the given time (x-axis), not including timeouts/unknowns. In this case, we also include a "virtual best" tool, obtained by taking the best among rlive-inf and αL2S on each instance. Additional information is provided in the table under the plots, where for each tool we show the number of solved instances (distinguishing also between safe and unsafe ones), the difference in number of solved instances wrt. rlive-inf, the number of instances gained (i.e. solved by the given tool but not by rlive-inf) and lost, and the total execution time taken on solved instances. In all cases, both algorithms agreed on their answers and no memouts occurred.

From the results, we can conclude that rlive-inf outperforms αL2S both in terms of number of solved instances (solving 22 more instances than αL2S) and in terms of runtime efficiency (with an average speedup of 6.47x on instances solved by both tools). From the plot on the right, we can see that the efficiency advantage remains regardless of the selected time limit (within the overall timeout of 1200 s used to run the experiments), shown by the fact that the rlive-inf curve always dominates the one corresponding to αL2S. Interestingly however, the two techniques compared show a high degree of complementarity, as highlighted by the scatter plot on the left and by the strong results obtained by the "virtual best" configuration both in terms of number of solved instances (34 more than rlive-inf alone) and of runtime efficiency. We believe that our results demonstrate the practical contributions of our new procedure to advancing the state of the art in LTL verification for infinite-state systems.

9 Conclusions and Future Work

We have presented rlive-inf, an generalisation of the rlive liveness model checking algorithm from finite- to infinite-state symbolic transition systems. By integrating predicate abstraction, invariant checking, and termination techniques based on well-founded relations, rlive-inf provides an efficient, fully-symbolic LTL model checker that outperforms the state of the art on a variety of benchmarks.

Regarding future work, we intend to address the limitation described in Sect. 6 concerning the integration of well-founded relations in the rlive search. We will also investigate the use of improved strategies for refinement, leveraging additional techniques for raking function synthesis such as [45], since this is often a limiting factor in the effectiveness of the approach. Finally, we intend to integrate techniques for the discovery of non-looping counterexamples for violated properties [10], and to study the problem of generating proof certificates for correctness.

Acknowledgements. A. Cimatti, A. Griggio and S. Tonetta have been supported by the PNRR project FAIR - Future AI Research (PE00000013), under the NRRP MUR program funded by the NextGenerationEU and the PNRR MUR project VITALITY (ECS00000041), Spoke 2 ASTRA - Advanced Space Technologies and Research Alliance. C. Johannsen and K.Y. Rozier have been supported by NSF:CCRI Award #2016592.

Disclosure of Interests. The authors have no competing interests to declare that are relevant to the content of this article.

References

1. Alur, R., Dang, T., Ivancic, F.: Counterexample-guided predicate abstraction of hybrid systems. Theor. Comput. Sci. **354**(2), 250–271 (2006)
2. Barrett, C.W., Sebastiani, R., Seshia, S.A., Tinelli, C.: Satisfiability modulo theories. In: Handbook of Satisfiability. Frontiers in Artificial Intelligence and Applications, vol. 336, pp. 1267–1329. IOS Press (2021)
3. Biere, A., Artho, C., Schuppan, V.: Liveness checking as safety checking. In: Proceedings of the 7th International Workshop on Formal Methods for Industrial Critical Systems. Electronic Notes in Theoretical Computer Science, vol. 66:2 (2002)
4. Birgmeier, J., Bradley, A.R., Weissenbacher, G.: Counterexample to induction-guided abstraction-refinement (CTIGAR). In: Biere, A., Bloem, R. (eds.) CAV 2014. LNCS, vol. 8559, pp. 831–848. Springer, Cham (2014). https://doi.org/10.1007/978-3-319-08867-9_55
5. Bjørner, N., Gurfinkel, A., McMillan, K., Rybalchenko, A.: Horn clause solvers for program verification. In: Beklemishev, L.D., Blass, A., Dershowitz, N., Finkbeiner, B., Schulte, W. (eds.) Fields of Logic and Computation II. LNCS, vol. 9300, pp. 24–51. Springer, Cham (2015). https://doi.org/10.1007/978-3-319-23534-9_2
6. Bliudze, S., et al.: Formal verification of infinite-state BIP models. In: Finkbeiner, B., Pu, G., Zhang, L. (eds.) ATVA 2015. LNCS, vol. 9364, pp. 326–343. Springer, Cham (2015). https://doi.org/10.1007/978-3-319-24953-7_25
7. Bombardelli, A., Cimatti, A., Griggio, A., Tonetta, S.: Another look at LTL modulo theory over finite and infinite traces. In: Principles of Verification (1), vol. 15260. LNCS, pp. 419–443. Springer (2024)
8. Bradley, A.R., Somenzi, F., Hassan, Z., Zhang, Y.: An incremental approach to model checking progress properties. In: 2011 Formal Methods in Computer-Aided Design (FMCAD), pp. 144–153. IEEE (2011)
9. Brockschmidt, M., Cook, B., Fuhs, C.: Better termination proving through cooperation. In: Sharygina, N., Veith, H. (eds.) CAV 2013. LNCS, vol. 8044, pp. 413–429. Springer, Heidelberg (2013). https://doi.org/10.1007/978-3-642-39799-8_28
10. Cimatti, A., Griggio, A., Magnago, E.: LTL falsification in infinite-state systems. Inf. Comput. **289**(Part), 104977 (2022)
11. Cimatti, A., Griggio, A., Mover, S., Roveri, M., Tonetta, S.: Verification modulo theories. Formal Methods Syst. Des. **60**(3), 452–481 (2022)
12. Cimatti, A., Griggio, A., Mover, S., Tonetta, S.: Verifying LTL properties of hybrid systems with K-Liveness. In: Biere, A., Bloem, R. (eds.) CAV 2014. LNCS, vol. 8559, pp. 424–440. Springer, Cham (2014). https://doi.org/10.1007/978-3-319-08867-9_28

13. Cimatti, A., Griggio, A., Mover, S., Tonetta, S.: Infinite-state invariant checking with IC3 and predicate abstraction. Formal Methods Syst. Des. **49**(3), 190–218 (2016). https://doi.org/10.1007/s10703-016-0257-4
14. Cimatti, A., Griggio, A., Schaafsma, B.J., Sebastiani, R.: The MathSAT5 SMT solver. In: Piterman, N., Smolka, S.A. (eds.) TACAS 2013. LNCS, vol. 7795, pp. 93–107. Springer, Heidelberg (2013). https://doi.org/10.1007/978-3-642-36742-7_7
15. Cimatti, A., Griggio, A., Tonetta, S.: The VMT-LIB language and tools. In: SMT, volume 3185 of CEUR Workshop Proceedings, pp. 80–89. CEUR-WS.org (2022)
16. Claessen, K., Sörensson, N.: A liveness checking algorithm that counts. In: 2012 Formal Methods in Computer-Aided Design (FMCAD), pp. 52–59. IEEE (2012)
17. Clarke, E., Grumberg, O., Hamaguchi, K.: Another look at LTL model checking. In: Dill, D.L. (ed.) CAV 1994. LNCS, vol. 818, pp. 415–427. Springer, Heidelberg (1994). https://doi.org/10.1007/3-540-58179-0_72
18. Clarke, E.M., Grumberg, O., Jha, S., Yuan, L., Veith, H.: Counterexample-guided abstraction refinement for symbolic model checking. J. ACM **50**(5), 752–794 (2003)
19. Cook, B., Gotsman, A., Podelski, A., Rybalchenko, A., Vardi, M.Y.: Proving that programs eventually do something good. ACM SIGPLAN Not. **42**(1), 265–276 (2007)
20. Cook, B., Khlaaf, H., Piterman, N.: On automation of CTL* verification for infinite-state systems. In: International Conference on Computer Aided Verification, pp. 13–29. Springer (2015)
21. Cook, B., Koskinen, E., Vardi, M.: Temporal property verification as a program analysis task. In: Gopalakrishnan, G., Qadeer, S. (eds.) CAV 2011. LNCS, vol. 6806, pp. 333–348. Springer, Heidelberg (2011). https://doi.org/10.1007/978-3-642-22110-1_26
22. Cook, B., Podelski, A., Rybalchenko, A.: Termination proofs for systems code. ACM Sigplan Not. **41**(6), 415–426 (2006)
23. Daniel, J., Cimatti, A., Griggio, A., Tonetta, S., Mover, S.: Infinite-state liveness-to-safety via implicit abstraction and well-founded relations. In: Chaudhuri, S., Farzan, A. (eds.) CAV 2016. LNCS, vol. 9779, pp. 271–291. Springer, Cham (2016). https://doi.org/10.1007/978-3-319-41528-4_15
24. Dietsch, D., Heizmann, M., Langenfeld, V., Podelski, A.: Fairness modulo theory: a new approach to LTL software model checking. In: Kroening, D., Păsăreanu, C.S. (eds.) CAV 2015. LNCS, vol. 9206, pp. 49–66. Springer, Cham (2015). https://doi.org/10.1007/978-3-319-21690-4_4
25. Doose, D., Brunel, J.: Simple LTL model checking on finite and infinite traces over concrete domains. In: International Conference on Formal Engineering Methods, pp. 375–390. Springer (2024)
26. Giacobbe, M., Kroening, D., Pal, A., Tautschnig, M.: Neural model checking. In: Advances in Neural Information Processing Systems 37 (NeurIPS 2024). NeurIPS (2024)
27. Giacobbe, M., Kroening, D., Parsert, J.: Neural termination analysis. In: Proceedings of the 30th ACM Joint European Software Engineering Conference and Symposium on the Foundations of Software Engineering, pp. 633–645 (2022)
28. Graf, S., Saïdi, H.: Construction of abstract state graphs with PVS. In: CAV, pp. 72–83 (1997)
29. Hajdu, Á., Tóth, T., Vörös, A.: A survey on CEGAR-based model checking. Master's thesis, Budapest University of Technology and Economics (2015)
30. Heizmann, M., Hoenicke, J., Leike, J., Podelski, A.: Linear ranking for linear lasso programs. In: Van Hung, D., Ogawa, M. (eds.) ATVA 2013. LNCS, vol. 8172, pp. 365–380. Springer, Cham (2013). https://doi.org/10.1007/978-3-319-02444-8_26

31. Heizmann, M., Hoenicke, J., Leike, J., Podelski, A.: Linear ranking for linear lasso programs. In: Van Hung, D., Ogawa, M. (eds.) ATVA 2013. LNCS, vol. 8172, pp. 365–380. Springer, Cham (2013). https://doi.org/10.1007/978-3-319-02444-8_26
32. Henzinger, T.A., Jhala, R., Majumdar, R., McMillan, K.L.: Abstractions from proofs. In: POPL, pp. 232–244 (2004)
33. Hoder, K., Bjørner, N.: Generalized property directed reachability. In: International Conference on Theory and Applications of Satisfiability Testing, pp. 157–171. Springer (2012)
34. ic3ia webpage. https://es-static.fbk.eu/people/griggio/ic3ia/
35. Ivrii, A., Nevo, Z., Baumgartner, J.: k-FAIR= k-LIVENESS+ FAIR revisiting SAT-based liveness algorithms. In: 2018 Formal Methods in Computer Aided Design (FMCAD), pp. 1–5. IEEE (2018)
36. Jhala, R., Podelski, A., Rybalchenko, A.: Predicate abstraction for program verification. In: Handbook of Model Checking, pp. 447–491. Springer (2018)
37. Komuravelli, A., Gurfinkel, A., Chaki, S.: SMT-based model checking for recursive programs. Formal Methods Syst. Des. **48**(3), 175–205 (2016). https://doi.org/10.1007/s10703-016-0249-4
38. McMillan, K.L.: Interpolation and model checking. In: Handbook of Model Checking, pp. 421–446. Springer (2018)
39. Niemetz, A., Preiner, M., Biere, A.: Turbo-charging lemmas on demand with don't care reasoning. In: 2014 Formal Methods in Computer-Aided Design (FMCAD), pp. 179–186. IEEE (2014)
40. Podelski, A., Rybalchenko, A.: A complete method for the synthesis of linear ranking functions. In: International Workshop on Verification, Model Checking, and Abstract Interpretation, pp. 239–251. Springer (2004)
41. Podelski, A., Rybalchenko, A.: Transition invariants. In: Proceedings of the 19th Annual IEEE Symposium on Logic in Computer Science, pp. 32–41. IEEE (2004)
42. Podelski, A., Rybalchenko, A.: Transition predicate abstraction and fair termination. ACM Trans. Program. Lang. Syst. **29**(3), 15–es (2007)
43. Schuele, T., Schneider, K.: Bounded model checking of infinite state systems. Form. Methods Syst. Des. **30**, 51–81 (2007)
44. Tonetta, S.: Abstract model checking without computing the abstraction. In: Cavalcanti, A., Dams, D.R. (eds.) FM 2009. LNCS, vol. 5850, pp. 89–105. Springer, Heidelberg (2009). https://doi.org/10.1007/978-3-642-05089-3_7
45. Urban, C., Gurfinkel, A., Kahsai, T.: Synthesizing ranking functions from bits and pieces. In: Chechik, M., Raskin, J.-F. (eds.) TACAS 2016. LNCS, vol. 9636, pp. 54–70. Springer, Heidelberg (2016). https://doi.org/10.1007/978-3-662-49674-9_4
46. Vardi, M.Y.: An automata-theoretic approach to linear temporal logic. In: Logics for Concurrency: Structure Versus Automata, pp. 238–266 (2005)
47. Xia, Y., Cimatti, A., Griggio, A., Li, J.: Avoiding the shoals - a new approach to liveness checking. In: International Conference on Computer Aided Verification, pp. 234–254. Springer (2024)

Open Access This chapter is licensed under the terms of the Creative Commons Attribution 4.0 International License (http://creativecommons.org/licenses/by/4.0/), which permits use, sharing, adaptation, distribution and reproduction in any medium or format, as long as you give appropriate credit to the original author(s) and the source, provide a link to the Creative Commons license and indicate if changes were made.

The images or other third party material in this chapter are included in the chapter's Creative Commons license, unless indicated otherwise in a credit line to the material. If material is not included in the chapter's Creative Commons license and your intended use is not permitted by statutory regulation or exceeds the permitted use, you will need to obtain permission directly from the copyright holder.

Deeply Optimizing the SAT Solver for the IC3 Algorithm

Yuheng Su[1,2], Qiusong Yang[1,3(✉)], Yiwei Ci[1], Yingcheng Li[1,2], Tianjun Bu[1,2], and Ziyu Huang[4]

[1] Institute of Software, Chinese Academy of Sciences, Beijing, China
gipsyh.icu@gmail.com, {yiwei,qiusong}@iscas.ac.cn
[2] University of Chinese Academy of Sciences, Beijing, China
{liyingcheng18,butianjun24}@mails.ucas.ac.cn
[3] Advanced Computing and Intelligence Engineering, Wuxi, China
[4] Beijing Forestry University, Beijing, China
fyy0007@bjfu.edu.cn

Abstract. The IC3 algorithm, also known as PDR, is a SAT-based model checking algorithm that has significantly influenced the field in recent years due to its efficiency, scalability, and completeness. It utilizes SAT solvers to solve a series of SAT queries associated with relative induction. In this paper, we introduce several optimizations for the SAT solver in IC3 based on our observations of the unique characteristics of these SAT queries. By observing that SAT queries do not necessarily require decisions on all variables, we compute a subset of variables that need to be decided before each solving process while ensuring that the result remains unaffected. Additionally, noting that the overhead of binary heap operations in VSIDS is non-negligible, we replace the binary heap with buckets to achieve constant-time operations. Furthermore, we support temporary clauses without the need to allocate a new activation variable for each solving process, thereby eliminating the need to reset solvers. We developed a novel lightweight CDCL SAT solver, GipSAT, which integrates these optimizations. A comprehensive evaluation highlights the performance improvements achieved by GipSAT. Specifically, the GipSAT-based IC3 demonstrates an average speedup of 3.61 times in solving time compared to the IC3 implementation based on MiniSat.

Keywords: Model Checking · IC3/PDR · SAT

1 Introduction

Model checking [16,17] is a powerful formal verification technique widely used in system design. Given a transition system and a property describing the desired system behavior, it can efficiently and automatically detect bugs or prove system correctness.

Recent significant advancements in SAT solvers, particularly the introduction of the Conflict Driven Clause Learning algorithm (CDCL) [35], have led to breakthroughs in model checking through SAT-based algorithms. Among these, IC3 [12] (also known as PDR [19]) stands out as a highly influential SAT-based model checking algorithm, widely used for hardware verification. IC3 efficiently searches for inductive invariants without requiring model unrolling. Compared to Bounded Model Checking (BMC) [10], IC3 offers completeness, and it demonstrates superior scalability over Interpolation-based Model Checking (IMC) [31] and K-Induction [34]. As a result, IC3 is widely regarded as the state-of-the-art algorithm and serves as the core engine in many efficient model checkers [15,24,30].

IC3 works by constructing SAT problems regarding the overapproximate reachable states of the model being verified. With the help of a SAT solver, solving these problems yields answers that facilitate the verification process. Therefore, currently, almost all implementations of IC3 essentially have a two-layer structure: the top layer is the IC3 algorithm layer, which drives the verification process by posing a series of SAT queries, and the bottom layer is the SAT solver layer, which handles the queries posed by the algorithm layer.

IC3 has been successfully applied to verify some industrial designs [23]. However, it still faces challenges due to the problem of state space explosion. Therefore, enhancing the performance and scalability of the IC3 algorithm to efficiently verify larger-scale models continues to be an important research direction. Most studies aiming to improve the IC3 algorithm focus on optimizing at the algorithm layer by proposing various variants or enhancing the efficiency of intermediate steps [27,33,36,40]. Only a very few studies focus on the SAT solver layer: [14] compared the performance of different SAT solver management strategies at the algorithm layer. [22] proposed a simple and easily implementable approach that enables the addition of a temporary clause without the need for activation literals, eliminating the need for IC3 to reset the SAT solver.

In this paper, we propose several optimizations for the SAT solver used in IC3, based on our analysis of the unique characteristics of SAT queries. We introduce a lightweight SAT solver, **GipSAT**, which incorporates these optimizations to enhance its efficiency in processing SAT queries within IC3. The key contributions of this paper are summarized as follows:

- We analyzed the characteristics of SAT queries in IC3 and observed that it is not necessary to make decisions on all variables. Additionally, the overhead of binary heap operations in VSIDS is non-negligible.
- We propose a method that, before each solving step, analyzes a subset of variables that need to be decided, ensuring that the result remains unaffected, thus reducing the number of decisions.
- We introduce a novel data structure that replaces the binary heap, enabling VSIDS operations to be performed in constant time.
- We propose a method that supports temporary clauses by reusing the same activation variable instead of allocating a new one before each solving process, thus eliminating the need for SAT solver resetting.
- We introduce a novel lightweight SAT solver, GipSAT, which incorporates these optimizations. We provide a detailed interface for GipSAT.

- We conduct a comprehensive performance evaluation of GipSAT. The experimental results demonstrate that GipSAT significantly enhances the efficiency and scalability of the IC3 algorithm.

2 Preliminaries

2.1 Basics and Notations

We use notations such as x, y for Boolean variables, and X, Y for sets of Boolean variables. The terms x and $\neg x$ are referred to as literals. A cube is a conjunction of literals, while a clause is a disjunction of literals. A Boolean formula in Conjunctive Normal Form (CNF) is a conjunction of clauses. It is often convenient to treat a clause or a cube as a set of literals, and a CNF as a set of clauses. For instance, given a CNF formula F, a clause c, and a literal l, we write $l \in c$ to indicate that l occurs in c, and $c \in F$ to indicate that c occurs in F. A formula F implies another formula G, if every satisfying assignment of F satisfies G, denoted as $F \Rightarrow G$. We use $\mathcal{V}(F)$ to represent the set of all variables appeared in formula F.

A transition system, denoted as S, can be defined as a tuple $\langle X, Y, I, T \rangle$. Here, X and X' represent the sets of state variables for the current state and the next state, respectively, while Y represents the set of input variables. The Boolean formula $I(X)$ represents the initial states, and $T(X, Y, X')$ describes the transition relation. State s_2 is a successor of state s_1 if and only if $(s_1, s_2') \Rightarrow T$. A safety property $P(X)$ is a Boolean formula over X. A system S satisfies P if and only if all reachable states of S satisfy P.

Without loss of generality, circuits are commonly represented in the form of And-Inverter Graph (AIG) [28]. An AIG is a directed acyclic graph, which includes primary inputs/outputs and two input and-nodes with optional inverter marks on the fanin edges. The Cone of Influence (COI) of a node is the set of all nodes that could potentially influence its value, which can be obtained by recursively traversing its fanins. When T is derived from an AIG, X and Y correspond to the primary inputs, while X' corresponds to the primary outputs. It exhibits the functional characteristic where each next state variable is assigned by a function of current states and inputs, $x_i' \leftrightarrow f_i(X, Y)$. Therefore, T is a conjunction of all assignment functions, $\bigwedge x_i' \leftrightarrow f_i(X, Y)$. The transformation of an AIG to CNF typically involves Tseitin encoding [37], where each node in the AIG is mapped to a variable in the CNF.

2.2 Incremental CDCL SAT Solver

Conflict Driven Clause Learning (CDCL) [35] is a powerful and widely used algorithm that employs conflict analysis and clause learning techniques to efficiently solve SAT problems. Modern CDCL SAT solvers typically rely on the Variable State Independent Decaying Sum (VSIDS) branching heuristic [32]. It calculates a score for each variable and selects the variable with the highest score during decision. This is typically maintained by a binary heap [21]. An incremental SAT solver efficiently solves a series of related formulas and typically provides the following interfaces:

- `add_clause`(*clause*): adds the *clause* to the solver.
- `solve`(*assumption*): checks the satisfiability under the given *assumption*.
- `get_model`(): retrieves the variable assignments from the previous SAT call.
- `unsat_core`(): retrieves the unsatisfiable core from the assumptions of the previous UNSAT call.

2.3 IC3 Algorithm

IC3 is a SAT-based model checking algorithm that does not require unrolling the system [12]. It attempts to prove that S satisfies P by finding an inductive invariant $INV(X)$ such that:
- $I(X) \Rightarrow INV(X)$
- $INV(X) \wedge T(X, Y, X') \Rightarrow INV(X')$
- $INV(X) \Rightarrow P(X)$

To achieve this objective, it maintains a monotone CNF sequence $F_0, F_1 \ldots F_k$. Each *frame* F_i is a Boolean formula over X, which represents an over-approximation of the states reachable within i transition steps. Each clause c in F_i is called *lemma* and the index i is called *level*. IC3 maintains the following invariant:

- $F_0 = I$
- $F_{i+1} \subseteq F_i$
- $F_i \wedge T \Rightarrow F'_{i+1}$
- for all $i < k, F_i \Rightarrow P$

A lemma c is said to be *inductive relative* to F_i if, starting from states that satisfy both F_i and c, all states reached in a single transition satisfy c. This condition can be expressed as a SAT query $sat(F_i \wedge c \wedge T \wedge \neg c')$. If this query is satisfiable, it indicates that c is not inductive relative to F_i, as we can find a counterexample where a state satisfying $F_i \wedge c$ and transitions to a state that does not satisfy c. If lemma c is inductive relative to F_i, it can also be said that the cube $\neg c$ is blocked in F_{i+1}.

Algorithm 1 provides an overview of the IC3 algorithm. This algorithm incrementally constructs frames by iteratively performing the blocking phase and the propagation phase. During the blocking phase, the IC3 algorithm focuses on making $F_k \Rightarrow P$. It iteratively get a cube c such that $c \Rightarrow \neg P$, and block it recursively. This process involves attempting to block the cube's predecessors if it cannot be blocked directly. It continues until the initial states cannot be blocked, indicating that $\neg P$ can be reached from the initial states in k transitions, which violates the property. In cases where a cube can be confirmed as blocked, IC3 proceeds to expand the set of blocked states through a process called generalization. This involves dropping literals and ensuring that the

Algorithm 1. Overview of IC3

```
 1: function get_predecessor()
 2:     model := get_model()
 3:     return {l ∈ model | var(l) ∈ X}
 4:
 5: function generalize(cube b, level i)
 6:     for each l ∈ b do
 7:         cand := b \ {l}
 8:         if I ⇒ ¬cand and ¬sat(F_{i-1} ∧ ¬cand ∧ T ∧ cand') then    ▷ Q_{gen}
 9:             b := unsat_core()
10:     return b
11:
12: function block(cube c, level i)
13:     if i = 0 then
14:         return false
15:     while sat(F_{i-1} ∧ ¬c ∧ T ∧ c') do                            ▷ Q_{block}
16:         p := get_predecessor()
17:         if ¬block(p, i − 1) then
18:             return false
19:     c := unsat_core()
20:     lemma := ¬generalize(c, i)
21:     for 1 ≤ j ≤ i do
22:         F_j := F_j ∪ {lemma}
23:     return true
24:
25: function propagate(level k)
26:     for 1 ≤ i < k do
27:         for each c ∈ F_i \ F_{i+1} do
28:             if ¬sat(F_i ∧ T ∧ ¬c') then                           ▷ Q_{push}
29:                 F_{i+1} := F_{i+1} ∪ {c}
30:         if F_i = F_{i+1} then
31:             return true
32:     return false
33:
34: procedure IC3(I, T, P)
35:     F_0 := I, k := 1, F_k := ⊤
36:     while true do
37:         while sat(F_k ∧ ¬P) do                                    ▷ Q_{bad}
38:             c := get_predecessor()
39:             if ¬block(c, k) then
40:                 return unsafe
41:         k := k + 1, F_k := ⊤
42:         if propagate(k) then
43:             return safe
```

resulting clause remains relatively inductive, with the objective of obtaining a minimal inductive clause. The propagation phase tries to push lemmas to the top frame. If a lemma c in $F_i \setminus F_{i+1}$ is also inductive relative to F_i, then push it into F_{i+1}. During this process, if two consecutive frames become identical ($F_i = F_{i+1}$), then the inductive invariant is found and the safety of this model can be proved.

The IC3 algorithm involves four different types of SAT queries, as denoted in Algorithm 1. Since $c \in F_i$, the query Q_{push} can be expressed as $sat(F_i \wedge c \wedge T \wedge \neg c')$. Consequently, Q_{gen}, Q_{block}, and Q_{push} are essentially the same and can be uniformly represented as $sat(F_i \wedge c \wedge T \wedge \neg c')$, where c is a clause and $\neg c'$ is a cube. This representation captures the inductiveness of c relative to F_i, which we denote as Q_{relind}.

3 Motivations

Table 1. The average solving time, number of calls, and average length of c in Q_{relind} were calculated for various SAT queries, yielding an overall average across all cases.

	Avg. solving time(ms)	#Calls	Avg. c length
Q_{gen}	1.099	110794.41	6.775
Q_{block}	0.600	12814.11	104.202
Q_{push}	0.712	87831.33	4.643
Q_{bad}	1.655	247.48	-

We analyzed the characteristics of SAT queries in Minisat-based rIC3 [9]. The analysis was conducted on the complete benchmarks of the 2020 and 2024 Hardware Model Checking Competition (HWMCC). For a detailed description of the experimental setup, please refer to Sect. 6. The results are presented in Table 1. It can be observed that the SAT queries generated by IC3 exhibit unique characteristics: they are solved quickly, with an average solving time of less than 1ms, but the number of queries is very large. Additionally, we have the following observations:

- **Observation 1:** Q_{relind}: $sat(F_i \wedge c \wedge T \wedge \neg c')$ represents whether there exists a predecessor of any state in $\neg c$ (where $\neg c$ is a cube, representing a set of states) that satisfies F_i but is not in $\neg c$. We have observed that solving Q_{relind} does not require considering assignments for all variables. Figure 1 shows an AIG model. The values of variables in c' are determined solely by $COI(c')$, as illustrated by the shaded region. The values of variables outside the shaded region do not affect the result. From the last column of Table 1, it can be observed that the c in Q_{gen} and Q_{push} is typically very small in size. Consequently, the size of $COI(c')$ is likely to be small compared to the total number of variables. We also calculated the average percentage of variables in $COI(c')$ for all Q_{relind} relative to the total number of variables, as shown in Fig. 2. It can be observed that, in most cases, the number of variables that need to be determined is only around 20% of the total number of variables. We may be able to use this information to reduce the number of variables that need to be assigned in each solving iteration. However, regular SAT solvers can only obtain the CNF representation of the AIG and cannot capture the dependency relationships between variables.

– **Observation 2:** SAT solvers utilize VSIDS (Variable State Independent Decaying Sum) to guide variable decisions. Typically, VSIDS employs a binary heap, where variables with higher scores are prioritized and popped out first. We also measured the overhead of VSIDS operations, as illustrated in Fig. 3. The results show that the overhead of VSIDS operations is non-negligible, with the majority of cases exhibiting an overhead of around 30%. This phenomenon may be attributed to the simplicity of the queries posed by IC3, which involve fewer conflicts during solving and may only require variable assignments in decision and BCP (Boolean Constraint Propagation). Due to the logarithmic time complexity of binary heap operations, compared to the constant time required for assignments, the overhead becomes significant.

– **Observation 3:** It can be observed that Q_{relind} requires the addition of a temporary clause c to the SAT solver, which only takes effect in the next solving iteration. However, most state-of-the-art SAT solvers do not support the direct removal of a clause, as removing a clause from the formula would necessitate removing every learned clause derived from it. One common approach to address this issue involves the use of activation variables [20], which most IC3 implementations adopt. Let a be an activation literal, which is a free variable that does not occur within the original formula. By incorporating $c \vee a$ into the formula and assuming $\neg a$, we effectively achieve the same result as directly adding c. To remove c, we can simply add the clause consisting of the single literal a to the formula. However, solving Q_{relind} each time requires creating a new activation variable. As the number of activation variables increases, their presence can negatively impact the performance of the SAT solver [14,22]. A common solution to this problem is to periodically reset the SAT solver with a fresh instance, though this approach has the drawback of clearing all learned clauses and heuristic scores. Our goal is to support temporary clauses while avoiding the need for such resets.

We can potentially leverage these distinctive characteristics to optimize the SAT solver for the IC3 algorithm to improve its performance.

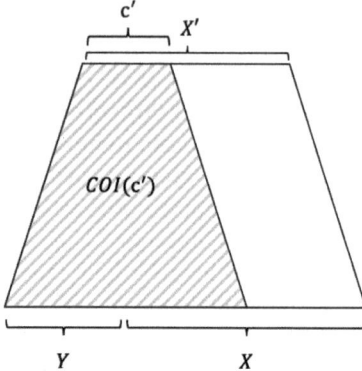

Fig. 1. The diagram of an AIG model. The entire trapezoid represents the transition relations T, and the shaded region represents the subset of relations required by c'.

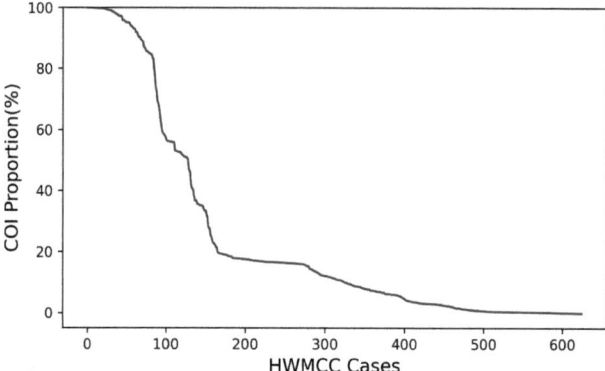

Fig. 2. The number of cases (x-axis) in which the average percentage of variables in $COI(c')$ relative to the total number of variables in Q_{relind} exceeds a given value (y-axis).

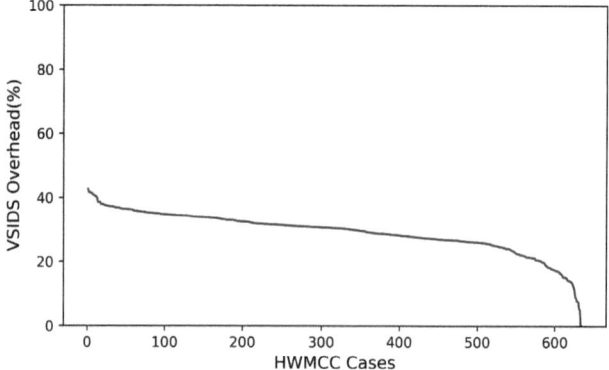

Fig. 3. The number of cases (x-axis) in which the overhead of VSIDS operations exceeds a given value (y-axis).

4 Optimizations

4.1 Decide and Propagate in Domain

Observation 1 shows that it is unnecessary to consider all variables when solving Q_{relind}. We analyze which variables need to be considered through the following theorems. Considering the formula Q_{relind}: $sat(F_i \wedge c \wedge T \wedge \neg c')$, we can analyze the subset of variables that need to be taken into account without affecting the satisfiability. To determine the satisfiability of $F_i \wedge c$, we only need to consider the variables that appear in this formula, which are $\mathcal{V}(F_i) \cup \mathcal{V}(c)$. Similarly, for the satisfiability of $T \wedge \neg c'$, the values of the variables in $\neg c'$ are solely determined by the $COI(c')$. Therefore only the variables in $COI(c')$ need to be considered. As a result, by considering only the variables in $\mathcal{V}(F_i) \cup \mathcal{V}(c) \cup COI(c')$, we can determine the satisfiability of the formula Q_{relind}.

We refer to the set of variables that need to be considered during solving as the *domain*. For solving Q_{relind}, it is sufficient to use $\mathcal{V}(F_i) \cup \mathcal{V}(c) \cup COI(c')$ as the domain, instead of all variables. This significantly reduces the number of variables that the SAT solver needs to decide and assign during BCP.

We use a hash table to record whether each variable belongs to the domain, allowing constant-time queries for domain information. Before each solving process, we need to compute the domain relevant to that instance. For $\mathcal{V}(F_i)$, the variables are permanently stored in the hash table, and new domain variables are added whenever a new lemma is introduced. For $\mathcal{V}(c)$, we simply extract all variables that appear in clause c. Finally, $COI(c')$ is computed by recursively traversing the fanins of c'. After computing $\mathcal{V}(c)$ and $COI(c')$, we also temporarily record them in the domain hash table, but they are removed after each solving process.

After computing the domain for the current solving instance, we push all domain variables into the VSIDS decision-required set to ensure they are considered for decisions. During BCP, if a clause contains a variable that is not in the current domain, it is considered irrelevant to the current solving process. Since out-of-domain variables are not eligible for assignment, any clause involving them cannot contribute to further propagation. When BCP attempts to find a new unassigned variable to serve as the watch literal, if that variable lies outside the domain, we simply ignore the clause and proceed to the next one, without performing any variable assignments based on that clause. This approach guarantees that out-of-domain variables are never assigned during BCP. Furthermore, by restricting assignments to domain variables only, we eliminate propagation involving irrelevant variables, thereby reducing BCP overhead.

It can also be noticed that the difference between c' in every two adjacent Q_{gen} is only one literal. This suggests that calculating $COI(c')$ for every Q_{gen} is unnecessary. Instead, We perform this calculation initially during generalization and upon successful drops, as depicted in Algorithm 2. We recalculate it upon successful drops because sometimes the unsat core can drop multiple variables at once compared to before.

Algorithm 2. Generalize with Domain

1: **function** $generalize$(cube b, level i)
2:     $set\_domain(\mathcal{V}(F_{i-1} \wedge \neg b) \cup COI(b'))$
3:     **for** each $l \in b$ **do**
4:        $cand := b \setminus \{l\}$
5:        **if** $I \Rightarrow \neg cand$ and $\neg sat(F_{i-1} \wedge \neg cand \wedge T \wedge cand')$ **then**   ▷ Q_{gen}
6:           $b := unsat\_core()$
7:           $set\_domain(\mathcal{V}(F_{i-1} \wedge \neg b) \cup COI(b'))$
8:     $unset\_domain()$
9:     **return** b

Algorithm 3. VSIDS by Bucket

1: $IntervalHeap$ $iheaps[NumBucket]$ ▷ Interval heap for each bucket
2: Map var_bucket ▷ Hash table maps variables to buckets
3: $Queue$ $queue[NumBucket]$ ▷ Variable queue for each bucket
4:
5: **function** $update$(Var v)
6:     $b := var\_bucket[v]$
7:     **while** $b > 0$ **do**
8:        **if** $iheaps[b].max().score > iheaps[b-1].min().score$ **then**
9:           $vmax := iheaps[b].pop\_max()$
10:           $vmin := iheaps[b-1].pop\_min()$
11:           $iheaps[b].push(vmin)$
12:           $iheaps[b-1].push(vmax)$
13:           $var\_bucket[vmin] = b$
14:           $var\_bucket[vmax] = b - 1$
15:        **else**
16:           **break**
17:        $b = b - 1$
18:
19: **function** $push$(Var v)
20:     $bucket := var\_bucket[v]$
21:     $queue[bucket].push\_back(v)$
22:     $head = min(head, bucket)$
23:
24: **function** $pop()$
25:     **while** $head < NumBucket$ **do**
26:        **if** $queue[head].size() > 0$ **then**
27:           **return** $queue[head].pop\_front()$
28:        $head = head + 1$
29:     **return** $None$

4.2 VSIDS by Bucket

Observation 2 highlights that the overhead of VSIDS is non-negligible, and reducing this overhead could potentially enhance overall performance. Inspired by bucket sorting, we introduce a novel data structure for VSIDS, that enables both push and pop operations to be performed in constant time. We predefine a fixed number of buckets (defaulting to 15) and assign each variable to a specific bucket. This design ensures that variables in lower-numbered buckets have higher VSIDS scores than those in higher-numbered buckets.

To maintain this guarantee amid dynamic changes in variable scores, we utilize an interval heap for each bucket. The interval heap is a double-ended priority queue that can efficiently pop either the maximum or minimum value in logarithmic time [29]. Each bucket's interval heap stores all the variables belonging to that bucket, using their scores as the sorting criterion. When the score of variable v increases, the *update* function in Algorithm 3 is invoked. This function first locates the bucket b where v resides. Then, it checks whether the maximum score in bucket b is greater than the minimum score in bucket $b - 1$. If so, it pops the variable with the maximum score from bucket b and pushes it into bucket $b-1$. Next, it pops the variable with the minimum score from bucket $b - 1$ and pushes it into bucket b. This process is repeated on bucket $b - 1$ to ensure the monotonicity of scores across buckets.

The interval heap is used to maintain the bucket corresponding to each variable, with changes occurring only when the score is updated. Additionally, we create a queue for each bucket to store the variables waiting to be decided within that bucket. The variables in the queue are unordered. During variable decision, the *pop* function in Algorithm 3 selects a variable from the non-empty queue of the smallest bucket. During backtracking, the *push* function places unassigned variables back into their respective queues based on their buckets.

This approach retains logarithmic time complexity for score updates while reducing the time complexity of the push and pop operations in VSIDS from logarithmic to constant time. However, this improvement comes at the cost of reduced accuracy in VSIDS, as the variable selected each time is from the bucket with the highest score but not necessarily the highest-scoring variable within that bucket. Nonetheless, since the queries are relatively simple, very high accuracy may not be critical.

4.3 Without Resetting

Observation 3 indicates that the SAT solver requires periodic resets due to the activation variables. However, this process also results in the loss of all learned clauses and heuristic scores. The key to supporting temporary clauses is to identify and remove all learned clauses that are directly or indirectly derived from temporary clauses after each solving process. We establish the following theorem:

Theorem 1. *To solve Q_{relind} with a temporary clause $\mathbf{c}$ by utilizing the activation variable $\mathbf{a}$, we consider the formula: $sat(F_i \wedge (c \vee a) \wedge T \wedge \neg c' \wedge \neg a)$, where $\neg c' \wedge \neg a$ serves as the temporary assumption. If a learned clause $\mathbf{lc}$ is derived from $c \vee a$, then $\mathbf{lc}$ must contain the literal $\mathbf{a}$.*

Proof. In a CDCL solver, every learned clause is the result of a sequence of resolution steps [13,39]. We prove this theorem by mathematical induction. Initially, the only clause containing a is $c \vee a$, and we assume that no clause contains the literal $\neg a$. Any learned clause derived from $c \vee a$ is either a direct or indirect resolvent of $c \vee a$. Since we assume that no clause contains $\neg a$, a cannot be used as a pivot in resolution. Consequently, every resolution step involving $c \vee a$ must preserve the literal a, implying that all learned clauses derived from $c \vee a$ must contain a. Furthermore, clauses not derived from $c \vee a$ cannot contain either a or $\neg a$, ensuring that our assumption remains valid throughout the process.

Theorem 1 states that learned clauses derived from the temporary clause contain the activation variable. Therefore, if all learned clauses containing the activation variable are identified and removed after each solving process, the temporary clause can also be safely deleted.

We use only one activation variable to support the temporary clause. A fixed variable is allocated in advance and serves as the activation variable for every query. During conflict clause analysis, if the learned clause contains this variable, it is recorded in a special vector. After each solving process, all learned clauses stored in this vector are removed from the clause database, along with the temporary clause itself. As a result, both the temporary clause and all its derived learned clauses are eliminated, ensuring that the activation variable does not appear in any remaining clauses. This frees the variable, making it available for reuse in the next solving process. Since this approach requires only a single additional variable, it eliminates the need to reset the SAT solver.

5 Implementation

Instead of implementing these optimizations on an existing SAT solver, we developed a new lightweight CDCL-based SAT solver from scratch, called GipSAT. It is implemented in Rust, a modern programming language designed to offer both performance and safety.

In many current implementations of IC3 [1,6,9], a separate SAT solver is created for each frame. GipSAT is designed based on this assumption, as each GipSAT instance corresponds to a specific frame. Since GipSAT is specifically optimized for the IC3 algorithm, it requires more information than other regular SAT solvers, such as the transition relation and awareness of which clauses belong to a frame for computing and maintaining the domain. Consequently, its interface differs from that of regular SAT solvers. The interfaces provided by GipSAT are as follows:

- new(*model*): Creates a new instance of GipSAT based on the provided transition system *model*. The transition relation T of *model* is represented in CNF format, with variable dependency information derived from AIG to compute the COI.
- add_lemma(*lemma*): Adds the given *lemma* to the solver. GipSAT maintains the lemmas of each frame. The add_clause method has been replaced with this, as users only need to add lemmas after creating a GipSAT instance. A

lemma is a clause that involves variables in X and has no dependent variables. Adding a clause with dependent variables could affect the correctness of domain maintenance. Therefore, only the add_lemma interface is provided.
- solve($assumption, constraint, droot$): Checks the satisfiability under the specified $assumption$ and $constraint$ within the domain COI($droot$) $\cup \mathcal{V}(F)$, where F represents the lemmas maintained by GipSAT. Users should ensure that $\mathcal{V}(assumption) \cup \mathcal{V}(constraint) \subseteq$ COI($droot$) $\cup \mathcal{V}(F)$.
- unsat_core(): Retrieves the UNSAT core from the previous UNSAT call.
- get_model(): Retrieves the variable assignments from the previous SAT call.
- set_domain($droot$): Configures GipSAT to use $\mathcal{V}(F) \cup$ COI($droot$) as the domain for subsequent solving processes, bypassing the need to recompute the domain before each solving step.
- unset_domain(): Resets the previously configured domain setting.

Meanwhile, GipSAT also provides encapsulated interfaces for the IC3 algorithm by leveraging the aforementioned functionalities. These interfaces include:

- relind(c): Checks the satisfiability of Q_{relind}, which is functionally equivalent to solve($\neg c', c, \mathcal{V}(c) \cup \mathcal{V}(c')$).
- inductive_core(): The inductive core is the UNSAT core produced by the previous relind(c), and an extra condition ensures that it does not overlap with the initial state I.
- has_bad(): Checks the satisfiability of Q_{bad}, which is functionally equivalent to solve($P, true, \mathcal{V}(P)$).

6 Evaluation

6.1 Experiment Setup

We integrated GipSAT into rIC3 [9], an implementation of the IC3 algorithm in Rust, which boasts competitive performance. We use the version based on Minisat. For comparison, we evaluated the performance of rIC3 with some state-of-the-art SAT solvers:

- **Minisat 2.2.0** [7]: Minisat is a popular SAT solver that serves as the underlying framework for many other SAT solvers.
- **CaDiCaL 2.1.2** [4]: CaDiCaL is a state-of-the-art SAT solver that has achieved high rankings in recent SAT Competitions [11].
- **CryptoMinisat 5.11.21** [5]: CryptoMinisat was the winner of the incremental track in the 2020 SAT Competition (no incremental track has been held since 2020).

We also considered the IC3 implementations in state-of-the-art model checkers, such as ABC [1] and nuXmv 2.1.0 [8], using their default configurations.

We conducted all configurations using the full benchmark suite from the two most recent Hardware Model Checking Competitions (HWMCC'20 and

Table 2. Total number of cases solved for different configurations. The additional cases solved and the geometric mean of the solving time ratio relative to GipSAT are presented, along with the PAR-2 score for each configuration.

Configuration	#Solved	ΔSolved	#Safe	#Unsafe	Avg. ST Ratio	PAR-2
rIC3-GipSAT	392	0	326	66	x1.00	2843.50
rIC3-Minisat	369	−23	309	60	x3.61	3140.95
rIC3-CryptoMinisat	364	−28	310	54	x4.83	3216.31
rIC3-CaDiCaL	366	−26	311	55	x5.99	3189.09
ABC	357	-	305	52	-	3258.97
nuXmv	353	-	301	52	-	3289.72

HWMCC'24), totaling 635 cases (after removing duplicates) in AIGER format [2]. All experiments were performed under identical resource constraints (16 GB memory and a 3600 s time limit) on an AMD EPYC 7532 processor running at 2.4 GHz. To ensure the accuracy of the results, we verified the results across different checkers to ensure consistency. To ensure reproducibility, we have made the implementations of our experiments available at [3].

6.2 Experimental Results

Table 2 and Fig. 4 present the summary of results and the number of cases solved over time by various configurations. The comparison shows that rIC3 performs well relative to state-of-the-art systems like ABC and nuXmv, making it a suitable choice as the experimental foundation. Notably, GipSAT solved 23 more cases than the best-performing regular solver, Minisat, greatly enhancing the capability of the IC3 algorithm. The last column of Table 2 lists the geometric mean speedup in solving time of GipSAT relative to regular solvers. GipSAT achieves a significant improvement in efficiency, with an average speedup of 3.61 times compared to Minisat in rIC3. Figure 5 shows scatter plots comparing the solving times of GipSAT with those of regular solvers in rIC3. It is clear that, with GipSAT, the solving time for most cases has decreased substantially. This experimental result clearly highlights the effectiveness of GipSAT in improving the efficiency and scalability of the IC3 algorithm.

6.3 Analysis

To better demonstrate the effectiveness of GipSAT, we measured the average solving time of queries using GipSAT and Minisat in rIC3, as described in Fig. 6. It is evident that, in the majority of cases, GipSAT demonstrates a significant reduction in solving time for queries when compared to Minisat. We also compared the proof-obligation length, number of frames, and invariant size between GipSAT and Minisat, as shown in Fig. 7. For cases solved by both GipSAT and Minisat, these values are largely the same from a statistical perspective, indicating that our approach primarily accelerates SAT solving without significantly

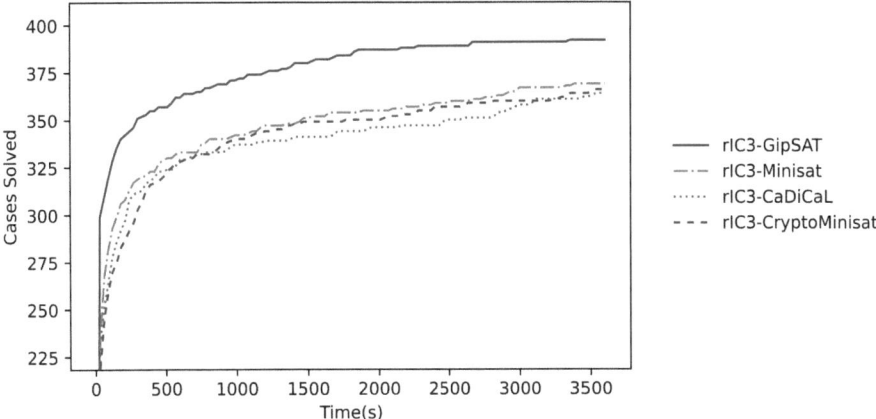

Fig. 4. The number of cases solved by different SAT solvers over time.

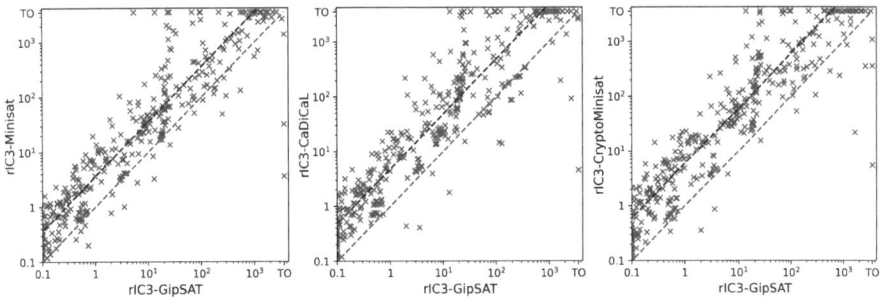

Fig. 5. The comparison of solving time(s) between GipSAT and other solvers in rIC3. Points above the gray solid line indicate that GipSAT performs better. The purple dashed line represents the geometric mean of the speedup. (Color figure online)

affecting the algorithm itself. For cases where GipSAT and Minisat do not both solve the problem, the frame depth of GipSAT is slightly larger. This is because GipSAT's faster solving speed allows the algorithm to reach deeper frames more quickly within the given time limit.

To assess the impact of each optimization, we evaluated rIC3-GipSAT under different optimization combinations:

- The **dm** flag determines whether domain optimization is enabled.
- The **bkt** flag indicates whether buckets are used to maintain VSIDS; if not, a binary heap is used instead.
- The **wr** flag represents whether the optimization described in Sect. 4.3 is applied; otherwise, a new activation variable is created before each solving, and the solver is reset every 1000 activation variables.

The results are presented in Table 3, where we also include the results of rIC3-Minisat for comparison. In the table, rIC3-GipSAT-noopt refers to the version

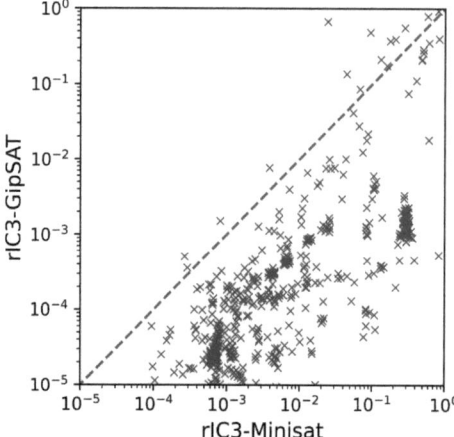

Fig. 6. The comparison of average solving time(s) for queries between GipSAT and Minisat in rIC3. Points below the gray diagonal indicate that GipSAT performs better.

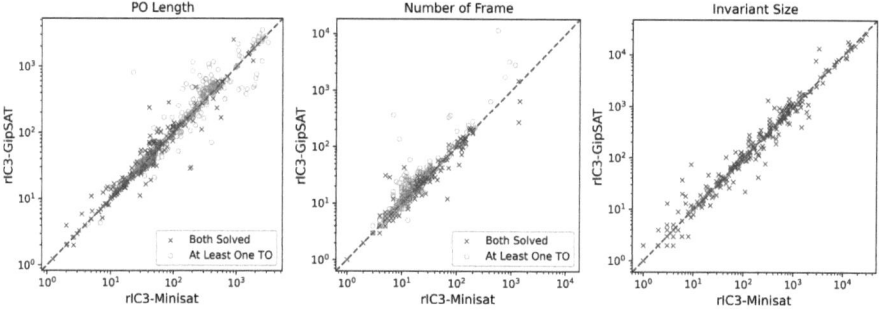

Fig. 7. The comparison of proof-obligation length, number of frames, and invariant size (safe instances) between GipSAT and Minisat in rIC3.

with all optimizations disabled. As shown, without any optimizations, rIC3-GipSAT-noopt performs similarly to rIC3-Minisat as GipSAT's CDCL framework is inspired by Minisat. Additionally, it can be observed that enabling optimizations leads to performance improvements, demonstrating the effectiveness of deciding in the domain, using buckets in VSIDS, and eliminating resetting, respectively. For further comparison, we also implemented the method from [22] on GipSAT (rIC3-GipSAT-fmcad21), which performs slightly better than ours. This method sequentially treats each literal in the constraint as an assumption, resulting in support for only one temporary clause, whereas our method allows for multiple temporary clauses.

7 Discussion

The IC3 algorithm involves a large number of relatively simple SAT problems, so improving the efficiency of each SAT call is essential for enhancing overall performance. The first optimization significantly boosts performance by reducing the number of decision variables, which leads to substantial improvements in many cases. However, when domain variables make up a large portion of the total variables, the effectiveness of this optimization becomes limited. The second optimization replaces the binary heap with a bucket-based approach to reduce the overhead of the VSIDS heuristic, while the third reuses activation literals to avoid unnecessary resets. Nonetheless, compared to the first optimization, the performance gains from the second and third optimizations are relatively modest. Overall, GipSAT significantly improves the SAT solving efficiency of the IC3 algorithm, enabling more cases to be solved within a limited time. However, it does not alter the IC3 algorithm itself, so cases that are unsolvable due to theoretical limitations remain unsolved.

Table 3. The total number of cases of different conditions. Using rIC3-GipSAT-noopt as the baseline, the additional solved cases and the geometric mean of the solving time improvement compared to the baseline are presented.

Configuration	#Solved	ΔSolved	Avg. ST Imprv
rIC3-GipSAT-noopt	370	0	x1.00
rIC3-Minisat	369	−1	x0.98
rIC3-GipSAT-dm	384	+14	x2.62
rIC3-GipSAT-bkt	374	+4	x1.24
rIC3-GipSAT-wr	373	+3	x1.13
rIC3-GipSAT-fmcad21	373	+3	x1.21
rIC3-GipSAT-bkt-wr	379	+9	x1.42
rIC3-GipSAT-dm-wr	386	+16	x2.84
rIC3-GipSAT-dm-bkt	390	+20	x3.17
rIC3-GipSAT-dm-bkt-wr	392	+22	x3.52

8 Related Work

Since the introduction of IC3 [12], numerous efforts have been dedicated to enhancing its performance. Most of these studies focus on the algorithm layer. For instance, [27] attempts to block counterexamples to generalization (CTG) to improve generalization. [38] proposes a variant of IC3 that integrates interpolation, while [33] introduces under-approximation to expedite bug detection. The algorithm in [40] drops literals that do not appear in any subsumed lemmas from the previous frame, thereby increasing the likelihood of propagating to the next frame. In [36], the authors aim to predict the outcome before generalization, which could potentially reduce overhead if successful. In [18], the authors leverage the internal signals of the circuit to represent invariants more concisely. [26] presents a flexible algorithmic framework that integrates IC3 with k-induction. Additionally, [25] aggressively pushes lemmas to the top by adding may-proof-obligation.

Only a few studies have focused on the SAT solver layer. [14] analyzed the results of different SAT solver management strategies at the algorithm layer, including SAT solver allocation, loading, and clean-up. [22] proposed a method that eliminates the need for activation literals in temporary clauses. Instead, it iteratively assumes a literal in the temporary clause before solving, thereby avoiding the need to reset the SAT solver, which means it can only support one temporary clause. Similarly, GipSAT also eliminates the need to reset the SAT solver, but it differs significantly in its approach. GipSAT uses the same activation literal in every query by promptly removing both the temporary clause and its derived learned clauses after each solving, allowing multiple temporary clauses. In Minisat, the `release_var` interface can avoid restarts by passing the activation variables. The principle behind it is to first add the activation variable clause and then periodically clean up satisfied clauses (since the occur list is not maintained for performance reasons, it can only be lazily cleaned up). Once all clauses containing released variables are cleared, the activation variables can be reused. Compared to this approach, our method not only avoids restarts but also promptly removes temporary clauses. In SMT, temporary constraints can be supported through `push` and `pop`, but more complex data structures are needed to maintain them.

9 Conclusion and Future Work

In this paper, we present GipSAT, a SAT solver specifically designed for the IC3 algorithm. GipSAT reduces the number of variables that need to be decided by precomputing the domain. It achieves constant-time operations by utilizing buckets in VSIDS. Moreover, it avoids resetting the solvers by eliminating the requirement for allocating an activation literal before each solving. The experimental results demonstrate that GipSAT significantly reduces the solving time of SAT queries posed by IC3, consequently leading to a substantial performance improvement compared to state-of-the-art regular SAT solvers. In the future, we will continue to optimize GipSAT and explore the possibility of designing an SMT solver for the word-level IC3 algorithm.

Acknowledgement. This work was supported by the Beijing Municipal Natural Science Foundation (Grant No. 4252024), the Foundation of Laboratory for Advanced Computing and Intelligence Engineering (Grant No. 2023-LYJJ-01-013), the Basic Research Projects from the Institute of Software, Chinese Academy of Sciences (Grant No. ISCAS-JCZD-202307) and the National Natural Science Foundation of China (Grant No. 62372438).

Disclosure of Interests. The authors have no competing interests to declare that are relevant to the content of this article.

References

1. Abc. https://github.com/berkeley-abc/abc
2. Aiger. https://fmv.jku.at/aiger
3. Artifact. https://github.com/gipsyh/GipSAT-CAV25
4. Cadical. https://github.com/arminbiere/cadical
5. Cryptominisat. https://github.com/msoos/cryptominisat
6. IC3ref. https://github.com/arbrad/IC3ref
7. MiniSat. http://minisat.se
8. nuXmv. https://nuxmv.fbk.eu
9. RIC3. https://github.com/gipsyh/rIC3, branch: satif
10. Biere, A., Cimatti, A., Clarke, E., Zhu, Y.: Symbolic model checking without BDDs. In: Cleaveland, W.R. (ed.) TACAS 1999. LNCS, vol. 1579, pp. 193–207. Springer, Heidelberg (1999). https://doi.org/10.1007/3-540-49059-0_14
11. Biere, A., Fazekas, K., Fleury, M., Heisinger, M.: CaDiCaL, Kissat, Paracooba, Plingeling and Treengeling entering the SAT competition 2020. In: Balyo, T., Froleyks, N., Heule, M., Iser, M., Järvisalo, M., Suda, M. (eds.) Proceedings of SAT Competition 2020 – Solver and Benchmark Descriptions. Department of Computer Science Report Series B, vol. B-2020-1, pp. 51–53. University of Helsinki (2020)
12. Bradley, A.R.: SAT-based model checking without unrolling. In: Jhala, R., Schmidt, D. (eds.) VMCAI 2011. LNCS, vol. 6538, pp. 70–87. Springer, Heidelberg (2011). https://doi.org/10.1007/978-3-642-18275-4_7
13. Buss, S., Nordström, J.: Proof complexity and SAT solving. In: Biere, A., Heule, M., van Maaren, H., Walsh, T. (eds.) Handbook of Satisfiability - Second Edition, Frontiers in Artificial Intelligence and Applications, vol. 336, pp. 233–350. IOS Press (2021). https://doi.org/10.3233/FAIA200990
14. Cabodi, G., Camurati, P.E., Mishchenko, A., Palena, M., Pasini, P.: SAT solver management strategies in IC3: an experimental approach. Formal Methods Syst. Des. **50**(1), 39–74 (2017). https://doi.org/10.1007/s10703-017-0272-0
15. Cavada, R., et al.: The NUXMV symbolic model checker. In: Biere, A., Bloem, R. (eds.) CAV 2014. LNCS, vol. 8559, pp. 334–342. Springer, Cham (2014). https://doi.org/10.1007/978-3-319-08867-9_22
16. Clarke, E.M., Grumberg, O., Kroening, D., Peled, D.A., Veith, H.: Model Checking, 2nd edn. MIT Press (2018). https://mitpress.mit.edu/books/model-checking-second-edition
17. Clarke, E.M., Henzinger, T.A., Veith, H., Bloem, R.: Handbook of Model Checking, 1st edn. Springer, Cham (2018). https://doi.org/10.1007/978-3-319-10575-8
18. Dureja, R., Gurfinkel, A., Ivrii, A., Vizel, Y.: IC3 with internal signals. In: Formal Methods in Computer Aided Design, FMCAD 2021, New Haven, CT, USA, 19–22 October 2021, pp. 63–71. IEEE (2021). https://doi.org/10.34727/2021/ISBN.978-3-85448-046-4_14
19. Eén, N., Mishchenko, A., Brayton, R.K.: Efficient implementation of property directed reachability. In: Bjesse, P., Slobodová, A. (eds.) International Conference on Formal Methods in Computer-Aided Design, FMCAD 2011, Austin, TX, USA, 30 October–02 November 2011, pp. 125–134. FMCAD Inc. (2011). http://dl.acm.org/citation.cfm?id=2157675

20. Eén, N., Sörensson, N.: Temporal induction by incremental SAT solving. In: Strichman, O., Biere, A. (eds.) First International Workshop on Bounded Model Checking, BMC@CAV 2003, Boulder, Colorado, USA, 13 July 2003. Electronic Notes in Theoretical Computer Science, vol. 89, pp. 543–560. Elsevier (2003). https://doi.org/10.1016/S1571-0661(05)82542-3
21. Forsythe, G.E.: Algorithms. Commun. ACM **7**(6), 347–349 (1964). https://doi.org/10.1145/512274.512284
22. Froleyks, N., Biere, A.: Single clause assumption without activation literals to speed-up IC3. In: Formal Methods in Computer Aided Design, FMCAD 2021, New Haven, CT, USA, 19–22 October 2021, pp. 72–76. IEEE (2021). https://doi.org/10.34727/2021/ISBN.978-3-85448-046-4_15
23. Goel, A., Sakallah, K.A.: Empirical evaluation of IC3-based model checking techniques on Verilog RTL designs. In: Teich, J., Fummi, F. (eds.) Design, Automation & Test in Europe Conference & Exhibition, DATE 2019, Florence, Italy, 25–29 March 2019, pp. 618–621. IEEE (2019). https://doi.org/10.23919/DATE.2019.8715289
24. Goel, A., Sakallah, K.: AVR: abstractly verifying reachability. In: TACAS 2020. LNCS, vol. 12078, pp. 413–422. Springer, Cham (2020). https://doi.org/10.1007/978-3-030-45190-5_23
25. Gurfinkel, A., Ivrii, A.: Pushing to the top. In: Kaivola, R., Wahl, T. (eds.) Formal Methods in Computer-Aided Design, FMCAD 2015, Austin, Texas, USA, 27–30 September 2015, pp. 65–72. IEEE (2015). https://doi.org/10.1109/FMCAD.2015.7542254
26. Gurfinkel, A., Ivrii, A.: K-induction without unrolling. In: Stewart, D., Weissenbacher, G. (eds.) 2017 Formal Methods in Computer Aided Design, FMCAD 2017, Vienna, Austria, 2–6 October 2017, pp. 148–155. IEEE (2017). https://doi.org/10.23919/FMCAD.2017.8102253
27. Hassan, Z., Bradley, A.R., Somenzi, F.: Better generalization in IC3. In: Formal Methods in Computer-Aided Design, FMCAD 2013, Portland, OR, USA, 20–23 October 2013, pp. 157–164. IEEE (2013). https://ieeexplore.ieee.org/document/6679405/
28. Kuehlmann, A., Krohm, F.: Equivalence checking using cuts and heaps. In: Yoffa, E.J., Micheli, G.D., Rabaey, J.M. (eds.) Proceedings of the 34st Conference on Design Automation, Anaheim, California, USA, Anaheim Convention Center, 9–13 June 1997, pp. 263–268. ACM Press (1997). https://doi.org/10.1145/266021.266090
29. van Leeuwen, J., Wood, D.: Interval heaps. Comput. J. **36**(3), 209–216 (1993). https://doi.org/10.1093/COMJNL/36.3.209
30. Mann, M., et al.: **Pono**: a flexible and extensible SMT-based model checker. In: Silva, A., Leino, K. (eds.) CAV 2021. LNCS, vol. 12760, pp. 461–474. Springer, Cham (2021). https://doi.org/10.1007/978-3-030-81688-9_22
31. McMillan, K.L.: Interpolation and SAT-based model checking. In: Hunt, W.A., Somenzi, F. (eds.) CAV 2003. LNCS, vol. 2725, pp. 1–13. Springer, Heidelberg (2003). https://doi.org/10.1007/978-3-540-45069-6_1
32. Moskewicz, M.W., Madigan, C.F., Zhao, Y., Zhang, L., Malik, S.: Chaff: engineering an efficient SAT solver. In: Proceedings of the 38th Design Automation Conference, DAC 2001, Las Vegas, NV, USA, 18–22 June 2001, pp. 530–535. ACM (2001). https://doi.org/10.1145/378239.379017

33. Seufert, T., Scholl, C., Chandrasekharan, A., Reimer, S., Welp, T.: Making PROGRESS in property directed reachability. In: Finkbeiner, B., Wies, T. (eds.) VMCAI 2022. LNCS, vol. 13182, pp. 355–377. Springer, Cham (2022). https://doi.org/10.1007/978-3-030-94583-1_18
34. Sheeran, M., Singh, S., Stålmarck, G.: Checking safety properties using induction and a SAT-solver. In: Hunt, W.A., Johnson, S.D. (eds.) FMCAD 2000. LNCS, vol. 1954, pp. 127–144. Springer, Heidelberg (2000). https://doi.org/10.1007/3-540-40922-X_8
35. Silva, J.P.M., Sakallah, K.A.: GRASP - a new search algorithm for satisfiability. In: Rutenbar, R.A., Otten, R.H.J.M. (eds.) Proceedings of the 1996 IEEE/ACM International Conference on Computer-Aided Design, ICCAD 1996, San Jose, CA, USA, 10–14 November 1996, pp. 220–227. IEEE Computer Society / ACM (1996). https://doi.org/10.1109/ICCAD.1996.569607
36. Su, Y., Yang, Q., Ci, Y.: Predicting lemmas in generalization of IC3. In: De, V. (ed.) Proceedings of the 61st ACM/IEEE Design Automation Conference, DAC 2024, San Francisco, CA, USA, 23–27 June 2024, pp. 208:1–208:6. ACM (2024). https://doi.org/10.1145/3649329.3655970
37. Tseitin, G.S.: On the complexity of derivation in propositional calculus. In: Automation of Reasoning: 2: Classical Papers on Computational Logic 1967–1970, pp. 466–483. Springer, Heidelberg (1983). https://doi.org/10.1007/978-3-642-81955-1_28
38. Vizel, Y., Gurfinkel, A.: Interpolating property directed reachability. In: Biere, A., Bloem, R. (eds.) CAV 2014. LNCS, vol. 8559, pp. 260–276. Springer, Cham (2014). https://doi.org/10.1007/978-3-319-08867-9_17
39. Vizel, Y., Weissenbacher, G., Malik, S.: Boolean satisfiability solvers and their applications in model checking. Proc. IEEE **103**(11), 2021–2035 (2015). https://doi.org/10.1109/JPROC.2015.2455034
40. Xia, Y., Becchi, A., Cimatti, A., Griggio, A., Li, J., Pu, G.: Searching for I-good lemmas to accelerate safety model checking. In: Enea, C., Lal, A. (eds.) Computer Aided Verification - 35th International Conference, CAV 2023, Paris, France, 17–22 July 2023, Proceedings, Part II. LNCS, vol. 13965, pp. 288–308. Springer, Cham (2023). https://doi.org/10.1007/978-3-031-37703-7_14

Open Access This chapter is licensed under the terms of the Creative Commons Attribution 4.0 International License (http://creativecommons.org/licenses/by/4.0/), which permits use, sharing, adaptation, distribution and reproduction in any medium or format, as long as you give appropriate credit to the original author(s) and the source, provide a link to the Creative Commons license and indicate if changes were made.

The images or other third party material in this chapter are included in the chapter's Creative Commons license, unless indicated otherwise in a credit line to the material. If material is not included in the chapter's Creative Commons license and your intended use is not permitted by statutory regulation or exceeds the permitted use, you will need to obtain permission directly from the copyright holder.

Property Directed Reachability with Extended Resolution

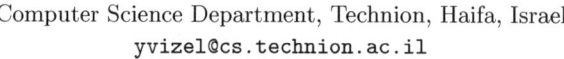

 Computer Science Department, Technion, Haifa, Israel
yvizel@cs.technion.ac.il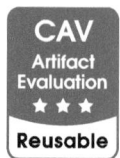

Abstract. Property Directed Reachability (PDR), also known as IC3, is a state-of-the-art model checking algorithm widely used for verifying safety properties. While PDR is effective in finding inductive invariants, its underlying proof system, Resolution, limits its ability to construct short proofs for certain verification problems.

This paper introduces PDRER, a novel generalization of PDR that uses Extended Resolution (ER), a proof system exponentially stronger than Resolution, when constructing a proof of correctness. PDRER leverages ER to construct shorter bounded proofs of correctness, enabling it to discover more compact inductive invariants. While PDRER is based on PDR, it includes algorithmic enhancements that had to be made in order to efficiently use ER in the context of model checking.

We implemented PDRER in a new open-source verification framework and evaluated it on the Hardware Model Checking Competition benchmarks from 2019, 2020 and 2024. Our experimental evaluation demonstrates that PDRER outperforms PDR, solving more instances in less time and uniquely solving problems that PDR cannot solve within a given time limit. We argue that this paper represents a significant step toward making strong proof systems practically usable in model checking.

1 Introduction

Property Directed Reachability (PDR), a.k.a. IC3 [5,18], is a state-of-the-art model checking algorithm, which is widely used by many verification tools. Given a model and a safety property to be verified, PDR is especially effective in finding an inductive invariant that establishes the correctness of that property w.r.t. the given model. Intuitively, one can view PDR as a proof-search algorithm, which searches for a proof, i.e. an inductive invariant, in order to establish the validity of the property. It is therefore natural to consider the underlying proof-system PDR uses during this process.

Proof-systems are a central concept in the theory of Computer Science and are a powerful tool when applying logic in automated reasoning. A proof-system P is a set of axioms and inference rules such that a derivation of a statement in P is a proof for the validity of that statement under the given set of axioms. A well-known proof-system is Resolution [16,24], which forms the theoretical foundation of Boolean Satisfiability (SAT) [15,16,27,28]. In fact, Resolution is the underlying proof-system in many SAT-based model checking algorithms [12, 26,31–33], including PDR [2].

In PDR, during the search for an inductive invariant the algorithm constructs a bounded proof of correctness, in Conjunctive Normal Form (CNF), that proves that the property holds up to a given bound. In fact, this bounded proof can be simulated by a Resolution proof [2]. More precisely, for a bounded proof of correctness $\vec{F}$ constructed by PDR, there exists a Resolution proof polynomial in the size of $\vec{F}$. By that, the bounded proofs PDR constructs are limited by the strength of the Resolution proof-system.

The strength of a proof-system P is determined by the length of the shortest proof it admits for a valid statement. The shorter the proofs in P, the stronger P is. In the case of Resolution, there exist formulas for which Resolution admits no "short" proofs, i.e. it admits no proof polynomial in the size of the formula. A notable example is the pigeonhole problem, which admits only exponential size Resolution proofs [21]. Since the bounded proof of correctness PDR constructs can be simulated by Resolution, this means that there exist models and properties, for which PDR admits no short bounded proof of correctness. This fact limits the performance of PDR. Moreover, it implies that there exist models and properties that PDR necessarily cannot solve in a reasonable time.

In this paper we present a novel model checking algorithm, PDRER, which generalizes PDR with Extended Resolution (ER) [30] as its underlying proof-system. ER is a strong proof-system that is *exponentially stronger* than Resolution. For example, there are polynomial size ER proofs for the pigeonhole problem [14]. Hence, if PDRER can efficiently utilize ER, it has the potential to construct shorter bounded and unbounded proofs of correctness.

ER generalizes Resolution with the addition of *the extension rule*. It enables the addition of an auxiliary variable along with its definition to the formula. For example, given a formula $\varphi(x_1, \ldots, x_n)$, applying the extension rule may add $y \leftrightarrow (x_1 \vee x_2)$ to φ, where y is a fresh variable. This results in the formula $\psi(x_1, \ldots, x_n, y) := \varphi(x_1, \ldots, x_n) \wedge (y \leftrightarrow (x_1 \vee x_2))$.

There is a trade-off between the strength of a proof system and the ability to implement an efficient proof-search algorithm for it. Hence, while ER is exponentially stronger than Resolution, the addition of the extension rule makes proof-search algorithms for ER intractable, since there is no guidance as to which auxiliary variables and definitions should be added.

The complexity in implementing an efficient proof-search algorithm for ER also manifests itself in PDRER. Therefore, the following three key aspects must be addressed for PDRER to be efficient: (i) the extension rule should add the "right" auxiliary variables and definitions; (ii) applying the extension rule should be efficient; and (iii) the model checking algorithm needs to be adjusted to account for the added auxiliary variables. The first two points are also true in the context of SAT. Hence, we draw our intuition from techniques that utilize ER in SAT-solvers, which had some limited success [1,25]. PDRER uses a pre-defined set of templates that guides the addition of auxiliary variables. The templates are used to match clauses from the bounded proof maintained by PDR. If a set of clauses in the proof matches a given template, an auxiliary variable is added and the matched clauses are replaced with a new *smaller* set of clauses. For example, assume the proof consists of the following clauses $(l_1 \vee l_2 \vee A)$ and $(\neg l_1 \vee \neg l_2 \vee A)$. When these clauses are identified, PDRER can add a fresh auxiliary variable y such that $y \leftrightarrow (l_1 \oplus l_2)$, and replace the above two clauses with $(y \vee A)$, effectively re-encoding the bounded proof of correctness with the addition of an auxiliary variable. Intuitively, this is somewhat similar to "ghost code" addition [10,22], only that in this case it is done *automatically*.

Using this mechanism in PDRER reduces the size of the bounded proof PDRER maintains. As it turns out, this reduction causes PDRER to learn redundant clauses, causing performance degradation. Hence, by preventing PDRER from learning redundant clauses its performance can be improved. This is where the third point mentioned above becomes relevant.

Using ER and adding auxiliary variables in PDR break many of its nice properties. For example, syntactic subsumption checks are no longer effective and may cause the proof to include many redundant clauses. This becomes a bottleneck when the number of such redundant clauses grows large. Another example comes from *propagation*. If PDRER uses the same propagation mechanism as in PDR it results in PDRER re-learning many of the clauses that already exist in the bounded proof it maintains. Thus, while PDRER is based on PDR, in order to make it efficient, the algorithm had to be modified such that it takes into account the existence of auxiliary variables that are introduced by ER.

We implemented PDRER in an open-source tool and evaluated it on the last three Hardware Model Checking Competition [4] benchmarks from 2019, 2020 and 2024 (HWMCC'19/20/24). We compared PDRER against our own implementation of PDR as well as the implementation of PDR in ABC. Our experimental evaluation shows that PDRER is *superior* to PDR. It solves many problems that are not solvable by PDR and performs better overall in terms of runtime and number of solved instances. In addition, it produces shorter proofs on almost all instances. This leads us to conclude that PDRER is the first step in making strong proof systems *efficiently usable* in model checking algorithms.

1.1 Related Work

The ER proof system received attention from the SAT community due to its strength. If SAT-solvers can efficiently utilize ER, the impact can be enormous. There have been a few works that tried to incorporate ER into SAT-solvers [1, 9,20,23,25,29]. While these works are in the context of SAT-solvers and proofs of unsatisfiability, our template-based algorithm for applying the extension rule draws intuition from [1,25]. In both these works the extension rule is applied on two clauses of the form $(l_1 \vee A)$ and $(l_2 \vee A)$, driving the addition of an auxiliary variable $x \leftrightarrow l_1 \wedge l_2$. Our algorithm extends this approach and can identify other templates that can also introduce an auxiliary variable of the form $x \leftrightarrow l_1 \oplus l_2$. Moreover, while all of these approaches operate on a given formula in Conjunctive Normal Form (CNF) and try to speed up satisfiability checking, in the case of PDRER, it operates on a number of formulas in CNF that change as the algorithm makes progress when searching for an inductive invariant.

The closest work to ours is [17]. It extends PDR to allow it to express inductive invariants over both state variables and internal signals. While this work allows PDR to use auxiliary variables when searching for the inductive invariant, the set of possible auxiliary variables is limited only to these variables that appear in the verified model. In contrast, PDRER does not have this limitation and it can add auxiliary variables that are defined by an arbitrary Boolean function. Moreover, the algorithm presented in [17] does not perform better than PDR overall and has only shown better performance on a specific class of verification problems. Unlike [17], PDRER outperforms PDR.

Another line of work that uses a similar principle is based on "ghost code" addition [3,10,11,13,19,22]. Ghost code augments programs with verification-specific constructs (e.g., ghost variables or assertions) that enable concise proofs without affecting runtime behavior. Intuitively, this is similar to the addition of auxiliary variables by ER.

2 Preliminaries

Given a set U of Boolean variables, a *literal* ℓ is a variable $u \in U$ or its negation $\neg u$, $var(l)$ denotes the associated variable of the literal l, and we denote by $Lits(U)$ the set of all literals over U. A *clause* is a disjunction of literals, and a formula in *Conjunctive Normal Form* (CNF) is a conjunction of clauses. It is convenient to treat a clause as a set of literals, and a CNF as a set of clauses. We refer to a conjunction of literals as a *cube*.

Safety Verification: A transition system T is a tuple $(\bar{v}, Init, Tr, Bad)$, where $\bar{v}$ is a set of variables that defines the states of T (i.e., all valuations to $\bar{v}$), $Init$ and Bad are formulas with variables in $\bar{v}$ denoting the set of initial states and bad states, respectively, and Tr is a formula with free variables in $\bar{v} \cup \bar{v}'$, denoting the transition relation. A state $s \in T$ is said to be reachable if and only if (iff) there exists a state $s_0 \in Init$, and $(s_i, s_{i+1}) \in Tr$ for $0 \le i < N$, and $s = s_N$.

A transition system T is UNSAFE iff there exists a state $s \in Bad$ s.t. s is reachable. When T is UNSAFE and $s_N \in Bad$ is the reachable state, the path from $s_0 \in Init$ to s_N is called a *counterexample* (CEX).

A transition system T is SAFE iff all reachable states in T do not satisfy Bad. Equivalently, there exists a formula Inv, called a *safe inductive invariant*, satisfying: $Init(\bar{v}) \rightarrow Inv(\bar{v})$, $Inv(\bar{v}) \wedge Tr(\bar{v}, \bar{v}') \rightarrow Inv(\bar{v}')$ and $Inv(\bar{v}) \rightarrow \neg Bad(\bar{v})$. A *safety* verification problem is to decide whether a transition system T is UNSAFE or SAFE, i.e., whether there exists an initial state in $Init$ that can reach a bad state in Bad, or synthesize a safe inductive invariant.

In SAT-based model checking, the verification problem is determined by computing over-approximations of the states reachable in T and, by that, trying to either construct an invariant or find a CEX.

Relative Induction: Given two formulas $F(\bar{v})$ and $G(\bar{v})$, G is *inductive relative to* F iff the following two conditions hold:

$$Init(\bar{v}) \rightarrow G(\bar{v}) \qquad (F(\bar{v}) \wedge G(\bar{v})) \wedge Tr(\bar{v}, \bar{v}') \rightarrow G(\bar{v}') \qquad (1)$$

3 Property Directed Reachability

In this section, we give a brief overview of PDR [5,18]. While PDR is well-known, we present the necessary details for the rest of the paper. Let us fix a transition system $T = (\bar{v}, Init, Tr, Bad)$.

The main data-structure maintained by PDR is a sequence of formulas $\vec{F} = [F_0, \ldots, F_N]$, called an *inductive trace*, or simply a *trace*. An inductive trace $\vec{F} = [F_0, \ldots, F_N]$ satisfies the following two properties:

$$Init(\bar{v}) = F_0(\bar{v}) \qquad \forall 0 \leq i < N \cdot F_i(\bar{v}) \wedge Tr(\bar{v}, \bar{v}') \rightarrow F_{i+1}(\bar{v}') \qquad (2)$$

The *size* of $\vec{F} = [F_0, \ldots, F_N]$ is $|\vec{F}| = N$. An element F_i of a trace is called a *frame*. The index of a frame is called a *level*. $\vec{F}$ is *clausal* when all its elements are in CNF. We abuse notation and treat every frame F_i as a set of clauses.

An inductive trace is *safe* if each F_i is safe: $F_i \rightarrow \neg Bad$; *monotone* if $\forall 0 \leq i < N$, $F_i \rightarrow F_{i+1}$; and *closed* if $\exists 1 \leq i \leq N \cdot F_i \rightarrow \left(\bigvee_{j=0}^{i-1} F_j\right)$.

A transition system:

Lemma 1. *If a transition system T admits a safe trace $\vec{F}$ of size $|\vec{F}| = N$, then T does not admit counterexamples of length less than, or equal to N.*

We refer to such a trace as *a bounded proof of correctness*. For an unbounded proof of correctness, the trace also needs to be closed:

Theorem 1. *A transition system T is SAFE iff it admits a safe closed trace.*

Thus, safety verification is reduced to searching for a safe closed trace or finding a CEX. In particular, PDR iteratively extends $\vec{F}$ such that $\vec{F}$ is safe. This procedure continues until $\vec{F}$ is either closed or it cannot be extended and remain safe. In the latter case, PDR can construct a counterexample that shows why $\vec{F}$ cannot be extended. It is important to note that the trace $\vec{F}$ PDR constructs is *syntactically monotone*, namely $\forall 0 < i < N$, $F_i \supseteq F_{i+1}$. Hence, $\vec{F}$ is closed when there exists a level $0 < i < N$ such that $F_i = F_{i+1}$. We note that in most implementations, due to the monotonicity of $\vec{F}$, it is often represented using a *delta-trace*. Given a monotone trace $\vec{F}$ of size N, the *delta*-trace of $\vec{F}$ is defined as $\vec{D} = [D_0, \ldots, D_N]$ such that $D_0 = F_0$, $D_i = F_i \setminus F_{i+1}$ for $0 < i < N$ and $D_N = F_N$. In what follows we use $\vec{F}$ and $\vec{D}$ interchangeably.

Algorithm 1 presents a high level view of PDR's main loop. We only present the details that are required for this paper. PDR starts by initializing an inductive trace $\vec{F} = [F_0]$ where $F_0 = Init$ (line 1). The main loop iteratively extends the trace $\vec{F}$ and tries to make it safe (line 3). If it fails, then a counterexample is returned (line 5). Otherwise, a new frame is added to $\vec{F}$ and it is initialized to $\top$. Once a new frame is added, PDR tries *propagating* clauses by adding clauses that exist in the frame F_i into the subsequent frame F_{i+1} (line 7). If after propagation there exists a frame that equals its subsequent frame, a safe inductive invariant is found and PDR terminates. Otherwise, it moves to the next iteration.

Redundancy: During the execution of MKSAFE(), PDR adds clauses to $\vec{F}$. When inserting a new clause c into a frame $F_i \in \vec{F}$, PDR removes subsumed clauses. This is done with a simple syntactic subsumption check. Namely, for every $0 < j \leq i$, if there exists a clause $d \in F_j$ such that $c \subseteq d$, d is removed from F_j.

Propagation: PDR performs propagation in order to construct a *closed* trace. Recall that $\vec{F}$ is *syntactically monotone*. Therefore, if all clauses in $F_i \setminus F_{i+1}$ (i.e. in D_i) can be *propagated* to F_{i+1} then $\vec{F}$ becomes closed and PDR terminates. Propagation is performed by checking if a clause $c \in D_i$ satisfies the following condition: $F_i \wedge Tr \rightarrow c'$. If this condition holds, c can be added to F_{i+1}.

Generalization: In a monotone trace $\vec{F}$, a frame $F_i \in \vec{F}$ over-approximates the set of states reachable in up to i steps of the Tr. Since $\vec{F}$ is clausal and F_i is in CNF, every clause $c \in F_i$ blocks states that are *necessarily unreachable* in up to i steps. Assume a set of states is represented by the cube φ. If PDR identifies that the states in φ are unreachable in up to i steps, it can add the clause $c = \neg \varphi$ to F_i. This means that the formula $(F_{i-1} \wedge c) \wedge Tr \rightarrow c'$ is valid. PDR uses this fact and tries to construct a *stronger clause* $d \subseteq c$ such that $Init \rightarrow d$ and $(F_{i-1} \wedge d) \wedge Tr \rightarrow d'$ are valid. By that, it can deduce that a larger set of states is unreachable in up to i steps. PDR refers to this process as *inductive generalization* as it is based on the fact that c is *relatively inductive* w.r.t. F_{i-1}.

Algorithm 1: PDR

Input: Transition System
Output: Proof or counterexample
1 Initially: $\vec{F} = [Init]$
2 while *true* do
3     $\vec{F} = \text{MKSAFE}(\vec{F})$;
4   if $\neg \vec{F}$.ISSAFE() then
5   return cex;
6     $\vec{F}$.EXTEND($\top$);
7     $\vec{F}$.PROPAGATE();
8     $N = \vec{F}$.SIZE();
9   if $\exists 0 \leq i < N \cdot F_i = F_{i+1}$ then
10   return F_i;

Algorithm 2: PDRER

Input: Transition System
Output: Proof or counterexample
1 Initially: $\vec{G} = [Init]$
2 size = 0;
3 while *true* do
4     $\vec{G} = \text{MKSAFE}(\vec{G})$;
5   if $\neg \vec{G}$.ISSAFE() then
6   return cex;
7   if $\vec{G}$.NUMCLAUSES() $>$ size $+ \Delta$ then
8        $\vec{G}$.REENCODE();
9   size = $\vec{G}$.NUMCLAUSES();
10     $\vec{G}$.EXTEND($\top$);
11     $\vec{G}$.PROPAGATE();
12     $N = \vec{G}$.SIZE();
13   if $\exists 0 \leq i < N \cdot G_i = G_{i+1}$ then
14   return G_i;

4 Applying the Extension Rule

In this section we describe how we apply the *extension rule* in PDRER.

The goal of using ER in PDRER is to enable it to construct shorter bounded proofs of correctness, and by that, construct a smaller inductive invariant. When applying the extension rule, PDRER introduces auxiliary variables along with their definitions, and by that re-encodes the trace it maintains. We draw intuition from SAT-solvers that take advantage of ER [1,20,25].

Our algorithm is based on *template-matching*. It uses a pre-defined set of templates and tries to match clauses in the trace against these templates. When a template is matched, a new auxiliary variable is added along with its definition, and the clauses that match the template are replaced with new clauses, which contain the auxiliary variable. Next we give formal definitions for a template and a matched set of clauses.

Let $\mathcal{V}$ be a set of template variables (disjoint from variables of the transition system T). A template is defined as $\tau \subseteq \mathcal{P}(Lits(\mathcal{V}))$. Let C be a set of clauses, the literals appearing in all clauses in C are denoted as $L(C) = \cup C$.

Definition 1 (Match). *Let C be a set of clauses and $\tau \subseteq \mathcal{P}(Lits(\mathcal{V}))$ a template. We say that C matches τ iff there exists an injective substitution $\sigma : \mathcal{V} \to L(C)$ and a bijective function $m : \tau \to C$ such that:*

1. *Match rule:* $\forall M \in \tau, \exists c \in C \cdot (m(M) = c) \land (M[\sigma] \subseteq c)$[1]
2. *Exclusivity rule:* $\forall M_1, M_2 \in \tau, \forall c_1, c_2 \in C \cdot (m(M_1) = c_1 \land m(M_2) = c_2) \to ((c_1 \setminus M_1[\sigma]) = (c_2 \setminus M_2[\sigma]))$

For simplicity of presentation, let us define the set of template variables as $\mathcal{V} = \{\alpha, \beta, \gamma, \delta\}$. We use the following three templates when applying the extension rule: (1) AND-template: $\tau_\land = \{\{\alpha\}, \{\beta\}\}$; (2) XOR-template: $\tau_\oplus = \{\{\alpha, \beta\}, \{\neg\alpha, \neg\beta\}\}$; (3) HALFADDER-template: $\tau_{ha} = \{\{\alpha, \beta, \gamma\}, \{\alpha, \beta, \delta\}, \{\neg\alpha, \neg\beta, \gamma, \delta\}\}$.

Definition 2 (Instantiation). *Given a set of clauses C, assume C matches τ_* where $* \in \{\land, \oplus, ha\}$. The instantiation of τ_* is:*

1. $\sigma[\tau_\land] = \{\{\sigma(\alpha)\}, \{\sigma(\beta)\}\}$ *when* $\tau_* = \tau_\land$.
2. $\sigma[\tau_\oplus] = \{\{\sigma(\alpha), \sigma(\beta)\}, \{\neg\sigma(\alpha), \neg\sigma(\beta)\}\}$ *when* $\tau_* = \tau_\oplus$.
3. $\sigma[\tau_{ha}] = \{\{\sigma(\alpha), \sigma(\beta), \sigma(\gamma)\}, \{\sigma(\alpha), \sigma(\beta), \sigma(\delta)\}, \{\neg\sigma(\alpha), \neg\sigma(\beta), \sigma(\gamma), \sigma(\delta)\}\}$ *when* $\tau_* = \tau_{ha}$.

The AND-template and XOR-template require two clauses for a match. The clauses should be of the following form: $\{(\alpha \lor A), (\beta \lor A)\}$ for $\tau_\land$ (two clauses that are similar except for one literal) and $\{(\alpha \lor \beta \lor A), (\neg\alpha \lor \neg\beta \lor A)\}$ for $\tau_\oplus$. When a set of clauses is matched with either $\tau_\land$ or $\tau_\oplus$, a new auxiliary variable x can be added such that $x \leftrightarrow \sigma(\alpha) \land \sigma(\beta)$ or $x \leftrightarrow \sigma(\alpha) \oplus \sigma(\beta)$, respectively. Note that σ is the substitution function for the match (see Definition 1). The matched clauses are then replaced with the clause $(x \lor A)$.

---

[1] $M[\sigma] = \{\sigma(l) | l \in M, l = var(l)\} \cup \{\neg\sigma(var(l)) | l \in M, l = \neg var(l)\}$.

$$
\begin{array}{lll}
(a \vee l_1 \vee l_2) & (\neg a \vee b \vee l_1 \vee l_2) & \\
(b \vee l_1 \vee l_2) & (a \vee \neg b \vee l_1 \vee l_2) & (a \vee b \vee c \vee l_1 \vee l_2) \\
(a \vee l_3) & (a \vee \neg b \vee l_3) & (a \vee b \vee d \vee l_1 \vee l_2) \\
(b \vee l_3) & (\neg a \vee b \vee l_3) & (\neg a \vee \neg b \vee c \vee d \vee l_1 \vee l_2) \\
(a \vee l_4 \vee l_5 \vee l_6) & (a \vee b \vee l_4 \vee l_5 \vee l_6) & \downarrow \\
(b \vee l_4 \vee l_5 \vee l_6) & (\neg a \vee \neg b \vee l_4 \vee l_5 \vee l_6) & (x \vee y \vee d \vee l_1 \vee l_2) \\
\downarrow & \downarrow & (x \vee z \vee c \vee l_1 \vee l_2) \\
(x \vee l_1 \vee l_2) & (\neg x \vee l_1 \vee l_2) & (x \leftrightarrow a \oplus b) \\
(x \vee l_3) & (\neg x \vee l_3) & (y \leftrightarrow a \wedge b) \\
(x \vee l_4 \vee l_5 \vee l_6) & (x \vee l_4 \vee l_5 \vee l_6) & (z \leftrightarrow y \wedge d) \\
(x \leftrightarrow a \wedge b) & (x \leftrightarrow a \oplus b) & \text{(c) } \tau_{ha} \\
\text{(a) } \tau_\wedge & \text{(b) } \tau_\oplus &
\end{array}
$$

Fig. 1. Clauses at the top match $\tau_\wedge$, $\tau_\oplus$ and τ_{ha} from left to right, respectively. Applying the extension rule transform them into the clauses at the bottom. The instantiations are $\{\{a\}, \{b\}\}$ for $\tau_\wedge$, $\{\{a,b\}, \{\neg a, \neg b\}\}$ for $\tau_\oplus$ and $\{\{a,b,c\}, \{a,b,d\}, \{\neg a, \neg b, c, d\}\}$ for τ_{ha}.

The third template, τ_{ha}, is more complex. Unlike $\tau_\wedge$ and $\tau_\oplus$, this template requires three clauses of the following form: $\{(\alpha \vee \beta \vee \gamma \vee A), (\alpha \vee \beta \vee \delta \vee A), (\neg \alpha \vee \neg \beta \vee \gamma \vee \delta \vee A)\}$. When a set of clauses is matched with τ_{ha}, three new auxiliary variables x, y, z can be added such that $x \leftrightarrow \sigma(\alpha) \oplus \sigma(\beta)$, $y \leftrightarrow \sigma(\alpha) \wedge \sigma(\beta)$, and $z \leftrightarrow y \wedge \sigma(\delta)$. The matched clauses are then replaced with the clauses $(x \vee y \vee \delta \vee A), (x \vee z \vee \gamma \vee A)$. Figure 1 presents examples of sets of clauses that match $\tau_\wedge$, $\tau_\oplus$ and τ_{ha}, respectively.

4.1 Matching Templates on an Inductive Trace

In this section we describe the algorithm that analyzes the inductive trace PDR maintains in order to match templates and apply the extension rule.

Using ER as part of PDR is different from using ER in SAT for the following reasons: (i) there are multiple formulas in CNF that need to be considered (a trace $\vec{F}$ contains multiple formulas); (ii) the CNF formulas change throughout the run of the algorithm; and (iii) the operations performed by PDR during its execution must be taken into account.

Multiple CNFs: When an auxiliary variable is added to $\vec{F}$, a set of clauses is re-encoded and replaced with other clauses. As an example, consider two clauses $c_1 = (a \vee b \vee l_1)$ and $c_2 = (\neg a \vee \neg b \vee l_1)$ that match $\tau_\oplus$. A new auxiliary variable $x \leftrightarrow a \oplus b$ is added, and a new clause $c = (x \vee l_1)$ replaces c_1 and c_2. Note that c represents *a set of clauses*, namely it replaces the conjunction $c_1 \wedge c_2$. Now, let us assume that $c_1, c_2 \in F_i$ while $c_2 \notin F_{i+1}$. This could be due to PDR propagating c_1 from level i to $i + 1$, while failing to propagate c_2 from level i to $i + 1$. If we consider $\vec{F}$ as the union of all clauses that appear in it and perform matching on this union, then x and c are used to re-encode $\vec{F}$ as a whole. In this case c_1 and c_2 are removed from $\vec{F}$, and therefore c_1 must be removed from F_{i+1}. Such an operation causes information loss. In order to avoid such a scenario, when ER is applied to $\vec{F}$, each frame is considered independently. Since $\vec{F}$ is monotone, the algorithm analyzes only the difference between the frames, namely the delta-trace.

Evolving CNF: Since the inductive trace $\vec{F}$ changes during the execution of PDR, the addition of auxiliary variables must not be aggressive. Consider the case where an auxiliary variable x is added and $\vec{F}$ is re-encoded, resulting in $\vec{F}^x$. Later, PDR continues and adds the set of clauses C to $\vec{F}^x$. Some templates may not match on $\vec{F}^x \cup C$, while they can be matched if the matching algorithm is applied on $\vec{F} \cup C$. This is due to the fact that template matching is *syntactic*. Hence, we apply re-encoding periodically based on a heuristic that inspects the number of clauses in $\vec{F}$ (see Sect. 5).

Matching Algorithm: Matching the given templates can be done in polynomial time. A naïve implementation tries all combinations of two ($\tau_\wedge$ and $\tau_\oplus$) or three (τ_{ha}) clauses, resulting in $O(n^2)$ or $O(n^3)$ complexity, respectively. However, such an implementation is time consuming, and in practice, not efficient.

In order to efficiently implement the template matching algorithm, we partition the clauses in a CNF into buckets, where each bucket contains clauses of a similar size (i.e. with the same number of literals). This is based on the following observation. In order for two clauses c_1 and c_2 to match $\tau_\wedge$ and $\tau_\oplus$, they must be of the same size ($|c_1| = |c_2|$). In addition, for three clauses c_1, c_2 and c_3 to match τ_{ha}, it must hold that $|c_1| = |c_2| = |c_3| - 1$. The template matching algorithm uses these conditions. It searches in a given bucket when trying to match $\tau_\wedge$ and $\tau_\oplus$, and searches in two consecutive buckets when trying to match τ_{ha}.

Algorithm 3: REENCODE

```
Input:  D⃗, a delta-trace
Output: a delta-trace
1  for D_i ∈ D⃗ do
2      M = M ∪ MATCHT(D_i);
   /* Cluster matches by their
      instantiations          */
3  clusters = HASHMAP();
4  for m ∈ M do
5      key = m.INSTANTIATION();
6      clusters[key] = clusters[key] ∪ m;
   /* Choose best template to use
                               */
7  key = choose(clusters);
8  if key == None then
9      return D⃗;
   /* Perform the re-encoding  */
10 for m ∈ clusters[key] do
11     D_i = m.GETCNF();
12     D_i = D_i \ m.GETMATCHEDCLAUSES();
13     D_i = D_i ∪ m.APPLYEXTENSION();
14 return D⃗;
```

Algorithm 4: IMPLICATIONER

```
Input:  c_1(v⃗, ā), c_2(v⃗, ā): clauses
Output: Boolean true/false
Ensures    : Returns true iff c_1 → c_2
1  if c_1 ⊆ c_2 then
2      return true;
3  if (c_1 ∪ c_2) ∩ Lits(ā) == ∅ then
4      return false;
5  if ∃l ∈ c_1 · coi(l) ∩ coi(c_2) = ∅ then
6      return false;
7  bdd_1 = cachedBuildBDD(c_1);
8  bdd_2 = cachedBuildBDD(c_2);
9  return (bdd_1 → bdd_2) = ⊤;
```

The overall procedure for adding auxiliary variables and re-encoding $\vec{F}$ appears in Algorithm 3. The algorithm starts by iterating over all elements of the delta-trace $\vec{D}$, and applying the matching algorithm (line 2). Once all templates are identified across the different frames, the algorithm tries to detect templates that correspond to multiple frames. By that, an added auxiliary variable can be used in multiple frames and as a result, a better reduction in the number of overall clauses is achieved. The algorithm clusters all matches using their template instantiation (lines 3–6). Once all matches are clustered, the algorithm chooses a match according to a pre-defined heuristic (line 7). For example, throughout our experiments we noticed the $\tau_\oplus$ is usually preferable over other templates, even when other templates may result in a more significant reduction in the number of clauses in $\vec{D}$. Lastly, the algorithm iterates over all matches for the selected instantiation and performs the re-encoding of $\vec{D}$. More precisely, it adds a new auxiliary variable along with its definition, and replaces the corresponding clauses according to the type of template (lines 10–13).

Note that while the presented algorithm only uses one instantiation, in practice we can choose a number of instantiations and thus introduce many new auxiliary variables at each invocation of REENCODE.

5 PdrER

In this section we describe a new model checking algorithm, PDRER, which is based on PDR. PDRER uses ER to re-encode the trace and includes other algorithmic modifications that take into account the added auxiliary variables. We emphasize that simply using ER to re-encode the trace does not use the full power of ER. Moreover, once the auxiliary variables are added, many of the nice features of PDR break. For example, syntactic subsumption is no longer effective, this results in redundant clauses that slow down PDR. Before describing the details of PDRER we generalize the notion of an invariant and an inductive trace to take into account the addition of auxiliary variables.

Definition 3 (Auxiliary Circuit). *Let $T = (\bar{v}, Init, Tr, Bad)$ be a transition system and let $\bar{a} = \{a_1, \ldots, a_m\}$ be a set of auxiliary variables. The auxiliary circuit for $\bar{a}$ is the formula $E(\bar{v}, \bar{a}) = \bigwedge_{i=1}^{m} (a_i \leftrightarrow l_{i_1} \star_i l_{i_2})$ such that*

$$\forall 1 \leq i \leq m \cdot (\star_i \in \{\wedge, \oplus\}) \wedge (l_{i_1}, l_{i_2} \in Lits(\bar{v} \cup \{a_j | a_j \in \bar{a} \wedge j < i\}))$$

We define the cone-of-influence (COI) of a literal $l \in Lits(\bar{v} \cup \bar{a})$ as

$$coi(l) = \begin{cases} var(l) & var(l) \in \bar{v} \\ coi(l_1) \cup coi(l_2) & var(l) \in \bar{a} \wedge var(l) \leftrightarrow l_1 \star l_2 \end{cases} \quad (3)$$

Intuitively, the COI includes all the variables in $\bar{v} \cup \bar{a}$ that are used to define l in $E(\bar{v}, \bar{a})$.

From this point on, let us fix a transition system $T = (\bar{v}, Init, Tr, Bad)$, a set of auxiliary variables $\bar{a} = \{a_1, \ldots, a_m\}$ and its auxiliary circuit $E(\bar{v}, \bar{a})$.

When using ER and auxiliary variables, a safe inductive invariant is no longer expressed only in terms of $\bar{v}$, but also includes the added auxiliary variables. We therefore generalize the definition of a safe inductive invariant:

Definition 4 (Generalized Invariant). *A generalized safe inductive invariant is a formula $Inv(\bar{v}, \bar{a})$ (over $\bar{v} \cup \bar{a}$) that satisfies:*

$$Init(\bar{v}) \wedge E(\bar{v}, \bar{a}) \to Inv(\bar{v}, \bar{a}) \quad (4)$$

$$Inv(\bar{v}, \bar{a}) \wedge E(\bar{v}, \bar{a}) \wedge Tr(\bar{v}, \bar{v}') \wedge E(\bar{v}', \bar{a}') \to Inv(\bar{v}', \bar{a}') \quad (5)$$

$$Inv(\bar{v}, \bar{a}) \wedge E(\bar{v}, \bar{a}) \to \neg Bad(\bar{v}) \quad (6)$$

Lemma 2. *Given a formula $\varphi(\bar{v}, \bar{a})$ over $\bar{v} \cup \bar{a}$ and assume $a_n \leftrightarrow l_1 \star l_2$ where $\star \in \{\wedge, \oplus\}$. Let $\bar{a}^* = \bar{a} \setminus \{a_n\}$ and $E^*(\bar{v}, \bar{a}^*)$ be its auxiliary circuit such that $E(\bar{v}, \bar{a}) = E^*(\bar{v}, \bar{a}^*) \wedge (a_n \leftrightarrow l_1 \star l_2)$. Let us define $\psi(\bar{v}, \bar{a}^*) := \varphi[a_n \leftarrow l_1 \star l_2]$, namely, every occurrence of a_n in φ is substituted by its definition $l_1 \star l_2$. Given an assignment $z^* : \bar{v} \cup \bar{a}^* \to \{0, 1\}$ over $\bar{v} \cup \bar{a}^*$ and an assignment $z : \bar{v} \cup \bar{a} \to \{0, 1\}$ over $\bar{v} \cup \bar{a}$, which satisfy the following conditions: $z(x) = z^*(x)$ for $x \in \bar{v} \cup \bar{a}^*$ and $z(a_n) = z^*(l_1) \star z^*(l_2)$. Then, $z \models \varphi \wedge E(\bar{v}, \bar{a})$ if and only if $z^* \models \psi \wedge E^*(\bar{v}, \bar{a}^*)$.*

Proof. The proof is immediate from the structure of the formulas. $z \models \varphi(\bar{v} \cup \bar{a}) \wedge E(\bar{v} \cup \bar{a})$ iff $z \models \varphi(\bar{v} \cup \bar{a}) \wedge E^*(\bar{v} \cup \bar{a}^*) \wedge a_n \leftrightarrow l_1 \star l_2$, iff $z \models \varphi(\bar{v} \cup \bar{a})$ and $z \models E^*(\bar{v} \cup \bar{a}^*)$ and $z \models a_n \leftrightarrow l_1 \star l_2$. Note that since z and z^* agree on $\bar{v} \cup \bar{a}^*$, and by the fact E^* is only over $\bar{v} \cup \bar{a}^*$, we get that $z \models E^*(\bar{v} \cup \bar{a}^*)$ iff $z^* \models E^*(\bar{v} \cup \bar{a}^*)$. Hence we only consider $z \models \varphi \wedge a_n \leftrightarrow l_1 \star l_2$.

We prove that $z \models \varphi(\bar{v} \cup \bar{a}) \wedge a_n \leftrightarrow l_1 \star l_2$ iff $z^* \models \psi(\bar{v} \cup \bar{a}^*)$ by induction on the structure of φ. For the base case, φ is simply a variable. If that variable is in $\bar{v} \cup \bar{a}^*$, we immediately conclude $z^* \models \psi$ since $\psi = \varphi$ and z agrees with z^* on $\bar{v} \cup \bar{a}^*$. If the variable is a_n then $\psi = l_1 \star l_2$, and by definition and the fact $z \models a_n \leftrightarrow l_1 \star l_2$ we get that $z^* \models \psi$. For the induction step, assume $\varphi = \varphi_1 \wedge \varphi_2$. By the induction hypothesis $z \models \varphi_i$ iff $z^* \models \varphi_i[a_n \leftarrow l_1 \star l_2]$, for $i \in \{1, 2\}$. Hence, it immediately follows that $z^* \models \varphi_1[a_n \leftarrow l_1 \star l_2] \wedge \varphi_2[a_n \leftarrow l_1 \star l_2]$, i.e. $z^* \models \psi$. A similar proof is applicable for other connectives, such as $\neg, \vee, \oplus$ etc. □

Lemma 3 (Auxiliary Variable Elimination). *If $Inv_1(\bar{v}, \bar{a})$ is a generalized safe inductive invariant w.r.t. T, where $\bar{a} = \{a_1, \ldots, a_n\}$ for $n \geq 1$, then there exists a generalized safe inductive invariant $Inv_2(\bar{v}, \bar{a}^*)$ where $\bar{a}^* = \bar{a} \setminus \{a_n\}$.*

Proof (Sketch). Assume $a_n \leftrightarrow l_1 \star l_2$ where $\star \in \{\wedge, \oplus\}$. Let $E^*(\bar{v}, \bar{a}^*)$ be the auxiliary circuit for $\bar{a}^*$, and let $E(\bar{v}, \bar{a}) = E^*(\bar{v}, \bar{a}^*) \wedge (a_n \leftrightarrow l_1 \star l_2)$ be the auxiliary circuit for $\bar{a}$. Let us define $Inv_2(\bar{v}, \bar{a}^*) = Inv_1(\bar{v}, \bar{a})[a_n \leftarrow l_1 \star l_2]$. We need to show that Inv_2 is a generalized safe inductive invariant, namely that Eqs. 4–6 hold for Inv_2. This can be shown using Lemma 2. □

Lemma 4. *If $Inv_g(\bar{v}, \bar{a})$ is a generalized safe inductive invariant w.r.t. T, then there exists a safe inductive invariant $Inv(\bar{v})$ w.r.t. T.*

Proof. By induction on the size of $\bar{a}$. If $|\bar{a}| = 0$ then $\bar{a} = \emptyset$ and $Inv_g(\bar{v}, \bar{a})$ is a formula over $\bar{v}$. Therefore, $Inv(\bar{v}) = Inv_g(\bar{v}, \bar{a})$ is a safe inductive invariant.

For the induction step, assume that for a generalized inductive invariant $Inv_g^*(\bar{v}, \bar{a}^*)$, where $|\bar{a}^*| = n$, there exists a safe inductive invariant $Inv^{\bar{a}^*}(\bar{v})$. Next, assume $Inv_g(\bar{v}, \bar{a})$ is a generalized safe inductive invariant where $\bar{a} =$

$\{a_1, \ldots, a_{n+1}\}$. Clearly, $|\bar{a}| = n+1$. Note that $a_{n+1} \in \bar{a}$ is the last auxiliary variable in $\bar{a}$ (recall that $\bar{a}$ is ordered). Let $\bar{a}^* = \bar{a} \setminus \{a_{n+1}\}$, by Lemma 3 there exists a generalized safe inductive invariant $Inv_g^*(\bar{v}, \bar{a}^*)$. By the induction hypothesis, there exists a safe inductive invariant $Inv^{\bar{a}^*}(\bar{v})$. □

Since PDRER maintains an inductive trace like PDR, we also generalize the definition of an inductive trace:

Definition 5 (Generalized Inductive Trace). *A generalized inductive trace* $\vec{G} = [G_0, \ldots, G_N]$ *satisfies the following properties:*

$$Init(\bar{v}) \wedge E(\bar{v}, \bar{a}) \rightarrow G_0(\bar{v}, \bar{a}) \quad (7)$$

$$\forall 0 \leq i < N \cdot G_i(\bar{v}, \bar{a}) \wedge E(\bar{v}, \bar{a}) \wedge Tr(\bar{v}, \bar{v}') \wedge E(\bar{v}', \bar{a}') \rightarrow G_{i+1}(\bar{v}', \bar{a}') \quad (8)$$

Theorem 2. *T is SAFE iff it admits a safe closed generalized trace.*

Proof. Assume T is SAFE. By Theorem 1 T admits a safe closed trace F. F is a generalized trace where $\bar{a} = \emptyset$ and $E(\bar{v}, \bar{a}) = \top$. Hence, this direction is trivial.

Assume T admits a safe closed generalized trace G of size N. Since G is closed, there exists $1 \leq j < N$ such that $G_j = G_{j+1}$, and G_j is a generalized safe inductive invariant. By Lemma 4 there exists a safe inductive invariant for T, and hence T is SAFE. □

Note that relative induction and implication checks are adjusted accordingly. For example, checking if a clause $c \in G_i$ can be propagated to G_{i+1} is done by checking if the following formula is valid

$$G_i(\bar{v}, \bar{a}) \wedge E(\bar{v}, \bar{a}) \wedge Tr(\bar{v}, \bar{v}') \wedge E(\bar{v}', \bar{a}') \rightarrow c(\bar{v}', \bar{a}')$$

PDRER maintains a generalized trace $\vec{G}$. Its main loop is similar to the main loop of PDR and appears in Algorithm 2. The only difference in the main loop is that $\vec{G}$ is periodically re-encoded by applying the extension rule and adding auxiliary variables (as described in Sect. 4). The frequency of re-encoding is based on a heuristic captured by the parameter Δ (lines 7–9). As we mentioned above, this change alone can reduce the number of clauses in $\vec{G}$ but this reduction does not necessarily translate to better performance overall. Next, we describe the algorithmic modifications that separate PDRER from PDR.

There are three main differences between PDRER and PDR due to the fact that $\vec{G}$ is over $\bar{v} \cup \bar{a}$: (i) clause redundancy checks cannot be syntactic; (ii) auxiliary variables are explicitly used for generalization; and (iii) clauses that include auxiliary variables and fail to propagate must be handled differently.

5.1 Redundant Clauses

In PDR, when a new clause c is added to F_i, a subsumption check is performed. Every clause $d \in D_j$, for $0 < j \leq i$, subsumed by c is removed. Since in PDR $\vec{F}$ is only over state variables, this subsumption check is performed by checking if

$c \subseteq d$ holds. However, for a generalized trace like the one maintained by PDRER, this simple check does not suffice. For example, consider the clauses $c_1 = y \vee l_1$ and $c_2 = a \vee l_1 \vee l_2$, where y is an auxiliary variable defined as $y \leftrightarrow a \wedge b$. Clearly, $c_1 \rightarrow c_2$, but a simple syntactic subsumption check fails to identify this fact. Hence, a semantic implication check must be performed. In order to perform efficient implication checks we use Binary Decision Diagrams (BDDs) [8].

Algorithm 4 presents how PDRER checks for implication between two clauses. It starts by performing the standard (syntactic) subsumption check (line 1). Then, it checks if the two clauses contain auxiliary variables (line 3). If they do not contain auxiliary variables and the initial subsumption check failed, it returns false. If the clauses contain auxiliary variables, the algorithm checks if there exists a literal $l \in c_1$ such that its COI does not intersect the COI of c_2 (lines 5–6). Note that if there exists such a literal $l \in c_1$, an assignment that satisfies c_1 but not c_2 can be constructed. Hence implication does not hold and the algorithm returns false. Lastly, if all syntactic checks fail, BDDs are used for the implication check. If the BDD representing $c_1 \rightarrow c_2$ is evaluated to $\top$, the algorithm returns true; otherwise, it returns false. Note that a clause over $\bar{v} \cup \bar{a}$ corresponds to a Boolean function over $\bar{v}$. Hence, BDD construction for such a clause may be computationally expensive. Since implication checks are performed frequently, IMPLICATIONER caches BDDs to avoid reconstructing the same BDD multiple times.

We emphasize that the use of BDDs in this case is crucial. As it turns out, trying to use a SAT-solver for these checks results in decreased performance.

Algorithm 5: GENERALIZEER

Input: $\varphi(\bar{v})$: cube, i: int
Output: $c(\bar{v}, \bar{a})$: clause
Requires: $G_{i-1}(\bar{v}, \bar{a}) \wedge E(\bar{v}, \bar{a}) \wedge Tr(\bar{v}, \bar{v}') \wedge E(\bar{v}', \bar{a}') \rightarrow \neg \varphi'$
Ensures: $G_{i-1}(\bar{v}, \bar{a}) \wedge E(\bar{v}, \bar{a}) \wedge c \wedge Tr(\bar{v}, \bar{v}') \wedge E(\bar{v}', \bar{a}') \rightarrow c'$

1 $c(\bar{v}) = \text{INDGEN}(i, \neg \varphi)$;
2 **for** $a \in \bar{a}$ where $a \leftrightarrow l_1 \star l_2$ **do**
3 $\quad d = None$;
4 $\quad$ **if** $(\star = \wedge)$ **then**
5 $\quad \quad$ **if** $(l_1 \in c) \wedge (l_2 \notin c)$ **then**
   $\quad \quad \quad d = (c \setminus \{l_1\}) \cup \{a\}$ **else if**
   $\quad \quad (l_1 \notin c) \wedge (l_2 \in c)$ **then**
   $\quad \quad \quad d = (c \setminus \{l_2\}) \cup \{a\}$
6 $\quad$ **if** $(\star = \oplus)$ **then**
7 $\quad \quad$ **if** $(l_1 \in c) \wedge (\neg l_2 \in c)$ **then**
8 $\quad \quad \quad d = (c \setminus \{l_1, \neg l_2\}) \cup \{\neg a\}$
9 $\quad \quad$ **else if** $(\neg l_1 \in c) \wedge (l_2 \in c))$ **then**
10 $\quad \quad \quad d = (c \setminus \{\neg l_1, l_2\}) \cup \{\neg a\}$
11 $\quad \quad$ **else if** $(l_1 \in c) \wedge (l_2 \in c))$ **then**
12 $\quad \quad \quad d = (c \setminus \{l_1, l_2\}) \cup \{a\}$
13 $\quad \quad$ **else if** $(\neg l_1 \in c) \wedge (\neg l_2 \in c))$ **then**
14 $\quad \quad \quad d = (c \setminus \{\neg l_1, \neg l_2\}) \cup \{a\}$
15 $\quad$ **if** $d = None$ **then continue**
   /* Is d inductive relative to G_{i-1}? */
16 $\quad$ **if** $Init(\bar{v}) \wedge E(\bar{v}, \bar{a}) \rightarrow d(\bar{v}, \bar{a})$ **then**
17 $\quad \quad$ **if** $(G_{i-1}(\bar{v}, \bar{a}) \wedge E(\bar{v}, \bar{a}) \wedge d(\bar{v}, \bar{a})) \wedge Tr(\bar{v}, \bar{v}') \wedge E(\bar{v}', \bar{a}') \rightarrow d(\bar{v}', \bar{a}')$ **then**
18 $\quad \quad \quad c = d$;
19 **return** c;

Algorithm 6: PROPAGATEER

Input: c : a clause to propagate, i: int
Requires: $c \in G_i$ and $\vec{G}^* = \vec{G}$ where $\vec{G}^*$ holds the initial state of $\vec{G}$ for the post-condition
Ensures: $\vec{G}$ is a generalized trace s.t. $\forall j \leq |\vec{G}| \cdot G_j \rightarrow G_j^*$

1 $\mathcal{A} = \emptyset$;
2 **while** $True$ **do**
3 $\quad$ **if**
   $\quad \quad G_i(\bar{v}, \bar{a}) \wedge E(\bar{v}, \bar{a}) \wedge Tr(\bar{v}, \bar{v}') \wedge E(\bar{v}', \bar{a}') \rightarrow c(\bar{v}', \bar{a}')$ **then**
4 $\quad \quad \vec{G}.\text{INSERT}(i+1, c)$;
5 $\quad \quad$ **break**;
6 $\quad$ **else**
   $\quad \quad$ /* extract assignment from SAT-solver */
7 $\quad \quad \varphi(\bar{v}', \bar{a}') = \text{GETASSIGNMENT}()$;
8 $\quad \quad \mathcal{A} = \mathcal{A} \cup \{\varphi\}$
9 $\quad \quad found = false$;
10 $\quad \quad$ **for** $a \in c$ where $var(a) \in \bar{a}$ **do**
11 $\quad \quad \quad C = c.\text{EXPAND}(a)$;
12 $\quad \quad \quad$ choose $d \in C$ such that $(\vee \mathcal{A}) \not\models \neg d'$;
13 $\quad \quad \quad$ **if** $d \neq Null$ **then**
14 $\quad \quad \quad \quad c = d$;
15 $\quad \quad \quad \quad found = true$;
16 $\quad \quad \quad \quad$ **break**;
17 $\quad \quad$ **if** $found = false$ **then break**

5.2 Generalization with Auxiliary Variables

Auxiliary variables are introduced when $\vec{G}$ is re-encoded. Assume that $\bar{a}$ is a set of auxiliary variables added by re-encoding $\vec{G}$. Since an inductive invariant can now be expressed in terms of $\bar{v} \cup \bar{a}$, it is important to allow PDRER to generate clauses over $\bar{v} \cup \bar{a}$. In PDR, new clauses are added to the trace by a generalization procedure. Next, we present GENERALIZEER, which is the generalization procedure used by PDRER that allows it to generate clauses over $\bar{v} \cup \bar{a}$.

Recall that PDR iteratively tries to prove that a given state[2] is unreachable in i steps, for some i. Such a state is referred to as a *proof obligation* at level i and it is represented by a cube and the level as $(\varphi(\bar{v}), i)$. PDR invokes generalization when it identifies that a proof obligation is unreachable. The generalization procedure starts from $\neg\varphi(\bar{v})$ as a candidate to be added to the trace at level i. Then, it tries to find a new clause $c(\bar{v}) \subseteq \neg\varphi(\bar{v})$ by dropping literals from $\neg\varphi$ such that c is inductive relative to frame $i-1$ in the trace. This process is usually referred to as *inductive generalization* [5,6]. The resulting clause c is then added to the trace at level i.

PDRER does not change the procedure that generates proof obligations. Hence, GENERALIZEER also starts from a proof obligation $(\varphi(\bar{v}), i)$ that is known to be unreachable. As a first step, GENERALIZEER also uses inductive generalization. Assume that $c(\bar{v}) \subseteq \neg\varphi(\bar{v})$ is the result of inductive generalization. GENERALIZEER tries to generalize c further, by replacing literals that appear in c with literals over auxiliary variables. Recall that a clause that includes auxiliary variables represents a *set of clauses*. Hence, such an operation is a *generalization* as it produces a *stronger* clause.

Example 1. Assume $c = (l_1 \vee l_2 \vee l_3)$ and there exists an auxiliary variable y such that $y \leftrightarrow l_3 \wedge l_4$. Now assume GENERALIZEER replaces l_3 with y resulting in $d = (l_1 \vee l_2 \vee y)$. Since $((y \leftrightarrow l_3 \wedge l_4) \wedge d) \rightarrow c$, in the context of PDRER, d is a generalization of c.

The generalization procedure GENERALIZEER, used by PDRER, is presented in Algorithm 5. The input to GENERALIZEER is an unreachable proof obligation $(\varphi(\bar{v}), i)$. First, inductive generalization is used in order to generate a clause $c \subseteq \neg\varphi$ (line 1). Then, in order to replace literals in c that are over $\bar{v}$ with literals over $\bar{a}$, GENERALIZEER iterates over $\bar{a}$ in order, starting from a_1. Recall that for $a_i, a_j \in \bar{a}$, if $j > i$ then a_i may appear in the COI of a_j but a_j cannot be in the COI of a_i (see Definition 3). For each auxiliary variable $a \leftrightarrow l_1 \star l_2$, GENERALIZEER performs the following. If $\star = \wedge$ then it checks if *only one* of the literals l_1 or l_2 are in c (lines 4–6). Assume, w.l.o.g., that $l_1 \in c$ and $l_2 \notin c$. Then, GENERALIZEER creates a clause d, which is similar to c but with l_1 substituted by a. If $\star = \oplus$ similar checks are performed (lines 7–15). For example, if $l_1 \in c$ and $l_2 \in c$, then l_1 and l_2 are substituted by a. In case such a substitution is performed, GENERALIZEER then checks if the resulting clause d is inductive relative to G_{i-1}. If it is, then c is updated to be d (lines 17–19), and the loop

---

[2] In practice, it can be a set of states.

continues with the next auxiliary variable. In case d is not inductive relative to G_{i-1}, generalization through the current auxiliary variable failed and c remains unchanged. Here too the loop continues with the next auxiliary variable.

Note that this process substitutes literals over $\bar{v} \cup \bar{a}$ with literals over $\bar{a}$ in a *bottom-up* fashion. A similar procedure can be performed *top-down*, however, our experiments show that the bottom-up procedure performs better in practice.

5.3 Fractional Propagation

One of the key procedures in PDR is *propagation*. During propagation PDR tries to "push" a clause to a higher level in the trace. Since PDRER uses a generalized trace $\vec{G}$, a clause in some frame G_i may include auxiliary variables. Let $c(\bar{v}, \bar{a})$ be such a clause. Since c is over $\bar{v} \cup \bar{a}$, it represents a *set of clauses* over $\bar{v}$. Hence, trying to propagate c is akin to propagating a set of clauses simultaneously. If one clause in that set cannot be propagated, c itself cannot be propagated. Intuitively, this reduces the likelihood of such a clause to be propagated.

Example 2. Consider the clause $c = (y \vee A)$ where $c \in G_i$ and y is an auxiliary variable such that $y \leftrightarrow l_1 \oplus l_2$. In this case c represents the clauses $c_1 = (l_1 \vee l_2 \vee A)$ and $c_2 = (\neg l_1 \vee \neg l_2 \vee A)$. Assume that

$$G_i(\bar{v}, \bar{a}) \wedge E(\bar{v}, \bar{a}) \wedge Tr(\bar{v}, \bar{v}') \wedge E(\bar{v}', \bar{a}') \not\rightarrow c(\bar{v}', \bar{a}') \tag{9}$$

$$G_i(\bar{v}, \bar{a}) \wedge E(\bar{v}, \bar{a}) \wedge Tr(\bar{v}, \bar{v}') \wedge E(\bar{v}', \bar{a}') \not\rightarrow c_1(\bar{v}', \bar{a}') \tag{10}$$

$$G_i(\bar{v}, \bar{a}) \wedge E(\bar{v}, \bar{a}) \wedge Tr(\bar{v}, \bar{v}') \wedge E(\bar{v}', \bar{a}') \rightarrow c_2(\bar{v}', \bar{a}') \tag{11}$$

The clause c cannot be propagated because c_1 cannot be propagated. However, c_2 can be propagated to G_{i+1}. If the propagation procedure does not treat auxiliary variables specifically, it can miss the fact c_2 can be propagated. As a result, PDRER is likely to relearn c_2 in higher levels during MKSAFE, which is less efficient than propagation.

PROPAGATEER is designed to specifically take into account auxiliary variables during propagation. Unlike the propagation procedure in PDR, if PROPAGATEER fails to propagate a clause $c(\bar{v}, \bar{a})$, it tries to identify a subset of the set of clauses c represents (a "fraction") that can be propagated. In order to understand the intuition behind PROPAGATEER, let us reconsider Example 2. From Eq. 9 we can conclude that $G_i(\bar{v}, \bar{a}) \wedge E(\bar{v}, \bar{a}) \wedge Tr(\bar{v}, \bar{v}') \wedge E(\bar{v}', \bar{a}') \wedge \neg c(\bar{v}', \bar{a}')$ is satisfiable. Let us denote by $\varphi(\bar{v}', \bar{a}')$ the cube such that $\varphi \models \neg c(\bar{v}', \bar{a}')$. Such a cube can be extracted from the satisfying assignment that shows why c cannot be propagated. Since $\varphi \models \neg c(\bar{v}', \bar{a}')$, it is easy to show that $\varphi \models (\neg c_1(\bar{v}', \bar{a}') \vee \neg c_2(\bar{v}', \bar{a}')) \wedge (y' \leftrightarrow l_1' \oplus l_2')$. By that, $\varphi \models \neg c_1(\bar{v}', \bar{a}') \wedge (y' \leftrightarrow l_1' \oplus l_2')$ or $\varphi \models \neg c_2(\bar{v}', \bar{a}') \wedge (y' \leftrightarrow l_1' \oplus l_2')$. PROPAGATEER uses such a cube (i.e. the assignment) to identify elements in the set of clauses c represents, that cannot be propagated. For this example, let us assume that $\varphi \models \neg c_1(\bar{v}', \bar{a}') \wedge (y' \leftrightarrow l_1' \oplus l_2')$ and $\varphi \not\models \neg c_2(\bar{v}', \bar{a}') \wedge (y' \leftrightarrow l_1' \oplus l_2')$. In this case, PROPAGATEER determines c_1 cannot be propagated and explicitly checks if c_2 can be propagated.

This exploration performed by PROPAGATEER depends on the number of auxiliary variables a clause depends on. At each propagation attempt that fails PROPAGATEER uses the satisfying assignment returned by the SAT-solver to choose an auxiliary variable to expand (i.e. replace it by its definition), and eliminate a subset of clauses that cannot be propagated. Note that it may be possible for an assignment to rule out the entire set of clauses.

The procedure PROPAGATEER, which implements fractional propagation, is described in Algorithm 6. PROPAGATEER receives as input a clause c and the level i. PDRER enters a loop where at each iteration it tries to push c to level $i+1$ (line 3). If it succeeds, then the clause is added to the corresponding frame and the procedure terminates. If it fails, it extracts the assignment from the SAT-solver and stores it in $\mathcal{A}$ (line 8). Then, it iterates over auxiliary literals in c. For such a literal a, PROPAGATEER retrieves the set of clauses c represents by expanding the definition of a (line 11). Next, it chooses a clause d in that set that is not ruled out by all previous assignments that were found during failed propagation attempts (line 11). If such a clause is found, c is updated to d and now represents a "fraction", and the algorithm starts a new iteration, trying to propagate the fraction. If no such clause is found for all auxiliary literals in c, the procedure terminates, without propagating any fraction of c.

We note that some implementation details are omitted for the simplicity of presentation. For example, if PROPAGATEER finds a fraction clause that can be propagated, it makes sure that this clause is not already implied at higher levels. It is also important to note that this procedure does not necessarily identify all fractions that can be propagated.

6 Experimental Evaluation

We implemented both PDR and PDRER in a new tool from the ground up[3] For SAT solving, we used CaDiCal 2.0, a state-of-the-art open-source SAT solver. For BDD operations, we used CUDD, a well-established open-source BDD library.

To isolate the impact of ER within PDR, we implemented PDRER as an extension of our PDR implementation, minimizing differences beyond the core algorithmic changes described in this paper. We used the PDR implementation in ABC [7], a widely used open-source hardware synthesis and verification tool, as a baseline. In the following, PDR and PDRER refer to the implementation in our tool, while ABC-PDR refers to ABC's PDR implementation.

6.1 HWMCC

We conducted a series of experiments comparing the performance of these three implementations on various Hardware Model Checking Competitions benchmarks (HWMCC); HWMCC'19/20/24, which include 317, 324 and 318

---
[3] https://github.com/TechnionFV/CAV_2025_artifact.

instances, respectively.[4] All experiments were executed on machines with AMD EPYC 74F3 CPU and 32GB of memory, under a timeout of 3600 s.

Figure 2 summarizes the results of our experiments, where in all three sets PDRER outperforms both PDR and ABC-PDR, particularly on SAFE instances. The difference is particularly apparent in HWMCC'24 where PDRER not only solves significantly more instances than PDR, but also achieves significantly more unique wins than the other solvers, and has a significantly lower average runtime.

Set	Solver	# Solved	#UNSAFE	#SAFE	# Unique	Avg. Time
HWMCC'19	ABC-PDR	212	27	185	2	1274.6
	PDR	233	**40**	193	1	1104.4
	PDRER	**236**	**40**	**196**	2	**1082.4**
	VB	239	43	196		1026.9
HWMCC'20	ABC-PDR	221	34	187	3	1274.4
	PDR	231	**43**	188	4	1144.0
	PDRER	**236**	41	**195**	6	**1095.4**
	VB	243	46	197		1038.4
HWMCC'24	ABC-PDR	157	27	130	3	1920.5
	PDR	175	33	142	0	1702.3
	PDRER	**188**	**36**	**152**	9	**1622.5**
	VB	191	36	155		1569.4

Fig. 2. HWMCC results, average runtime is in seconds

Runtime: Figure 3 compares PDRER and PDR on the entire benchmark set (VB stands for Virtual Best). Runtime comparison for PDRER and PDR appears in Fig. 3a. Instances where PDRER outperforms PDR appear below the parity diagonal, highlighting its advantage. The plot demonstrates that PDRER achieves substantial runtime improvements across numerous benchmarks while successfully solving a significant subset of problems that PDR fails to solve within the time limit. Some instances exhibit a faster runtime under PDR, which we associate with the computational overhead of identifying and using auxiliary variables, particularly those that ultimately prove ineffective for the proof. Overall, PDRER performs better than PDR as is evident in Fig. 3b. Note that PDRER solves 550 instances in 1500 s while PDR takes 2200 s to solve the same amount of instances. Moreover, we can see for the harder instances (runtime of over 500 s), PDRER has a clear advantage over PDR. Lastly, PDRER is very close to VB. This leads us to conclude that PDRER is overall better than PDR and in addition its performance does not degrade due to the use of ER.

Auxiliary Variables: In order to evaluate the effect ER has on the proofs generated by PDRER, we first evaluate the auxiliary variables PDRER uses. Note that for trivial instances (i.e., those that are solved quickly), PDRER never re-encodes the trace and therefore it does not use auxiliary variables. Figure 4

---

[4] HWMCC'24 officially includes 319 instances but one is malformed.

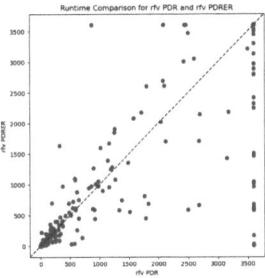
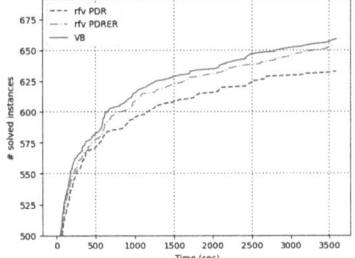

(a) Runtime comparison: PDR (X-axis) vs. PDRER (Y-axis).

(b) Y-axis represents number of solved instances. VB stands for Virtual Best.

Fig. 3. HWMCC'19/20/24

presents the instances that use auxiliary variables and the average number of auxiliary variables used in each instance. Considering SAFE instances, the table presents how many invariants use auxiliary variables and what is the average number of auxiliary variables used to express the invariants.

Set	#Instances	#Instances using AVs	Average AVs	%⊕	Invariants using AVs	Average AVs in Invariants	%⊕
HWMCC'19	317	199	59	85%	94	23	78%
HWMCC'20	324	207	56	85%	105	17	78%
HWMCC'24	318	185	76	74%	61	39	73%

Fig. 4. Auxiliary Variables (AVs) added and used by PDRER. %⊕ stand for percentage of AVs using ⊕ in their definition.

Proof Size: In order to evaluate our conjecture regarding the ability of PDRER to produce shorter proofs due to the use of ER, we analyzed and compared the proofs generated by both PDRER and PDR. Figure 5a and Fig. 5d compare the size of the invariants for HWMCC'24 and HWMCC'19/20, respectively. As can be seen from the table in Fig. 2, PDRER outperforms PDR considerably on HWMCC'24, while on HWMCC'19/20 the margin in favor of PDRER is smaller. A close analysis of the proofs generated by PDRER vs. those generated by PDR reveals that on HWMCC'24, the proofs generated by PDRER are *shorter*.

Figure 5b and Fig. 5e compare the number of clauses in the trace maintained by PDRER ($\vec{G}$) and PDR ($\vec{F}$) for HWMCC'24 and HWMCC'19/20, respectively. The plots show a clear advantage for PDRER, which generates shorter bounded proofs for the majority of instances. The advantage is more apparent on HWMCC'24, which can explain why PDRER is considerably better on that set. This is also in accordance with the data that appears in Fig. 4. To further establish the advantage of PDRER, Fig. 5c and Fig. 5f compare the number of proof obligations generated by PDRER and PDR. This metric demonstrates that PDRER explores the state-space more efficiently.

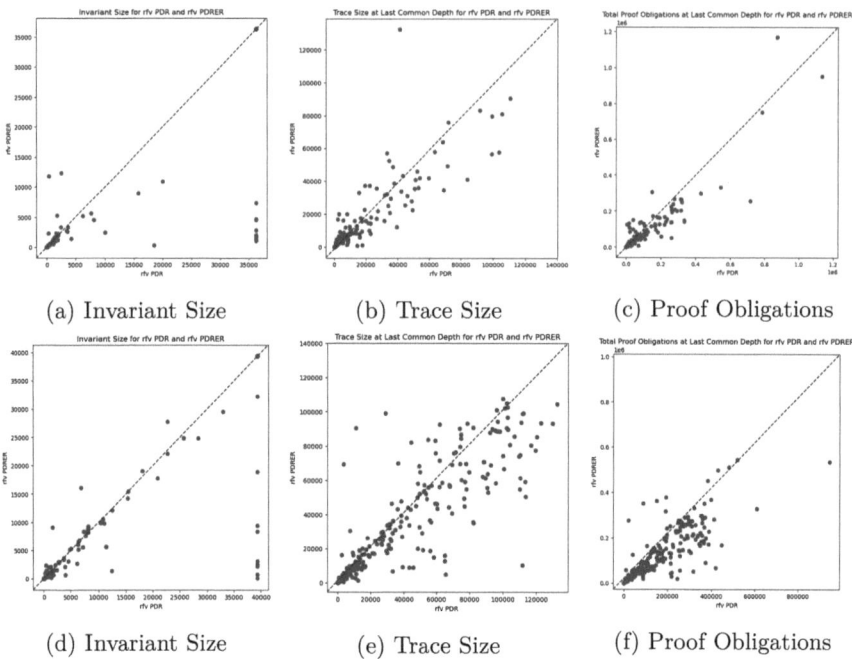

Fig. 5. Proof comparison: PDRER vs. PDR. X-axis is PDR across all plots. (5a)–(5c) HWMCC'24, (5d)–(5f) HWMCC'19/20.

6.2 The Effect of ImplicationER, GeneralizeER and PropagateER

In order to understand the importance of the adaptions made to the different parts of PDR, we analyze the impact these modifications have on performance.

Table 1 summarizes the contribution of each of these functions to PDRER on the entire benchamrk set (HWMCC'19/20/24). The letters "G", "F", and "I" stands for GENERALIZEER, PROPAGATEER and IMPLICATIONER, respectively. The second row in the table (PDRER without "G", "F", and "I") represents PDRER without any modifications to core PDR functions. This version of PDRER only uses ER to re-encode the trace, and uses the standard PDR generalization, propagation and subsumption checks. As can be seen from the table, it solves the least number of instances and has the highest runtime. Adding GENERALIZEER (PDRER-F-I) improves the number of solved instances and the runtime. Similarly, adding PROPAGATEER and IMPLICATIONER increases the number of solved instances. Interestingly, considering the entire benchmark, PDRER-F performs the best in terms of runtime. We believe that this is only due to the implementation and can be improved.

BDDs and IMPLICATIONER: As mentioned in Sect. 5, syntactic subsumption checks are insufficient when extension variables are used. On this benchmark set, syntactic checks in IMPLICATIONER are only sufficient in 40% of the cases (*true* is returned due to line 1). Other syntactic checks (lines 1–6) are successful in 94% of the times, and BDDs are only used in 6% of the calls to IMPLICATIONER.

Table 1. Performance with and without PDRER modifications.

Configuration	Number of Solved Instances	Average Runtime [s]
PDR	639	1316
PDRER-G-F-I	652	1297
PDRER-F-I	655	1264
PDRER-I	657	1273
PDRER-F	**660**	**1234**
PDRER	660	1283

6.3 Exponential Invariant in CNF

The closest work to ours is [17], where PDR is extended such that inductive invariants can be expressed in terms of $\bar{v}$ as well as logical connectives appearing in Tr (i.e., internal signals). Since the tool (IC3-INN) developed in [17] is not open-source and not available, we could not compare PDRER against it. However, we did evaluate PDRER on the examples described in Section III of [17]. The examples admit only an exponential invariant in CNF and are therefore challenging for PDR, but can be solved by IC3-INN. We confirm that PDRER can solve these examples by finding compact inductive invariants, as expected.

Furthermore, we identified instances where the inductive invariant cannot be expressed compactly by $\bar{v}$ and internal signals. For such examples, IC3-INN does not provide a benefit over PDR. Let us consider vis_arrays_bufferAlloc from HWMCC'19. It implements a buffer allocation protocol that works as follows. Assume that the buffer has k cells, a user can either request to allocate a cell on the buffer, or free a specific cell, not necessarily in order. Whenever a cell is allocated or de-allocated, a counter is being incremented or decremented by 1, respectively. In addition, a bit-array, called busy, tracks which cells are used and which are free. A simple safety property for such a protocol states that the counter is always in the range $[0, k]$. While this protocol is fairly simple, PDR struggles with it since the invariant requires $O(2^k)$ clauses. For example, for $k = 16$, PDR requires almost an hour to find the invariant, and the invariant contains more than 65,000 clauses. In contrast, PDRER solves this instance in 10 min, finding an invariant with around 5000 clauses. We emphasize that while we could not evaluate this example with IC3-INN, the invariant cannot be expressed in terms of internal signals, and hence we conjecture that IC3-INN should perform similarly to PDR.

7 Conclusion

We presented PDRER, the *first* model checking algorithm that efficiently uses Extended Resolution as its underlying proof-system. PDRER generalizes PDR and includes many algorithmic enhancements that enable an efficient integration of ER in model checking. Due to the use of ER, PDRER produces shorter proofs for the majority of instances from HWMCC'19/20/24. In addition, and most importantly, the use of ER in PDRER does not lead to performance degradation in the general case and outperforms PDR in most instances we evaluated. Moreover, it admits short proofs for problems for which PDR can only admit proofs of exponential size. We strongly believe that PDRER demonstrates that strong proof systems can be used efficiently in model checking.

References

1. Audemard, G., Katsirelos, G., Simon, L.: A restriction of extended resolution for clause learning SAT solvers. In: Fox, M., Poole, D. (eds.) Proceedings of the Twenty-Fourth AAAI Conference on Artificial Intelligence, AAAI 2010, Atlanta, Georgia, USA, 11–15 July 2010, pp. 15–20. AAAI Press (2010)
2. Bayless, S., Val, C.G., Ball, T., Hoos, H.H., Hu, A.J.: Efficient modular SAT solving for IC3. In: Formal Methods in Computer-Aided Design, FMCAD 2013, Portland, OR, USA, 20–23 October 2013, pp. 149–156. IEEE (2013)
3. Becker, B., Marché, C.: Ghost code in action: automated verification of a symbolic interpreter. In: Chakraborty, S., Navas, J.A. (eds.) VSTTE 2019. LNCS, vol. 12031, pp. 107–123. Springer, Cham (2020). https://doi.org/10.1007/978-3-030-41600-3_8
4. Biere, A., van Dijk, T., Heljanko, K.: Hardware model checking competition. In: Stewart, D., Weissenbacher, G. (eds.) 2017 Formal Methods in Computer Aided Design, FMCAD 2017, Vienna, Austria, 2–6 October 2017, p. 9. IEEE (2017)
5. Bradley, A.R.: SAT-based model checking without unrolling. In: Jhala, R., Schmidt, D. (eds.) VMCAI 2011. LNCS, vol. 6538, pp. 70–87. Springer, Heidelberg (2011). https://doi.org/10.1007/978-3-642-18275-4_7
6. Bradley, A.R., Manna, Z.: Checking safety by inductive generalization of counterexamples to induction. In: Formal Methods in Computer-Aided Design, 7th International Conference, FMCAD 2007, Austin, Texas, USA, 11–14 November 2007, Proceedings, pp. 173–180. IEEE Computer Society (2007)
7. Brayton, R., Mishchenko, A.: ABC: an academic industrial-strength verification tool. In: Touili, T., Cook, B., Jackson, P. (eds.) CAV 2010. LNCS, vol. 6174, pp. 24–40. Springer, Heidelberg (2010). https://doi.org/10.1007/978-3-642-14295-6_5
8. Bryant, R.E.: Binary decision diagrams. In: Handbook of Model Checking, pp. 191–217. Springer, Cham (2018). https://doi.org/10.1007/978-3-319-10575-8_7
9. Bryant, R.E., Heule, M.J.H.: Generating extended resolution proofs with a BDD-based SAT solver. ACM Trans. Comput. Log. **24**(4), 31:1–31:28 (2023)
10. Chang, B.-Y.E., Leino, K.: Abstract interpretation with alien expressions and heap structures. In: Cousot, R. (ed.) VMCAI 2005. LNCS, vol. 3385, pp. 147–163. Springer, Heidelberg (2005). https://doi.org/10.1007/978-3-540-30579-8_11
11. Chevalier, M., Feret, J.: Sharing ghost variables in a collection of abstract domains. In: Beyer, D., Zufferey, D. (eds.) VMCAI 2020. LNCS, vol. 11990, pp. 158–179. Springer, Cham (2020). https://doi.org/10.1007/978-3-030-39322-9_8
12. Clarke, E.M.: SAT-based counterexample guided abstraction refinement in model checking. In: Baader, F. (ed.) CADE 2003. LNCS (LNAI), vol. 2741, p. 1. Springer, Heidelberg (2003). https://doi.org/10.1007/978-3-540-45085-6_1
13. Clochard, M., Marché, C., Paskevich, A.: Deductive verification with ghost monitors. Proc. ACM Program. Lang. **4**(POPL), 2:1–2:26 (2020)
14. Cook, S.A.: A short proof of the pigeon hole principle using extended resolution. SIGACT News **8**(4), 28–32 (1976)

15. Davis, M., Logemann, G., Loveland, D.: A machine program for theorem-proving. Commun. ACM **5**(7), 394–397 (1962)
16. Davis, M., Putnam, H.: A computing procedure for quantification theory. J. ACM **7**(3), 201–215 (1960)
17. Dureja, R., Gurfinkel, A., Ivrii, A., Vizel, Y.: IC3 with internal signals. In: Formal Methods in Computer Aided Design, FMCAD 2021, New Haven, CT, USA, 19–22 October 2021, pp. 63–71. IEEE (2021)
18. Eén, N., Mishchenko, A., Brayton, R.K.: Efficient implementation of property directed reachability. In: Bjesse, P., Slobodová, A. (eds.) International Conference on Formal Methods in Computer-Aided Design, FMCAD 2011, Austin, TX, USA, 30 October–02 November 2011, pp. 125–134. FMCAD Inc. (2011)
19. Filliâtre, J.-C., Gondelman, L., Paskevich, A.: The spirit of ghost code. Formal Methods Syst. Des. **48**(3), 152–174 (2016). https://doi.org/10.1007/s10703-016-0243-x
20. Haberlandt, A., Green, H., Heule, M.J.H.: Effective auxiliary variables via structured reencoding. In: Mahajan, M., Slivovsky, F. (eds.) 26th International Conference on Theory and Applications of Satisfiability Testing, SAT 2023, 4–8 July 2023, Alghero, Italy. LIPIcs, vol. 271, pp. 11:1–11:19. Schloss Dagstuhl - Leibniz-Zentrum für Informatik (2023)
21. Haken, A.: The intractability of resolution. Theor. Comput. Sci. **39**, 297–308 (1985)
22. Halbwachs, N., Péron, M.: Discovering properties about arrays in simple programs. In: Gupta, R., Amarasinghe, S.P. (eds.) Proceedings of the ACM SIGPLAN 2008 Conference on Programming Language Design and Implementation, Tucson, AZ, USA, 7–13 June 2008, pp. 339–348. ACM (2008)
23. Huang, J.: Extended clause learning. Artif. Intell. **174**(15), 1277–1284 (2010)
24. Knuth, D.E.: The Art of Computer Programming, Volume I: Fundamental Algorithms, 3rd edn. Addison-Wesley (1997)
25. Manthey, N., Heule, M., Biere, A.: Automated reencoding of Boolean formulas. In: Biere, A., Nahir, A., Vos, T. (eds.) HVC 2012. LNCS, vol. 7857, pp. 102–117. Springer, Heidelberg (2013). https://doi.org/10.1007/978-3-642-39611-3_14
26. McMillan, K.L.: Interpolation and SAT-based model checking. In: Hunt, W.A., Somenzi, F. (eds.) CAV 2003. LNCS, vol. 2725, pp. 1–13. Springer, Heidelberg (2003). https://doi.org/10.1007/978-3-540-45069-6_1
27. Moskewicz, M.W., Madigan, C.F., Zhao, Y., Zhang, L., Malik, S.: Chaff: engineering an efficient SAT solver. In: Proceedings of the 38th Design Automation Conference, DAC 2001, Las Vegas, NV, USA, 18–22 June 2001, pp. 530–535. ACM (2001)
28. Silva, J.P.M., Sakallah, K.A.: GRASP - a new search algorithm for satisfiability. In: Rutenbar, R.A., Otten, R.H.J.M. (eds.) Proceedings of the 1996 IEEE/ACM International Conference on Computer-Aided Design, ICCAD 1996, San Jose, CA, USA, 10–14 November 1996, pp. 220–227. IEEE Computer Society/ACM (1996)
29. Sinz, C., Biere, A.: Extended resolution proofs for conjoining BDDs. In: Grigoriev, D., Harrison, J., Hirsch, E.A. (eds.) CSR 2006. LNCS, vol. 3967, pp. 600–611. Springer, Heidelberg (2006). https://doi.org/10.1007/11753728_60
30. Tseitin, G.S.: On the complexity of derivation in propositional calculus (1983)
31. Vizel, Y., Grumberg, O.: Interpolation-sequence based model checking. In: Proceedings of 9th International Conference on Formal Methods in Computer-Aided Design, FMCAD 2009, 15–18 November 2009, Austin, Texas, USA, pp. 1–8. IEEE (2009)

32. Vizel, Y., Gurfinkel, A.: Interpolating property directed reachability. In: Biere, A., Bloem, R. (eds.) CAV 2014. LNCS, vol. 8559, pp. 260–276. Springer, Cham (2014). https://doi.org/10.1007/978-3-319-08867-9_17
33. Vizel, Y., Weissenbacher, G., Malik, S.: Boolean satisfiability solvers and their applications in model checking. Proc. IEEE **103**(11), 2021–2035 (2015)

Open Access This chapter is licensed under the terms of the Creative Commons Attribution 4.0 International License (http://creativecommons.org/licenses/by/4.0/), which permits use, sharing, adaptation, distribution and reproduction in any medium or format, as long as you give appropriate credit to the original author(s) and the source, provide a link to the Creative Commons license and indicate if changes were made.

The images or other third party material in this chapter are included in the chapter's Creative Commons license, unless indicated otherwise in a credit line to the material. If material is not included in the chapter's Creative Commons license and your intended use is not permitted by statutory regulation or exceeds the permitted use, you will need to obtain permission directly from the copyright holder.

Introducing Certificates to the Hardware Model Checking Competition

Nils Froleyks[1](✉), Emily Yu[2], Mathias Preiner[3], Armin Biere[4], and Keijo Heljanko[5,6]

[1] Johannes Kepler University, Linz, Austria
Nils.froleyks@gmail.com
[2] Institute of Science and Technology Austria, Klosterneuburg, Austria
[3] Stanford University, Stanford, CA, USA
[4] University of Freiburg, Freiburg, Germany
[5] University of Helsinki, Helsinki, Finland
[6] Helsinki Institute for Information Technology, Helsinki, Finland

Abstract. Certification was made mandatory for the first time in the latest hardware model checking competition. In this case study, we investigate the trade-offs of requiring certificates for both passing and failing properties in the competition. Our evaluation shows that participating model checkers were able to produce compact, correct certificates that could be verified with minimal overhead. Furthermore, the certifying winner of the competition outperforms the previous non-certifying state-of-the-art model checker, demonstrating that certification can be adopted without compromising model checking efficiency.

1 Introduction

Competitions have played a key role in advancing the state of the art in automated reasoning tools by enabling direct performance comparisons across a wide range of solvers, offering challenging benchmarks, and fostering new research. However, many of these tools operate as black boxes by providing only *true* or *false* as an output. Certification addresses this limitation by requiring a counterexample when verification fails and a proof when it succeeds. Since certificates can be independently validated, they significantly enhance confidence in the correctness of verification results, thereby improving the reliability of solvers.

One goal of using certificates in hardware model checking is to repeat the success story of proof certificates in SAT for this automated reasoning domain with a large industrial user base. Besides increasing trust in verification results, certificates enable more complex design optimizations, allow to continue using legacy code and can streamline and improve efficiency of tool development in both verification and synthesis. The simple proof certificate format used in SAT still allows to capture a wide range of solving optimizations at industrial scale. In this case study, we investigate whether the simple model checking certificate format employed in the recent hardware model checking competition has the potential to achieve the same in the field of hardware model checking.

The Hardware Model Checking Competition (HWMCC) has its roots in a rather lively discussion at the 2nd Alpine Verification Meeting (AVM) in 2006 among Daniel Kröning, Dirk Beyer and Armin Biere. The debated question was if and how model checking research as well as industrial applications can benefit from competitions in the same way the SAT competitions were instrumental in advancing SAT. Daniel Kröning and Armin Biere argued to focus on hardware gate-level models with simple and clear semantics.[1]

This argument prompted the development of the AIGER format [3] used in the first (hardware) model checking competition, affiliated to CAV'07. This first version of AIGER (20071012) came with a library for parsing and other essential tools, including a translator from SMV and BLIF to AIGER. The challenge of the first competitions in 2007, 2008 and 2010 was to collect benchmarks.

For the 2011 competition the first major revision of the AIGER 1.9 format [6] included *liveness* properties and *constraints*. The following competitions from 2012–2015 [8] and in 2017 [4] included a *deep bound track* to emphasize the common industrial practice of relying on incomplete but deep bounded model checking. In 2019 a word-level track was established based on the BTOR 2.0 format [22] proposed at CAV'18. After focusing on word-level in 2020 the organizers decided in 2024 [5] to reintroduce a bit-level track but take the chance to force all participating model checkers to produce certificates.

The introduction of mandatory certification in HWMCC'24 significantly impacted participation and competition dynamics. The 2024 competition saw a record nine participants, up from three in the previous edition, reflecting growing interest and accessibility. Discussions with participants revealed that new rules, *particularly the requirement for certification*, leveled the playing field by encouraging the development of verifiable solvers. Feedback indicated that participants successfully implemented certificate generation based on our published results [14, 29–31]. It was also noted that implementing correct model checking algorithms demanded substantially more effort than generating certificates.

The certificate format itself has undergone several iterations with the ultimate aim of its use in the competition. In HWMCC'24, all participating model checkers were required to produce proofs alongside the model checking results for both safe and unsafe instances. For unsafe instances, the certificate is a trace serving as a counterexample, which can be validated via simulation; as for safe instances, it is a proof witness circuit. For the competition we use an extended version of the witness format defined in [14], that supports constraints, an essential feature of AIGER 1.9.

In this case study, we first describe the certificate format used in the competition, then present experimental findings. We investigate the overhead introduced by certificate checking in model checking and results show that it accounts for only *a fraction of the total verification time*. Moreover, we compare the

---

[1] Dirk Beyer proposed to use C as input language, which is much harder to master, due to its complex semantics. Accordingly the first SV-COMP took place in 2012.

certifying winner of HWMCC'24, RIC3, against the state-of-the-art model checker ABC which does not support certificate generation. Results show that RIC3 outperforms ABC even when including the time required for witness validation.

2 Related Work

Certification in other Competitions. Certification has been an essential part in many other competitions. In SAT competitions [13], certification has been mandatory for almost a decade, as a fundamental requirement. Solvers must produce certificates for both SAT and UNSAT instances: a satisfying truth assignment for SAT and a proof in the DRAT [28] format for UNSAT. A solver is disqualified from the main track if a singe certificate is found invalid. The software verification community is following suit. At SV-COMP'24, it is the second year of having a dedicated track for witness validation, with a range of participating witness validators [2]. The MaxSAT Evaluation [1] has also taken a step forward in 2024 by requesting proofs for the first time. In QBF Evaluations [25], there used to be a dedicated Evaluate & Certify track, where solvers are required to produce proofs that are easier to check than the solving task; however, as the organizers pointed out, only a few QBF solvers support certificate generation. SMT competitions (SMT-COMP) [27] and ATP System Competitions (CASC) [26] feature a wide variety of theories and have yet to adopt a universal certification standard. Classical Planning is similar to verification, but usually more focused on finding solutions (plans). Nevertheless, a deductive certificate format [11] has been introduced, and extended to support UNSAT certificates produced by an underlying SAT solver [10].

Related Work in Model Checking Certification. Deductive proof systems have been used for generating proofs of model checking. For example, the author of [21] addresses μ-calculus, while the authors of [15] focus on liveness and several pre-processing techniques. These approaches require model checkers to provide deductive proofs. The works in [7,16] explore the use of inductive invariants as certificates for k-induction. Notably, the certificate format employed in HWMCC'24 is also compatible with these inductive invariants. The authors of [18] use liveness-to-safety reduction techniques to certify liveness properties. The problem of certifying model checking has also been addressed in infinite-state systems [9,19] where SMT solvers are leveraged for unbounded state spaces. An alternative approach to providing certificates, is to formally verify the model checker itself, as demonstrate in [12].

3 Certificate Format

We assume the standard notions and terminology of Boolean logic. In the following, we consider hardware designs modeled as Boolean circuits encoded as sequential and-inverter graphs (AIGs) [3,6,17,20]. Such a Boolean circuit is given as a tuple $M = (I, L, R, F, P, C)$ where I is an ordered set of inputs, L is an ordered set of latches, R defines the set of reset states, represented as a reset predicate that holds when every latch $l \in L$ equals its reset function r_l; F is the transition predicate that refers to two consecutive states, and encodes that each latch in one state is equal to its corresponding transition function f_l applied to the previous state; P and C are predicates that define the set of good states and the set of states valid under the *constraint*, respectively. These predicates, along with the reset and transition functions, are encoded in the circuits as binary AND-gates with possible negation at the incoming gates.

We use the notion of a reset predicate R being stratified; for space reasons we refer to [30] for formal definitions. In essence, it means that the dependencies that the reset functions introduce among the latches are acyclic. For $K \subseteq L$, $R\{K\}$ and $F\{K\}$ restrict these predicates so only the latches in K are required to be equal to their reset or transition. When referencing a sequence of states, we use indices on the predicates to represent the corresponding copy of the predicate at a certain state in the sequence.

A trace of length n is a sequence of $n + 1$ states, where the first state needs to satisfy R, every pair of consecutive states satisfies F (written $F_{i,i+1}$ for the i-th and its successor state) and all states satisfy the constraint C. If the last state violates P, the trace is bad. Thus a satisfying assignment to the following formula *certifies* that a circuit is *unsafe*:

$$R_0 \wedge \bigwedge_{i \in [0,n)} F_{i,i+1} \wedge \bigwedge_{i \in [0,n]} C_i \wedge \neg P_n.$$

For *safe* instances, the certificate format employed in HWMCC'24 takes the form of witness circuits, defined as follows.

Definition 1 (Witness Circuit). *The circuit* $W = (I', L', R', F', P', C')$ *is a witness circuit of* $M = (I, L, R, F, P, C)$, *if* R' *is stratified and for* $K = L \cap L'$:

1. *Reset:* $R\{K\} \wedge C \Rightarrow R'\{K\} \wedge C'$;
2. *Transition:* $F_{0,1}\{K\} \wedge C_0 \wedge C_1 \wedge C'_0 \Rightarrow F'_{0,1}\{K\} \wedge C'_1$;
3. *Property:* $(C \wedge C') \Rightarrow (P' \Rightarrow P)$;
4. *Base:* $R'\{L'\} \wedge C' \Rightarrow P'$;
5. *Step:* $P'_0 \wedge F'_{0,1}\{L'\} \wedge C'_0 \wedge C'_1 \Rightarrow P'_1$.

The five conditions described above are simple SAT checks. An additional polynomial-time check is required to verify that R' is stratified. If all checks pass, M' is a valid certificate for M, certifying its safety property. The first three conditions in Definition 1 establish a simulation relation between two circuits, such that if M' is safe, M is also safe. The intuition is that an initial state in the original circuit M corresponds to an initial state in the witness circuit, and each valid transition in M corresponds to a transition in M'.

Property P' is a strengthening of P. Consequently, safety of M' implies safety of M. In summary, a bad trace in M corresponds to a bad trace in M'. A sketch of the traces for both M and M' is provided in Fig. 1. The latter two checks

(Definition 1.4 and Definition 1.5) prove P' to be an inductive invariant, entailing the safety of M'. We provide a high-level intuitive illustration of Definition 1 in Fig. 1.

This is a slight extension to the format in [14], as it supports constraints and now covers all AIGER 1.9 [6] features except liveness. In HWMCC'24, witness circuits are also produced as AIGER files. The witness circuit validation is implemented in the certificate checker CERTIFAIGER[2] used for the competition, but has not been described in detail before. For efficient certification, CERTIFAIGER leverages the SAT solver Kissat 4.0.0, winner of the SAT competition 2024.

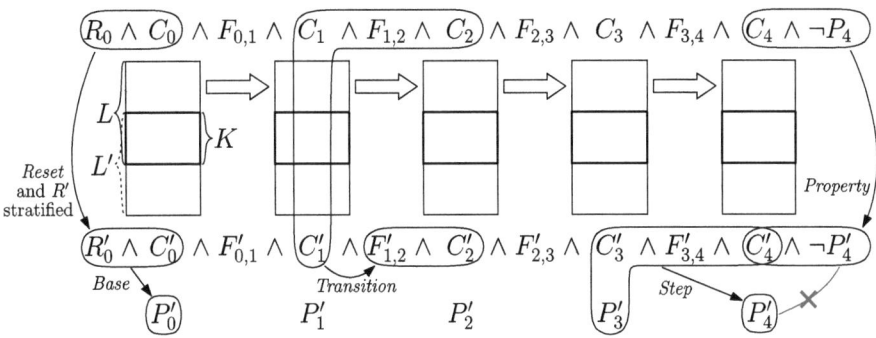

Fig. 1. An illustration for the correctness of Definition 1. Assuming that a circuit M with a valid witness M' has a bad trace leads to a contradiction. Depicted are the overlapping sets of variables and how conditions of the witness check are used to construct a bad trace in M', and arrive at a contradiction. For *Transition* and *Step* only one application is illustrated.

3.1 Soundness of the Certificate Format

We present a proof that the existence of a witness circuit as defined in Definition 1 indeed certifies the safety of a model. The proof extends what is presented in [14] by considering constraints.

Theorem 1. *Given two circuits M and M', with $M = (I, L, R, F, P, C)$, and $M' = (I', L', R', F', P', C')$. If M' is a valid witness circuit for M, then M is safe.*

Before proving the main theorem, we first introduce some additional notation: An assignment maps a subset of the gates to true or false, and is always consistent with the valuation of the AND-gates. Extending an assignment means assigning more gates while leaving previously assigned gates unchanged. We refer to the reset gate associated with latch l as r_l and the primed version r'_l, when referencing the reset gates used by R'.

---

[2] https://github.com/Froleyks/certifaiger.

Every gate g refers to the Boolean function defined by its fan-in cone, and we write $g(s)$ to denote that we consider the function under an assignment s, i.e., the variables in g which are assigned by s are replaced with the corresponding constants. A function g *semantically depends* on a variable v if an assignment exists under which $g(s_v)$ and $g(s_{\neg v})$ evaluate to different truth values.

We first show that a reset state in M corresponds to a reset state in M'.

Lemma 1. *For circuits $M = (I, L, R, F, P, C)$ and $M' = (I', L', R', F', P', C')$ satisfying the reset check (Definition 1.1) and R' stratified, any assignment to $I \cup L$ satisfying $R\{K\} \wedge C$, where $K = L \cap L'$, can be extended to satisfy $R'\{L'\} \wedge C'$.*

Proof. Assuming the reset check passes and R' is stratified, let s be an arbitrary but fixed assignment to $I \cup L$ satisfying $R\{K\} \wedge C$. The assumptions of the Lemma further imply that s satisfies $R'\{K\} \wedge C'$. To show that s can be extended to satisfy $R'\{L'\}$, we first prove for each latch $l \in K$, $r'_l(s)$ has no semantic dependency outside $(I \cup L) \cap (I' \cup L')$. Assume, for contradiction, there is a latch $l \in K$ with $r'_l(s) \not\Leftrightarrow r'_l(s_u)$ where s_u is the same as s except for the value of some gate $u \in (I' \cup L') \setminus (I \cup L)$. We have $l \not\Leftrightarrow r'_l(s_u)$ and therefore $R'\{K\}$ does not hold under s_u. However, u is not in $I \cup L$ and $R\{K\} \wedge C$ still evaluates to true under s_u, thus implying $R'\{K\}$, and leading to the desired contradiction.

Since R' is stratified, the semantic dependencies of the reset gates r'_l can be seen as a topologically sorted graph. Given the above result, when considering $r'_l(s)$, the remaining dependency graph can be sorted topologically such that the variables in $(I \cup L) \cap (I' \cup L')$ are at the bottom. Thus, s can be extended to satisfy $R'\{L'\}$ by assigning the remaining latches in the reverse of that order. The extended assignment still satisfies $R\{K\} \wedge C$ and thereby C'.

We can now move on to prove the correctness of the certificate format, i.e., the proof of the main Theorem 1. Refer to Fig. 1 for a visualization of the proof.

Proof. Suppose, for contradiction, M is unsafe. Then there is a bad trace of some finite length n in the form of an assignment to $n + 1$ copies of $I \cup L$ satisfying:

$$R_0\{L\} \wedge C_0 \wedge F_{0,1}\{L\} \wedge C_1 \wedge \cdots \wedge C_{n-1} \wedge F_{n-1,n}\{L\} \wedge C_n \wedge \neg P_n.$$

We extend this assignment to each copy of the gates in $I' \setminus I \cup L' \setminus L$ that satisfies:

$$R'_0\{L'\} \wedge C'_0 \wedge F'_{0,1}\{L'\} \wedge C'_1 \wedge \cdots \wedge C'_{n-1} \wedge F'_{n-1,n}\{L'\} \wedge C'_n \wedge \neg P'_n.$$

Let $X' = (I' \cup L') \setminus (I \cup L)$. The assignment satisfying $R_0\{K\} \wedge C_0$ can by Lemma 1 can be extended to X'_0 satisfying $R'_0\{L'\} \wedge C'$. With that and the transition check $F'_{0,1}\{K\} \wedge C'_1$ is satisfied and the assignment can be extended to X'_1 satisfying $F'_{0,1}\{L'\} \wedge C'_1$ by the definition of transition functions.

Applying the same argument n times yields an assignment to $(I \cup L \cup I' \cup L')^n$ satisfying $F'_{i,i+1}\{L\}$ for $i \in [0, n)$ and C_i for $i \in [0, n]$. Lastly, the property check guarantees $\neg P'_n$, giving us the desired assignment. However, the base and step check together ensure that the property P' holds on all reachable states of M', thus contradicting the initial assumption that a bad trace exists in M.

4 Evaluation

In this section, we present a comprehensive analysis of the competition results[3], focusing on the overhead of certificate generation and checking. Specifically, we address the following three questions:

1. What is the runtime overhead associated with validating certificates?
2. What is the space overhead associated with storing certificates?
3. How do certifying model checkers compare to the state of the art?

Experimental Setup. The 2024 competition ran on a cluster of 48 compute nodes equipped with an AMD Ryzen 9 7950X 16-core processor at 4.5 GHz and 128 GB or RAM, running Ubuntu 20.04 LTS. For fairness, the experiment described in Sect. 4.3 ran on the cluster used for the last competition in 2020. Each node has access to two Xeon E5-2620 v4 CPUs, for a total of 16 cores running at 2.1 GHz, and 128 GB of RAM.

We focus on (all) the 319 bit-level benchmarks of HWMCC'24, which were translated from the word-level (BTOR/bit-vector) track of HWMCC'24. The majority of the benchmarks (250) are new benchmarks submitted in 2024 by three different groups, including benchmarks for checking safety properties of open source RISC-V cores, sequential equivalence checking, branch coverage problems, as well as software verification problems, which were translated from SV-COMP'24 [2]. The remaining 69 benchmarks were selected randomly from previous competition years (2019 and 2020). Each model checker had exclusive access to a node, with a 120 GB memory limit and a one-hour wall-clock limit. A separate limit of 10 h was imposed for certificate checking.

Note that for precision and reliability of measurements, the competition cluster uses `runexec` to measure resource consumption of the model checkers. We further rely on it to properly isolate the processes and to enforce both the time and memory resource limits.

4.1 Certificate Checking Overhead

We now evaluate the overhead introduced by certificate checking. For each solver, we consider the model checking time, t_{MC}, the time required to validate the produced certificate, t_{CERT}, and the total time $t_{\text{TOTAL}} = t_{\text{MC}} + t_{\text{CERT}}$. The certificate checking overhead for a model checker refers to the additional time required to run all benchmarks when certification is enabled. Note that benchmarks unsolved by the model checker are excluded from this metric. The results are displayed in Fig. 2 where both safe and unsafe instances are considered.

The clear winner of the competition is RIC3, demonstrating superior performance on both safe and unsafe benchmarks. When considering only safe benchmarks, the ranking remains virtually unchanged, with FRIC3 narrowly outperforming SUPERCAR. As for unsafe instances, which constitute approximately 30%

---
[3] https://hwmcc.github.io/2024.

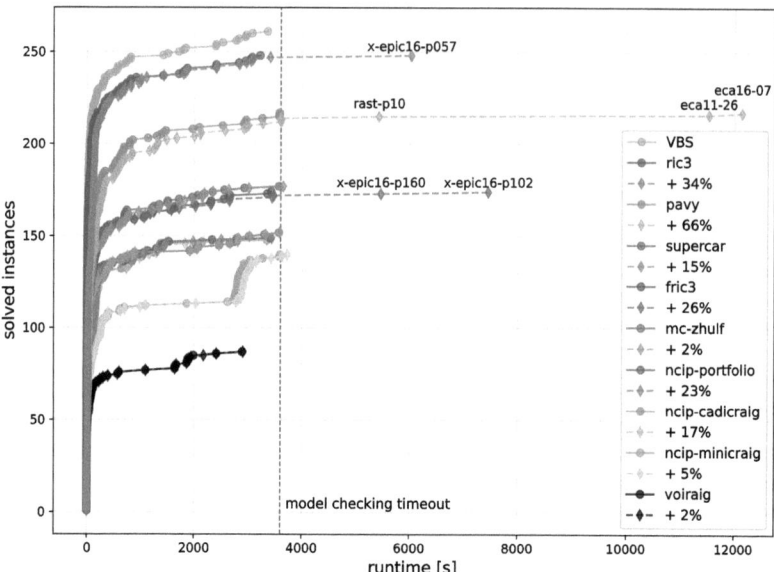

Fig. 2. HWMCC'24 results (319 benchmarks). The plots show the number of solved instances as a function of time. For each model checker, we present (1) the model checking time and (2) the total time for model checking and certificate validation. Diamonds represents the time taken to model check a circuit and validate the produced witness, while dots indicate model checking time only. Benchmarks whose certificates were especially time-consuming to verify are labeled. The Virtual Best Solver (VBS) indicates the top solver performance on each instance. The legend includes the overall certification overhead. The results clearly indicate, that certificate validation only adds minimal overhead.

of solved benchmarks, SUPERCAR slightly outperforms PAVY. In both scenarios, RIC3 maintains its lead and performs impressively close to the virtual best solver.

In Fig. 2, we also identify six outliers where the combined model checking and certification time exceeded the one-hour model checking timeout by more than 5%. The difficulty in their certification seems to be related to the witness circuit generation process *within* the model checker, as for each of these instances, another model checker found a witness circuit, which could be validated under 100 s. An exception is the x-epic16-p057 benchmark, which was solved exclusively by RIC3. Certificate checking never exceeded the 10-hour limit.

As Fig. 2 shows, the overall certification overhead only gives rise to a small fraction of the model checking time, which is highly promising and highlights the effectiveness of the certificate format. For instance, when using RIC3 to model check all 248 instances it solved, the total time is increased by only 34% when all produced certificates are validated. In general, validating certificates for safe instances is a more challenging task than validating simulation traces for unsafe ones, a trend similar as in SAT solving. In fact, simulation time accounts for only 2% of the overhead in RIC3, and even less for all other solvers.

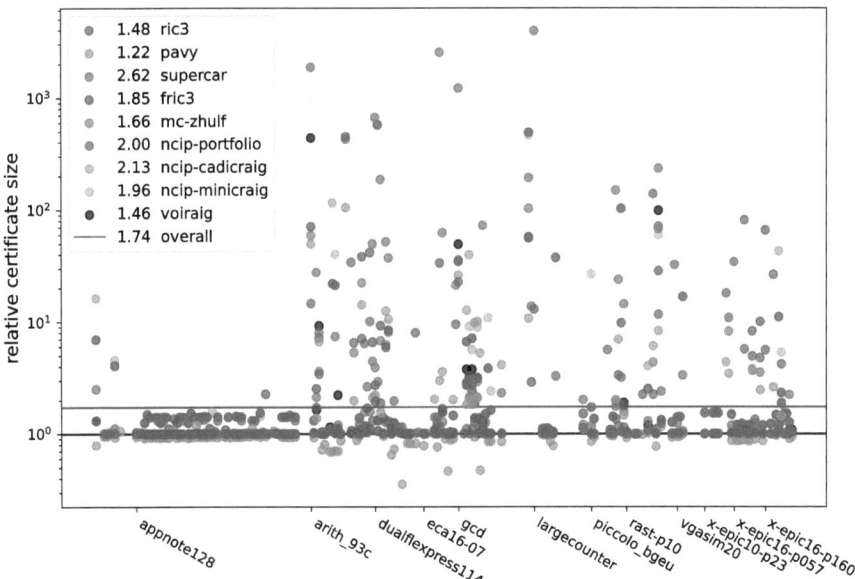

Fig. 3. Size of produced witness circuits relative to their original model circuit. The x-axis represents the set of benchmarks, sorted alphabetically, whereas the y-axis indicates the certificate size (gates) relative to the model. The legend also shows the geometric mean of the relative certificate size for each model checker and all produced certificates combined. Dots stacked vertically correspond to the same benchmark. Since the x-axis is sorted by benchmark name, neighboring instances are likely to belong to the same family. For clarity and space reasons, only a select few benchmarks are explicitly labeled. We observe an overall relative certificate size of 1.74, which indicates the compactness of the certificates.

4.2 Certificate Size

Next, we evaluate the size of witness circuits for safe instances, where circuit size is measured in terms of gates, which includes the number of inputs, latches, and AND-gates. The relative certificate size is defined as $\frac{\text{certificate size}}{\text{model size}}$. Figure 3 presents the relative certificate sizes for all solved instances. Note that appnote and x-epic families, comprising 52 and 13 benchmarks respectively, depicted in the plot, include several multi-property benchmarks. In these cases, the benchmarks represent the same model, differing only in the property to be checked.

We observe that PAVY produces smallest witnesses, with a geometric mean ratio of 1.22, whereas SUPERCAR exhibits the highest ratio of 2.62. Overall, more than 80% of the produced witnesses are less than twice as large as the certified model, with a geometric mean ratio of 1.74 across all produced witness circuits.

It further turns out that PAVY consistently generates witnesses substantially smaller than their corresponding models. Notably, this was not possible in earlier versions of the certificate format [29–31], which required the entire model to be embedded within the witness circuit. The original format was revised in [14]

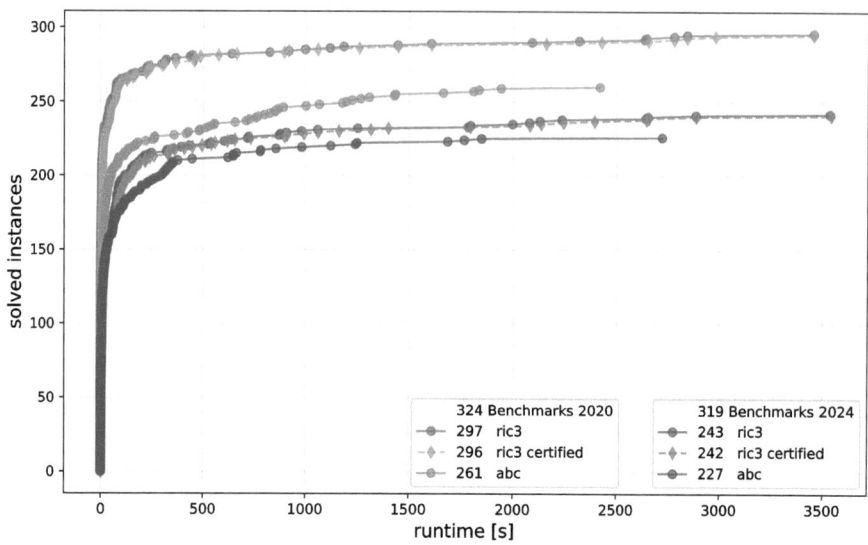

Fig. 4. Comparing RIC3 (2024 winner) with ABC (2020 winner). The same HWMCC'20 hardware setup is used, for both benchmarks sets (2020 and 2024). RIC3 is also run in a fully certified mode, where each result is confirmed by checking the certificate. Note that for these certified runs the shown run-time not only includes model checking time but also certificate production and certificate checking time. We observe that on both sets RIC3 consistently outperforms ABC, even when accounting for certificate validation time.

and went through another update for the competition, which is described in Sect. 3. This version allows, beside constraints, optimized witnesses that focus on a subset of the certified model, enabling significant reduction in witness size.

Witness size only correlates weakly with validation time. The biggest witness, produced by SUPERCAR for the largecounter benchmark, contains over 7 million gates for a model with fewer than 2 thousand gates, yet is verified within 900 s, which is 30% faster than model checking. Conversely, the two difficult-to-check eca witnesses produced by PAVY are 20% smaller than the model.

4.3 Comparison to State of the Art

Since participating model checkers in HWMCC'24 generate certificates, i.e., are *certifying model checkers*, it remains to show data on how certificate generation affects solver speed. We thus compare RIC3, the HWMCC'24 winner, with the state-of-the-art model checker ABC, the winner of the previous HWMCC edition in 2020, where witness circuits were not yet introduced. It is worth noting that the industrial-strength model checker ABC has dominated the bit-level track of the HWMCC since its debut in 2008. However, it could not participate in the 2024 competition, as certificates are now mandatory.

For our experiment, we use the version of ABC, which was submitted to the HWMCC'20, and was tailored specifically for the competition thus distinct from its public releases. To ensure that ABC is used with the same hardware specifications as expected by the participants in 2020 we run our experiment on the HWMCC'20 hardware. Note that this hardware is significantly older than the cluster used for HWMCC'24.

Note that the benchmarks from HWMCC'20 and HWMCC'24 were both included (there was no competition in between). The two sets are mostly distinct with only 8 benchmarks in common. This is following the SAT competition practice: HWMCC uses mostly new benchmarks every year, adhering to the SAT Practitioner's Manifesto.

Figure 4 shows that RIC3 convincingly outperforms ABC on both benchmark sets. Notably, in 2020, RIC3 solves 36 more benchmarks and is faster on 247 out of the 256 benchmarks solved by both model checkers. For RIC3, we also include a certified version, which represents its performance if it did internal certificate validation, and every benchmark is only reported as solved after the certificate has been successfully validated. Even in its certified mode, RIC3 still holds a clear lead, losing only one instance per year due to certificate validation exceeding the remaining time before the one-hour model checking timeout.

One minor exception is the performance on the 2024 benchmarks within the first 30 s, where the certificate checking adds a significant enough overhead for ABC to catch up to the certified version. Nevertheless, certificate production introduces *no measurable overhead* to overall model checking performance. These results demonstrate that RIC3, is a robust and efficient model checker, that presents superior performance while providing added benefits of certifying.

Invalid Certificates. In HWMCC'24 and the experiments presented above, producing an invalid certificate causes the benchmark to count as unsolved. Out of the 1536 certificates generated during the competition, 44 were found to be incorrect. They were produced by four model checkers: SUPERCAR (20), NCIP-MINICRAIG (9), NCIP-PORTFOLIO (8), FRIC3 (7). The incorrect certificates produced by SUPERCAR are all simulation traces, notably 8 of them are for benchmarks which have been proven *safe* by other model checkers. In addition to 3 more incorrect simulation traces from FRIC3, all other invalid certificates were witness circuits failing one of the checks outlined in Definition 1.

Many of the invalid certificates stemmed from bugs uncovered by the organizers before the competition through extensive fuzz testing. The fuzzer and subsequent delta-debugging helped identify minimal failing circuits, shared subsequently with the model checker developers for fixes. Initially, all model checkers produced invalid certificates. After extensive feedback, most solvers passed thousands of fuzzer-generated test cases with correct certificates. This process highlights the benefits of certifying model checkers to improve their robustness.

Summary of Results. Our experimental evaluation entails the following key findings. (i) Minimal overhead: certification adds only a small runtime overhead, representing a fraction of the total model checking time. (ii) Compact certificates: optimized certificate formats reduced storage requirements, with over 80% of certificates being less than twice the size of the certified model. (iii) Impact on performance: RIC3, the 2024 winner, outperformed the 2020 winner ABC, even when all certificates are verified, demonstrating that certifying approaches can simultaneously provide correctness guarantees and strong performance.

5 Conclusion

HWMCC'24 marks the first time that the Hardware Model Checking Competition has mandated certification for all participating solvers. Our case study confirms that certification can be integrated with minimal overhead while significantly improving confidence in verification results, illustrating the practical benefits of mandatory certification in hardware model checking.

Looking ahead, we call on more participants and model checker developers—both in academia and industry—to adopt and support certification. Building on the success of HWMCC'24, we intend to extend certification to the word-level track, for which a certificate checker CERBOTOR is already publicly available. However, challenges remain, including the need to develop techniques for generating certificates tailored to word-level-specific methods and addressing the use of trustworthy SMT solvers, which require SMT-based certificates.

On the other hand, a certifying liveness track is under planning, although this endeavor requires certificate generation for liveness checking algorithms, which remains another open research challenge. Another direction concerns the degree of trust we can place in the certificate checker. Ultimately, achieving a fully verified certificate checker would ensure an end-to-end correctness in the verification process, further increasing confidence.

Beyond increasing trust in model checkers, certificates have broader applications. An ongoing industry collaboration explores the integration of certifying model checkers as hammers in interactive theorem provers such as Isabelle [23] via Sledgehammer [24]. This entails, the theorem prover encoding an open proof as a model checking problem, invoking a model checker, and lifting the certificate back into the theorem prover.

Acknowledgements. This work is supported in part by the ERC-2020-AdG 101020093, the LIT AI Lab funded by the State of Upper Austria, the Research Council of Finland under the project 336092, and a gift from Intel Corporation.

Furthermore we of course also owe a big thank-you to the submitters of model checkers and benchmarks to the competition over all these years. Without their enthusiasm and support neither the competition nor this study would exist.

Disclosure of Interests. The authors have no competing interests to declare that are relevant to the content of this paper.

References

1. Bacchus, F., Berg, J., Järvisalo, M., Martins, R.: MaxSAT evaluation 2020: solver and benchmark descriptions (2020)

2. Beyer, D.: State of the art in software verification and witness validation: SV-COMP 2024. In: Finkbeiner, B., Kovács, L. (eds.) TACAS 2024. LNCS, vol. 14572, pp. 299–329. Springer, Cham (2024). https://doi.org/10.1007/978-3-031-57256-2_15
3. Biere, A.: The AIGER And-Inverter Graph (AIG) format version 20071012. Technical report, 07/1, Institute for Formal Models and Verification, Johannes Kepler University, Altenbergerstr. 69, 4040 Linz, Austria (2007). https://doi.org/10.35011/fmvtr.2007-1
4. Biere, A., van Dijk, T., Heljanko, K.: Hardware model checking competition 2017. In: Stewart, D., Weissenbacher, G. (eds.) Formal Methods in Computer-Aided Design, FMCAD 2017, Vienna, Austria, 02–06 October 2017, p. 9. IEEE (2017)
5. Biere, A., Froleyks, N., Preiner, M.: Hardware model checking competition 2024. In: Narodytska, N., Rümmer, P. (eds.) Proceedings 24th International Conference on Formal Methods in Computer-Aided Design (FMCAD 2024), p. 7. TU Wien Academic Press (2024). https://doi.org/10.34727/2024/isbn.978-3-85448-065-5_6
6. Biere, A., Heljanko, K., Wieringa, S.: AIGER 1.9 and beyond. Technical report, 11/2, Institute for Formal Models and Verification, Johannes Kepler University, Altenbergerstr. 69, 4040 Linz, Austria (2011). https://doi.org/10.35011/fmvtr.2011-2
7. Bjørner, N., Gurfinkel, A., McMillan, K., Rybalchenko, A.: Horn clause solvers for program verification. In: Beklemishev, L.D., Blass, A., Dershowitz, N., Finkbeiner, B., Schulte, W. (eds.) Fields of Logic and Computation II. LNCS, vol. 9300, pp. 24–51. Springer, Cham (2015). https://doi.org/10.1007/978-3-319-23534-9_2
8. Cabodi, G., et al.: Hardware model checking competition 2014: an analysis and comparison of solvers and benchmarks. J. Satisf. Boolean Model. Comput. **9**(1), 135–172 (2014). https://doi.org/10.3233/SAT190106
9. Conchon, S., Mebsout, A., Zaïdi, F.: Certificates for parameterized model checking. In: Bjørner, N., de Boer, F. (eds.) FM 2015. LNCS, vol. 9109, pp. 126–142. Springer, Cham (2015). https://doi.org/10.1007/978-3-319-19249-9_9
10. Eriksson, S., Helmert, M.: Certified unsolvability for SAT planning with property directed reachability. In: Proceedings of the International Conference on Automated Planning and Scheduling, vol. 30, pp. 90–100 (2020). https://doi.org/10.1609/icaps.v30i1.6649
11. Eriksson, S., Röger, G., Helmert, M.: Unsolvability certificates for classical planning. In: Barbulescu, L., Frank, J., Mausam, Smith, S.F. (eds.) Proceedings of the Twenty-Seventh International Conference on Automated Planning and Scheduling, ICAPS 2017, Pittsburgh, Pennsylvania, USA, 18–23 June 2017, pp. 88–97. AAAI Press (2017)
12. Esparza, J., Lammich, P., Neumann, R., Nipkow, T., Schimpf, A., Smaus, J.G.: A fully verified executable LTL model checker. Arch. Formal Proofs **2014** (2014)
13. Froleyks, N., Heule, M., Iser, M., Järvisalo, M., Suda, M.: SAT competition 2020. Artif. Intell. **301**, 103572 (2021)
14. Froleyks, N., Yu, E., Biere, A., Heljanko, K.: Certifying phase abstraction. In: Benzmüller, C., Heule, M.J.H., Schmidt, R.A. (eds.) IJCAR 2024. LNCS, vol. 14739, pp. 284–303. Springer, Cham (2024). https://doi.org/10.1007/978-3-031-63498-7_17
15. Griggio, A., Roveri, M., Tonetta, S.: Certifying proofs for SAT-based model checking. Formal Methods Syst. Des. **57**(2), 178–210 (2021). https://doi.org/10.1007/s10703-021-00369-1
16. Gurfinkel, A., Ivrii, A.: K-induction without unrolling. In: 2017 Formal Methods in Computer Aided Design (FMCAD), pp. 148–155. IEEE (2017)

17. Kuehlmann, A., Paruthi, V., Krohm, F., Ganai, M.K.: Robust Boolean reasoning for equivalence checking and functional property verification. IEEE Trans. Comput. Aided Des. Integr. Circuits Syst. **21**(12), 1377–1394 (2002). https://doi.org/10.1109/TCAD.2002.804386
18. Kuismin, T., Heljanko, K.: Increasing confidence in liveness model checking results with proofs. In: Bertacco, V., Legay, A. (eds.) HVC 2013. LNCS, vol. 8244, pp. 32–43. Springer, Cham (2013). https://doi.org/10.1007/978-3-319-03077-7_3
19. Mebsout, A., Tinelli, C.: Proof certificates for SMT-based model checkers for infinite-state systems. In: FMCAD, pp. 117–124. IEEE (2016)
20. Mishchenko, A., Chatterjee, S., Brayton, R.K.: DAG-aware AIG rewriting a fresh look at combinational logic synthesis. In: Sentovich, E. (ed.) Proceedings of the 43rd Design Automation Conference, DAC 2006, San Francisco, CA, USA, 24–28 July 2006, pp. 532–535. ACM (2006). https://doi.org/10.1145/1146909.1147048
21. Namjoshi, K.S.: Certifying model checkers. In: Berry, G., Comon, H., Finkel, A. (eds.) CAV 2001. LNCS, vol. 2102, pp. 2–13. Springer, Heidelberg (2001). https://doi.org/10.1007/3-540-44585-4_2
22. Niemetz, A., Preiner, M., Wolf, C., Biere, A.: BTOR2, BtorMC and Boolector 3.0. In: Chockler, H., Weissenbacher, G. (eds.) CAV 2018. LNCS, vol. 10981, pp. 587–595. Springer, Cham (2018). https://doi.org/10.1007/978-3-319-96145-3_32
23. Nipkow, T., Wenzel, M., Paulson, L.C.: Isabelle/HOL: A Proof Assistant for Higher-Order Logic. Springer, Heidelberg (2002)
24. Paulson, L., Nipkow, T.: The Sledgehammer: let automatic theorem provers write your Isabelle scripts (2023)
25. Pulina, L., Seidl, M.: The 2016 and 2017 QBF solvers evaluations (QBFEVAL'16 and QBFEVAL'17). Artif. Intell. **274**, 224–248 (2019)
26. Sutcliffe, G.: Proceedings of the 12th IJCAR ATP System Competition (CASC-J12) (2024)
27. Weber, T., Conchon, S., Déharbe, D., Heizmann, M., Niemetz, A., Reger, G.: The SMT competition 2015–2018. J. Satisfiability Boolean Model. Comput. **11**(1), 221–259 (2019)
28. Wetzler, N., Heule, M., Hunt, W.A.: DRAT-trim: efficient checking and trimming using expressive clausal proofs. In: Sinz, C., Egly, U. (eds.) SAT 2014. LNCS, vol. 8561, pp. 422–429. Springer, Cham (2014). https://doi.org/10.1007/978-3-319-09284-3_31
29. Yu, E., Biere, A., Heljanko, K.: Progress in certifying hardware model checking results. In: Silva, A., Leino, K. (eds.) CAV 2021. LNCS, vol. 12760, pp. 363–386. Springer, Cham (2021). https://doi.org/10.1007/978-3-030-81688-9_17
30. Yu, E., Froleyks, N., Biere, A., Heljanko, K.: Stratified certification for K-Induction. In: Griggio, A., Rungta, N. (eds.) 22nd Formal Methods in Computer-Aided Design, FMCAD 2022, Trento, Italy, 17–21 October 2022, pp. 59–64. IEEE (2022). https://doi.org/10.34727/2022/ISBN.978-3-85448-053-2_11
31. Yu, E., Froleyks, N., Biere, A., Heljanko, K.: Towards compositional hardware model checking certification. In: Nadel, A., Rozier, K.Y. (eds.) Formal Methods in Computer-Aided Design, FMCAD 2023, Ames, IA, USA, 24–27 October 2023, pp. 1–11. IEEE (2023). https://doi.org/10.34727/2023/ISBN.978-3-85448-060-0_12

Open Access This chapter is licensed under the terms of the Creative Commons Attribution 4.0 International License (http://creativecommons.org/licenses/by/4.0/), which permits use, sharing, adaptation, distribution and reproduction in any medium or format, as long as you give appropriate credit to the original author(s) and the source, provide a link to the Creative Commons license and indicate if changes were made.

The images or other third party material in this chapter are included in the chapter's Creative Commons license, unless indicated otherwise in a credit line to the material. If material is not included in the chapter's Creative Commons license and your intended use is not permitted by statutory regulation or exceeds the permitted use, you will need to obtain permission directly from the copyright holder.

BTOR2-SELECT: Machine Learning Based Algorithm Selection for Hardware Model Checking

Zhengyang Lu[1](✉), Po-Chun Chien[2](✉), Nian-Ze Lee[2,3](✉), Arie Gurfinkel[1](✉), and Vijay Ganesh[4](✉)

[1] University of Waterloo, Waterloo, Canada
z52lu@uwaterloo.ca
[2] LMU Munich, Munich, Germany
[3] National Taiwan University, Taipei, Taiwan
[4] Georgia Institute of Technology, Atlanta, USA

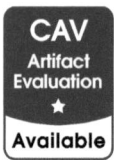

Abstract. In recent years, a diverse variety of hardware model-checking tools and techniques that exhibit complementary strengths and distinct weaknesses have been proposed. This state of affairs naturally suggests the use of algorithm-selection techniques to select the right tool for a given instance. To automate this process, we present BTOR2-SELECT, a machine learning-based algorithm-selection framework for the hardware model-checking problem described in the word-level modeling language BTOR2. The framework offers an efficient and effective machine-learning pipeline for training an algorithm selector. BTOR2-SELECT also enables the use of the trained selector to predict the most suitable off-the-shelf model checker for a given verification task and automatically invoke it to solve the task. Evaluated on a comprehensive BTOR2 benchmark suite coupled with a set of state-of-the-art model checkers, BTOR2-SELECT trained an algorithm selector that successfully closed over 65 % of the PAR-2 performance gap between the best single tool and the idealized virtual selector. Moreover, the selector outperformed a portfolio model checker that runs three complementary verification engines in parallel. BTOR2-SELECT offers a simple, systematic, and extensible solution to harness the complementary strengths of diverse model checkers. With its fast and highly configurable training procedure, BTOR2-SELECT can be easily integrated with new tools and applied to various application domains.

Keywords: Algorithm selection · Machine learning · Model checking · Formal verification · Word-level circuit · BTOR2 · SMT · SAT

1 Introduction

Hardware model checking is now an extensively adopted verification methodology used primarily for ensuring the correctness and reliability of industrial

---

A preliminary version of this work appeared as a student abstract at AAAI 2025 [32].

© The Author(s) 2025
R. Piskac and Z. Rakamarić (Eds.): CAV 2025, LNCS 15931, pp. 296–311, 2025.
https://doi.org/10.1007/978-3-031-98668-0_15

hardware systems [17]. As digital systems become increasingly integrated into everyday life, even minor design errors can have severe consequences, particularly in safety-critical domains such as autonomous vehicles and aerospace. Yet, model checking is computationally hard [24], and there is no "silver bullet" to all model-checking instances arising from a diversity of applications.

Over the years, researchers have developed a range of model-checking algorithms, such as bounded model checking (BMC) [8], k-induction [50], and property-directed reachability (IC3/PDR) [9,21]. These algorithms have been implemented in various verification tools. As is common with computationally challenging problems, different algorithms and tools exhibit complementary strengths and varying weaknesses across different classes of instances.

Practitioners have sought to harness such complementary strengths. One approach is to handcraft selection heuristics based on expert knowledge, as done in SUPER_PROVE [11]. However, such approaches demand significant expertise and effort, and may fail to scale with the growing number of tools and their configurations. Early automation attempts used expert systems [13,27,40], but they still rely on manually crafted rules that may generalize poorly and are hard to maintain as new tools are introduced.

In this paper, we explore the use of machine learning (ML)-based algorithm selection [28] for hardware model checking. ML-based algorithm selection is a systematic, data-driven approach that learns to predict the best algorithm for a given problem instance, based on a historical performance dataset of different algorithms on a set of training instances. It has achieved significant success in areas closely related to hardware model checking, such as SAT [55,56] and SMT [35,44,49]. Over the past decade, it has also been applied to software verification [20,31,46,47,54]. In the context of hardware verification, an early work from 2012 explored ML techniques for selecting multiple verification heuristics for parallel execution [48]. Our work distinguishes itself by building on the rapid advances in ML techniques and applications over the past decade, and by selecting from a comprehensive set of state-of-the-art hardware model checkers.

We present BTOR2-SELECT, an automated ML-based algorithm-selection framework for hardware model checking in the word-level language BTOR2 [42]. It builds on a fast yet effective algorithm-selection paradigm: pairwise classification (PWC) [56] with the Support Vector Machine (SVM) [56] classifiers, using structural features of circuits to represent BTOR2 instances. Our empirical experiments found that, even with a simple feature representation that only counts the frequency of BTOR2 keywords, the PWC-SVM approach delivers robust performance. With more sophisticated feature representations, such as the Weisfeiler-Lehman graph kernel [51], the selector's performance can be further improved. Moreover, the SVM model's simplicity enables better generalization than more complex models like XGBOOST [14], which tends to overfit.

Our Contributions

- **BTOR2-SELECT, an ML-based algorithm-selection framework.** We present a simple yet effective ML-based algorithm-selection framework for

hardware model checking. Specifying a set of off-the-shelf verifiers and providing their performance upon a sample BTOR2 instance set, users can use BTOR2-SELECT to efficiently learn a reliable algorithm selector, thanks to the efficiency and effectiveness of the PWC-SVM approach. Our framework is highly configurable, allowing easy integration of new verifiers and adaptation to different application domains.
- **Strong experimental results with SOTA verifiers and a comprehensive benchmark suite.** We evaluated BTOR2-SELECT on a comprehensive BTOR2 benchmark suite, using state-of-the-art open-source model checkers as backend engines for selection. After training, BTOR2-SELECT successfully closed 65.3 % and 67.8 % of the PAR-2[1] performance gap between the virtual best solver and the single best solver for bit-vector-only and array-involved tasks, respectively. Additionally, in our evaluation, BTOR2-SELECT, which executes only one selected engine, achieved comparable walltime performance to award-winning parallel-portfolio model checkers, while using considerably fewer CPU resources.

2 Preliminaries

Word-Level Hardware Model Checking and BTOR2. One of the main goals of hardware model checking is to ensure the safety properties of digital systems, which assert that certain undesirable states, referred to as *bad states*, are unreachable. BTOR2 [42] is a prevailing word-level language for modeling such systems as *sequential circuits*, and has been adopted by HWMCC since 2019 [6]. Figure 1a illustrates an example BTOR2 task. A corresponding graph representation of this example is shown in Figure 1b, where the edges indicate the propagation of values through operations. Many advanced model checkers natively support BTOR2 [23,36,42], while translations into the bit-level AIGER circuits [7,41] or C programs [4] enable access to an even broader set of tools, further enhancing the extensibility and versatility of this ecosystem.

Machine Learning-Based Algorithm Selection. Let V be a set of available off-the-shelf verifiers for the model-checking problem. An algorithm selector f maps an instance x to a verifier $f(x) \in V$. The objective is to find an optimal algorithm selector f^* that maximizes its performance over an instance distribution D of interest. The ML approach starts with drawing a training instance set S from D, and collects the performance of every (v, s) pair, where $v \in V$ and $s \in S$. Using the collected performance dataset, an algorithm selector $\hat{f}$ is trained to maximize its performance over S, with the expectation that $\hat{f}$ also generalizes well over D. Otherwise, we say that $\hat{f}$ is *overfitting* to S.

An algorithm selector is typically evaluated by comparing its performance to the *virtual best solver* (VBS) and the *single best solver* (SBS). The VBS

---
[1] The PAR-2 score is equal to the runtime if the instance is successfully solved within the resource limit; otherwise, it is set to twice the time limit as a penalty.

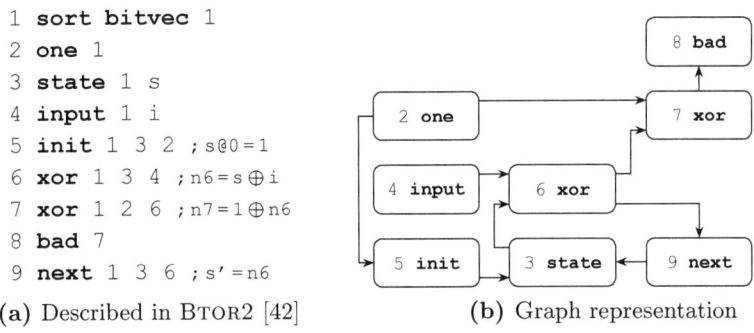

Fig. 1. An example word-level hardware model-checking task

represents an idealized perfect selector that always picks the best verifier for each instance, providing an upper bound on achievable performance. The SBS is the single verifier from the portfolio with the best overall performance on a given instance set. It is expected that a well-designed algorithm selector outperforms the SBS. Thus, a common evaluation metric for algorithm selectors is the fraction of the VBS-SBS performance gap closed by the selector.

Cost-sensitive pairwise classification (PWC) [56] is a common approach to algorithm selection. During training, a binary classifier is built for each pair of verification engines in the portfolio, predicting which engine performs better on a given instance. Training samples are *cost-sensitive*, assigning greater weight to instances with larger performance gaps. At inference time, given a new instance, each classifier votes for the better engine in its pair, and the engine with the most votes is selected.

Weisfeiler-Lehman (WL) Graph Kernel. The WL graph kernel [51] is a broadly used method for measuring graph similarities by capturing structural patterns in a computationally efficient way. At its core, the WL kernel represents graphs as sets of subgraph patterns derived from an iterative *node relabeling* process. At each iteration, every node is relabeled by concatenating its current label with a multiset of its neighbors' labels. This iterative process continues for a specified number of iterations, gradually encoding higher-order structural information. After relabeling, graph similarity is then computed by comparing the distributions of node labels across iterations.

3 BTOR2-SELECT: Framework and Implementation

BTOR2-SELECT is an ML-based algorithm-selection framework designed for model checking in the BTOR2 format. An overview of its architecture and workflow is shown in Figure 2. During the training phase in Figure 2a, BTOR2-SELECT takes as input a set of off-the-shelf verifier engines and a set of BTOR2 instances sampled from the target application domain. An algorithm selector is learned from the

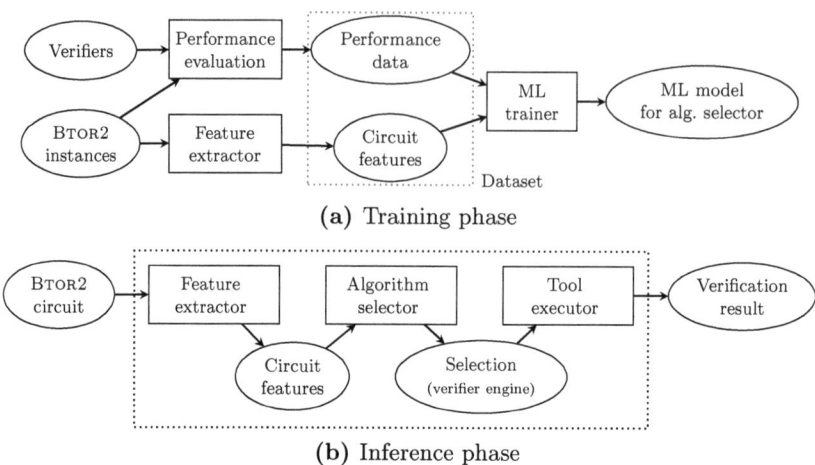

Fig. 2. Overview of BTOR2-SELECT

performance data of the provided verifier engines on the sample BTOR2 instances with their extracted circuit features. During the inference phase in Figure 2b, the algorithm-selection-based model checker works as follows: the trained algorithm selector makes predictions according to the circuit features of an input BTOR2 task, and the selected verifier is invoked by a tool executor.

BTOR2-SELECT is an open-source framework[2] implemented in Python, allowing convenient prototyping for various application scenarios and integration with standard machine-learning libraries. The three main components of BTOR2-SELECT, i.e., feature extraction, selector training, and tool execution, will be described in the following.

3.1 Feature Representation

BTOR2-SELECT supports two types of BTOR2 feature representation: Bag-of-Keywords (BoKW) and the Weisfeiler-Lehman (WL) graph kernel.

The BoKW representation encodes a BTOR2 instance by counting the occurrences of the 69 BTOR2 keywords, such as add, and, and xor, in the instance. Thus, each instance is represented by a 69-dimensional integer vector, where each entry indicates the number of occurrences of a specific keyword. For example, the BoKW representation of the BTOR2 instance in Figure 1a assigns the values 0, 1, and 2 to the dimensions add, input, and xor, respectively.

The WL graph kernel extends BoKW by incorporating structural information beyond individual node labels in a BTOR2 circuit. Operating on the graph representation of a BTOR2 instance with nodes labeled by keywords (as illustrated in Figure 1b), the WL kernel iteratively aggregates information from the neighboring nodes to relabel each graph node. More iterations enable the WL

---

[2] Available at https://gitlab.com/sosy-lab/software/btor2-select.

kernel to progressively capture richer structural information from the BTOR2 instance. We compute graph kernels using the library GRAKEL [52].

The BoKW and WL kernel features present a tradeoff between efficient extraction and expressive representation. BoKW is a lightweight yet tested-effective representation, while the WL kernel effectively captures more circuit structural information at a slightly higher computation cost. The expressiveness and efficiency are particularly relevant for algorithm selection, as many algorithm-selection approaches rely on the premise that similar instances exhibit similar solver performance [26,56]. BTOR2-SELECT offers the BoKW and WL kernel representations to cater to different application scenarios.

Time Limits for Extracting WL Kernel Features. Computing WL-graph-kernel features requires first converting the text representation of a BTOR2 instance into a graph representation, which can be time-consuming for large instances. Long feature-extraction times lead to a significant increase in both training and inference times, degrading the overall performance of algorithm selection. To mitigate this, BTOR2-SELECT allows users to specify a time limit for feature extraction. During training, instances that exceed this limit are excluded from the ML model training. Instead, a fallback solver is determined based on the performance across all engines on these timed-out instances. At inference time, if feature extraction runs into timeout for a given instance, BTOR2-SELECT directly invokes the fallback solver, bypassing the ML model. The default time limit is set to 1 s, which is sufficient for most BTOR2 instances. This limit can also be fine-tuned through the cross-validation procedure described in Section 3.2.

3.2 Selector Training

To prepare the performance data for selector training, we leverage BENCHEXEC [5], a widely used and reliable benchmarking framework, for its precise resource measurement and convenient tooling for processing the data.

BTOR2-SELECT adopts the PWC approach for algorithm selection. BTOR2 instances are represented by BoKW or the WL graph kernel with a specified number of iterations. In the PWC training scheme, a separate classifier is trained for each pair of verification engines, and training samples are weighted by the performance difference between the pair. The default and recommended classifier in BTOR2-SELECT is SVM [19], implemented by the SCIKIT-LEARN library [43].

K-Fold Cross-Validation. As ML approaches are data-dependent, different feature representations may suit different application scenarios. A k-fold cross-validation step is provided in BTOR2-SELECT to help users choose the most suitable feature representation for their problem. K-fold cross-validation [29] is a common ML technique that splits the dataset into k equal folds. Each fold is used for validation once while the remaining $(k-1)$ folds train the model. The process repeats k times, and the validation performances are averaged across the k runs.

Table 1. Benchmarked verification tools and algorithms (tools or algorithms that are only benchmarked on the `bitvec` set are marked with ^{bv})

Input	Tool	Version	Algorithms
AIGER	ABC^{bv}	af1de4fa	BMC, IMC, PDR, sc-IMC, sc-PDR
	RIC3^{bv}	HWMCC24	BMC, KI, IC3
BTOR2	AVR	bdbfc83b	BMC, KI, IC3sa
	BTORMC	6603ed7	BMC, KI, KI-sp
	PONO	508b380	BMC, KI-sp, IMC, IC3^{bv}, IC3ia
C	CBMC	5.95.1	BMC, KI
	ESBMC	7.4.0	BMC, KI^{bv}

3.3 Integration with Backend Model Checkers

BTOR2-SELECT reuses existing components in the BENCHEXEC [5] framework to achieve a modular integration with the backend model checkers. Our implementation leverages the so-called *tool-info modules* from BENCHEXEC, which provides the necessary functionality to assemble command lines for executing model checkers and to parse their output for extracting verification results. This modular approach ensures compatibility with a wide range of model checkers and allows easy extension to integrate new tools as needed.

4 Benchmarks, Verifiers, and Performance Data Collection

To evaluate our proposed algorithm selector framework BTOR2-SELECT, we collected a comprehensive benchmark suite of BTOR2 model-checking tasks, included a diverse set of state-of-the-art open-source verification tools and algorithmic implementations, and measured their performance on the collected tasks.[3]

Benchmark Tasks. We collected verification tasks in BTOR2 format from a wide range of domains. The sources include the benchmark sets used in HWMCC 2019, 2020, and 2024 [1,6,45], as well as other sources. Following the same practice as in HWMCC, the collected benchmarks were divided into two categories: tasks with only bit-vector sorts (denoted as the `bitvec` set) and the ones additionally involving arrays (denoted as the `array` set). In total, there are 3 498 BTOR2 tasks, where the `bitvec` set contains 1 977 and the `array` set contains 1 521.

---

[3] The benchmark suite, verifiers, and performance data are available at https://gitlab.com/sosy-lab/research/data/perf-eval-hwmc.

Verification Tools and Algorithms. Our study includes a portfolio of state-of-the-art open-source verifiers in symbolic model checking. Notably, the evaluated tools were the winners and top contenders of previous editions of HWMCC and SV-COMP. Table 1 lists the included tools and their employed algorithms.

We benchmarked the following tools on the collected BTOR2 tasks: (1) bit-level hardware model checkers for AIGER: ABC [10] and RIC3 [53], (2) word-level hardware model checkers for BTOR2: AVR [23], BTORMC [42], and PONO [36], and (3) software verifiers for C programs: CBMC [18] and ESBMC [38]. Task translators BTOR2AIGER [41] (at commit a1bb6932) and BTOR2C [4] (at commit 7cf65f00) are bundled with the verifiers for AIGER and C, respectively, to translate the BTOR2 tasks to the input formats of these tools.

For each verifier, different verification algorithms are considered, including BMC [8], k-induction (KI) [50], interpolation-based model checking (IMC) [37], and IC3/PDR [9,21]. Each algorithm may be combined with additional techniques (denoted with a prefix or suffix), such as simple-path constraints ("-sp"), syntax-guided abstraction ("sa") [22], implicit predicate abstraction ("ia") [16], or speculative reduction ("sc-") [39]. Several verifier-algorithm combinations were executed only on the `bitvec` set (as indicated in Table 1), due to missing support or unsound behavior on tasks involving arrays. In the following, we use "<verifier>·<algorithm>" to denote a verifier-algorithm combination.

Performance Data Collection. For each pair of BTOR2 task and verification tool running a specific algorithm, we collected the verification results produced by the tool, along with the consumed CPU time, walltime, and memory. The executions were conducted on machines running Ubuntu 24.04 (64-bit, Linux 6.8.0), each equipped with a 3.4 GHz CPU (Intel Xeon E3-1230 v5) with 8 processing units and 33 GB of RAM. Each run was limited to one CPU core, 900 s of CPU time, and 15 GB of memory. To facilitate large-scale and reliable performance benchmarking, the platform BENCHCLOUD [3] was employed, which leverages BENCHEXEC [5] to accurately limit and measure resource consumption. Upon the `bitvec` benchmarks, we found that ABC·sc-PDR is the SBS, correctly solving 1 306 among the 1 977 tasks, while the VBS solved 1 541. For the `array` benchmarks, AVR·KI was the SBS, correctly solving 797 out of 1 521 tasks, whereas the VBS solved 943. These gaps highlight the potential for "smart" algorithm selection to fill. An overview of each verification engine's performance is provided in a supplementary technical report [15].

5 Evaluation

To evaluate the effectiveness of BTOR2-SELECT and to demonstrate its usage, we conducted experiments on the `bitvec` and `array` benchmark sets. The same procedure was applied to both sets. For each set, the benchmarking instances were randomly split into training and testing sets with an 80-20 ratio. A 4-fold cross-validation was performed on the training set to determine the best feature representation. For comparison, we included the Empirical Hardness

Model (EHM) approach [55] in cross-validation. EHM is an intuitive regression-based algorithm-selection approach that predicts solvers' runtime to select the best one. We also tried other ML models, e.g., XGBoost, in this stage. During cross-validation, selector performance was estimated: given a BTOR2 task, the selector chooses a backend engine to run, and the selector's performance is assessed based on the recorded performance of the selected engine for that task, along with the selection overhead (including the feature extraction and ML model inference time).

After cross-validation, an algorithm selector with the chosen configuration was trained on the entire training set and evaluated on the held-out testing set. All comparison baselines described below were also evaluated on this same testing set. During testing (see Section 5.2), BTOR2-SELECT integrated the trained selector with the backend engines to perform end-to-end model checking.

All ML models were trained on a Linux machine, equipped with 2 TB of RAM and two 2.0 GHz AMD EPYC 7713 CPUs with 128 processing units each. The testing setup was the same as described in Section 3.3.

Parallel-Portfolio Baselines. Parallel-portfolio model checkers are widely adopted in hardware verification. Therefore, we also compared BTOR2-SELECT, which executes only one single selected engine, with some parallel-portfolio tools. We included super_prove [11] (at commit c7a4df4f; built with ABC at commit 806a996b[4]) in our comparison, which is an expert-designed portfolio model checker based on ABC. In addition, we evaluated the parallel-portfolio configurations of rIC3 and AVR, which were the respective winners of bitvec and array tracks in HWMCC 2024 [6]. Note that not all engines used in the portfolios of super_prove, AVR, and rIC3 were part of our performance dataset (see Section 3.3). As a result, these three baselines may have outperformed the VBS by solving additional tasks or achieving lower runtimes on certain tasks.

We also implemented a simple parallel-portfolio solver, BTOR2-PARA, which runs three verification engines in parallel. These engines were selected from the same pool used by BTOR2-SELECT, but the selection was not instance-specific, that is, the same three engines were used for all instances. To select the engines, a greedy strategy based on marginal contribution to the combined VBS was employed: starting with the SBS on the training set, we iteratively included the engine that offered the largest additional improvement to the VBS when combined with those already selected. In our experiments, the three selected engines were ABC·sc-PDR, rIC3·KI, and AVR·IC3sa for bitvec, and AVR·KI, AVR·IC3sa, and Pono·BMC for array. All parallel-portfolio baselines were allocated additional computing resources: 4 CPU cores, 3600 s of CPU time, 900 s of walltime, and 15 GB of memory.

---

[4] Due to compatibility issues, super_prove cannot be built with the ABC version in Table 1, and was executed inside an Ubuntu 22.04 container during the evaluation.

5.1 Cross-Validation Results

Feature Representation. The cross-validation results are summarized in Table 2, with all measurements averaged over four folds and accompanied by standard deviations. The WL-based models used a feature-extraction time limit of 1 s. Although extended limits of 5 s and 10 s were also evaluated, the 1-s setting consistently yielded higher validation performance and lower training time. Therefore, we report only these results in Table 2.

Table 2. 4-fold cross-validation results (superscript $^{(k)}$: number of WL iterations)

Model	Feat.	bitvec Gap closed (%) Training	bitvec Gap closed (%) Validation	bitvec Train time (min)	array Gap closed (%) Training	array Gap closed (%) Validation	array Train time (min)
	BoKW	87.5 ± 1.3	54.1 ± 14.2	2.5	87.3 ± 2.0	**74.1** ± 4.2	1.5
	WL$^{(1)}$	90.4 ± 1.2	59.7 ± 10.5	2.3	87.5 ± 1.4	72.9 ± 6.5	1.9
BTOR2-SELECT	WL$^{(2)}$	92.9 ± 1.3	60.3 ± 10.5	2.3	88.8 ± 1.4	71.3 ± 5.4	2.2
PWC-SVM	WL$^{(3)}$	94.1 ± 0.6	**61.4** ± 10.5	3.1	89.3 ± 1.3	72.7 ± 4.0	2.6
	WL$^{(4)}$	94.2 ± 0.5	58.3 ± 12.8	3.6	89.8 ± 1.3	73.6 ± 6.5	3.2
	WL$^{(5)}$	94.5 ± 0.6	56.3 ± 12.9	4.2	92.3 ± 1.5	71.6 ± 7.4	3.8
PWC-XGB	BoKW	96.1 ± 0.6	50.7 ± 6.6	4.4	93.0 ± 0.9	68.5 ± 7.3	3.6
EHM-XGB	BoKW	95.3 ± 0.4	38.7 ± 14.4	2.4	92.6 ± 1.0	55.6 ± 11.0	2.6

Our adopted method, PWC with SVM classifiers (PWC-SVM), effectively closed up to 61.4 % of the PAR-2 VBS-SBS gap on average on the `bitvec` validation set, and up to 74.1 % on the `array` set. As expected, more complex feature representations consistently improved training performance. However, these improvements did not always translate to better validation results. Overall, WL$^{(3)}$ achieved the best performance on `bitvec`, while the simple BoKW performed best on `array`. We also observe that validation performance improves with increasing WL iteration up to a certain point, after which it declines, suggesting potential overfitting.

Additionally, thanks to the simplicity of the SVM models, the selection overhead, which includes the feature extraction and ML model inference time, was relatively low. For example, the average selection overhead for the most complex PWC-SVM-WL$^{(5)}$ model was only 0.44 s on the `bitvec` validation set.

Training Scalability and Incrementality. BTOR2-SELECT is designed to be scalable and adaptable to changes in the portfolio of backend engines. The use of fast-to-train SVM classifiers keeps the overall training time manageable, even for relatively large portfolios. For the training times shown in Table 2, the majority was spent on feature extraction, which is independent of the portfolio size. The time spent on the SVM training was relatively negligible. For example, training all the SVM models for PWC-SVM-WL$^{(3)}$ took only 1.1 s. More importantly, the training process is incremental: if an BTOR2-SELECT model is already trained, adding a new engine only requires training classifiers between the new engine and the existing ones, while all previously trained classifiers remain reusable.

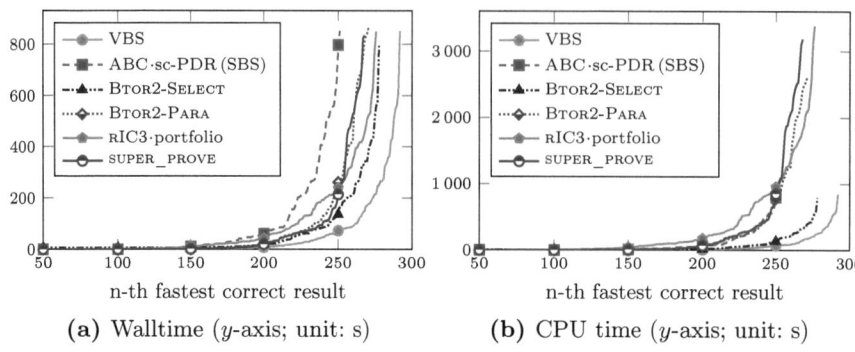

Fig. 3. Cactus plots comparing runtime on the `bitvec` test set

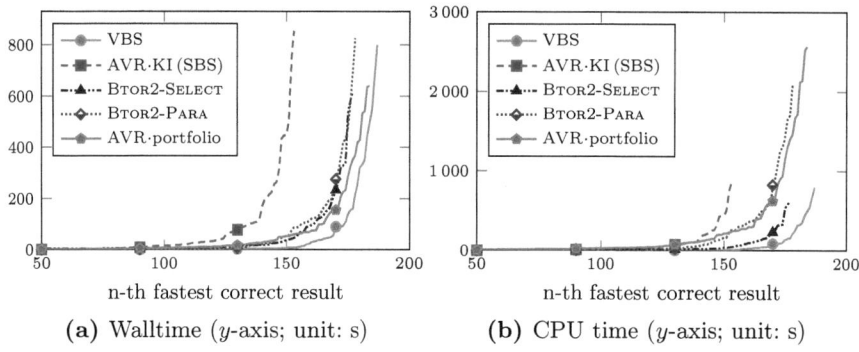

Fig. 4. Cactus plot comparing runtime on the `array` test set

Alternative Algorithm-Selection Approaches. We compared PWC-SVM with alternative methods in cross-validation. PWC-XGBoost-BoKW had higher training performance than its SVM counterpart, but its validation performance was worse. EHM-XGBoost-BoKW performed even worse on the validation set. In general, we found that more complicated ML models, such as XGBoost, were more prone to overfitting in our problem setting. Other ML models and techniques, including Random Forest [12], Deep Neural Network [30], and Principle Component Analysis [25], were also explored, but they either performed worse or showed similar overfitting patterns. Their results are omitted due to space constraints.

5.2 Test Results

We selected PWC-SVM-WL[(3)] for the `bitvec` set and PWC-SVM-BoKW for the `array` set as the final selector configurations due to their highest average cross-validation performance. The algorithm selectors were then trained on the entire training sets and integrated with the backend verification engines. Btor2-Select was evaluated using the environment and resource limits specified in Section 3.3.

Figures 3 and 4 show cactus plots comparing BTOR2-SELECT, VBS, SBS, and other parallel-portfolio baselines on the `bitvec` and `array` test sets, respectively. In each plot, a data point (x, y) indicates that there are x tasks, each of which can be solved by the respective engine within a time bound of y seconds. To improve clarity and focus on the most relevant performance range, the x-axis of each plot begins at 50. On the `bitvec` set, BTOR2-SELECT outperformed all the other baselines in terms of both the number of solved instances and the runtime. On the `array` test set, BTOR2-SELECT clearly outperformed the SBS and solved a comparable number of tasks to BTOR2-PARA but with lower runtime. Although it did not surpass AVR's parallel portfolio in terms of total number of solved instances, it was more efficient in terms of CPU time.

Notably, BTOR2-SELECT was able to close a significant portion of the VBS-SBS gap in terms of PAR-2: 65.3 % on `bitvec` set and 67.8 % on `array` set, demonstrating the effectiveness of the proposed framework.

6 Related Work, Conclusion, and Future Work

While early work relied on handcrafted heuristics [11] or expert systems [13, 27, 40] to select or tune model checkers from a portfolio of tools, ML has recently emerged as a data-driven approach for this task. A noticeable trend in this area is the shift towards more sophisticated learning representations and models. Early work in this area [20, 48, 54] usually relied on handcrafted features, more recent approaches have adopted graph kernels [46], attention mechanisms [47], and GNNs [31]. However, our work demonstrates that simple ML models can also support effective algorithm selection while mitigating overfitting, consistent with the learning-theoretical findings [2].

The work closely related to ours is PESCO [46], which uses graph kernels to represent C programs for software verification. Beyond the clear distinction that we focus on hardware model checking, BTOR2-SELECT prioritizes the practical performance boost brought by algorithm selection and an easy-to-use integrated system, while PESCO mostly focused on increasing the selection accuracy.

Built on state-of-the-art model checkers and trained on a comprehensive benchmark suite, BTOR2-SELECT demonstrates strong performance in our evaluation. With its fast and user-friendly training process, we expect BTOR2-SELECT to help practitioners easily integrate their own tool portfolios and adapt to different problem scenarios. Although BTOR2-SELECT currently supports executing only a single selected backend engine, our experiments show that it achieves wall-time performance comparable to advanced parallel-portfolio verifiers while using significantly fewer CPU resources, which is advantageous in resource-constrained environments. Future work will focus on extending BTOR2-SELECT into a parallel-portfolio verifier and investigating the interpretability of its selection decisions.

Funding Statement. This project was funded in part by the Deutsche Forschungsgemeinschaft (DFG) – 536040111 (Bridge) and the Google Summer of Code program 2024.

Data-Availability Statement. All model-checking tasks, tools, and experimental results from our evaluation are available in the reproduction package [33,34]. More information about this work is available on the supplementary webpage: https://www.sosy-lab.org/research/btor2-select/.

References

1. Hardware model-checking competition (HWMCC). https://hwmcc.github.io/. Accessed 14 Jan 2025
2. Balcan, M.F., Sandholm, T., Vitercik, E.: Generalization in portfolio-based algorithm selection. In: Proc. AAAI, vol. 35, pp. 12225–12232. AAAI Press (2021). https://doi.org/10.1609/aaai.v35i14.17451
3. Beyer, D., Chien, P.C., Jankola, M.: BENCHCLOUD: A platform for scalable performance benchmarking. In: Proc. ASE, pp. 2386–2389. ACM (2024). https://doi.org/10.1145/3691620.3695358
4. Beyer, D., Chien, P.C., Lee, N.Z.: Bridging hardware and software analysis with BTOR2C: A word-level-circuit-to-C translator. In: Sankaranarayanan, S., Sharygina, N. (eds.) TACAS 2023. LNCS, vol. 13994, pp. 152–172. Springer, Cham (2023). https://doi.org/10.1007/978-3-031-30820-8_12
5. Beyer, D., Löwe, S., Wendler, P.: Reliable benchmarking: Requirements and solutions. Int. J. Softw. Tools Technol. Transfer **21**(1), 1–29 (2017). https://doi.org/10.1007/s10009-017-0469-y
6. Biere, A., Froleyks, N., Preiner, M.: Hardware model checking competition 2024. In: Proc. FMCAD, p. 7. TU Wien Academic Press (2024). https://doi.org/10.34727/2024/isbn.978-3-85448-065-5_6
7. Biere, A., Heljanko, K., Wieringa, S.: AIGER 1.9 and beyond. Technical report, 11/2, Institute for Formal Models and Verification, Johannes Kepler University (2011). https://doi.org/10.35011/fmvtr.2011-2
8. Biere, A., Cimatti, A., Clarke, E.M., Strichman, O., Zhu, Y.: Bounded model checking. Adv. Comput. **58**, 117–148 (2003). https://doi.org/10.1016/S0065-2458(03)58003-2
9. Bradley, A.R.: SAT-based model checking without unrolling. In: Jhala, R., Schmidt, D. (eds.) VMCAI 2011. LNCS, vol. 6538, pp. 70–87. Springer, Heidelberg (2011). https://doi.org/10.1007/978-3-642-18275-4_7
10. Brayton, R., Mishchenko, A.: ABC: An academic industrial-strength verification tool. In: Touili, T., Cook, B., Jackson, P. (eds.) CAV 2010. LNCS, vol. 6174, pp. 24–40. Springer, Heidelberg (2010). https://doi.org/10.1007/978-3-642-14295-6_5
11. Brayton, R.K., Eén, N., Mishchenko, A.: Using speculation for sequential equivalence checking. In: Proc. IWLS (2012)
12. Breiman, L.: Random forests. Mach. Learn. **45**(1), 5–32 (2001). https://doi.org/10.1023/A:1010933404324
13. Cabodi, G., Nocco, S., Quer, S.: Benchmarking a model checker for algorithmic improvements and tuning for performance. Formal Methods Syst. Des. **39**(2), 205–227 (2011). https://doi.org/10.1007/S10703-011-0123-3
14. Chen, T., Guestrin, C.: XGBoost: A scalable tree boosting system. In: Proc. KDD, pp. 785–794. ACM (2016). https://doi.org/10.1145/2939672.2939785
15. Chien, P.C., Lee, N.Z., Lu, Z.: Performance dataset for hardware model checking on BTOR2 benchmarks (technical report, May 2025). Zenodo (2025). https://doi.org/10.5281/zenodo.15605218

16. Cimatti, A., Griggio, A., Mover, S., Tonetta, S.: IC3 modulo theories via implicit predicate abstraction. In: Ábrahám, E., Havelund, K. (eds.) TACAS 2014. LNCS, vol. 8413, pp. 46–61. Springer, Heidelberg (2014). https://doi.org/10.1007/978-3-642-54862-8_4
17. Clarke, E.M., Grumberg, O., Peled, D.A.: Model Checking. MIT (1999). https://mitpress.mit.edu/books/model-checking
18. Clarke, E., Kroening, D., Lerda, F.: A tool for checking ANSI-C programs. In: Jensen, K., Podelski, A. (eds.) TACAS 2004. LNCS, vol. 2988, pp. 168–176. Springer, Heidelberg (2004). https://doi.org/10.1007/978-3-540-24730-2_15
19. Cortes, C., Vapnik, V.: Support-vector networks. Mach. Learn. **20**(3), 273–297 (1995). https://doi.org/10.1007/BF00994018
20. Demyanova, Y., Pani, T., Veith, H., Zuleger, F.: Empirical software metrics for benchmarking of verification tools. Formal Methods Syst. Des. **50**(2-3), 289–316 (2017). https://doi.org/10.1007/s10703-016-0264-5
21. Eén, N., Mishchenko, A., Brayton, R.K.: Efficient implementation of property directed reachability. In: Proc. FMCAD, pp. 125–134. FMCAD Inc. (2011). https://dl.acm.org/doi/10.5555/2157654.2157675
22. Goel, A., Sakallah, K.: Model checking of Verilog RTL using IC3 with syntax-guided abstraction. In: Badger, J.M., Rozier, K.Y. (eds.) NFM 2019. LNCS, vol. 11460, pp. 166–185. Springer, Cham (2019). https://doi.org/10.1007/978-3-030-20652-9_11
23. Goel, A., Sakallah, K.: AVR: Abstractly verifying reachability. In: TACAS 2020. LNCS, vol. 12078, pp. 413–422. Springer, Cham (2020). https://doi.org/10.1007/978-3-030-45190-5_23
24. Heljanko, K.: Model checking with finite complete prefixes is PSPACE-complete. In: Palamidessi, C. (ed.) CONCUR 2000. LNCS, vol. 1877, pp. 108–122. Springer, Heidelberg (2000). https://doi.org/10.1007/3-540-44618-4_10
25. Jolliffe, I.T.: Principal Component Analysis, 1 edn. Springer, New York (1986). https://doi.org/10.1007/978-1-4757-1904-8
26. Kadioglu, S., Malitsky, Y., Sabharwal, A., Samulowitz, H., Sellmann, M.: Algorithm selection and scheduling. In: Lee, J. (ed.) CP 2011. LNCS, vol. 6876, pp. 454–469. Springer, Heidelberg (2011). https://doi.org/10.1007/978-3-642-23786-7_35
27. Kamhi, G., Fix, L., Binyamini, Z.: Symbolic model checking visualization. In: Gopalakrishnan, G., Windley, P. (eds.) FMCAD 1998. LNCS, vol. 1522, pp. 290–302. Springer, Heidelberg (1998). https://doi.org/10.1007/3-540-49519-3_19
28. Kerschke, P., Hoos, H.H., Neumann, F., Trautmann, H.: Automated algorithm selection: Survey and perspectives. Evol. Comput. **27**(1), 3–45 (2019). https://doi.org/10.1162/evco_a_00242
29. Kohavi, R.: A study of cross-validation and bootstrap for accuracy estimation and model selection. In: Proc. IJCAI, pp. 1137–1145. Morgan Kaufmann (1995). http://ijcai.org/Proceedings/95-2/Papers/016.pdf
30. LeCun, Y., Bengio, Y., Hinton, G.: Deep learning. Nature **521**(7553), 436–444 (2015). https://doi.org/10.1038/nature14539
31. Leeson, W., Dwyer, M.B.: Algorithm selection for software verification using graph neural networks. ACM Trans. Softw. Eng. Methodol. **33**(3) (2024). https://doi.org/10.1145/3637225
32. Lu, Z., Chien, P.C., Lee, N.Z., Ganesh, V.: Algorithm selection for word-level hardware model checking (student abstract). In: Proc. AAAI, vol. 39, pp. 29426–29427 (2025). https://doi.org/10.1609/aaai.v39i28.35275

33. Lu, Z., Chien, P.C., Lee, N.Z., Gurfinkel, A., Ganesh, V.: Reproduction package for CAV 2025 article 'Btor2-Select: machine learning based algorithm selection for hardware model checking'. Zenodo (2025). https://doi.org/10.5281/zenodo.15485472
34. Lu, Z., Chien, P.C., Lee, N.Z., Gurfinkel, A., Ganesh, V.: Reproduction package for CAV 2025 submission 'Btor2-Select: machine learning based algorithm selection for hardware model checking'. Zenodo (2025). https://doi.org/10.5281/zenodo.15338910
35. Lu, Z., Siemer, S., Jha, P., Day, J., Manea, F., Ganesh, V.: Layered and staged Monte Carlo tree search for SMT strategy synthesis. In: Proc. IJCAI, pp. 1907–1915. IJCAI Org (2024). https://doi.org/10.24963/ijcai.2024/211
36. Mann, M., Irfan, A., Lonsing, F., Yang, Y., Zhang, H., Brown, K., Gupta, A., Barrett, C.W.: Pono: a flexible and extensible SMT-based model checker. In: Silva, A., Leino, K. (eds.) CAV 2021. LNCS, vol. 12760, pp. 461–474. Springer, Cham (2021). https://doi.org/10.1007/978-3-030-81688-9_22
37. McMillan, K.L.: Interpolation and SAT-based model checking. In: Hunt, W.A., Somenzi, F. (eds.) CAV 2003. LNCS, vol. 2725, pp. 1–13. Springer, Heidelberg (2003). https://doi.org/10.1007/978-3-540-45069-6_1
38. Menezes, R., Aldughaim, M., Farias, B., Li, X., Manino, E., Shmarov, F., Song, K., Brauße, F., Gadelha, M.R., Tihanyi, N., Korovin, K., Cordeiro, L.: ESBMC v7.4: Harnessing the power of intervals (competition contribution). In: Finkbeiner, B., Kovács, L. (eds.) TACAS 2024. LNCS, vol. 14572, pp. 376–380. Springer, Cham (2024). https://doi.org/10.1007/978-3-031-57256-2_24
39. Mony, H., Baumgartner, J., Mishchenko, A., Brayton, R.: Speculative reduction-based scalable redundancy identification. In: Proc. DATE, pp. 1674–1679. IEEE (2009). https://doi.org/10.1109/DATE.2009.5090932
40. Mony, H., Baumgartner, J., Paruthi, V., Kanzelman, R., Kuehlmann, A.: Scalable automated verification via expert-system guided transformations. In: Hu, A.J., Martin, A.K. (eds.) FMCAD 2004. LNCS, vol. 3312, pp. 159–173. Springer, Heidelberg (2004). https://doi.org/10.1007/978-3-540-30494-4_12
41. Niemetz, A., Preiner, M., Wolf, C., Biere, A.: Source-code repository of BTOR2 tools. https://github.com/hwmcc/btor2tools. Accessed 01 May 2025
42. Niemetz, A., Preiner, M., Wolf, C., Biere, A.: BTOR2, BtorMC and Boolector 3.0. In: Chockler, H., Weissenbacher, G. (eds.) CAV 2018. LNCS, vol. 10981, pp. 587–595. Springer, Cham (2018). https://doi.org/10.1007/978-3-319-96145-3_32
43. Pedregosa, F., Varoquaux, G., Gramfort, A., Michel, V., Thirion, B., Grisel, O., Blondel, M., Prettenhofer, P., Weiss, R., Dubourg, V., Vanderplas, J., Passos, A., Cournapeau, D., Brucher, M., Perrot, M., Duchesnay, É.: Scikit-learn: Machine learning in Python. J. Mach. Learn. Res. **12**(85), 2825–2830 (2011). http://jmlr.org/papers/v12/pedregosa11a.html
44. Pimpalkhare, N., Mora, F., Polgreen, E., Seshia, S.A.: MedleySolver: Online SMT algorithm selection. In: Li, C.-M., Manyà, F. (eds.) SAT 2021. LNCS, vol. 12831, pp. 453–470. Springer, Cham (2021). https://doi.org/10.1007/978-3-030-80223-3_31
45. Preiner, M., Froleyks, N., Biere, A.: HWMCC '24 benchmarks and results. Zenodo (2024). https://doi.org/10.5281/zenodo.14156844
46. Richter, C., Hüllermeier, E., Jakobs, M.C., Wehrheim, H.: Algorithm selection for software validation based on graph kernels. Autom. Softw. Eng. **27**(1), 153–186 (2020). https://doi.org/10.1007/s10515-020-00270-x

47. Richter, C., Wehrheim, H.: Attend and represent: A novel view on algorithm selection for software verification. In: Proc. ASE, pp. 1016–1028 (2020). https://doi.org/10.1145/3324884.3416633
48. Safe, G.P., Coelho, C., Vieira, L., Val, C., Nacif, J., Fernandes, A.O.: Selection of formal verification heuristics for parallel execution. Int. J. Softw. Tools Technol. Transf. **14**(1), 95–108 (2012). https://doi.org/10.1007/S10009-011-0204-Z
49. Scott, J., Niemetz, A., Preiner, M., Nejati, S., Ganesh, V.: Algorithm selection for SMT: MachSMT: Machine learning driven algorithm selection for SMT solvers. Int. J. Softw. Tools Technol. Transfer **25**(2), 219–239 (2023). https://doi.org/10.1007/s10009-023-00696-0
50. Sheeran, M., Singh, S., Stålmarck, G.: Checking safety properties using induction and a SAT-solver. In: Hunt, W.A., Johnson, S.D. (eds.) FMCAD 2000. LNCS, vol. 1954, pp. 127–144. Springer, Heidelberg (2000). https://doi.org/10.1007/3-540-40922-X_8
51. Shervashidze, N., Schweitzer, P., van Leeuwen, E.J., Mehlhorn, K., Borgwardt, K.M.: Weisfeiler-Lehman graph kernels. J. Mach. Learn. Res. **12**, 2539–2561 (2011). https://dl.acm.org/doi/10.5555/1953048.2078187
52. Siglidis, G., Nikolentzos, G., Limnios, S., Giatsidis, C., Skianis, K., Vazirgiannis, M.: GRAKEL: A graph kernel library in Python. J. Mach. Learn. Res. **21**(54), 1–5 (2020). http://jmlr.org/papers/v21/18-370.html
53. Su, Y., Yang, Q., Ci, Y.: Predicting lemmas in generalization of IC3. In: Proc. DAC. ACM (2024). https://doi.org/10.1145/3649329.3655970
54. Tulsian, V., Kanade, A., Kumar, R., Lal, A., Nori, A.V.: MUX: Algorithm selection for software model checkers. In: Proc. MSR, pp. 132–141. ACM (2014). https://doi.org/10.1145/2597073.2597080
55. Xu, L., Hutter, F., Hoos, H.H., Leyton-Brown, K.: SATzilla: Portfolio-based algorithm selection for SAT. J. Artif. Intell. Res. **32**, 565–606 (2008). https://doi.org/10.1613/JAIR.2490
56. Xu, L., Hutter, F., Hoos, H., Leyton-Brown, K.: Evaluating component solver contributions to portfolio-based algorithm selectors. In: Cimatti, A., Sebastiani, R. (eds.) SAT 2012. LNCS, vol. 7317, pp. 228–241. Springer, Heidelberg (2012). https://doi.org/10.1007/978-3-642-31612-8_18

Open Access This chapter is licensed under the terms of the Creative Commons Attribution 4.0 International License (http://creativecommons.org/licenses/by/4.0/), which permits use, sharing, adaptation, distribution and reproduction in any medium or format, as long as you give appropriate credit to the original author(s) and the source, provide a link to the Creative Commons license and indicate if changes were made.

The images or other third party material in this chapter are included in the chapter's Creative Commons license, unless indicated otherwise in a credit line to the material. If material is not included in the chapter's Creative Commons license and your intended use is not permitted by statutory regulation or exceeds the permitted use, you will need to obtain permission directly from the copyright holder.

Cryptography and Security

Automated Verification of Consistency in Zero-Knowledge Proof Circuits

Jon Stephens[1,2](✉)[iD], Shankara Pailoor[2][iD], and Isil Dillig[1,2][iD]

[1] The University of Texas at Austin, Austin, USA
{jon,isil}@cs.utexas.edu
[2] Veridise Inc., Austin, USA
shankara@veridise.com

Abstract. Circuit languages like Circom and Gnark have become essential tools for programmable zero-knowledge cryptography, allowing developers to build privacy-preserving applications. These domain-specific languages (DSLs) encode both the computation to be verified (as a *witness generator*) and the corresponding *arithmetic circuits*, from which the prover and verifier can be automatically generated. However, for these programs to be correct, the witness generator and the arithmetic circuit need to be mutually consistent in a certain technical sense, and inconsistencies can result in security vulnerabilities. This paper formalizes the consistency requirement for circuit DSLs and proposes the first automated technique for verifying it. We evaluate the method on hundreds of real-world circuits, demonstrating its utility for both automated verification and uncovering errors that existing tools are unable to detect.

1 Introduction

Zero-knowledge (ZK) proofs are cryptographic protocols that allow a prover to convince a verifier of the truth of a statement without disclosing confidential information. These protocols have become crucial building blocks in implementing privacy-preserving applications. Recent advancements in cryptography have introduced a powerful class of *succinct* zero-knowledge proofs [1,2] that enable verification of complex computations while keeping both proof sizes and verification times minimal. This innovation has enabled a wide range of applications, including anonymous whistleblowing [3], image authentication [4], private digital transactions [5], and ensuring computational integrity in blockchains [6].

However, successfully integrating zero-knowledge proofs into an application requires developers to create two interdependent artifacts: (1) a set of constraints, formulated as polynomial equations over a finite field and (2) a *witness generator* that produces satisfying values for these constraints. Crucially, a fundamental assumption about these artifacts is that the constraints should only accept values that are produced by the witness generator. Failure to meet this requirement can lead to severe security vulnerabilities, allowing true statements to become unprovable or, even more seriously, false statements to be incorrectly verified.

To aid developers in defining these two artifacts, several domain-specific languages (DSLs) have been developed. These "circuit DSLs", such as Circom and

Gnark, streamline the process of maintaining consistency between constraints and witness generators. For example, several DSLs include constructs that allow developers to define constraints and assignments simultaneously, reducing the risk of errors. Despite these tools, inconsistencies remain a major challenge, with over 95% of known ZK vulnerabilities arising from such issues [7].

This paper aims to address these challenges by introducing a formal definition of consistency between constraints and witness computation and presenting the first automated algorithm to verify this notion of consistency in circuit DSLs. Informally, a circuit is *consistent* if its constraints accept only those witnesses generated by the witness generator. While prior work has focused on detecting specific instances of inconsistency (such as non-determinism) [8–11], none have provided an automated solution for verifying the stronger notion consistency formalized in this paper.

From a technical perspective, the consistency verification problem poses two key challenges. First, it requires proving a relational property between a witness generator and an arithmetic circuit, which oftentimes defines non-linear finite field equations that tend to challenge SMT solvers. Second, both of these artifacts are typically derived from *templates* containing arrays and complex loops, necessitating the inference of complex quantified loop invariants.

This paper tackles the consistency verification problem through a two-step approach. First, given a *product program* that simultaneously performs constraint generation and witness construction, our approach uses lightweight static reasoning to infer pair-wise equivalences between array elements and simplifies the initial product program as much as possible. In the subsequent verification step, our method infers more complicated quantified invariants over arrays to discharge the verification conditions needed for proving equivalence.

We have implemented our method in a tool called ZEQUAL, which verifies consistency of circuit templates written in Circom, a widely-used circuit DSL and the target language of several other ZK circuit verifiers and bug-finding tools in prior literature [8–10,12]. We evaluate ZEQUAL on hundreds of real-world benchmarks taken from popular projects and show that ZEQUAL can verify consistency in a majority of these templates. We also demonstrate that ZEQUAL is capable of finding bugs that cannot be detected using prior methods.

To summarize, contributions of this paper include: (1) a formal definition of the *consistency verification problem* for ZK circuits; (2) first automated technique for verifying consistency of ZK circuit templates; (3) evaluation of the method on several hundred real-world circuit templates.

2 Background

Zero-Knowledge Proofs (ZKPs) are protocols that allow a prover to demonstrate the truth of a statement to a verifier without revealing any additional information beyond the statement's validity. Traditionally, ZKPs were developed for specific statements such as the three-coloring problem or graph isomorphism; however, new advancements in Programmable ZKP have enabled greater flexibility.

For example, proof frameworks like zk-SNARKs [1] or zk-STARKs [2] can generate verifiable proofs that $P(x) = y$ for some computation P and private input x. A key property of programmable ZKPs is that a prover and verifier can be automatically generated from a set of polynomial equations over a finite field $\mathcal{F}_p$. The variables in these equations are referred to as signals, and addition and multiplication are performed modulo a large prime p. The details of how the prover and verifier are generated are beyond the scope of this paper, but we refer the interested reader to [1,13,14] for additional background.

Once the prover and verifier are set up, proofs are generated and verified as illustrated in Fig. 1. The process begins with the witness generator, a program that produces a *witness*—a mapping of signals to values that satisfy the constraints. Conceptually, the witness generator executes the computation P for which the user seeks to prove correctness. The prover then uses this witness, along with the constraints, to generate a proof, which is sent to the verifier. Crucially, the proof conceals the values of all private signals. The verifier receives the proof and only the *public* values, verifying its correctness or rejecting it. Notably, witnesses do not need to be generated solely by running the witness generator; any satisfying assignment to the constraints can produce a verifiable proof. As a result, it is essential that the constraints accurately reflect the intended computation and align with the witness generator. Inconsistencies between these artifacts could lead to invalid proofs being accepted or valid computations failing to produce verifiable proofs. Indeed, most security vulnerabilities in real-world implementations of these protocols stem from such inconsistencies [7].

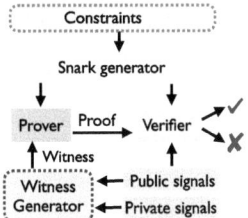

Fig. 1. ZK workflow.

Circom DSL. Manually encoding a computation as a set of constraints is a time-consuming and error-prone task. To address these challenges, several domain-specific languages have been developed [15–17], with Circom being one of the most popular [16]. Circom allows developers to specify the witness generation logic and constraints in a unified language (with concepts similar to a hardware description language (HDL)), and the compiler automatically generates the witness generator along with the constraints. Tools like SnarkJS [18] can then be used to generate the prover and verifier from these constraints.

A Circom program consists of a list of *templates* with one template distinguished as the entry point. A template is similar to a sub-circuit module in a HDL as it defines a reusable block of code that is instantiated upon invocation by connecting the declared input and output signals within the caller. All output signals in Circom are public and other signals are private by default unless otherwise specified. Witness generation is expressed using the `<--` and `-->` operators for signal assignment, while the `===` operator expresses constraints. Additionally, the `==>` and `<==` operators can be used to combine assignment and constraint declaration when the left and right hand sides are polynomials, helping developers maintain consistency between computation and constraints.

```
1  template MultiMux() {
2     signal input x[5]; // Constants
3     signal input y[5]; // Constants
4     signal input s; // Selector
5     signal output out[5];
6     for (var i=0; i<5; i++) {
7        out[i] <== (x[i] - y[i])*s + x[i];
8     }
9  }
```

```
1  template IsZero() {
2     signal input in;
3     signal output out;
4     signal inv;
5     inv <-- in!=0 ? 1/in : 0;
6     out <== -in*inv +1;
7     in*out === 0; }
```

Fig. 2. Examples of Circom templates.

```
1  template Divide() {
2     signal input numerator, denominator;
3     signal output remainder, quotient;
4     isZero := IsZero();
5     isZero.in <== denominator;
6     isZero.out === 0; // ensure denominator is non-zero
7     remainder <-- numerator % denominator;
8     quotient <-- numerator \ denominator;
9     numerator === denominator * quotient + remainder;
10 }
```

```
1  template Reward() {
2
3     signal input inp;
4     signal output out;
5     var gwei = 10 ** 6;
6     out <-- inp \ gwei;
7     out * gwei === inp;
8  }
9
```

Fig. 3. Non-determinism bug on left; inconsistency bug on right.

For example, the program on the left in Fig. 2 only performs addition and multiplication over signals—operations that are directly expressible as polynomials over finite fields. As such, it is able to exclusively use the <== operator, keeping the witness generation and constraints consistent. In contrast, the program in Fig. 2(b) does not use the <== operator because comparisons cannot be expressed directly as polynomials. Instead, the corresponding constraints utilize an intermediate signal, inv, relying on the field axiom that every nonzero element has a multiplicative inverse.

Circuit Bugs. Languages like Circom help developers maintain consistency between witness generation and constraints, but implementations often contain bugs due to discrepancies. A common issue, known as "Unintended Nondeterminism" or "Underconstrained Circuits", arises when constraints $C(in, out)$ allow multiple outputs o and o' for the same input i. The program on the left of Fig. 3 provides an example of a nondeterminism bug: the template takes a numerator and denominator as inputs and returns the quotient and remainder. The witness generation code performs this logic directly using the integer division operator \ and the modulo operator %. However, the constraints only assert that quotient * numerator + remainder = numerator, lacking a crucial check that the remainder is *less than* the denominator when interpreted as integers. Without this check, there are multiple solutions for a given input.

However, not all discrepancies manifest themselves as nondeterminism bugs: constraints can be deterministic, yet their satisfying assignments may still diverge from the witness values, as illustrated on the right of Fig. 3[1]. This program takes an input currency amount inp, and the witness generator returns

---

[1] This example was taken from [9] and is a simplified version of a bug found in a real-world closed-source project.

a reward out by dividing inp by a constant gwei using integer division. Here, the computation and constraints only align when inp is a multiple of gwei but diverge in all other cases. For instance, if inp is 1, the witness will assign out to 0, while the satisfying assignment for the constraints sets out to $gwei^{-1}$. This results in the output (as defined by the constraints) being even larger than the input, which could allow gaining more reward than intended.

```
1 template DecomposeProduct(N) {
2   signal input u8_xs[N], u8_ys[N];
3   signal u16s[N];
4   signal output high[N], low[N];
5   component bits_low[N], bits_high[N];
6
7   for (var i = 0; i < N; i++) {
8     u16s[i] <== u8_xs[i] * u8_ys[i];
9     low[i] <- u16s[i] % 0x100;
10    bits_low[i] = Num2Bits(8);
11    bits_low[i].in <== low[i];
12    high[i] <- (u16s[i] \ 0x100) % 0x100;
13    bits_high[i] = Num2Bits(8);
14    bits_high[i].in <== high[i];
15    u16s[i] === low[i] + 0x100 * high[i];
16  }
17 }
```

Fig. 4. Code for motivating example

```
1 template DecomposeProduct_Expanded(N) {
2   signal input u8_xs[N], u8_ys[N];
3   signal u16s_w[N], u16s_c[N];
4   signal output high_w[N], high_c[N];
5   signal output low_w[N], low_c[N];
6   component bits_low[N], bits_high[N];
7
8   for (var i = 0; i < N; i++) {
9     u16s_w[i] <- u8_xs[i] * u8_ys[i];
10    u16s_c[i] === u8_xs[i] * u8_ys[i];
11    low_w[i] <- u16s_w[i] % 0x100;
12    bits_low[i] = Num2Bits(8);
13    bits_low[i].in_w <- low_w[i];
14    bits_low[i].in_c === low_c[i];
15    high_w[i] <- (u16s_w[i] \ 0x100) % 0x100;
16    bits_high[i] = Num2Bits(8);
17    bits_high[i].in_w <- high_w[i];
18    bits_high[i].in_c === high_c[i];
19    u16s_c[i] === low_c[i] + 0x100 * high_c[i];
20  }
21 }
```

Fig. 5. Product program

3 Motivating Example

Figure 4 presents a Circom template which takes two arrays, u8_xs and u8_ys of length N, each containing field elements whose integer representation is an unsigned 8-bit integer. The template computes the element-wise product, capturing the result as 16-bit unsigned integers in u16s. Each entry in u16s is then decomposed into two output arrays, low and high, which store the lower and higher 8 bits, respectively.

At first glance, it is not immediately obvious why the witness generator and the constraints expressed by this program align with each other. For instance, the witness generator computes the low and high bytes in a standard way using integer division and the modulo operator (lines 9, 12), whereas the constraints enforce this decomposition at the bit level, validating each byte component individually through binary representations (Num2Bits) (lines 10, 13). Given the nontrivial differences between the witness generator and the constraints, establishing their equivalence over all possible template instantiations is challenging. In the following discussion, we explain the key ideas that enable ZEQUAL to perform verification successfully, along with the observations that inspired these ideas.

Observation #1: *Many circuit DSLs provide a "pseudo-product-program" with good alignment.* A common approach to verifying equivalence is to reduce the relational verification task to checking assertions in a *product program* [19]. A crucial step in this reduction is establishing a suitable *alignment*—a mapping that pairs corresponding operations between the two programs. In general-purpose languages, achieving this alignment can be difficult because the program structures may differ significantly.

Fortunately, circuit DSLs like Circom, Gnark, and Zirgen implicitly define a "pseudo-product-program" with good alignment where corresponding operations between the witness and constraint components are grouped within the same basic block. We call this a *pseudo-product* because it uses the *same variables* to represent signals in both the constraints and the witness generator even when they may *not* be equivalent. Hence, in order to instrument the program with suitable assertions that ensure equivalence, our method modifies the Circom program by introducing two copies s_c, s_w for each (non-input) signal. For instance, as shown in Fig. 5, high[N] is replaced with two arrays high_w[N] and high_c[N] denoting the constraint and witness generation components respectively.

Observation #2: *Lightweight static analysis can help infer pair-wise equivalence between signals, simplifying the verification task.* As mentioned in Sect. 2, circuit DSLs often include constructs that generate equivalent witness generation logic and constraints from a single statement. For instance, in Circom, the statement x <== e serves as shorthand for both the assignment x <-- e and the constraint x === e. Other circuit languages also have similar features.[2]

This duality between witness generator logic and constraints is commonly leveraged by circuit developers to maintain consistency across the two artifacts. This makes it feasible to infer pair-wise equality between the two copies s_c, s_w of a signal s through *lightweight static analysis* of the product program. For example, at line 9 of Fig. 5, u16s_w[i] is assigned to some expression e and line 10 includes constraint u16s_c[i] === e using the same expression e. Because e only involves input signals, we can conclude that u16s_w[i] and u16s_c[i] are pair-wise equivalent and then propagate this information to potentially prove equivalence of more signals. Finally, for any pair of signals proven equivalent, we can simplify the product program by deleting assignments and replacing the two copies of a signal with a single variable. In this example, we can delete the assignment at line 9 and replace u16s_w and u16s_c with a single variable u16s.

Observation #3: *Invariants needed for verification often have a particular shape.* After simplifying the product program, our approach instruments it with assumptions and assertions (see Fig. 6) and tries to discharge the latter. However, because circuit programs often contain loops, ZEQUAL needs to synthesize quantified array invariants. While this is a challenging problem in general, most required invariants involve predicates of the form $\forall \bar{i}.\ \phi(\bar{i}) \to s_w[f(\bar{i})] = s_c[f(\bar{i})]$ where ϕ is a guard predicate over the loop counters and f is an arithmetic function. Our method generates candidate invariants of this shape through static

---

[2] For example, in Gnark and Cairo, every operation, *by default*, is translated both into a statement (in the witness generator) and a field equation; when this is not possible, the developer needs to employ so-called "hints". Similarly, in Zirgen, computation performed in a component generates equivalent witness generator logic and constraints while computation performed in an extern is only performed in the witness generator.

```
1 template DecomposeProduct_Instrumented(N) {
2     signal input u8_xs[N], u8_ys[N];
3     signal u16s[N];
4     signal output high_w[N], high_c[N];
5     signal output low_w[N], low_c[N];
6     component bits_low[N], bits_high[N];
7
8     for (var i = 0; i < N; i++) {
9         assume(u16s[i] = u8_xs[i]*u8_ys[i]);
10        low_w[i] <- u16s_w[i] % 0x100;
11        bits_low[i] = Num2Bits(8);
12        bits_low[i].in_w <- low_w[i];
13        assume(bits_low[i].in_c = low_c[i]);
14        assert(bits_low[i].in_w = low_w[i]);
15        high_w[i] <- (u16s_w[i] \ 0x100) % 0x100;
16        bits_high[i] = Num2Bits(8);
17        bits_high[i].in_w <- high_w[i];
18        assume(bits_high[i].in_c = high_c[i]);
19        assert(bits_low[i].in_w = low_w[i]);
20        assume(u16s[i] = low_c[i] + 0x100 * high_c[i]);
21        assert(u16s[i] = low_w[i] + 0x100 * high_w[i]);
22    }
23    assert(low_w = low_c && high_w = high_c);
24 }
```

Fig. 6. Instrumented product

analysis and computes the strongest conjunction over this universe of predicates through monomial predicate abstraction [20]. For our example, the following invariant is sufficient for successful verification:

$$\forall x.\ 0 \leq x < i \leq N \rightarrow (\text{low\_w}[x] = \text{low\_c}[x] \wedge \text{high\_w}[x] = \text{high\_c}[x])$$

4 Problem Statement

In this paper, we adopt a formalization that captures commonalities between most circuit DSLs, such as Circom [16], Gnark [15], Zirgen [21], and Zokrates [22].

Definition 1 (Circuit program). *A ZK circuit program P is a tuple $(\Gamma, \mathcal{F}_p, \Phi, \omega)$ where:*

- Γ *is a set of signal declarations $s : \tau$, where $\tau \in \{\text{In}, \text{Out}, \text{Temp}\}$;*
- $\mathcal{F}_p$ *is the prime field of the circuit – i.e., $s \in \mathcal{F}_p$ for any signal s;*
- *Constraint Φ is a formula in the theory of finite fields [23]. The precise language for such formulas is shown on the left side of Fig. 7.*
- *Witness computation ω is a loop-free program over signals in Γ. The language for expressing witness computation is shown on the right side of Fig. 7.*

Given a program $P = (\Gamma, \mathcal{F}_p, \Phi, \omega)$, we write P_Φ, P_ω to denote Φ and ω respectively, and, for a signal s, $\Gamma(s)$ denotes the type of s. We refer to signals of type Ins, Out, and Temp as input, output, and intermediate signals respectively. Witness computation ω can *only* perform assignments to output and intermediate signals but never to inputs. Furthermore, ω can never perform multiple assignments to the same signal within the same execution.

$$\begin{aligned}&\text{Constraints } \Phi ::= \Phi_1 \wedge \Phi_2 \mid P_1 == P_2\\&\text{Polynomial } P ::= P_1 + P_2\\&\qquad\qquad\quad\mid P_1 * P_2 \mid s \mid c\end{aligned}$$

$$\begin{aligned}&\text{Program } \omega \quad ::= s \leftarrow E \mid \omega_1;\omega_2\\&\qquad\qquad\qquad\mid \text{if}(C)\ \omega_1\ \text{else}\ \omega_2\\&\text{Conditional } C ::= E_1 \otimes E_2 \mid \neg C\\&\text{Expression } E \ ::= E_1 \oplus E_2 \mid s \mid c \mid E^{-1}\end{aligned}$$

Fig. 7. (Left) Arithmetic circuit DSL. P is a polynomial equation over a finite field $\mathcal{F}_p$. (Right) Witness generation DSL over $\mathcal{F}_p$. E^{-1} computes the multiplicative inverse of E, and $\oplus, \otimes$ denote arithmetic and logical operators respectively.

The semantics of ZK circuit programs are defined over *signal valuations* σ that map signals to concrete values. The output of a program is a tuple (b, σ') where b is a boolean and σ' is the output valuation. Given a program $P = (\Gamma, \mathcal{F}_p, \Phi, \omega)$ we write $(\sigma, P) \Downarrow (b, \sigma')$ iff $[\![\Phi]\!](\sigma)$ evaluates to b and executing ω on σ yields new environment σ'. Next, we define a notion of *agreement* between the witness computation and constraint in ZK circuit programs.

Definition 2 (Agreement). *Let $P = (\Gamma, \mathcal{F}_p, \Phi, \omega)$ be a program and let σ be a signal valuation such that $(\sigma, P) \Downarrow (b, \sigma')$. We say that constraint Φ and witness computation ω agree on σ, denoted $\sigma \vdash \Phi \sim \omega$, iff the following holds:*

$$b \rightarrow ([\![\Phi]\!](\sigma') \wedge \forall (s : \mathsf{Out}) \in \Gamma.\ \sigma(s) = \sigma'(s)) \tag{1}$$

According to this definition, if the constraint Φ "accepts" some valuation σ (meaning b is true), then (1) the output valuation σ' produced by the witness generator should also be accepted by Φ, and (2) the two valuations σ and σ' should agree on the values of all output signals. In other words, if a given witness σ with inputs I is accepted by the constraints Φ, then the witness generator ω should also be able to produce a satisfying witness σ' with the same inputs I such that the output signals in σ and σ' match. This ensures that the constraints will only accept valuations that are produced by the witness generator, which in turn captures the desired behavior of a ZK circuit program.

Definition 3 (Consistency). *Let $P = (\Gamma, \mathcal{F}_p, \Phi, \omega)$ be a ZK circuit program. P is correct iff for all $\sigma \in \mathcal{F}_p^{|\Gamma|}$, we have $\sigma \vdash \Phi \sim \omega$.*

The definition of consistency expresses the desired notion of correctness as it states that the constraint Φ agrees with the witness computation function ω for all possible signal valuations. This definition is similar to the definition of *strong safety* from prior work [16]. In particular, strong safety states that for every input to the circuit, (a) there is exactly one solution to the constraints and (b) that solution is equal to the witness produced by the witness generator on that input. However, we note that *strong safety* is too strong a requirement in practice: for many real world circuits, there can be multiple witnesses that satisfy the constraints which disagree on their assignment to the *intermediate signals* but agree on their assignments to the output signals. In contrast, our notion of consistency allows the two witnesses to disagree on the assignment to intermediate signals as long as both witnesses satisfy the constraints.

```
Skeleton  𝒫 ::= D; S
Var Decl  D ::= var v[E]; | D₁; D₂
Statement S ::= □ᵢ | v ← E | S₁; S₂ | if(C) S₁ else S₂ | while(C) S
Expression E ::= E₁ ⊕ E₂ | s | v | α | E₁[E₂] | c
Conditional C ::= E₁ ⊗ E₂ | ¬C
```

Fig. 8. Template syntax. c, s, v, α denote constants, signals, variables, and parameters respectively where $\oplus \in \{+, -, *, /, \&, |\}$ and $\otimes \in \{\leq, <, >, \geq, \neq, =\}$. Holes are instantiated with terms from Figs. 9 and 10.

```
Constraint  φ  ::= E₁' == E₂'
Expression  E' ::= s | v | α | c | E₁'[E₂']
                 | E₁' + E₂' | E₁' * E₂'
```

Fig. 9. Constraint DSL

```
Assignments   A ::= L ← E | A; A
LHS Expression L ::= s | L[E]
```

Fig. 10. Witness DSL

ZK Circuit Templates. While ZK circuit programs cannot contain unbounded constraints or computation, many DSLs *do* allow developers to implement *templates* containing loops as long as these templates can be instantiated to ZK circuit programs at *compile time*. However, in general, it is often desirable to reason about the correctness of the template itself rather than its specific instantiations. For example, many libraries provide circuit templates that are instantiated by clients of that library, so reasoning about the correctness of a library in isolation requires the ability to reason about template correctness. Thus, we also generalize our formalization to circuit templates as follows.

Definition 4 (Template). *A template* $\mathcal{T}$ *is a tuple* $(V, \Gamma, \mathcal{F}_p, \mathcal{P}, , \sum_\omega)$ *where:*

- V *is a set of template parameters;*
- Γ *is a set of signal declarations* $s : \tau$, *and* $\mathcal{F}_p$ *is the prime field for the circuit;*
- $\mathcal{P}$ *is a program with holes belonging to the syntax of Fig. 8;*
- *is a mapping from holes in* $\mathcal{P}$ *to constraints, as defined in Fig. 9;*
- $\sum_\omega$ *is a mapping from holes in* $\mathcal{P}$ *to statements, as defined in Fig. 10*

We refer to $\mathcal{P}[]$ as a constraint template and $\mathcal{P}[\sum_\omega]$ as a witness template.

Template parameters $\alpha \in V$ are instantiated at compile-time; thus, they can never be modified. Signals can have type $\mathsf{Array}(\tau)$, and we refer to a type τ as an *input type*, denoted $\mathsf{IsInput}(\tau)$, if $\tau = \mathsf{Ins}$ or $\tau = \mathsf{Array}(\tau')$ and $\mathsf{IsInput}(\tau')$.

In most DSLs, the constraint and witness templates are required to have the same control flow structure; thus, we represent them using a shared *control-flow skeleton* $\mathcal{P}$. As shown in Fig. 8, the skeleton involves loops, conditionals, constants, and importantly, *mutable* data variables denoted v. Typically, data variables are used as loop counters and for configuring different parts of the circuit. The constraint and witness templates are obtained by filling the holes in the shared control-flow skeleton with constraints (Fig. 9) or statements that manipulate signals (Fig. 10) respectively. Statements in the witness DSL can

```
 1: procedure VERIFYCIRCUITTEMPLATE(T)
    input: A ZK circuit template T = (V, Γ, F_p, P, , Σ_ω)
 2:   # Step 1: Construct product of circuit and witness programs
 3:   S ← {s | (s : τ) ∈ Γ, ¬IsInput(τ)}
 4:   P_⊗ ← P[{(□_i ↦ A_i[S_w/S]; φ_i[S_c/S]) | [□_i] = φ_i ∧ Σ_ω[□_i] = A_i}]
 5:   # Step 2: Perform static analysis to simplify P_⊗ into P_⋆
 6:   E ← INFEREQUIVALENCES(P_⊗, S)
 7:   P_⋆ ← SIMPLIFY(P_⊗, E)
 8:   # Step 3: Verify product program
 9:   P_I ← INSTRUMENT(P_⋆)
10:   return VERIFYPRODUCT(P_I)
```

Fig. 11. Top-level algorithm. Given signals S, we write S_x to denote $\{v_x | v \in S\}$

only perform assignments to signals, but not to data variables, which can only be modified in the shared control-flow skeleton.

Definition 5 (Instantiation). *A template instantiation is a pair* (T, ν) *where* T *is a template, and* ν *maps template parameters* V *to values in* $\mathcal{F}_p$, *and* $(T, \nu) \hookrightarrow P$ *indicates that* P *is the ZK circuit program obtained by evaluating* T *under* ν.

Definition 6 (Correctness of template). *A ZK circuit template* T *is correct if, for every* ν *such that* $(T, \nu) \hookrightarrow P$, P *is correct according to Definition 3.*

5 Verification Algorithm

Figure 11 shows our top-level algorithm for verifying the correctness of a circuit template. The algorithm starts by constructing a *product program* [19] that encodes the simultaneous execution of both the witness template $\mathcal{P}[\Sigma_\omega]$ and the constraint template $\mathcal{P}[]$ (lines 3–4). Because circuit languages force programmers to write constraint and witness templates with the same shared control-flow structure, constructing a suitable product program is very easy: We introduce two different copies S_c, S_w of the *non-input* signals and replace each hole $\square_i$ in $\mathcal{P}$ with $A_i[S_w/S]; \phi_i[S_c/S]$ where $A_i = \Sigma_\omega[\square_i]$ and $\phi_i = [\square_i]$.

The second step of the algorithm statically analyzes the constructed product program $\mathcal{P}_\otimes$ and tries to infer invariants of the form $s_c = s_w$ establishing that two copies of the same signal s have the same value. If so, we can treat signal s as an input signal after deleting all assignments to s_w and renaming the different copies s_c and s_w in $\mathcal{P}_\otimes$ both as s (performed by SIMPLIFY at line 7). Finally, the algorithm instruments the resulting program to contain suitable assertions and assumptions by calling INSTRUMENT at line 9 and attempts to discharge the assertions by calling VERIFYPRODUCT at line 10.

Assumptions. The rest of this section assumes that all signals and data variables are modeled as (possibly flattened) single-dimensional arrays. Following existing circuit languages, we also disallow multiple assignments to signals.

```
1: procedure INFEREQUIVALENCES(P_⊗, S)
2:     Σ ← CONSTRUCTSYMBOLICSTORE(P_⊗);   ℰ ← ∅
3:     for s ∈ S do
4:         if ISEQUIVALENT(Σ, s_w, s_c) then ℰ ← ℰ ∪ {s}
5:     return ℰ
```

Fig. 12. Algorithm for inferring equivalent signals

$$\frac{\varsigma \text{ fresh variable}}{\Sigma \vdash \star : \varsigma} \text{(UNKNOWN)} \qquad \frac{\Sigma \vdash E : \varphi \quad (v, \varphi) \in dom(\Sigma)}{\Sigma \vdash v[E] : \Sigma(v, \varphi)} \text{(ARR-1)}$$

$$\frac{\Sigma \vdash E : \varphi \quad (v, \varphi) \notin dom(\Sigma) \quad \neg \mathsf{IsInput}(v) \quad \Sigma \vdash \star : \varphi'}{\Sigma \vdash v[E] : \varphi'} \text{(ARR-2)} \qquad \frac{\Sigma \vdash E : \varphi \quad (v, \varphi) \notin dom(\Sigma) \quad \mathsf{IsInput}(v)}{\Sigma \vdash v[E] : v[\varphi]} \text{(ARR-3)}$$

$$\frac{\mathsf{IsConst}(E) \vee \mathsf{IsTemplParam}(E)}{\Sigma \vdash E : E} \text{(BASIC)} \qquad \frac{\Sigma \vdash E_i : \varphi_i}{\Sigma \vdash f(E_1, \ldots, E_n) : f(\varphi_1, \ldots, \varphi_n)} \text{(ARITH)}$$

Fig. 13. Look-up rules. Every application of Unknown produces a fresh variable.

5.1 Inference of Equivalent Signals via Static Analysis

In this section, we present the INFEREQUIVALENCES algorithm from Fig. 12, which uses lightweight static analysis to infer equivalent signal pairs $(s_c, s_w) \in (S_w \times S_c)$. The algorithm first constructs a so-called *symbolic store* Σ to represent values of array elements as symbolic expressions over the inputs (line 2) and then checks pair-wise equality between them (line 4). The symbolic expressions φ in our analysis are defined by the grammar:

$$\varphi := \alpha \mid c \mid \varsigma \mid s_{in}[\varphi] \mid \varphi \oplus \varphi$$

Here, s_{in} is an input signal, α a template parameter, c a constant, ς an unknown, and $\oplus$ an arithmetic operator. Symbolic expressions represent immutable values, ensuring that syntactically identical expressions are equal. To improve precision and enable relational reasoning, fresh variables ς are used to represent unknowns instead of the standard top element $\top$ in abstract interpretation. For a symbolic expression φ, Unknown(φ) indicates that it corresponds to a fresh variable ς.

The symbolic store Σ maps array elements (v, φ) to symbolic expressions, where v is a signal or data variable, and φ represents an array index. For instance, $(s_w, 0) \mapsto s_{in}[1]$ indicates that index 0 of s_w is (transitively) assigned to the second element of s_{in}. Figure 14 defines a flow-sensitive analysis for constructing Σ, using lookup rules from Fig. 13 to perform on-demand initialization of input arrays, as their sizes are not statically known. In Fig. 14, the rule ASGN-SIG processes assignments to *signals*, updating the entry (s_w, φ_1) with φ_2 via a *strong update* [24], since circuit languages ensure signals are assigned only once. For data variables, the ASGN-VAR rule adopts a conservative approach, handling potential aliasing by updating (v, φ) and invalidating other entries (v, φ_i) that might alias φ. The CSTR rule tracks equality constraints on signals s_c. The final

$$\frac{\Sigma \vdash E_1 : \varphi_1 \quad \Sigma \vdash E_2 : \varphi_2}{\Sigma \vdash s_w[E_1] \leftarrow E_2 : \Sigma[(s_w, \varphi_1) \leftarrow \varphi_2]}(\text{Asgn-Sig})$$

$$\frac{\Sigma \vdash \star : \varphi'}{\Sigma \vdash \mathsf{Havoc}(v, \varphi) : \Sigma[(v, \varphi) \leftarrow \varphi']}(\text{Havoc})$$

$$\frac{\begin{array}{c}\Sigma \vdash E_1 : \varphi \quad \Sigma \vdash E_2 : \varphi' \\ \Theta = \{(\varphi_i \mid (v, \varphi) \in \mathsf{Dom}(\Sigma) \wedge \mathsf{SAT}(\varphi = \varphi_i)\} \\ \Sigma \vdash \mathsf{Havoc}(v, \varphi_1); \ldots; \mathsf{Havoc}(v, \varphi_{|\Theta|}) : \Sigma'\end{array}}{\Sigma \vdash v[E_1] \leftarrow E_2 : \Sigma'[(v, \varphi) \leftarrow \varphi']}(\text{Asgn-Var})$$

$$\frac{\Sigma \vdash E : \varphi \quad \Sigma \vdash E' : \varphi' \quad \Sigma' = \Sigma[(s_c, \varphi) \leftarrow \varphi']}{\Sigma \vdash s_c[E] == E' : \Sigma'}(\text{Cstr})$$

$$\frac{\Sigma \vdash S_1 : \Sigma_1 \quad \Sigma_1 \vdash S_2 : \Sigma_2}{\Sigma \vdash S_1; S_2 : \Sigma_2}(\text{Seq}) \quad \frac{\Sigma \vdash S_1 : \Sigma_1 \quad \Sigma \vdash S_2 : \Sigma_2 \quad \Sigma' \leftarrow \Sigma_1 \sqcup \Sigma_2}{\Sigma \vdash \mathsf{if}(C)\ S_1\ \mathsf{else}\ S_2 : \Sigma'}(\text{If}) \quad \frac{\Sigma \sqsubseteq \Sigma_1 \quad \Sigma_1 \vdash S : \Sigma_2 \quad \Sigma_2 \sqsubseteq \Sigma_1}{\Sigma \vdash \mathsf{while}(C)\ S : \Sigma_1}(\text{While})$$

Fig. 14. Symbolic store construction. $\Sigma_1 \subseteq \Sigma_2$ holds if, for all elements $(v, \varphi) \in \mathsf{Dom}(\Sigma_1), \Sigma_1(v, \varphi)$. $\varphi_1 \subseteq \varphi_2$ holds if $\varphi_1 = \varphi_2$ or $\mathsf{Unknown}(\varphi_2)$.

$$\frac{\varphi_1 = \varphi_2}{\varphi_1 \sqcup \varphi_2 = \varphi_1}(\text{SymExp-1}) \quad \frac{\varphi_1 \neq \varphi_2 \quad \Sigma \vdash \star : \varphi}{\varphi_1 \sqcup \varphi_2 : \varphi}(\text{SymExp-2})$$

$$\frac{(v, \varphi) \notin \mathsf{Dom}(\Sigma_i) \quad \Sigma_i \vdash \star : \varphi'}{(\Sigma_1 \sqcup \Sigma_2)[(v, \varphi)] = \varphi'}(\text{One}) \quad \frac{(v, \varphi) \in \mathsf{Dom}(\Sigma) \cap \mathsf{Dom}(\Sigma')}{(\Sigma \sqcup \Sigma')[(v, \varphi)] = \Sigma[(v, \varphi)] \sqcup \Sigma'[(v, \varphi)]}(\text{Both})$$

Fig. 15. Rules defining join operation on symbolic stores

three rules handle sequencing, conditionals, and loops, where the join operator is defined in Fig. 15. Finally, the WHILE rule requires the symbolic store Σ_1 to be a fixed-point solution for the loop.

Once the symbolic store is constructed, the IsEQUIVALENT procedure (summarized in Fig. 16) uses these symbolic expressions to deduce that two signals s_c, s_w are equivalent, denoted $\Sigma \vdash s_c \sim s_w$. According to Fig. 16, signals s_c, s_w are equivalent if (a) they have the same set of written indices and (b) their values at these indices are equal. Here, we use the notation $\varphi \equiv \varphi'$ to indicate that φ and φ' are equivalent expressions (e.g., $\alpha + 1 \equiv 1 + \alpha$). The theorems stating the soundness of our analysis can be found in the extended version of the paper [25], along with their proofs.

$$\frac{\forall (s_w, \varphi) \in dom(\Sigma).\ \exists (s_c, \varphi') \in dom(\Sigma).\ \varphi \equiv \varphi' \wedge \Sigma(s_c, \varphi) \equiv \Sigma(s_w, \varphi)}{\forall (s_c, \varphi) \in dom(\Sigma).\ \exists (s_w, \varphi') \in dom(\Sigma).\ \varphi \equiv \varphi' \wedge \Sigma(s_w, \varphi) \equiv \Sigma(s_c, \varphi)}(\text{Sig-Equiv})$$
$$\Sigma \vdash s_c \sim s_w$$

Fig. 16. Rule describing the IsEquivalent procedure

$$\frac{S = \{s \mid s \in \mathsf{Sigs}(E) \land s \in \mathcal{E}\}}{\mathcal{E} \vdash E \rightsquigarrow E[S/S_c, S/S_w]} \text{ (S-Expr)} \quad \frac{s \in \mathcal{E}}{\mathcal{E} \vdash s[E_1] \leftarrow E_2 \rightsquigarrow \mathsf{skip}} \text{ (S-Asg1)}$$

$$\frac{s \notin \mathcal{E} \quad \mathcal{E} \vdash E_1 \rightsquigarrow E_1' \quad \mathcal{E} \vdash E_2 \rightsquigarrow E_2'}{\mathcal{E} \vdash s[E_1] \leftarrow E_2 \rightsquigarrow s[E_1'] \leftarrow s[E_2']} \text{ (S-Asg2)}$$

Fig. 17. SIMPLIFY procedure. $\mathsf{Sigs}(E)$ returns the normalized (i.e., without c, w subscripts) versions of the signals in E. We omit the trivial rules (e.g., for sequencing).

5.2 Product Program Simplification and Instrumentation

The next step in the algorithm uses the static analysis results to simplify the product program. Figure 17 presents the SIMPLIFY procedure as inference rules $\mathcal{E} \vdash S \to S'$, where S simplifies to S' under inferred equivalences $\mathcal{E}$. The procedure deletes assignments like $s_w[E] \leftarrow E$ if s_w and s_c are equivalent (S-Asg1) and substitutes all occurrences of s_c and s_w with s for any $s \in \mathcal{E}$ (S-Expr). Next, given the simplified program $\mathcal{P}_\star$, the INSTRUMENT procedure generates the instrumented program $\mathcal{P}_I$ such that $\mathcal{P}_I$ is safe if and only if the original template is correct. This procedure is summarized in Fig. 18 and appends an assertion at the end of the product program stating pair-wise equivalence between the output signals. It also recursively instruments the body of $\mathcal{P}_\star$, as summarized in the first three rows of Fig. 18. In particular, constraints of the form $e_1[S_c] == e_2[S_c']$ are rewritten into an assertion $\mapsto (e_1[S_w] = e_2[S_w'])$ on the witness variables and an assumption $\mathsf{assume}(e_1[S_c] = e_2[S_c'])$ on the constraint variables. The assumption ensures counterexamples are limited to executions where $[\![\Phi]\!](\sigma)$ holds, enforcing the antecedent in Def. 2. On the other hand, the assertion enforces that witnesses satisfy constraints $[\![\Phi]\!](\sigma')$, corresponding to the first conjunct in the consequent Definition 2. Finally, the second conjunct in the consequent of Definition 2 is enforced by the assertions placed at the end of the product program.

5.3 Verification of Instrumented Product Program

$$\begin{aligned}
\mathsf{Instr}(e_1[S_c] == e_2[S_c']) &\triangleq \mathsf{assume}(e_1[S_c] = e_2[S_c']) \vdash (e_1[S_w] = e_2[S_w']); \\
\mathsf{Instr}(s[E_1] \leftarrow E_2) &\triangleq s[E_1] \leftarrow E_2 \\
\mathsf{Instr}(S_1; S_2) &\triangleq \mathsf{Instr}(S_1); \mathsf{Instr}(S_2) \\
\textsc{Instrument}(P_\otimes) &\triangleq \mathsf{Instr}(P_\otimes); \vdash (\forall s \in \mathsf{OutputSignals}(P_\otimes).\ s_w \equiv s_c)
\end{aligned}$$

Fig. 18. Instrumentation procedure, INSTRUMENT

The verification algorithm (Fig. 19) operates in two phases. In the first phase, it populates an environment Λ with information about loop counters, calling InferBounds (line 7) to compute lower and upper bounds for each counter κ via interval analysis [26] and invoking InferStepSize to determine κ's step size. The

1: **procedure** VERIFYPRODUCT($P_\otimes$)
2:     # $\mathcal{J}, \Psi$ map each loop to their invariant and pre-conditions respectively
3:     $(\mathcal{J}, \Psi) \leftarrow (\emptyset, \emptyset); \Lambda \leftarrow \emptyset$
4:     # Phase 1: Infer information about loop counters
5:     **for** $L \in \mathsf{Loops}(P_\otimes)$ **do**
6:        $(\kappa, \mathcal{J}[L]) \leftarrow (\mathsf{InferLoopCounter}(L), \mathsf{true})$
7:        $\Lambda[\kappa] \leftarrow (\mathsf{InferBounds}(\kappa, L), \mathsf{InferStepSize}(\kappa, L))$
8:     # Phase 2: Weaken invariants until they are sound
9:     done $\leftarrow$ false; first $\leftarrow$ true
10:    **while** ¬done **do**
11:        $(\Psi, \mathsf{done}) \leftarrow (\mathsf{ComputeSP}(P_\otimes, \mathcal{J}), \mathsf{true})$
12:        **for** $L \in \mathsf{Loops}(P_\otimes)$ **do**
13:           $I \leftarrow$ INFERLOOPINV$(L, \Psi[L], \Lambda, \neg\mathsf{first})$
14:           **if** $I \neq \mathcal{J}[L]$ **then** done $\leftarrow$ false; $\mathcal{J}[L] \leftarrow I$
15:        first $\leftarrow$ false
16:     # Generate VCs and check their validity
17:     **return** $\mathsf{Valid}(\mathsf{GenVC}(P_\otimes, \mathcal{J}))$

Fig. 19. Verification algorithm; procedures in sans serif font are explained in text.

1: **procedure** INFERLOOPINV($L, \psi, \Lambda,$ check-pre)
    input: Loop L with condition C and body B, pre-condition ψ,
2:          counter environment Λ, boolean check-pre
3:     # Conjecture predicates that are likely to be part of the invariant
4:     $\Pi \leftarrow$ CONJECTUREPREDICATES(L, Λ)
5:     # Remove predicates not implied by pre-condition
6:     **if** check-pre **then** $\Pi \leftarrow \{\varphi \mid \varphi \in \Pi \land \psi \Rightarrow \varphi\}$
7:     # Houdini-style fixed-point computation; done initialized to false
8:     **while** ¬done **do**
9:        done $\leftarrow$ true
10:    **for** $\varphi \in \Pi$ **do**
11:        **if** $\nvdash \{C \land \bigwedge_{p_i \in \Pi} p_i\} B \{\varphi\}$ **then** $\Pi \leftarrow \Pi \setminus \{\varphi\}$; done $\leftarrow$ false
12:    **return** $\bigwedge_{p \in \Pi} p$

Fig. 20. Invariant inference algorithm. If Π is empty, then we define $\bigwedge_{p \in \Pi} p$ to be True.

second phase (lines 9–15) computes inductive loop invariants, initializing them in the first iteration and weakening each invariant until soundness is ensured. Specifically, for each loop L, INFERLOOPINV is invoked at line 13 to compute an inductive invariant for L *assuming* that $\Psi[L]$ over-approximates L's true precondition. These loop pre-conditions (Ψ) are computed through standard post-condition computation, using invariants $\mathcal{J}$ for preceding loops. However, since the "invariants" computed in the first iteration may be stronger than the true invariant, these pre-conditions may also be too strong. Hence, the algorithm weakens both the pre-conditions and the invariants until a fixed-point is reached. Upon convergence, it generates verification conditions and checks their validity.

1: **procedure** CONJECTUREPREDICATES(L, Λ)
   input: Loop L and counter environment Λ
   output: Candidate guarded array equality predicates Π
2: $\quad \mathcal{W} \leftarrow$ SignalWrites(L) $\quad \Pi \leftarrow \{\}$;
3: $\quad$ **for** $(s_w, f(\kappa_1, \ldots, \kappa_n)) \in \mathcal{W}$ **do**
4: $\quad\quad$ # Infer constraints over counters $\kappa_1, \ldots, \kappa_n$, sorted outermost to innermost
5: $\quad\quad (\varphi, \varphi_a) \leftarrow$ (false, true)
6: $\quad\quad$ **for** $\kappa_i \in [\kappa_1, \ldots, \kappa_n]$ **do**
7: $\quad\quad\quad$ # generate constraints φ_{κ_i} on κ_i assuming $\varphi_a = \bigwedge_{i=1}^{n} x_i = \kappa_i$
8: $\quad\quad\quad (l_i, u_i, s_i) \leftarrow \Lambda[\kappa_i]$
9: $\quad\quad\quad \varphi_{\kappa_i} \leftarrow \phi_a \wedge (l_i \leq x_i < \kappa \leq u_i \wedge x_i - l_i \bmod s_i = 0)$
10: $\quad\quad\quad$ **for** $\kappa_j \in [\kappa_{i+1}, \ldots, \kappa_n]$ **do**
11: $\quad\quad\quad\quad (l_j, u_j, s_j) \leftarrow \Lambda[\kappa']$
12: $\quad\quad\quad\quad \varphi_{\kappa_i} \leftarrow \varphi_{\kappa_i} \wedge (l_j \leq x_j < u_j \wedge x_j - l_j \bmod s_j = 0)$
13: $\quad\quad\quad$ # Add constraints φ_{κ_i} to φ and add assumption $x_i = \kappa_i$ to φ_a
14: $\quad\quad\quad (\varphi, \varphi_a) \leftarrow (\varphi \vee \varphi_\kappa, \varphi_a \wedge x_i = \kappa_i)$;
15: $\quad\quad \Pi \leftarrow \Pi \cup \{\forall x_1, \ldots, x_n. \ \varphi \rightarrow s_w[f(x_1, \ldots, x_n)] = s_c[f(x_1, \ldots, x_n)]\}$
16: $\quad$ **return** Π

Fig. 21. Algorithm for generating guarded array equality predicates.

Inferring Loop Invariants. Figure 20 outlines our procedure for generating loop invariants, based on a standard Houdini-style approach [27] with two distinguishing features. First, it uses a novel technique (CONJECTUREPREDICATES) to construct the predicate universe; second, it includes a boolean parameter check-pre to control whether predicates are filtered using pre-condition ψ. During the first invocation, check-pre is **false**, so the inferred invariant could be too strong (satisfying consecution but not initiation). In subsequent calls, check-pre is **true**, ensuring that predicates failing initiation are eventually filtered out.

CONJECTUREPREDICATES. (Figure 21) generates candidate predicates for a loop L, returning a set of *guarded array equality* (GAE) predicates which are of the form $\forall \overline{x}. \ \phi(\overline{x}) \rightarrow s_c[f(\overline{x})] = s_w[f(\overline{x})]$. To explain our algorithm, we utilize the example in Fig. 22 for which the required invariant is:

$$\forall x, y. \ (0 \leq x < i \leq N \wedge 0 \leq y < M) \vee (x = i \wedge 0 \leq y < j \leq M) \rightarrow$$
$$s_w[N * x + y] = s_c[N * x + y]$$

Here, the guard captures all loop counter values c_x, c_y for which $s_w[N * c_x + c_y]$ was written before the current iteration. To infer such predicates, the algorithm first identifies all writes in the loop (line 2), represented as tuples $(s_w, f(\kappa_i, \ldots, \kappa_j))$, where $f(\kappa_i, \ldots, \kappa_j)$ is the symbolic expression for the index written in s_w. In this example, the only write is to s_w at $N * i + j$, so the algorithm conjectures $s_w[N * i + j] = s_c[N * i + j]$ as the array equality component of the GAE predicate.

```
for (var i = 0; i < N; i++) {
  for (var j = 0; j < M; j++) {
    s_w[N*i + j] <- a;
    s_c[N*i + j] == a;}}
```

Fig. 22. Loop Example

For each inferred array equality predicate, the algorithm constructs its guard φ by iterating over loop counter variables from outermost to innermost. For each counter κ_i, it synthesizes a predicate φ_{κ_i} capturing all feasible values for counters $[\kappa_i, \ldots, \kappa_n]$, assuming parent counters hold their current iteration values (φ_a). Lines 10–14 compute φ_{κ_i} using loop bounds and step sizes from Λ, ensuring the predicate accounts for all inner counter values during successful executions of prior iterations. The final guard φ is updated as $\varphi \vee \varphi_{\kappa_i}$, while φ_a adds the assumption $x_i = \kappa_i$. Going back to the example, the counter environment maps i to $[0, N)$ and step size 1, and j to $[0, M)$ and step size 1. The procedure first generates φ_i as $0 \leq x_i < i \leq N \wedge 0 \leq x_j < M$. Next, it updates φ_a with $x_i = i$ and computes φ_j for the inner loop as $x_i = i \wedge 0 \leq x_j < j \leq M$. Finally, φ becomes $\varphi_i \vee \varphi_j$, yielding the desired guard:

$$(0 \leq x_i < i \leq N \wedge 0 \leq x_j < M) \vee (x_i = i \wedge 0 \leq x_j < j \leq M)$$

We refer the interested reader to the extended version of the paper [25] for an example demonstrating a more complex loop invariant.

6 Implementation

We implemented our approach in a tool called ZEQUAL and built it on top of the Circom compiler [28]. ZEQUAL discharges SMT queries via Z3 [29] in the theory of integers. Finite field operations are modeled by performing all operations modulo the BN254 prime. For expressions composed of additions, subtractions, or multiplications, the modulo reduction is moved to the outermost expression to reduce the number of large mod operations. In cases where an operation is not supported by the theory of integers (e.g. bitwise arithmetic, exponentiation, finite field inverse), we model these operations with uninterpreted functions and include appropriate axioms.

Although Sect. 5 describes our procedure as operating on a single product program, real-world circuits and witness generators are often composed of sub-circuit invocations. ZEQUAL verifies such circuits by assuming the consistency of any invoked subcircuit. A circuit can therefore be verified by checking the consistency of all invoked sub-circuits in addition to the circuit itself.

7 Evaluation

In this section, we present the results of an experimental evaluation that is designed to answer the following research questions: (1) Can ZEQUAL be used to verify real-world circuits? (2) Does ZEQUAL uncover buggy ZK circuit templates in the wild? (3) How important is the proposed static analysis for successful verification? (4) Can static analysis be used *on its own* to prove consistency? To answer questions (1) and (2), we analyze what percentage of circuits ZEQUAL can verify/falsify. To answer the latter two questions, we perform two ablation studies that disable static analysis and deductive verification respectively.

Table 1. Results. The column called "#verified" shows the number of benchmarks for which ZEQUAL is able to prove correctness, "# cex" shows the number of benchmarks for which ZEQUAL is unable to prove the validity of the generated VC and "# failed" shows the number of benchmarks for which ZEQUAL times out or returns unknown. The last column called "verif. time" shows the average running time of ZEQUAL for those benchmarks that were successfully verified.

Project	# templates	LoC	# verified	# cex	# failed	Verif. time
tornado-core	5	vtc	5 (100%)	0 (0%)	0 (0%)	0.40
semaphore	2	vsem	2 (100%)	0 (0%)	0 (0%)	2.41
circomlib	103	vcl	69 (67%)	24 (23%)	10 (10%)	7.28
maci	52	vmci	40 (77%)	9 (17%)	3 (6%)	1.74
stealthdrop	36	vsd	17 (47%)	13 (36%)	6 (17%)	13.58
circom-ecdsa	63	vdsa	36 (57%)	22 (35%)	5 (8%)	1.65
hydra-s1-zkps	4	vhsz	4 (100%)	0 (0%)	0 (0%)	2.31
zkshield	5	vzks	2 (40%)	1 (20%)	2 (40%)	6.14
circomlib-ml	37	vcml	34 (92%)	3 (8%)	0 (0%)	5.75
eigen-zkvm	21	vevm	11 (52%)	6 (29%)	4 (19%)	10.85
zk-nullifier-sig	44	vzns	24 (55%)	13 (30%)	7 (16%)	16.49
tornado-nova	7	vtn	5 (71%)	2 (29%)	0 (0%)	1.77
darkforest-eth	22	vdf	13 (59%)	8 (36%)	1 (5%)	3.84
ed25519-circom	20	vec	8 (40%)	10 (50%)	2 (10%)	3.86
unirep	14	vuni	12 (86%)	1 (7%)	1 (7%)	1.42
zk-hunt	29	vzh	24 (83%)	4 (14%)	1 (3%)	1.68
Overall	464	292,163	306 (66%)	116 (25%)	42 (9%)	5.71

Benchmarks. We evaluate ZEQUAL on Circom programs gathered from the 20 most popular Circom projects (measured by GitHub stars). After excluding four repositories that use unsupported features (e.g., incompatible with ZEQUAL's version of the Circom compiler), we retain 464 templates from 16 unique repositories, spanning over 290K lines of code. Collectively, these projects span a variety of applications, including cryptographic primitives, games, and machine learning components. For all projects, ZEQUAL attempts to verify the consistency of each template declared within the source code. Since all templates rely on primitives provided by circomlib, which serves as a foundational library for Circom development, ZEQUAL employs stubs of circomlib circuits when analyzing other projects. These stubs capture the behavior of circomlib components, enabling ZEQUAL to reason about templates in other repositories without requiring their full implementation. To evaluate ZEQUAL on these benchmarks, we make *minor* semantics-preserving modifications to a small subset of the templates in order to ensure that they comply with ZEQUAL's assumptions (e.g., our implementation assumes that array sizes only reference template parameters rather than local variables).

Experimental Setup. The experiments were conducted on a MacBook Pro® with an M1 Max CPU, 64 GB of memory, and MacOS 12.3.1. Each benchmark was allocated a runtime of 10 min. Each experiment requires verifying the correctness of a specific template, assuming all external templates are correct.

Main Results. Table 1 summarizes the results of our evaluation. Out of 464 benchmarks, ZEQUAL successfully verifies the correctness of 306 templates, meaning it can verify correctness for *any* instantiation of the templates in 66% of the benchmarks. ZEQUAL is also highly efficient, with an average verification time of just 5.71 seconds per template. For the remaining 158 benchmarks, verification does not succeed. In 42 cases (9%), ZEQUAL exceeds the 10-minute time limit or the tool returns unknown, primarily due to the Z3 timing out on SMT queries. In the remaining 116 benchmarks (25%), ZEQUAL identifies counterexamples to the validity of the generated VC. These counterexamples occur for two reasons: (1) some template instantiations are genuinely incorrect, or (2) the template is correct, but verification fails due to analysis imprecision, such as weak loop invariants.

Failure Analysis. Next, we examine the scenarios in which ZEQUAL is unable to prove correctness. The findings from this failure analysis are summarized in Fig. 23. Among the cases where verification fails, 22% are true positives, which are discussed in more detail below. For the remaining benchmarks, ZEQUAL fails to verify correctness for four primary reasons:

Reason for failure	# (%)
True positive	26 (22%)
Insufficient loop invariant	61 (53%)
Imprecise loop bound	10 (9%)
Imprecise template stub	8 (7%)
Imprecise operation modeling	11 (9%)

Fig. 23. Results of the failure analysis.

- *Insufficient loop invariant:* For 61 of the failure cases (53% of false positives), the loop invariant inferred by ZEQUAL is too weak. For instance, several benchmarks require invariants that capture precise valuations of s_c and s_w to establish the consistency of a signal s across *multiple* loops. We refer the interested reader to the extended version of the paper [25] for a representative example.
- *Imprecise loop bounds:* Recall that our approach relies on static analysis of loop counters to infer bounds and step sizes as a precursor to loop invariant generation. 10 of the failure cases (i.e., 9% of false positives) are due to imprecision in the static analysis of loop counters.
- *Imprecise template stubs:* Recall that our approach utilizes stubs of circomlib templates when analyzing other projects. In some cases, the stubs are not sufficiently precise, accounting for 7% of false positives.

– *Imprecise modeling:* As discussed in Sect. 6, ZEQUAL uses uninterpreted functions to model operations that are not supported by the theory of integers. Roughly 9% of false positives are caused by imprecision in the SMT encoding.

True Positive Analysis. Among the 116 potentially vulnerable circuits we manually inspected, 26 were confirmed to correspond to real bugs. However, since ZEQUAL assumes that external template invocations are safe, these 26 templates could also have cascading effects on other benchmarks. We therefore reran ZEQUAL without this assumption, and identified an additional 20 buggy benchmarks. Hence, ZEQUAL identified a total of 46 buggy templates in the wild.

Of the 46 falsified templates, 41 exhibit violations of the determinism property explored in prior work [8,10] under *some* instantiation of the template parameters. On the other hand, 5 benchmarks are incorrect despite being deterministic and fail to properly validate their inputs. In practice, an attacker can easily take advantage of such bugs in the validation logic to trick the verifier into accepting proofs that should be classified as invalid. An example of an incorrect but deterministic benchmark can be found in the extended version of the paper [25].

Comparison with Prior Work . As discussed previously, 41 out of the 46 incorrect templates also violate the determinism property studied in prior work [8,10]. Therefore, *in principle*, these 41 bugs could be uncovered by an existing tools like QED^2 and CIVER, which specialize in refuting determinism. However, existing tools for determinism checking are limited to analyzing fully instantiated circuits and cannot directly handle *templates*.

To evaluate how ZEQUAL compares with existing determinism checkers, we instantiated the 41 non-deterministic templates with the *smallest* parameter values that expose the bug. This approach avoids scalability issues caused by larger parameter values while ensuring that the bug remains detectable. Using state-of-the-art tools, QED^2 and CIVER, we then attempted to identify the non-determinism bugs within a time limit of 10 min. Among the 41 non-deterministic circuits, QED^2 successfully detected the issue in 22 (54%) circuits but failed to do so for the remaining 19 (46%) cases. Similarly, CIVER successfully detected the issue in 27 (66%) circuits but failed to do so for the remaining 14 (34%) cases.

These results highlight a significant limitation of existing open source determinism checking tools: their ability to refute determinism diminishes in practice due to scalability challenges, even when working with specific circuit instantiations. In contrast, ZEQUAL directly analyzes templates and verifies a much stronger property for *any* instantiation, without requiring manually-crafted parameter templates. However, ZEQUAL cannot automatically refute correctness, even when restricted to determinism, making it a complementary approach rather than a replacement.

Ablation Study. To assess the significance of the key design choices in ZEQUAL, we compare its performance against two ablated versions:

– **Zequal-nsa**: This variant disables the static analysis described in Sect. 5.1. Without static analysis, Zequal-nsa bypasses simplifications of the product program and directly invokes the verification procedure. This evaluation highlights the contribution of static analysis in reducing verification complexity.
– **Zequal-osa**: This variant relies solely on the static analysis results to determine correctness. Specifically, it uses the IsEquivalent procedure to verify whether *all* signals in the ZK circuit are equivalent. If this equivalence holds, all instrumented assertions reduce to *true*, and the circuit is deemed correct. This approach examines the standalone utility of static analysis without leveraging the full verification pipeline in Zequal.

The results of the ablation study, shown in Fig. 24, highlight the importance of both the static analysis and the proposed verification pipeline. Specifically, Zequal-nsa verifies over 100 fewer benchmarks than Zequal due to the increased complexity of the product program, which leads to a significantly higher number of timeouts. On the other hand, Zequal-osa is much faster since it relies solely on lightweight static analysis, but it verifies only half as many benchmarks as Zequal. These results demonstrate that static analysis alone is insufficient for proving correctness, reinforcing the necessity of the full verification pipeline.

Tool	# verified
Zequal-nsa	205 (44%)
Zequal-osa	150 (32%)
Zequal	306 (66%)

Fig. 24. Ablation study

8 Related Work

Formal Verification of ZK Circuits. Recent work has explored using formal verification to check the correctness of ZK circuits [8,10–12,30–33]. One line of work uses interactive theorem provers to verify functional correctness [12,30,31]. For example, CODA [12] uses a custom circuit DSL embedded in Coq which is equipped with a rich type system for specifying circuit properties. Its type checker uses a combination of tactics along with manually proved lemmas to check correctness in Coq. Another line of work uses SMT solvers for automated verification [8,10,11,32,33], focusing on specific circuit properties rather than full functional correctness. The most related work to ours is QED^2 [8], which checks the determinism of ZK circuits using a combination of static analysis and SMT solvers like Zequal. However, unlike Zequal, QED^2 checks a weaker property and is limited to instantiated circuits (without loops), whereas Zequal can directly analyze circuit templates.

Relational Verification. Checking relational properties between programs often involves building product programs [34–38], and a key challenge is determining a suitable alignment between programs. For instance, Churchill et al. [35] check program equivalence by using manually provided tests to generate program traces and synthesize alignment predicates from the trace states. They then lift the alignment predicates back to the source code to construct the product program. In contrast, ZEQUAL leverages the natural alignment between constraints and witness generators in circuit DSLs and performs static analysis to substantially simplify the product program.

Array Invariants. There is an extensive body of work on generating quantified invariants for loops with array variables [39–44]. For example, Flanagan et al. [40] use predicate abstraction and Skolemization to construct quantified invariants, while Gulwani et al. [42] employ a quantified abstract domain to express universally quantified formulas over arrays. Although these techniques could be applied in our setting, we leverage a domain-specific insight: Most loop invariants express equality between the witness and constraint components of signal arrays. This allows us to generate high-quality templates and efficiently construct loop invariants in most cases.

9 Conclusion

This paper presents ZEQUAL, a framework for verifying the consistency of zero-knowledge circuit templates by combining static analysis and deductive verification. ZEQUAL formalizes the consistency requirement for circuit DSLs and introduces a verification method that directly operates on templates, providing guarantees for any circuit instantiated from them. We have evaluated the proposed approach through an extensive experimental study on 464 real-world benchmarks drawn from popular Circom projects. The results show that ZEQUAL terminates on 91% of the benchmarks within a 10-minute time limit and successfully verifies 72% of the cases where it terminates. For benchmarks where verification fails, a systematic failure analysis reveals that roughly 22% of counterexamples correspond to true positives. ZEQUAL also uncovers several bugs that a state-of-the-art tool, QED^2, cannot detect. This capability arises from two key advantages: First, ZEQUAL is not limited to verifying determinism, and, second, it can reason about all possible instantiations of the template in a scalable manner. Additionally, ablation studies validate the design choices behind ZEQUAL, showing that the combination of lightweight static analysis and deductive verification is critical for making the approach effective.

Acknowledgements. This work was conducted in a research group supported by NSF awards CCF-1762299, CCF-1918889, CNS-1908304, CCF-1901376, CNS-2120696, CCF- 2210831, and CCF-2319471.

Disclosure of Interests. All authors are employed by Veridise, a company that provides formal verification services. The authors have no other competing interests to declare that are relevant to the content of this article.

References

1. Groth, J.: Short non-interactive zero-knowledge proofs. In: Abe, M. (ed.) ASIACRYPT 2010. LNCS, vol. 6477, pp. 341–358. Springer, Heidelberg (2010). https://doi.org/10.1007/978-3-642-17373-8_20
2. Ben-Sasson, E., Bentov, I., Horesh, Y., Riabzev, M.: Scalable, transparent, and post-quantum secure computational integrity. Cryptology ePrint Archive, Paper 2018/046 (2018)
3. Jie, K.W.: Openclimate-sg/datawhistleblowing: Work done for the yale open climate collabathon
4. Datta, T., Chen, B., Boneh, D.: VerITAS: Verifying image transformations at scale. Cryptology ePrint Archive, Paper 2024/1066 (2024)
5. Ben Sasson, E., et al.: Zerocash: decentralized anonymous payments from bitcoin. In: 2014 IEEE Symposium on Security and Privacy, pp. 459–474 (2014)
6. Smith, C.:Zero-knowledge rollups
7. Chaliasos, S., Ernstberger, J., Theodore, D., Wong, D., Jahanara, M., Livshits, B.: Sok: What don't we know? understanding security vulnerabilities in snarks (2024)
8. Pailoor, S., et al.: Automated detection of underconstrained circuits for zero-knowledge proofs. Cryptology ePrint Archive, Paper 2023/512 (2023)
9. Wen, H., et al.:Practical security analysis of zero-knowledge proof circuits.' Cryptology ePrint Archive, Paper 2023/190 (2023)
10. Isabel, M., Rodriguez-Nunez, C., Rubio, A.: Scalable Verification of Zero-Knowledge Protocols. In: 2024 IEEE Symposium on Security and Privacy (SP), (Los Alamitos, CA, USA), pp. 1794–1812. IEEE Computer Society, (May 2024)
11. Soureshjani, F.H., Hall-Andersen, M., Jahanara, M., Kam, J., Gorzny, J., Ahmadvand, M.: Automated analysis of halo2 circuits. Cryptology ePrint Archive, Paper 2023/1051 (2023)
12. Liu, J., et al.: Certifying zero-knowledge circuits with refinement types. In: 2024 IEEE Symposium on Security and Privacy (SP), pp. 1741–1759 (2024)
13. Parno, B., Gentry, C., Howell, J., Raykova, M.: Pinocchio: Nearly practical verifiable computation. Cryptology ePrint Archive, Paper 2013/279 (2013). https://eprint.iacr.org/2013/279
14. Buterin, V.: Quadratic arithmetic programs: From zero to hero (Dec 2016). https://medium.com/@VitalikButerin/quadratic-arithmetic-programs-from-zero-to-hero-f6d558cea649
15. ConsenSys, gnark: A Framework for Zero-Knowledge Proofs (2024). Documentation for circuit concepts in gnark
16. Bellés-Muñoz, M., Isabel, M., Muñoz-Tapia, J.L., Rubio, A., Baylina, J.: Circom: a circuit description language for building zero-knowledge applications. IEEE Trans. Dependable Secure Comput. **20**(6), 4733–4751 (2022)
17. halo2 - the halo2 book. https://zcash.github.io/halo2/index.html
18. iden3, Iden3/snarkjs: Zksnark implementation in javascript and wasm. https://github.com/iden3/snarkjs
19. Barthe, G., Crespo, J.M., Kunz, C.: Relational verification using product programs. In: Butler, M., Schulte, W. (eds) FM 2011. LNCS, vol. 6664, pp. 200–214. Springer, Heidelberg (2011). https://doi.org/10.1007/978-3-642-21437-0_17
20. Lahiri, S.K., Qadeer, S.: Complexity and algorithms for monomial and clausal predicate abstraction. In: Schmidt, R.A. (ed.) CADE 2009. LNCS (LNAI), vol. 5663, pp. 214–229. Springer, Heidelberg (2009). https://doi.org/10.1007/978-3-642-02959-2_18

21. RISC Zero, ZirGen: Risc zero circuit generator (2024). https://github.com/risc0/zirgen. Accessed 1 Nov 2024
22. ZoKrates Team, ZoKrates: A Toolbox for zkSNARKs on Ethereum. Official Documentation (2024)
23. Ax, J.: The elementary theory of finite fields. Ann. Math. **88**(2), 239–271 (1968)
24. Dillig, I., Dillig, T., Aiken, A.: Fluid updates: beyond strong vs. weak updates. In: Gordon, A.D. (ed.) ESOP 2010. LNCS, vol. 6012, pp. 246–266. Springer, Heidelberg (2010). https://doi.org/10.1007/978-3-642-11957-6_14
25. Stephens, J., Pailoor, S., Dillig, I.: Automated verification of consistency in zero-knowledge proof circuits. Cryptology ePrint Archive, Paper 2025/916 (2025). https://eprint.iacr.org/2025/916
26. Cousot, P., Cousot, R.: Abstract interpretation: a unified lattice model for static analysis of programs by construction or approximation of fixpoints. In: Proceedings of the 4th ACM SIGACT-SIGPLAN Symposium on Principles of Programming Languages, pp. 238–252 (1977)
27. Flanagan, C., Leino, K.: Houdini, an annotation assistant for ESC/Java. In: Oliveira, J.N., Zave, P. (eds.) FME 2001. LNCS, vol. 2021, pp. 500–517. Springer, Heidelberg (2001). https://doi.org/10.1007/3-540-45251-6_29
28. Circom compiler. https://github.com/iden3/circom
29. de Moura, L., Bjørner, N.: Z3: an efficient SMT solver. In: Ramakrishnan, C.R., Rehof, J. (eds.) TACAS 2008. LNCS, vol. 4963, pp. 337–340. Springer, Heidelberg (2008). https://doi.org/10.1007/978-3-540-78800-3_24
30. Coglio, A., McCarthy, E., Smith, E., Chin, C., Gaddamadugu, P., Dellepere, M.: Compositional formal verification of zero-knowledge circuits. Cryptology ePrint Archive, Paper 2023/1278 (2023)
31. Kwan, C., Dao, Q., Thaler, J.: Verifying jolt zkVM lookup semantics. Cryptology ePrint Archive, Paper 2024/1841 (2024)
32. Stronati, M., Firsov, D., Locascio, A., Livshits, B.: Clap: a semantic-preserving optimizing edsl for plonkish proof systems (2024)
33. Chen, H., Li, G., Chen, M., Liu, R., Gao, S.: Ac4: Algebraic computation checker for circuit constraints in zkps (2024)
34. Sharma, R., Schkufza, E., Churchill, B., Aiken, A.: Data-driven equivalence checking. SIGPLAN Not. **48**, 391–406 (2013)
35. Churchill, B., Padon, O., Sharma, R., Aiken, A.: Semantic program alignment for equivalence checking. In: Proceedings of the 40th ACM SIGPLAN Conference on Programming Language Design and Implementation, PLDI 2019, pp. 1027–1040. Association for Computing Machinery, New York (2019)
36. Dahiya, M., Bansal, S.: Black-Box equivalence checking across compiler optimizations. In: Chang, B.-Y.E. (ed.) APLAS 2017. LNCS, vol. 10695, pp. 127–147. Springer, Cham (2017). https://doi.org/10.1007/978-3-319-71237-6_7
37. Dickerson, R., Mukherjee, P., Delaware, B.: Kestrel: Relational verification using e-graphs for program alignment (2024)
38. Chen, J., Wei, J., Feng, Y., Bastani, O., Dillig, I.: Relational verification using reinforcement learning. Proc. ACM Program. Lang. **3** (2019)
39. Gulwani, S., Tiwari, A.: An abstract domain for analyzing heap-manipulating low-level software. In: Damm, W., Hermanns, H. (eds.) CAV 2007. LNCS, vol. 4590, pp. 379–392. Springer, Heidelberg (2007). https://doi.org/10.1007/978-3-540-73368-3_42
40. Flanagan, C., Qadeer, S.: Predicate abstraction for software verification. SIGPLAN Not. **37**, 191–202 (2002)

41. Gopan, D., Reps, T., Sagiv, M.: A framework for numeric analysis of array operations. SIGPLAN Not. **40**, 338–350 (2005)
42. Gulwani, S., McCloskey, B., Tiwari, A.: Lifting abstract interpreters to quantified logical domains. SIGPLAN Not. **43**, 235–246 (2008)
43. Kovács, L., Voronkov, A.: Finding loop invariants for programs over arrays using a theorem prover. In: Chechik, M., Wirsing, M. (eds.) FASE 2009. LNCS, vol. 5503, pp. 470–485. Springer, Heidelberg (2009). https://doi.org/10.1007/978-3-642-00593-0_33
44. Dillig, I., Dillig, T., Aiken, A.: Symbolic heap abstraction with demand-driven axiomatization of memory invariants. SIGPLAN Not. **45**, 397–410 (2010)

Open Access This chapter is licensed under the terms of the Creative Commons Attribution 4.0 International License (http://creativecommons.org/licenses/by/4.0/), which permits use, sharing, adaptation, distribution and reproduction in any medium or format, as long as you give appropriate credit to the original author(s) and the source, provide a link to the Creative Commons license and indicate if changes were made.

The images or other third party material in this chapter are included in the chapter's Creative Commons license, unless indicated otherwise in a credit line to the material. If material is not included in the chapter's Creative Commons license and your intended use is not permitted by statutory regulation or exceeds the permitted use, you will need to obtain permission directly from the copyright holder.

Integer Reasoning Modulo Different Constants in SMT

Elizaveta Pertseva[1(✉)], Alex Ozdemir[1], Shankara Pailoor[2], Alp Bassa[2], Sorawee Porncharoenwase[4], Işıl Dillig[2,3], and Clark Barrett[1]

[1] Stanford University, Stanford, USA
pertseva@stanford.edu
[2] Veridise, Austin, USA
[3] The University of Texas at Austin, Austin, USA
[4] Amazon Web Services, Seattle, USA

Abstract. This paper presents a new refutation procedure for multi-modular systems of integer constraints that commonly arise when verifying cryptographic protocols. These systems, involving polynomial equalities and disequalities modulo different constants, are challenging for existing solvers due to their inability to exploit multimodular structure. To address this issue, our method partitions constraints by modulus and uses lifting and lowering techniques to share information across subsystems, supported by algebraic tools like weighted Gröbner bases. Our experiments show that the proposed method outperforms existing state-of-the-art solvers in verifying cryptographic implementations related to Montgomery arithmetic and zero-knowledge proofs.

1 Introduction

Throughout history, cryptosystems have been defined using modular arithmetic. The first symmetric cipher— the Caesar cipher— used arithmetic modulo the alphabet size. The first public key exchange (Diffie-Hellman [24]) used arithmetic modulo a large prime. The first digital signature (RSA [72]) used arithmetic modulo a large biprime. More recently, cryptosystems that *compute* on secret data, such as homomorphic encryption [37], multiparty computation [83], and zero-knowledge proofs (ZKPs) [38], often perform computation modulo a prime.

The relationship between integer arithmetic systems with *different* moduli plays a central role in *implementing* cryptography. Generally, this is because the cryptosystem is defined using a modulus that is different from the one natively supported by the computational model. For example, microprocessors efficiently perform arithmetic modulo powers of two (e.g., $2^{16}, 2^{32}, 2^{64}, \ldots$), but elliptic-curve cryptosystems require arithmetic modulo ≈256-bit primes. To bridge the gap, implementations use techniques such as Montgomery and Barrett reduction [7,56]. Similar problems (and solutions) arise in other contexts, such as when using ZKPs. ZKPs often only support arithmetic modulo a large prime [78] and

---
S. Porncharoenwase—Work done while at Veridise.

Fig. 1. Overview of our refutation procedure. Integer-reasoning interacts with modules for reasoning about equations modulo constants, e.g. (in this figure, modulo 2 and 7).

must then find ways to express and prove any properties that are not natively defined modulo that prime.

Thus, when the correctness of a cryptosystem is expressed as a logical formula, such as a Satisfiability Modulo Theories (SMT) formula, it often contains equations with different moduli. Some of the equations express the cryptographic *specification* (e.g., modulo the prime $2^{255} - 19$), and others express the *operations* performed by the implementation (e.g., modulo 2^{64}). We call such sets of constraints *multimodular systems*.

Unfortunately, such multimodular systems are hard for existing SMT solvers. One approach is to use a theory that explicitly supports the modulus operator, such as integers or bit-vectors. In practice, this leads to poor performance because the solvers for these theories are designed for *general* modular reduction (i.e., where the modulus could be a variable) and are not optimized for the special case of many constraints with constant moduli. Another approach is to combine theories optimized for different constant moduli, such as bit-vectors (modulo a power of two) and finite fields (modulo a prime). This also performs poorly because existing combination mechanisms cannot exchange sufficiently powerful lemmas between the theories.

The primary contribution of this paper is a novel refutation procedure for multimodular systems. The procedure, illustrated in Fig. 1, partitions constraints into *subsystems* based on their moduli and then does local reasoning within each subsystem to detect conflicts. *Global reasoning* is done by exchanging lemmas across subsystems. This is facilitated by two key techniques: *lifting*, which promotes modular constraints to the integer domain, and *lowering*, which projects integer constraints into specific moduli. The derivation and exchange of lemmas is further supported by two complementary strategies. First, range analysis is used to verify whether a literal can be soundly lifted or lowered without altering the satisfiability of the overall system. Second, the procedure identifies additional literals *implied* by a given subsystem using algebraic techniques, such as weighted Gröbner bases and integer linear programming, to uncover constraints that enhance cross-subsystem reasoning.

We apply our procedure to unsatisfiable benchmarks based on three kinds of cryptographic implementations. The implementations include Montgomery arithmetic [56], non-native field arithmetic for a ZKP [64,75], and multi-precision bit-vector arithmetic for a ZKP [49]. We implement our procedure in cvc5 [3], and show that it significantly outperforms prior solvers on these benchmarks. To summarize, our contributions are:

1. a refutation procedure for multimodular systems;
2. two algorithms for finding shareable lemmas, one using a weighted monomial order and the other using integer linear constraints; and
3. multimodular benchmarks from cryptographic verification applications.

The rest of the paper is organized as follows. We give a motivating example in Sect. 2, provide background in Sect. 3, introduce a logic for multimodular systems in Sect. 4, explain our refutation procedure in Sect. 5 and its implementation in Sect. 6, present benchmarks and experiments in Sect. 7, discuss related work in Sect. 8, and conclude in Sect. 9.

2 Motivating Example

Consider the following system of constraints Φ, which is based on code from a zero-knowledge proof library written by Succinct Labs [75]:

$$\Phi \triangleq \quad xy \equiv r_1 + c_1 p \mod q \quad \wedge \quad 0 \leq r_1, c_1 < p \quad \wedge$$
$$r_1 y \equiv r_2 + c_2 p \mod q \quad \wedge \quad 0 \leq r_2, c_2 < p \quad \wedge$$
$$x + r_2 \equiv r_3 + c_3 p \mod q \quad \wedge \quad 0 \leq r_3, c_3 < p$$

Here, p and q are concrete primes of 32 and 256 bits respectively, but their specific values are not important. Φ is designed to ensure a correctness condition $C \triangleq (x + xy^2 \equiv r_3 \mod p)$, assuming bounds on the inputs x and y: $B \triangleq (0 \leq x, y < p)$. Formally, proving Φ is correct is equivalent to proving the validity of $(\Phi \wedge B) \Rightarrow C$, or to proving the unsatisfiability of:

$$\Phi \wedge B \wedge \neg C \tag{1}$$

It is easy enough to refute Formula (1) by hand. First, observe that the range constraints in B and Φ ensure that none of the equivalences in Φ can overflow mod q— so the equivalences hold over the integers. Second, observe that said equivalences must also hold mod p:

$$xy \equiv r_1 \mod p \quad \wedge \quad r_1 y \equiv r_2 \mod p \quad \wedge \quad x + r_2 \equiv r_3 \mod p$$

Third, these equivalences imply $x + xy^2 \equiv r_3 \pmod{p}$, which contradicts $\neg C$.

However, existing SMT solvers fail to do this refutation. For example, when Formula (1) is encoded in QF_NIA using explicit modular reductions, state-of-the-art SMT solvers (including cvc5, z3, MathSAT, and Yices) fail to solve it. And when the formula is encoded in QF_BV using 512-bit bit-vectors, none of cvc5, z3, nor bitwuzla can solve it.[1] QF_FF solvers (cvc5 and Yices) do not apply because they cannot encode a variable modulo more than one prime.

The key ingredients in the manual refutation were lifting equalities from a modular space into the integers— and then lowering them back to a different modular space. In this paper, we show how to design a procedure that performs this lifting and lowering automatically.

---
[1] All tests were run with a time limit of 20 min and a memory limit of 8 GB.

3 Background

In this section, we define notation and provide a brief overview of algebra [54], ideals [22], and SMT [6]. More details can be found in the cited work.

3.1 Algebra

Sets, Intervals, and Functions. Let $\mathbb{Z}$ be the integers, $\mathbb{Z}_{\geq 0}$ the non-negative integers, and $\mathbb{Z}^+$ the positive integers. Let $\mathbb{Z}_\infty^+$ be $\mathbb{Z}^+ \cup \{\infty\}$, and let $\mathbb{Z}_n$ be the non-negative integers less than n. X denotes the set of variables $\{x_1, \ldots, x_k\}$. For a set S and some t, the notation S,t abbreviates $S \cup \{t\}$. $[i, j]$ denotes the closed integer interval from i to j. Interval intersection is defined in the usual way: $[a, b] \cap [c, d] = [\max(a, c), \min(b, d)]$. For an interval, pair, or sequence t, we denote by t_i the ith element of t, e.g., $(a, b)_1 = a$. We use two variants of the modulo function. $a \bmod n$, for $a \in \mathbb{Z}$ and $n \in \mathbb{Z}^+$, is the unique $r \in \mathbb{Z}_n$ such that $a = qn + r$ for some $q \in \mathbb{Z}$ (as in SMT-LIB [5]). The signed variant $a \operatorname{smod} n$ is defined as $a \bmod n$ if that value is at most $\frac{n}{2}$ and $(a \bmod n) - n$ otherwise.

Polynomial Rings. Let R be a ring [25]. We overload $\mathbb{Z}$ to also denote the integer ring and $\mathbb{Z}_n$ to also denote the ring over $\{0, \ldots, n-1\}$, with addition and multiplication modulo n. Both $\mathbb{Z}$ and $\mathbb{Z}_n$ are principal ideal rings (PIR), and if n is prime, $\mathbb{Z}_n$ is also a *field*. Let $R[X]$ denote the ring of polynomials with variables in X and coefficients in R. In this paper, we focus on the following rings: (1) $\mathbb{Z}[X]$, which is the ring of polynomials with integer coefficients, and (2) $\mathbb{Z}_n[X]$, which is the ring of polynomials with integer coefficients modulo n. In ring $R[X]$, a *monomial* is a polynomial of the form $x_1^{e_1} \cdots x_k^{e_k}$, with $e_i \in \mathbb{Z}_{\geq 0}$. When $e_i = 0$ for every i, we denote the monomial as 1. A *term* is a monomial multiplied by a coefficient. Polynomials are written as a sum of terms with distinct monomials.

Monomial Orders. A *monomial order* $\leq$ is a total order on monomials that satisfies the following properties: (i) $1 \leq m$ for every monomial m; and (ii) for all monomials m_1, m_2, m, if $m_1 \leq m_2$, then $m_1 m \leq m_2 m$. Examples of monomial orders for a monomial of the form $x_1^{e_1} \cdots x_k^{e_k}$ include the following: *lexicographic order* compares monomials by (lexicographically) comparing their exponent tuples $(e_1, \ldots, e_k)$, *graded reverse lexicographic order* by comparing $(\sum_{i=1}^k e_i, -e_k, \ldots, -e_1)$, and *weighted reverse lexicographic order* by comparing $(\sum_{i=1}^k w_i e_i, -e_k, \ldots, -e_1)$ for a fixed tuple of weights $(w_1 \ldots w_k)$. Given a monomial order, the *leading monomial* of a polynomial p, denoted $lm(p)$, is the largest monomial occurring in p with respect to the monomial order. The leading term, denoted $lt(p)$, is that monomial's term.

3.2 Ideals

For a set of polynomials $S = \{f_1, \ldots, f_n\} \subset R[X]$, $I(S) = \{g_1 f_1 + \cdots + g_n f_n \mid g_i \in R[X]\}$ is the *ideal generated by* S. In order to disambiguate which ring R

is meant in the definition of an ideal, we use the notation $I_n(S)$, with $n \in \mathbb{Z}_\infty^+$. The meaning of $I_n(S)$ is either the ideal generated by S with $g_i \in \mathbb{Z}_n[X]$, when $n \in \mathbb{Z}^+$, or the ideal generated by S with $g_i \in \mathbb{Z}[X]$, when $n = \infty$.

A *solution* to the polynomial system $S \subset R[X]$, is $\mathbf{a} \in R^k$ such that for all $f \in S$, $f(a_1, \ldots, a_k) = 0$. The set of all solutions is called the *variety* of S, denoted $\mathcal{V}(S)$. As above, we use the subscript n to distinguish among rings. Thus $\mathcal{V}_n(S)$ for $n \in \mathbb{Z}^+$ is a subset of $\mathbb{Z}_n^k$ and $\mathcal{V}_\infty(S)$ is a subset of $\mathbb{Z}^k$. If $1 \in I_n(S)$, then $\mathcal{V}_n(S) = \emptyset$, i.e., S has no solution. However, the converse does not hold.

One incomplete test for ideal membership is *reduction*. For the polynomials p, g, and $r \in R[X]$, where R is a PIR, p reduces to r modulo g, written $p \to_g r$, if some term t of p is divisible by $lt(g)$ with $r = p - \frac{t}{lt(g)} g$ [27]. If R is a field, then $p \to_g r$, if some term t of p is divisible by $lm(g)$. Reduction is also defined for a set of polynomials S, written as $p \to_S r$. p reduces to r modulo S if there is a sequence of reductions from p to r, each modulo some polynomial in S, and no further reduction of r modulo S is possible. If p reduces to 0 modulo S then p belongs to the ideal generated by S. However, once again, the converse does not hold.

Gröbner Bases. A *Gröbner basis* [13] is a set of polynomials with special properties, including that reduction is a complete test for ideal membership: p reduces to 0 modulo a Gröbner basis iff p belongs to the ideal generated by the Gröbner basis. There exist numerous algorithms for computing Gröbner bases, including Buchberger's algorithm [13], F4 [32], and F5 [33]. We use $\mathtt{GB}_{n,\leq}$ with $n \in \mathbb{Z}_\infty^+$ to refer to a Gröbner basis computation. The subscript n indicates which ring the Gröbner basis is computed in ($n \in \mathbb{Z}^+$ means $\mathbb{Z}_n[X]$ and $n = \infty$ means $\mathbb{Z}[X]$), while $\leq$ indicates which monomial order to use. In this paper, we assume Gröbner bases are *strong* and *reduced*, meaning that $\mathtt{GB}_{n,\leq}$ is always deterministic, producing a single unique basis.

3.3 SMT

In addition to the algebraic domains above, we also work in the logical setting of many-sorted first-order logic with equality [29]. Σ denotes a signature with a set of sort symbols (including Bool), a symbol family $\approx_\sigma$ with sort $\sigma \times \sigma \to$ Bool for all sorts $\sigma \in \Sigma$,[2] and a set of interpreted function symbols. We assume the usual definitions of well-sorted Σ-terms and literals, and refer to Σ-terms of sort Bool as formulas. To distinguish logical Σ-terms from algebraic terms in polynomials (defined above), we write Σ-*term* to refer to the former, where Σ is the signature. A *theory* is a pair $\mathcal{T} = (\Sigma, \mathbf{I})$, where Σ is a signature and $\mathbf{I}$ is a class of Σ-interpretations. A *logic* is a theory together with a syntactic restriction on formulas. A formula ϕ is *satisfiable* if it evaluates to true in some interpretation in $\mathbf{I}$. Otherwise, ϕ is *unsatisfiable*.

The CDCL($\mathcal{T}$) framework of SMT aims to determine if a formula ϕ is *satisfiable*. At a high level, a *core* module explores the propositional abstraction of ϕ

---
[2] We drop the σ subscript when it is clear from context.

Symbol	Arity
$n \in \mathbb{Z}$	Int
$-, +, \times$	Int × Int → Int
mod	Int × Int → Int
$\approx$	Int × Int → Bool
$\leq, \geq$	Int × Int → Bool

(a) Signature used by QF_MIA.

```
Op     → × | + | -
Exp    → (Exp Op Exp) | Var | Int
BExp   → Var ≤ Int | Var ≥ Int
EqExp  → Exp ≈ 0 | Exp mod Int ≈ 0
Atom   → BExp | EqExp
Literal → Atom | ¬Atom
```

(b) QF_MIA grammar; Int $\in \mathbb{Z}$ and Var $\in X$.

Fig. 2. The signature and grammar for QF_MIA, a fragment of QF_NIA.

and forwards literals corresponding to the current propositional assignment to the *theory solver*. A *theory solver*, specialized for a particular theory $\mathcal{T}$, checks if there exists an interpretation that satisfies the received set of literals. We focus on three main theories. The theory of finite fields (defined in [65]), which we refer to as $\mathcal{T}_{FF}$, reasons about finite fields, i.e., rings $\mathbb{Z}_n[X]$ where n is prime. We also make use of the standard SMT-LIB [5] theories of bit-vectors, which we denote $\mathcal{T}_{BV}$, and integer arithmetic, which we denote $\mathcal{T}_{Int}$. For two $\mathcal{T}_{Int}$ terms s, t, we abbreviate the literal $\neg(s \approx t)$ as $s \not\approx t$. We use $\bowtie$ to refer to an operator in the set $\{\approx, \not\approx\}$. QF_NIA refers to the SMT-LIB logic that uses the theory $\mathcal{T}_{Int}$ and restricts formulas to be quantifier-free.

4 A Multimodular Logic

Previous work on verifying arithmetic modulo large primes [65,66] encodes constraints using $\mathcal{T}_{FF}$. However, the signature of $\mathcal{T}_{FF}$ does not support non-prime moduli or constraints that share variables and use different moduli, limiting the range of problems that can be encoded. Instead, we encode multimodular constraints directly in $\mathcal{T}_{Int}$. However, we restrict the syntax of $\mathcal{T}_{Int}$ by defining a logic called QF_MIA (multimodular integer arithmetic), which is a fragment of QF_NIA. Importantly, QF_MIA is not *semantically* weaker than QF_NIA; it includes integer polynomials and predicates, so all of QF_NIA can be encoded in QF_MIA via standard rewrites. Rather, QF_MIA is a syntactic restriction of QF_NIA that is designed to make the multimodular structure of queries clearer so that our procedure can leverage that structure.

The subset of the signature of $\mathcal{T}_{Int}$ used by QF_MIA is shown in Fig. 2a. From now on, we use Σ to denote this signature. A grammar for the syntactic fragment of QF_MIA is shown in Fig. 2b. We assume a set $\mathcal{X} = \{x_1, \ldots, x_k\}$ of logical variables of sort Int and define corresponding categories of Σ-terms as follows. A QF_MIA *expression* (produced by Exp) is either an integer constant, a variable (in $\mathcal{X}$), or an application of one of the operators $-$, $+$, or $\times$ to two expressions. For simplicity, we often represent multiplication with juxtaposition (e.g., ab instead of $a \times b$) and leave out parentheses when clear from context (i.e., when they can be inferred from standard operator precedence rules). A QF_MIA *atom* (produced by Atom) is an inequality (between a variable and a constant), an equality between an expression and 0, or an equality between an expression modulo some integer constant and zero. A QF_MIA *literal* (produced by Literal) is either an atom or the negation of an atom. From now on, unless otherwise noted, expressions, atoms, and literals are QF_MIA expressions, atoms, and literals. We also assume that interpretations are $\mathcal{T}_{\text{Int}}$-interpretations and all notions of satisfiability are modulo $\mathcal{T}_{\text{Int}}$. Since we need to work in both the algebraic and the logical domains, we assume a bijection from logical variables in $\mathcal{X}$ to algebraic variables in X and define an operator $[\![\cdot]\!]$ that takes a logical Σ-term and returns the corresponding polynomial in $\mathbb{Z}[X]$ (distributing multiplication and combining like terms as necessary to obtain a sum of terms, each with a unique monomial).

5 Refutation Procedure

In this section, we describe our refutation procedure. First we describe our approach at a high level, and then we discuss its key technical ingredients.

5.1 Key Ideas

A naive approach to solving a multimodular system of constraints is to use a standard encoding in QF_NIA, introducing an auxiliary variable for each modular constraint. For instance, $x \equiv y \pmod{n}$ would be encoded as $x \approx y + n \cdot k$ using an auxiliary integer variable k. While sound, this naive approach scales poorly, as we show experimentally in Sect. 7. Our key insight is that this limitation can often be overcome by *partitioning* the original system into a *set* of different subsystems, one for each specific modulus. Reasoning in each subsystem can be done efficiently, and if any subsystem is unsatisfiable, then so is the original set of constraints. However, since the converse is not true, our procedure seeks to exchange as much information as possible between the different subsystems, with the goal of improving our ability to detect unsatisfiable constraints. To enable the exchange of information between the different subsystems, we employ the concepts of *lifting* and *lowering*.

Definition 1 (Liftable). *Let C be a set of QF_MIA literals. A literal of the form $e \bmod n \bowtie 0$ is liftable (in C) if $C \cup \{e \bmod n \bowtie 0\}$ is equisatisfiable to $C \cup \{e \bmod n \bowtie 0, e \bowtie 0\}$.*

In other words, a constraint is liftable if adding the constraint without the modulus n maintains equisatisfiability.

Definition 2 (Lowerable). *Let C be a set of QF_MIA literals. A literal the form $e \bowtie 0$ is lowerable (in C) with respect to n if $C \cup \{e \bowtie 0\}$ and $C \cup \{e \bowtie 0, e \bmod n \bowtie 0\}$ are equisatisfiable.*

In other words, a constraint is *lowerable* w.r.t. n if adding it with a modular reduction maintains equisatisfiability.

Remark 1. If the literal $e \bmod n \bowtie 0$ is implied by C, then the lifting definition reduces to: C and $C \cup \{e \bowtie 0\}$ must be equisatisfiable. Similarly, if the literal $e \bowtie 0$ is implied by C, it is lowerable w.r.t. n if C and $C \cup \{e \bmod n \bowtie 0\}$ are equisatisfiable. In the remainder of the paper, we rely on these simpler versions of the definitions.

Lifting provides a way for each subsystem containing modular constraints to share information in a common language without adding new variables. Lowering adds constraints to individual subsystems and can often result in significant simplifications: when we lower an equation with respect to n, all integer constants divisible by n can be replaced by 0. For example, lowering $x_1 - 6x_2 \approx 0$ with respect to 6 adds a new equality $x_1 \approx 0$ to the subsystem with modulus 6. We denote by $simp_n(e)$ the result of replacing every integer constant c in e by c smod n^3 and simplifying.

As expected, not all constraints are liftable or lowerable. In order to facilitate the inference of liftable and lowerable constraints, our method splits the constraint system into the following subsystems, for $n \in \mathbb{Z}_\infty^+$:

- **Modulus-n equality subsystems** are sets of expressions $\{e_1, \ldots, e_m\}$. Each e_i represents the constraint $e_i \bmod n \approx 0$ when $n \neq \infty$ or the constraint $e_i \approx 0$ when $n = \infty$. We write $R_n^\approx$ to denote the set of expressions.
- **Modulus-n disequality subsystems** are sets of expressions $\{e_1, \ldots, e_m\}$. Each e_i represents the constraint $e_i \bmod n \not\approx 0$ when $n \neq \infty$ or the constraint $e_i \not\approx 0$ when $n = \infty$. We write $R_n^{\not\approx}$ to denote the set of expressions.

$$\text{ModExp} \frac{\bowtie \in \{=, \neq\} \quad (e \bmod n \bowtie 0) \in C}{C := C \setminus \{e \bmod n \bowtie 0\} \quad R_n^\bowtie := R_n^\bowtie, simp_n(e)}$$

$$\text{IntExp} \frac{\bowtie \in \{=, \neq\} \quad (e \bowtie 0) \in C}{C := C \setminus \{e \bowtie 0\} \quad R_\infty^\bowtie := R_\infty^\bowtie, e}$$

$$\text{GEQ} \frac{(\mathsf{x} \geq n) \in C}{C := C \setminus \{\mathsf{x} \geq n\} \quad B(\mathsf{x})_1 := \max(B(\mathsf{x})_1, n)}$$

$$\text{LEQ} \frac{(\mathsf{x} \leq n) \in C}{C := C \setminus \{\mathsf{x} \leq c\} \quad B(\mathsf{x})_2 := \min(B(\mathsf{x})_2, n)}$$

$$\text{nGEQ} \frac{\neg(x \geq n) \in L}{C := C \setminus \{\neg(\mathsf{x} \geq n)\} \quad B(\mathsf{x})_2 := \min(B(\mathsf{x})_2, n-1)}$$

$$\text{nLEQ} \frac{\neg(\mathsf{x} \leq n) \in L}{C := C \setminus \{\neg(\mathsf{x} \leq n) \quad B(\mathsf{x})_1 := \max(B(\mathsf{x})_1, n+1)}$$

Fig. 3. Encoding rules for a multimodular system C, where e is an expression and $n \in \mathbb{Z}_\infty^+$.

---

[3] We use smod instead of mod to reduce the magnitude of coefficients of $simp_n(e)$ and increase the likelihood that $simp_n(e)$ is liftable according to Lemma 1.

- **Variable bounds:** Our method also maintains a mapping B from each variable in $\mathcal{X}$ to its lower and upper bound (with $-\infty/\infty$ denoting unbounded variables). As we will see shortly, this bound information is crucial for identifying lowerable and liftable equations.

Given a multimodular system C, we assume that it is encoded as a tuple $(B, R_\infty^\approx, R_\infty^{\not\approx}, R_{n_1}^\approx, R_{n_1}^{\not\approx}, \ldots, R_{n_k}^\approx, R_{n_k}^{\not\approx})$, where $\{n_1, \ldots, n_k\}$ is the set of all integer constants greater than 1 appearing anywhere in a literal in C. For example, for a multimodular system $\{2x \bmod 3 \approx 0, x < 5\}$, the resulting tuple would be $(B, R_\infty^\approx, R_\infty^{\not\approx}, R_2^\approx, R_2^{\not\approx}, R_3^\approx, R_3^{\not\approx}, R_5^\approx, R_5^{\not\approx})$. A set of rules for accomplishing the encoding is included in Fig. 3.

Going forward, we use C to refer both to the original set of constraints and to the tuple encoding. We also define $\texttt{CalcBds}(B, e)$ as a function that returns the maximum and minimum possible values that expression e can take when evaluated at the variable assignments permitted by the variable bounds map B, based on standard interval arithmetic [45]. For example, given an equality $x_1 x_2 \bmod 6 \approx 0$ and variable bounds $B = \{x_1 : [0,6], x_2 : [0,6]\}$, $\texttt{CalcBds}(B, x_1 x_2)$ would return the interval $[0, 36]$. Using this machinery, we now state the following lemmas that help identify liftable and lowerable constraints. We include the proofs in the extended version of the paper [69]. Recall that I_n computes the ideal generated by a set of polynomials.

Lemma 1. *Let C be a multimodular system with bounds B and modulus-n equality subsystem $R_n^\approx$, with $n \in \mathbb{Z}^+$. Then, an equality $e \bmod n \approx 0$ is liftable in C if (1) $[\![e]\!] \in I_n([\![R_n^\approx]\!])$ and (2) $\texttt{CalcBds}(B, e) \subseteq [1 - n, n - 1]$.*

This lemma is useful in two ways. First, if e is in $R_n^\approx$, then certainly, $[\![e]\!]$ is in $I_n([\![R_n^\approx]\!])$; thus, checking whether the constraint represented by an element of $R_n^\approx$ is liftable reduces to computing $\texttt{CalcBds}(B, e)$, which can be done in linear time. Second, this lemma gives a way to find *additional* liftable equalities that are not part of the original constraint system by identifying polynomials that are in the ideal of $[\![R_\infty^\approx]\!]$. While listing all the polynomials in an ideal is infeasible, later subsections (Sects. 5.4 and 5.5) explore effective methods to identify useful polynomials that are in the ideal. The next lemma states that disequalities are always liftable.

Lemma 2. *Let C be a multimodular system with modulus-n disequality subsystem $R_n^{\not\approx}$, with $n \in \mathbb{Z}^+$. Then a disequality $e \bmod n \not\approx 0$ is liftable in C w.r.t. n if $e \in R_n^{\not\approx}$.*

This lemma states that all of the original disequalities are liftable. However, unlike the equality case, we cannot infer *additional* disequalities using ideals, as disequalities are not preserved under the operations used to construct the elements of an ideal. The next two lemmas are dual to Lemmas 1 and 2, but are for lowerability instead of liftability.

Lemma 3. *Let C be a multimodular system with integer equalities $R_\infty^\approx$. If e is an expression and $[\![e]\!] \in I_\infty([\![R_\infty^\approx]\!])$, then $e \approx 0$ is lowerable w.r.t. every $n \in \mathbb{Z}^+$.*

Lemma 4. *Let C be a multimodular system with integer disequalities $R_\infty^{\not\approx}$ and bounds B. Then, if $n \in \mathbb{Z}^+$, a disequality $e \not\approx 0$ is lowerable in C w.r.t. to n if (1) $e \in R_\infty^{\not\approx}$ and (2) $\mathtt{CalcBds}(B,e) \subseteq [1-n, n-1]$.*

5.2 Refutation Calculus

Next, we leverage the notions of liftability and lowerability defined in the previous subsection to formulate our *refutation calculus* (presented in Fig. 4). The rules in our calculus serve four main roles. First, they establish whether a specific subsystem is unsatisfiable. Second, they attempt to tighten existing bounds and learn new equalities from these bounds. Third, they leverage Lemmas 1–4 to exchange information between different subsystems via lifting and lowering. Finally, they simplify unliftable equalities via branching.

We present the calculus as rules that modify *configurations*, as is common in SMT procedures [50,74]. Here, a configuration is the representation of the system of constraints C as the tuple $(B, R_\infty^\approx, R_\infty^{\not\approx}, R_{n_1}^\approx, R_{n_1}^{\not\approx}, \ldots, R_{n_k}^\approx, R_{n_k}^{\not\approx})$ as described in Sect. 5.1. The rules are presented in *guarded assignment form*, where the premises describe the conditions on the current configuration under which the rule can be applied, and the conclusion is either unsat or indicates how the configuration is modified. A rule may have multiple alternative conclusions separated by ||. An application of a rule is *redundant* if it does not change the configuration in any way. A configuration other than unsat is *saturated* if every possible application is redundant. A *derivation tree* is a tree where each node is a configuration and its children, if any, are obtained by a non-redundant application of a rule of the calculus. A derivation tree is closed if all of its leaves are unsat. A *derivation* is a sequence of derivation trees in which each element in the sequence (after the first) is obtained by expanding a single leaf node in the previous tree. We explain each class of rules in the calculus in more detail below.

Checking Unsatisfiability. UnsatOne is used to conclude unsatisfiability using algebraic techniques: As explained in Sect. 3, if some ideal $[\![R_n^\approx]\!]$ contains the polynomial 1, this indicates that the constraints represented by $R_n^\approx$ have no common solution in the modulus-n subsystem. Hence, we can conclude that the whole system is unsatisfiable. UnsatDiseq checks if any of the polynomials in the ideal of $[\![R_n^\approx]\!]$ match an expression in $R_n^{\not\approx}$. Finally, UnsatBds concludes unsat if some variable's lower bound exceeds its upper bound.

Tightening Bounds. ConstrBds tightens bounds based on equations in $R_\infty^\approx$. Suppose e is an expression, with $[\![e]\!] \in I_\infty([\![R_\infty^\approx]\!])$, consisting of the sum of ax_i and some other expression e'. ConstrBds uses e to compute new bounds for x_i and then intersects these with the current bounds for x_i. InfEq uses the bounds information to infer new equalities: When a variable's upper and lower bounds become equal, we can obtain a new equality.

Lifting/Lowering. The lifting and lowering rules are directly based on the lemmas stated in Sect. 5.1. The rules LiftEq and LiftDiseq *lift* (dis)equalities from

$$\text{UnsatOne} \; \frac{1 \in I_n(\llbracket R_n^{\approx} \rrbracket)}{\text{unsat}} \qquad \text{UnsatDiseq} \; \frac{e \in R_n^{\not\approx} \quad \llbracket e \rrbracket \in I_n(\llbracket R_n^{\approx} \rrbracket)}{\text{unsat}}$$

$$\text{UnsatBds} \; \frac{B(x_i)_1 > B(x_i)_2}{\text{unsat}}$$

$$\text{ConstrBds} \; \frac{\llbracket e \rrbracket \in I_\infty(\llbracket R_\infty^{\approx} \rrbracket) \quad e = ax_i + e' \quad x_i \notin e' \quad B(x_i)_1 \leq B(x_i)_w}{B(x_i) := \text{CalcBds}(B, -\frac{1}{a}(e - ax_i)) \cap B(x_i)}$$

$$\text{InfEq} \; \frac{B(x_i)_1 = B(x_i)_2 \quad \llbracket x_i - B(x_i)_1 \rrbracket \notin I_\infty(\llbracket R_\infty^{\approx} \rrbracket)}{R_\infty^{\approx} := R_\infty^{\approx}, x_i - B(x_i)_1}$$

$$\text{LiftEq} \; \frac{n \neq \infty \quad \llbracket e \rrbracket \in I_n(\llbracket R_n^{\approx} \rrbracket) \quad \text{CalcBds}(B, e) \subseteq [1 - n, n - 1] \quad \llbracket e \rrbracket \notin I_\infty(\llbracket R_\infty^{\approx} \rrbracket)}{R_\infty^{\approx} := R_\infty^{\approx}, e}$$

$$\text{LiftDiseq} \; \frac{n \neq \infty \quad e \in R_n^{\not\approx} \quad e \notin R_\infty^{\not\approx}}{R_\infty^{\not\approx} := R_\infty^{\not\approx}, e}$$

$$\text{LowerEq} \; \frac{\llbracket e \rrbracket \in I_\infty(\llbracket R_\infty^{\approx} \rrbracket) \quad n \neq \infty \quad \llbracket simp_n(e) \rrbracket \notin I_n(\llbracket R_n^{\approx} \rrbracket) \quad R_n^{\approx} \in C}{R_n^{\approx} := R_n^{\approx}, simp_n(e)}$$

$$\text{LowerDiseq} \; \frac{e \in R_\infty^{\not\approx} \quad n \neq \infty \quad \text{CalcBds}(B, e) \subseteq [1 - n, n - 1] \quad simp_n(e) \notin R_n^{\not\approx} \quad R_n^{\not\approx} \in C}{R_n^{\not\approx} := R_n^{\not\approx}, simp_n(e)}$$

$$\text{RngLift} \; \frac{\begin{array}{c}\llbracket e \rrbracket \in I_n(\llbracket R_n^{\approx} \rrbracket) \quad n \neq \infty \\ \text{CalcBds}(B, e) \not\subseteq [1 - n, n - 1] \quad \text{CalcBds}(B, e) \subseteq [1 - 2n, 2n - 1] \\ \llbracket e - n \rrbracket \notin I_\infty(\llbracket R_\infty^{\approx} \rrbracket) \quad \llbracket e \rrbracket \notin I_\infty(\llbracket R_\infty^{\approx} \rrbracket) \quad \llbracket e + n \rrbracket \notin I_\infty(\llbracket R_\infty^{\approx} \rrbracket)\end{array}}{R_\infty^{\approx} := R_\infty^{\approx}, e - n \; || \; R_\infty^{\approx} := R_\infty^{\approx}, e \; || \; R_\infty^{\approx} := R_\infty^{\approx}, e + n}$$

$$\text{ZeroOrOne} \; \frac{\llbracket e \rrbracket \in I_n(\llbracket R_n^{\approx} \rrbracket) \quad \llbracket e \rrbracket = s^2 - s \quad n \neq \infty \quad \text{IsPrime}(n) \quad \llbracket s \rrbracket \notin I_n(\llbracket R_n^{\approx} \rrbracket) \quad \llbracket s - 1 \rrbracket \notin I_n(\llbracket R_n^{\approx} \rrbracket)}{R_n^{\approx} := R_n^{\approx}, s \; || \; R_n^{\approx} := R_n^{\approx}, s - 1}$$

Fig. 4. Derivation rules. e, s are expressions, $a \in \mathbb{Z}$, and $n \in \mathbb{Z}_\infty^+$.

$R_n^{\bowtie}$ to $R_\infty^{\bowtie}$, by relying on Lemmas 1 and 2. We also check entailment (polynomial ideal containment for equalities and set containment for disequalities) to avoid adding redundant information. Dually, the rules LowerEq and LowerDiseq *lower* (dis)equalities from from $R_\infty^{\bowtie}$ to $R_n^{\bowtie}$ by relying on Lemmas 3 and 4.

Branching Rules. When encountering equations that are *almost* liftable, we rely on branching rules to either lift or simplify them. For example, if $\text{CalcBds}(B, x) = [0, 7]$, $x \mod 6 \approx 0$ is *almost* liftable, as its range exceeds the liftable range only slightly. RngLift branches on possible values for e that are within $|n|$ of the liftable range. ZeroOrOne detects when the value of a variable

In: A set of constraints C
Out: unsat/unknown

```
1 def REFUTE(C):
2     (B, R_∞^≈, R_∞^≉ ... R_n^≈, R_n^≉) ← Split(C)  // Figure 3
3     while Exchange((B, R_∞^≈, R_∞^≉ ... R_n^≈, R_n^≉))  // Section 5.2-5.5
4     do
5         if CheckUnsat((B, R_∞^≈, R_∞^≉ ... R_n^≈, R_n^≉))  // Section 5.2
6         then
7             return unsat
8         if S ← Branch((B, R_∞^≈, R_∞^≉ ... R_n^≈, R_n^≉)) then
9             for c_i ∈ S do
10                if REFUTE(c_i) == unknown then
11                    return unknown
12            return unsat
13    return unknown
```

Algorithm 1: Overview of the Refutation Procedure

can only be 0 or 1; it applies only to prime moduli because other moduli have zero divisors.

We state *soundness* and *termination* theorems for our calculus and include the proofs in the extended version of the paper [69]. However, the calculus is *not* complete—a saturated leaf in a derivation tree does not necessarily mean that the constraints at the root of the tree are satisfiable.

Theorem 1. *Soundness: If T is a closed derivation tree with root node C, then C is unsatisfiable in $\mathcal{T}_{\text{Int}}$.*

Theorem 2. *Termination: Every derivation starting from a finite configuration C where every variable is bounded is finite.*

5.3 Refutation Algorithm

Our implementation of the calculus follows the following strategy. It first performs lifting via the LiftEq and LiftDiseq rules to exhaustion (i.e., until these rules no longer apply) and then attempts to refute each subsystem using the UnsatOne and UnsatDiseq rules for each $R_n^{\approx}$, $n \neq \infty$. If this fails, it applies the bounds-related rules (ConstrBds, InfEq, UnsatBds) and lowering rules (LowerEq and LowerDiseq), also to exhaustion. It then once again attempts refutation, but with $n = \infty$. If that also fails, it applies a branching rule, if applicable (trying first ZeroOrOne, then RngLift), and then the entire strategy repeats.

Algorithm 1 presents an algorithmic view of the overall process. Given constraints C, the procedure starts by encoding C into a configuration using the Split routine, which creates the tuple encoding described in Sect. 5.1 and applies the rules from Fig. 3. The main refutation procedure consists of the while loop in lines 3–7 and works as follows. First, it exchanges expressions between the different subsystems via lifting and lowering and tightens bounds or learns new equations from bounds (line 3). Since lifting requires finding additional polynomials that are in the ideal, the implementation of the Exchange procedure utilizes the methods described in Sects. 5.4 and 5.5 to find additional polynomials corresponding to exchangeable expressions. The methods can be used individually or in combination, and we defer the discussion of their ordering to Sect. 7. Next, at line 5, the algorithm invokes CheckUnsat to attempt to refute any of the subsystems. If CheckUnsat returns true, the algorithm terminates with unsat. Otherwise, the algorithm attempts to apply a branching rule (lines 8–12). If successful, it recursively calls the REFUTE procedure on a new set of constraints and returns unsat if *all* recursive calls perform successful refutation. Since our algorithm is intended only for refutation rather than model construction, it returns unknown in all other cases.

5.4 Finding Liftable Equalities via Weighted Gröbner Bases

Recall that several rules in our refutation calculus require finding liftable or lowerable constraints that correspond to a polynomial in the ideal of some existing set of polynomials. As explained earlier, finding *additional* liftable/lowerable constraints is useful because they can make it easier to prove unsatisfiability. However, since ideals are infinite, we need some algorithm for selecting which polynomials to target. In this section, we present a method for computing "useful" polynomials—those that are likely to correspond to liftable constraints. We focus on the liftability of equalities only, because all equalities are already lowerable, and disequalities do not form an ideal and thus are easy to enumerate.

Based on Lemma 1, a polynomial's bound endpoints are the most important indicators of liftability. As a result, we target polynomials that we call *near-zero polynomials*, or polynomials with a bound whose endpoints have small absolute value. Based on this definition, a polynomial with a bound $[-5, 5]$ is *closer to zero* than a polynomial with a bound of $[-50, 50]$ or $[49, 50]$.

Since we cannot enumerate the ideal, one possibility is to construct a basis for the ideal that contains polynomials that are more likely to refer to liftable constraints. As discussed in Sect. 3, one possible basis is a Gröbner basis, which uses a monomial order. A Gröbner basis is computed via an algorithm that often eliminates larger monomials with respect to the order. Our idea is to compute a Gröbner basis using a carefully chosen monomial order in which monomials that are closer to zero are smaller than those farther from zero. The insight is that polynomials with near-zero monomials are generally (though not always) more likely to be liftable. To achieve this, our monomial order must encode information about bounds on the monomials. To this end, we first take the maximum of the absolute values of the lower and upper bounds on each variable. Additionally, since weighted monomial orders are determined by the dot product of variable exponents and assigned weights, we apply logarithmic scaling to ensure that the influence of a bound is appropriately adjusted by each variable's degree. Based on this intuition, we use a *weighted reverse lexicographic* monomial order

(Sect. 3), with weights:[4]

$$\texttt{weights} \leftarrow [\log(\max(|B(\mathsf{x}_i)_1|, |B(\mathsf{x}_i)_2|) + \epsilon) \mid \mathsf{x}_i \in \mathcal{X}] \qquad (2)$$

When applying the `LiftEq` rule in the refutation calculus our algorithm computes a Gröbner basis according to the order defined by (2) and only checks the liftability of the polynomials in this Gröbner basis.

Ideally, when we apply the `LiftEq` rule, we want to find a *complete* set of liftable equations—that is, any other liftable constraint should be implied by the ones inferred by our technique. Our weighted Gröbner basis method does not have this completeness guarantee in general, but the following theorem states a weaker completeness guarantee that it *does* provide:

Theorem 3. *Let C be a constraint system containing a modulus-n equality subsystem $R_n^{\approx}$ and variable bounds B s.t. for all $\mathsf{x}_i \in \mathcal{X}$, $0 \in B(\mathsf{x}_i)$. Let $G = GB_{n,\leq}(\llbracket R_n^{\approx} \rrbracket)$ be a Gröbner basis computed with a weighted reverse lexicographical order with weights from Eq. 2.*

Finding liftable equalities derived from $I(R_n^{\approx})$ by computing G is complete if every generator $\llbracket e \rrbracket \in G$ that has a leading monomial $\llbracket m \rrbracket$ s.t. $\texttt{CalcBds}(B, m) \subseteq [1-n, n-1]$ corresponds to a liftable expression $e \mod n$ in C.

Completeness implies that the ideal generated by the generators of G, which correspond to liftable expressions, contains all polynomials corresponding to liftable expressions from $I_n(\llbracket R_n^{\approx} \rrbracket)$.

Intuitively, completeness means $\{\llbracket p \rrbracket : \texttt{CalcBds}(B, p) \subseteq [1-n, n-1] \wedge \llbracket p \rrbracket \in I_n(\llbracket R_n^{\approx} \rrbracket)\} \subseteq I_n(\{\llbracket g \rrbracket : \texttt{CalcBds}(B, g) \subseteq [1-n, n-1] \wedge \llbracket g \rrbracket \in G\})$. A detailed proof can be found in the extended version of the paper [69]. This theorem is useful because it allows us to identify cases when additional heuristics for identifying liftable polynomials might be useful.

5.5 Finding Liftable Equalities via Integer Linear Constraints

Now we present another method, complementary to the one in Sect. 5.4, for finding liftable constraints. This new method is motivated by the following observation: In many cases, liftable equalities can be obtained from *linear combinations* of existing expressions—i.e., they are of the form $e' = \sum_{i=1}^{l} a_i e_i$ for existing expressions e_i and constant coefficients a_i. The method proposed here aims to find these unknown coefficients $a_1, \ldots, a_n$ by setting up an auxiliary *integer linear constraint*. If this linear constraint is feasible, then the inferred equality is guaranteed to satisfy the conditions from Lemma 1.

To emphasize that the coefficients a_i are the unknowns being solved for, we depict them using a bold font below. Our goal is to encode the condition $\texttt{CalcBds}(B, e') \subset [1-n, n-1]$ in the generated constraint. Since $\texttt{CalcBds}$ depends on e''s coefficients, we express those coefficients in terms of the $\mathbf{a}_i$.

---

[4] The ϵ serves to avoid $\log(0)$ which is undefined.

Let $[\![m_1]\!], \ldots, [\![m_t]\!]$ be all the monomials present in $[\![R_n^\approx]\!]$, including the constant monomial $1 \in \mathbb{Z}[X]$. Moreover, let $[\![e_i]\!]$ have coefficients $c_{i,j}$, such that $[\![e_i]\!] = \sum_{j=1}^t c_{i,j}[\![m_j]\!]$. Then, the coefficient of $[\![m_j]\!]$ in $[\![e']\!]$, denoted coef_j, is the linear polynomial, $\text{coef}_j \triangleq \sum_{i=1}^t \mathbf{a}_i c_{i,j}$.

We can now express the relevant bounds. The lower and upper bounds on each monomial m_j can be concretely computed as $u_j \triangleq \text{CalcBds}(B, m_j)_1$ and $l_j \triangleq \text{CalcBds}(B, m_j)_0$. Then, the lower and upper bounds on e' itself are respectively:

$$\text{lb} \triangleq \sum_{j=1}^t (l_j \cdot \text{ReLU}(\text{coef}_j) - u_j \cdot \text{ReLU}(-\text{coef}_j))$$
$$\text{ub} \triangleq \sum_{j=1}^t (u_j \cdot \text{ReLU}(\text{coef}_j) - l_j \cdot \text{ReLU}(-\text{coef}_j)),$$

where $\text{ReLU}(a)$ is $\max(a, 0)$. ReLU constraints capture how negating a monomial affects its upper and lower bounds: if $\text{coef}_j > 0$, u_j contributes to the upper bound of e'; otherwise, it contributes to the lower bound. These constraints can be encoded using binary variables when the upper and lower bounds are known [76]. Since the operations are performed modulo n, all coefficients must lie within the interval $[1-n, n-1]$. Our encoding Φ is then:

$$\Phi \triangleq \quad \text{lb} > -n \quad \wedge \quad \text{ub} < n \quad \wedge \quad \sum_{i=1}^k (\text{ReLU}(\text{coef}_j) + \text{ReLU}(-\text{coef}_j)) > 0$$

The first two conditions ensure e' is liftable, and the last ensures that $e' \neq 0$.

Theorem 4. *Let C be a constraint system containing modulus-n equality subsystem $R_n^\approx$ and variable bounds B. Φ is satisfiable iff there exists a linear combination of the form $e' = \sum_{i=1}^l a_i e_i$, $a_i \in \mathbb{Z}$ and $e_i \in R_n^\approx$, s.t. e' is liftable in C and $e' \neq 0$.*

In the case that Φ is satisfiable, we seek to find all linearly independent solutions, as different solutions correspond to different liftable equations, all of which may be useful for proving unsatisfiability. Thus, we add constraints ruling out linear combinations of solutions found so far and iterate until ϕ is unsatisfiable.

6 Implementation

We implemented our refutation procedure in the cvc5 SMT solver [3] as an alternative to the existing nonlinear integer solver. We use Singular v4.4.0 [23] for the algebraic components of our procedure and glpk [52] v4.6.0 for solving the integer linear constraints problems from Sect. 5.5. Below we describe the key details in our implementation.

Rewrites. Our implementation disables all rewrites for the mod operator but retains the remaining cvc5 rewrites and pre-processing passes.

Ideal Membership Check. To check if a polynomial version of an expression is in $I_n(\llbracket R_n^\approx \rrbracket)$ we compute a Gröbner basis (GB) of $\llbracket R_n^\approx \rrbracket$ using *graded reverse lexicographic order* unless $\llbracket R_n^\approx \rrbracket$ is already a GB. (Recall that reduction by a GB is a complete ideal membership test.)

To prevent GB computation from becoming a bottleneck, we impose a 30-second timeout. If a timeout occurs, we only check inclusion in the set instead of the ideal.

Liftable Equalities via Integer Linear Constraints. Experimental results showed that integer linear constraint solvers perform poorly on problems with large integer constants. To address this issue, our implementation uses an approximate version where we scale constants using signed log defined as $\text{slog}_2(a) = \frac{|a|}{a} \log_2(a)$ and use a 30-second timeout. Details of our approximation, including empirical results that motivate this approximation can be found in the extended version of the paper [69]. All experimental results reported in the paper use this relaxation of the encoding.

7 Experiments

Our experiments are designed to answer two key empirical questions 1. How does our refutation procedure compare to the state of the art? 2. Do our lifting algorithms (Sect. 5.4 and 5.5) improve performance? All of our expriments are run on a cluster with Intel Xeon E5-2637 v4 CPUs. Each run is limited to one physical core, 8GB memory, and 20 min.

7.1 Benchmarks

The benchmarks used in our experimental evaluation consist of logical formulas encoding the correctness of simulating arithmetic operations in a given *specification* domain using arithmetic in a corresponding *base* domain. Each domain is either a finite field ($\mathbb{F}_p$ or $\mathbb{F}_q$) or a bit-vector domain ($\mathbb{Z}_{2^b}$). Implementations that represent values in the specification domain as multiple *limbs* in the base domain are referred to as *multiprecision* (m), while those using a single representation are classified as *single precision* (s).

As summarized in Table 1, our benchmarks fall under the following categories:

- f/b(s) encode the correctness of single-precision *Montgomery arithmetic* [56], which implements arithmetic modulo p using bit-vector operations, without mod-p reductions, and is common in prime field CPU implementations. The benchmarks verify the correctness of the REDC subroutine and the end-to-end correctness of Montgomery's approach for evaluating expressions mod p.

- f/b(m) encode correctness of multi-precision Montgomery arithmetic.

Table 1. Our benchmarks, which verify arithmetic implementations with various specification domains, base domains and numeric precisions.

Family	Spec.	Base	Reference
f/b(s)	$\mathbb{F}_p$	$\mathbb{Z}_{2^b}$	Montgomery arithmetic [56]
f/b(m)	$\mathbb{F}_p$	$\mathbb{Z}_{2^b}$	Montgomery arithmetic [56]
f/f(s)	$\mathbb{F}_p$	$\mathbb{F}_q$	Succinct labs [43,75]
f/f(m)	$\mathbb{F}_p$	$\mathbb{F}_q$	o1-labs [64]
b/f(m)	$\mathbb{Z}_{2^b}$	$\mathbb{F}_p$	xjSnark [49]

- f/f(s) encode implementations of arithmetic modulo the 31-bit Goldilocks prime [43] modulo a 255-bit prime (the order of the BLS 12–381 elliptic curve [4,10]).
  The benchmarks model a Succinct labs implementation [75] that is used for recursive zero-knowledge proofs (ZKPs).
- f/f(m) encode the correctness of implementations of arithmetic modulo one 255-bit prime using arithmetic modulo another 255-bit prime.
  Multiple limbs are used to avoid unintended overflow in the base domain.
  The benchmarks model an o1-labs implementation [64] used for recursive ZKPs.
- b/f(m) encode correctness of multi-precision implementations of bit-vector arithmetic modulo a 255-bit prime.
  The benchmarks model techniques from the xjSnark ZKP compiler [49] that are used to check RSA signatures.

Determinism. We include *determinism* [66] benchmarks in addition to correctness for families with a finite field base domain. Determinism is a weaker property than correctness but rules out most bugs in practice [15]. We do not include determinism f/f(m) benchmarks because they are correct but **non**deterministic. Additional benchmark statistics are included in the extended version of the paper [69].

7.2 State of the Art Comparison

Baselines Our benchmarks are SMT problems in QF_MIA (Sect. 4). Since all variables have finite bounds, our benchmarks can also be encoded in QF_BV. Our determinism benchmarks contain only variable bounds and equations modulo one prime and can thus be encoded in QF_FF using standard $\mathbb{F}$ encodings of range constraints [49]. As a result, the baselines for our work are existing solvers for QF_NIA, QF_BV, and QF_FF. We compare against Yices v2.6.5 [26], cvc5 v1.2.2 [3], bitwuzla v0.5.0 [60], and z3 v4.13.1 [57], which are state of the art for these logics. We evaluate bitwuzla with and without abstraction [62] and cvc5's QF_FF solver with and without split Gröbner bases [66].

Table 2. Solved benchmarks. Here, cor stands for correctness and det for determinism. – indicates the benchmark family cannot be encoded into the logic.

		Family						
		f/b(s)	f/b(m)	f/f(s)		f/f(m)	b/f(m)	
Solver/Logic		cor	cor	cor	det	cor	cor	det	Total
ours QF_MIA		**53**	14	**10**	**84**	**50**	**24**	**20**	**255**
z3 QF_NIA		49	21	3	34	40	22	21	190
cvc5 QF_NIA		40	35	0	19	**50**	14	8	166
yices QF_NIA		32	24	0	2	10	13	8	89
bitwuzla(abst.) QF_BV		49	**49**	0	2	25	9	8	142
bitwuzla QF_BV		49	**49**	0	0	0	9	8	115
cvc5 QF_BV		43	48	0	0	0	9	7	107
z3 QF_BV		48	37	0	0	0	9	8	102
cvc5 QF_FF		–	–	–	1	–	–	**23**	24
yices QF_FF		–	–	–	0	–	–	20	20
cvc5 (split GB) QF_FF		–	–	–	2	–	–	9	11
# Benchmarks		72	58	10	98	50	24	24	336

Table 3. Results with different lifting algorithms

	Family								
	f/b(s)	f/b(m)	f/f(s)		f/f(m)	b/f(m)			
Ablation	cor	cor	cor	det	cor	cor	det	Total	Uniq.
Weighted GB	53	14	**10**	**84**	**50**	**24**	20	**255**	11
Unweighted GB	41	**25**	**10**	61	**50**	17	20	223	1
Lin. Constraints	37	18	0	7	0	7	3	72	3
Weighted GB & Lin.	**54**	23	**10**	73	**50**	**24**	20	254	**12**
# Benchmarks	72	58	10	98	50	24	24	336	

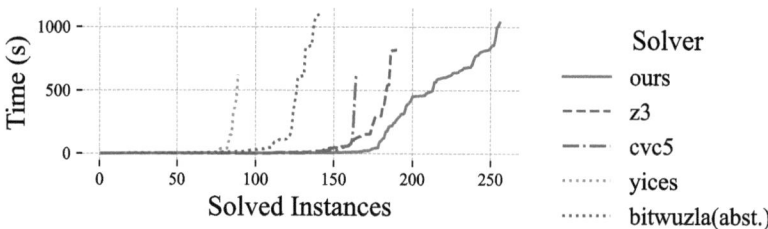

Fig. 5. Benchmarks solved over time for top 5 solvers: ours (QF_MIA), z3 (QF_NIA), cvc5 (QF_NIA), yices (QF_NIA), and bitwuzla w/ abstractions (QF_BV)

Comparison. Table 2 shows the number of unsat benchmarks solved by family, type, logic, and tool, and Fig. 5 shows the performance for the top 5 solvers. Here, 'ours' stands for the best version of our solver: one with a lifting algorithm based on a weighted Gröbner basis (Sect. 5.4). This configuration outperforms existing tools on 5 out of the 7 categories, as well as in total benchmarks solved. It is also the most efficient and has the most unique solves, with 76 benchmarks not solved by any other solver. Of the 81 benchmarks our tool fails to solve, 27 remain unsolved by any solver. For these 81 benchmarks, 10 run out of memory, 29 time out, and 42 return unknown. Our solver performs the worst on the f/b(m) family; it accounts for 34 of the unknown benchmarks. We believe the poor performance in this domain is due to our algorithm's inability to find liftable equalities necessary to detect unsatisfiability, even though such equalities exist in the ideal.

7.3 Evaluation of Lifting Methods

Recall that our method relies on identifying liftable equations, with Sects. 5.4 and 5.5 introducing two potentially complementary approaches for this purpose. We now present the results of an evaluation comparing these lifting methods. As summarized in Table 3, the weighted Gröbner basis method achieves the best overall performance. However, on the f/b(m) benchmark family, the unweighted Gröbner basis method outperforms the weighted variant, supporting our hypothesis that the weighted Gröbner basis's inability to find certain liftable equalities contributes to its weaker performance in this category. Lifting based on integer linear constraints performs the poorest, identifying almost no liftable equalities required for refutation. Nevertheless, when combined with the weighted Gröbner basis method (in cases where the Gröbner basis method is not guaranteed to be complete per Theorem 3), this hybrid approach has the most unique solves (12).

8 Related Work

There are many SMT theory solvers for different kinds of modular integer arithmetic. Some solvers target theories of non-linear integer arithmetic with an explicit modulus operator, such as the theory of integers [2,8,14,17,19,35,46–48,53,58,77,80], and the theory of bit-vectors [11,39,59,61,62]. These solvers can be used to solve multimodular systems, but generally perform poorly because they are designed to support *general* modular reduction (i.e., reduction modulo a variable) rather than reduction by constants. There are solvers that efficiently support reduction by a single constant or *class* of constants. For example, finite field solvers [40–42,65,66] support reduction modulo primes, while bit-vector solvers support reduction modulo powers of two. But, none of these can reason simultaneously about equations modulo a large prime and powers of two. The Omega test reasons about equations modulo arbitrary constants—but the equations must be linear [71]. Our procedure supports non-linear equations modulo arbitrary constants.

Some of the above solvers use Gröbner bases: an algebraic tool for understanding polynomial systems [12]. For example, most similar to our refutation procedure, cvc5's finite field solver [65,66] also relies on a Gröbner basis to detect unsatisfiability of constraint subsystems. However, unlike our approach, it does not separate bounds or apply lifting, lowering, or weighted ordering techniques to share expressions across subsystems.

Many computer algebra systems (CASs) implement algorithms for computing different kinds of Gröbner bases [1,9,21,23,27,28,36,44,55,82,84]. Following in this vein, our procedure uses strong Gröbner bases [63], and our implementation uses the Singular CAS [23].

Formal methods for modular arithmetic have a long history of applications to cryptography. Interactive theorem provers (ITPs) have been used to verify many cryptographic implementations [31,70,73], including the Fiat cryptography library, which is used in all major web-browsers [30]. ITPs have also been used to verify zero-knowledge proofs (ZKPs) [16,18,34,51]. But ITP-based verification requires significant manual effort and expertise. SMT solvers for finite fields [67,68] and static analyses [20,79,81] have been used to verify ZKPs automatically, but these tools are limited by challenging tradeoffs between scalability and generality.

9 Conclusion and Future Work

In this paper we presented a novel refutation procedure for multimodular constraints and two algorithms for sharing lemmas: one based on a weighted Gröbner basis and another utilizing integer linear constraints. Our experiments demonstrate improvement over state-of-the-art solvers on benchmarks that arise from verifying cryptographic implementations. They also show the promise of lifting algorithms, both individually and in combination. Nevertheless, substantial future work remains.

First, as discussed in Sects. 5.4 and 5.5, none of our lifting algorithms are complete. Exploring solutions with more completeness guarantees could boost the performance of our method. Second, as shown in the extended version of the paper [69], lifting using linear integer constraints shows poor performance due to the limitations of existing solvers. A custom solver tailored to our encoding could lead to better results. Third, our method focuses on unsatisfiable benchmarks and does not address model construction for satisfiable instances. However, we believe that leveraging the subsystem structure could also be beneficial for restricting the search space of possible assignments for satisfiable multimodular problems. Finally, our method treats Gröbner basis computation as a black box. Exploring more iterative methods based on s-polynomials could also boost performance.

Acknowledgements. We thank Ben Sepanski and Kostas Ferles for helpful conversations. We acknowledge funding from NSF grant number 2110397, the Stanford Center for Automated Reasoning, and the Simons foundation.

Disclosure of Interests. Shankara Pailoor, Alp Bassa, and Isil Dillig are employed at Veridise. Alex Ozdemir and Sorawee Porncharoenwase previously worked at Veridise. Sorawee Porncharoenwase is currently employed at Amazon Web Services (AWS). Clark Barrett is an Amazon Scholar.

References

1. Abbott, J., Bigatti, A.M.: CoCoALib: A C++ library for computations in commutative algebra... and beyond. In: International Congress on Mathematical Software (2010)
2. Ábrahám, E., Davenport, J.H., England, M., Kremer, G.: Deciding the consistency of non-linear real arithmetic constraints with a conflict driven search using cylindrical algebraic coverings. J. Logical Algebraic Methods Program. **119** (2021)
3. Barbosa, H., et al.: cvc5: A versatile and industrial-strength SMT solver. In: TACAS (2022)
4. Barreto, P.S., Lynn, B., Scott, M.: Constructing elliptic curves with prescribed embedding degrees. In: SCN (2003)
5. Barrett, C., Fontaine, P., Tinelli, C.: The Satisfiability Modulo Theories Library (SMT-LIB). www.SMT-LIB.org (2016)
6. Barrett, C., Tinelli, C.: Satisfiability modulo theories. In: Handbook of Model Checking, pp. 305–343. Springer, Cham (2018). https://doi.org/10.1007/978-3-319-10575-8_11
7. Barrett, P.: Implementing the rivest shamir and adleman public key encryption algorithm on a standard digital signal processor. In: CRYPTO (1986)
8. Bjørner, N., Nachmanson, L.: Arithmetic solving in z3. In: CAV (2024)
9. Bosma, W., Cannon, J., Playoust, C.: The Magma algebra system I: the user language. J. Symb. Comput. **24**(3–4), 235–265 (1997)
10. Bowe, S.: BLS12-381: New zk-snark elliptic curve construction (Mar. 2017). https://electriccoin.co/blog/new-snark-curve/
11. Brummayer, R., Biere, A.: Boolector: An efficient SMT solver for bit-vectors and arrays. In: TACAS (2009)
12. Buchberger, B.: Ein Algorithmus zum Auffinden der Basiselemente des Restklassenringes nach einem nulldimensionalen Polynomideal. PhD thesis, University of Innsbruck (1965)
13. Buchberger, B.: A theoretical basis for the reduction of polynomials to canonical forms. SIGSAM Bulletin (1976)
14. Caviness, B.F., Johnson, J.R.: Quantifier elimination and cylindrical algebraic decomposition. Springer Science & Business Media (2012)
15. Chaliasos, S., Ernstberger, J., Theodore, D., Wong, D., Jahanara, M., and Livshits, B.: SoK: what don't we know? understanding security vulnerabilities in SNARKs. In: USENIX Security (2024)
16. Chin, C., Wu, H., Chu, R., Coglio, A., McCarthy, E., Smith, E.: Leo: A programming language for formally verified, zero-knowledge applications (2021). Preprint at https://ia.cr/2021/651
17. Cimatti, A., Griggio, A., Irfan, A., Roveri, M., Sebastiani, R.: Incremental linearization for satisfiability and verification modulo nonlinear arithmetic and transcendental functions. ACM TOCL **19**(3) (2018)
18. Coglio, A., McCarthy, E., Smith, E., Chin, C., Gaddamadugu, P., Dellepere, M.: Compositional formal verification of zero-knowledge circuits (2023). https://ia.cr/2023/1278

19. Corzilius, F., Kremer, G., Junges, S., Schupp, S., Ábrahám, E.: SMT-RAT: an open source C++ toolbox for strategic and parallel SMT solving. SAT (2015)
20. Dahlgren, F.: It pays to be Circomspect (2022). https://blog.trailofbits.com/2022/09/15/it-pays-to-be-circomspect/. Accessed 15 October 2023
21. Davenport, J.: The axiom system (1992)
22. David, C.: Ideals, Varieties, and Algorithms-An Introduction to Computational Algebraic Geometry and Commutative Algebra. Undergraduate Texts in Mathematics (1991)
23. Decker, W., Greuel, G.-M., Pfister, G., Schönemann, H.: Singular 4-4-0 — A computer algebra system for polynomial computations (2024). http://www.singular.uni-kl.de
24. Diffie, W., Hellman, M.E.: New directions in cryptography. IEEE Trans. Inform. Theory **22**(6) (1976)
25. Dummit, D.S., Foote, R.M.: Abstract algebra, vol. 3. Wiley Hoboken (2004)
26. Dutertre, B.: Yices 2.2. In: CAV (2014)
27. Eder, C., Hofmann, T.: Efficient Gröbner bases computation over principal ideal rings. J. Symb. Comput. **103**, 1–13 (2021)
28. Eisenbud, D., Grayson, D.R., Stillman, M., Sturmfels, B.: Computations in algebraic geometry with Macaulay 2, vol. 8. Springer Science & Business Media (2001)
29. Enderton, H.B.: A mathematical introduction to logic. Elsevier (2001)
30. Erbsen, A., Philipoom, J., Gross, J., Sloan, R., Chlipala, A.: Systematic generation of fast elliptic curve cryptography implementations. Technical report, MIT (2018)
31. Erbsen, A., Philipoom, J., Gross, J., Sloan, R., Chlipala, A.: Simple high-level code for cryptographic arithmetic: with proofs, without compromises. ACM SIGOPS Operating Syst. Rev. **54**(1) (2020)
32. Faugére, J.C.: A new efficient algorithm for computing Gröbner bases (f4). J. Pure Appl. Algebra **139**(1), 61–88 (1999)
33. Faugére, J.C.: A new efficient algorithm for computing Gröbner bases without reduction to zero (f5). In: ISSAC. ACM (2002)
34. Fournet, C., Keller, C., Laporte, V.: A certified compiler for verifiable computing. In: CSF (2016)
35. Fränzle, M., Herde, C., Teige, T., Ratschan, S., Schubert, T.: Efficient solving of large non-linear arithmetic constraint systems with complex boolean structure. J. Satisfiability, Boolean Model. Comput. **1**(3–4) (2006)
36. GAP – Groups, Algorithms, and Programming, Version 4.13dev. https://www.gap-system.org, this year
37. Gentry, C.: Fully homomorphic encryption using ideal lattices. In: STOC (2009)
38. Goldwasser, S., Micali, S., Rackoff, C.: The knowledge complexity of interactive proof systems. SIAM J. Comput. **18**(1), 186–208 (1989)
39. Graham-Lengrand, S., Jovanović, D., Dutertre, B.: Solving bitvectors with MCSAT: explanations from bits and pieces. In: IJCAR (2020)
40. Hader, T.: Non-linear SMT-reasoning over finite fields. MS Thesis (TU Wein) (2022)
41. Hader, T., Kaufmann, D., Kovács, L.: SMT solving over finite field arithmetic. In: LPAR (2023)
42. Hader, T., Kovács, L.: Non-linear SMT-reasoning over finite fields. In: SMT. Extended Abstract (2022)
43. Hamburg, M.: Ed448-goldilocks, a new elliptic curve (2015).https://ia.cr/2015/625
44. Heck, A., Koepf, W.: Introduction to MAPLE, vol. 1993 (1993)
45. Hickey, T., Ju, Q., Van Emden, M.H.: Interval arithmetic: from principles to implementation. ACM **48**(5), 1038–1068 (2001)

46. Jovanović, D.: Solving nonlinear integer arithmetic with MCSAT. In: VMCAI (2017)
47. Jovanović, D., De Moura, L.: Solving non-linear arithmetic. ACM Commun. Comput. Algebra **46**(3/4) (2013)
48. Jovanović, D., Moura, L.d.: Cutting to the chase solving linear integer arithmetic. In: CADE (2011)
49. Kosba, A., Papamanthou, C., Shi, E.: xJsnark: A framework for efficient verifiable computation. In: IEEE S&P (2018)
50. Liang, T., Reynolds, A., Tinelli, C., Barrett, C., Deters, M.: A DPLL(T) theory solver for a theory of strings and regular expressions. In: Biere, A., Bloem, R. (eds.) CAV 2014. LNCS, vol. 8559, pp. 646–662. Springer, Cham (2014). https://doi.org/10.1007/978-3-319-08867-9_43
51. Liu, J., et al.: Certifying zero-knowledge circuits with refinement types (2023). https://ia.cr/2023/547
52. Makhorin, A.: GNU linear programming kit version 4.6.0 (2024). http://www.gnu.org/software/glpk/glpk.html
53. Maréchal, A., Fouilhé, A., King, T., Monniaux, D., Périn, M.: Polyhedral approximation of multivariate polynomials using handelman's theorem. In: VMCAI (2016)
54. McCoy, N.H.: Rings and ideals, vol. 8. American Mathematical Soc. (1948)
55. Meurer, A., et al.: Sympy: symbolic computing in python. PeerJ Comput. Sci. **3**, e103 (2017)
56. Montgomery, P.L.: Modular multiplication without trial division. Math. Comput. **44**(170), 519–521 (1985)
57. Moura, L.d., Bjørner, N.: Z3: An efficient SMT solver. In: TACAS (2008)
58. Moura, L.d., Jovanović, D.: A model-constructing satisfiability calculus. In: VMCAI (2013)
59. Niemetz, A., Preiner, M.: Ternary propagation-based local search for more bit-precise reasoning. In: FMCAD (2020)
60. Niemetz, A., Preiner, M.: Bitwuzla. In: CAV (2023)
61. Niemetz, A., Preiner, M., Reynolds, A., Zohar, Y., Barrett, C., Tinelli, C.: Towards bit-width-independent proofs in SMT solvers. In: CADE (2019)
62. Niemetz, A., Preiner, M., Zohar, Y.: Scalable bit-blasting with abstractions. In: CAV (2024)
63. Norton, G.H., Sălăgean, A.: Strong Gröbner bases for polynomials over a principal ideal ring. Bull. Aust. Math. Soc. **64**(3), 505–528 (2001)
64. o1-labs. Foreign field multiplication gate (2024). https://github.com/o1-labs/rfcs/blob/eeb8070c9901c611c9a557464022bbf9237900b9/0006-ffmul-revised.md
65. Ozdemir, A., Kremer, G., Tinelli, C., Barrett, C.: Satisfiability modulo finite fields. In: CAV (2023)
66. Ozdemir, A., Pailoor, S., Bassa, A., Ferles, K., Barrett, C., Dillig, I.: Split Gröbner Bases for satisfiability modulo finite fields. In: CAV (2024)
67. Ozdemir, A., Wahby, R.S., Brown, F., Barrett, C.: Bounded verification for finite-field-blasting. In: CAV (2023)
68. Pailoor, S., et al.: Automated detection of under-constrained circuits in zero-knowledge proofs. In: PLDI (2023)
69. Pertseva, E., et al.: Integer reasoning modulo different constants in smt (2025). https://arxiv.org/abs/2505.14998
70. Philipoom, J.: Correct-by-construction finite field arithmetic in Coq PhD thesis, Massachusetts Institute of Technology (2018)
71. Pugh, W.: The Omega test: a fast and practical integer programming algorithm for dependence analysis. In: SC (1991)

72. Rivest, R.L., Shamir, A., Adleman, L.: A method for obtaining digital signatures and public-key cryptosystems. Commun. ACM **21**(2), 120–126 (1978)
73. Schwabe, P., Viguier, B., Weerwag, T., Wiedijk, F.: A Coq proof of the correctness of X25519 in TweetNaCl. In: CSF (2021)
74. Sheng, Y., et al.: Reasoning about vectors using an SMT theory of sequences. In: IJCAR (2022)
75. Succinct Labs. Gnark Plonky2 recursive verifier: The goldilocks field implementation (2024). https://github.com/succinctlabs/gnark-plonky2-verifier/tree/7025b2efd67b5ed30bd85f93c694774106d21b3d/goldilocks
76. Tsay, C., Kronqvist, J., Thebelt, A., Misener, R.: Partition-based formulations for mixed-integer optimization of trained relu neural networks. NeurIPS (2021)
77. Tung, V.X., Khanh, T.V., Ogawa, M.: raSAT: an SMT solver for polynomial constraints. In: IJCAR (2016)
78. Walfish, M., Blumberg, A.J.: Verifying computations without reexecuting them. Commun. ACM **58**(2), 74–84 (2015)
79. Wang, F.: Ecne: Automated verification of ZK circuits (2022). https://0xparc.org/blog/ecne
80. Weispfenning, V.: Quantifier elimination for real algebra–the quadratic case and beyond. Applicable Algebra Eng. Commun. Comput. **8**(2) (1997)
81. Wen, H., et al.: Practical security analysis of zero-knowledge proof circuits (2023). https://ia.cr/2023/190
82. Wolfram, S.: Mathematica: a system for doing mathematics by computer. Addison Wesley Longman Publishing Co., Inc (1991)
83. Yao, A.C.: Protocols for secure computations. In: FOCS (1982)
84. Zimmermann, P., et al.: Computational mathematics with SageMath. SIAM (2018)

Open Access This chapter is licensed under the terms of the Creative Commons Attribution 4.0 International License (http://creativecommons.org/licenses/by/4.0/), which permits use, sharing, adaptation, distribution and reproduction in any medium or format, as long as you give appropriate credit to the original author(s) and the source, provide a link to the Creative Commons license and indicate if changes were made.

The images or other third party material in this chapter are included in the chapter's Creative Commons license, unless indicated otherwise in a credit line to the material. If material is not included in the chapter's Creative Commons license and your intended use is not permitted by statutory regulation or exceeds the permitted use, you will need to obtain permission directly from the copyright holder.

Structural Operational Semantics for Functional and Security Verification of Pipelined Processors

Robert J. Colvin[1,2] and Roger C. Su[3]

[1] Defence Science and Technology Group, Brisbane, Australia
r.colvin@uq.edu.au
[2] University of Queensland, Brisbane, Australia
[3] School of Computing, Australian National University, Canberra, Australia

Abstract. The design of computer microarchitectures is a challenging task, involving a trade-off between efficiency and security. In the literature, two concerns which are affected by the details of the microarchitecture – formal assembly semantics, and vulnerability discovery and mitigation – are often addressed separately. In this paper we provide a structural operational semantics for pipelined microprocessors (Arm, x86, RISC-V) that is based on a regular understanding of microarchitectural features (pipelines, branch prediction, caches, privilege checks), conforms to established memory consistency models, and exposes the Spectre and Meltdown vulnerabilities. A key point is that the operational rules correspond to stages of the pipeline and are based almost entirely on syntactic aspects of fetched instructions, as is generally understood to be the case in real pipelines. We develop a model checker based closely on the semantics, which we use to experimentally validate the model and to provide the basis for security analyses.

1 Introduction

Pipelined and superscalar processors allow out-of-order execution of assembly instructions. This feature can improve performance by, e.g., utilising multiple arithmetic units, and allowing incremental evaluation of instructions while waiting for relatively slow interactions with main memory to complete. However, out-of-order execution, including speculative execution (evaluation of instructions down paths before knowing if they will be selected), has been shown to allow information leakage via a cache side-channel: out-of-order loads leave an imprint in the cache which an attacker on a parallel core may be able to access.

To design a secure, efficient chip with provable properties requires a formal model of low-level microarchitectural features. In reality a chip is unlikely to be completely secure, but can at least provide an accurate assessment of where vulnerabilities may arise. Low-level systems code, e.g., kernel features, device drivers, and efficient cryptographic algorithms, are particularly exposed to microarchitectural effects, since they provide the foundation for security and efficiency for entire systems.

In the literature usually the two concerns – functional correctness and security – are considered separately. Functional correctness of programs impacted by out-of-order execution is addressed by formal weak memory models, often representing behaviours using partial orders on memory events, and providing a powerful level of abstraction away from the microarchitecture [5,6,37,38]. However, this abstraction, while allowing hardware developers to experimentally validate their implementations, does not immediately admit the possibility of formally analysing and simulating specific microarchitectural constructs. Security analyses often have more microarchitectural detail, but typically focus on smaller sets of instruction types [17,32,63]. In this paper we complement abstract formal models of architecture behaviours with a more detailed structural operational semantics, of use during earlier stages of hardware design. We found that a classical understanding and encoding of pipelined execution, based around explicit checks for dependence on previous instructions in the pipeline and branch prediction, naturally gives rise to observable out-of-order execution consistent with modern hardware and abstract models. Furthermore these foundational concepts, once extended with known microarchitectural detail, also expose security vulnerabilities associated with speculative execution and caches.

More specifically the contributions of this paper are the following.

- A generic assembly language and semantics, pline, that parallelises computation of multiple instructions. It covers instruction types such as loads, stores, fences, atomics, branches and jumps. The semantics aligns with the well-understood pipelining model of execution [34,50]: instructions are first fetched and decoded; then execution proceeds incrementally by reading the values of registers and/or at addresses in main memory; before finally either updating registers or main memory, or evaluating a condition and jumping to other parts of the codebase. As an example, the execution of a single instruction r := x + 1 could involve three individual steps before completing and becoming a no-op.

$$\texttt{r := x + 1} \xrightarrow{\text{load x = 2}} \texttt{r := 2 + 1} \xrightarrow{\text{eval. expr.}} \texttt{r := 3} \xrightarrow{\text{update r}} \texttt{nop}$$

Within a pipeline multiple instructions may be incrementally executed in parallel. Fetching of branch instructions involves an encoding of prediction and hence speculative execution.
- Straightforward extensions of the foundational framework to include known microarchitectural features that expose the Spectre and Meltdown vulnerabilities [39,43]: caches, which may be updated after a load; and a micro-operation encoding a privilege check on loaded addresses.
- A simulator/model checker for the semantics written in Haskell, which has close correspondence to the abstract semantics presented in the paper and can be used to analyse reachable states. The tool is used to experimentally validate the semantics for the Arm, RISC-V, and x86 architectures.

A fundamental limitation of such an approach is that it may expose only those vulnerabilities that arise from the particular features modelled; however, we hope to have demonstrated that the `pline` framework is extensible to further features (e.g., the transaction lookaside buffer and branch prediction buffer), while still being efficient for reachability analysis via model checking.

We present the operational semantics of `pline` in Sect. 2. In Sect. 3 we extend the base model with caches and privilege checks and demonstrate how Spectre and Meltdown vulnerabilities emerge. In Sect. 4 we report on the tool that implements the operational rules and their experimental evaluation.

2 Pipelined Processor Semantics

2.1 Multicore System Structure

A multicore system (1) consists of memory, `mem` (a mapping from shared variables or addresses to values), shared between n individual cores operating in parallel (the scope of `mem` is indicated by an overbrace). Each $core_i$ is a quadtuple formed from its registers, $regs_i$ (a mapping from local variables to values), its codebase, c_i (a static sequence of instructions), current program counter, pc_i (an index into the codebase), and the dynamic pipeline, p_i (a sequence of instructions). To aid readability we write cores and pipelines vertically, with segments of pipelines or individual instructions inside boxes. Where a pipeline segment `p` appears we indicate this via dashed edges.

$$\overbrace{\begin{array}{c} regs_1 \\ c_1@pc_1 \\ p_1 \end{array} \| \cdots \| \begin{array}{c} regs_n \\ c_n@pc_n \\ p_n \end{array}}^{\text{mem}} \quad (1)$$

Instructions `i` (type Instr) and memory operations `op` (type MOp) are the foundational primitives of the system. Instructions are fetched into the pipeline and incrementally evaluated/executed, interacting with main memory via memory operations.

$$\begin{array}{rl} \mathtt{i} ::= & \mathtt{nop} \mid \mathtt{x} := \mathtt{e} \mid \mathtt{barrier} \mid \mathtt{br}\ \mathtt{e} : \mathtt{l} \mid \mathtt{jump}(\mathtt{e}) \mid \mathtt{swp}(\mathtt{x},\mathtt{r}) \\ \mathtt{barrier} ::= & \mathtt{fence} \mid \mathtt{fence.st} \mid \mathtt{fence.ld} \mid \ldots \\ \mathtt{op} ::= & \mathtt{R}(\mathtt{x},\mathtt{v}) \mid \mathtt{W}(\mathtt{x},\mathtt{v}) \mid \mathtt{RW}(\mathtt{x},\mathtt{v},\mathtt{v}') \end{array}$$

The instruction types covered by `pline` include: no-ops (`nop`); assignments (`x := e`, e.g., stores, loads, and register operations); barriers, which may be a full fence (both store and load), store-only fence, load-only fence, or many other kinds; branches `br e : l`, where `e` is a condition to check and `l` the program label from where to continue if `e` evaluates to true (`tt`); jumps `jump(e)`, where `e` may be a program label or an expression that evaluates to a label; or an atomic swap `swp(x,r)`, where `x` is updated to the value in `r`, and additionally `r` is updated to the current value of `x`. We also address release/acquire annotations and several other types of atomic operations (such as compare-and-swap and fetch-and-increment) but omit their rules for brevity; they are included in and evaluated by the model checker. Note that the branch instruction type br e : l has a different semantics when fetched into the pipeline and decoded: the label is overwritten with the target label in case of evaluation to false (ff) rather than true. Hence when used in the pipeline (rather than the codebase) we instead write branch instructions as $e\,?\,l$. The reasons for this change in meaning are due to speculative execution described in detail later (see, e.g., (R16) and Sect. 2.5).

$\sigma[\mathtt{x}]$	Lookup the value of x in the state σ
$\sigma[\mathtt{x} := \mathtt{v}]$	Update state σ so that x maps to v
$\mathtt{i}_{\langle e \rangle}$	An instruction i that contains a subexpression e for evaluation
reads(.)	Variables read by expression/instruction/pipeline
writes(.)	Variables written to by instruction/pipeline
vars(.)	= reads(.) ∪ writes(.)
svars(.)	vars() restricted to Shared.

Fig. 1. Additional notation

Memory operations may be a read R(x,v), indicating the current value of x in main memory is v, a write W(x,v), updating the value of x to v, or an atomic combination of both, RW(x,v,v'). Additionally many steps of a core do not interact with main memory, which we decorate with the 'silent' step, τ.

We distinguish between local variables, Local – corresponding to registers – and shared variables, Shared – corresponding to memory addresses. We do not arbitrarily constrain expressions e, appearing in assignments and branch conditions, though for a real system they will be restricted to what the ISA provides (arithmetic and logical operations), and will typically involve at most one shared variable.

Additional notation is given in Fig. 1, covering standard notions of reading and updating a state, and the notation $\mathtt{i}_{\langle e \rangle}$ to indicate an instruction i that contains a (sub)expression e (typically a variable or immediate value). We also make use of several functions defined inductively over the structure of expressions and instructions. Functions reads(.) and vars(.) are overloaded to apply to expressions, instructions, and pipelines. And writes(.) applies to instructions and pipelines. All of these functions return a set of variables; i.e. a subset of Local ∪ Shared. Some instruction types behave differently for local and shared variables, the latter of which are collected in svars(.).

We collect the set of all fence, branch, etc., instructions that can be constructed using the syntax in the sets barriers, branches, etc., respectively. For a particular pipeline p we define, e.g., branches(p) = branches ∩ elems(p), where elems(p) is the set of instructions in p. Such abstract set-based definitions can be implemented straightforwardly by induction over lists and syntactic checks on instructions.

2.2 Semantics of Register Operations, Stores, Loads and Fences

The operational semantics of register-only, non-branching instructions is given in Fig. 2. The *fetch* phase of the instruction lifecycle is given by (R2); given the codebase c and current program counter pc, if the instruction i at c[pc] is non-branching then i is simply placed at the end of the current pipeline, p, and the program counter is incremented.

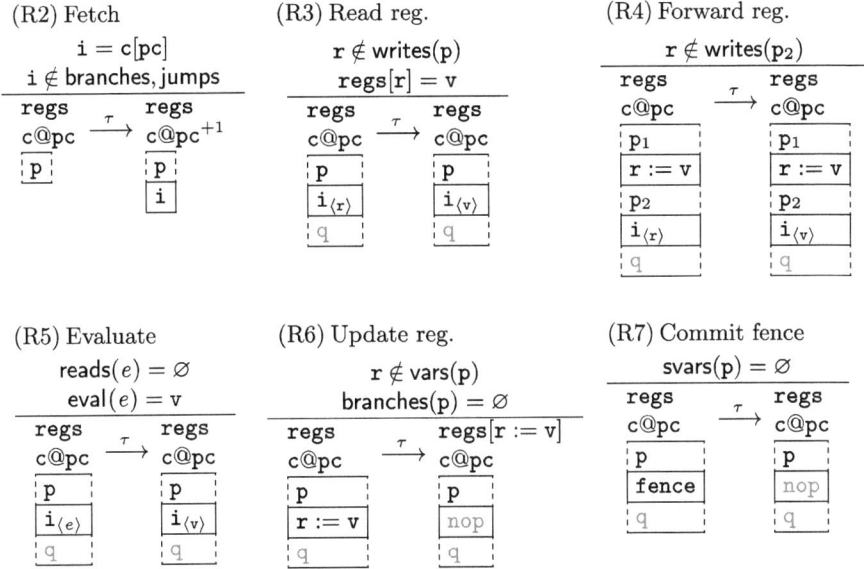

Fig. 2. Fetch, fence, and register-based instruction execution

Instructions that refer to registers must be incrementally evaluated by replacing registers with the appropriate value, which can either be found by looking up their value on the chip or by using a previously calculated value in the *pipeline*. Rule (R3) generically applies to any instruction type i (assignment, branch, swap, etc.) that requires evaluation of register r (written i(r)), retrieving it by looking up the value of r in the registers, regs[r]. If the value of r is v then this replaces r in i. Note that this lookup is only valid if r is not written to (modified) by some instruction earlier in the pipeline, as any such write would potentially overwrite v, *before* i takes place.

As an alternative to looking up the value of a register – which, as with committing a value to a register, is a relatively expensive operation – the most recently calculated value for r in the pipeline can be used, as shown in (R4). That is, given an earlier instruction r := v before i, and given no intervening writes to r, the value v may be safely used in place of r. This mechanism is called *forwarding* or *bypassing*, and, along with many other concepts to do with out-of-order execution, originated at least as early as the 1960s [58,59].

An expression e which contains no references to registers or memory addresses can be evaluated to a value (e.g., via an ALU) as given by (R5). This reduces a potentially complex expression to a single value. When an update of a register r is the earliest use of that register in the pipeline it may be committed to regs as in (R6), provided there are no earlier branch instructions. This restriction is required because an uncompleted branch instruction indicates that any later instructions in the pipeline are *speculative* or *transient*; until the branch is resolved no state changes should occur (as these would require significant book-keeping to roll back). However, through forwarding (R4) it is possible to continue to incrementally evaluate later instructions in transient contexts.

Rule (R7) allows a full fence to be removed from the pipeline once there are no earlier references to *shared* variables. As shown later, accesses to shared memory may be blocked by particular fence instructions, so (R7) in combination with those rules enforces strict ordering between memory operations. Similar rules apply specifically for load and store fences, where only loads or stores block execution. As with (R6) these committed instructions are replaced with nop in the pipeline (an alternative is to wait until these instructions bubble to the front and then remove them). Additionally, leading nop can be straightforwardly removed from the pipeline. Of note is that in all of these rules, aside from expression evaluation and standard interactions with the local state, the conditions on the rules are all determined syntactically by the content of preceding instructions.

2.3 Accessing Main Memory

The rules for instructions that access main memory are given in Fig. 3, and are essentially the same as the corresponding rules governing register accesses in Fig. 2, but with stronger constraints. (R8) replaces a reference to a shared variable x in an instruction with its value in main memory, provided x is neither read nor written previously in the pipeline, and there are no load fences. This strengthens the conditions of the corresponding (R3), since reads of shared memory are kept in program order in most practical weak memory models [6]. The read interacts with main memory via a read event, R(x,v), where v is the current value of x. (R9) corresponds to (R4); note that forwarding can occur across fences and branches. (R10) states that a store x := v can be committed provided there are no earlier references to x in the pipeline, and there are no store fences or branches. Interaction with main memory is via the W(x, v) event.

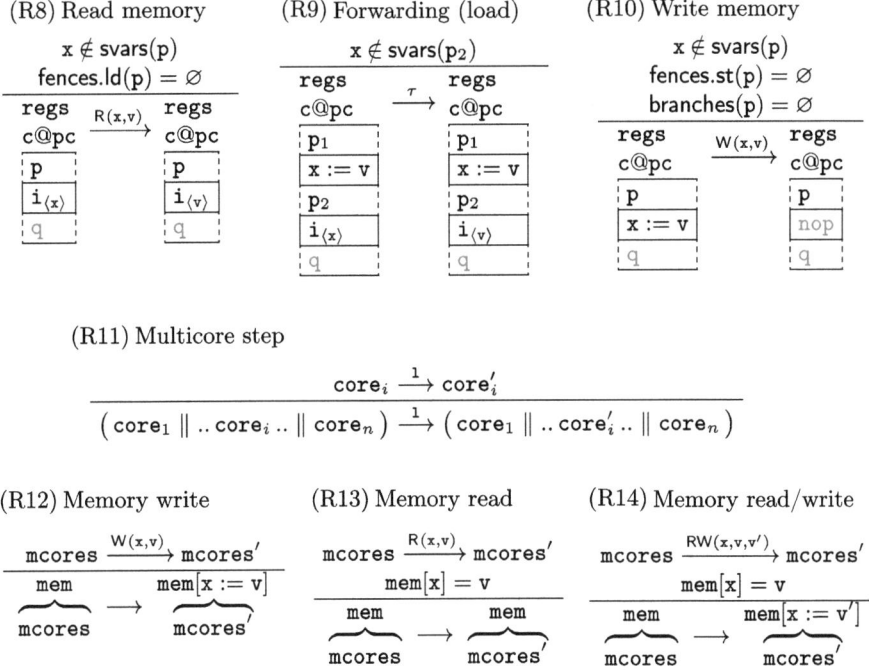

Fig. 3. Instructions accessing main memory

An atomic swap operation, involving both a read-from and write-to main memory, is governed by (R15). A RW(x, v, v′) operation on main memory includes v, the current value of x, and v′, its new value. Hence, a swp(x, r′) instruction updates x to the value in r, which is then updated, separately, with the original value of x.

Note that (R10) and (R15), which involve a write to main memory, require the absence of previous branches in the pipeline, while (R8) (for loads) does not, and (R9) does not consider branches at all. These relaxations allows forwarding to be used for incremental evaluation of instructions without committing their effects, and for values to be speculatively read from main memory; the latter feature is one of the sources of the Spectre vulnerability discussed in Sect. 3.

A multicore system mcores consisting of n cores operating in parallel takes a step if any individual core takes a step, as given in (R11). Main memory is updated according to the memory operations emitted by the cores as shown in (R12)–(R14).

2.4 Control Flow Instructions

Execution of branches and jumps are shown in Fig. 4. A branch instruction "br e : 1" *in the codebase* says that if condition e evaluates to true then execution should continue from label 1, otherwise continue from the next instruction (pc^{+1}). Since condition e may take some time to evaluate (e.g., due to a dependence on an earlier read from main memory), rather than stall with an unknown program counter, the core may make a *prediction* of either true (R16) or false (R17). In either case the core's program counter pc is updated to the corresponding predicted label, while the alternative label overwrites the original label *in the pipeline*. We distinguish the pipelined version of an instruction (where the label holds the target in case of failure) by different syntax, namely, "$e?1$" instead of "br e : 1". Note that when predicting an evaluation to false the condition $\neg e$ is used rather than e (corresponding to flipping a bit in the opcode).

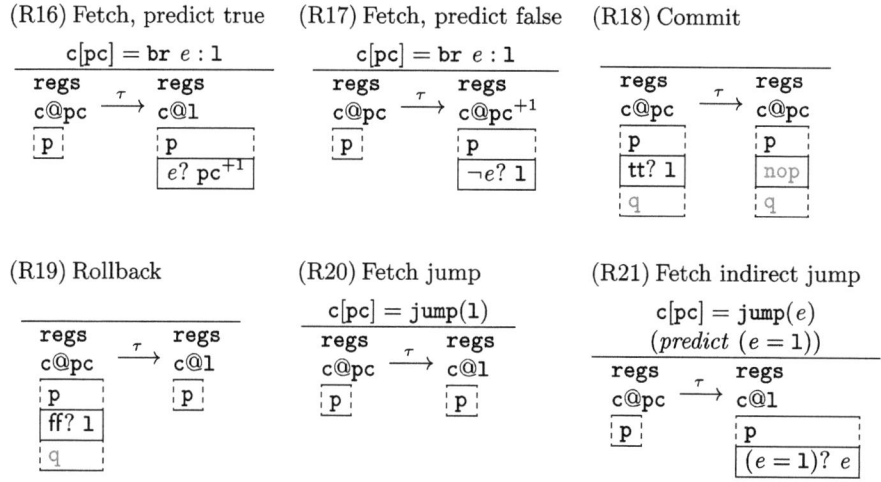

Fig. 4. Fetch, prediction, and execution of branch and jump instructions

If the prediction is eventually found to have been correct, that is, if the condition evaluates (via the earlier expression evaluation rules) to true (tt), then nothing more needs to be done and the branch can be eliminated (R18). As shown in (R19), if instead the evaluation was mispredicted (evaluated to false (ff)), all instructions that have been (speculatively) fetched since the branch point must be removed from the pipeline, and the program counter is updated so that fetching now restarts from the fail-case label recorded in the instruction. The constraints in earlier rules include checking for branches in the pipeline,

$$
\begin{array}{rl}
& \texttt{regs}, \texttt{c@}l_0, \quad \boxed{\texttt{empty}} \\
(\text{R2}) \longrightarrow & \texttt{regs}, \texttt{c@}l_1, \quad \boxed{\texttt{r1} := \texttt{x}} \\
(\text{R17}) \longrightarrow & \texttt{regs}, \texttt{c@}l_2, \quad \boxed{\texttt{r1} := \texttt{x}} \boxed{\texttt{r1} \neq 0?\, l_5} \\
(\text{R2})_{\times 2} \longrightarrow & \texttt{regs}, \texttt{c@}l_4, \quad \boxed{\texttt{r1} := \texttt{x}} \boxed{\texttt{r1} \neq 0?\, l_5} \boxed{\texttt{y} := 1} \boxed{\texttt{r2} := \texttt{z}} \\
(\text{R20}) \longrightarrow & \texttt{regs}, \texttt{c@end}, \quad \boxed{\texttt{r1} := \texttt{x}} \boxed{\texttt{r1} \neq 0?\, l_5} \boxed{\texttt{y} := 1} \boxed{\texttt{r2} := \texttt{z}} \boxed{\texttt{jump}(\texttt{end})} \\
(\text{R8}) \xrightarrow{R(z,1)} & \texttt{regs}, \texttt{c@end}, \quad \boxed{\texttt{r1} := \texttt{x}} \boxed{\texttt{r1} \neq 0?\, l_5} \boxed{\texttt{y} := 1} \boxed{\texttt{r2} := 1} \\
(\text{R8}) \xrightarrow{R(x,0)} & \texttt{regs}, \texttt{c@end}, \quad \boxed{\texttt{r1} := 0} \boxed{\texttt{r1} \neq 0?\, l_5} \boxed{\texttt{y} := 1} \boxed{\texttt{r2} := 1} \\
(\text{R4}) \longrightarrow & \texttt{regs}, \texttt{c@end}, \quad \boxed{\texttt{r1} := 0} \boxed{0 \neq 0?\, l_5} \boxed{\texttt{y} := 1} \boxed{\texttt{r2} := 1} \\
(\text{R5}) \longrightarrow & \texttt{regs}, \texttt{c@end}, \quad \boxed{\texttt{r1} := 0} \boxed{\texttt{ff}?\, l_5} \boxed{\texttt{y} := 1} \boxed{\texttt{r2} := 1} \\
(\text{R19}) \longrightarrow & \texttt{regs}, \texttt{c@}l_5, \quad \boxed{\texttt{r1} := 0} \\
(\text{R2})_{\times 2} \longrightarrow & \texttt{regs}, \texttt{c@end}, \quad \boxed{\texttt{r1} := 0} \boxed{\texttt{y} := 2} \boxed{\texttt{r2} := 0} \\
(\text{R10}) \xrightarrow{W(y,2)} & \texttt{regs}, \texttt{c@end}, \quad \boxed{\texttt{r1} := 0} \boxed{\texttt{nop}} \boxed{\texttt{r2} := 0} \\
(\text{R6})_{\times 2} \longrightarrow & \texttt{regs}[\texttt{r1} := 0][\texttt{r2} := 0], \texttt{c@end}, \boxed{\texttt{nop}} \boxed{\texttt{nop}} \boxed{\texttt{nop}}
\end{array}
$$

Fig. 5. An example of pipelined execution.

and hence no registers can have been written to, nor shared address updated, by instructions coming after an unresolved branch point. However, loads from main memory may have occurred, as these are not prevented by earlier branch instructions (see (R8)).

If the next instruction is an unconditional jump to label l then the program counter is immediately updated, and the instruction need not enter the pipeline (R20). If instead the jump target is given by an expression (e.g., held in a register) the target may be predicted, as shown in (R21). A jump target l is selected (we leave the method for this choice underspecified), and fetching continues from that label, but that choice and any subsequent writes to registers or main memory will be committed only if e evaluates to l. This is implemented by using a branch instruction, where the target in case of misprediction is simply given by e itself. Both instances of e in the instruction are evaluated at the same time (in a true pipeline, only one copy would of course be used, but we keep both for clarity). If the branch target prediction is wrong all subsequently fetched instructions are removed via (R19) and fetching will resume from the calculated label for e.

2.5 Example

Consider the codebase c on the left below, for which we show two possible outcomes from multiple fetchings before any instruction execution takes place.

Codebase c:
l_0 : r1 := x
l_1 : br r1 = 0 : l_5
l_2 : y := 1
      r2 := z
l_4 : jump(end)
l_5 : y := 2
      r2 := 0
end :

$\xrightarrow{\text{fetched as:}}$

Predict true
| r1 := x |
| r1 = 0? l_2 |
| y := 2 |
| r2 := 0 |

or

Predict false
| r1 := x |
| r1 ≠ 0? l_5 |
| y := 1 |
| r2 := z |
| jump(end) |

```
r1 := x ;
if r1 ≠ 0
  y := 1 ;
  r2 := z
else
  y := 2 ;
  r2 := 0
```

Each instruction in c is labelled (though we omit some to avoid clutter), including label end (an alias for l_7) marking the end of the codebase. In all cases we assume $l_i^{+1} = l_{i+1}$. This assembly could be generated by compiling the code to the right (the choice of branch condition and order of branches depends on factors including optimisation level). When the branch instruction br r1 = 0 : l_5 is fetched, the condition r1 = 0 is predicted to eventually evaluate to true or to false, with subsequent fetches proceeding from the branch target (l_5) in the true case, or falling through to the next instruction (l_2) in the false case. Note, however, that when (decoded and) fetched into the pipeline the branch instruction is modified to record the *alternative* label in case of misprediction. That is, if predicted to evaluate to true, the instruction is decoded to r1 = 0 ? l_2, and if predicted to evaluate to false, the instruction is decoded to r1 ≠ 0 : l_5. We give an example of pipelined execution of c, involving (mis)prediction and rollback, in Fig. 5. For space reasons we present the pipelines horizontally rather than vertically. The register state is given by regs, which changes only in the final step of this execution.

The execution starts at label l_0 with an empty pipeline. First the leading assignment to r1 is fetched into the pipeline (R2), and then the branch instruction br r1 = 0 : l_5 is fetched and predicted to evaluate to false (R17); the current program counter is updated to fall through to the next instruction (l_2) while the instruction in the pipeline reflects the prediction (r1 ≠ 0) and records the location from which to restart fetching in case of misprediction (l_5). Two more instructions are fetched (R2), setting the program counter to l_4, which is the jump instruction jump(end). This causes a change in program counter to end by (R20) (we indicate the "ghost" jump instruction in the figure). At this stage no more fetching is possible. The value of z in the final instruction is loaded (R8), despite being inside a speculative branch (whereas, by the premise branches(p) = ∅ of (R10), the store to y is not enabled). Now x is loaded (R8), then forwarded to the branch instruction (R4). The condition becomes 0 ≠ 0, which evaluates to ff (R5), indicating a misprediction, and so the pipeline is cleared from that point onwards, and the program counter is updated to the alternative branch, l_5 (R19). Execution continues by fetching (two) instructions from l_5. Execution continues by updating main memory and registers ((R10) and (R6)). Note that although never used, the value for z was (speculatively) loaded; this aspect is relevant to security analysis in Sect. 3.

2.6 Address Space and Dereferences

For simplicity above we have treated the components of main memory as individual variables, but in reality main memory is indexed by addresses. This requires a straightforward generalisation to include dereferenced expressions. Whereas we would write x := 1 for an update, this becomes [rx] := 1, where rx is a register that holds an address into main memory; similarly memory operations such as W(x, 1) become W(addr, 1), where addr is an address. We allow general expressions to be dereferenced, e.g., [e], where e is successively evaluated to a single address addr using the rules in Fig. 2, before being read or written. We say a dereference expression [e] is *unresolved* if e contains registers; for instance, [addr + r] is unresolved, and represents a common pattern where addr marks the start of an array, and r holds the index to be accessed. Any unresolved dereference blocks later stores and loads, to avoid potentially violating coherence. That is, consider consecutive instructions [$addr_1$ + r] and [$addr_2$]; until r is resolved to a value it is unknown if $addr_1$ + r = $addr_2$, and if they are equal then the accesses should be kept in program order. The test for unresolved dereferences is straightforwardly added to the relevant rules in Fig. 3 (these definitions plus the existing syntactic checks combine to give axiomatic *address dependencies* [6]).

3 Extensions for Cache-Based Security Vulnerabilities

In this section we show that the Meltdown and Spectre exploits [39,43] emerge from the operational rules of pline, due in-part to out-of-order execution in the pipeline and branch prediction. To expose the relevant behaviours requires two modest extensions to include the relevant microarchitectural details: a) tracking loads in an explicit cache (Sect. 3.1), and b) adding a micro-operation to check the local core has the right access privileges for the target address of a load (Sect. 3.2). Similarly, we show how one of the (many) proposed mitigations [15, 16,18,66] – inserting a load fence at the correct point – can prevent Spectre behaviours.

3.1 Caches

A memory system typically includes several levels of *caches*, which record parts of main memory accessed by cores, and can be specific to a single core or shared between cores. Caches can provide a speed-up for repeated loads of the same address, at the cost of keeping values across shared memory and multiple levels of caches consistent. For this paper we abstract from the details of the sizes of caches, cache lines, and coherence, and simply keep track of values as they are loaded (updates to the cache as a result of stores are straightforward to

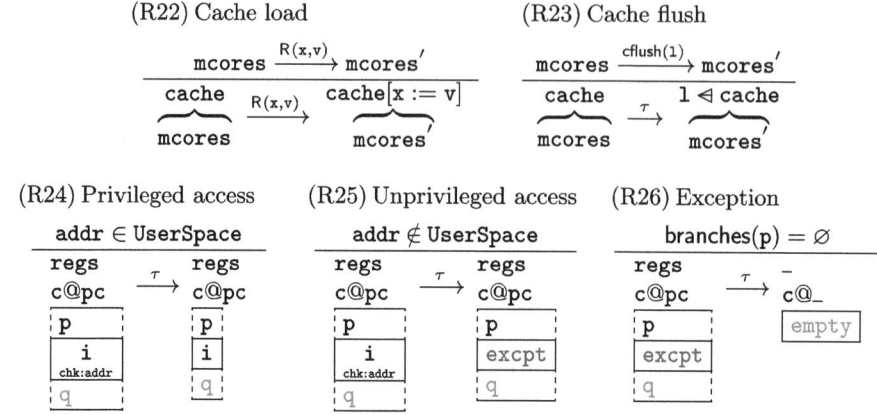

Fig. 6. Caches, privilege checks, and exceptions

encode, as required to model, e.g., SpectrePrime [62]). We write $\underbrace{\text{cache}}_{\text{mcores}}$ to indicate a cache that is shared by one or more cores in mcores, where the cache itself is a partial mapping from variables (addresses) to values. Because it is a partial function some requested values may not be in the domain, and hence such requests trigger a further interaction with main memory (a cache miss). Multiple levels of cache can be modelled by nesting caches.

A minimal set of operational rules covering caches are given in Fig. 6. A read event emitted from any core triggers an update in the cache, as shown in (R22).[1] Some processors allow a flush of a cache line, cflush(l), where l is some subset of addresses, as in (R23). The flushed line is removed from (the domain of) the cache (◁); this is a crucial facility to enable cache side-channel attacks.

3.2 Privilege Checking

A typical constraint on stores and loads of an address addr is that the thread has the necessary *privilege* to access that address. The kernel may of course access any address, but user threads will typically be restricted. We treat a privilege check of an address addr as a micro-operation to determine if addr is within a valid range. For instance, given a load instruction r := [rx] in the codebase, when fetched and decoded it becomes $\underset{r:=[rx]}{\text{chk}:rx}$ in the pipeline, where the loaded address is explicitly marked for checking via the 'chk : rx' tag. This composite instruction is partly evaluated within the pipeline as before (in particular, register rx is resolved to an address), however, it will not write to register r, nor allow any

---

[1] This rule could be extended to include details such as using a value already in the cache for x, avoiding the interaction with main memory; similarly writes could also interact with the cache. This level of precision necessitates further details to trigger cache refreshes when main memory changes, and is outside the scope of this paper.

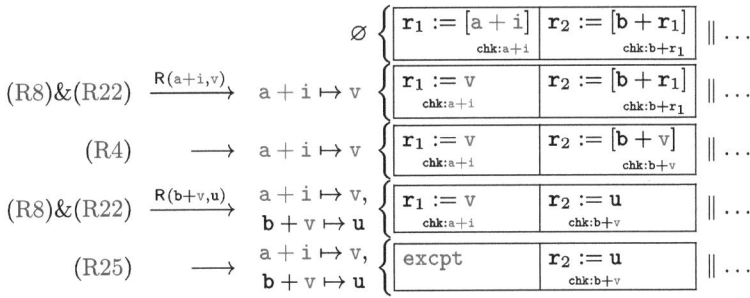

Fig. 7. Execution for Meltdown (27).

later writes to memory or registers, unless the privilege check succeeds. That is, a load with an unresolved chk : rx micro-operation blocks later instructions in exactly the same way as a branch instruction: loads may proceed, but stores and writes to registers may not. This is enforced formally by extending the premises of (R10) and (R6) to include a condition $\mathrm{chks}(p) = \varnothing$, where $\mathrm{chks}(p)$ syntactically extracts any privilege checks in the same way as $\mathrm{fences}(p)$.

As shown in Fig. 6, assuming the range of valid addresses for the thread is given by 'UserSpace', (R24) states that a privilege check is resolved if addr is within that range, and removed. If, on the other hand, addr is not in the allowed range, the instruction becomes an *exception* (R25). In this paper we treat an exceptional instruction excpt as one that wipes the registers, program counter, and pipeline (R26), provided it is not executing speculatively; other versions could also be modelled, in particular where an exception generates an event that is trapped by the core.

A key aspect of the privilege check associated with a load instruction is that the check may occur *after* the value at the invalid address is retrieved from main memory. For example, if rx holds address addr, which is outside the allowed range, the following sequence of steps may occur.

$$r := [\mathrm{rx}] \underset{\mathrm{chk:rx}}{\longrightarrow} r := [\mathrm{addr}] \underset{\mathrm{chk:addr}}{\xrightarrow{R(\mathrm{addr},v)}} r := v \underset{\mathrm{chk:addr}}{\longrightarrow} \mathrm{excpt}$$

The first step retrieves the value addr for rx ((R3) or (R4)), then reads the value at addr from main memory (R8), before finally raising an exception (R25).

3.3 Meltdown

Caches and privilege checks combine to expose the Meltdown vulnerability. An attacker, given execution access on the target machine, may run the assembly in (27). Here i is an integer that can be controlled by the attacker, and is used

$$\begin{aligned} r_1 &:= [a + i] \\ r_2 &:= [b + r_1] \end{aligned} \quad (27)$$

as an offset to some address a, and is deliberately chosen by the attacker to be large and hence fall outside the allowed address range.[2]

The architectural intention is that the access of [a + i] will trigger an exception due to a privilege violation, wiping the information in the core and preventing any leakage. However, a second core that shares a cache can still determine the value at the illegal address.

We depict one possible execution of (27) in Fig. 7. After being fetched and decoded, the two loads in the pipeline include explicit privilege checks.

Initially the cache is empty, having been flushed by the attacker which shares the cache (the attacker is a sibling core within the ellipses (...)). Before the check of a + i occurs, the value, v, at that address is brought into the pipeline (R8), and hence into the cache (R22). (Recall that we assume that i has been chosen such that a + i $\notin$ UserSpace.) After forwarding via (R4) the value v is used to index into b, and, as above, the value at b + v is brought into the cache. The privilege check now proceeds and raises an exception by (R25), which effectively clears the problematic value v from the core. However, it remains, indirectly accessible, in the cache shared with the attacker.

The attacker's core is unable to directly read any values from the cache, but is able to determine, through a timing analysis, whether a particular address is in the cache or not (loads of values stored in the cache complete much more quickly than loads that access main memory). By iterating over the possible offsets of b and timing the loads of each corresponding element, the attacker can determine that none of the addresses b, ..., b + (v − 2), b + (v − 1), b + (v + 1), ... have been accessed, but, uniquely, b + v has been added to the cache. The attacker may therefore deduce that the value at illegal address a + i is v. The attacker now flushes the cache and reruns the code with input i + 1, and is able to read arbitrarily large sections of memory.

Because an unresolved privilege check blocks stores, and will wipe registers once an exception is raised, there is no other (currently known) direct way for a concurrent core to observe the value v. The timing attack relies on the fact that values retrieved from the cache return much faster than values that must be retrieved from main memory (this is indeed the rationale for using caches in the microarchitecture).

3.4 Spectre

Whereas Meltdown requires the ability to run arbitrary code on the target machine, Spectre instead requires access to, for instance, a routine offered by the target that fits a similar pattern, or 'gadget', such as that in

$$\begin{aligned} &\text{br } i \geq n : l \\ &r_1 := [a + i] \\ &r_2 := [b + r_1] \end{aligned} \quad (28)$$

---

[2] The assembly in (27) could be compiled from high-level code such as, $r_1 := A[i]$; $r_2 := B[r_1]$, where A and B are arrays starting at addresses A and B, respectively; for brevity we omit details such as the calculation of a + i = &A+(sizeof($A[0]$)∗i), cache line sizes, etc.; the square brackets indicate array indexing in higher level code, rather than address dereferencing.

(28).³ In this case the potentially out-of-bounds access a + i is preceded by a bounds check, and will be skipped over if outside some bound n on offsets to a. However, speculative execution with a misprediction still allows speculative loads to proceed.

$$
\begin{array}{rl}
 & \varnothing \left\{ \begin{array}{|l|l|l|} \hline \texttt{i < n? l} & \texttt{r}_1 := [\texttt{a} + \texttt{i}] & \texttt{r}_2 := [\texttt{b} + \texttt{r}_1] \\ & \text{chk:}\texttt{a}+\texttt{i} & \text{chk:}\texttt{b}+\texttt{r}_1 \\ \hline \end{array} \right\| \ldots \\[2ex]
(\text{R8})\&(\text{R22}) \xrightarrow{R(\texttt{a}+\texttt{i},\texttt{v})} & \texttt{a} + \texttt{i} \mapsto \texttt{v} \left\{ \begin{array}{|l|l|l|} \hline \texttt{i < n? l} & \texttt{r}_1 := \texttt{v} & \texttt{r}_2 := [\texttt{b} + \texttt{r}_1] \\ & \text{chk:}\texttt{a}+\texttt{i} & \text{chk:}\texttt{b}+\texttt{r}_1 \\ \hline \end{array} \right\| \ldots \\[2ex]
(\text{R4}) \longrightarrow & \texttt{a} + \texttt{i} \mapsto \texttt{v} \left\{ \begin{array}{|l|l|l|} \hline \texttt{i < n? l} & \texttt{r}_1 := \texttt{v} & \texttt{r}_2 := [\texttt{b} + \texttt{v}] \\ & \text{chk:}\texttt{a}+\texttt{i} & \text{chk:}\texttt{b}+\texttt{v} \\ \hline \end{array} \right\| \ldots \\[2ex]
(\text{R8})\&(\text{R22}) \xrightarrow{R(\texttt{b}+\texttt{v},\texttt{u})} & \begin{array}{l}\texttt{a}+\texttt{i} \mapsto \texttt{v}, \\ \texttt{b}+\texttt{v} \mapsto \texttt{u}\end{array} \left\{ \begin{array}{|l|l|l|} \hline \texttt{i < n? l} & \texttt{r}_1 := \texttt{v} & \texttt{r}_2 := \texttt{u} \\ & \text{chk:}\texttt{a}+\texttt{i} & \text{chk:}\texttt{b}+\texttt{v} \\ \hline \end{array} \right\| \ldots \\[2ex]
(\text{R19}) \longrightarrow & \begin{array}{l}\texttt{a}+\texttt{i} \mapsto \texttt{v}, \\ \texttt{b}+\texttt{v} \mapsto \texttt{u}\end{array} \left\{ \begin{array}{|l|} \hline \texttt{empty} \\ \hline \end{array} \right\| \ldots
\end{array}
$$

Fig. 8. Execution for Spectre (28).

A possible execution of (28) is shown in Fig. 8. We assume the attacker shares the cache with the problematic code (within the ellipses), and can control the input i. After being fetched and a prediction of false is made for the branch condition (i.e., predicting that i is less than the bound n, a value that must be retrieved from main memory) the loads are decoded to include the relevant privilege checks. Speculative execution proceeds as with the Meltdown case, reading values for both a + i and b+v into the cache. However, before (or after) the privilege check raises the corresponding exception, the branch prediction is found to have been erroneous (i ≥ n). As such the pipeline is cleared by (R19), and fetching proceeds from some other location l. However, as with Meltdown, the attacker may infer the value v via a timing attack on the shared cache. Note that although an exception may be raised in the pipeline, because i < n was mispredicted the exception will be removed from the pipeline via (R19), and prevented from otherwise being raised by the precondition of (R26).

The insertion of a load fence (lfence on x86) into the code as in (29) prevents the problematic behaviour.

To define the behaviour of lfence we introduce a rule that states that it is blocked by preceding branches, and we generalise (R8) to require the absence of lfence for a read to proceed. This prevents the problematic load of address a + i from proceeding before the privilege check completes. However, this mitigation also prevents all other prefetched loads, potentially impacting performance.

$$
\begin{array}{l}
\texttt{br i} \geq \texttt{n} : \texttt{l} \\
\texttt{lfence} \\
\texttt{r}_1 := [\texttt{a} + \texttt{i}] \\
\texttt{r}_2 := [\texttt{b} + \texttt{r}_1]
\end{array} \quad (29)
$$

---

[3] The assembly in (28) could be compiled from high-level code such as if i < n then r₁ := A[i]; r₂ := B[r₁]. To avoid distraction we allow the shared address n to be directly included in the branch condition, but in most assembly languages it would need to be loaded into a register first.

4 Experimental Evaluation

In this section we describe how we empirically validated the semantics of Sect. 2 against other models, including the official Arm model, and hardware. We also address the detection of vulnerabilities related to cache side channels (Sect. 3).

4.1 Haskell Encoding

We chose the functional programming language Haskell to implement the operational rules of Sect. 2. Our development focussed on correspondence, rather than efficiency. As an example, (R7) is encoded as follows.

```
rule core@Core { pipeline = Pt (p, Fence Full, q)} | svars p == [] =
    [(fenceEv (Fence Full), core { pipeline = P (p ++ q)} )]
```

This function clause pattern matches with a core (named `core`) with a partitioned (`Pt`) pipeline that contains a full fence as an instruction, preceded by pipeline segment `p` and succeeded by pipeline segment `q`. Provided the list of shared variables (`svars`) in `p` is empty, this clause applies, returning (a singleton list formed of) a pair consisting of a fence event and a new core, which in this case is the original `core` updated so that its (unpartitioned) pipeline is the concatenation of `p` and `q`. (This slight difference with (R7) is because we immediately remove `nop` from the pipeline in the interests of reducing the state space.) The code includes other corresponding operational `rules` such as this, which return a *list* of event/core pairs (the transition event and the new core state). A list is used to model nondeterminism associated with multiple possible next steps for a given instruction (for instance, multiple steps are possible when fetching a branch instruction). The returned list is empty if the rule does not apply, e.g., when a particular instruction is blocked from completing by earlier instructions in the pipeline.

We use symbolic execution on each individual core, where symbols record values read from main memory, generating an execution tree by recursively applying the rules. These trees are then interleaved and executed on the global state, from where all final states can be retrieved.

4.2 Validation Against Litmus Tests

The primary way to test conformance to weak memory models is via litmus tests, small assembly programs that involve the interaction of at least two processes (cores), with a final predicate tested for reachability. A classic example is the "store buffer" pattern, as shown below. We assume the shared variables x and y are initially 0. The final state of interest is $r1 = 0 \land r2 = 0$, that is, whether the registers in each core can both have the final value of 0 – a final state that is not reachable under a strict sequential execution of the instructions.

$$\begin{array}{cc}
\{r1 \mapsto 0\} & \{r2 \mapsto 0\} \\
sb_1@\_ & sb_2@\_ \\
\boxed{x := 1} & \boxed{y := 1} \\
\boxed{r1 := y} & \boxed{r2 := x}
\end{array} \quad \xrightarrow{R(x,0)}_{(R8)} \cdots \xrightarrow{R(y,0)}_{(R8)} \quad \begin{array}{cc}
\{r1 \mapsto 0\} & \{r2 \mapsto 0\} \\
sb_1@\_ & sb_2@\_ \\
\boxed{x := 1} & \boxed{y := 1} \\
\boxed{r1 := 0} & \boxed{r2 := 0}
\end{array}$$

In both cores the target of the load instruction is independent of the target of the preceding store, so both may read the initial values of x and y by (R8). Eventually the stores will commit but regardless the registers will both be 0.

The herdtools7 package, based on theory developed for axiomatic specifications of weak memory models [6], can be used to work with litmus tests: generation (diy7), model-based testing (herd7), and execution (litmus7). Using diy7 we generate tests based on "relaxation candidates" (relations) that correspond to axiomatic definitions controlling the instruction types of pline. For our experiments the tests were formed from up to four concurrent processes (cores), each containing up to five instructions, and cycles (potential violations of relaxation candidates spanning the instructions of multiple processes) of up to length six.

After generating a representative set of tests they can be run using herd7 according to the semantics of theoretical models, returning a result of Never, Sometimes, or Always for the given final state. For example, the store buffer litmus test above returns a result of Sometimes on any of the x86, Arm, or RISC-V models that come with herdtools7. The same tests can be run on specific machines using litmus7, generating actual results on hardware.

We set up our testing framework around reachability testing, in line with herd7. The main source of state space explosion is from branch instructions, which each generate four behaviours: correct and incorrect prediction that the condition will evaluate to true, and correct and incorrect prediction that the condition will evaluate to false. For running a large number of tests we therefore introduced some simplifications to reduce nondeterminism (in addition to early elimination of nops), as outlined below. In summary, no discrepancies with expected results were found when running without these simplifications and using a timeout to eliminate larger tests.

Maximal-Fetching: as many instructions as possible are fetched at once into the pipeline, including down speculative paths, before any execution of the fetched instructions begins. (Misprediction may still result in more fetching during execution, however.) This special case of execution significantly speeds up the model checking, which would otherwise be burdened with many equivalent traces; for example, compare the sequence fetch i_1/fetch i_2/single evaluation step of i_1, vs. fetch i_1/single evaluation step of i_1/fetch i_2. To check whether this special case of execution affects outcomes we ran the model checker on the set of Arm tests with this option switched off; 64% of tests still completed within 2 s, giving the expected results (the remainder timed out). We take this as reasonable justification for including this speed-up while investigating architectures. As test size increases we expect the computational penalty for not making this simplification would become untenable.

Preferential Execution of Register Operations: when an instruction involving zero or one registers is enabled (usually an evaluated assignment or branch), we preferentially execute that instruction before considering nondeterminism associated with instructions that involve shared variables, i.e., we give preference to rules such as (R6). As above for maximal fetching, we ran the Arm test set with this option off, and recorded a 98.5% completion rate within 2 s, and a 99.6% completion rate within 30 s.

Table 1. Results summary, pline vs. available models and hardware.

Arch.	#tests	time	herd7 conformance	Hardware conformance
Arm	239,724	0.004s/4.372s	100%	100% (Apple M1 Pro)
RISC-V	126,863	0.007s/3.899s	100%	–
x86	31,006	0.004s/0.032s	100%	100% (AMD Ryzen 7 3700X)

Column headings: #tests: numbers of tests (generated by diy7) evaluated. time: Average and maximum completion times given as indication of practicality of pline, compiled with ghc with multithreading and optimization level -O2, running on an Apple M1 chip with 8 cores and 16 GB memory. herd7: conformance with expected outcomes obtained by running the tests with the herd7 simulator. Hardware: conformance with expected outcomes obtained by running the tests on hardware using litmus7 (1 million runs per test).

We summarise our results in Table 1. Every test agreed with the axiomatic model available with herdtools7, and we did not detect any discrepancies with hardware. Note that a given manufactured chip will not necessarily display all possible behaviours allowed by a theoretical model, but must not display any that are forbidden. We discuss some notable aspects of our evaluation below.

Arm. The herdtools7 axiomatic model is the official model endorsed by Arm [5,7]. We automatically derived litmus tests based on the relationships defined in that model, and as outlined at [4]. We cover 58 different instruction mnemonics and variants involving release/acquire semantics (both strong and weak versions, e.g., ldar vs ldapr). Additionally the tests cover Arm's isb, dmb.st, dmb.ld, and dsb fences, the rules for which are straightforward to encode (see [44, B2.3.7]): an isb fence is blocked by preceding branches and unresolved dereferences, and blocks succeeding loads; the dmb.st (store) and dmb.ld (load) fences are blocked by preceding stores/loads and block succeeding stores/loads; and we interpret a dsb fence as equivalent to dmb – the architecture manual states that dsb is stronger [44, B2.6.9], but the tests we generated using herd7 do not expose this difference. Compare-and-swap and several other 3-place atomic operations were also tested (e.g., [44, C6.2.156]).

RISC-V. The semantics for RISC-V is similar to that for Arm; however the default, and only, release/acquire semantics is the weaker version (RC_{pc} from [27]); Arm provides both options. We handle RISC-V's fence instruction type which has 2-place r/w/rw specifications, e.g., fence.r.w. This defines whether the fence is blocked by (left-side), or blocks (right-side), instruction types involving either or both of a read of (r) or a write to (w) main memory. For the purposes of testing we interpreted fence.i as a nop, and fence.iorw as fence.rw.rw (a full fence); the tests we generated did not reveal a discrepancy. The only operational rule that required a special case for RISC-V (as opposed to Arm) was for forwarding (R4) from a `swp` instruction (`amoswap` in RISC-V) to a load, which is not permitted under the axiomatic model of `herd7`. The authors were unable to obtain access to a multicore RISC-V processor for testing `pline` directly against hardware.

x86. The x86 architecture is a version of *total store order* (TSO), and was originally described formally and mechanised in highly influential research [49,57]. The model was described using *write buffers*, which would temporarily hold stores generated by the program, potentially delaying their effect and allowing later loads to proceed or access the buffered values – this is essentially a specialised form of pipeline. x86 is a stronger memory model than either Arm or RISC-V, because, as the name TSO implies, independent stores are kept in program order; furthermore loads are kept in order with respect to each other. These extra constraints ($\mathtt{svars(p)} = \varnothing$) were straightforward to add to the premises of the corresponding rules for loads and stores ((R8) and (R10)), selected via an execution option specifying x86 semantics.

4.3 Observing Cache Side-Channels

To encode the Meltdown and Spectre vulnerabilities we extend each core with its own (optional) cache as in Sect. 3.1, where any read events generated by the application of a rule result in an update of the cache as in (R22). Privilege checks are (optionally) fetched when a load is encountered in the codebase; in the tool we treat them as a separate instruction (micro-operation) in the pipeline, which block register updates and write events. Running the code as given in (27) and (28) we observe, as expected, a core that has generated an exception, and a core that has taken the false case, respectively; no values are visible in the register state of the core, but an illegal value taken from outside the valid range of addresses appears as the index into array B, in the cache. The insertion of a load fence (x86's `lfence` instruction) after the branch instruction as in (29), straightforwardly encoded operationally to be blocked by earlier branches and to block later loads, prevents the leak. We tested multiple other variants based on a similar structure [15], with the expected results as above.

5 Related Work

The typical approach to weak memory model semantics is via axiomatic definitions controlling the shape of global traces of memory operations (MOp), perhaps best exemplified by [6]. This approach has been extended to model and detect Spectre variants and their mitigations [41] (but not Meltdown), at a similarly high level of abstraction. Abstracting away from specific microarchitectural details is clearly advantageous where possible [25]; in contrast our semantics exposes these details, at a level of more relevance to hardware designers rather than software developers, similarly to [14,24,57].

Other approaches to model weak memory model effects operationally vary in their abstract data structures [26,29,38,53,54,57,64]. The closest to `pline` include [26,55], which specify detailed instruction evaluation and execution, however the formalisation is not presented structurally (compositionally), and they do not consider security vulnerabilities due to the cache. Syntax-based rules for comparing instructions within a higher-level language and describing Spectre are given in [19–21], but do not model the details of assembly-level languages.

Our semantics of speculative execution and prediction is influenced by works such as [17,32,63], which include instructions fetched into a pipeline for execution, with rollback in case of misprediction. Those works are aimed at speculative execution specifically, and as such are not designed for full weak memory semantics (multiple fence types, release/acquire constraints, explicit forwarding, etc.). Given there are significant underlying similarities with the models of branch prediction, the security analyses in [17,32,63], and related approaches such as [30,31], should be compatible with `pline`, alongside functional correctness.

The *Check* suite of tools [45–48,60,61] provides both a detailed, multi-stage instruction-level semantics, as well as explicit caches used to address security flaws in the microarchitecture. At its core the Check suite leverages axiomatic memory model definitions to establish preserved program order, and uses a graph representation of memory operations, constructed algorithmically, giving significant power for describing a wide range of behaviours. In contrast the `pline` framework explains many behaviours of weak memory models and microarchitectural vulnerabilities fully operationally and syntactically.

A significant body of work has been devoted to developing efficient model checkers for weak memory models, including general reachability and decidability results [1–3,10,11] (but not vulnerability detection). We hope to replicate such results for `pline` by mapping into that framework and potentially formally eliminating the pipeline similar to the elimination of write buffers for x86 [12].

6 Conclusions

We have a presented a semantics for pipelines, a well-studied microarchitectural feature [34,50], showing that instruction-level parallelism (based on syntactic checks of variables accessed by instructions) and speculated branches exhibit many of the behaviours observed on modern x86, Arm and RISC-V multicore processors. Additionally, modest extensions (privilege checks and caches) give rise naturally to cache vulnerabilities, building on branch prediction and relatively weak constraints on the execution of load instructions. The low-level nature of `pline` is both its strength and its weakness: for hardware designers this level of specification can provide a bridge where specific details of a microarchitecture may be related to expected memory consistency model specifications, up to the register transfer level; however compiler writers and software developers should not be exposed to specific implementation details. We see `pline` sitting between those two levels, in particular where security vulnerabilities arise as a result of microarchitectural features.

We plan to encode the operational rules in a theorem prover so that properties of processors, both functional and security-related, may be formally established. This can complement the model-checking approach developed in this paper, for instance to formally justify compiler transformations [51], and to justify the execution simplifications described in Sect. 4.2 (e.g., maximal fetching). Building on this, the operational nature of the semantics means that programs may be denoted as sets of traces, from which can be derived compositional, algebraic properties of both assembly and microarchitectural layouts in a process-algebraic style [19,33,35,36]. Further extensions where we believe a framework such as `pline` may be of benefit include analysis of potential vulnerabilities in other microarchitectural features. For example, the ZombieLoad vulnerability [56] arises in part due to hyperthreading (multiple threads executing in parallel on a single core), which we believe can be incorporated relatively straightforwardly in `pline` by maintaining multiple codebases and pc values in each core, and the behaviour of the line-fill buffer of the cache system, which will require extension of the cache representation in pline, guided by other formalisation efforts [13,52]. We are also analysing proposed architectural mitigations for Spectre and variants targeting other parts of the microarchitecture [28,42,65]. To establish further correspondence with real architectures requires extending the operational rules to take into account detailed instruction semantics, e.g., including condition flags and other aspects of control [8,9,22,23,40].

Acknowledgments. We thank Alistair Michael for helpful comments and proof reading. This project was funded by Department of Defence and administered through the Advanced Strategic Capabilities Accelerator.

Disclosure of Interests. The authors have no competing interests to declare that are relevant to the content of this article.

References

1. Abdulla, P., Atig, M.F., Bouajjani, A., Kumar, K.N., Saivasan, P.: Verification under Intel-x86 with persistency. Proc. ACM Program. Lang. **8**(PLDI) (2024). https://doi.org/10.1145/3656425
2. Abdulla, P.A., Atig, M.F., Bouajjani, A., Ngo, T.P.: Context-bounded analysis for POWER. In: TACAS '17. LNCS, vol. 10206, p. 56–74. Springer, Heidelberg (2017). https://doi.org/10.1007/978-3-662-54580-5_4
3. Abdulla, P.A., Atig, M.F., Jonsson, B., Leonardsson, C.: Stateless model checking for POWER. In: Chaudhuri, S., Farzan, A. (eds.) Computer Aided Verification, pp. 134–156. Springer, Cham (2016)
4. Alglave, J.: How to generate litmus tests automatically with the diy7 tool (2020). https://community.arm.com/developer/ip-products/processors/b/processors-ip-blog/posts/generate-litmus-tests-automatically-diy7-tool. Accessed Oct 2024
5. Alglave, J., Deacon, W., Grisenthwaite, R., Hacquard, A., Maranget, L.: Armed cats: formal concurrency modelling at Arm. ACM Trans. Program. Lang. Syst. **43**(2) (2021). https://doi.org/10.1145/3458926,

6. Alglave, J., Maranget, L., Tautschnig, M.: Herding cats: modelling, simulation, testing, and data mining for weak memory. ACM Trans. Program. Lang. Syst. **36**(2), 7:1–7:74 (2014). https://doi.org/10.1145/2627752
7. Arm Ltd.: Herd7 simulator (online) (2024). https://developer.arm.com/herd7. Accessed Oct 2024
8. Armstrong, A., et al.: ISA semantics for ARMv8-a, RISC-V, and CHERI-MIPS. Proc. ACM Program. Lang. **3**(POPL) (2019). https://doi.org/10.1145/3290384
9. Armstrong, A., Campbell, B., Simner, B., Pulte, C., Sewell, P.: Isla: Integrating full-scale ISA semantics and axiomatic concurrency models. In: Silva, A., Leino, K. (eds.) Computer Aided Verification, pp. 303–316. Springer International Publishing, Cham (2021)
10. Atig, M.F., Bouajjani, A., Burckhardt, S., Musuvathi, M.: On the verification problem for weak memory models. In: POPL 2010, pp. 7–18. ACM (2010). https://doi.org/10.1145/1706299.1706303
11. Atig, M.F., Bouajjani, A., Burckhardt, S., Musuvathi, M.: What's decidable about weak memory models? In: Seidl, H. (ed.) Programming Languages and Systems, pp. 26–46. Springer, Heidelberg (2012)
12. Atig, M.F., Bouajjani, A., Parlato, G.: Getting rid of store-buffers in TSO analysis. In: Gopalakrishnan, G., Qadeer, S. (eds.) Computer Aided Verification, pp. 99–115. Springer, Heidelberg (2011)
13. Bijo, S., Johnsen, E.B., Pun, K.I., Tapia Tarifa, S.L.: A Maude framework for cache coherent multicore architectures. In: Lucanu, D. (ed.) Rewriting Logic and Its Applications, pp. 47–63. Springer, Cham (2016)
14. Burch, J.R., Dill, D.L.: Automatic verification of pipelined microprocessor control. In: Dill, D.L. (ed.) Computer Aided Verification, pp. 68–80. Springer, Heidelberg (1994)
15. Canella, C., et al.: A systematic evaluation of transient execution attacks and defenses. In: 28th USENIX Security Symposium (USENIX Security 19), pp. 249–266 (2019)
16. Carruth, C.: Speculative Load Hardening: A Spectre variant #1 mitigation technique (2018). https://llvm.org/docs/SpeculativeLoadHardening.html. Accessed Oct 2024
17. Cauligi, S., et al.: Constant-time foundations for the new spectre era. In: PLDI, PLDI 2020, New York, NY, USA, pp. 913–926. Association for Computing Machinery (2020). https://doi.org/10.1145/3385412.3385970,
18. Cauligi, S., Disselkoen, C., Moghimi, D., Barthe, G., Stefan, D.: SoK: practical foundations for software Spectre defenses. In: 2022 IEEE Symposium on Security and Privacy (SP), pp. 666–680 (2022). https://doi.org/10.1109/SP46214.2022.9833707
19. Colvin, R.J.: Parallelized sequential composition and hardware weak memory models. In: SEFM, pp. 201–221 (2021). https://doi.org/10.1007/978-3-030-92124-8_12
20. Colvin, R.J.: A fine-grained semantics for arrays and pointers under weak memory models. In: FM, pp. 301–320 (2023). https://doi.org/10.1007/978-3-031-27481-7_18
21. Colvin, R.J., Winter, K.: An abstract semantics of speculative execution for reasoning about security vulnerabilities. In: Sekerinski, E., et al. (eds.) Formal Methods 2019 International Workshops, pp. 323–341. Springer (2020)
22. Coughlin, N., Michael, A., Lam, K.: Lift-offline: Instruction lifter generators. In: Giacobazzi, R., Gorla, A. (eds.) Static Analysis, pp. 86–119. Springer, Cham (2025)

23. Craaijo, J., Verbeek, F., Ravindran, B.: liblisa: Instruction discovery and analysis on x86-64. Proc. ACM Program. Lang. **8**(OOPSLA2) (2024). https://doi.org/10.1145/3689723
24. Damm, W., Pnueli, A.: Verifying Out-of-Order Executions, pp. 23–47. Springer, Boston (1997). https://doi.org/10.1007/978-0-387-35190-2_3
25. Disselkoen, C., Jagadeesan, R., Jeffrey, A., Riely, J.: The code that never ran: modeling attacks on speculative evaluation. In: 2019 IEEE Symposium on Security and Privacy (SP), pp. 1238–1255 (2019). https://doi.org/10.1109/SP.2019.00047
26. Flur, S., et al.: Modelling the ARMv8 architecture, operationally: concurrency and ISA. In: POPL 2016, New York, NY, USA, pp. 608–621. ACM (2016). https://doi.org/10.1145/2837614.2837615,
27. Gharachorloo, K., Lenoski, D., Laudon, J., Gibbons, P., Gupta, A., Hennessy, J.: Memory consistency and event ordering in scalable shared-memory multiprocessors. In: ISCA, pp. 15–26 (1990). https://doi.org/10.1145/325164.325102
28. Godbole, A., Cheang, K., Manerkar, Y.A., Seshia, S.A.: Lifting micro-update models from RTL for formal security analysis. In: Proceedings of the 29th ACM International Conference on Architectural Support for Programming Languages and Operating Systems. ASPLOS '24, New York, NY, USA, vol. 2, pp. 631–648. Association for Computing Machinery (2024). https://doi.org/10.1145/3620665.3640418
29. Gray, K.E., Kerneis, G., Mulligan, D., Pulte, C., Sarkar, S., Sewell, P.: An integrated concurrency and core-ISA architectural envelope definition, and test oracle, for IBM POWER multiprocessors. In: Proceedings of the 48th International Symposium on Microarchitecture. MICRO-48, New York, NY, USA, pp. 635–646, Association for Computing Machinery (2015). https://doi.org/10.1145/2830772.2830775
30. Guanciale, R., Balliu, M., Dam, M.: Inspectre: Breaking and fixing microarchitectural vulnerabilities by formal analysis. In: Proceedings of the 2020 ACM SIGSAC Conference on Computer and Communications Security. CCS '20, New York, NY, USA, pp. 1853–1869, Association for Computing Machinery (2020). https://doi.org/10.1145/3372297.3417246,
31. Guarnieri, M., Köpf, B., Morales, J.F., Reineke, J., Sánchez, A.: Spectector: Principled detection of speculative information flows. In: 2020 IEEE Symposium on Security and Privacy (SP), pp. 1–19 (2020). https://doi.org/10.1109/SP40000.2020.00011
32. Guarnieri, M., Köpf, B., Reineke, J., Vila, P.: Hardware-software contracts for secure speculation. In: 2021 IEEE Symposium on Security and Privacy (SP), pp. 1868–1883 (2021). https://doi.org/10.1109/SP40001.2021.00036
33. Hayes, I.J., Colvin, R.J., Meinicke, L.A., Winter, K., Velykis, A.: An algebra of synchronous atomic steps. In: FM, pp. 352–369 (2016). https://doi.org/10.1007/978-3-319-48989-6_22
34. Hennessy, J.L., Patterson, D.A.: Computer Architecture: A Quantitative Approach. Elsevier (2011)
35. Hoare, C.: Communicating Sequential Processes. Prentice-Hall Inc, Upper Saddle River (1985)
36. Hoare, C.A.R., Möller, B., Struth, G., Wehrman, I.: Concurrent Kleene algebra. CONCUR 2009, pp. 399–414. Springer (2009). https://doi.org/10.1007/978-3-642-04081-8_27
37. Jeffrey, A., Riely, J., Batty, M., Cooksey, S., Kaysin, I., Podkopaev, A.: The leaky semicolon: Compositional semantic dependencies for relaxed-memory concurrency. Proc. ACM Program. Lang. **6**(POPL) (2022). https://doi.org/10.1145/3498716

38. Kang, J., Hur, C.K., Lahav, O., Vafeiadis, V., Dreyer, D.: A promising semantics for relaxed-memory concurrency. In: POPL, pp. 175–189 (2017). https://doi.org/10.1145/3009837.3009850
39. Kocher, P., et al.: Spectre attacks: exploiting speculative execution. In: Security and Privacy, pp. 1–19. IEEE (2019)
40. Lam, K., Coughlin, N.: Lift-off: Trustworthy ARMv8 semantics from formal specifications. In: Nadel, A., Rozier, K.Y. (eds.) Formal Methods in Computer-Aided Design, FMCAD 2023, Ames, IA, USA, October 24-27, 2023. pp. 274–283. IEEE (2023). https://doi.org/10.34727/2023/ISBN.978-3-85448-060-0_36
41. Ponce de León, H., Kinder, J.: Cats vs. spectre: an axiomatic approach to modeling speculative execution attacks. In: 2022 IEEE Symposium on Security and Privacy (SP), pp. 235–248. IEEE (2022)
42. Li, T., Hopkins, B., Parameswaran, S.: SIMF: single-instruction multiple-flush mechanism for processor temporal isolation (2022). https://arxiv.org/abs/2011.10249
43. Lipp, M., et al.: Meltdown: reading kernel memory from user space. In: 27th USENIX Security Symposium (USENIX Security 18) (2018)
44. Arm Ltd.: Arm® Architecture Reference Manual (for A-profile architecture) (11 2024). https://developer.arm.com/documentation/ddi0487/la/, document number: ARM DDI 0487. Accessed May 2025
45. Lustig, D., Pellauer, M., Martonosi, M.: PipeCheck: specifying and verifying microarchitectural enforcement of memory consistency models. In: 47th Annual IEEE/ACM International Symposium on Microarchitecture, pp. 635–646 (2014)
46. Lustig, D., Sethi, G., Martonosi, M., Bhattacharjee, A.: COATCheck: verifying memory ordering at the hardware-OS interface. In: Proceedings of the Twenty-First International Conference on Architectural Support for Programming Languages and Operating Systems. ASPLOS '16, New York, NY, USA, pp. 233–247. Association for Computing Machinery (2016). https://doi.org/10.1145/2872362.2872399,
47. Manerkar, Y.A., Lustig, D., Martonosi, M., Gupta, A.: PipeProof: automated memory consistency proofs for microarchitectural specifications. In: 51st Annual IEEE/ACM International Symposium on Microarchitecture, pp. 788–801 (2018)
48. Manerkar, Y.A., Lustig, D., Pellauer, M., Martonosi, M.: CCICheck: using μHB graphs to verify the coherence-consistency interface. In: Proceedings of the 48th International Symposium on Microarchitecture. MICRO-48, New York, NY, USA, pp. 26–37. Association for Computing Machinery (2015). https://doi.org/10.1145/2830772.2830782,
49. Owens, S., Sarkar, S., Sewell, P.: A better x86 memory model: x86-TSO. In: Berghofer, S., Nipkow, T., Urban, C., Wenzel, M. (eds.) Theorem Proving in Higher Order Logics, pp. 391–407. Springer, Heidelberg (2009)
50. Patterson, D.A., Hennessy, J.L.: Computer Organization and Design ARM Edition: The Hardware Software Interface. Morgan Kaufmann (2016)
51. Podkopaev, A., Lahav, O., Vafeiadis, V.: Bridging the gap between programming languages and hardware weak memory models. Proc. ACM Program. Lang. **3**(POPL) (2019). https://doi.org/10.1145/3290382
52. Pong, F., Dubois, M.: Verification techniques for cache coherence protocols. ACM Comput. Surv. **29**(1), 82–126 (1997). https://doi.org/10.1145/248621.248624
53. Pulte, C., Pichon-Pharabod, J., Kang, J., Lee, S.H., Hur, C.K.: Promising-ARM/RISC-V: a simpler and faster operational concurrency model. In: PLDI. PLDI 2019, pp. 1–15. ACM (2019). https://doi.org/10.1145/3314221.3314624,

54. Raad, A., Maranget, L., Vafeiadis, V.: Extending Intel-x86 consistency and persistency: formalising the semantics of Intel-x86 memory types and non-temporal stores. Proc. ACM Program. Lang. **6**(POPL) (2022). https://doi.org/10.1145/3498683
55. Sarkar, S., Sewell, P., Alglave, J., Maranget, L., Williams, D.: Understanding POWER multiprocessors. In: Proceedings of the 32nd ACM SIGPLAN Conference on Programming Language Design and Implementation. PLDI '11, New York, NY, USA, pp. 175–186. Association for Computing Machinery (2011). https://doi.org/10.1145/1993498.1993520,
56. Schwarz, M., et al.: ZombieLoad: cross-privilege-boundary data sampling. In: Proceedings of the 2019 ACM SIGSAC Conference on Computer and Communications Security. CCS '19, New York, NY, USA, pp. 753–768. Association for Computing Machinery (2019). https://doi.org/10.1145/3319535.3354252,
57. Sewell, P., Sarkar, S., Owens, S., Zappa Nardelli, F., Myreen, M.O.: x86-TSO: a rigorous and usable programmer's model for x86 multiprocessors. Commun. ACM **53**(7), 89–97 (2010). https://doi.org/10.1145/1785414.1785443
58. Thornton, J.E.: Parallel operation in the control Data 6600. In: Proceedings of the October 27–29, 1964, Fall Joint Computer Conference, Part II: Very High Speed Computer Systems. p. 33–40. AFIPS '64 (1964). https://doi.org/10.1145/1464039.1464045
59. Tomasulo, R.M.: An efficient algorithm for exploiting multiple arithmetic units. IBM J. Res. Dev. **11**(1), 25–33 (1967)
60. Trippel, C., Lustig, D., Martonosi, M.: Security verification via automatic hardware-aware exploit synthesis: the CheckMate approach. IEEE Micro **39**(3), 84–93 (2019). https://doi.org/10.1109/MM.2019.2910010
61. Trippel, C., Manerkar, Y.A., Lustig, D., Pellauer, M., Martonosi, M.: Full-stack memory model verification with TriCheck. IEEE Micro **38**(3), 58–68 (2018). https://doi.org/10.1109/MM.2018.032271062
62. Trippel, C., Lustig, D., Martonosi, M.: MeltdownPrime and SpectrePrime: automatically-synthesized attacks exploiting invalidation-based coherence protocols. CoRR abs/1802.03802 (2018), http://arxiv.org/abs/1802.03802
63. Vassena, M., et al.: Automatically eliminating speculative leaks from cryptographic code with Blade. Proc. ACM Program. Lang. **5**(POPL) (2021). https://doi.org/10.1145/3434330,
64. Wickerson, J., Batty, M., Beckmann, B.M., Donaldson, A.F.: Remote-scope promotion: clarified, rectified, and verified. SIGPLAN Not. **50**(10), 731–747 (2015). https://doi.org/10.1145/2858965.2814283
65. Yavarzadeh, H., et al.: Pathfinder: high-resolution control-flow attacks exploiting the conditional branch predictor. In: ASPLOS. ASPLOS '24, New York, NY, USA, pp. 770–784. Association for Computing Machinery (2024). https://doi.org/10.1145/3620666.3651382,
66. Zhao, Z.N., Ji, H., Morrison, A., Marinov, D., Torrellas, J.: Pinned loads: taming speculative loads in secure processors. In: Proceedings of the 27th ACM International Conference on Architectural Support for Programming Languages and Operating Systems, ASPLOS '22, New York, NY, USA, pp. 314–328. Association for Computing Machinery (2022). https://doi.org/10.1145/3503222.3507724,

Open Access This chapter is licensed under the terms of the Creative Commons Attribution 4.0 International License (http://creativecommons.org/licenses/by/4.0/), which permits use, sharing, adaptation, distribution and reproduction in any medium or format, as long as you give appropriate credit to the original author(s) and the source, provide a link to the Creative Commons license and indicate if changes were made.

The images or other third party material in this chapter are included in the chapter's Creative Commons license, unless indicated otherwise in a credit line to the material. If material is not included in the chapter's Creative Commons license and your intended use is not permitted by statutory regulation or exceeds the permitted use, you will need to obtain permission directly from the copyright holder.

Relational Hoare Logic for Realistically Modelled Machine Code

Denis Mazzucato[1], Abdalrhman Mohamed[2], Juneyoung Lee[3](✉),
Clark Barrett[2], Jim Grundy[3], John Harrison[3], and Corina S. Păsăreanu[1]

[1] Carnegie Mellon University, Pittsburgh, USA
{dmazzuca,pcorina}@andrew.cmu.edu
[2] Stanford University, Stanford, USA
{abdal,barrettc}@stanford.edu
[3] Amazon Web Services, Seattle, USA
{lebjuney,jmgruj,jargh}@amazon.com

Abstract. Many security- and performance-critical domains, such as cryptography, rely on low-level verification to minimize the trusted computing surface and allow code to be written directly in assembly. However, verifying assembly code against a realistic machine model is a challenging task. Furthermore, certain security properties—such as constant-time behavior—require relational reasoning that goes beyond traditional correctness by linking multiple execution traces within a single specification. Yet, relational verification has been extensively explored at a higher level of abstraction. In this work, we introduce a Hoare-style logic that provides low-level, expressive relational verification. We demonstrate our approach on the s2n-bignum library, proving both constant-time discipline and equivalence between optimized and verification-friendly routines. Formalized in HOL Light, our results confirm the real-world applicability of relational verification in large assembly codebases.

Keywords: Relational Verification · Machine Code · Mechanized Proofs

1 Introduction

Verification of low-level program properties is paramount for security-critical systems. This applies to microkernels [25], where processors and other hardware may have effects that are not captured by high-level abstractions, as well as cryptographic libraries [6,13], which aim to minimize the trusted computing base and build-toolchain dependencies. Additionally, performance-critical code is often written directly in assembly to maximize performance.

Many challenges arise when verifying low-level code, as programs execute on machines with finite memory, bounded integers, unstructured control flow, and memory space that is shared between data and code. In contrast, high-level

---

D. Mazzucato and A. Mohamed—Contributed equally to this work.

© The Author(s) 2025
R. Piskac and Z. Rakamarić (Eds.): CAV 2025, LNCS 15931, pp. 389–413, 2025.
https://doi.org/10.1007/978-3-031-98668-0_19

verification uses abstractions that simplify reasoning and hide hardware-specific details. For instance, low-level verification must consider that primitives, when storing data, need to have free memory space. Furthermore, the verification process becomes much harder when dealing with *relational properties* [16]. Relational properties link multiple execution traces together within a single property specification. They are necessary for critical applications, such as proving that a cryptographic routine runs in constant time with respect to secret data, or that two versions of a program are functionally equivalent.

In this work, we target the s2n-bignum library,[1] a cryptographic library written in assembly for ARM and x86 architectures. It includes mathematical operations on large integers, such as modular multiplication, as well as more cryptographic-oriented operations, such as elliptic curve operations. As part of the AWS's TLS/SSL implementation, these arithmetic routines are both performance- and security-critical. The library features both highly optimized routines that are hard to verify as well as verification-friendly variants that are easier to verify but slower in practice. By verifying the latter and proving that they are functionally equivalent to the former, we can ensure that the high-performance versions do not compromise correctness. We also aim to ensure that the high-performance routines execute in constant time, a property necessary to prevent timing side-channel attacks, which could compromise sensitive data.

A number of works previously studied Hoare-style logics for realistically modelled machine code [4,14,29,37,42,48]. Hoare-style reasoning has also been pervasively studied for relational properties [9,12,45]. However, relational verification for low-level code remains underexplored, especially for machine code with realistic features such as finite memory and unstructured control flow. Ideally, a binary verification toolkit would use a robust Hoare-style logic that supports realistic machine code, can express relational properties, provides sound and complete proof rules, and retains key properties that users naturally expect. These include, for instance, commutativity, as well as the ability to weaken and strengthen pre- and postconditions and to unify contracts across different contexts. Such *natural properties* enable modular reasoning, support multiple proof strategies, and make the framework practical for real-world applications. To the best of our knowledge, no existing work has presented a relational Hoare logic for realistically modelled machine code that satisfies all these properties.

In this paper, we fill that gap by introducing a novel Hoare-style logic for low-level, relational verification. Our framework, fully formalized in the HOL Light theorem prover [18,19], offers proof rules designed to meet users' natural expectations. We demonstrate our approach via two major case studies: in the first, we show how our framework can be used to verify constant-time behavior of various routines; in the second, we show it can be used to prove the functional equivalence of two different implementations of the same routine (e.g., one optimized for speed and the other optimized for verifiability). These case studies are conducted on the s2n-bignum cryptographic library. Results show that our logic scales to large assembly programs and yields practical value.

---

[1] https://github.com/awslabs/s2n-bignum.

While our primary application is the s2n-bignum library, the generality of our relational Hoare logic extends beyond cryptographic code. It supports low-level features including indirect branches and self-modifying code, even though cryptographic libraries such as s2n-bignum may not employ these features.

We summarize our contributions as follows:

i) A novel relational Hoare logic tailored to realistically modelled machine code, formalized in HOL Light.
ii) A first case study on constant-time behavior of cryptographic routines in the s2n-bignum library, including the copy and modular inversion routines.
iii) A second case study involving equivalence proofs between optimized and verification-friendly implementations of s2n-bignum routines.

2 Related Work

Hoare-Style Reasoning for Realistically Modelled Machine Code. Verifying realistically modelled machine code is challenging due to unstructured control flow, which traditional Hoare logics [20] struggle to handle. While Affeldt [2] uses Hoare logic to verify low-level arithmetic routines, their work is limited to assembly fragments with structured control flow. Several approaches address unstructured control flow, such as the inductive assertion method [39, Section 2] used by Barthe et al. [7] and Lehner and Muller [28] to generate verification conditions, and the program logic by Tan et al. [47] based on continuation-passing style reasoning [8]. However, these methods often fail to specify pre- and postconditions with shared continuation labels.

Other notable efforts include a logic for total correctness of communicating unstructured programs [4,21,22], formalized in Isabelle/HOL, and one for reasoning about MIPS assembly in Coq [30]. However, these logics are compositional only for nonoverlapping fragments. Full compositionality is critical for modular reasoning, which, in turn, is needed for scalability.

Wang [48] proposes a logic for total correctness of unstructured programs with multi-exit postconditions, but it does not guarantee postconditions upon first encounter. Unstructured programs may, in fact, go through the last instruction, jump back, and then meet the postcondition later. While this might seem misleading, we argue that functional specifications are generally confined to function boundaries, where the final instruction is a return statement. This ensures the program cannot continue execution and revisit the postcondition later, effectively solving the issue of first-met postconditions.

Myreen and Gordon [38] introduce a logic for unstructured code applied in the verified CakeML compiler [27], leveraging decompilation into logic [33–37]. Despite its major impact in verifying seL4 compilation [46] and realistic executables [47], it lacks a conjunction rule, a property that is naturally expected from a Hoare-style logic in order to unify contracts over different postconditions. The lack of a conjunction rule significantly increases the proof burden.

For instance, this assembly program increments x0 by 1 until it reaches 3, then halts. Let $P = (\text{x0} = 1)$, $Q = (\text{x0} = 2)$, and $Q' = (\text{x0} = 3)$. The program satisfies Q and Q' separately, on line 3, after two and three iterations, respectively, but Q and Q' cannot possibly hold simultaneously. In Sect. 5, we show how to handle such cases.

```
0    mov  x0,xzr
1  loop:
2    add  x0,x0,#1
3    cmp  x0,#3
4    bne  loop
```

Ray et al. [43] address conjunction rules and first-met postconditions by tracking execution steps, while Lundberg et al. [29] extend this to handle multi-exit locations, ensuring postconditions hold at the first encounter. However, their approaches assume deterministic semantics, incompatible with architectures like x86. Jensen et al. [23] addresses this gap by using separation logic [40,44] but only for a subset of x86 code. Furthermore, EverCrypt [42] verifies cryptographic primitives using a Hoare-style logic through C and assembly code interoperability, but it does not support ARM architecture. Similar to our embedding of relational to unary Hoare triples, exploiting the event list, EverCrypt is able to prove constant-time. Fiat-Crypto [17] generates verified cryptographic code from high-level specifications with applications to big-number arithmetic, in scope similar to the s2n-bignum library. All these approaches lack a robust foundation for generic relational properties—not only the ones reducible to unary properties.

Relational Hoare Logics. Relational Hoare logics [39] extend unary Hoare triples to reason about multiple execution traces. Benton [9] gives a relational Hoare logic for two execution traces, later generalized by Blatter et al. [12] to any number of traces. While Benton also covers relational properties of low-level unstructured code [8], their logic relies on an idealized computational model. We propose a generic framework for manual proof of relational properties.

In credible compilation, Rinard [45] developed relational logics for pointer allocation, and Benton [10] proposes a sound-but-incomplete fully automatic tool for equivalence preservation of compiled programs with minor differences. They verify HHVM bytecode, which is not a high-level language but not as low as assembly; for instance, they do not handle physical registers. Instead, our approach sacrifices automation, gaining both soundness and completeness.

Barthe et al. [5] propose product program constructions for equivalence reasoning, later extended [3,11] to support equivalence across multiple programs. Kang et al. [24] describe a relational logic for LLVM code which lacks support for indirect branches and self-modifying code. Pit-Claudel et al. [41] further extend relational verification to low-level stack machines. Our logic handles relational properties but does not trade off any low level features of assembly code.

3 Running Example

We use the program compare, shown in Fig. 1 (left), as a running example for the rest of the paper. It compares byte-by-byte the contents of a key buffer k and a data buffer x of length n. It takes as input the buffer length n and the memory addresses of the buffers k and x, provided via the registers n, k, and

Program 1.1. compare

```
1   cbz n, eq
2   loop:
3     sub n, n, #1
4     ldr kn, [k, n, lsl #3]
5     ldr xn, [x, n, lsl #3]
6     cmp kn, xn
7     bne neq
8     cbnz n, loop
9   eq:
10    mov res, #1
11    ret
12  neq:
13    mov res, xzr
14    ret
```

Program 1.2. cst-compare

```
1     mov diff, xzr
2     cbz n, end
3   loop:
4     sub n, n, #1
5     ldr kn, [k, n, lsl #3]
6     ldr xn, [x, n, lsl #3]
7     eor temp, kn, xn
8     orr diff, diff, temp
9     cbnz n, loop
10  end:
11    cmp diff, xzr
12    cset res, eq
13    ret
```

Fig. 1. Two programs to perform byte-by-byte comparison of buffers. The program compare (left) is not constant-time, while the program compare-constant (right) is.

x, respectively. Temporary values are stored in the registers kn, xn, diff, and temp, while the result is stored in res. The private data is the content of the key buffer. The program compare iterates backwards, comparing corresponding elements from both buffers. If a mismatch is detected, the program jumps to the label neq and sets res to 0. Otherwise, if all elements match, it reaches the label eq and sets res to 1. This behavior results in variable execution time depending on the buffer contents. An attacker can exploit this timing variation to deduce the position of mismatches and reconstruct the secret buffer k in linear time.

To address this issue, program cst-compare in Fig. 1 (right) implements a constant-time comparison. It always iterates over the entire buffer length, regardless of mismatches, accumulating possible differences in diff. The program's execution time is constant for any buffer content, ensuring no timing leaks and preventing attackers from inferring secret information. Furthermore, the two programs are functionally equivalent.

4 Unary Hoare Logic $\mathcal{L}_1$

This section provides background on an unary Hoare logic used in the verification framework described in [29,38]. We refer to this logic as $\mathcal{L}_1$. The definitions and theorems of $\mathcal{L}_1$ have been fully mechanized in HOL Light by previous researchers.

States. Let Σ denote a set of machine states, represented as the set of functions mapping observable resources $\mathbb{L}$ (e.g., memory, registers, program counter) to their values. For example, in the ARM architecture, the resources $\mathbb{L}_{\text{ARM}}$ include a 64-bit program counter pc, 32 general-purpose registers regs_i, flags flags_k, and memory memory_h, indexed accordingly by i, k, and h. Similarly, the x86 architecture has resources like an instruction pointer (rip) and extended flags. To generalize across different architectures, the label instr refers to the address of the next instruction, where instr = pc for ARM and instr = rip for x86. We use $s(l)$ for the value of resource $l \in \mathbb{L}$ in the state $s \in \Sigma$ and $s[l \mapsto v]$ for the updated state. Resource values depend on the architecture; e.g., for ARM, $s(\texttt{pc}) \in \texttt{int64}$, $s(\texttt{regs}_i) \in \texttt{int64}$, and $s(\texttt{memory}_h) \in \texttt{byte}$, where $\texttt{byte} \stackrel{\text{def}}{=} \{0,1\}^8$ and $\texttt{int}n \stackrel{\text{def}}{=} \{0,1\}^n$.

Properties. A property P is a subset of machine states Σ. A state s satisfies the property $P \subseteq \Sigma$ if $s \in P$. The execution of a single instruction is modelled as the small-step operational semantics $\tau \subseteq \Sigma \times \Sigma$, where $s \xrightarrow{\tau} s'$ describes the fetch-decode-execute cycle, updating state s to s' and advancing $\texttt{instr}$. The composition of two relations τ_1, τ_2 is defined as $\tau_1 \circ \tau_2 \stackrel{\text{def}}{=} \{(s, s'') \mid \exists s'.\ s \xrightarrow{\tau_1} s' \xrightarrow{\tau_2} s''\}$. The n-th composition of τ is τ^n. The decoding function $\textsc{decode}^\tau(s, i)$ maps bytes in the memory at address i either to an instruction or to $\bot$ if undecodable. ARM instructions have a length of 4 bytes and are 4-byte aligned. X86 instructions have variable lengths. We write $\textsc{length}^\tau(C)$ for the number of bytes that the program C occupies in the memory without padding for alignment. Execution halts when the first undecodable instruction is encountered, denoted by $\textsc{end}^\tau(s, i) \stackrel{\text{def}}{\iff} s(\texttt{instr}) = i \land \textsc{decode}^\tau(s, i) = \bot$.

We use $\textsc{align}^\tau(s, i_0, C)$ in this paper to denote that the program C is stored in memory starting from the address i_0 where $s(\texttt{instr}) = i_0$ and i_0 satisfies the alignment constraint of a program if the architecture is ARM. The predicate $\textsc{align}^\tau(s, i_0, C)$ may appear as a conjunctive clause in P to describe the program of interest. The notation $\texttt{prog}(P)$ refers to the program C constrained by P.

The `eventually` *Property.* Assume that a machine state $s \in \Sigma$ satisfies a precondition. A postcondition $Q \subseteq \Sigma$ must eventually hold after a finite number of steps from s. To represent such s, $\texttt{eventually}^\tau(Q)$ defines the set of states from which Q eventually holds along every possible path through τ.

Definition 1 (Eventually). *Given an operational semantics $\tau \subseteq \Sigma \times \Sigma$ and a property $Q \subseteq \Sigma$, the property $\texttt{eventually}^\tau(Q) \subseteq \Sigma$ is defined inductively as:*

$$\frac{s \in Q}{s \in \texttt{eventually}^\tau(Q)} \qquad \frac{\exists s'.\ s \xrightarrow{\tau} s' \quad \forall s'.\ s \xrightarrow{\tau} s' \implies s' \in \texttt{eventually}^\tau(Q)}{s \in \texttt{eventually}^\tau(Q)}$$

The second inference rule expands $\texttt{eventually}^2$ if every next state s' is in $\texttt{eventually}^\tau(Q)$. This notion of $\texttt{eventually}$ is essential for reasoning about nondeterministic operational semantics, such as in X86, where certain instructions exhibit nondeterministic behavior. For instance, the $\texttt{mul}$ instruction[3] nondeterministically sets the $\texttt{SF}$ flag to either 0 or 1. A simplified small-step semantics for $\texttt{mul}$ is as follows:

$$\frac{s(\texttt{instr}) = i \quad \textsc{decode}^{\tau\text{x86}}(s, i) = \texttt{mul } r \quad r \in \texttt{int16} \quad s(r) = x \quad sf \in \{0,1\}}{s \xrightarrow{\tau\text{x86}} s\,[\texttt{EAX} \mapsto s(\texttt{AX}) \cdot x,\ \texttt{SF} \mapsto sf,\ \texttt{instr} \mapsto i + \textsc{length}^\tau(\texttt{mul } r)]} \text{ MUL}$$

---

[2] We omit the τ symbol when the operational semantics is clear from the context.
[3] https://www.felixcloutier.com/x86/mul#flags-affected.

Example 1. Consider a program C consisting of the instructions `mul ax`, `sets dl`, and `imul edx, eax`. The program starts at instruction register i_0, where AX (the least significant 16 bits of EAX) is multiplied by itself, setting SF to 0 or 1. In the second instruction, the least significant byte of EDX, referred to as DL, is set to SF. After then, the values of EAX and EDX are multiplied, and the truncated result up to 32 bits is stored in EDX. The program terminates at $i_0 + 9$ because each of the x86 instructions is 3 bytes, and EDX is equal to either 0 or x^2. The postcondition can be expressed as: $\{s' \mid \text{END}^{\tau_{x86}}(s', i_0 + 9) \land (s'(\text{EDX}) = x^2 \lor s'(\text{EDX}) = 0)\}$. It holds under a precondition requiring AX to initially be equal to x and EDX to 0.

Unary Hoare Triple. Reasoning about machine code differs from reasoning about high-level languages in several ways. First, the machine code is not represented as a syntactic program but instead as a set of instructions in the memory space. Second, a machine code may modify anything during its execution, including itself and callee-save registers. To denote unwanted modifications after the program execution, a *frame condition* $F \subseteq \Sigma \times \Sigma$ bounds allowed changes of state components between the input and output states. We explain the formal definition of the predicate `ensures` which is the Hoare triple in $\mathcal{L}_1$. The notation used in this paper follows the convention you may find in the s2n-bignum library.

Definition 2 (Ensures). *Given an operational semantics $\tau \subseteq \Sigma \times \Sigma$, a precondition $P \subseteq \Sigma$, a postcondition $Q \subseteq \Sigma$, and a frame condition $F \subseteq \Sigma \times \Sigma$, we define the predicate* `ensures`$^\tau(P, Q, F)$ *as follows:*

$$\text{ensures}^\tau(P, Q, F) \overset{\text{def}}{\iff}$$
$$\forall s.\ s \in P \implies s \in \text{eventually}^\tau(\{s' \mid s' \in Q \land (s, s') \in F\})$$

Example 2. Consider the program C from Example 1, starting from the precondition $\{s \mid \text{ALIGN}^{\tau_{x86}}(s, i_0, C) \land s(\text{AX}) = x \land s(\text{EDX}) = 0\}$, ensuring that the memory is aligned with C and AX is equal to x. By application of the operational semantics, we eventually satisfy the postcondition where C terminates with EDX equal to 0 or x^2.

During execution, C may modify EAX, EDX, and the sign flag SF. We denote by MAYCHANGE : $\wp(\mathbb{L}) \to \wp(\Sigma \times \Sigma)$ the resources that the program may modify. Formally, MAYCHANGE$(L) \overset{\text{def}}{=} \{(s, s') \mid \forall l \in \mathbb{L}.\ l \notin L \implies s(l) = s'(l)\}$. Thus, the frame condition can be written as MAYCHANGE$(\{\text{instr}, \text{EAX}, \text{EDX}, \text{SF}\})$. The correctness of C is captured by:

$$\text{ensures}^{\tau_{x86}} \begin{pmatrix} \{s \mid \text{ALIGN}^{\tau_{x86}}(s, i_0, C) \land s(\text{AX}) = x \land s(\text{EDX}) = 0\}, \\ \{s \mid \text{END}^{\tau_{x86}}(s, i_0 + 12) \land (s(\text{EDX}) = x^2 \lor s(\text{EDX}) = 0)\}, \\ \text{MAYCHANGE}(\{\text{instr}, \text{EAX}, \text{EDX}, \text{SF}\}) \end{pmatrix}$$

Recall that the frame rule in separation logic [40,44] states that if $\{P\}\ C\ \{Q\}$ holds, then for a disjoint memory region R, $\{P * R\}\ C\ \{Q * R\}$ also holds. Similarly, in our logic, if R is invariant under MAYCHANGE(L), i.e., $\forall s, s'.\ (s, s') \in$

MAYCHANGE(L) $\implies$ ($s \in R \iff s' \in R$) then ensures($P, Q,$ MAYCHANGE(L)) implies ensures($P \cap R, Q \cap R,$ MAYCHANGE(L)). Therefore, $\mathcal{L}_1$ supports modular verification while preserving the simplicity of first-order predicates, enabling efficient proof automation.

The logic $\mathcal{L}_1$ is equipped with the usual derivation rules for reasoning about the program execution [32, Appendix A]. The logic core and tactics are implemented in 10k lines of HOL Light [18]. It is currently used to verify functional safety properties of the s2n-bignum library, comprising 615 arithmetic routines written in ARM and X86 assembly languages for P-256/384/521, x25519/ed25519 and RSA. A total of 1013 functional properties have been verified, amounting to 860k lines of proofs.

5 Program Logic $\mathcal{L}_2$ for Relational Verification

In this section, we first introduce a stronger variant of the eventually predicate. Then, we present the relational logic $\mathcal{L}_2$ as a natural extension of $\mathcal{L}_1$. We show how to prove a unary Hoare triple from a relational one and vice versa. This last step is essential in demonstrating the robustness of our logic and allows proofs to transition between $\mathcal{L}_1$ and $\mathcal{L}_2$. We highlight the main extensions that allow us to prove relational properties and leave a discussion about the details of the challenges in Appendix B [32].

5.1 Unary Hoare Triples with Number of Steps

Building on [43], we propose a stronger eventually operator that explicitly specifies the number of steps required to reach a given postcondition.

Definition 3 (Stronger Eventually). *Given an operational semantics $\tau \subseteq \Sigma \times \Sigma$ and a number of steps $n \in \mathbb{N}$, for any postcondition $Q \subseteq \Sigma$, we define:*

$$\texttt{eventuallyn}_n^\tau(Q) \stackrel{\text{def}}{=} \left\{ s \in \Sigma \;\middle|\; \begin{array}{l} \forall s'.\; s \xrightarrow{\tau^n} s' \implies s' \in Q \;\land \\ \forall s', l \in \mathbb{N}.\; l < n \land s \xrightarrow{\tau^l} s' \implies \exists s''.\; s' \xrightarrow{\tau} s'' \end{array} \right\}$$

That is, it defines the set of states such that for all states reachable in n steps, the postcondition Q must hold, and for all states reachable in less than n steps, there must exist a successor state.

There are two merits in specifying the number of steps n. First, it makes the conjunction rule sound. In low-level languages, a program execution that failed to satisfy the postcondition at instr may continue as long as it encounters decodable instructions, and then branch back prior to instr and eventually satisfy the postcondition. Therefore, writing multiple postconditions at instr that hold at different steps but not together would break the conjunction rule as shown in Sect. 2. Explicitly stating the exact number of steps to arrive at the postcondition as an additional constraint resolves such problem. Second, it retains soundness of the commutativity and composition of nested eventuallyn operators, which are similarly important for proving natural properties of relational Hoare triples. When a low-level program exhibits nondeterministic behavior, each trace may meet the postcondition after different numbers of steps.[4] The definition of eventuallyn is stronger than eventually, cf. Definition 1.

Lemma 1. $\forall Q \subseteq \Sigma, n \in \mathbb{N}.\ \text{eventuallyn}_n(Q) \subseteq \text{eventually}(Q)$

The stronger eventually operator supports the following properties:

Conjunction. As we require postconditions to hold after exactly n steps, we can unify contracts stating different postconditions on the final states.

$$\frac{s \in \text{eventuallyn}_n(Q) \qquad s \in \text{eventuallyn}_n(Q')}{s \in \text{eventuallyn}_n(Q \cap Q')} \text{ CONJ}$$

Commutativity. Nested eventually operators commute, implying that the order of the two programs specified by the relational property will not matter. Whenever $Q^\times \subseteq \Sigma \times \Sigma$ is eventually satisfied in n_0 and n_1 steps, for the first and second components of $Q^\times$, the inverse $\{(s_1, s_0) \mid (s_0, s_1) \in Q^\times\}$ is satisfied in n_1 and n_0 steps, respectively.

$$\frac{s_0 \in \text{eventuallyn}_{n_0}\left(\left\{s'_0 \mid s_1 \in \text{eventuallyn}_{n_1}\left(\dot{Q}^\times_{\pi_0 = s'_0}\right)\right\}\right)}{s_1 \in \text{eventuallyn}_{n_1}\left(\left\{s'_1 \mid s_0 \in \text{eventuallyn}_{n_0}\left(\dot{Q}^\times_{\pi_1 = s'_1}\right)\right\}\right)} \text{ COMM}$$

Here, $\dot{Q}^\times_{\pi_i = s_x} \subseteq \Sigma$ contains all states that satisfy Q together with s_x in the i-th component, i.e., $\dot{Q}^\times_{\pi_i = s_x} \stackrel{\text{def}}{=} \{\pi_{1-i}(s, s') \mid \pi_i(s, s') = s_x \wedge (s, s') \in Q^\times\}$. The projection π_i retrieves the i-th component of a pair of states (zero indexed). Projections are lifted to sets of states by $\pi_i(Q^\times) \stackrel{\text{def}}{=} \{\pi_i(s, s') \mid (s, s') \in Q^\times\}$.

Composition. Two fragments reaching $Q^\times$ and $R^\times$ in n_0, n_1 and m_0, m_1 steps, respectively, can be composed to reach $R^\times$ in $n_0 + m_0$ and $n_1 + m_1$ steps.

$$\frac{\begin{array}{c} s_0 \in \text{eventuallyn}_{n_0}\left(\left\{s \mid s_1 \in \text{eventuallyn}_{n_1}\left(\dot{Q}^\times_{\pi_0 = s}\right)\right\}\right) \\ \forall s'_0, s'_1.(s'_0, s'_1) \in Q \implies s'_1 \in \text{eventuallyn}_{m_0}\left(\left\{s \mid s'_0 \in \text{eventuallyn}_{m_1}\left(\dot{R}^\times_{\pi_0 = s}\right)\right\}\right) \end{array}}{s_0 \in \text{eventuallyn}_{n_0 + m_0}\left(\left\{s \mid s_1 \in \text{eventuallyn}_{n_1 + m_1}\left(\dot{R}^\times_{\pi_0 = s}\right)\right\}\right)} \text{ COMP}$$

With the three properties of eventuallyn (cf. CONJ, COMM, and COMP), we can define a unary Hoare triple that maintains the properties that users would naturally expect from a Hoare logic. To do so, we employ a step function $\textit{fn} : \Sigma \to \mathbb{N}$ to make the number of steps dependent on a given state.

---

[4] https://github.com/awslabs/s2n-bignum/blob/c747b1b66801e3975a8da502e18962838d3be945/common/relational2.ml#L86-L243.

Definition 4 (Stronger Ensures). *Given an operational semantics $\tau \subseteq \Sigma \times \Sigma$, a precondition $P \subseteq \Sigma$, a postcondition $Q \subseteq \Sigma$, a frame condition $F \subseteq \Sigma \times \Sigma$, and a step function $fn : \Sigma \to \mathbb{N}$, a unary Hoare triple is a statement of the form $\texttt{ensuresn}_{fn}(P, Q, F)$, where:*

$$\texttt{ensuresn}_{fn}(P, Q, F) \stackrel{\text{def}}{\iff}$$
$$\forall s.\ s \in P \implies s \in \texttt{eventuallyn}^{\tau}_{fn(s)}(\{s' \mid s' \in Q \land (s, s') \in F\})$$

Whenever precondition P holds for state s, postcondition Q holds for any state s' that is related by $fn(s)$ steps of the execution of the program $\texttt{prog}(P)$, and $\texttt{prog}(P)$ modifies only the memory locations specified by the frame condition F.

As a consequence of Lemma 1, the unary Hoare triple $\texttt{ensuresn}_{fn}(P, Q, F)$ is stronger than $\texttt{ensures}$, cf. Definition 2.

Theorem 1. $\forall P, Q, F, fn.\ \texttt{ensuresn}_{fn}(P, Q, F) \implies \texttt{ensures}(P, Q, F)$

The other direction of the implication is not always true; in fact, it holds only for deterministic programs. The reason is that the program may branch based on a nondeterministic choice, and the postcondition may hold in a different number of steps than the one specified in the Hoare triple.

Theorem 2. *For any operational semantics τ, precondition P, postcondition Q, frame condition F, if τ is deterministic, then:*

$$\texttt{ensures}^{\tau}(P, Q, F) \implies \exists fn.\ \texttt{ensuresn}^{\tau}_{fn}(P, Q, F)$$

5.2 Relational Hoare Triples

We now define the relational Hoare triple $\texttt{ensures2}_{fn_0, fn_1}(P^{\times}, Q^{\times}, F^{\times})$ that allows us to reason about the behavior of two programs. Whenever the precondition $P^{\times} \subseteq \Sigma \times \Sigma$ holds for a pair of states (s_0, s_1), the postcondition $Q^{\times} \subseteq \Sigma \times \Sigma$ should eventually hold for any pair of states (s'_0, s'_1) that are related by respectively fn_0 and fn_1 steps of the execution of the two programs C_0 and C_1. As for the logic $\mathcal{L}_1$, the two programs are not explicitly given but instead are constrained in the memory space by P, i.e., $C_0 = \texttt{prog}(\pi_0(P))$ and $C_1 = \texttt{prog}(\pi_1(P))$. The frame condition $F^{\times} \subseteq (\Sigma \times \Sigma) \times (\Sigma \times \Sigma)$ specifies the memory locations that can be modified by the two programs. Formally:

Definition 5 (Relational Ensures). *Given operational semantics $\tau \subseteq \Sigma \times \Sigma$, a precondition $P^{\times} \subseteq \Sigma \times \Sigma$, a postcondition $Q^{\times} \subseteq \Sigma \times \Sigma$, and a frame condition $F^{\times} \subseteq (\Sigma \times \Sigma) \times (\Sigma \times \Sigma)$, two step functions $fn_0, fn_1 : \Sigma \to \mathbb{N}$, a relational Hoare triple is a statement of the form $\texttt{ensures2}_{fn_0, fn_1}(P^{\times}, Q^{\times}, F^{\times})$, where:*

$$\texttt{ensures2}_{fn_0, fn_1}(P^{\times}, Q^{\times}, F^{\times}) \stackrel{\text{def}}{\iff} \forall s_0, s_1.\ (s_0, s_1) \in P^{\times} \implies s_0 \in M_{s_0, s_1}$$

$$\text{where } M_{s_0, s_1} \stackrel{\text{def}}{=} \texttt{eventuallyn}_{fn_0(s_0)}(\{s'_0 \mid s_1 \in N_{s_0, s_1, s'_0}\})$$

$$\text{and } N_{s_0, s_1, s'_0} \stackrel{\text{def}}{=} \texttt{eventuallyn}_{fn_1(s_1)}(\{s'_1 \mid (s'_0, s'_1) \in Q^{\times} \land ((s_0, s_1), (s'_0, s'_1)) \in F^{\times}\})$$

The definitions of M_{s_0,s_1} and $N_{s_0,s_1,s_0'}$ nest eventuallyn requirements: M_{s_0,s_1} includes all the states where the program C_0 reaches a state s_0' within $fn_0(s_0)$ steps, and $N_{s_0,s_1,s_0'}$ includes all the states where the program C_1 reaches a state s_1' where $(s_0', s_1') \in Q^\times$ and $((s_0, s_1), (s_0', s_1')) \in F^\times$ hold within $fn_1(s_1)$ steps.

As this definition is based on nested eventuallyn operators, thanks to its properties CONJ, COMM, and COMP, it follows that the relational Hoare triple ensures2 commutes, is compositional, and allows contract unification.

Lemma 2 (Commutativity). *Given precondition $P^\times$, postcondition $Q^\times$, frame condition $F^\times$, and step functions fn_0, fn_1, the relational Hoare triple commutes:*

$$\text{ensures2}_{fn_0, fn_1}(P^\times, Q^\times, F^\times) \iff \text{ensures2}_{fn_1, fn_0}(P^S, Q^S, F^S)$$

where the swapped versions are defined as $X^S \stackrel{\text{def}}{=} \{(s_1, s_0) \mid (s_0, s_1) \in X^\times\}$.

This symmetry above ensures that the relational logic is invariant to the program orders, allowing their roles to be interchanged without affecting the triple's validity.

Lemma 3 (Compositional). *Given three properties $P^\times, R^\times, Q^\times$, two frame conditions $F_0^\times, F_1^\times$, and four step numbers n_0, n_1, m_0, m_1, it holds that two relational Hoare triples can be composed transitively:*

$$\text{ensures2}_{\lambda s. n_0, \lambda s. m_0}(P^\times, R^\times, F_0^\times) \wedge \text{ensures2}_{\lambda s. n_1, \lambda s. m_1}(R^\times, Q^\times, F_1^\times)$$
$$\implies \text{ensures2}_{\lambda s. n_0+n_1, \lambda s. m_0+m_1}(P^\times, Q^\times, F_0^\times \circ F_1^\times)$$

Similarly, also the frame condition can be transitively composed. This is essential in Sect. 7 for the composition of program equivalences.

Lemma 4 (Compositional of Frame Conditions). *Given two preconditions P, P', two postconditions Q, Q', and three frame conditions F_0, F_1, F_2, and three step functions fn_0, fn_1, fn_2, it holds that two relational Hoare triples can be composed transitively with respect to the frame conditions:*

$$\frac{\text{ensures2}_{fn_0, fn_1}(P, Q, \{((s_0, s_1), (s_0', s_1')) \mid (s_0, s_0') \in F_0 \wedge (s_1, s_1') \in F_1\})}{\text{ensures2}_{fn_1, fn_2}(P', Q', \{((s_0, s_1), (s_0', s_1')) \mid (s_0, s_0') \in F_1 \wedge (s_1, s_1') \in F_2\})}{\text{ensures2}_{fn_0, fn_2}(P \circ P', Q \circ Q', \{((s_0, s_1), (s_0', s_1')) \mid (s_0, s_0') \in F_0 \wedge (s_1, s_1') \in F_2\})}$$

Lemma 4 formalizes equivalence transitivity: when a program C_0 is equivalent to C_1 and C_1 is equivalent to C_2, then C_0 is equivalent to C_2. This Lemma is vital in the equivalence proofs because proving the correctness of each optimization step independently is easier than directly proving the equivalence of the original and optimized program.

Lemma 5 (Conjunction). *Given two preconditions $P_0^\times, P_1^\times$, two postconditions $Q_0^\times, Q_1^\times$, and a frame condition $F^\times$, two contracts can be unified with a conjunction:*

$$\text{ensures2}_{fn_0, fn_1}(P_0^\times, Q_0^\times, F^\times) \wedge \text{ensures2}_{fn_0, fn_1}(P_1^\times, Q_1^\times, F^\times)$$
$$\implies \text{ensures2}_{fn_0, fn_1}(P_0^\times \cap P_1^\times, Q_0^\times \cap Q_1^\times, F^\times)$$

All these properties of our Hoare triples enable us to reason about the behavior of two programs, while maintaining the natural properties of a Hoare logic. Appendix C [32] presents the additional properties of our program logic $\mathcal{L}_2$, including the weakening and strengthening of pre-, post-, and frame conditions. Implemented in HOL Light, the core of the relational verification amounts to 1704 lines of code.

5.3 Connection with Unary Hoare Triples

We compare the relational Hoare triple ensures2 with the unary counterpart ensuresn, demonstrating two key transformations: (1) deriving relational Hoare triples from two unary ones, and (2) extracting a unary Hoare triple from a *hybrid* relational one. These transformations serve a dual purpose. First, deriving a relational triple from unary ones enables reasoning about the behavior of two programs by analyzing each independently:

Theorem 3. *Given two sets of pre-, post-, and frame conditions P, P', Q, Q', F, F', and two step functions fn_0, fn_1, it holds that:*

$$\text{ensuresn}_{fn_0}(P, Q, F) \wedge \text{ensuresn}_{fn_1}(P', Q', F')$$
$$\implies \text{ensures2}_{fn_0, fn_1}(P \times P', Q \times Q', F \times F')$$

Second, extracting a unary triple from a hybrid relational one allows results obtained in the unary logic to be seamlessly promoted to the relational framework. A hybrid relational triple is a relational triple where the pre-, post-, and frame conditions relate to unary pre-, post-, and frame conditions, respectively. The goal is to be able to extract a unary Hoare triple from a relational one; hence: (*i*) the relational precondition should always have a satisfying pair (s_0, s_1) when s_1 satisfies the unary precondition; (*ii*) if a pair (s_0, s_1) satisfies the relational postcondition, then s_1 should satisfy the unary postcondition; and (*iii*) the frame condition should be satisfied for the product relation whenever the second component satisfies the frame condition of the unary relation.

Definition 6 (Hybrid Relational Ensures). *Given the pre-, post-, and frame conditions for the product relation $P^\times, Q^\times, F^\times$, and unary pre-, post-, and frame conditions P, Q, F, and two step functions $fn_0, fn_1 : \Sigma \to \mathbb{N}$, a* hybrid *relational Hoare triple*, written $h\mathsf{ensures2}_{fn_0,fn_1}(P^\times, Q^\times, F^\times \mid P, Q, F)$, holds if:

$$\mathsf{ensures2}_{fn_0,fn_1}(P^\times, Q^\times, F^\times)$$
$$\land \forall s_1.\ s_1 \in P \implies \exists s_0.\ (s_0, s_1) \in P^\times \qquad (i)$$
$$\land \forall s_0, s_1, (s_0, s_1) \in Q^\times \implies s_1 \in Q \qquad (ii)$$
$$\land \exists F'.\ \forall s_0, s_1, s_0', s_1'.\ \begin{pmatrix} ((s_0', s_1'), (s_0, s_1)) \in F^\times \iff \\ (s_0', s_1') \in F' \land (s_0, s_1) \in F \end{pmatrix} \qquad (iii)$$

Employing the hybrid relational triple $h\mathsf{ensures2}$ (with the prefix h denoting "hybrid") simplifies the verification process and makes the logic more robust. For instance, it enables translating correctness proofs for one program to another, equivalent program without having to reprove them, saving time and effort. The next result shows that a hybrid relational Hoare triple can be transformed into a unary Hoare triple.

Theorem 4. $h\mathsf{ensures2}_{fn_0,fn_1}(P^\times, Q^\times, F^\times \mid P, Q, F) \implies \mathsf{ensuresn}_{fn_1}(P, Q, F)$.

6 Constant-Time Behavior

In this section, we show how our relational logic $\mathcal{L}_2$ can be applied to reason about constant-time behavior. As is customary in security analysis, we discriminate between public and private input data by partitioning the state labels into two disjoint sets, i.e., $\mathbb{L} = \mathbb{L}_{\text{pub}} \cup \mathbb{L}_{\text{pri}}$ and $\mathbb{L}_{\text{pub}} \cap \mathbb{L}_{\text{pri}} = \emptyset$. Public and private data induce equivalence relations on states, i.e., $\simeq_{\text{pub}}$ and $\simeq_{\text{pri}}$ respectively. The public data is accessible to the attacker, while the private data is kept secret. A program is constant-time if, for the same public input data, any two executions terminate with the same number of clock cycles. As a result, private data does not influence the execution time of the program.

Constant-Time via Events Accumulation. It is not practical to specify constant-time behavior by ensuring that the number of steps is equivalent in executions with the same public data, as it is highly dependent on the underlying hardware. Due to microarchitectural effects, such as memory access patterns or branch prediction, the number of clock cycles can vary significantly between executions. Instead, we can safely reason about constant-time behavior by employing a stronger notion of timing security: a program is *constant-time* if—for the same public input data—any two executions of the program induce *the same trace of microarchitectural events*.

To observe these events, we extend the state space Σ with an events component in $\mathbb{L}_e \stackrel{\text{def}}{=} \mathbb{L} \cup \{\mathsf{events}\}$. The events component records an ordered list of events, such as memory accesses ($\mathsf{load}\ x, n$ or $\mathsf{store}\ x, n$; where x is the accessed address and n the operation size in bytes), and branch jumps ($\mathsf{branch}\ x, y$; where

x and y are the current and the destination program counter, respectively), Any other variable-time instruction, such as division or floating point operations can also be included in the event trace. In our case studies, these operations are intentionally left unresolved by the operational semantics, and thus not included in the event trace. These events are public data, i.e., $\text{events} \in \mathbb{L}_{\text{pub}}$. The extended state space is Σ_e with operational semantics τ^e. For instance, loading a memory address x into a 16 bit register r collects a load event of 2 bytes:

$$\frac{\begin{array}{c}s(\texttt{instr}) = i \quad \text{DECODE}(s,i) = \texttt{load } r, \, x \\ s(\texttt{memory}_x) = v \quad s(\texttt{events}) = e \quad \text{LENGTH}(r) = 16\end{array}}{s \xrightarrow{\tau^e} s\,[r \mapsto v, \, \texttt{events} \mapsto (e \, \texttt{++} \, \texttt{load } x, 2), \, \texttt{instr} \mapsto i + \text{LENGTH}^\tau(\texttt{load } r, x)]} \text{ LOAD}$$

Therefore, we are now able to specify constant-time behavior by ensuring that the list of microarchitectural events is the same in both executions. Our approach can be easily extended to include other side-channels, such as power consumption.

While we do not include opcode-level information in our events, instruction opcodes can influence the number of cycles (e.g., the cbz and b.ne instructions in ARM). This relies on an assumption that a program is public information, and therefore the events do not need to carry opcode information. This assumption can be broken if a program runs assembly instructions that are separately stored in a private input buffer. We prove that such things do not happen individually.

Definition 7 (Constant-Time via Event Accumulation). *Let $\tau^e \subseteq \Sigma_e \times \Sigma_e$ be an operational semantics that collects the microarchitectural events, $P \subseteq \Sigma_e$ be a precondition, $Q \subseteq \Sigma_e$ a postcondition, $F \subseteq \Sigma_e \times \Sigma_e$ a frame condition, and $fn_0, fn_1 : \Sigma_e \to \mathbb{N}$ two step functions. The program $\texttt{prog}(P)$ is constant-time with respect to private data $\mathbb{L}_{\text{pri}}$ if it holds that:*

$$\texttt{ensures2}^{\tau^e}_{fn_0, fn_1} \begin{pmatrix} \{(s_0, s_1) \in P \times P \mid s_0(\mathbb{L}_{\text{pub}}) = s_1(\mathbb{L}_{\text{pub}})\}, \\ \{(s_0, s_1) \in Q \times Q \mid s_0(\texttt{events}) = s_1(\texttt{events})\}, \\ F \times F \end{pmatrix}$$

Note that, by constraining the public data to be equal in the precondition, we also require that states share the same event trace before executing the program.

Example 3. The program cst-compare in Fig. 1 (right) is constant-time with respect to the microarchitectural events of Definition 7. Indeed, cst-compare first branches on the length n of the buffers if $n = 0$ at Line 2; otherwise, it compares the buffers byte-by-byte. Assuming registers of 32 bits, each iteration collects two 4-bytes load events: one for each buffer at Lines 5 and 6. Then, it branches to start the next iteration at Line 9 until the end of the buffers, no matter what the comparison result is. Hence, for any public input value, cst-compare induces the same event trace.

In contrast, the program compare in Fig. 1 (left) is not constant-time since the event trace may be different for two executions. Consider the following counterexample, where $n = 1$ and the buffers are $k = 10$ and $x = 20$. In memory, the two executions contain $s_0(\text{memory}_{10}) = 0$ and $s_0(\text{memory}_{20}) = 0$; and $s_1(\text{memory}_{10}) = 0$ and $s_1(\text{memory}_{20}) = 1$ respectively. The two traces differ at the first mismatch, as the loop in the second execution is terminated early. For brevity, the following event traces are simplified omitting the address of branch instructions with the evaluation of the condition:

$s_0(\text{events}) = [\text{branch FALSE}, \text{load } 10, 4, \text{load } 20, 4, \text{branch FALSE}, \text{branch FALSE}]$
$s_1(\text{events}) = [\text{branch FALSE}, \text{load } 10, 4, \text{load } 20, 4, \text{branch TRUE}]$

Constant-Time via Unary to Relational Embedding. We can employ unary Hoare logic to prove constant-time behavior by showing that private data does not influence the event trace generated during program execution. In other words, it is sufficient to provide a witness trace that depends only on public data.

Definition 8 (Constant-Time via Unary to Relational Embedding). *Let τ^e be an operational semantics that collects the microarchitectural events, P be a precondition, Q a postcondition, and F a frame condition. The program $\text{prog}(P)$ is constant-time with respect to private data $\mathbb{L}_{\text{pri}}$ if there exists a function $f : \Sigma_e(\mathbb{L}_{\text{pub}}) \to \mathbb{E}$ such that:*

$$\forall v_{\text{pub}}, e_0.\ \text{ensuresn}_{fn}^{\tau^e} \begin{pmatrix} \{s \in P \mid v_{\text{pub}} = s(\mathbb{L}_{\text{pub}}) \land e_0 = s(\text{events})\}, \\ \{s \in Q \mid s(\text{events}) = e_0 +\!\!+ f(v_{\text{pub}})\}, \\ F \end{pmatrix}$$

where $\Sigma_e(\mathbb{L}_{\text{pub}})$ is the partial projection of states Σ_e on public data $\mathbb{L}_{\text{pub}}$, and $+\!\!+$ is the list concatenation.

This approach eliminates the need to run the symbolic simulation tactic twice, but requires providing an explicit witness for the event trace function f. Since this approach proves a statement about a single program execution, the proof structure is very similar to the correctness proof. Therefore, we can merge the two proofs for correctness and constant-time behavior into a single one; thus eliminating the computational effort of checking each proof separately and greatly reducing the overhead of writing and maintaining them. We can retrieve the relational definition by instantiating Theorem 3 with two instances of the same ensuresn proof, renamed accordingly.

Example 4. Using list comprehension, for a given public input v_{pub}, the witness f for the program cst-compare in Fig. 1 is defined as:

$$[\text{branch } (v_{\text{pub}}(\texttt{n}) = 0)] +\!\!+ \begin{bmatrix} \text{load } (v_{\text{pub}}(\texttt{x}) + v_{\text{pub}}(\texttt{n}) - 1 - i), 4 \\ \text{load } (v_{\text{pub}}(\texttt{y}) + v_{\text{pub}}(\texttt{n}) - 1 - i), 4 \\ \text{branch } (i < v_{\text{pub}}(\texttt{n})) \end{bmatrix} i \in [0, v_{\text{pub}}(\texttt{n}))$$

where n, x, and y are public data and therefore accessible in v_{pub}.

Note that, routines in the s2n-bignum library can be proven constant-time by instantiating either Definition 7 or Definition 8, the two are equivalent.

7 Equivalence Checking

In this section, we demonstrate the application of our relational Hoare logic framework to equivalence checking between performance and verification-friendly implementations of the same routine in the s2n-bignum library.

Equivalence Between Two Programs. Two programs are considered functionally equivalent if they produce the same output states starting from equivalent input states. When dealing with assembly-level programs, we must carefully define what it means for two states to be "equal". For instance, two equal input states should not require the exact same code in memory; otherwise, only identical programs could be compared. Similarly, because the calling convention allows callee-save registers to hold different values, the value of these registers should not be constrained.

On the output side, certain registers or memory regions may differ if they are not designated as outputs. For example, eliminating dead stores to the stack frame is a valid optimization because the stack frame is not used after function returned. Two equivalent output states must allow those parts of memory to contain different data.

As a consequence, the equivalence checking takes as a parameter the equivalence relations $\simeq_{in} \subseteq \Sigma \times \Sigma$ and $\simeq_{out} \subseteq \Sigma \times \Sigma$ that define when input and output states are considered equivalent. This relation has to be defined manually for each pair of programs to be compared.

Example 5. Consider the two programs compare and cst-compare in Fig. 1. Assuming a proof of correctness for compare already exists, our goal is to prove that the secure constant-time version is functionally equivalent to the original program, without needing to reprove the correctness of cst-compare from scratch. To do so, we define the input equivalence $\simeq_{in}$, relating the program counter, input registers, and relevant part of the memory as follows:

$$\simeq_{in} = \text{MAYCHANGE}\left(\mathbb{L} \setminus \begin{pmatrix} \{\texttt{instr}, \texttt{n}, \texttt{x}, \texttt{y}\} \cup \\ \{\texttt{memory}_i \mid i \in [x, x+n) \vee i \in [y, y+n)\} \end{pmatrix}\right)$$

Note the use of the MAYCHANGE operator to define a relation that allows two states to differ in all labels but the ones specified. For output equivalence $\simeq_{out}$, we relate only the output register, i.e., $\simeq_{out} = \text{MAYCHANGE}(\mathbb{L} \setminus \{\texttt{res}\})$.

Definition 9 (Equivalence). *Let $P_0, P_1 \subseteq \Sigma$ be two preconditions, $Q_0, Q_1 \subseteq \Sigma$ two postconditions, $F_0, F_1 \subseteq \Sigma \times \Sigma$ two frame conditions, and $fn_0, fn_1 : \Sigma \to \mathbb{N}$ two step functions. Given the input and output equivalences $\simeq_{in}, \simeq_{out} \subseteq \Sigma \times \Sigma$, the programs $\texttt{prog}(P_0)$ and $\texttt{prog}(P_1)$ are equivalent if it holds that:*

$$\texttt{ensures2}_{fn_0, fn_1} \begin{pmatrix} \{(s_0, s_1) \in P_0 \times P_1 \mid s_0 \simeq_{in} s_1\}, \\ \{(s_0, s_1) \in Q_0 \times Q_1 \mid s_0 \simeq_{out} s_1\}, \\ F_0 \times F_1 \end{pmatrix}$$

Example 6. We can prove that the constant-time program `cst-compare` is equivalent to the original program in `compare` by applying Definition 9 with the input and output equivalences defined in Example 5. Along the lines of the pre- and postconditions defined in Sect. 6, we define:

$$P' = \left\{ s \,\middle|\, \begin{array}{l} s(\mathtt{n}) = n \wedge s(\mathtt{x}) = x \wedge s(\mathtt{y}) = y \wedge \\ \forall i \leq n.\ s(\mathtt{memory}_{x+i}) = x_i \wedge s(\mathtt{memory}_{y+i}) = y_i \end{array} \right\},$$

$$P_0 = \{s \in P' \,|\, \text{ALIGN}^\tau(s, i_0, \mathtt{cst\text{-}compare})\}, P_1 = \{s \in P' \,|\, \text{ALIGN}^\tau(s, i_0, \mathtt{compare})\},$$
$$Q_0 = \{s \,|\, \text{END}^\tau(s, \text{LENGTH}^\tau(\mathtt{cst\text{-}compare}))\}, Q_1 = \{s \,|\, \text{END}^\tau(s, \text{LENGTH}^\tau(\mathtt{compare}))\},$$
$$F_0 = \text{MAYCHANGE}(\{\mathtt{instr}, \mathtt{n}, \mathtt{xn}, \mathtt{yn}\}),$$
$$F_1 = \text{MAYCHANGE}(\{\mathtt{instr}, \mathtt{n}, \mathtt{xn}, \mathtt{yn}, \mathtt{diff}, \mathtt{temp}\}),$$
$$fn_0(s) = \text{LARGESTPREFIX}_n(s, x, y), \text{ and } fn_1(s) = s(\mathtt{n}),$$

where $\text{LARGESTPREFIX}_n(s, x, y)$ is the length of the largest prefix among the two given memory addresses x and y of length n. In conclusion, Definition 9 provides the specification for the equivalence proof between the two programs.

Composition of Program Equivalences. We slightly abuse notation and define eqensures as a shorthand for the equivalence of two programs C_0, C_1 with $\simeq_{\text{in}}$ in the precondition starting from $\mathtt{pc}_0, \mathtt{pc}_1$, eventually reaching $\simeq_{\text{out}}$ in the postcondition at $\mathtt{pc}'_0, \mathtt{pc}'_1$: $\text{eqensures}_{\mathtt{pc}_0, \mathtt{pc}'_0, \mathtt{pc}_1, \mathtt{pc}'_1}(C_0, C_1, \simeq_{\text{in}}, \simeq_{\text{out}})$. Notably, Lemma 3 proves that the sequential composition of two equivalence proofs is sound if $\forall s, s'.\ s \simeq_{\text{out}} s' \implies s \simeq_{\text{in}}' s'$. Formally, the *sequential composition* of two equivalences is defined as follows:

$$\frac{\text{eqensures}_{\mathtt{pc}_0, \mathtt{pc}'_0, \mathtt{pc}_1, \mathtt{pc}'_1}(C_0, C_1, \simeq_{\text{in}}, \simeq_{\text{out}}) \quad \text{eqensures}_{\mathtt{pc}'_0, \mathtt{pc}''_0, \mathtt{pc}'_1, \mathtt{pc}''_1}(C_0, C_1, \simeq_{\text{in}}', \simeq_{\text{out}}')}{\text{eqensures}_{\mathtt{pc}_0, \mathtt{pc}''_0, \mathtt{pc}_1, \mathtt{pc}''_1}(C_0, C_1, \simeq_{\text{in}}, \simeq_{\text{out}}')}$$

Lemma 4 instead proves the soundness of the transitive composition of two equivalences, only if the result input and output equivalences preserve the existence of an intermediate state, i.e., $s \simeq_{\text{in}}' s' \iff \exists s''.(s \simeq_{\text{in}} s'' \wedge s'' \simeq_{\text{in}}' s')$ and $s \simeq_{\text{out}}' s' \iff \exists s''.(s \simeq_{\text{out}} s'' \wedge s'' \simeq_{\text{out}}' s')$. Formally, the *transitive composition* of two equivalences is defined as follows:

$$\frac{\text{eqensures}_{\mathtt{pc}_0, \mathtt{pc}'_0, \mathtt{pc}_1, \mathtt{pc}'_1}(C_0, C_1, \simeq_{\text{in}}, \simeq_{\text{out}}) \quad \text{eqensures}_{\mathtt{pc}_1, \mathtt{pc}'_1, \mathtt{pc}_2, \mathtt{pc}'_2}(C_1, C_2, \simeq_{\text{in}1}, \simeq_{\text{out}1})}{\text{eqensures}_{\mathtt{pc}_0, \mathtt{pc}'_0, \mathtt{pc}_2, \mathtt{pc}'_2}(C_0, C_2, \simeq_{\text{in}}', \simeq_{\text{out}}')}$$

Combining Equivalence and Correctness Proofs. In the following, we show how to reuse a correctness proof of an original program to obtain a correctness proof of an optimized program through program equivalence. Indeed, given the functional correctness of the original program in the form of an ensuresn proof, we can apply it to the optimized program by proving the equivalence of the two via the relational Hoare triple ensures2. The correctness proof of the optimized program is given in the form of a hybrid relational Hoare triple $h$ensures2, presented in Definition 6.

Theorem 5 (Transfer of Correctness through Equality).

$$\texttt{ensuresn}^\tau_{fn_0}(P, Q, F) \wedge \texttt{ensures2}^\tau_{fn_0,fn_1}(P^\times, Q^\times, F^\times)$$

$$\implies h\texttt{ensures2}^\tau_{fn_0,fn_1}\begin{pmatrix}\{(s_0,s_1) \in P^\times \mid s_0 \in P\}, \\ \{(s_0,s_1) \in Q^\times \mid s_0 \in Q\}, \\ \{((s_0,s_1),(s'_0,s'_1)) \in F^\times \mid (s_0,s'_0) \in F\}\end{pmatrix}\begin{vmatrix}P, \\ Q, \\ F\end{vmatrix}$$

Let $P_0 \subseteq \Sigma$ be the precondition, $Q_0 \subseteq \Sigma$ the postcondition, $F_0 \subseteq \Sigma \times \Sigma$ the frame condition, and $fn_0 : \Sigma \to \mathbb{N}$ the step function. We state functional correctness as: $\texttt{ensuresn}_{fn_0}(\{s \in P_0 \mid s(\texttt{pc}) = x_0\}, \{s \in Q_0 \mid s(\texttt{pc}) = x_\omega\}, F_0)$. Afterwards, from Definition 9, given the two input-output equivalences $\simeq_{\text{in}}$ and $\simeq_{\text{out}}$, the equivalence between two programs is achieved by proving:

$$\texttt{ensures2}_{fn_0,fn_1}\begin{pmatrix}\{(s_0,s_1) \in P_0 \times P_1 \mid s_0 \simeq_{\text{in}} s_1\}, \\ \{(s_0,s_1) \in Q_0 \times Q_1 \mid s_0 \simeq_{\text{out}} s_1\}, \\ F_0 \times F_1\end{pmatrix}$$

where P_1, Q_1, F_1 are the pre-, post-, and frame conditions of the second program, respectively. Theorem 5 transfers the correctness and equivalence proofs to the following hybrid relational Hoare triple:

$$h\texttt{ensures2}_{fn_0,fn_1}\begin{pmatrix}\{(s_0,s_1) \in P_0 \times P_1 \mid s_0 \simeq_{\text{in}} s_1 \wedge s_0(\texttt{pc}) = x_0\}, \\ \{(s_0,s_1) \in Q_0 \times Q_1 \mid s_0 \simeq_{\text{out}} s_1 \wedge s_0(\texttt{pc}) = x_\omega\}, \\ F_0 \times F_1\end{pmatrix}\begin{vmatrix}\{s \in P_1 \mid s(\texttt{pc}) = x_0\}, \\ \{s \in Q_1 \mid s(\texttt{pc}) = x_\omega\}, \\ F_1\end{vmatrix}$$

Finally, by applying Theorem 4, we obtain the correctness proof of the new program: $\texttt{ensuresn}_{fn_1}(\{s \in P_1 \mid s(\texttt{pc}) = x_0\}, \{s \in Q_1 \mid s(\texttt{pc}) = x_\omega\}, F_1)$. In Appendix D [32], we provide the steps required to promote a correctness proof that was originally written via the `ensures` operator—without an explicit number of steps—to a proof that uses the `ensuresn` operator. The majority of functional correctness proofs already available in the s2n-bignum library are written using the `ensures` operator. In total, the core of the equivalence checking proofs is 2629 lines of HOL Light code.

8 Obtaining Proofs for the Hol-Bignum Library

8.1 Case Study: Bignum Copy and Inversion Modulo Routine

We apply the constant-time verification to the s2n-bignum library, notably on the copy program of large integers, cf. `bignum_copy`, and the inversion modulo a prime $p = 2^{255} - 19$, cf. `bignum_inv_p25519`. The following should provide guidance on which proof approach to apply depending on the program size and complexity.

The `bignum_copy` routine is relatively small, comprising 16 instructions that copy the content of buffer k to the buffer z, padding z with zeros if it is bigger than k. Despite its size, `bignum_copy` has the most complex program flow in the library, making it a good candidate for constant-time verification. The functional correctness proof is 180 lines. The constant-time proof, using Definition 7, is 276 lines: it does not require an explicit event trace and is fairly easy to prove correct. On the other hand, the unary constant-time proof using Definition 8 is 245 lines, and requires an explicit event trace. Although the event trace is small and intuitive, this parameter makes the proof more complex as it requires a nontrivial induction on list comprehensions. Notably, we can combine correctness and constant-time proofs together via Theorem 3 in a single, 277-line proof, which yields the lowest proof size overhead.

The `bignum_inv_p25519` routine instead is a 1033-instruction program that finds the inverse of a big integer modulo a prime $p = 2^{255} - 19$. The functional correctness proof is 2303 lines long. The constant-time proof, using the unary embedding of Definition 8 combining correctness and constant-time proofs, is 2633 lines long. Most of the additions in the proof are due to the explicit definition of the event trace, which contains 90 memory events alone. However, after defining the event trace, extending the correctness proof with the constant-time proof was effortless. All the mechanized proofs are available in the artifact.[5] In future work, we plan to automate the generation of the event trace, which will significantly reduce the required level of manual effort.

8.2 Case Study: Elliptic Curves and Montgomery Reduction

We utilized program equivalence to verify the functional correctness of optimized implementations for (1) *field and point operations* of NIST elliptic curves (specifically, curves P-256, P-384, and P-521), and (2) *Montgomery reduction*, an algorithm that allows efficient modular arithmetic when the modulus is large. These optimizations were achieved using an *autovectorizer*, a constraint solver-based instruction scheduler called SLOTHY [1], and the point operations of NIST curves were optimized using a custom memory instruction optimizer for the ARM architecture. We also have similar equivalence checking tactics for the X86 architecture. Overall, we checked the equivalence for 15 pairs of arithmetic routines, amounting to a total of 19k lines of proofs.

The autovectorizer replaces sequences of 64-bit scalar multiplication instructions, such as `mul` and `umulh`, with their equivalent NEON vector instructions. This optimization targets the ARM Neoverse N1 architecture, whose microarchitecture contains only one multiplication pipeline. The `mul`/`umulh` instructions stall this pipeline for a few cycles when executing scalar multiplication instructions. SLOTHY employs a constraint solver and cost model to find the optimal instruction scheduling, significantly reducing these stalls. Specifically, SLOTHY improves the scheduling of straight-line code in the main basic blocks of NIST curves' field operations, and also improves the software pipelining optimization in the main loop of the Montgomery reduction. The memory instruction optimizer performs two key tasks in the ARM architecture: store-to-load forwarding and dead store elimination. Store-to-load forwarding replaces load instructions with

---

[5] https://doi.org/10.5281/zenodo.15309209.

stored values, eliminating redundant memory accesses. Dead store elimination removes store instructions with results that are never used.

Tactics for Program Equivalence Proofs. To automate the writing of equivalence proofs, we developed proof tactics that can be used for two different classes of optimizations: small localized updates and instruction reordering.

For local optimizations that update only small portions of the original program, such as autovectorization, we implemented the tactic EQUIV_STEPS_TAC. This tactic takes as input a list of line ranges and annotations describing whether each range is optimized or left identical. For the identical portion, the tactic performs lock-step symbolic simulation and eagerly abbreviates the common outputs of the instructions with fresh variables to avoid exponential explosion of the sizes of the output expressions. For optimized ranges, the tactic employs stuttering simulation, which executes the corresponding sections of each program step-by-step. To help EQUIV_STEPS_TAC automatically converge on complex cases, users can register custom bit-vector equality theorems for output expressions.

For optimizations involving instruction reordering, we implemented two additional tactics: STEPS_ABBREV_TAC and STEPS_REWRITE_TAC. The first tactic performs stuttering symbolic simulation for the first program, storing the symbolic output expressions to an OCaml array. The second tactic takes as input an instruction index mapping between the two programs, along with the symbolic output generated by STEPS_ABBREV_TAC. Then, it simulates the second program step-by-step, proving that the symbolic output of each instruction is equal to the symbolic expression in the first program, according to the instruction mapping.

Software Pipelining of Montgomery Reduction. The Montgomery reduction is heavily used in cryptographic operations performing modular exponentations. Its original implementation in the s2n-bignum library includes a nested loop structure, where the outer loop consists of three basic blocks: loop entry, inner loop (which consists of a single basic block), and loop exit. A faster version was achieved by: caching repetitive calculations, vectorizing mul and umulh in all basic blocks, applying software pipelining optimizations to the inner loop, and rescheduling instructions using SLOTHY.

We verified the functional correctness of the optimized Montgomery reduction by *transitively* composing equivalence proofs with the original correctness proof after each optimization stage. For each optimization, we applied *sequential* composition of equivalences between each basic block pair and induced the equivalence of the whole loop. In the case of software pipelining, which transforms the control flow graph by adding loop prologue and epilogue blocks, equivalence composition has been applied between each block.

Overall, the optimized field operations of NIST curves achieved throughput speedups up to 38%, and integrating these improvements into point operations alongside memory optimizations resulted in up to 23% throughput gains. These enhancements demonstrate the substantial impact of the new optimizations.

9   Conclusion

This work presents a novel relational Hoare logic framework for verifying realistically modelled machine code, while preserving natural properties expected from Hoare-style reasoning. Fully formalized in HOL Light, the framework is applied in two case studies involving the s2n-bignum cryptographic library, a key component of a TLS/SSL implementation. Our results show that the logic scales to large assembly programs and yields practical value in the verification of cryptographic codebases.

While Mazzucato et al. [31] have investigated constant-time verification for libraries similar to s2n-bignum, their approach relies on abstraction-dependent methods through an untrusted computing base to decompile assembly into C. In contrast, our framework operates directly on the assembly level, ensuring higher reliability of the verification results as it reduces the trusted computing base to the minimal core of the HOL Light theorem prover and to the operational semantics implementations. As future work, we plan to increase coverage of relational properties on the s2n-bignum library and improve proof automation to handle repetitive tasks. As a natural extension to constant-time proofs, we aim to address speculative execution vulnerabilities [15, 26].

Acknowledgements. We would like to thank Hanno Becker for his help in improving the Montgomery reduction implementation, and the anonymous reviewers of CAV 2025 for their valuable feedback.

Disclosure of Interests. Research reported in this publication was supported by an Amazon Research Award, Fall 2023.

References

1. Abdulrahman, A., Becker, H., Kannwischer, M.J., Klein, F.: Fast and Clean: Auditable high-performance assembly via constraint solving. Cryptology ePrint Archive, Paper 2022/1303 (2022)
2. Affeldt, R.: On construction of a library of formally verified low-level arithmetic functions. In: Proceedings of the 27th Annual ACM Symposium on Applied Computing, SAC 2012, pp. 1326–1331. Association for Computing Machinery, New York (2012). ISBN 978-1-4503-0857-1. https://doi.org/10.1145/2245276.2231986
3. Antonopoulos, T., Gazzillo, P., Hicks, M., Koskinen, E., Terauchi, T., Wei, S.: Decomposition instead of self-composition for proving the absence of timing channels. In: Proceedings of the 38th ACM SIGPLAN Conference on Programming Language Design and Implementation, PLDI 2017, pp. 362–375. Association for Computing Machinery, New York (2017). ISBN 978-1-4503-4988-8. https://doi.org/10.1145/3062341.3062378
4. Bartels, B., Jähnig, N.: Mechanized, compositional verification of low-level code. In: Badger, J.M., Rozier, K.Y. (eds.) NFM 2014. LNCS, vol. 8430, pp. 98–112. Springer, Cham (2014). https://doi.org/10.1007/978-3-319-06200-6_8
5. Barthe, G., Crespo, J.M., Kunz, C.: Relational verification using product programs. In: Butler, M., Schulte, W. (eds.) FM 2011. LNCS, vol. 6664, pp. 200–214. Springer, Heidelberg (2011). https://doi.org/10.1007/978-3-642-21437-0_17

6. Barthe, G., Gregoire, B., Laporte, V.: Secure compilation of side-channel countermeasures: the case of cryptographic "constant-time". In: 2018 IEEE 31st Computer Security Foundations Symposium (CSF 2018), pp. 328–343. IEEE (2018)
7. Barthe, G., Rezk, T., Saabas, A.: Proof obligations preserving compilation. In: Dimitrakos, T., Martinelli, F., Ryan, P., Schneider, S. (eds.) FAST 2005. LNCS, vol. 3866, pp. 112–126. Springer, Heidelberg (2006). https://doi.org/10.1007/11679219_9
8. Benton, N.: A typed, compositional logic for a stack-based abstract machine. In: Yi, K. (ed.) APLAS 2005. LNCS, vol. 3780, pp. 364–380. Springer, Heidelberg (2005). https://doi.org/10.1007/11575467_24
9. Benton, N.: Simple relational correctness proofs for static analyses and program transformations. In: Proceedings of the 31st ACM SIGPLAN-SIGACT Symposium on Principles of Programming Languages, POPL 2004, pp. 14–25. Association for Computing Machinery, New York (2004). ISBN 978-1-58113-729-3. https://doi.org/10.1145/964001.964003
10. Benton, N.: Semantic equivalence checking for HHVM bytecode. In: Proceedings of the 20th International Symposium on Principles and Practice of Declarative Programming, PPDP 2018, pp. 1–8. Association for Computing Machinery, New York (2018). ISBN 978-1-4503-6441-6. https://doi.org/10.1145/3236950.3236975
11. Beringer, L.: Relational decomposition. In: van Eekelen, M., Geuvers, H., Schmaltz, J., Wiedijk, F. (eds.) ITP 2011. LNCS, vol. 6898, pp. 39–54. Springer, Heidelberg (2011). https://doi.org/10.1007/978-3-642-22863-6_6
12. Blatter, L., Kosmatov, N., Prevosto, V., Le Gall, P.: Certified verification of relational properties. In: Integrated Formal Methods: 17th International Conference, IFM 2022, Lugano, Switzerland, 7–10 June 2022, Proceedings, pp. 86–105. Springer, Heidelberg (2022). ISBN 978-3-031-07726-5. https://doi.org/10.1007/978-3-031-07727-2_6
13. Bond, B., et al.: Vale: verifying high-performance cryptographic assembly code. In: 26th USENIX Security Symposium (USENIX Security 2017), pp. 917–934 (2017). ISBN 978-1-931971-40-9
14. Bosamiya, J., Gibson, S., Li, Y., Parno, B., Hawblitzel, C.: Verified transformations and hoare logic: beautiful proofs for ugly assembly language. In: Christakis, M., Polikarpova, N., Duggirala, P.S., Schrammel, P. (eds.) NSV/VSTTE -2020. LNCS, vol. 12549, pp. 106–123. Springer, Cham (2020). https://doi.org/10.1007/978-3-030-63618-0_7
15. Cauligi, S., Disselkoen, C., Moghimi, D., Barthe, G., Stefan, D.: SoK: practical foundations for software spectre defenses. In: 2022 IEEE Symposium on Security and Privacy (SP), pp. 666–680. IEEE Computer Society (2022). ISBN 978-1-66541-316-9. https://doi.org/10.1109/SP46214.2022.9833707
16. Clarkson, M.R., Schneider, F.B.: Hyperproperties. In: 2008 21st IEEE Computer Security Foundations Symposium, pp. 51–65 (2008). https://doi.org/10.1109/CSF.2008.7
17. Erbsen, A., Philipoom, J., Gross, J., Sloan, R., Chlipala, A.: Simple high-level code for cryptographic arithmetic - with proofs, without compromises. In: 2019 IEEE Symposium on Security and Privacy (SP), pp. 1202–1219 (2019). https://doi.org/10.1109/SP.2019.00005
18. Harrison, J.: HOL light: an overview. In: Berghofer, S., Nipkow, T., Urban, C., Wenzel, M. (eds.) TPHOLs 2009. LNCS, vol. 5674, pp. 60–66. Springer, Heidelberg (2009). https://doi.org/10.1007/978-3-642-03359-9_4
19. Harrison, J.: HOL Light Tutorial (for Version 2.20) (2011)

20. Hoare, C.: An axiomatic basis for computer programming. Commun. ACM **12**(10), 576–580 (1969)
21. Jähnig, N., Gothel, T., Glesner, S.: A denotational semantics for communicating unstructured code (2015)
22. Jähnig, N., Göthel, T., Glesner, S.: Refinement-based verification of communicating unstructured code. In: De Nicola, R., Kühn, E. (eds.) SEFM 2016. LNCS, vol. 9763, pp. 61–75. Springer, Cham (2016). https://doi.org/10.1007/978-3-319-41591-8_5
23. Jensen, J.B., Benton, N., Kennedy, A.: High-level separation logic for low-level code. In: Proceedings of the 40th Annual ACM SIGPLAN-SIGACT Symposium on Principles of Programming Languages, POPL 2013, pp. 301–314. Association for Computing Machinery, New York (2013). ISBN 978-1-4503-1832-7. https://doi.org/10.1145/2429069.2429105
24. Kang, J., et al.: Crellvm: verified credible compilation for LLVM. In: Proceedings of the 39th ACM SIGPLAN Conference on Programming Language Design and Implementation, PLDI 2018, pp. 631–645. Association for Computing Machinery, New York (2018). ISBN 978-1-4503-5698-5. https://doi.org/10.1145/3192366.3192377
25. Klein, G., et al.: Formal verification of an OS kernel. In: Proceedings of the ACM SIGOPS 22nd Symposium on Operating Systems Principles, pp. 207–220 (2009)
26. Kocher, P., et al.: Spectre attacks: exploiting speculative execution. In: 2019 IEEE Symposium on Security and Privacy (SP), pp. 1–19 (2019). ISSN 2375-1207. https://doi.org/10.1109/SP.2019.00002
27. Kumar, R., Myreen, M., Norrish, M., Owens, S.: Cakeml: a verified implementation of ml. ACM SIGPLAN Not. **49**(1), 179–191 (2014)
28. Lehner, H.: Muller: formal translation of bytecode into BoogiePL. Electron. Notes Theor. Comput. Sci. **190**(1), 35–50 (2007)
29. Lundberg, D., Guanciale, R., Lindner, A., Dam, M.: Hoare-style logic for unstructured programs. In: de Boer, F., Cerone, A. (eds.) SEFM 2020. LNCS, vol. 12310, pp. 193–213. Springer, Cham (2020). https://doi.org/10.1007/978-3-030-58768-0_11
30. Marti, N.: Formal verification of low-level software. Ph.D. thesis, University of Tokyo (2008)
31. Mazzucato, D., Campion, M., Urban, C.: Quantitative static timing analysis. In: 31st Static Analysis Symposium (SAS 2024), Roberto Giacobazzi and Alessandra Gorla and Marco Campion, Pasadena, CA, United States (2024). https://doi.org/10.1007/978-3-031-74776-2_11
32. Mazzucato, D., et al.: Relational hoare logic for realistically modelled machine code (2025). https://arxiv.org/abs/2505.14348
33. Myreen, M., Curello, G.: Formal verification of machine-code programs. In: Lundberg, D. (ed.) International Conference on Certified Programs and Proofs, p. 20. University of Cambridge, Computer Laboratory (2009)
34. Myreen, M., Gordon, M.: Verification of machine code implementations of arithmetic functions for cryptography. In: Theorem Proving in Higher Order Logics: Emerging Trends Proceedings, Department of Computer Science, University of Kaiserslautern (2007)
35. Myreen, M., Gordon, M., Slind, K.: Machine-code verification for multiple architectures-an application of decompilation into logic. In: 2008 Formal Methods in Computer-Aided Design, pp. 1–8. IEEE (2008)
36. Myreen, M., Gordon, M., Slind, K.: Decompilation into logic—improved. In: 2012 Formal Methods in Computer-Aided Design (FMCAD, pp. 78–81. IEEE (2012)

37. Myreen, M.O., Fox, A., Gordon, M.: Hoare logic for ARM machine code. In: Arbab, F., Sirjani, M. (eds.) FSEN 2007. LNCS, vol. 4767, pp. 272–286. Springer, Heidelberg (2007). https://doi.org/10.1007/978-3-540-75698-9_18
38. Myreen, M.O., Gordon, M.: Hoare logic for realistically modelled machine code. In: Grumberg, O., Huth, M. (eds.) TACAS 2007. LNCS, vol. 4424, pp. 568–582. Springer, Heidelberg (2007). https://doi.org/10.1007/978-3-540-71209-1_44
39. Naumann, D.A.: Thirty-seven years of relational hoare logic: remarks on its principles and history. In: Margaria, T., Steffen, B. (eds.) ISoLA 2020. LNCS, vol. 12477, pp. 93–116. Springer, Cham (2020). https://doi.org/10.1007/978-3-030-61470-6_7
40. O'Hearn, P., Reynolds, J., Yang, H.: Local reasoning about programs that alter data structures. In: Proceedings of Computer Science Logic (2001)
41. Pit-Claudel, C., Philipoom, J., Jamner, D., Erbsen, A., Chlipala, A.: Relational compilation for performance-critical applications: extensible proof-producing translation of functional models into low-level code. In: Proceedings of the 43rd ACM SIGPLAN International Conference on Programming Language Design and Implementation, PLDI 2022, pp. 918–933. Association for Computing Machinery, New York (2022). ISBN 978-1-4503-9265-5. https://doi.org/10.1145/3519939.3523706
42. Protzenko, J., et al.: EverCrypt: a fast, verified, cross-platform cryptographic provider. In: 2020 IEEE Symposium on Security and Privacy (SP), pp. 983–1002 (2020). ISSN 2375-1207. https://doi.org/10.1109/SP40000.2020.00114
43. Ray, S., Hunt, W.A., Matthews, J., Moore, J.S.: A mechanical analysis of program verification strategies. J. Autom. Reason. **40**(4), 245–269 (2008). ISSN 1573-0670. https://doi.org/10.1007/s10817-008-9098-1
44. Reynolds, J.: Separation logic: a logic for shared mutable data structures. In: Proceedings of 17th IEEE Symposium on Logic in Computer Science (LICS) (2002)
45. Rinard, M.: Credible Compilation (1999)
46. Sewell, T., Myreen, M., Klein, G.: Translation validation for a verified OS kernel. In: Proceedings of the 34th ACM SIGPLAN Conference on Programming Language Design and Implementation, pp. 471–482 (2013)
47. Tan, J., Tay, H.J., Gandhi, R., Narasimhan, P.: AUSPICE: automatic safety property verification for unmodified executables. In: Gurfinkel, A., Seshia, S.A. (eds.) VSTTE 2015. LNCS, vol. 9593, pp. 202–222. Springer, Cham (2016). https://doi.org/10.1007/978-3-319-29613-5_12
48. Wang, A.: An axiomatic basis for proving total correctness of goto-programs. BIT Numer. Math. **16**(1), 88–102 (1976). ISSN 1572-9125. https://doi.org/10.1007/BF01940782

Open Access This chapter is licensed under the terms of the Creative Commons Attribution 4.0 International License (http://creativecommons.org/licenses/by/4.0/), which permits use, sharing, adaptation, distribution and reproduction in any medium or format, as long as you give appropriate credit to the original author(s) and the source, provide a link to the Creative Commons license and indicate if changes were made.

The images or other third party material in this chapter are included in the chapter's Creative Commons license, unless indicated otherwise in a credit line to the material. If material is not included in the chapter's Creative Commons license and your intended use is not permitted by statutory regulation or exceeds the permitted use, you will need to obtain permission directly from the copyright holder.

Correction to: Efficient Probabilistic Model Checking for Relational Reachability

Lina Gerlach, Tobias Winkler, Erika Ábrahám, Borzoo Bonakdarpour, and Sebastian Junges

Correction to:
Chapter 6 in: R. Piskac and Z. Rakamarić (Eds.):
(Computer Aided) Verification, **LNCS 15931**,
https://doi.org/10.1007/978-3-031-98668-0_6

The original version of this book chapter was inadvertently published without Algorithm 1. This has been corrected.

The updated version of this chapter can be found at
https://doi.org/10.1007/978-3-031-98668-0_6

Open Access This chapter is licensed under the terms of the Creative Commons Attribution 4.0 International License (http://creativecommons.org/licenses/by/4.0/), which permits use, sharing, adaptation, distribution and reproduction in any medium or format, as long as you give appropriate credit to the original author(s) and the source, provide a link to the Creative Commons license and indicate if changes were made.

The images or other third party material in this chapter are included in the chapter's Creative Commons license, unless indicated otherwise in a credit line to the material. If material is not included in the chapter's Creative Commons license and your intended use is not permitted by statutory regulation or exceeds the permitted use, you will need to obtain permission directly from the copyright holder.

Author Index

A
Ábrahám, Erika   127

B
Barrett, Clark   339, 389
Bassa, Alp   339
Biere, Armin   281
Bonakdarpour, Borzoo   127
Bu, Tianjun   185, 237

C
Chen, Hanyue   162
Chien, Po-Chun   296
Ci, Yiwei   185, 237
Cimatti, Alessandro   215
Colvin, Robert J.   363

D
Dhavala, Venkata   148
Dillig, Isil   315
Dillig, Işil   339

E
Eilers, Marco   107
Esen, Zafer   56

F
Faella, Marco   3
Froleyks, Nils   281

G
Ganesh, Vijay   296
Gerlach, Lina   127
Griggio, Alberto   215
Grundy, Jim   389
Gupta, Ekanshdeep   56, 81
Gurfinkel, Arie   296

H
Harrison, John   389
Heljanko, Keijo   281
Hojjat, Hossein   56

Hovland, Paul D.   148
Huang, Ziyu   185, 237
Hückelheim, Jan   148

J
Jiang, Hongjian   200
Johannsen, Christopher   215
Junges, Sebastian   127

L
Lee, Juneyoung   389
Lee, Nian-Ze   296
Li, Yingcheng   237
Lin, Anthony W.   200
Lu, Zhengyang   296
Luka, Andrew   258

M
Markgraf, Oliver   200
Mazzucato, Denis   389
Mohamed, Abdalrhman   389
Müller, Peter   107

O
Ozdemir, Alex   339

P
Pailoor, Shankara   315, 339
Parlato, Gennaro   3
Păsăreanu, Corina S.   389
Patel, Nisarg   81
Pertseva, Elizaveta   339
Porncharoenwase, Sorawee   339
Preiner, Mathias   281

R
Rozier, Kristin Yvonne   215
Rümmer, Philipp   56, 200

S
Schwerhoff, Malte   107
Siegel, Stephen F.   148

© The Editor(s) (if applicable) and The Author(s) 2025
R. Piskac and Z. Rakamarić (Eds.): CAV 2025, LNCS 15931, pp. 415–416, 2025.
https://doi.org/10.1007/978-3-031-98668-0

Sotoudeh, Matthew 29
Stan, Daniel 200
Stephens, Jon 315
Su, Roger C. 363
Su, Yuheng 185, 237
Summers, Alexander J. 107

T
Tonetta, Stefano 215

V
Vaandrager, Frits 162
Vizel, Yakir 258

W
Wies, Thomas 56, 81
Winkler, Tobias 127
Wolff, Sebastian 56

Y
Yang, Qiusong 185, 237
Yu, Emily 281

Z
Zhang, Miaomiao 162

MIX
Papier aus verantwortungsvollen Quellen
Paper from responsible sources
FSC® C105338

If you have any concerns about our products,
you can contact us on
ProductSafety@springernature.com

In case Publisher is established outside the EU,
the EU authorized representative is:
**Springer Nature Customer Service Center GmbH
Europaplatz 3, 69115 Heidelberg, Germany**

Printed by Libri Plureos GmbH
in Hamburg, Germany